CENTRAL TEXAS COLLEGE EDITION

THE LONGMAN READER

JUDITH NADELL
JOHN LANGAN
ELIZA A. COMODROMOS

Taken from:

The Longman Reader, Eighth Edition
by Judith Nadell, John Langan, and Eliza A. Comodromos

CENTRAL TEXAS COLLEGE

PEARSON
Custom
Publishing

PEARSON
Longman

Cover image: *Moraine Lake, Canada* courtesy of Tom Kirila.

Taken from:
The Longman Reader, Eighth Edition
by Judith Nadell, John Langan, and Eliza A. Comodromos
Copyright © 2007 by Pearson Education, Inc.
Published by Longman
New York, New York 10036

This special edition published in cooperation with Pearson Custom
Publishing.

Printed in the United States of America

10   9

ISBN 0-536-38612-9

2007240111

LH

Please visit our web site at *www.pearsoncustom.com*

PEARSON CUSTOM PUBLISHING
75 Arlington Street, Suite 300, Boston, MA 02116
A Pearson Education Company

The Pathway to Success in Your College Courses

Your journey through college can be winding, filled with detours and potholes, or it can be relatively straight and smooth. The information below will help you have a pleasant experience along the way.

Time Management

> *I am definitely going to take a course on time management . . . just as soon as I can work it into my schedule.*
> — Louis E. Boone

The time you spend preparing to study relates directly to a successful outcome. But time, or lack thereof, is a common complaint. How often do you comment that you don't have enough time to accomplish everything you wish to do?

How Do You Spend Your Time?

The first step in time management is to see how you currently spend your time. Have you ever taken the time to add up all of the hours you spend on your regular activities? Take a moment to write down everything you do during a seven-day period. These questions will help you consider all of the activities you do.

- You may spend 40 hours a week on your job, but what about commute time?
- You have to fuel your body. How many hours a week do you spend eating?
- Good grooming is essential. How many hours a week do you spend bathing and dressing?
- How much time do you give to your friends and family?

Remember, there are only 168 hours in a week. Is there any time left to sleep?

How Can I Make More Time?

You can't add hours to the day or days to the week, but if you learn to plan your time wisely, you should be able to make better use of the time you have. As an added bonus, you should feel less stress. Scheduling your time is a step in the right direction.

Develop schedules:

Long term
- Include fixed commitments only
- Include weekly obligations-job, classes, church, meetings, etc.
- Plan enough time for study-as a minimum, use two hours for every one hour in the classroom.
- Plan for weekly reviews-at least one hour each week for each class.

Intermediate

- One per week
- List major events and amount of work to be accomplished in each subject.
- Try to study at the same time every day.
- Make use of free hours between classes.
- Include non-study activities.

Short term

- Daily
- Use small note card you can carry with you.
- Write specifically what you need to accomplish that day.
- Mark out each item as it is completed.

Study Environment

Where you study and how you study is as important as how often you study.

- Identify a quiet place with a desk or table, a chair, and good lighting.
- Your bed might be inviting, but remember your goal is to stay awake and concentrate.
- Although music or some type of background noise might be ok, avoid the TV.
- It's too easy to get engrossed in a show rather than your course work.
- Watching CSI can be interesting, but it probably won't help you with your Introduction to Criminal Justice final exam.
- Make sure you have everything you need: your textbooks, notes, paper and pencil, and a clock.
- Why a clock? To help you manage your time.
- And, don't forget to take regular breaks.

Learning Styles

- If you are assembling a toy or using a new computer program, do you put instructions aside and refer to them only when you run into trouble?
- Do you have to see a name or address in writing in order to remember it?
- Do you enjoy audio books, or do you find your mind wandering as you listen?

Your answers to these questions relate to your preferred learning style, and like clothing, one learning style doesn't fit all. If you have access to the Internet, you can take a learning style inventory at *http://www.vark-learn.com/english/index.asp* and then view helpsheets at *http://www.vark-learn.com/english/page.asp?p=helpsheets* related to your preferred learning style.

Visual Learners

- learn through seeing
- need to see the teacher's body language and facial expression to fully understand the content of a lesson.
- tend to prefer sitting at the front of the classroom to avoid visual obstructions (e.g. people's heads).
- may think in pictures and learn best from visual displays including: diagrams, illustrated text books, overhead transparencies, videos, flip charts and hand-outs.
- During a lecture or classroom discussion, visual learners often prefer to take detailed notes to absorb the information.

If you are a visual learner, here are some suggestions just for you:

- use visual materials such as pictures, charts, maps, graphs, etc.
- have a clear view of your teachers when they are speaking so you can see their body language and facial expression
- use color to highlight important points in text
- take notes or ask your teacher to provide handouts
- illustrate your ideas as a picture or brainstorming bubble before writing them down
- write a story and illustrate it
- use multi-media (e.g. computers, videos, and filmstrips)
- study in a quiet place away from verbal disturbances
- read illustrated books
- visualize information as a picture to aid memorization

Aural Learners

- learn through listening
- learn best through verbal lectures, discussions, talking things through and listening to what others have to say.
- interpret the underlying meanings of speech through listening to tone of voice, pitch, speed and other nuances. Written information may have little meaning until it is heard.
- often benefit from reading text aloud and using a tape recorder.

If you are an aural learner, here are some suggestions just for you:

- participate in class discussions/debates
- make speeches and presentations
- use a tape recorder during lectures instead of taking notes
- read text out aloud
- create musical jingles to aid memorization
- create mnemonics to aid memorization
- discuss your ideas verbally
- dictate to someone while they write down your thoughts
- use verbal analogies, and story telling to demonstrate your point

Read/Write Learners

- learn through reading and writing
- learn best by reading and re-reading the textbook and their notes, writing and rewriting their notes, and in general, organizing items into lists.

Kinesthetic Learners

- learn through moving, doing, and touching
- learn best through a hands-on approach, actively exploring the physical world around them.
- may find it hard to sit still for long periods and may become distracted by their need for activity and exploration.

If you are a tactile/kinesthetic learner, here are some suggestions just for you:

- take frequent study breaks

- move around to learn new things (e.g. read while on an exercise bike, mold a piece of clay to learn a new concept)
- work at a standing position
- chew gum while studying
- use bright colors to highlight reading material
- dress up your work space with posters
- if you wish, listen to music while you study
- skim through reading material to get a rough idea what it is about before settling down to read it in detail.

Multimodal Learners

- don't have a single preferred learning style.
- learn best through combinations.

If you have multiple preferences, you are in the majority as somewhere between fifty and seventy percent of any population seems to fit into that group.

Reading Skills and Strategies

Good reading skills are essential to your success in your college-level classes. Here are a couple of reasons why:

- In high school, you may have been able to get good grades without reading much of the text. Now that you're in college, professors will expect you to read the textbook and they may test you on information not discussed in class but covered in the reading. In fact, many professors test on assigned readings as a check to make sure students are using their texts.
- The average freshman is assigned over 250 pages of reading each week, so clearly you're going to need to keep up with your reading assignments. If you do not read during week one, that means that you will need to read 500 pages the next week-just to stay caught up! If you choose not to read during the second week either . . . well, you can see how the work can just snowball.

Improving Your Reading Skills and Applying Reading Strategies

A good reader:

- seizes the main ideas.
- thinks about what the author is saying
- is active, not passive.
- concentrates on what is being read.
- remembers as much as possible.
- applies what is being read to personal experience.

Go to *http://www.how-to-study.com/pqr.htm* for more on reading skills.

SQ3R is one recommended method for improving your reading comprehension. The letters in the name stand for these five steps:

Survey: Before you read, scan the titles, headings, pictures, and summaries. Consider using the heading and subheadings as an outline for notes as you read.

Question: Ask yourself questions based on Step 1 and look for answers as you complete Step 3. For example, if a subheading is entitled "Basic Concepts of Reading," change it to read, "What are the Basic Concepts of Reading?"

Read: Read and take notes.

Recall: Without referring to the book or your notes, think about what you have read. See if your questions were answered. Could you explain the content to someone else? Try putting major concepts in your own words.

Review: Look at your questions, answers, notes and book to see how well you did recall. Observe carefully the points stated incorrectly or omitted. Fix carefully in mind the logical sequence of the entire idea, concepts, or problem. Finish up with a mental picture of the WHOLE.

Another method is **PQR3**, which stands for

Preview: Preview what you are going to read.

Question: Question what you are going to learn after the preview.

Read: Read the assignment.

Recite: Stop every once in a while, look up from the book, and put in your own words what you have just read.

Review: After you have finished, review the main points.

(Sounds similar to SQ3R, doesn't it?) Go to *http://www.how-to-study.com/pqr.htm* to learn more about this method.

There is even a related study method known as **M.U.R.D.E.R.**

Mood: Set a positive mood for yourself to study in.

Understand: Mark any information you don't understand in a particular unit and keep a focus on one unit or a manageable group of exercise.

Recall: After studying the unit, stop and put what you have learned into your own words.

Digest: Go back to what you did not understand and reconsider the information. Contact external expert sources (e.g., other books or an instructor) if you still cannot understand it.

Expand: ask three kinds of questions concerning the studied material:

- If I could speak to the author, what questions would I ask or what criticism would I offer?
- How could I apply this material to what I am interested in?
- How could I make this information interesting and understandable to other students?

Review: Go over the material you've covered. Review what strategies helped you understand and/or retain information in the past and apply these to your current studies.

Check this system out at *http://www.studygs.net/murder.htm*.

Notetaking

Why take notes?

- It triggers basic lecturing processes and helps you to remember information.
- It helps you to concentrate in class.
- It helps you prepare for tests.
- Your notes are often a source of valuable clues for what information the instructor thinks most important (i.e., what will show up on the next test).
- Your notes often contain information that cannot be found elsewhere (i.e., in your textbook).

Evaluate your present notetaking system. Ask yourself:

- Did I use complete phrases or sentences that mean something to me later?
- Did I use any form at all?
- Are my notes clear or confusing?
- Did I capture main points and all subpoints?
- Did I streamline using abbreviations and shortcuts?

If you answered "no" to any of these questions, you may need to develop some new notetaking skills!

Guidelines for Taking Notes

- Concentrate on the lecture or on the reading material.
- Take notes consistently.
- Take notes selectively.
  - Do NOT try to write down every word.
  - Remember that the average lecturer speaks approximately 125-140 words per minute, and the average note-taker writes at a rate of about 25 words per minute.
- Translate ideas into your own words.
- Organize notes into some sort of logical form.
- Be brief. Write down only the major points and important information.
- Write legibly. Notes are useless if you cannot read them later!
- Don't be concerned with spelling and grammar.

There are many reasons for taking lecture notes.

- Making yourself take notes forces you to listen carefully and test your understanding of the material.
- When you are reviewing, notes provide a gauge to what is important in the text.
- Personal notes are usually easier to remember than the text.
- The writing down of important points helps you to remember then even before you have studied the material formally.

Instructors usually give clues to what is important to take down. Some of the more common clues are:

- Material written on the blackboard.
- Repetition
- Emphasis
  - Emphasis can be judged by tone of voice and gesture.
  - Emphasis can be judged by the amount of time the instructor spends on points and the number of examples he or she uses.
- Word signals (e.g. "There are **two points of view** on . . . " "The **third** reason is . . . " " In **conclusion** . . . ")
- Summaries given at the end of class.
- Reviews given at the beginning of class.

Each student should develop his or her own method of taking notes, but most students find the following suggestions helpful:

- Make your notes brief.
  - Never use a sentence where you can use a phrase. Never use a phrase where you can use a word.

- –Use abbreviations and symbols, but be consistent.
- Put most notes in your own words. However, the following should be noted exactly:
  - –Formulas
  - –Definitions
  - – Specific facts
- Use outline form and/or a numbering system. Indention helps you distinguish major from minor points.
- Date your notes. Perhaps number the pages.
- If you miss a statement, write key words, skip a few spaces, and get the information later.
- Don't try to use every space on the page. Leave room for coordinating your notes with the text after the lecture. (You may want to list key terms in the margin or make a summary of the contents of the page.)

Here are some hints ("Do not's") regarding taking notes on classroom lectures that can save time for almost any student.

Do not plan to rewrite or type your notes later. To do so is to use a double amount of time; once to take the original notes a second to rewrite them. The advice is simple: DO IT RIGHT THE FIRST TIME!

Do not take notes in shorthand. Though shorthand is a valuable tool for a secretary, it is almost worthless for a student doing academic work. Here's why. Notes in shorthand cannot be studied in that form. They must first be transcribed. The act of transcribing notes takes an inordinate amount of time and energy but does not significantly contribute to their mastery. It is far better to have taken the notes originally in regular writing and then spend the time after that in direct study and **recitation** of the notes.

Do not record the lesson on a cassette tape or any other tape. The lecture on tape precludes flexibility. This statement can be better understood when seen in the light of a person who has taken his/her notes in regular writing. Immediately after taking the notes this person can study them in five minutes before the next class as s/he walks toward the next building, as s/he drinks his/her coffee, or whatever. Furthermore, this student, in looking over his/her notes, may decide that the notes contain only four worthwhile ideas which s/he can highlight, relegating the rest of the lecture to obscurity. Whereas the lecture on tape has to be listened to in its entirety including the worthwhile points as well as the "garbage," handwritten notes may be studied selectively. A student who takes the easy way out - recording the lecture on tape as he or she sits back doing nothing—will box him or herself into inflexibility.

Learning to make notes effectively will help you to improve your study and work habits and to remember important information. Often, students are deceived into thinking that because they **understand** everything that is said in class they will therefore remember it. This is dead wrong! Write it down.

As you make notes, you will develop skill in selecting important material and in discarding unimportant material. The secret to developing this skill is practice. Check your results constantly. Strive to improve. Notes enable you to retain important facts and data and to develop an accurate means of arranging necessary information.

Hints on Note Making

- Don't write down everything that you read or hear.
  - –Be alert and attentive to the main points.
  - –Concentrate on the "meat" of the subject and forget the trimmings.
- Notes should consist of key words or very short sentences. If a speaker gets sidetracked it

is often possible to go back and add further information.

- Take accurate notes.
  - –You should usually use your own words, but try not to change the meaning.
  - –If you quote **directly** from an author, quote **correctly**.
- Think a minute about your material before you start making notes.
  - –Don't take notes just to be taking notes!
  - –Take notes that will be of real value to you when you look over them at a later date.
- Have a uniform system of punctuation and abbreviation that will make sense to you.
  - –Use a skeleton outline and show importance by indenting.
  - –Leave lots of white space for later additions.
- Omit descriptions and full explanations.
  - –Keep your notes short and to the point.
  - –Condense your material so you can grasp it rapidly.
- Don't worry about missing a point.
- Don't keep notes on oddly shaped pieces of paper.
  - –Keep notes in order and in one place.
- Shortly after making your notes, go back and rework (not redo) your notes by adding extra points and spelling out unclear items.
  - – Remember, we forget rapidly. Budget time for this vital step just as you do for the class itself.
- Review your notes regularly. This is the only way to achieve lasting memory.

These are only a few of the many methods for taking notes.

- the Cornell Method
- the Outline Method
- the Mapping Method (or Mindmapping)
- the Charting Method
- the Sentence Method

For details on these methods, go to *http://www.sas.calpoly.edu/asc/ssl/notetaking.systems.html*. Also check out this resource about note taking: *http://www.how-to-study.com/Taking%20Notes%20in%20Class.htm*

Memory Techniques

We hope that the information on preparing to study has been helpful, but do you feel that your real problem is remembering? Don't worry. There are ways to help you build your memory skills too.

Acronym

- An *acronym* is defined as "a word formed from the initial letters of a name," such as PCS for permanent change of station or SOC for Servicemembers Opportunity Colleges, "or by combining initial letters or parts of a series of words," as radar for radio detecting and ranging.
- Can you think of other acronyms?

Mnemonic

- A *mnemonic* is defined as "a device, such as a formula or rhyme, used as an aid in remembering."

Examples

As a child, you might have determined the number of days in a given month

- by reciting the rhyme "Thirty days hath September, April, June, and November . . . ." or
- by using your knuckles ("peaks" have 31 days and "valleys" have 30, except February, of course).

If you have studied music, you might have used these techniques for remembering the names of the notes:

- FACE represents the names of the notes in the spaces on the staff.
- The first letters of the words in sentence "Every good boy does fine" represent the names of the notes on the lines on the staff.

A mnemonic used to recall the steps for simplifying algebraic expressions is "Please excuse my dear Aunt Sally."

- Perform operations within the innermost parentheses and work outward.
- Evaluate all exponential expressions.
- Perform multiplications and divisions as they occur, working from left to right.
- Perform additions and subtractions as they occur, working from left to right.

Use the sentence "My Very Educated Mother Just Served Us Nine Pizzas" to recall the order of the planets from the sun

- Mercury
- Venus
- Earth
- Mars
- Jupiter
- Saturn
- Uranus
- Neptune
- Pluto

Big Brown Rabbits Often Yield Great Big Vocal Groans When Gingerly Slapped for the color codes for resistors

- Black
- Brown
- Red
- Orange
- Yellow
- Green
- Blue
- Violet
- Gray
- White
- Gold
- Silver

Preparing For and Taking Tests

If you have practiced the strategies we have outlined in this orientation, you should be reviewing on a regular basis as you study rather than waiting to cram right before a test.

- Try to anticipate what is important and will be on the test, and use any review materials that are available, such as practice tests or review sheets.
- This doesn't mean that you don't need to study right before a test, but you shouldn't have to stay up all night to prepare for it, and you should feel more confident when you take the test.

Do You Suffer From Test Anxiety?

- Do you do great on homework assignments, but you dread test days?
- Do you forget everything you know when you sit down to take a test?
- Does it seem like what you studied has nothing to do with the test you are taking?

Once you are sitting in the hot spot with your pencil in hand, use the DETER strategy for taking tests as described at *http://www.how-to-study.com/A%20Strategy%20for%20Taking%20Tests.htm.*

Directions: Read and understand the test directions.
Examine: Examine the entire test to see what is required.
Time: Determine how much time to allow for each item.
Easiest: Answer the easiest items first.
Review: Allow time to review the test to check your answers for accuracy and completeness.

Again, practice makes perfect. There are several web sites for taking practice tests. Here are a few:

- *http://www.actstudent.org/testprep/index.html*
- *http://4tests.com/*
- *http://www.collegeboard.com/*
- *http://www.ets.org/*

Computer Basics

For many classes, you need to know the basics about using a computer and possibly even surfing the Internet in order to complete certain assignments. If you are taking a distance learning class, you MUST have some basic knowledge of computers and the Internet.

You must be able to

- prepare, save, and retrieve files
- send and receive emails with attachments
- deposit files in an electronic drop box
- locate and navigate web sites
- download software and plug ins
- participate in discussion boards.

A good resource for learning about these items is *http://www.learnthenet.com/english/index.html.*

- Once you have reached this site, note the "How To" list at the left side of the screen.
- If you are a novice, you might want to start with "How to Use this Site."
- Otherwise, start with "Master the Basics" and then work your way down the list.

You will find information ranging from making the connection to the Internet to building your own web site.

- Click on each underlined word or title to access the information.
- This information is also available as the "Animated Internet."

Jan's Illustrated Computer Literacy 101 at *http://www.jegsworks.com/Lessons/index.html* includes lessons on the topics listed on the next screens, and the approach is very detailed yet easy to understand. Even if you have never touched a mouse before, you should be able to follow along.

Do you want to learn about specific items; i.e., WindowsXP or MSWord2003?

- These are Microsoft products.
- You can go to *http://www.microsoft.com/* and find training on just about every product produced by Microsoft—even older versions.

The information above is just a teaser. We have included only a few websites because websites come and go. To learn more, check out the Internet and use a search engine, such as GOOGLE (*www.google.com*), to find sites on the topics we have referenced.

ABOUT THE
AUTHORS

Judith Nadell was until several years ago Associate Professor of Communications at Rowan University (New Jersey). During her eighteen years at Rowan, she coordinated the introductory course in the Freshman Writing Sequence and served as Director of the Writing Lab. In the past several years, she has developed a special interest in grassroots literacy. Besides designing an adult-literacy project, a children's reading-enrichment program, and a family-literacy initiative, she has worked as a volunteer tutor and a tutor trainer in the programs. A Phi Beta Kappa graduate of Tufts University, she received a doctorate from Columbia University. She is author of *Becoming a Read-Aloud Coach* (Townsend Press) and coauthor of *Doing Well in College* (McGraw-Hill), *Vocabulary Basics* (Townsend Press), and *The Longman Writer.* The recipient of a New Jersey award for excellence in the teaching of writing, Judith Nadell lives with her coauthor husband, John Langan, near Philadelphia.

John Langan has taught reading and writing courses at Atlantic Cape Community College near the New Jersey shore for more than twenty years. He earned an advanced degree in reading at Glassboro State College and another in writing at Rutgers University. Active in a mentoring program, he designed a reading-enrichment program for inner-city high school students and wrote a motivational and learning skills guidebook, *Ten Skills You Really Need to Succeed in School,* for urban youngsters. Coauthor of *The Longman Writer* and author of a series of college textbooks on both reading and writing, he has published widely with McGraw-Hill Book Company, Townsend Press, and Longman. His books include *English Skills, Reading and Study Skills,* and *College Writing Skills.*

Eliza A. Comodromos has taught composition and developmental writing in the English Departments of both Rutgers University and John Jay College of Criminal Justice. After graduating with a B.A. in English and in French from La Salle University, she did graduate work at the City University of New York Graduate School and went on to earn an advanced degree at Rutgers University, New Brunswick. A freelance editor and textbook consultant, Eliza Comodromos has delivered numerous papers at language and literature conferences around the country. She lives with her husband, Paul, and daughters, Anna Maria and Sophia Mae, near Philadelphia.

CONTENTS

3 DESCRIPTION   71

Having battled poverty and prejudice himself, writer-photographer
Gordon Parks visits a Brazilian slum and finds, among the wretched
thousands forgotten by the outside world, a dying yet smiling boy.

Three weeks after Hurricane Katrina, an environmentalist tours
New Orleans and the Gulf Coast to assess damage and the prospects
for recovery.

Hidden deep within herself after the trauma of a rape, a young girl is
escorted back into life by the grand lady of a small town.

Past, present, and future merge when White returns to a beloved
boyhood spot.

With wistful affection, the author recalls the laughter and lessons of the
late-afternoon gathering of women in her family.

4 NARRATION   123

5 EXEMPLIFICATION   169

7 PROCESS ANALYSIS   280

8 COMPARISON-CONTRAST   335

10 DEFINITION   432

11 ARGUMENTATION-PERSUASION 477

APPENDIX A: A CONCISE GUIDE TO FINDING AND DOCUMENTING SOURCES 607

APPENDIX B: AVOIDING TEN COMMON WRITING ERRORS 634

THEMATIC
CONTENTS

COMMUNICATION AND LANGUAGE

EDUCATION AND WORK

ETHICS AND MORALITY

FAMILY AND CHILDREN

GOVERNMENT AND LAW

HEALTH AND MEDICINE

HUMAN GROUPS AND SOCIETY

HUMOR AND SATIRE

MEANING IN LIFE

MEDIA AND TECHNOLOGY

MEMORIES AND AUTOBIOGRAPHY

MEN AND WOMEN

NATURE AND SCIENCE

PREFACE

The landscape of the college classroom has certainly evolved since the publication of the first edition of this book. The Internet has transformed not only how students acquire and communicate information but even how many instructors teach. Still, despite the forward march of technology, some things in education remain the same. Perhaps the most fundamental of these is the need for students to develop sound writing skills. It's to this mission that we continue to be committed.

When we first began working on *The Longman Reader,* we aimed for a different kind of text—one that would offer fresh examples of professional prose, one that would take a more active role in helping students become stronger readers, thinkers, and writers.

As in the first seven editions, our primary goal in the eighth edition has been to enliven the mix of selections commonly appearing in readers. *The Longman Reader* continues to include widely read and classic essays, as well as fresh new pieces, such as David Helvarg's "The Storm This Time" and Leslie Savan's "Black Talk and Pop Culture." We've been careful to choose selections that range widely in subject matter and approach, from the humorous to the informative, from personal meditation to polemic. We've also made sure that each selection captures students' interest and clearly illustrates a specific pattern of development or combination of patterns.

Our second concern has remained the quality of instruction in the book. As before, our objective has been to help students bridge the gap between the product and process approaches to reading and writing. Throughout, we describe possible sequences and structures but emphasize that such steps and formats are not meant to be viewed as rigid prescriptions; rather, they are strategies for helping students discover what works best in a particular situation. Buoyed by compliments about the previous editions' teachability, we haven't tinkered with the book's underlying format. Such a structure, we've been told, does indeed help students read more critically, think more logically, and write more skillfully. Here is the book's basic format.

- **Chapter 1, "The Reading Process,"** is designed to reflect current theories about the interaction of reading, thinking, and writing. The chapter provides guided practice in a three-part process for reading with close attention and a high level of interpretive skill. This step-by-step process sharpens students' understanding of the book's selections and promotes the rigorous thinking needed to write effective essays. An activity at the end of the chapter gives students a chance to use the three-step process. First, they read an essay by the journalist Ellen Goodman. The essay has been annotated both to show students the reading process in action and to illustrate how close critical reading can pave the way to promising writing topics. Then they respond to sample questions and writing assignments, all similar to those accompanying each of the book's selections. The chapter thus does more than just tell students how to sharpen their reading abilities; it guides them through a clearly sequenced plan for developing critical reading skills.
- **Chapter 2, "The Writing Process,"** introduces students to essay writing. To make the composing process easier for students to grasp, we provide a separate section for each of the following stages: prewriting, identifying a thesis, supporting the thesis with evidence, organizing the evidence, writing the first draft, and revising. From the start, we point out that the stages are fluid. Indeed, the case history of an evolving student paper illustrates just how recursive and individualized the writing process can be. Guided activities at the end of each section give students practice taking their essays through successive stages in the composing process.

  To illustrate the link between reading and writing, the writing chapter presents the progressive stages of a student paper written in response to Ellen Goodman's "Family Counterculture," the selection presented in Chapter 1. An easy-to-spot symbol in the margin ( ) makes it possible to locate—at a glance—this evolving student essay. Commentary following the student paper highlights the essay's strengths and points out spots that could use additional work. In short, by the end of the second chapter, the entire reading-writing process has been illustrated, from reading a selection to writing about it.

• **Chapters 3–11** of *The Longman Reader* contain selections grouped according to **nine patterns of development:** description, narration, exemplification, division-classification, process analysis, comparison-contrast, cause-effect, definition, and argumentation-persuasion. The sequence progresses from the more personal and expressive patterns to the more public and analytic. However, because each chapter is self-contained, the patterns may be covered in any order. Instructors preferring a thematic approach will find the Thematic Contents helpful.

The Longman Reader treats the patterns separately because such an approach helps students grasp the distinctive characteristics of each pattern. At the same time, the book continually shows the way writers usually combine patterns in their work. We also encourage students to view the patterns as strategies for generating and organizing ideas. Writers, we explain, rarely set out to compose an essay in a specific pattern. Rather, they choose a pattern or combination of patterns because it suits their purpose, audience, and subject.

Each of the nine pattern-of-development chapters follows this format:

1. **A detailed explanation of the pattern** begins the chapter. The explanation includes (a) a definition of the pattern, (b) a description of the way the pattern helps a writer accommodate his or her purpose and audience, and (c) step-by-step guidelines for using the pattern.

2. Next, we present **an annotated student essay** using the pattern. Written in response to one of the professional selections in the chapter, each essay illustrates the characteristic features of the pattern discussed in the chapter.

3. **Commentary** after each student essay points out the blend of patterns in the piece, identifies the paper's strengths, and locates areas needing improvement. "First draft" and "revised" versions of one section of the essay reveal how the student writer went about revising, thus illustrating the relationship between the final draft and the steps taken to produce it.

4. The **professional selections** in the pattern-of-development chapters are accompanied by these items.

   • *A biographical note and "Pre-Reading Journal Entry"* give students a perspective on the author and create interest in the piece. The journal assignment "primes" students for the selection by encouraging them to explore—in a loose, unpressured way—their thoughts about an issue that will be raised in the selection. The journal entry thus motivates students to read the piece with extra care, attention, and personal investment.

- *Questions for Close Reading,* five in all, help students dig into and interpret the selection. The first question asks them to identify the selection's thesis; the last provides work on vocabulary development.
- *Questions About the Writer's Craft,* four in all, deal with such matters as purpose, audience, tone, organization, sentence structure, diction, and figures of speech. The first question in the series (labeled "The Pattern") focuses on the distinctive features of the pattern used in the selection. And usually there's another question (labeled "Other Patterns") that asks students to analyze the writer's use of additional patterns in the piece.
- *Writing Assignments,* five in all, follow each selection. Packed with suggestions on how to proceed, the assignments use the selection as a springboard. The first two assignments ask students to write an essay using the same pattern as the one used in the selection; the next two assignments encourage students to experiment with a combination of patterns in their own essay; the last assignment helps students turn the raw material in their pre-reading journal entries into fully considered essays. By the time students reach this final assignment, the rough ideas in their journals will have been enriched by a careful reading of the selection, setting the stage for more rigorously conceived essays. *The value of collaborative learning is underscored throughout,* as many assignments encourage students to investigate various sides of an issue by brainstorming with classmates, questioning friends, speaking with family members, or interviewing "experts." Such assignments help students formulate sound, well-reasoned opinions and steer them away from reflexive, off-the-cuff positions. Frequently, the assignments are preceded by the symbol ∞, indicating a cross-reference to at least one other selection in the book. By encouraging students to make connections among readings, such assignments broaden students' perspective and give them additional material to draw on when they write. These "paired assignments" will be especially welcome to instructors stressing recurring ideas and themes. In other cases, assignments are preceded by the symbol 💻, indicating that students might benefit from conducting library and/or Internet research.

5. **Prewriting and revising activities,** placed in shaded boxes at the end of each chapter, help students understand the unique demands posed by the pattern being studied.

6. At the end of each pattern-of-development chapter are two sets of **Additional Writing Assignments:** "General Assignments" and "Assignments With a Specific Purpose, Audience, and Point of

View." The first set provides open-ended topics that prompt students to discover the best way to use a specific pattern; the second set develops their sensitivity to rhetorical context by asking them to apply the pattern in a real-world situation.

- **Chapter 12, "Combining the Patterns,"** offers a sample student essay as well as two essays each by three very different prose stylists. Annotations on the student essay and on one of the professional selections show how writers often blend patterns of development in their work. The chapter also provides guidelines to help students analyze this fusing of patterns.
- **Appendix A, "A Concise Guide to Finding and Documenting Sources,"** provides guidelines for conducting library and Internet research and for citing print and electronic sources.
- **Appendix B, "Avoiding Ten Common Writing Errors,"** targets common problem areas in student writing and offers quick, accessible solutions for each.

The Longman Reader also includes a glossary that lists all the key terms presented in the text.

WHAT'S NEW IN THE EIGHTH EDITION

In preparing this edition, we looked closely at the questionnaires completed by instructors using the book. Their comments helped us identify new directions the book might take. Here are some of the new features of this edition of *The Longman Reader.*

- *Striking new visuals now open every pattern-of-development chapter.* Far from being just window dressing, these visuals have *real pedagogical value.* Chapters (3–11) begin with an engaging photo, which reappears in thumbnail form following the "How [*name of pattern*] Fits Your Purpose and Audience" section. There, the image prompts a pattern-related writing activity that encourages students to consider issues of purpose and audience in a piece of real-world writing.
- *In other ways, too, the book's design is more attractive and user-friendly than ever. A new vibrant color format makes key information, such as annotations, more accessible.*
- *Nearly one-fifth of the selections are new.* Many of these readings were suggested by instructors across the country; others were chosen after a lengthy search through print and online magazines, nonfiction collections, newspapers, autobiographies, and the like. Whether written by a well-known figure such as Stanley Fish ("Free-Speech Follies") or a relative newcomer such as Charmie Gholson ("Charity Display?"), the

new selections are bound to stimulate strong writing on a variety of topics—family life, education, technology, race, mass culture, and morality, to name a few. When selecting new readings, we took special care to include pieces written from the first- and the second-person point of view (for example, David Shipley's "Talk About Editing") as well as those written from the third-person point of view (for example, Natalie Angier's "The Cute Factor"). Honoring the requests of many instructors, we also made an effort to find compelling pieces on education and on technology. David Brooks' "Psst! 'Human Capital' " is one such piece. Finally, we're pleased to include thought-provoking selections examining the issue of illegal immigration. For example, a new set of paired essays (Roberto Rodriguez's "The Border on Our Backs" and Star Parker's "*Se Habla* Entitlement") debates the hotly contested question of how the U.S. government should handle the nation's large number of illegal immigrants.

- *The comprehensive argumentation-persuasion chapter further expands coverage of refutation strategies by presenting a provocative new pair of professional essays on illegal immigration.*
- The *research paper* has been *updated* to reflect the *most recent MLA guidelines regarding the use of electronic sources.*
- *Appendix A, "A Concise Guide to Finding and Documenting Sources," has been updated and includes additional citation examples for students.* This chapter includes *up-to-date information on both library and Internet research, highlighting the most useful and authoritative research tools and sources.* The sample MLA bibliographic entries have been revised to reflect the most recent guidelines regarding the documentation of print and electronic sources.

Supplements for Students and Instructors

A comprehensive *Instructor's Manual* contains the following: in-depth answers to the "Questions for Close Reading" and "Questions About the Writer's Craft"; suggested activities; pointers about using the book; a detailed syllabus; and an analysis of the blend of patterns in the selections in the "Combining the Patterns" chapter.

A *Companion Website* (www.ablongman.com/nadell), written by Karen Grandy, offers a number of *helpful features,* including review and writing exercises and thematic groupings of links to other sites of interest. The Instructor's Resources section includes links of interest to instructors, a sample syllabus, and sample grading rubrics.

ACKNOWLEDGMENTS

At Longman, our thanks go to Lauren Finn for her perceptive editorial guidance and enthusiasm for *The Longman Reader.* We're also indebted to Linda

Stern, our Development Editor, and to Heather Johnson of Elm Street Publishing Services, Inc., and Eric Jorgensen of Longman for their skillful handling of the never-ending complexities of the production process.

Over the years, many writing instructors have reviewed *The Longman Reader* and responded to detailed questionnaires about its selections and pedagogy. Their comments have guided our work every step of the way. To the following reviewers we are indeed grateful: Donald W. Adams, Chipola Junior College; James C. Addison, Jr., Western Carolina University; Rebecca L. Allen, Louisburg College; Joseph A. Alvarez, Central Piedmont Community College; Ken Anania, Massasoit Community College; Chris Anson, University of Minnesota; Bruce J. Ardinger, Columbus State Community College; Martha R. Bachman, Camden County College; Constantina Rhodes Bailly, Hillsborough Community College; Mary Beth Bamforth, Wake Technical Community College; B. G. Bardin, Rogers State College; A. M. Belmont, Southern Arkansas University; Robert P. Berman, Wake Technical Community College; Carol Bledsoe, Florida Gulf Coast University; Wilson C. Boynton, Holyoke Community College; Susan Buchler, Montgomery County Community College; John S. Capps, Virginia Western Community College; Ursula Carfagno, Montgomery County Community College; Barbara Carr, Stephen F. Austin State University; Amy M. Clarke, Sierra College; Bruce Coad, Mountain View College; David Cole, Quinnipaic College; Viralene J. Coleman, University of Arkansas, Pine Bluff; Howard J. Coughlin, Jr., Eastern Connecticut University; George Cox, Johnston Community College; Charles R. Croghan, Jr., Indian River Community College; Michael Cross, Tulsa Junior College; Laurie Culbreth, Chipola Junior College; F. Marino D'Amato, Manchester Community College; Lincoln Davis, Imperial Valley College; Betty Keating Dietz, Ohlone College; Benjamin B. Edwards, Tulsa Junior College; Mary Faraci, Florida Atlantic University; Benjamin Fiester, Wilkes College; Raymond W. Foster, Scottsdale Community College; Sister Pauline Fox, Mt. Mercy College; Margaret Franson, Valparaiso University; Nancy N. Frazer, Fairmont State College; Lois Friesen, Butler County Community College; Ann Mace Futrell, Louisiana Technical University; Loris D. Galford, McNeese State University; Anita Gandolfo, West Virginia University; Michael G. Gessner, Central Arizona College; Casey Gilson, Broward Community College; Roberta Grantham, Chipola Junior College; Patricia Graves, Georgia State University; Michael Gress, Vincennes University; Chrysanthy M. Grieco, Seton Hall University; Gary Griswold, California State University, Long Beach; Harrabeth A. Haidusek, Lamar University; Mary M. Hatcher, Burlington County College; Betty Boyd Heard, Averett College; Angela Hilterbrand, Ashland Community College; Jean Hodgin, North Shore Community College; Patricia Hummel, Albright College; Ginger A. Hurajt, Northern Essex Community College; Mary L. Hurst, Cuyahoga Community College; Eleanor D. James, Montgomery County Community College;

Wanda L. Jared, Tennessee Technological University; Shakuntala Jayswal, University of New Haven; Scott P. Johnson, Bethel College; Kellie Jones, University of Tennessee at Martin; David Kelly, Dyersburg State Community College; Elaine Kromhout, Indian River Community College; Jennifer Lane, Glendale Community College; Sue V. Lape, Columbus State Community College; Stephen Larson, Wake Technical Community College; Kristin LaTour, Central Texas College; Robert Lesman, Northern Virginia Community College; Carol Liebscher, Montgomery County Community College; Teri Maddox, Jackson State Community College; Barry Maid, University of Arkansas at Little Rock; Paul Marx, University of New Haven; Catherine Mau, Leeward Community College; Joseph F. McCadden, Burlington County College; Mary Ann McCandless, Butler County Community College; Brian McRea, University of Florida; Elizabeth Metzger, University of South Florida; Teresa Miller, Rogers State University; Kathy Mincey, Morehead State University; R. H. Moody, Madison Area Tech College; Robert Mugford, Scottsdale Community College; Roxanne Munch, Joliet Junior College; Allison Murray, Long Beach City College; Monique E. Neal, University of Delaware; Grace C. Ocasio, Central Piedmont Community College; Steve Odden, University of Wisconsin at Stevens Point; Thomas B. O'Grady, University of Massachusetts, Boston; Michael G. O'Hara, Muscatine Community College; Daniel Olson, North Harris College; Richard Pepp, Massasoit Community College; Lillian Polak, Nassau Community College; Barbara J. Porter, Canisius College; Patricia M. Price, Virginia Western Community College; M. Cathleen Raymond, Florida Atlantic University; Taryn Rice, Johnston Community College; John Rogers, Vincennes University; Rhonda Lemke Sanford, Fairmont State College; Irene Schiller, Camden County College; Susan Schmeling, Vincennes University; Marcia Bundy Seabury, University of Hartford; Marie Secor, Pennsylvania State University; Rita J. Self, Lamar University; Mary L. Simpson, Central Texas College; Carl Singleton, Fort Hays State University; Carolyn Smith, University of Florida; Eric R. Smith, SUNY College at Cortland; James Gregory Smith, Lamar University; Margo Smith, Rogers State College; Cynthia Somin, Long Beach City College; Charles Staats, Broward Community College–North; Judith Stanford, Merrimack College; Jacqueline Stark, Los Angeles Valley College; Virginia Stein, Community College of Allegheny County; Suzanne St. Laurent, Broward Community College; George Stoll, Broward Community College–North; Ralph Sturm, Edinboro University of Pennsylvania; Charles Swannell, Burlington Community College; John W. Taylor, South Dakota State University; Merle Thompson, North Virginia Community College; Robert Thompson, Macomb County Community College; Vivian Tortorici, Hudson Valley Community College; Sinéad Waters Turner, Wake Technical Community College; Larry K. Uffelman, Mansfield University; Victor Uszerowicz, Miami-Dade Community College; Cyrilla M. Vessey, Northern Virginia Community College; Anna Villegas, San Joaquin

Delta College; Cheryl L. Ware, McNeese State University; Patricia M. Wheeler, Central Piedmont Community College; Deanna M. White, University of Texas at San Antonio; Mildred J. White, Ohlone College; Samuel W. Whyte, Montgomery County Community College; David Wickham, Mountain View College; Dorena Allen Wright, Loyola Marymount University; Wei-hsiung Kitty Wu, Bowie State University; Donnie Yeilding, Central Texas College; and Sam Zahran, Fayetteville Technical Community College.

We also thank the following reviewers for the valuable assistance they have provided during the preparation of the eighth edition of *The Longman Reader:* Shadric Baker, Delaware Technical and Community College; Carlos Campo, Community College of Southern Nevada; Mary Cantrell, Tulsa Community College; Brenda Cornell, Central Texas College; Anne Gowdy, University of Mississippi; Tammy Jabin, Chemeketa Community College; David A. James, Houston Community College–Northwest; Eleanor James, Montgomery County Community College; Donna Lad, Blue Ridge Community College; Philip Lane, Miami Dade College, Wolfson Campus; Richard Levesque, Fullerton College; Rebecca Mullen, Vincennes University; Sean Nighbert, St. Philips College; Susan Palmer, San Jacinto College North; Sharon Prince, Wharton County Junior College; Jim Sanderson, Lamar University; James R. Sodon, St. Louis Community College; Rosie Soy, Hudson County Community College; and April Van Camp, Indian River Community College.

Our work on this edition was influenced too by the many students who took advantage of the questionnaire at the back of the seventh edition to tell us which selections they preferred.

Thanks also go to Jennifer Druce and the staff of very knowledgeable research librarians at the Camden County Library in Voorhees, New Jersey, for sharing their expertise on library and Internet research.

Some individuals from our at-home office deserve special thanks. During the preparation of the eighth edition, Marion Castellucci provided valuable assistance with the apparatus. Finally, as always, we're thankful to our students. Their reaction to various drafts of material sharpened our thinking and helped focus our work. And we are especially indebted to the eleven students whose essays are included in the book. Their thoughtful, carefully revised papers dramatize the potential of student writing and the power of the composing process.

Judith Nadell
John Langan
Eliza A. Comodromos

THE
LONGMAN
READER

THE READING PROCESS

More than two hundred years ago, essayist Joseph Addison commented, "Of all the diversions of life, there is none so proper to fill up its empty spaces as the reading of useful and entertaining authors." Addison might have added that reading also challenges our beliefs, deepens our awareness, and stimulates our imagination.

Why, then, don't more people delight in reading? After all, most children feel great pleasure and pride when they first learn to read. As children grow older, though, the initially magical world of books is increasingly associated with homework, tests, and grades. Reading turns into an anxiety-producing chore. Also, as demands on a person's time accumulate throughout adolescence and adulthood, reading often gets pushed aside in favor of something that takes less effort. It's easier simply to switch on the television and passively view the ready-made images that flash across the screen. In contrast, it's almost impossible to remain passive while reading. Even a slick best-seller requires that the reader decode, visualize, and interpret what's on the page. The more challenging the material, the more actively involved the reader must be.

The essays we selected for this book call for active reading. Representing a broad mix of styles and subjects, the essays range from the classic to the contemporary. They contain language that will move you, images that will enlarge your understanding of other people, and ideas that will transform your views on complex issues.

The selections serve other purposes as well. For one thing, they'll help you develop a repertoire of reading skills—abilities that will benefit you throughout life. Second, as you become a better reader, your own writing style will become more insightful and polished. Increasingly, you'll be able to draw on the ideas presented in the selections and employ the techniques that professional writers use to express such ideas. As novelist Saul Bellow has observed, "A writer is a reader moved to emulation."

In the pages ahead, we outline a three-stage approach for getting the most out of this book's selections. Our suggestions will enhance your understanding of the book's essays, as well as help you read other material with greater ease and assurance.

STAGE 1: GET AN OVERVIEW OF THE SELECTION

Ideally, you should get settled in a quiet place that encourages concentration. If you can focus your attention while sprawled on a bed or curled up in a chair, that's fine. But if you find that being very comfortable is more conducive to daydreaming and dozing off than it is to studying, avoid getting too relaxed.

Once you're settled, it's time to read the selection. To ensure a good first reading, try the following hints.

☑ FIRST READING: A CHECKLIST

❑ Start by reading the biographical note that precedes the selection. By providing background information about the author, the biographical note helps you evaluate the writer's credibility as well as his or her slant on the subject. For example, if you know that Leslie Savan has written extensively about advertising, for major broadcast and print media, you can better assess whether she is a credible source for the material she presents in her essay "Black Talk and Pop Culture" (page 193).

❑ Do the *Pre-Reading Journal Entry* assignment, which precedes the selection. This assignment "primes" you for the piece by helping you to explore—in an easy, unpressured way—your thoughts about a key point raised in the selection. By preparing the journal entry, you're inspired to read the selection with special care, attention, and personal investment. (For more on pre-reading journal entries, see pages 14–16 and 654.)

❑ Consider the selection's title. A good title often expresses the essay's main idea, giving you insight into the selection even before you read it. For example, the title of Yuh Ji-Yeon's "Let's Tell the Story of All America's Cultures" (page 517) suggests that the piece will advocate multiculturalism. A title may also hint at a selection's tone. Paul Roberts's "How to Say Nothing in 500 Words" (page 314) points to an essay that's light in spirit, whereas George Orwell's "Shooting an Elephant" (page 143) suggests a piece with a serious mood.

❑ Read the selection straight through purely for pleasure. Allow yourself to be drawn into the world the author has created. Just as you first see a painting from the doorway of a room and form an overall impression without perceiving the details, you can have a preliminary, subjective feeling about a reading selection. Moreover, because you bring your own experiences and viewpoints to the piece, your reading will be unique. As Ralph Waldo Emerson said, "Take the book, my friend, and read your eyes out; you will never find there what I find."

❏ After this initial reading of the selection, focus your first impressions by asking yourself whether you like the selection. In your own words, briefly describe the piece and your reaction to it.

STAGE 2: DEEPEN YOUR SENSE OF THE SELECTION

At this point, you're ready to move more deeply into the selection. A second reading will help you identify the specific features that triggered your initial reaction.

There are a number of techniques you can use during this second, more focused reading. You may, for example, find it helpful to adapt some of the strategies that Mortimer Adler, a well-known writer and editor, wrote about in his 1940 essay "How to Mark a Book." There, Adler argues passionately for marking up the material we read. The physical act of annotating, he believes, etches the writer's ideas more sharply in the mind, helping readers grasp and remember those ideas more easily. And "best of all," Adler writes, the "marks and notes . . . stay there forever. You can pick up the . . . [material] the following week or year, and there are all your points of agreement, doubt, and inquiry. It's like resuming an uninterrupted conversation."

Adler goes on to describe various annotation techniques he uses when reading. Several of these techniques, adapted somewhat, are presented in the checklist below.

☑ SECOND READING: A CHECKLIST

Using a pen (or pencil) and highlighter, you might . . .

❏ Underline or highlight the selection's main idea, or thesis, often found near the beginning or end. If the thesis isn't stated explicitly, write down your own version of the selection's main idea.

❏ Place numbers in the margin to designate the main points that support the thesis.

❏ Circle or put an asterisk next to key ideas that are stated more than once.

❏ Take a minute to write "Yes," "No," or a brief comment beside points with which you strongly agree or disagree. Your reaction to these points often explains your feelings about the aptness of the selection's ideas.

❑ Return to any unclear passages you encountered during the first reading. The feeling you now have for the piece as a whole will probably help you make sense of initially confusing spots. However, this second reading may also reveal that, in places, the writer's thinking isn't as clear as it could be. If that's the case, you might put a question mark in the margin beside the unclear material.

❑ Put brackets around words whose meaning you need to check in a dictionary.

❑ Ask yourself if your initial impression of the selection has changed in any way as a result of this second reading. If your feelings *have* changed, try to determine why you reacted differently on this reading.

STAGE 3: EVALUATE THE SELECTION

Now that you have a good grasp of the selection, you may want to read it a third time, especially if the piece is long or complex. This time, your goal is to make judgments about the essay's effectiveness. Keep in mind, though, that you shouldn't evaluate the selection until after you have a strong hold on it. A negative or even a positive reaction is valid only if it's based on an accurate reading.

At first, you may feel uncomfortable about evaluating the work of a professional writer. But remember: Written material set in type only *seems* perfect; all writing can be finetuned. By identifying what does and doesn't work in others' writing, you're taking an important first step toward developing your own power as a writer. You might find it helpful at this point to get together with other students to discuss the selection. Comparing viewpoints often opens up a piece, enabling you to gain a clearer perspective on the selection and the author's approach.

To evaluate the essay, ask yourself the following questions.

☑ EVALUATING A SELECTION: A CHECKLIST

❑ *Where does support for the selection's thesis seem logical and sufficient? Where does support seem weak?* Which of the author's supporting facts, arguments, and examples seem pertinent and convincing? Which don't?

❑ *Is the selection unified? If not, why not?* Where does something in the selection not seem relevant? Where are there any unnecessary digressions or detours?

❑ *How does the writer make the selection move smoothly from beginning to end?* How does the writer create an easy flow between ideas? Are any parts of the essay abrupt and jarring? Which ones?

❑ *Which stylistic devices are used to good effect in the selection?* Which *pattern of development* or combination of patterns does the writer use to develop the piece? Why do you think those patterns were selected? How do paragraph development, sentence structure, and word choice contribute to the piece's overall effect? What *tone* does the writer adopt? Where does the writer use *figures of speech* effectively? (The next chapter and the glossary explain the terms shown here in italics.)

❑ *How does the selection encourage further thought?* What new perspective on an issue does the writer provide? What ideas has the selection prompted you to explore in an essay of your own?

It takes some work to follow the three-step approach just described, but the selections in *The Longman Reader* are worth the effort. Bear in mind that none of the selections sprang full-blown from the pen of its author. Rather, each essay is the result of hours of work—hours of thinking, writing, rethinking, and revising. As a reader, you should show the same willingness to work with the selections, to read them carefully and thoughtfully. Henry David Thoreau, an avid reader and prolific writer, emphasized the importance of this kind of attentive reading when he advised that "books must be read as deliberately and unreservedly as they were written."

To illustrate the multi-stage reading process just described, we've annotated the professional essay that follows: "Family Counterculture" by Ellen Goodman. Note that annotations are provided in the margin of the essay as well as at the end of the essay. As you read Goodman's essay, try applying the three-stage sequence. You can measure your ability to dig into the selection by making your own annotations on Goodman's essay and then comparing them to ours. You can also see how well you evaluated the piece by answering the questions in "Evaluating a Selection: A Checklist" and then comparing your responses to ours on pages 9–10.

Ellen Goodman

The recipient of a Pulitzer Prize, Ellen Goodman (1941–) worked for *Newsweek* and the *Detroit Free Press* before joining the staff of the *Boston Globe* in the mid-1970s. A resident of the Boston area, Goodman writes a popular syndicated column that provides insightful commentary on life in the United States. Her pieces have appeared in a number of national publications, including *The Village Voice* and *McCalls*. Collections of her columns have been published in *Close to Home* (1979), *Turning Points* (1979), *At Large* (1981), *Keeping in Touch* (1985), *Making Sense* (1989), and *Value Judgments* (1993). Most recently, she coauthored *I Know Just What You Mean* (1999), a book that examines the complex nature of women's friendships, and *Paper Trail* (2004). The following selection is from *Value Judgments*.

Pre-Reading Journal Entry

Television is often blamed for having a harmful effect on children. Do you think this criticism is merited? In what ways does TV exert a negative influence on children? In what ways does TV exert a positive influence on youngsters? Take a few minutes to respond to these questions in your journal.

Marginal Annotations

Family Counterculture

Interesting take on the term "counterculture"

Sooner or later, most Americans become card-carrying members of the counterculture. This is not an underground holdout of hippies. No beads are required. All you need to join is a child.

Time frame established

Light humor; easy, casual tone

At some point between Lamaze and the PTA, it becomes clear that one of your main jobs as a parent is to counter the culture. What the media delivers to children by the masses, you are expected to rebut one at a time.

Time frame picked up

Thesis, developed overall by cause-effect pattern

The latest evidence of this frustrating piece of the parenting job description came from pediatricians. This summer, the American Academy of Pediatrics called for a ban on television food ads. Their plea was hard on the heels of a study showing that one Saturday morning of TV cartoons contained 202 junk-food ads.

First research-based example to support thesis

The kids see, want, and nag. That is, after all, the theory behind advertising to children, since few six-year-olds

6

have their own trust funds. The end result, said the pediatricians, is obesity and high cholesterol.

5 Their call for a ban was predictably attacked by the grocers' association. But it was also attacked by people assembled under the umbrella marked "parental responsibility." We don't need bans, said these "PR" people, we need parents who know how to say "no."

Relevant paragraph? Identifies Goodman as a parent, but interrupts flow

6 Well, I bow to no one in my capacity for naysaying. I agree that it's a well-honed skill of child raising. By the time my daughter was seven, she qualified as a media critic.

Transition doesn't work but would if ¶6 were cut

7 But it occurs to me now that the call for "parental responsibility" is increasing in direct proportion to the irresponsibility of the marketplace. Parents are expected to protect their children from an increasingly hostile environment.

Series of questions and brief answers consistent with overall casual tone

8 Are the kids being sold junk food? Just say no. Is TV bad? Turn it off. Are there messages about sex, drugs, violence all around? Counter the culture.

Brief real-life examples support thesis

9 Mothers and fathers are expected to screen virtually every aspect of their children's lives. To check the ratings on the movies, to read the labels on the CDs, to find out if there's MTV in the house next door. All the while keeping in touch with school and, in their free time, earning a living.

Fragments

10 In real life, most parents do a great deal of this monitoring and just-say-no-ing. Any trip to the supermarket produces at least one scene of a child grabbing for something only to have it returned to the shelf by a frazzled parent. An extraordinary number of the family arguments are over the goodies—sneakers, clothes, games—that the young know only because of ads.

More examples

11 But at times it seems that the media have become the mainstream culture in children's lives. Parents have become the alternative.

Another weak transition—no contrast

Restatement of thesis

12 Barbara Dafoe Whitehead, a research associate at the Institute for American Values, found this out in interviews with middle-class parents. "A common complaint I heard from parents was their sense of being overwhelmed by the culture. They felt their voice was a lot weaker. And they felt relatively more helpless than their parents.

Second research-based example to support thesis

Citing an expert reinforces thesis

13 "Parents," she notes, "see themselves in a struggle for the hearts and minds of their own children." It isn't that they can't say no. It's that there's so much more to say no to.

Restatement of thesis

14 Without wallowing in false nostalgia, there has been a fundamental shift. Americans once expected parents to raise

Comparison-
contrast pattern—
signaled by
"once," "Today,"
"Once," and
"Now"

their children in accordance with the dominant cultural messages. Today they are expected to raise their children in opposition.

Once the chorus of cultural values was full of ministers, teachers, neighbors, leaders. They demanded more conformity, but offered more support. Now the messengers are Ninja Turtles, Madonna, rap groups, and celebrities pushing sneakers. Parents are considered "responsible" only if they are successful in their resistance.   15

Restatement
of thesis

It's what makes child raising harder. It's why parents feel more isolated. It's not just that American families have less time with their kids. It's that we have to spend more of this time doing battle with our own culture.   16

Conveys the
challenges that
parents face

It's rather like trying to get your kids to eat their green beans after they've been told all day about the wonders of Milky Way. Come to think of it, it's exactly like that.   17

Annotations at End of Selection

Thesis: First stated in paragraph 2 (". . . it becomes clear that one of your main jobs as a parent is to counter the culture. What the media delivers to children by the masses, you are expected to rebut one at a time.") and then restated in paragraphs 11 ("the media have become the mainstream culture in children's lives. Parents have become the alternative."); 13 (Parents are frustrated, not because ". . . they can't say no. It's that there's so much more to say no to."); and 16 ("It's not just that American families have less time with their kids. It's that we have to spend more of this time doing battle with our own culture.").

First reading: A quick take on a serious subject. Informal tone and to-the-point style gets to the heart of the media vs. parenting problem. Easy to relate to.

Second and third readings:
1. Uses the findings of the American Academy of Pediatrics, a statement made by Barbara Dafoe Whitehead, and a number of brief examples to illustrate the relentless work parents must do to counter the culture.
2. Uses cause-effect overall to support thesis and comparison-contrast to show how parenting nowadays is more difficult than it used to be.
3. Not everything works (reference to her daughter as a media critic, repetitive and often inappropriate use of "but" as a transition), but overall the essay succeeds.
4. At first, the ending seems weak. But it feels just right after an additional reading. Shows how parents' attempts to counter the culture are as commonplace as their attempts to get kids to eat vegetables. It's an ongoing and constant battle that makes parenting more difficult than it has to be and less enjoyable than it should be.
5. Possible essay topics: A humorous paper about the strategies kids use to get around their parents' saying "no" or a serious paper on the negative effects on kids of another aspect of television culture (cable television, MTV, tabloid-style talk shows, and so on).

The following answers to the questions in "Evaluating a Selection: A Checklist" on pages 4–5 will help crystallize your reaction to Goodman's essay.

1. *Where does support for the selection's thesis seem logical and sufficient? Where does support seem weak?*

Goodman begins to provide evidence for her thesis when she cites the American Academy of Pediatrics' call for a "ban on television food ads" (paragraphs 3–5). The ban followed a study showing that kids are exposed to 202 junk-food ads during a single Saturday morning of television cartoons. Goodman further buoys her thesis with a list of brief "countering the culture" examples (8–10) and a slightly more detailed example (10) describing the parent-child conflicts that occur on a typical trip to the supermarket. By citing Barbara Dafoe Whitehead's findings later on (12–13), Goodman further reinforces her point that the need for constant rebuttal makes parenting especially frustrating: Because parents have to say "no" to virtually everything, more and more family time ends up being spent "doing battle" with the culture (16).

2. *Is the selection unified? If not, why not?*

In the first two paragraphs, Goodman identifies the problem and then provides solid evidence of its existence (3–4, 8–10). But Goodman's comments in paragraph 6 about her daughter's skill as a media critic seem distracting. Even so, paragraph 6 serves a purpose because it establishes Goodman's credibility by showing that she, too, is a parent and has been compelled to be a constant naysayer with her child. From paragraph 7 on, the piece stays on course by focusing on the way parents have to compete with the media for control of their children. The concluding paragraphs (16–17) reinforce Goodman's thesis by suggesting that parents' struggle to counteract the media is as common—and as exasperating—as trying to get children to eat their vegetables when all the kids want is to gorge on candy.

3. *How does the writer make the selection move smoothly from beginning to end?*

The first two paragraphs of Goodman's essay are clearly connected: The phrase "sooner or later" at the beginning of the first paragraph establishes a time frame that is then picked up at the beginning of the second paragraph with the phrase "at some point between Lamaze and the PTA." And Goodman's use in paragraph 3 of the word *this* ("The latest evidence of *this* frustrating piece of the parenting job description . . .") provides a link to the preceding paragraph. Other connecting strategies can be found in the piece. For example, the words *once, Today, Once,* and *Now* in paragraphs 14–15 provide an easy-to-follow contrast between parenting in earlier times and parenting in this era. However, because paragraph 6 contains a distracting aside, the contrast implied by the word *But* at the beginning of paragraph 7 doesn't work. Nor does Goodman's use of the word *But* at the beginning of paragraph 11 work; the point there emphasizes rather than contrasts with the one made in paragraph 10. From this point on, though, the essay is tightly written and moves smoothly along to its conclusion.

4. *Which stylistic devices are used to good effect in the selection?*

Goodman uses several patterns of development in her essay. The selection as a whole shows the *effect* of the mass media on kids and their parents. In paragraphs 3 and 12, Goodman provides *examples in the form of research data* to support her thesis, while paragraphs 8–10 provide a series of *brief real-life examples*. Paragraphs 12–15 use *contrast*, and paragraph 17 makes a *comparison* to punctuate Goodman's concluding point. Throughout, Goodman's *informal, conversational tone* draws readers in, and her *no-holds-barred style* drives her point home forcefully. In paragraph 8, she uses a *question-and-answer format* ("Are the kids being sold junk food? Just say no.") and *short sentences* ("Turn it off" and "Counter the culture") to illustrate how pervasive the situation is. And in paragraph 9, she uses *fragments* ("To check the ratings . . ." and "All the while keeping in touch with school . . .") to focus attention on the problem. These varied stylistic devices help make the essay a quick, enjoyable read. Finally, although Goodman is concerned about the corrosive effects of the media, she leavens her essay with dashes of *humor*. For example, the image of parents as counterculturists (1) and the comments about green beans and Milky Ways (17) probably elicit smiles or gentle laughter from most readers.

5. *How does the selection encourage further thought?*

Goodman's essay touches on a problem most parents face at some time or another—having to counter the culture in order to protect their children. Her main concern is how difficult it is for parents to say "no" to virtually every aspect of the culture. Although Goodman offers no immediate solutions, her presentation of the issue urges us to decide for ourselves which aspects of the culture should be countered and which should not.

If, for each essay you read in this book, you consider the preceding questions, you'll be able to respond thoughtfully to the *Questions for Close Reading* and *Questions About the Writer's Craft* presented after each selection. Your responses will, in turn, prepare you for the writing assignments that follow the questions. Interesting and varied, the assignments invite you to examine issues raised by the selections and encourage you to experiment with various writing styles and organizational patterns.

Following are some sample questions and writing assignments based on the Goodman essay; all are similar to the sort that appear later in this book. Note that the final writing assignment paves the way for a student essay, the stages of which are illustrated in Chapter 2.

Questions for Close Reading

1. According to Goodman, what does it mean to "counter the culture"? Why is this harder now than ever before?
2. Which two groups, according to Goodman, protested the American Academy of Pediatrics's ban on television food ads? Which of these two groups does she take more seriously? Why?

Questions About the Writer's Craft

1. What audience do you think Goodman had in mind when she wrote this piece? How do you know? Where does she address this audience directly?

2. What word appears four times in paragraph 16? Why do you think Goodman repeats this word so often? What is the effect of this repetition?

Writing Assignments

1. Goodman believes that parents are forced to say "no" to almost everything the media offer. Write an essay illustrating the idea that not everything the media present is bad for children.

2. Goodman implies that, in some ways, today's world is hostile to children. Do you agree? Drawing upon but not limiting yourself to the material in your pre-reading journal, write an essay in which you support or reject this viewpoint.

The benefits of active reading are many. Books in general and the selections in *The Longman Reader* in particular will bring you face to face with issues that concern all of us. If you study the selections and the questions that follow them, you'll be on the way to discovering ideas for your own papers. Chapter 2, "The Writing Process," offers practical suggestions for turning those ideas into well-organized, thoughtful essays.

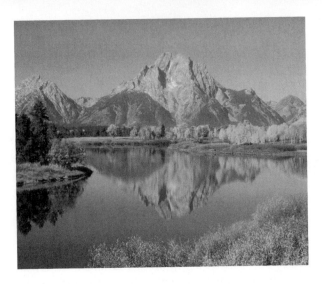

THE WRITING PROCESS

Not many people retire at age thirty-eight. But Michel Montaigne, a sixteenth-century French attorney, did exactly that. Montaigne retired at a young age because he wanted to read, think, and write about all the subjects that interested him. After spending years getting his ideas down on paper, Montaigne finally published his short prose pieces. He called them *essais*—French for "trials" or "attempts."

In fact, all writing is an attempt to transform ideas into words, thus giving order and meaning to life. By using the term *essais*—or *essays* in English—Montaigne acknowledged that a written piece is never really finished. Of course, writers have to stop at some point, especially if they have deadlines to meet. But, as all experienced writers know, even after they dot the final *i*, cross the final *t*, and say "That's it," there's always something that could have been explored further or expressed a little better.

Because writing is a process, shaky starts and changes in direction aren't uncommon. Although there's no way to eliminate the work needed to write effectively, certain approaches can make the process more manageable and rewarding. This chapter describes a sequence of steps for writing essays. Familiarity with a specific sequence develops your awareness of strategies and choices, making you feel more confident when it comes time to write. You're less likely to look at a blank piece of paper and think, "Help! Now what do I do?" During the sequence, you do the following:

1. Prewrite
2. Identify the thesis
3. Support the thesis with evidence
4. Organize the evidence

5. Write the first draft
6. Revise the essay

We present the sequence as a series of stages, but we urge you not to view it as a rigid formula that must be followed step by unchanging step. Most people develop personalized approaches to the writing process. Some writers mull over a topic in their heads and then move quickly into a promising first draft; others outline their essays in detail before beginning to write. Between these two extremes are any number of effective approaches. The sequence here can be streamlined, juggled around, or otherwise altered to fit individual writing styles as well as the requirements of specific assignments.

STAGE 1: PREWRITE

Prewriting refers to strategies you can use to generate ideas *before* starting the first draft of a paper. Prewriting techniques are like the warm-ups you do before going out to jog—they loosen you up, get you moving, and help you to develop a sense of well-being and confidence. Since prewriting techniques encourage imaginative exploration, they also help you discover what interests you most about your subject. Having such a focus early in the writing process keeps you from plunging into your initial draft without first giving some thought to what you want to say.

Prewriting can help in other ways, too. When we write, we often sabotage our ability to generate material because we continually critique what we put down on paper. During prewriting, you deliberately ignore your internal critic. Your purpose is simply to get ideas down on paper *without evaluating* their effectiveness. Writing without immediately judging what you produce can be liberating. Once you feel less pressure, you'll probably find that you can generate a good deal of material. And that can make your confidence soar.

Keep a Journal

Of all the prewriting techniques, keeping a journal (daily or almost daily) is the one most likely to make writing a part of your life. Some journal entries focus on a single theme; others wander from topic to topic. Your starting point may be a dream, a snippet of overheard conversation, a video on MTV, a political cartoon, an issue raised in class or in your reading—anything that surprises, interests, angers, depresses, confuses, or amuses you. You may also use a journal to experiment with your writing style—say, to vary your sentence structure if you tend to use predictable patterns.

Here is a fairly focused excerpt from a student's journal:

Today I had to show Paul around school. He and Mom got here by 9. I didn't let on that this was the earliest I've gotten up all semester! He got out of the car looking kind of nervous. Maybe he thought his big brother would be different after a couple of months of college. I walked him around part of the campus and then he went with me to Am. Civ. and then to lunch. He met Greg and some other guys. Everyone seemed to like him. He's got a nice, quiet sense of humor. When I went to Bio., I told him that he could walk around on his own since he wasn't crazy about sitting in on a science class. But he said "I'd rather stick with you." Was he flattering me or was he just scared? Anyway it made me feel good. Later when he was leaving, he told me he's definitely going to apply. I guess that'd be kind of nice, having him here. Mom thinks it's great and she's pushing it. I don't know. I feel kind of like it would invade my privacy. I found this school and have made a life for myself here. Let him find his own school! But it could be great having my kid brother here. I guess this is a classic case of what my psych teacher calls ambivalence. Part of me wants him to come, and part of me doesn't! (November 10)

Although some instructors collect students' journals, you needn't be overly concerned with spelling, grammar, sentence structure, or organization. While journal writing is typically more structured than freewriting (see page 22), you don't have to strive for entries that read like mini-essays. In fact, sometimes you may find it helpful to use a simple list (see the journal entry on page 21) when recording your thoughts about a subject. The important thing is to let your journal writing prompt reflection and new insights, providing you with material to draw upon in your writing. It is, then, a good idea to reread each week's entries to identify recurring themes and concerns. Keep a list of these issues at the back of your journal, under a heading like "Possible Essay Subjects." Here, for instance, are a few topics suggested by the preceding journal entry: deciding which college to attend, leaving home, sibling rivalry. Each of these topics could be developed in a full-length essay.

The Pre-Reading Journal.   To reinforce the value of journal writing, we've included a journal assignment before every selection in the book. This assignment, called *Pre-Reading Journal Entry,* "primes" you for the piece by encouraging you to explore—in a tentative fashion—your thoughts about an issue that will be raised in the selection. Here, once again, is the *Pre-Reading Journal Entry* assignment that precedes Ellen Goodman's "Family Counter-culture" (page 6):

Television is often blamed for having a harmful effect on children. Do you think this criticism is merited? In what ways does TV exert a negative influence on children? In what ways does TV exert a positive influence on youngsters? Take a few minutes to respond to these questions in your journal.

The following journal entry shows how one student, Harriet Davids, responded to the journal assignment. A thirty-eight-year-old college student and mother of two young teenagers, Harriet was understandably intrigued by the assignment. As you'll see, Harriet used a listing strategy to prepare her journal entry. She found that lists were perfect for dealing with the essentially "for or against" nature of the journal assignment.

TV's Negative Influence on Kids

Teaches negative behaviors (violence, sex, swearing, drugs, alcohol, etc.)

Cuts down on imagination and creativity

Cuts down on time spent with parents (talking, reading, playing games together)

Encourages parents' lack of involvement with kids

Frightens kids excessively by showing images of real-life violence (terrorist attacks, war, murders, etc.)

Encourages isolation (watching screen rather than interacting with other kids)

De-emphasizes reading and creates need for constant stimulation

Promotes materialism (commercials)

TV's Positive Influence on Kids

Teaches important educational concepts (Sesame Street, shows on The Learning Channel, etc.)

Exposes kids to new images and worlds (Dora the Explorer, Mister Rogers' Neighborhood)

Can inspire important discussions (about morals, sexuality, drugs, etc.) between kids and parents

Gives parents a needed break from kids

Educates kids about the painful realities in the world

Creates common ground among kids, basis of conversations and games

Encourages kids to slow down and read books based on a TV series or show (the Arthur and the Clifford, the Big Red Dog series, The Bookworm Bunch, etc.)

Can be used by parents to teach kids that they can't have everything they see

The journal assignment and subsequent journal entry do more than prepare you to read a selection with extra care and attention; they also pave the way to a full-length essay. Here's how. The final assignment following each selection is called *Writing Assignment Using a Journal Entry as a Starting Point*. This assignment helps you to translate the raw material in your journal entry into a thoughtful, well-considered essay. By the time you get to the assignment, the rough ideas in your journal entry will have been enriched by your reading of the selection. (For an example of a writing assignment that draws upon material in a pre-reading journal entry, turn to page 91.)

As you've just seen, journal writing can stimulate thinking in a loose, unstructured way; journal writing can also prompt the focused thinking required by a specific writing assignment. When you have a specific piece to write, you should approach prewriting in a purposeful, focused manner. You need to:

- Understand the boundaries of the assignment.
- Determine your purpose, audience, and tone.
- Discover your essay's limited subject.
- Generate raw material about your limited subject.
- Organize the raw material.

We'll discuss each of these steps in turn. But first, here's a practical tip: If you don't use a word processor during the prewriting stage, try using a pencil and scrap paper. They're less intimidating than pen, typewriter, and "official" paper; they also reinforce the notion that prewriting is tentative and exploratory.

Understand the Boundaries of the Assignment

You shouldn't start writing a paper until you know what's expected. First, clarify the *kind of paper* the instructor has in mind. Assume the instructor asks you to discuss the key ideas in an assigned reading. What does the instructor want you to do? Should you include a brief summary of the selection? Should you compare the author's ideas with your own view of the subject? Should you determine if the author's view is supported by valid evidence?

If you're not sure about an assignment, ask your instructor—not the student next to you, who may be as confused as you—to make the requirements clear. Most instructors are more than willing to provide an explanation. They would rather take a few minutes of class time to explain the assignment than spend hours reading dozens of student essays that miss the mark.

Second, find out *how long* the paper is expected to be. Many instructors will indicate the approximate length of the papers they assign. If no length requirements are provided, discuss with the instructor what you plan to cover and indicate how long you think your paper will be. The instructor will either give you the go-ahead or help you refine the direction and scope of your work.

Determine Your Purpose, Audience, and Tone

Once you understand the requirements for a writing assignment, you're ready to begin thinking about the essay. What is its *purpose*? For what *audience* will it be written? What *tone* will you use? Later on, you may modify your decisions about these issues. That's fine. But you need to understand the way these considerations influence your work in the early phases of the writing process.

Purpose.   The papers you write in college are usually meant to *inform* or *explain,* to *convince* or *persuade,* and sometimes to *entertain.* In practice, writing often combines purposes. You might, for example, write an essay trying to *convince* people to support a new trash recycling program in your community. But before you win readers over, you most likely would have to *explain* something about current waste disposal technology.

When purposes blend this way, the predominant one determines the essay's content, organization, emphasis, and choice of words. Assume you're writing about a political campaign. If your primary goal is to *entertain,* to take a gentle poke at two candidates, you might start with several accounts of one candidate's "foot-in-mouth" disease and then describe the attempts of the other candidate, a multimillionaire, to portray himself as an average Joe. Your language, full of exaggeration, would reflect your objective. But if your primary purpose is to *persuade* readers that the candidates are incompetent and shouldn't be elected, you might adopt a serious, straightforward style. Rather than poke fun at one candidate's gaffes, you would use them to illustrate her insensitivity to important issues. Similarly, the other candidate's posturing would be presented, not as foolish pretension, but as evidence of his lack of judgment.

Audience.   To write effectively, you need to identify who your readers are and to take their expectations and needs into account. An essay about the artificial preservatives in the food served by the campus cafeteria would take one form if submitted to your chemistry professor and a very different one if written for the college newspaper. The chemistry paper would probably be formal and technical, complete with chemical formulations and scientific data: "Distillation revealed sodium benzoate particles suspended in a gelatinous medium." But such technical material would be inappropriate in a newspaper column intended for general readers. In this case, you might provide specific examples of cafeteria foods containing additives—"Those deliciously smoky cold cuts are loaded with nitrates and nitrites, both known to cause cancer in laboratory animals"—and suggest ways to eat more healthily: "Pass by the deli counter and fill up instead on vegetarian pizza and fruit juices."

When analyzing your audience, ask yourself the following questions.

☑ ANALYZING YOUR AUDIENCE: A CHECKLIST

❏ What are my readers' age, sex, and educational level?
❏ What are their political, religious, and other beliefs?

❏ What interests and needs motivate my audience?

❏ How much do my readers already know about my subject?

❏ Do they have any misconceptions?

❏ What biases do they have about me, my subject, my opinion?

❏ How do my readers expect me to relate to them?

❏ What values do I share with my readers that will help me communicate with them?

Tone.   Just as your voice may project a range of feelings, your writing can convey one or more *tones,* or emotional states: enthusiasm, anger, resignation, and so on. Tone is integral to meaning; it permeates writing and reflects your attitude toward yourself, your purpose, your subject, and your readers. How do you project tone? You pay close attention to sentence structure and word choice.

Sentence structure refers to the way sentences are shaped. Although the two paragraphs that follow deal with exactly the same subject, note how differences in sentence structure create sharply dissimilar tones:

> During the 1960s, many inner-city minorities considered the police an occupying force and an oppressive agent of control. As a result, violence against police grew in poorer neighborhoods, as did the number of residents killed by police.

> An occupying force. An agent of control. An oppressor. That's how many inner-city minorities in the '60s viewed the police. Violence against police soared. Police killings of residents mounted.

Informative in its approach, the first paragraph projects a neutral, almost dispassionate tone. The sentences are fairly long, and clear transitions ("During the 1960s"; "As a result") mark the progression of thought. But the second paragraph, with its dramatic, almost alarmist tone, seems intended to elicit a strong emotional response; its short sentences, fragments, and abrupt transitions reflect the turbulence of earlier times.

Word choice also plays a role in establishing the tone of an essay. Words have *denotations,* neutral dictionary meanings, as well as *connotations,* emotional associations that go beyond the literal meaning. The word *beach,* for instance, is defined in the dictionary as "a nearly level stretch of pebbles and sand beside a body of water." This definition, however, doesn't capture individual responses to the word. For some, *beach* suggests warmth and relaxation; for others, it calls up images of hospital waste and sewage washed up on a once-clean stretch of shoreline.

Since tone and meaning are tightly bound, you must be sensitive to the emotional nuances of words. In a respectful essay about police officers, you wouldn't refer to *cops, narcs,* or *flatfoots;* such terms convey a contempt inconsistent with the tone intended. Your words must also convey tone clearly. Suppose you're writing a satirical piece criticizing a local beauty pageant. Dubbing the participants "livestock on view" leaves no question about your tone. But if you simply referred to the participants as "attractive young women," readers might be unsure of your attitude. Remember, readers can't read your mind, only your paper.

Discover Your Essay's Limited Subject

Once you have a firm grasp of the assignment's boundaries and have determined your purpose, audience, and tone, you're ready to focus on a limited aspect of the general assignment. Because too broad a subject can result in a diffuse, rambling essay, be sure to restrict your general subject before starting to write.

The following examples show the difference between general subjects that are too broad for an essay and limited subjects that are appropriate and workable. The examples, of course, represent only a few among many possibilities.

General Subject	Less General	Limited
Education	Computers in education	Computers in elementary school arithmetic classes
	High school education	High school electives
Transportation	Low-cost travel	Hitchhiking
	Getting around a metropolitan area	The transit system in a nearby city
Work	Planning for a career	College internships
	Women in the work force	Women's success as managers

How do you move from a general to a narrow subject? Imagine that you're asked to prepare a straightforward, informative essay for your writing class. Reprinted below is writing assignment 2 from page 11. The assignment, prompted by Ellen Goodman's essay "Family Counterculture," is an extension of the journal-writing assignment on page 6.

Goodman implies that, in some ways, today's world is hostile to children. Do you agree? Drawing upon but not limiting yourself to the material in your pre-reading journal, write an essay in which you support or reject this viewpoint.

You might feel unsure about how to proceed. But two techniques can help you limit such a general assignment. Keeping your purpose, audience, and tone in mind, you may *question* or *brainstorm* the general subject. These two techniques have a paradoxical effect. Although they encourage you to roam freely over a subject, they also help restrict the discussion by revealing which aspects of the subject interest you most.

1. Question the general subject. One way to narrow a subject is to ask a series of *who, how, why, where, when,* and *what* questions. The following example shows how Harriet Davids, the mother of two young teenagers, used this technique to limit the Goodman assignment.

You may recall that, before reading Goodman's essay, Harriet had used her journal to explore TV's effect on children (see page 15). After reading "Family Counterculture," Harriet concluded that she essentially agreed with Goodman; like Goodman, she felt that parents nowadays are indeed forced to raise their kids in an "increasingly hostile environment." She was pleased that the writing assignment gave her an opportunity to expand preliminary ideas she had jotted down in her journal.

Harriet soon realized that she had to narrow the Goodman assignment. She started by asking a number of pointed questions about the general topic. As she proceeded, she was aware that the same questions could have led to different limited subjects—just as other questions would have.

General Subject: We live in a world that is difficult, even hostile to children.

Question	**Limited Subject**
<u>Where</u> do kids go to escape?	Television, which makes the world seem even more dangerous (violence, sex, etc.). Also malls and the Internet
<u>Who</u> is to blame for the difficult conditions under which children grow up?	Parents' casual attitude toward child-rearing
<u>How</u> have schools contributed to the problems children face?	Not enough counseling programs for kids in distress
<u>Why</u> do children feel frightened?	Divorce
<u>When</u> are children most vulnerable?	The special problems of adolescents
<u>What</u> dangers or fears should parents discuss with their children?	AIDS, drugs, alcohol, war, terrorism

2. Brainstorm the general subject. Another way to focus on a limited subject is to list quickly everything about the general topic that pops into your mind. Working vertically down the page, jot down brief words, phrases, and abbreviations to capture your free-floating thoughts. Writing in complete sentences will slow you down. Don't try to organize or censor your ideas. Even the most fleeting, random, or seemingly outrageous thoughts can be productive.

Here's an example of the brainstorming that Harriet Davids generated in an effort to gather even more material on the Goodman assignment:

General Subject: We live in a world that is difficult, even hostile to children.

- TV--shows corrupt politicians, casual sex, drugs, alcohol, foul language, violence
- Real-life violence on TV, especially terrorist attacks and war, scares kids--have nightmares!
- Kids babysat by TV
- Not enough guidance from parents
- Kids raise themselves
- Too many divorces
- Parents squabbling over material goods in settlements
- Money too important
- Kids feel unimportant
- Families move a lot
- I moved in fourth grade--hated it
- Rootless feeling
- Nobody graduates from high school in the same district they went to kindergarten in
- Drug abuse all over, in little kids' schools
- Pop music glorifies drugs
- Kids not innocent--know too much
- Single-parent homes
- Day-care problems
- Abuse of little kids in day care
- TV coverage of day-care abuse frightens kids
- Perfect families on TV make kids feel inadequate

As you can see, questioning and brainstorming suggest many possible limited subjects. To identify especially promising ones, reread your material. What arouses your interest, anger, or curiosity? What themes seem to dominate and cut to the heart of the matter? Star or circle ideas with potential.

After marking the material, write several phrases or sentences summarizing the most promising limited subjects. These, for example, are just a few that emerged from Harriet Davids's questioning and brainstorming for the Goodman assignment:

- TV partly to blame for children having such a hard time
- Relocation stressful to children

- Schools also at fault
- The special problems that parents face raising children today

Harriet decided to write on the last of these limited subjects—the special problems that parents face raising children today. This topic, in turn, is the focus of our discussion in the pages ahead.

Generate Raw Material About Your Limited Subject

When a limited subject strikes you as having possibilities, your next step is to see if you have enough interesting and insightful things to say about the subject to write an effective essay. To find out if you do, you may use any or all of the following techniques.

1. Freewrite on your limited subject.   *Freewriting* means jotting down in rough sentences or phrases everything that comes to mind. To capture this continuous stream of thought, write nonstop for ten minutes or more. Don't censor anything; put down whatever pops into your head. Don't reread, edit, or pay attention to organization, spelling, or grammar. If your mind goes blank, repeat words until another thought emerges.

Here is part of the freewriting that Harriet Davids generated about her limited subject, "The special problems that parents face raising children today":

> Parents today have tough problems to face. Lots of dangers. Drugs and alcohol for one thing. Also crimes of violence against kids. Parents also have to keep up with cost of living, everything costs more, kids want and expect more. Television? The Internet? Another thing is <u>Playboy</u>, <u>Penthouse</u>. Internet sites featuring sex. Sexy ads on TV, movies deal with sex. Kids grow up too fast, too fast. Drugs. Witness real-life violence on TV, like terrorist attacks. Little kids can't handle knowing too much at an early age. Both parents at work much of the day. Finding good day care a real problem. Lots of latchkey kids. Another problem is getting kids to do homework, lots of other things to do. Especially playing on the computer and going to the mall! When I was young, we did homework after dinner, no excuses accepted by my parents.

2. Brainstorm your limited subject.   Let your mind wander freely, as you did when using brainstorming to narrow your subject. This time, though, list every idea, fact, and example that occurs to you about your limited subject. Use brief words and phrases so you don't get bogged down writing full sentences. For now, don't worry whether ideas fit together or whether the points listed make sense.

To gather additional material on her limited subject for the Goodman assignment ("The special problems that parents face raising children today"), Harriet Davids brainstormed the following list:

- Trying to raise kids when both parents work
- Prices of everything outrageous, even when both parents work
- Commercials make kids want <u>more</u> of everything
- Clothes so important
- Day care not always the answer--cases of abuse
- Day care very expensive
- Sex everywhere--TV, movies, magazines
- Sexy clothes on little kids. Absurd!
- Sexual abuse of kids
- Violence on TV, especially images of real-life terrorist attacks--scary for kids!
- Violence against kids when parents abuse drugs
- Acid, "Ecstasy," heroin, AIDS
- Schools have to teach kids about these things
- Schools doing too much--not as good as they used to be
- Not enough homework assigned--kids unprepared
- Distractions from homework--malls, TV, phones, stereos, MTV, Internet, computer games

3. Use group brainstorming.   Brainstorming can also be conducted as a group activity. Thrashing out ideas with other people stretches the imagination, revealing possibilities you may not have considered on your own. Group brainstorming doesn't have to be conducted in a formal classroom situation. You can bounce ideas around with friends and family anywhere— over lunch, at the student center, and so on.

4. Map out the limited subject.   If you're the kind of person who doodles while thinking, you may want to try *mapping,* sometimes called *diagramming* or *clustering.* Like other prewriting techniques, mapping proceeds rapidly and encourages the free flow of ideas. Begin by expressing your limited subject in a crisp phrase and placing it in the center of a blank sheet of paper. As ideas come to you, put them along lines or in boxes or circles around the limited subject. Draw arrows and lines to show the relationships among ideas. Don't stop there, however. Focus on each idea; as subpoints and details come to you, connect them to their source idea, again using boxes, lines, circles, or arrows to clarify how everything relates.

5. Use the patterns of development.   Throughout this book, we show how writers use various patterns of development (narration, process analysis, definition, and so on), singly or in combination, to develop and organize their ideas. Because each pattern has its own distinctive logic, the patterns encourage you, when you prewrite, to think about a subject in different ways, causing insights to surface that might otherwise remain submerged.

The various patterns of development are discussed in detail in Chapters 3–11. At this point, though, you should find the following chart helpful.

It not only summarizes the broad purpose of each pattern but also shows the way each pattern can generate different raw material for the limited subject of Harriet Davids's essay.

Limited Subject: The special problems that parents face raising children today.

Pattern	Purpose	Raw Material
Description	To detail what a person, place, or object is like	Detail the sights and sounds of a glitzy mall that attracts kids
Narration	To relate an event	Recount what happened when neighbors tried to forbid their kids from going to a rock concert
Exemplification	To provide specific instances or examples	Offer examples of family arguments. Can a friend known to use drugs visit? Can a child go to a party where alcohol will be served? Can parents outlaw MTV?
Division-classification	To divide something into parts or to group related things in categories	Identify components of a TV commercial that distorts kids' values Classify the kinds of commercials that make it difficult to teach kids values
Process analysis	To explain how something happens or how something is done	Explain step by step how family life can disintegrate when parents have to work all the time to make ends meet
Comparison-contrast	To point out similarities and/or dissimilarities	Contrast families today with those of a generation ago
Cause-effect	To analyze reasons and consequences	Explain why parents are not around to be with their kids: Industry's failure to provide day care and inflexibility about granting time off for parents with sick kids Explain the consequences of absentee parents: Kids feel unloved; they're undisciplined; they take on adult responsibility too early
Definition	To explain the meaning of a term or concept	What is meant by "tough love"?
Argumentation-persuasion	To win people over to a point of view	Convince parents to work with schools to develop programs that make kids feel safer and more secure

(For more on ways to use the patterns of development in different phases of the writing process, see pages 32–33, 40, and 574–576.)

6. Conduct research.   Depending on your topic, you may find it helpful to visit the library and/or to go online to identify books and articles about your limited subject. (See pages 607–633 for hints on conducting research.) At this point, you don't need to read closely the material you find. Just skim and perhaps take a few brief notes on ideas and points that could be useful.

In researching the Goodman assignment, for instance, Harriet Davids could look under such headings and subheadings as the following:

Day care
Drug abuse
Family
Parent-child relationship
    Child abuse
    Children of divorced parents
    Children of working mothers
School and home

Organize the Raw Material

Once you generate the raw material for your limited subject, you're ready to shape your rough, preliminary ideas. Preparing a *scratch outline* or *scratch list* is an effective strategy. On pages 42–45, we talk about the more formal outline you may need later on in the writing process. Here we show how a rough outline or scratch list can impose order on the tentative ideas generated during prewriting.

Reread your exploratory thoughts about the limited subject. Cross out anything not appropriate for your purpose, audience, and tone; add points that didn't originally occur to you. Star or circle compelling items that warrant further development. Then draw arrows between related items, your goal being to group such material under a common heading. Finally, determine what seems to be the best order for those headings.

By giving you a sense of the way your free-form material might fit together, a scratch outline makes the writing process more manageable. You're less likely to feel overwhelmed once you actually start writing because you'll already have some idea about how to shape your material into a meaningful statement. Remember, though, the scratch outline can, and most likely will, be modified along the way.

The following scratch outline shows how Harriet Davids began to shape her brainstorming (page 23) into a more organized format. Note the way she eliminated some items (for example, the points about outrageous prices and about real-life TV violence), added others (for example, the point about video arcades), and grouped the brainstormed items under four main headings, with the appropriate details listed underneath. (If you'd like to see Harriet's more formal outline and her first draft, turn to pages 42–45 and 58–59.)

Limited Subject: The special problems that parents face raising children today.

1. Day care for two-career families
   - Expensive
   - Before-school problems
   - After-school problems

2. Distractions from homework
   - Stereos, televisions, and computers in room at home
   - Places to go--malls, video arcades, fast-food restaurants, rock concerts

3. Sexually explicit materials
   - Magazines and books
   - Television shows
   - Internet
   - MTV
   - Movies
   - Rock posters

4. Life-threatening dangers
   - AIDS
   - Drugs
   - Drinking
   - Violence against children (by sitters, in day care, etc.)

The prewriting strategies just described provide a solid foundation for the next stages of your work. But invention and imaginative exploration don't end when prewriting is completed. As you'll see, remaining open to new ideas is crucial during all phases of the writing process.

Activities: Prewrite

1. Number the items in each set from 1 (*broadest subject*) to 5 (*most limited subject*):

Set A	Set B
Abortion	Business Majors
Controversial social issue	Students' majors
Cutting state abortion funds	College students
Federal funding of abortions	Kinds of students on campus
Social issues	Why many students major in business

2. Which of the following topics are too broad for an essay of two to five type-written pages: soap operas' appeal to college students; day care; trying to

"kick" the junk-food habit; male and female relationships; international terrorism?

3. Use the techniques indicated in parentheses to limit each general topic listed below. Then, identify a specific purpose, audience, and tone for the one limited subject you consider most interesting. Next, with the help of the patterns of development, generate raw material about that limited subject. (You may find it helpful to work with others when developing this material.) Finally, shape your raw material into a scratch outline—crossing out, combining, and adding ideas as needed. (Save your scratch outline so you can work with it further after reading about the next stage in the writing process.)

Friendship (*journal writing*)
Malls (*mapping*)
Leisure (*freewriting*)
Television (*brainstorming*)
Required courses (*group brainstorming*)
Manners (*questioning*)

STAGE 2: IDENTIFY THE THESIS

The process of prewriting—discovering a limited subject and generating ideas about it—prepares you for the next stage in writing an essay: identifying the paper's *thesis*, or controlling idea. Presenting your opinion on a subject, the thesis should focus on an interesting and significant issue, one that engages your energies and merits your consideration. You may think of the thesis as the essay's hub—the central point around which all the other material revolves. Your thesis determines what does and does not belong in the essay. The thesis, especially when it occurs early in an essay, also helps focus the reader on the piece's central point.

Sometimes the thesis emerges early in the prewriting stage, particularly if a special angle on your limited topic sparks your interest or becomes readily apparent. Often, though, you'll need to do some work to determine your thesis. For some topics, you may need to do some library research. For others, the best way to identify a promising thesis is to look through your prewriting and ask yourself questions such as these: "What statement does all this prewriting support? What aspect of the limited subject is covered in most detail? What is the focus of the most provocative material?"

For a look at the process of finding the thesis within prewriting material, glance back at the scratch outline (page 26) that Harriet Davids prepared for the limited subject "The special problems that parents face raising children today." Harriet devised the following thesis to capture the focus of this prewriting: "Being a parent today is much more difficult than it was a generation ago." (The full outline for Harriet's paper appears on pages 44–45; the first draft on pages 58–59; the final draft on pages 66–67.)

Writing an Effective Thesis

What makes a thesis effective? Generally expressed in one or two sentences, a thesis statement often has two parts. One part presents your paper's *limited subject;* the other presents your *point of view,* or *attitude,* about that subject. Here are some examples of the way you might move from general subject to limited subject to thesis statement. In each thesis statement, the limited subject is underlined once and the attitude twice.

General Subject	Limited Subject	Thesis
Education	Computers in elementary school arithmetic classes	Computer programs in arithmetic can individualize instruction more effectively than the average elementary school teacher can.
Transportation	A metropolitan transit system	Although the city's transit system still has problems, it has become safer and more efficient in the last two years.
Work	College internships	College internships provide valuable opportunities to students uncertain about what to do after graduation.
Our anti-child world	Special problems that parents face raising children today	Being a parent today is much more difficult than it was a generation ago.

 (*Reminder:* The last of these thesis statements is the one that Harriet Davids devised for the essay she planned to write in response to the assignment on page 11. Harriet's prewriting appears on pages 23 and 26. You can find her first draft on pages 58–59.)

Because identifying your thesis statement is an important step in writing a sharply focused essay, you need to avoid three common problems that lead to an ineffective thesis.

Don't make an announcement.   Some writers use the thesis statement merely to announce the limited subject of their paper and forget to indicate their attitude toward the subject. Such statements are announcements of intent, not thesis statements.

Compare the following three announcements with the thesis statements beside them.

Announcements	Thesis Statements
My essay will discuss whether a student pub should exist on campus.	This college should not allow a student pub on campus.
Handgun legislation is the subject of this paper.	Banning handguns is the first step toward controlling crime in the United States.
I want to discuss cable television.	Cable television has not delivered on its promise to provide an alternative to network programming.

Don't make a factual statement.   Your thesis and thus your essay should focus on an issue capable of being developed. If a fact is used as a thesis, you have no place to go; a fact generally doesn't invite much discussion.

Notice the difference between these factual statements and thesis statements:

Factual Statements	Thesis Statements
Many businesses pollute the environment.	Tax penalties should be levied against businesses that pollute the environment.
Nowadays, many movies are violent.	Movie violence provides a healthy outlet for aggression.
The population of the United States is growing older.	The aging of the U.S. population will eventually create a crisis in the delivery of health-care services.

Don't make a broad statement.   Avoid stating your thesis in vague, general, or sweeping terms. Broad statements make it difficult for readers to grasp your essay's point. Moreover, if you start with a broad thesis, you're saddled with the impossible task of trying to develop a book-length idea in an essay that runs only several pages.

The following examples contrast statements that are too broad with thesis statements that are focused effectively.

Broad Statements	Thesis Statements
Nowadays, high school education is often meaningless.	High school diplomas have been devalued by grade inflation.
Newspapers cater to the taste of the American public.	The success of *USA Today* indicates that people want newspapers that are easy to read and entertaining.

Broad Statements	Thesis Statements
The computer revolution is not all that we have been led to believe it is.	Home computers are still an impractical purchase for many people.

You have considerable freedom regarding the placement of the thesis in an essay. The thesis is often stated near the beginning, but it may be delayed, especially if you need to provide background information before it can be understood. Sometimes the thesis is reiterated—with fresh words—in the essay's conclusion or elsewhere. You may even leave the thesis unstated, relying on strong evidence to convey the essay's central idea.

One final point: Once you start writing your first draft, some feelings, thoughts, and examples may emerge that qualify, even contradict, your initial thesis. Don't resist these new ideas; they frequently move you toward a clearer statement of your main point. Remember, though, your essay must have a thesis. Without this central concept, you have no reason for writing.

Activities: Identify the Thesis

1. For each of the following limited subjects, four possible thesis statements are given. Indicate whether each is an announcement (*A*), a factual statement (*FS*), too broad a statement (*TB*), or an effective thesis (*OK*). Then, for each effective thesis, identify a possible purpose, audience, and tone.

   Limited Subject: The ethics of treating severely handicapped infants

   Some babies born with severe handicaps have been allowed to die.

   There are many serious issues involved in the treatment of handicapped newborns.

   The government should pass legislation requiring medical treatment for handicapped newborns.

   This essay will analyze the controversy surrounding the treatment of severely handicapped babies who would die without medical care.

   Limited Subject: Privacy and computerized records

   Computers raise some significant and crucial questions for all of us.

   Computerized records keep track of consumer spending habits, credit records, travel patterns, and other personal information.

   Computerized records have turned our private lives into public property.

   In this paper, the relationship between computerized records and the right to privacy will be discussed.

2. Each of the following sets lists the key points in an essay. Using the information provided, prepare a possible thesis for each essay.

Set A

- One evidence of this growing conservatism is the reemerging popularity of fraternities and sororities.
- Beauty contests, ROTC training, and corporate recruiting—once rejected by students on many campuses—are again popular.
- Most important, many students no longer choose risky careers that enable them to contribute to society but select, instead, safe fields with moneymaking potential.

Set B

- We do not know how engineering new forms of life might affect the earth's delicate ecological balance.
- Another danger of genetic research is its potential for unleashing new forms of disease.
- Even beneficial attempts to eliminate genetic defects could contribute to the dangerous idea that only perfect individuals are entitled to live.

3. Following are four pairs of general and limited subjects. Generate an appropriate thesis statement for each pair. Select one thesis, and determine which pattern of development would support it most effectively. Use that pattern to draft a paragraph developing the thesis. (Save the paragraph so you can work with it further after reading about the next stage in the writing process.)

General Subject	Limited Subject
Psychology	The power struggles in a classroom
Health	Doctors' attitudes toward patients
U.S. politics	Television's coverage of presidential campaigns
Work	Minimum-wage jobs for young people

4. Return to the scratch outline you prepared for activity 3 on page 27. After examining the outline, identify a thesis that conveys the central idea behind most of the raw material. Then, ask others to evaluate your thesis in light of the material in the outline. Finally, keeping the thesis—as well as your purpose, audience, and tone—in mind, refine the scratch outline by deleting inappropriate items, adding relevant ones, and indicating where more material is needed. (Save your refined scratch outline and thesis so you can work with them further after reading about the next stage in the writing process.)

STAGE 3: SUPPORT THE THESIS WITH EVIDENCE

After identifying a preliminary thesis, you should develop the evidence needed to support the central idea. Such supporting material grounds your essay, showing readers you have good reason for feeling as you do about your subject. Your evidence also adds interest and color to your writing. In college essays of five hundred to fifteen hundred words, you usually need at least three major points of evidence to develop your thesis. These major points—each focusing on related but separate aspects of the thesis—eventually become the supporting paragraphs in the body of the essay.

What Is Evidence?

By *evidence,* we mean a number of different kinds of support. *Examples* are just one option. To develop your thesis, you might also include *reasons, facts, details, statistics, anecdotes,* and *quotations from experts.* Imagine you're writing an essay with the thesis "People normally unconcerned about the environment can be galvanized to constructive action if they feel personally affected by an environmental problem." You could support this thesis with any combination of the following types of evidence:

- *Examples* of successful recycling efforts in several neighborhoods.
- *Reasons* why people got involved in a neighborhood recycling effort.
- *Facts* about other residents' efforts to preserve the quality of their well water.
- *Details* about the steps that people can take to get involved in environmental issues.
- *Statistics* showing the number of Americans concerned about the environment.
- An *anecdote* about your involvement in environmental efforts.
- A *quotation* from a well-known scientist about the impact that citizens can have on environmental legislation.

Where Do You Find Evidence?

Where do you find the examples, anecdotes, details, and other types of evidence needed to support your thesis? As you saw when you followed Harriet Davids's strategies for gathering material for an essay (pages 22–25), a good deal of evidence is generated during the prewriting stage. In this phase of the writing process, you tap into your personal experiences, draw upon other people's observations, perhaps interview a person with special knowledge about your subject. The library, with its abundant material, is another rich source of supporting evidence. In addition, the various patterns of development are a valuable source of evidence.

How the Patterns of Development
Help Generate Evidence

On pages 23–24, we discussed the way patterns of development help generate material about a limited subject. The same patterns also help develop support for a thesis. The following chart shows how they generate evidence for this thesis: "To those who haven't done it, babysitting looks easy. In practice, though, babysitting can be difficult, frightening, even dangerous."

Pattern	Evidence Generated
Description	Details about a child who, while being babysat, was badly hurt
Narration	Story about the time a friend babysat an ill child whose condition was worsened by the babysitter's actions
Exemplification	Examples of potential babysitting problems: an infant rolls off a changing table; a toddler sticks objects in an electric outlet; a school-age child is bitten by a neighborhood dog
Division-classification	A typical babysitting evening divided into stages: playing with the kids; putting them to bed; dealing with their nighttime fears once they're in bed
	Classify kids' nighttime fears: of monsters under their beds; of bad dreams; of being abandoned by their parents
Process analysis	Step-by-step account of what a babysitter should do if a child becomes ill or injured
Comparison-contrast	Contrast between two babysitters: one well-prepared, the other unprepared
Cause-effect	Why children have temper tantrums; the effect of such tantrums on an unskilled babysitter
Definition	What is meant by a *skilled* babysitter?
Argumentation-persuasion	A proposal for a babysitting training program

(For more on ways to use the patterns of development in different phases of the writing process, see pages 23–24, 40, and 574–576.)

Characteristics of Evidence

No matter how it is generated, all types of supporting evidence share the characteristics described in the following sections. You should keep these characteristics in mind as you review your thesis and scratch outline. That way, you can make the changes needed to strengthen the evidence gathered earlier. As you'll see shortly, Harriet Davids focused on many of these issues as she worked with the evidence she collected during the prewriting phase.

The evidence is relevant and unified.   All the evidence in an essay must clearly support the thesis. It makes no difference how riveting material might be; if it doesn't *relate directly* to the essay's central point, the material should be eliminated. Irrelevant material can weaken your position by implying that no relevant support exists. It also distracts readers from your controlling idea, thus disrupting the paper's overall unity.

The following paragraph, taken from an essay illustrating recent changes in Americans' television-viewing habits, demonstrates the importance of unified evidence. The paragraph focuses on people's reasons for switching from network to cable television. As you'll see, the paragraph lacks unity because it contains points (underlined) unrelated to its main idea. Specifically, the comments about cable's foul language should be deleted. Although these observations bring up interesting points, they shift the paragraph's focus. If the writer wants to present a balanced view of the pros and cons of cable and network television, these points *should* be covered, but in *another paragraph*.

Nonunified Support

Many people consider cable TV an improvement over network television. For one thing, viewers usually prefer the movies on cable. Unlike network films, cable movies are often only months old, they have not been edited by censors, and they are not interrupted by commercials. Growing numbers of people also feel that cable specials are superior to the ones the networks grind out. Cable viewers may enjoy such pop stars as Billy Joel, Mariah Carey, or Chris Rock in concert, whereas the networks continue to broadcast tired variety shows and boring awards ceremonies. There is, however, one problem with cable comedians. The foul language many of them use makes it hard to watch these cable specials with children. The networks, in contrast, generally present "clean" shows that parents and children can watch together. Then, too, cable TV offers viewers more flexibility since it schedules shows at various times over the month. People working night shifts or attending evening classes can see movies in the afternoon, and viewers missing the first twenty minutes of a show can always catch them later. It's not surprising that cable viewership is growing while network ratings have taken a plunge.

 Early in the writing process, Harriet Davids was aware of the importance of relevant evidence. Take a moment to compare Harriet's brainstorming (pages 21 and 23) and her scratch outline (page 26). Even though Harriet hadn't identified her thesis when she prepared the scratch outline, she realized she should delete a number of items on the reshaped version of her brainstorming—for example, the second item and third-to-last item ("prices of everything outrageous" and "schools doing too much"). Harriet eliminated these points because they weren't consistent with the focus of her limited subject.

The evidence is specific.   When evidence is vague and general, readers lose interest in what you're saying, become skeptical of your ideas' validity, and feel puzzled about your meaning. In contrast, *specific, concrete evidence* provides sharp *word pictures* that engage your readers, persuade them that your thinking is sound, and clarify meaning.

Consider, for example, the differences between the following two sentences: "The young man had trouble lifting the box out of an old car" and "Joe, only twenty years old but more than fifty pounds overweight, struggled to lift the heavy wooden crate out of the rusty, dented Chevrolet." The first sentence, filled with generalities, is fuzzy and imprecise while the second sentence, filled with specifics, is crisp and clear.

As the preceding sentences illustrate, three strategies can be used, singly or in combination, to make writing specific. First, you can provide answers to *who, which, what,* and similar *questions.* (The question "How does the car look?" prompts a change in which "an old car" becomes "a rusty, dented Chevrolet.") Second, you can use *vigorous verbs* ("had trouble lifting" becomes "struggled to lift"). Finally, you can replace *vague, abstract* nouns with *vivid, concrete* nouns or phrases ("the young man" becomes "Joe, only twenty years old but more than fifty pounds overweight").

Following are two versions of a paragraph from an essay about trends in the business community. Although both paragraphs focus on one such trend—flexible working hours—note how the first version's bland language fails to engage the reader and how its vague generalities leave the meaning unclear. What, for example, is meant by the term "flex-time scheduling"? The second paragraph answers this question (as well as several others) with clear specifics; it also uses strong, energetic language. As a result, the second paragraph is more informative and more interesting than the first.

Nonspecific Support

More and more companies have begun to realize that flex-time scheduling offers advantages. Several companies outside Boston have tried flex-time scheduling and are pleased with the way the system reduces the difficulties their employees face getting to work. Studies show that flex-time scheduling also increases productivity, reduces on-the-job conflict, and minimizes work-related accidents.

Specific Support

More and more companies have begun to realize that flex-time scheduling offers advantages over a rigid 9-to-5 routine. Along suburban Boston's Route 128, such companies as Compugraphics and Consolidated Paper now permit employees to schedule their arrival any time between 6 A.M. and 11 A.M. The corporations report that the number of rush-hour jams and accidents has fallen dramatically. As a result, employees no longer arrive at work weighed down by tension induced by choking clouds of exhaust fumes and the blaring horns of gridlocked drivers. Studies sponsored by the journal Business Quarterly show that this more mellow state of mind benefits corporations. Traffic-stressed employees begin their workday anxious and exasperated, still grinding their teeth at their fellow commuters, their frustration often spilling over into their performance at work. By contrast, stress-free employees work more productively and take fewer days off. They are more tolerant of coworkers and customers, and less likely to balloon minor irritations into major confrontations. Perhaps most importantly, employees arriving at work relatively free of stress can focus their attention on working safely. They rack up significantly fewer on-the-job accidents, such as falls and injuries resulting from careless handling of dangerous equipment. Flex-time improves employee well-being, and as well-being rises, so do company profits.

At this point, it will be helpful to compare once again Harriet Davids's brainstorming (pages 21 and 23) and her scratch outline (page 26). Note the way she added new details to make her brainstorming more specific. For example, to the item "Distractions from homework," she added the new examples "video arcades," "fast-food restaurants," and "rock concerts." And, as you'll see when you read Harriet's first and final drafts (pages 58–59 and 66–67), she added many more vigorous specifics during later stages of the writing process.

The evidence is adequate.   Readers won't automatically accept your thesis; you need to provide *enough specific evidence* to support your viewpoint. On occasion, a single extended example will suffice. Generally, though, you'll need various kinds of evidence: facts, examples, reasons, personal observations, expert opinion, and so on.

Following are two versions of a paragraph from a paper showing how difficult it is to get personal, attentive service nowadays at gas stations, super-markets, and department stores. Both paragraphs focus on the problem at gas stations, but one paragraph is much more effective. As you'll see, the first paragraph starts with good, specific support, yet fails to provide enough of it. The second paragraph offers additional examples, descriptive details, and dia-logue—all of which make the writing stronger and more convincing.

Inadequate Support

Gas stations are a good example of this impersonal attitude. At many stations, attendants have even stopped pumping gas. Motorists pull up to a combination convenience store and gas island where an attendant is enclosed in a glass booth with a tray for taking money. The driver must get out of the car, pump the gas, and walk over to the booth to pay. That's a real inconvenience, especially when compared with the way service stations used to be run.

Adequate Support

Gas stations are a good example of this impersonal attitude. At many stations, attendants have even stopped pumping gas. Motorists pull up to a combination convenience store and gas island where an attendant is enclosed in a glass booth with a tray for taking money. The driver must get out of the car, pump the gas, and walk over to the booth to pay. Even at stations that still have "pump jockeys," employees seldom ask, "Check your oil?" or wash windshields, although they may grudgingly point out the location of the bucket and squeegee. And customers with a balky engine or a nonfunctioning heater are usually out of luck. Why? Many gas stations have eliminated on-duty mechanics. The skillful mechanic who could replace a belt or fix a tire in a few minutes has been replaced by a teenager in a jumpsuit who doesn't know a carburetor from a charge card and couldn't care less.

Now take a final look at Harriet Davids's scratch outline (page 26). You'll see that Harriet realized she needed more than one block of supporting material to develop her limited subject; that's why she identified four separate blocks of evidence (day care, homework distractions, sexual material, and dangers). When Harriet prepared her first and final drafts (pages 58–59 and 66–67), she decided to eliminate the material about day care. But she added so many more specific and dramatic details that her evidence was more than sufficient.

The evidence is accurate.   When you have a strong belief and want readers to see things your way, you may be tempted to overstate or downplay facts, disregard information, misquote, or make up details. Suppose you plan to write an essay making the point that dormitory security is lax. You begin supporting your thesis by narrating the time you were nearly mugged in your dorm hallway. Realizing the essay would be more persuasive if you also mentioned other episodes, you decide to invent some material. Perhaps you describe several supposed burglaries on your dorm floor or exaggerate the amount of time it took campus security to respond to an emergency call from a residence hall. Yes, you've supported your point—but at the expense of truth.

The evidence is representative.   Using representative evidence means that you rely on the typical, the usual, to show that your point is valid. Contrary to the maxim, exceptions don't prove the rule. Perhaps you plan to write an essay contending that the value of seat belts has been exaggerated. To support your position, you mention a friend who survived a head-on collision without wearing a seat belt. Such an example isn't representative because the facts and figures on accidents suggest your friend's survival was a fluke.

Borrowed evidence is documented.   If you include evidence from outside sources (books, articles, interviews), you need to acknowledge where that information comes from. If you don't, readers may consider your evidence nothing more than your point of view, or they may regard as dishonest your failure to cite your indebtedness to others for ideas that obviously aren't your own.

For help in documenting sources in brief, informal papers, turn to page 485. For information on acknowledging sources in longer, more formal papers, refer to Appendix A (pages 607–633).

Strong supporting evidence is at the heart of effective writing. Without it, essays lack energy and fail to convey the writer's perspective. Such lifeless writing is more apt to put readers to sleep than to engage their interest and convince them that the points being made are valid. Taking the time to accumulate solid supporting material is, then, a critical step in the writing process.

Activities: Support the Thesis With Evidence

1. Each of the following sets includes a thesis statement and four points of support. In each set, identify the one point that is off target.

   Set A

   Thesis: Colleges should put less emphasis on sports.

   Encourages grade fixing
   Creates a strong following among former graduates
   Distracts from real goals of education
   Causes extensive and expensive injuries

   Set B

   Thesis: The United States is becoming a homogenized country.

   Regional accents vanishing
   Chain stores blanket country
   Americans proud of their ethnic identities
   Metropolitan areas almost indistinguishable from one another

2. For each of the following thesis statements, develop three points of relevant support. Then use the patterns of development to generate evidence for each point of support.

   Thesis: The trend toward disposable, throwaway products has gone too far.

   Thesis: The local (or college) library fails to meet the needs of those it is supposed to serve.

   Thesis: Television portrays men as incompetent creatures.

3. Choose one of the following thesis statements. Then identify an appropriate purpose, audience, and tone for an essay with this thesis. Using freewriting, mapping, or the questioning technique, generate at least three supporting points for the thesis. Last, write a paragraph about one of the points, making sure your evidence reflects the characteristics discussed in these pages. Alternatively, you may go ahead and prepare the first draft of an essay having the selected thesis. (If you choose the second option, you may want to turn to page 57 to see a diagram showing how to organize a first draft.) Save whatever you prepare so you can work with it further after reading about the next stage in the writing process.

   • Winning the lottery may not always be a blessing.
   • All of us can take steps to reduce the country's trash crisis.

- Drug education programs in public schools are (or are not) effective.

4. Select one of the following thesis statements. Then determine your purpose, audience, and tone for an essay with this thesis. Next, use the patterns of development to generate at least three supporting points for the thesis. Finally, write a paragraph about one of the points, making sure that your evidence demonstrates the characteristics discussed in these pages. Alternatively, you may go ahead and prepare a first draft of an essay having the thesis selected. (If you choose the latter option, you may want to turn to page 57 to see a diagram showing how to organize a first draft.) Save whatever you prepare so you can work with it further after reading about the next stage in the writing process.

- Teenagers should (or should not) be able to obtain birth control devices without their parents' permission.
- The college's system for awarding student loans needs to be overhauled.
- VCRs have changed for the worse (or the better) the way Americans entertain themselves.

5. Retrieve the paragraph you wrote in response to activity 3 on page 31. Keeping in mind the characteristics of effective evidence discussed in pages 33–38, make whatever changes are needed to strengthen the paragraph. (Save the paragraph so you can work with it further after reading about the next stage in the writing process.)

6. Look at the thesis and refined scratch outline you prepared in response to activity 4 on page 31. Where do you see gaps in the support for your thesis? By brainstorming with others, generate material to fill these gaps. If some of the new points generated suggest that you should modify your thesis, make the appropriate changes now. (Save this material so you can work with it further after reading about the next stage in the writing process.)

STAGE 4: ORGANIZE THE EVIDENCE

After you've generated supporting evidence, you're ready to *organize* that material. Even highly compelling evidence won't illustrate the validity of your thesis or achieve your purpose if readers have to plow through a maze of chaotic evidence. Some writers can move quickly from generating support to writing a clearly structured first draft. (They usually say they have sequenced their ideas in their heads.) Most, however, need to spend some time sorting out their thoughts on paper before starting the first draft; otherwise, they tend to lose their way in a tangle of ideas.

When moving to the organizing stage, you should have in front of you your scratch outline (see pages 25–26) and thesis plus any supporting material you've accumulated since you did your prewriting. To find a logical framework for all this material, you'll need to (1) determine which pattern of development is implied in your evidence, (2) select one of four basic approaches for organizing your evidence, and (3) outline your evidence. These issues are discussed in the pages ahead.

Use the Patterns of Development

As you saw on pages 23–25 and 32–33, the patterns of development (definition, narration, process analysis, and others) can help you develop prewriting material and generate evidence for a thesis. In the organizing stage, the patterns provide frameworks for presenting evidence in an orderly, accessible way. Here's how.

Each pattern of development has its own internal logic that makes it appropriate for some writing purposes but not for others. (You may find it helpful at this point to turn to pages 23–25 so you can review the broad purpose of each pattern.) Once you see which pattern (or combination of patterns) is implied by your purpose, you can block out your paper's general structure. Imagine that you're writing an essay *explaining why* some students drop out of college during the first semester. You might organize the essay around a three-part discussion of the key *causes* contributing to the difficulty that students have adjusting to college: (1) they miss friends and family, (2) they take inappropriate courses, and (3) they experience conflicts with roommates. As you can see, your choice of pattern of development significantly influences your essay's content and organization.

Some essays follow a single pattern, but most blend them, with a predominant pattern providing the piece's organizational framework. In our example essay, you might include a brief *description* of an overwhelmed first-year college student; you might *define* the psychological term "separation anxiety"; you might end the paper by briefly explaining a *process* for making students' adjustment to college easier. Still, the essay's overall organizational pattern would be *cause-effect* since the paper's primary purpose is to explain why students drop out of college. (For more information on the way patterns often blend in writing, see Chapter 12, "Combining the Patterns.")

Although writers often combine the patterns of development, your composition instructor may ask you to write an essay organized according to a single pattern. Such an assignment helps you understand a particular pattern's unique demands. Keep in mind, though, that most writing begins not with a specific pattern but with a specific *purpose*. The pattern or combination of patterns used to develop and organize an essay evolves out of that purpose.

Select an Organizational Approach

No matter which pattern(s) of development you select, you need to know four general approaches for organizing supporting evidence. These are explained below.

Chronological approach.   When an essay is organized *chronologically*, supporting material is arranged in a clear time sequence, usually starting with what happened first and ending with what happened last. Occasionally, chronological sequences can be rearranged to create flashback or flashforward effects, two techniques discussed in Chapter 4 on narration. Essays using narration (for example, an experience with prejudice) or process analysis (for instance, how to deliver an effective speech) are most likely to be organized chronologically. The paper on public speaking might use a time sequence to present its points: how to prepare a few days before the presentation is due; what to do right before the speech; what to concentrate on during the speech itself. (For examples of chronologically arranged student essays, turn to pages 131 and 288.)

Spatial approach.   When you arrange supporting evidence *spatially*, you discuss details as they occur in space, or from certain locations. This strategy is particularly appropriate for description. Imagine that you plan to write an essay describing the joyous times you spent as a child playing by a towering old oak tree in the neighborhood park. Using spatial organization, you start by describing the rich animal life (the plump earthworms, swarming anthills, and numerous animal tracks) you observed while hunkered down *at the base* of the tree. Next, you re-create the contented feeling you experienced sitting on a branch *in the middle* of the tree. Finally, you end by describing the glorious view of the world you had *from the top* of the tree.

Although spatial arrangement is flexible (you could, for instance, start with a description from the top of the tree), you should always proceed systematically. And once you select a particular spatial order, you should usually maintain that sequence throughout the essay; otherwise, readers may get lost along the way. (A spatially arranged student essay appears on page 78.)

Emphatic approach.   In *emphatic* order, the most compelling evidence is saved for last. This arrangement is based on the psychological principle that people remember best what they experience last. Emphatic order has built-in momentum because it starts with the least important point and builds to the most significant. This method is especially effective in argumentation-persuasion essays, in papers developed through examples, and in pieces involving comparison-contrast, division-classification, or causal analysis.

Consider an essay analyzing the negative effect that workaholic parents can have on their children. The paper might start with a brief discussion of relatively minor effects such as the family's eating mostly frozen or takeout foods. Paragraphs on more serious effects might follow: children get no parental help with homework; they try to resolve personal problems without parental advice. Finally, the essay might close with a detailed discussion of the most significant effect—children's lack of self-esteem because they feel unimportant in their parents' lives. (The student essays on pages 177, 343, and 439 all use an emphatic arrangement.)

Simple-to-complex approach.   A final way to organize an essay is to proceed from relatively *simple* concepts to more *complex* ones. By starting with easy-to-grasp, generally accepted evidence, you establish rapport with your readers and assure them that the essay is firmly grounded in shared experience. In contrast, if you open with difficult or highly technical material, you risk confusing and alienating your audience.

Assume you plan to write a paper arguing that your college has endangered students' health by not making an all-out effort to remove asbestos from dormitories and classroom buildings. It probably wouldn't be a good idea to begin with a medically sophisticated explanation of precisely how asbestos damages lung tissue. Instead, you might start with an observation that is likely to be familiar to your readers—one that is part of their everyday experience. You could, for example, open with a description of asbestos—as readers might see it—wrapped around air ducts and furnaces or used as electrical insulation and fireproofing material. Having provided a basic, easy-to-visualize description, you could then go on to explain the complicated process by which asbestos can cause chronic lung inflammation. (See page 390 for an example of a student essay using the simple-to-complex arrangement.)

    Depending on your purpose, any one of these four organizational approaches might be appropriate. For example, assume that you planned to write an essay developing Harriet Davids's thesis: "Being a parent today is much more difficult than it was a generation ago." To emphasize that the various stages in children's lives present parents with different difficulties, you'd probably select a *chronological* sequence. To show that the challenges that parents face vary depending on whether children are at home, at school, or in the world at large, you'd probably choose a *spatial* sequence. To stress the range of problems that parents face (from less to more serious), you'd probably use an *emphatic* sequence. To illustrate today's confusing array of theories for raising children, you might take a *simple-to-complex* approach, moving from the basic to the most sophisticated theories.

Prepare an Outline

Do you, if asked to submit an outline, prepare it *after* you've written the essay? If you do, we hope to convince you that having an outline—a skeletal version of your paper—*before* you begin the first draft makes the writing process much more manageable. The outline helps you organize your thoughts beforehand, and it guides your writing as you work on the draft. Even though ideas continue to evolve during the draft, an outline clarifies how ideas fit together, which points are major, which should come first, and so on. An outline may also reveal places where evidence is weak, underscoring the need, perhaps, for more prewriting.

Like previous stages in the writing process, outlining is individualized. Some people prepare highly structured outlines; others make only a few informal jottings. Sometimes outlining will go quickly, with points falling easily into place; at other times you'll have to work hard to figure out how points are related. If that happens, be glad you caught the problem while outlining rather than while writing the first draft.

To prepare an effective outline, you should reread and evaluate your scratch outline and thesis as well as any other evidence you've generated since the prewriting stage. Then decide which pattern of development (description, cause-effect, and so on) seems to be suggested by your evidence. Also determine whether your evidence lends itself to a chronological, a spatial, an emphatic, or a simple-to-complex order. Having done all that, you're ready to identify and sequence your main and supporting points.

The amount of detail in an outline will vary according to the paper's length and the instructor's requirements. A scratch outline (like the one on page 26) is often sufficient, but for longer papers, you'll probably need a more detailed and formal outline. In such cases, the suggestions in the accompanying checklist will help you develop a sound plan. Feel free to modify these guidelines to suit your needs.

☑ OUTLINING: A CHECKLIST

❏ Write your purpose, audience, tone, and thesis at the top of the outlining page.

❏ Below the thesis, enter the pattern of development that seems to be implied by the evidence you've accumulated.

❏ Also record which of the four organizational approaches would be most effective in sequencing your evidence.

❏ Reevaluate your supporting material. Delete anything that doesn't develop the thesis or that isn't appropriate for your purpose, audience, and tone.

❏ Add any new points or material. Group related items together. Give each group a heading that represents a main topic in support of your thesis.

❏ Label these main topics with roman numerals (I, II, III, and so on). Let the order of the numerals indicate the best sequence.

❏ Identify subtopics and group them under the appropriate main topics. Indent and label these subtopics with capital letters (A, B, C, and so on). Let the order of the letters indicate the best sequence.

❏ Identify supporting points (often, reasons and examples) and group them under the appropriate subtopics. Indent and label these supporting points with arabic numbers (1, 2, 3, and so on). Let the numbers indicate the best sequence.

❏ Identify specific details (secondary examples, facts, statistics, expert opinions, quotations) and group them under the appropriate supporting points. Indent and label these specific details with lowercase letters (a, b, c, and so on). Let the letters indicate the best sequence.

❏ Examine your outline, looking for places where evidence is weak. Where appropriate, add new evidence.

❏ Double-check that all main topics, subtopics, supporting points, and specific details develop some aspect of the thesis. Also confirm that all items are arranged in the most logical order.

 The sample outline that follows develops the thesis "Being a parent today is much more difficult than it was a generation ago." You may remember that this is the thesis that Harriet Davids devised for the essay she planned to write in response to the assignment on page 11. Harriet's scratch list appears on page 26. When you compare Harriet's scratch list and outline, you'll find some differences. On the whole, the outline contains more specifics, but it doesn't include all the material in the scratch list. For example, after reconsidering her purpose, audience, tone, and thesis, Harriet decided to omit from her outline the section on day care and the points about rock concerts, MTV, rock posters, and AIDS.

The plan shown below is called a *topic outline* because it uses phrases, or topics, for each entry. For a lengthier or more complex paper, a *sentence outline* would be more appropriate.

Purpose: To inform

Audience: Instructor as well as class members, most of whom are 18–20 years old

Tone: Serious and straightforward

Thesis: Being a parent today is much more difficult than it was a generation ago.

Pattern of development: Exemplification

Organizational approach: Emphatic order

  I. Distractions from homework
    A. At home
      1. Stereos, radios, tapes
      2. Television--esp. on MTV
      3. Computers--Internet

   B. Outside home
     1. Malls
     2. Video arcades
     3. Fast-food restaurants

II. Sexually explicit materials
   A. In print
     1. Sex magazines
       a. Playboy
       b. Penthouse
     2. Pornographic books
   B. In movies
     1. Seduction scenes
     2. Casual sex
   C. On television
     1. Soap operas
     2. R-rated comedians
     3. R-rated movies on cable
   D. Internet
     1. Easy-to-access adult chat rooms
     2. Easy-to-access pornographic websites

III. Increased dangers
   A. Drugs--peer pressure
   B. Alcohol--peer pressure
   C. Violent crimes against children

(If you'd like to see the first draft that resulted from Harriet's outline, turn
to pages 58–59. Hints for moving from an outline to a first draft appear on
page 47.)

Before starting to write your first draft, show your outline to several people
(your instructor, friends, classmates). Their reactions will indicate whether
your proposed organization is appropriate for your thesis, purpose, audience,
and tone. Their comments can also highlight areas needing additional work.
After making whatever changes are needed, you're in a good position to go
ahead and write the first draft of your essay.

Activities: Organize the Evidence

1. The thesis statement below is followed by a scrambled list of supporting
   points. Prepare an outline for a potential essay, making sure to distinguish
   between major and secondary points.

   Thesis: Our schools, now in crisis, could be improved in several ways.

   Certification requirements for teachers
   Schedules

Teachers
Longer school year
Merit pay for outstanding teachers
Curriculum
Better textbooks for classroom use
Longer school days
More challenging content in courses

2. Assume you plan to write an essay based on the following brief outline, which consists of a thesis and several points of support. Determine which pattern of development (page 40) you would probably use for the essay's overall framework. Also identify which organizational approach (pages 40–42) you would most likely adopt to sequence the points of support listed. Then, use one or more patterns of development to generate material to support those points. Having done that, review the material generated, deleting, adding, combining, and arranging ideas in logical order. Finally, make an outline for the body of the essay. (Save your outline so you can work with it further after reading about the next stage in the writing process.)

   Thesis: Friends of the opposite sex fall into one of several categories: the pal, the confidant, or the pest.

   • Frequently, an opposite-sex friend is simply a "pal."
   • Sometimes, though, a pal turns, step by step, into a confidant.
   • If a confidant begins to have romantic thoughts, he or she may become a pest, thus disrupting the friendship.

3. Retrieve the writing you prepared in response to activity 3, 4, or 5 on pages 38–39. As needed, reshape that material, applying the organizational principles discussed in these pages. Be sure, for example, that you select the approach (chronological, spatial, emphatic, or simple-to-complex) that would be most appropriate, given your main idea, purpose, audience, and tone. (Save whatever you prepare so you can work with it further after reading about the next stage in the writing process.)

4. Look again at the thesis and scratch outline you refined and elaborated in response to activity 6 on page 39. Reevaluate this material by deleting, adding, combining, and rearranging ideas as needed. Also, keeping your purpose, audience, and tone in mind, consider whether a chronological, a spatial, an emphatic, or a simple-to-complex approach will be most appropriate. Now prepare an outline of your ideas. Finally, ask at least one person to evaluate your organizational plan. (Save your outline. After reading about the next stage in the writing process, you can use it to write the essay's first draft.)

STAGE 5: WRITE THE FIRST DRAFT

After prewriting, deciding on a thesis, and developing and organizing evidence, you're ready to write a *first draft*—a rough, provisional version of your essay. Because of your work in the preceding stages, the first draft may flow quite smoothly. But don't be discouraged if it doesn't. You may find that your thesis has to be reshaped, that a point no longer fits, that you need to return to a prewriting activity to generate additional material. Such stopping and starting is to be expected. Writing the first draft is a process of discovery, involving the continual clarification and refining of ideas.

How to Proceed

There's no single right way to prepare a first draft. Some writers rely heavily on their scratch lists or outlines; others glance at them only occasionally. Some people write the first draft in longhand; others use a typewriter or a computer.

However you choose to proceed, consider the suggestions in the following checklist when moving from an outline or scratch list to a first draft.

☑ TURNING OUTLINE INTO FIRST DRAFT: A CHECKLIST

❑ Make the outline's *main topics* (I, II, III) the *topic sentences* of the essay's supporting paragraphs. (Topic sentences are discussed later, on page 49.)

❑ Make the outline's *subtopics* (A, B, C) the *subpoints* in each paragraph.

❑ Make the outline's *supporting points* (1, 2, 3) the key *examples* and *reasons* in each paragraph.

❑ Make the outline's *specific details* (a, b, c) the *secondary examples, facts, statistics, expert opinions,* and *quotations* in each paragraph.

(To see how one student, Harriet Davids, moved from outline to first draft, turn to pages 58–59.)
Although outlines and lists are valuable for guiding your work, don't be so dependent on them that you shy away from new ideas that surface during your writing of the first draft. If promising new thoughts pop up, jot them down in the margin. Then, at the appropriate point, go back and evaluate them: Do they support your thesis? Are they appropriate for your essay's purpose, audience, and tone? If so, go ahead and include the material in your draft.

It's easy to get bogged down while preparing the first draft if you try to edit as you write. Remember: A draft isn't intended to be perfect. For the time being, adopt a relaxed, noncritical attitude. Working as quickly as you can, don't stop to check spelling, correct grammar, or refine sentence structure. Save these tasks for later. One good way to help remind you that the first draft is tentative is to use scrap paper and pencil. Writing on alternate lines also underscores your intention to revise later on, when the extra space will make it easier to add and delete material. Similarly, writing on only one side of the paper can prove helpful if, during revision, you decide to move a section to another part of the paper.

What should you do if you get stuck while writing your first draft? Stay calm and try to write something—no matter how awkward or imprecise it may seem. Just jot a reminder to yourself in the margin ("Fix this," "Redo," or "Ugh!") to finetune the section later. Or leave a blank space to hold a spot for the right words when they finally break loose. It may also help to reread—out loud is best—what you've already written. Regaining a sense of the larger context is often enough to get you moving again. You might also try talking your way through a troublesome section. By speaking aloud, you tap your natural oral fluency and put it to work in your writing.

If a section of the essay strikes you as particularly difficult, don't spend time struggling with it. Move on to an easier section, write that, and then return to the challenging part. If you're still getting nowhere, take a break. Watch television, listen to music, talk with friends. While you're relaxing, your thoughts may loosen up and untangle the knotty section.

Because you read essays from beginning to end, you may assume that writers work the same way, starting with the introduction and going straight through to the conclusion. Often, however, this isn't the case. In fact, since an introduction depends so heavily on everything that follows, it's usually best to write the introduction *after* the essay's body.

When preparing your first draft, you may find it helpful to follow this sequence:

1. Write the supporting paragraphs.
2. Connect ideas in the supporting paragraphs.
3. Write the introduction.
4. Write the conclusion.
5. Write the title.

Write the Supporting Paragraphs

Drawn from the main sections in your outline or scratch list, each *supporting paragraph* should develop an aspect of your essay's thesis. Besides containing relevant, concrete, and sufficient evidence (see pages 33–37), a strong supporting paragraph is (1) often focused by a topic sentence and (2) organized around one or more patterns of development. We'll focus on both features in the pages ahead. As you read our discussion, though, keep in mind that you shouldn't expect your draft paragraphs to be perfect; you'll have a chance to revise them later on.

Use topic sentences.   Frequently, each supporting paragraph in an essay is focused by a *topic sentence* that functions as a kind of mini-thesis for the paragraph. Generally one or two sentences in length, the topic sentence usually appears at or near the beginning of the paragraph. However, it may also appear at the end, in the middle, or—with varied wording—several times within the paragraph.

Regardless of its length or location, the topic sentence states the paragraph's main idea. The other sentences in the paragraph provide support for this central point in the form of examples, facts, expert opinion, and so on. Like a thesis statement, the topic sentence *signals the paragraph's subject* and frequently *indicates the writer's attitude* toward that subject. In the topic sentences that follow, the subject of the paragraph is underlined once and the attitude toward that subject is underlined twice:

Some students select a particular field of study for the wrong reasons.
The ocean dumping of radioactive waste is a ticking time bomb.
Several contemporary rock groups show unexpected sensitivity to social
    issues.
Political candidates are sold like slickly packaged products.

As you work on the first draft, you may find yourself writing paragraphs without paying too much attention to topic sentences. That's fine, as long as you evaluate the paragraphs later on. When revising, you can provide a topic sentence for a paragraph that needs a sharper focus, recast a topic sentence for a paragraph that ended up taking an unexpected turn, even eliminate a topic sentence altogether if a paragraph's content is sufficiently unified to imply its point.

Use the patterns of development.   As you saw on page 40, an entire essay can be organized around one or more patterns of development (narration, process analysis, definition, and so forth). These patterns can also provide the organizational framework for an essay's supporting paragraphs. Assume you're writing an article for your town newspaper with the thesis "Year-round residents of an ocean community must take an active role in safeguarding the seashore environment." Your supporting paragraphs could develop this thesis through a variety of patterns, with each paragraph's topic sentence suggesting a specific pattern or combination of patterns. For example, one paragraph might start with the topic sentence "In a nearby ocean community, signs of environmental danger are everywhere" and go on to *describe* a seaside town with polluted waters, blighted trees, and diseased marine life. The next paragraph might have the topic sentence "Fortunately, not all seaside towns are plagued by such environmental problems" and continue by *contrasting* the troubled community with another, more ecologically sound shore town. A later paragraph, focused by the topic sentence "Residents can get involved in a variety of pro-environment activities," might use *division-classification* to elaborate on activities at the neighborhood, town, and municipal levels.

Connect Ideas in the Supporting Paragraphs

While writing the supporting paragraphs, you can try to smooth out the progression of ideas within and between paragraphs. In a *coherent* essay, the relationship between points is clear; readers can easily follow the development of your thoughts. (Sometimes, working on coherence causes a first draft to get bogged down; if this happens, move on, and wait until the revision stage to focus on such matters.)

The following paragraph lacks coherence for two main reasons. First, it sequences ideas improperly. (The idea about the toll attendants' being cut off from coworkers is introduced, dropped, then picked up again. References to motorists are similarly scattered throughout the paragraph.) Second, it doesn't indicate how individual ideas are related. (What, for example, is the connection between drivers who pass by without saying anything and attendants who have to work at night?)

Incoherent Support

Collecting tolls on the turnpike must be one of the loneliest jobs in the world. Each toll attendant sits in his or her booth, cut off from other attendants. Many drivers pass by each booth. None stays long enough for a brief "hello." Most don't acknowledge the attendant at all. Many toll attendants work at night, pushing them "out of synch" with the rest of the world. And sometimes the attendants have to deal with rude drivers who treat them like non-people, swearing at them for the long lines at the tollgate. Attendants also dislike how cut off they feel from their coworkers. Except for infrequent breaks, they have little chance to chat with each other and swap horror stories--small pleasures that would make their otherwise routine jobs bearable.

Coherent Support

Collecting tolls on the turnpike must be one of the loneliest jobs in the world. First of all, although many drivers pass by the attendants, none stays long enough for more than a brief "hello." Most drivers, in fact, don't acknowledge the toll collectors at all, with the exception of those rude drivers who treat the attendants like non-people, swearing at them for the long lines at the tollgate. Then, too, many toll attendants work at night, pushing them further "out of synch" with the rest of the world. Worst of all, attendants say, is how isolated they feel from their coworkers. Each attendant sits in his or her booth, cut off from other attendants. Except for infrequent breaks, they have little chance to chat with each other and swap horror stories--small pleasures that would make their otherwise routine jobs bearable.

To avoid the kinds of problems found in the incoherent paragraph, use—as the revised version does—two key strategies: (1) a clearly *chronological, spatial, emphatic* ("*Worst of all*, attendants say . . ."), or *simple-to-complex* approach and (2) *signal devices* ("*First of all*, although many drivers pass by . . .") to show how ideas are connected. For a discussion of the four organizational approaches, see pages 40–42. The following paragraphs describe signal devices.

Once you determine a logical approach for presenting your points, you need to make sure readers can follow the progression of those points. Signal devices provide readers with cues, reminding them where they have been and indicating where they are going.

Aim to include some signals—however awkward or temporary—in your first draft. If you find you *can't*, that's probably a warning that your ideas may not be arranged logically. A light touch should be your goal with such signals. Too many call attention to themselves, making the essay mechanical and plodding. In any case, here are some signaling devices to consider.

1. Transitions.   Words and phrases that ease readers from one idea to another are called *transitions*. The following chart lists a variety of such signals. (You'll notice that some transitions can be used for more than one purpose.)

TRANSITIONS

Time

first	immediately	afterward
before	at the same time	after
earlier	simultaneously	finally
next	in the meantime	later
then	meanwhile	eventually
now	subsequently	

Addition (or Sequence)

moreover	one . . . another	next
also	and	finally
furthermore	also	last
in addition	too	
first, . . . second, . . . third	besides	

Space

above	next to
below	behind

Examples

for instance   specifically
for example   namely
to illustrate

Contrast   **Comparison**

but   despite   similarly
however   even though   in the same way
yet   on the one (other) hand   also
in contrast   still   likewise
on the contrary   whereas   too
although   nevertheless   in comparison
otherwise   nonetheless
conversely

Cause or Effects   **Summary or Conclusion**

because   therefore
as a result   thus
consequently   in short
therefore   in conclusion
then
so
since

Here's an earlier paragraph from this chapter. Note how the italicized transitions show readers how ideas fit together.

> *After* you've generated supporting evidence, you're ready to organize that material. Even highly compelling evidence won't illustrate the validity of your thesis or achieve your purpose if the readers have to plow through a maze of chaotic evidence. Some writers can move quickly from generating support to writing a clearly structured first draft. (They usually say they have sequenced their ideas in their heads.) Most, *however,* need to spend some time sorting out their thoughts on paper before starting the first draft; *otherwise,* they tend to lose their way in a tangle of ideas.

2. Bridging sentences.   Although bridging sentences may be used within a paragraph, they are more often used to move readers from one paragraph to the next. Look again at the first sentence in the preceding paragraph. Note that the sentence consists of two parts: The first part reminds readers that the previous discussion focused on techniques for generating evidence; the second part tells readers that the focus will now be the organization of such evidence.

3. Repeated words, synonyms, and pronouns.   The repetition of important words maintains continuity, reassures readers that they are on the right track, and highlights key ideas. Synonyms—words similar in meaning to key words or phrases—also provide coherence, while making it possible to avoid unimaginative and tedious repetitions. Finally, pronouns (*he, she, it, they, this, that*) enhance coherence by causing readers to think back to the original word the pronoun replaces (antecedent). When using pronouns, however, be sure there is no ambiguity about antecedents.

Reprinted here is another paragraph from this chapter. Repeated words have been underlined once, synonyms underlined twice, and pronouns printed in italic type to illustrate how these techniques were used to integrate the paragraph's ideas.

> The process of prewriting—discovering a limited subject and generating ideas about *it*—prepares you for the next stage in writing an essay: identifying the paper's thesis or controlling idea. Presenting your opinion on a subject, the thesis should focus on an interesting and significant issue, *one* that engages your energies and merits your consideration. You may think of the thesis as the essay's hub—the central point around which all the other material revolves. Your thesis determines what does and does not belong in the essay. The thesis, especially when *it* occurs early in an essay, also helps focus the reader on the piece's central point.

Write the Introduction

Many writers don't prepare an introduction until they have started to revise; others feel more comfortable if their first draft includes in basic form all parts of the final essay. If that's how you feel, you'll probably write the introduction as you complete your first draft. No matter when you prepare it, keep in mind how crucial the introduction is to your essay's success. Specifically, the introduction serves three distinct functions: It arouses readers' interest, introduces your subject, and presents your thesis.

The length of your introduction will vary according to your paper's scope and purpose. Most essays you write, however, will be served best by a one- or two-paragraph beginning. To write an effective introduction, use any of the following methods, singly or in combination. The thesis statement in each sample introduction is underlined.

Broad Statement Narrowing to a Limited Subject

For generations, morality has been molded primarily by parents, religion, and schools. Children traditionally acquired their ideas about what is right and wrong, which goals are important in life, and how other people should be treated from these three sources collectively. But in the past few decades, a single force--television--has undermined the beneficial influence that parents, religion, and school have on children's moral development. Indeed, <u>television often implants in children negative values about sex, work, and family life.</u>

Brief Anecdote

At a local high school recently, students in a psychology course were given a hint of what it is like to be the parents of a newborn. Each "parent" had to carry a raw egg around at all times to symbolize the responsibilities of parenthood. The egg could not be left alone; it limited the "parents'" activities; it placed a full-time emotional burden on "Mom" and "Dad." This class exercise illustrates a common problem facing the majority of new mothers and fathers. <u>Most people receive little preparation for the job of being parents.</u>

Idea That Is the Opposite of the One Developed

We hear a great deal about divorce's disastrous impact on children. We are deluged with advice on ways to make divorce as painless as possible for youngsters; we listen to heartbreaking stories about the confused, grieving children of divorced parents. Little attention has been paid, however, to a different kind of effect that divorce may have on children. <u>Children from divorced families may become skilled manipulators, playing off one parent against the other, worsening an already painful situation.</u>

Series of Short Questions

What happens if a child is caught vandalizing school property? What happens if a child goes for a joyride in a stolen car and accidentally hits a pedestrian? Should parents be liable for their children's mistakes? Should parents have to pay what might be hundreds of thousands of dollars in damages? Adults have begun to think seriously about such questions because the laws concerning the limits of parental responsibility are changing rapidly. <u>With unfortunate frequency, courts have begun to hold parents legally and financially accountable for their children's misdeeds.</u>

Quotation

Educator Neil Postman believes that television has blurred the line between childhood and adulthood. According to Postman, "All the secrets that a print culture kept from children . . . are revealed all at once by media that do not, and cannot, exclude any audience." <u>This media barrage of information, once intended only for adults, has changed childhood for the worse.</u>

Refutation of a Common Belief

Adolescents care only about material things; their lives revolve around brand-name sneakers, designer jeans, the latest fad in stereo equipment. They resist education, don't read, barely know who is president, mainline rock 'n' roll, experiment with drugs, and exist on a steady diet of Ring-Dings, nachos, and beer. This is what many adults, including parents, seem to believe about the young. <u>The reality is, however, that young people today show more maturity and common sense than most adults give them credit for.</u>

Dramatic Fact or Statistic

Seventy percent of the respondents in a poll conducted by columnist Ann Landers stated that if they could live their lives over, they would choose not to have children. This startling statistic makes one wonder what these people believed parenthood would be like. <u>Most parents, it seems, have unrealistic expectations about their children.</u> Parents want their children to accept their values, follow their paths, and succeed where they failed.

Introductory paragraphs sometimes end with a *plan of development:* a quick preview of the essay's major points in the order in which those points will be discussed. The plan of development may be part of the thesis (as in the first sample introduction) or it may immediately follow the thesis (as in the last sample introduction). Because the plan of development outlines the essay's organizational structure, it helps prepare the reader for the essay's progression of ideas. In a brief essay, readers can often keep track of the ideas without this extra help. In a longer paper, though, a plan of development can be an effective unifying device since it highlights the main ideas the essay will develop.

Write the Conclusion

You may have come across essays that ended with jarring abruptness because they had no conclusions at all. Other papers may have had conclusions, but they sputtered to a weak close, a sure sign that the writers had run out of steam and wanted to finish as quickly as possible. Just as satisfying closes are an important part of everyday life (we feel cheated if dinner doesn't end with dessert or if a friend leaves without saying goodbye), a strong conclusion is an important part of an effective essay. Generally one or two paragraphs in length, the conclusion should give the reader a feeling of completeness and finality. One way to achieve this sense of "rounding off" is to return to an image, idea, or anecdote from the introduction. Because people tend to remember most clearly the points they read last, the conclusion is also a good place to remind readers of your thesis. You may also use the conclusion to make a final point about your subject. Be careful, though, not to open an entirely new line of thought at the essay's close.

Illustrated briefly here are several strategies for writing sound conclusions. These techniques may be used singly or in combination. The first strategy, the summary conclusion, can be especially helpful in long, complex essays since readers may appreciate a review of your points. Tacked onto a short essay, though, a summary conclusion often seems boring and mechanical.

Summary

Contrary to what many adults think, most adolescents are not only aware of the important issues of the times but also deeply concerned about them. They are sensitive to the plight of the homeless, the destruction of the environment, and the pitfalls of rampant materialism. Indeed, today's young people are not less mature and sensible than their parents were. If anything, they are more so.

Prediction

The growing tendency on the part of the judicial system to hold parents responsible for the actions of their wayward children can have a disturbing impact on all of us. Parents will feel bitter toward their own children and cynical about a system that holds them accountable for the actions of minors. Children, continuing to escape the consequences of their actions, will become even more lawless and destructive. Society cannot afford two such possibilities.

Quotation

The comic W. C. Fields is reputed to have said, "Anyone who hates children and dogs can't be all bad." Most people do not share Fields's cynicism. Viewing childhood as a time of purity, they are alarmed at the way television exposes children to the seamy side of life, stripping youngsters of their innocence and giving them a glib sophistication that is a poor substitute for wisdom.

Statistic

Granted, divorce may, in some cases, be the best thing for families torn apart by parents who battle one another. However, in longitudinal studies of children from divorced families, psychologist Judith Wallerstein found that only 10 percent of the youngsters felt relief at their parents' divorce; the remaining 90 percent felt devastated. Such statistics surely call into question parents' claims that they are divorcing for their children's sake.

Recommendation or Call for Action

It is a mistake to leave parenting to instinct. Instead, we should make parenting skills a required course in schools. In addition, a nationwide hotline should be established to help parents deal with crises. Such training and continuing support would help adults deal more effectively with many of the problems they face as parents.

Write the Title

Some writers say that they began a certain piece with only a title in mind. But for most people, writing a title is a finishing touch. Although creating a title for your paper is usually one of the last steps in writing an essay, it shouldn't be done haphazardly. It may take time to write an effective title— one that hints at the essay's thesis and snares the reader's interest.

Good titles may make use of the following techniques: repetition of sounds ("The Border on Our Backs"); questions ("Can You Be Educated From a Distance?"); and humor ("How to Say Nothing in 500 Words"). More often, though, titles are straightforward phrases derived from the essay's subject or thesis: "Shooting an Elephant" and "The Ways We Lie," for example.

Pull It All Together

Now that you know how to prepare a first draft, you might find it helpful to examine the accompanying illustration to see how the different parts of a draft can fit together. Keep in mind that not every essay you write will take this shape. As your purpose, audience, and tone change, so will your essay's structure. An introduction or conclusion, for instance, may be developed in more than one paragraph; the thesis statement may be implied or delayed until the essay's middle or end; not all paragraphs may have topic sentences; and several supporting paragraphs may be needed to develop a single topic sentence. Even so, the basic format presented here offers a strategy for organizing a variety of writing assignments—from term papers to lab reports. Once you feel comfortable with the structure, you have a foundation on which to base your variations. (This book's student and professional essays illustrate some possibilities.) Even when using a specific format, you always have room to give your spirit and imagination free play. The language you use, the details you select, the perspective you offer are uniquely yours. They are what make your essay different from everyone else's.

Sample First Draft

Here is the first draft of Harriet Davids's essay. (The assignment and prewriting for the essay appear on pages 11, 21–23, and 26.) Harriet wrote the draft in one sitting. Working at a computer, she started by typing her thesis at the top of the first page. Then, following the guidelines on page 47, she moved the material in her outline (pages 44–45) to her draft. Harriet worked rapidly; she started with the first body paragraph and wrote straight through to the last supporting paragraph.

By moving quickly, Harriet got down her essay's basic text rather easily. Once she felt she had captured in rough form what she wanted to say, she reread her draft to get a sense of how she might open and close the essay. Then she drafted her introduction and conclusion; both appear here, together with the body of the essay. The commentary following the draft will give you a clearer sense of how Harriet proceeded. (Note that the marginal annotations reflect Harriet's comments to herself about areas she needs to address when revising her first draft.)

Challenges for Today's Parents
by Harriet Davids

Thesis: Being a parent today is much more difficult than it was a generation ago.

Raising children used to be much simpler in the '50s and '60s. I remember TV images from that era showing that parenting involved simply teaching kids to clean their rooms,

ADD
SPECIFICS —————— do their homework, and_____. But being a parent today is much more difficult because nowadays parents have to shield/protect kids from lots of things, like distractions from schoolwork, from sexual material, from dangerous situations.

Parents have to control all the new distractions/temptations that turn kids away from schoolwork. These days many kids have stereos, computers, and televisions in their rooms. Certainly, my girls can't resist the urge to listen to MTV and go online, especially if it's time to do homework. Unfortunately, though, kids aren't assigned much homework and what is assigned too often is busywork. And there are even more distractions outside the home. Teens no longer hang out/ congregate on the corner where Dad and Mom can yell to them to come home and do homework. Instead they hang out at the mall, in video arcades, and fast-food restaurants. Obviously, parents and school can't compete with all this.

WEAK TRANS. ——— Also, parents have to help kids develop responsible sexual values even though sex is everywhere. Kids see sex magazines and dirty paperbacks in the corner store where they used to get candy and comic books. And instead of the artsy nude shots of

SP? ——— the past, kids see ronchey, explicit shots in Playboy and Penthouse. And movies have sexy stuff in them today. Teachers seduce students and people treat sex casually/as a sport. Not exactly traditional values. TV is no better. Kids see soap-opera characters in bed and cable shows full of nudity by

FIX ——— just flipping the dial. Even worse is what's on the Internet. Too easy for kids to access chat rooms and websites dealing with adult, sometimes pornographic material. The situation has gotten so out of hand that maybe the government should establish guidelines on what's permissible.

Worst of all are the life-threatening dangers that parents must help children fend off over the years. With older kids,

AWK. ——— drugs fall into place as a main concern. Peer pressure to try drugs is, bigger to kids than their parents' warnings. Other

WRONG WORD ——— kinds of warnings are common when children are small. Then parents fear violence since news shows constantly report stories of little children being abused. And when kids aren't

ADD SPECIFICS ——— much older, they have to resist the pressure to drink. Alcohol has always attracted kids, but nowadays they are drinking more and this can be deadly, especially when drinking is

REDO ——— combined with driving.

Most adults love their children and want to be good parents. But it's difficult because the world seems stacked against young people. Even Holden Caufield had trouble dealing

SP? ——— with society's confusing pressures. Parents must give their children some freedom but not so much that the kids lose sight of what's important.

Commentary

As you can see, Harriet's draft is rough. Because she knew she would revise later on (page 60), she "zapped out" the draft in an informal, colloquial style. For example, she occasionally expressed her thoughts in fragments ("Not exactly traditional values"), relied heavily on "and" as a transition, and used slangy expressions such as "kids," "dirty paperbacks," and "lots of things." She also used slashes between alternative word choices and left a blank space when wording just wouldn't come. Then, as Harriet reviewed the printed copy of this rough draft, she made handwritten marginal notes to herself in capital letters: "REDO" or "FIX" to signal awkward sentences; "ADD SPECIFICS" to mark overly general statements; "WRONG WORD" after an imprecise word; "SP?" to remind herself to check spelling in the dictionary; "WEAK TRANS." to indicate where a stronger signaling device was needed. (Harriet's final draft appears on pages 66–67.)

Writing a first draft may seem like quite a challenge, but the tips offered in these pages should help you proceed with confidence. Indeed, as you work on the draft, you may be surprised how much you enjoy writing. After all, this is your chance to get down on paper something you want to say.

Activities: Write the First Draft

1. Retrieve the writing you prepared in response to activity 3 on page 46. Applying the principles just presented, rework that material. If you wrote a single paragraph earlier, expand the material into a full essay draft. If you prepared an essay, strengthen what you wrote. In both cases, remember to consider your purpose, audience, and tone as you write the body of the essay as well as its introduction and conclusion. (Save your draft so you can rework it even further after reading about the next stage in the writing process.)

2. Referring to the outline you prepared in response to activity 2 or activity 4 on page 46, draft the body of your essay, making your evidence as strong as possible. As you work, keep your purpose, audience, and tone in mind. After reading what you've prepared, go ahead and draft a rough introduction, conclusion, and title. Finally, ask at least one other person to react to your draft by listing its strengths and weaknesses. (Save the draft so you can work with it further after reading about the next stage in the writing process.)

STAGE 6: REVISE THE ESSAY

By now, you've probably abandoned any preconceptions you might have had about good writers sitting down and creating a finished product in one easy step. Alexander Pope's comment that "true ease in writing comes from art, not chance" is as true today as it was more than two hundred years ago. Writing that seems effortlessly clear is often the result of sustained work, not of good luck or even inborn talent. And much of this work takes place during the final stage of the writing process when ideas, paragraphs, sentences, and words are refined and reshaped.

Professional writers—novelists, journalists, textbook authors—seldom submit a piece of writing that hasn't been revised. They recognize that rough, unpolished work doesn't do them justice. What's more, they often look forward to revising. Columnist Ellen Goodman puts it this way: "What makes me happy is rewriting. . . . It's like cleaning house, getting rid of all the junk, getting things in the right order, tightening up."

In a sense, revision occurs throughout the writing process: At some earlier stage, you may have dropped an idea, overhauled your thesis, or shifted paragraph order. What, then, is different about the rewriting that occurs in the revision stage? The answer has to do with the literal meaning of the word *revision*—to resee, or to see again. Genuine revision involves casting clear eyes on your work, viewing it as though you're a reader rather than the writer. Revision means that you go through your paper looking for trouble, ready to pick a fight with your own writing. And then you must be willing to sit down and make the changes needed for your writing to be as effective as possible.

Revision is not, as some believe, simply touch-up work—changing a sentence here or a word there, eliminating spelling errors, preparing a neat final copy. Revision means cutting deadwood, rearranging paragraphs, substituting new words for old ones, recasting sentences, improving coherence, even generating new material when appropriate. With experience, you'll learn how to streamline the process so you can focus on the most critical issues for a particular piece of writing. (For advice on correcting some common writing errors, see Appendix B on pages 634–646.)

Five Revision Strategies

Because revision is challenging, you may find yourself unsure about how to proceed. Keep in mind that there are no hard-and-fast rules about the revision process. Even so, the following pointers should help get you going if you balk at or feel overwhelmed by revising.

- *Set your draft aside for a while* before revising. When you pick up your paper again, you'll have a fresh, more objective point of view.
- *Work from typed or computer-generated material* whenever possible. Having your essay in neutral typed letters instead of in your own familiar writing helps you see the paper impartially, as if someone else had written it. Each time you make major changes, try to print out a copy of that section so that you can see it anew.
- *Read your draft aloud* as often as you can. Hearing how your writing sounds helps you pick up problems that you passed by before: places where sentences are awkward, meaning is ambiguous, words are imprecise. Even better, have another person read aloud to you what you have written. If the reader slows to a crawl over a murky paragraph or trips over a convoluted sentence, you know where you have to do some rewriting.
- *View revision as a series of steps*. Don't try to tackle all of a draft's problems at once; instead, proceed step by step, starting with the most pressing issues. Although there are bound to be occasions when you have time for only one quick pass over a draft, whenever possible, read

your draft several times; each time focus on different matters and ask yourself different questions. Move from a broad view of the draft to an up-close look at its mechanics.

* *Evaluate and respond to instructor feedback.* Often, instructors collect and respond to students' first drafts. Like many students, you may be tempted to look only briefly at your instructor's comments. Perhaps you've "had it" with the essay and don't want to think about revising the paper to reflect the instructor's remarks. But taking your instructor's comments into account when revising is often what's needed to turn a shaky first draft into a strong final draft.

When an instructor returns a final draft graded, you may think that the grade is all that counts. Remember, though: Grades are important, but comments are even more so. They can help you *improve* your writing—if not in this paper, then in the next one. If you don't understand or agree with the instructor's observations, don't hesitate to request a conference. Getting together gives both you and the instructor a chance to clarify your respective points of view.

Peer Review: An Additional Revision Strategy

Many instructors include in-class or at-home peer review as a regular part of a composition course. Peer review—the critical reading of another person's writing with the intention of suggesting changes—accomplishes several important goals. First, peer review helps you gain a more objective perspective on your work. When you write something, you're often too close to what you've prepared to evaluate it fairly; you may have trouble seeing where the writing is strong and where it needs to be strengthened. Peer review supplies the fresh, neutral perspective you need. Second, reviewing your classmates' work broadens your own composing options. You may be inspired to experiment with a technique you admired in a classmate's writing but wouldn't have thought of on your own. Finally, peer review trains you to be a better reader and critic of your *own* writing. When you get into the habit of critically reading other students' writing, you become more adept at critiquing your own.

The Peer Review/Revision Checklist on the inside front cover of this book will help focus your revision—whether you're reworking your own paper or responding to a peer's. Your instructor may have you respond to all questions on the checklist or to several selected items. What follows is a peer review worksheet that Harriet Davids's instructor prepared to help students respond to first drafts based on the assignment on page 11. Wanting students to focus on four areas (thesis statement, support for thesis statement, overall organization, and signal devices), the instructor drew upon relevant sections from the Peer Review/Revision Checklist. With this customized worksheet in hand, Harriet's classmate Frank Tejada was able to give Harriet constructive feedback on her first draft (see pages 58–59). (*Note:* Because Harriet didn't want to influence Frank's reaction, the draft she gave him didn't include her marginal notations to herself.)

Peer Review Worksheet

Essay Author's Name: <u>Harriet Davids</u> Reviewer's Name: <u>Frank Tejada</u>

1. **What is the essay's thesis? Is it explicit or implied? Does the thesis focus on a limited subject and express the writer's attitude toward that subject?**

   Thesis: "Being a parent today is much more difficult [than it used to be]." The thesis is limited and expresses a clear attitude. But the sentence the thesis appears in (last sentence of para. 1) is too long because it also contains the plan of development. Maybe put thesis and plan of development in separate sentences.

2. **What are the main points supporting the thesis? List the points. Is each supporting point developed sufficiently? If not, where is more support needed?**

   (1) Parents have to control kids' distractions from school.
   (2) Parents have to help kids develop responsible sexual values despite sex being everywhere.
   (3) Parents have to protect kids from life-threatening dangers.
      The supporting points are good and are explained pretty well, except for a few places. The "Unfortunately" sentence in para. 2 is irrelevant. Also, in para. 2, you use the example of your girls, but never again. Either include them throughout or not at all. In para. 3, the final sentence about the government guidelines opens a whole new topic; maybe steer away from this. The items in para. 4 seem vague and need specific examples. In the conclusion, omit Holden Caulfield; since he was from an earlier generation, this example undermines your thesis about parenting today.

3. **What overall format (chronological, spatial, emphatic, simple-to-complex) is used to sequence the essay's main points? Does this format work? Why or why not? What organizational format is used in each supporting paragraph? Does the format work? Why or why not?**

   The paper's overall emphatic organization seems good. Emphatic order also works in para. 3, and spatial order works well in para. 2. But the sentences in para. 4 need rearranging. Right now, the examples are in mixed-up chronological

> order, making it hard to follow. Maybe you should reorder the examples from young kids to older kids.

4. What signal devices are used to connect ideas within and between paragraphs? Are there too few signal devices or too many? Where?

> The topic sentence of para. 3 needs to be a stronger bridging sentence. Also, too many "and's" in para. 3. Try "in addition" or "another" in some places. I like the "worst of all" transition to para. 4.

As you can see, Frank flagged several areas that Harriet herself also noted needed work. (Turn to pages 58–59 to see Harriet's marginal comments on her draft.) But he also commented on entirely new areas (for example, the sequence problem in paragraph 4), offering Harriet a fresh perspective on what she needed to do to polish her draft. To see which of Frank's suggestions Harriet followed, take a look at her final draft on pages 66–67 and at the "Commentary" following the essay.

Becoming a skilled peer reviewer.   Even with the help of a checklist, preparing a helpful peer review is a skill that takes time to develop. At first, you, like many students, may be too easy or too critical. Effective peer review calls for rigor and care; you should give classmates the conscientious feedback that you hope for in return. Peer review also requires tact and kindness; feedback should always be constructive and include observations about what works well in a piece of writing. People have difficulty mustering the energy to revise if they feel there's nothing worth revising.

If your instructor doesn't include peer review, you can set up peer review sessions outside of class, with classmates getting together to respond to each other's drafts. Or you may select non-classmates who are objective (not a love-struck admirer or a doting grandparent) and skilled enough to provide useful commentary.

To focus your readers' comments, you may adapt the Peer Review/ Revision Checklist on the inside front cover of this book, or you may develop your own questions. If you prepare the questions yourself, be sure to solicit *specific* observations about what does and doesn't work in your writing. If you simply ask, "How's this?" you may receive a vague comment like "It's not very effective." What you want are concrete observations and suggestions: "I'm confused because what you say in the fifth sentence contradicts what you say in the second." To promote such specific responses, ask your readers targeted (preferably written) questions like "I'm having trouble moving from my second to my third point. How can I make the transition smoother?" Such questions require more than "yes" or "no" responses; they encourage readers to dig into your writing where you sense it needs work. (If it's feasible, encourage readers to *write* their responses to your questions.)

If you and your peer reviewer(s) can't meet in person, **e-mail** can provide a crucial means of contact. With a couple of clicks, you can simply send each other computer files of your work. Before you do so, determine whether your word-processing software is compatible; if so, you'll be able to send each other your computerized drafts as file attachments. If not, you can copy the text of your paper and paste it into the e-mail message box. (You'll likely lose the paper's format features, but the content is what matters most during peer review.) You and your reviewer(s) also need to decide exactly how to exchange comments about your drafts. You might conclude, for example, that you'll type your responses, perhaps in bold capitals, into the file itself. Or you might decide to print out the drafts and reply to the comments in writing, later exchanging the annotated drafts in person. No matter what you and your peer(s) decide, you'll probably find e-mail an invaluable tool in the writing process.

Evaluating and responding to peer review.   Accepting criticism isn't easy (even if you asked for it), and not all peer reviewers will be diplomatic. Even so, try to listen with an open mind to those giving you feedback. Take notes on their oral observations and/or have them fill out relevant sections from the Peer Review/Revision Checklist (on the inside front cover). Later, when you're ready to revise your paper, reread your notes. Which reviewer remarks seem valid? Which don't? Rank the problems and solutions that your reviewers identified, designating the most critical as number 1. Using the peer feedback, enter your own notes for revising in the margins of a clean copy of your draft. This way, you'll know exactly what changes need to be made in your draft as you proceed. Then, keeping the problems and remedies in mind, start revising. If you've been working on a computer, type in your changes, or handwrite changes directly on the draft above the appropriate line. (Rework extensive sections on a separate piece of paper.) When revising, always keep in mind that you may not agree with every reviewer suggestion. That's fine. It's *your* paper, and it's *your* decision to implement or reject the suggestions made by your peers.

STUDENT ESSAY

In this chapter, we've taken you through the various stages in the writing process. You've seen how Harriet Davids used prewriting (pages 21–23 and 26) and outlining (pages 44–45) to arrive at her first draft (pages 58–59). You've also seen how Harriet's peer reviewer, Frank Tejada, critiqued her first draft (pages 63–64). In the following pages, you'll look at Harriet's final draft—the paper she submitted to her instructor.

Harriet, a thirty-eight-year-old college student and mother of two teenagers, wanted to write an informative paper with a straightforward, serious tone. While preparing her essay, she kept in mind that her audience would include her course instructor as well as her classmates, many of them considerably younger than she. This is the assignment that prompted Harriet's essay:

> Goodman implies that, in some ways, today's world is hostile to children. Do you agree? Drawing upon but not limiting yourself to the material in your pre-reading journal, write an essay in which you support or reject this viewpoint.

Harriet's essay is annotated so that you can see how it illustrates the essay format described on page 57. As you read her essay, try to determine how well it reflects the principles of effective writing. The commentary following the paper will help you look at the essay more closely and give you some sense of the way Harriet went about revising her first draft.

Challenges for Today's Parents
by Harriet Davids

Introduction

Reruns of situation comedies from the 1950s and early 1960s dramatize the kinds of problems that parents used to have with their children. The Cleavers scold Beaver for not washing his hands before dinner; the Andersons ground Bud for not doing his homework; the Nelsons dock little Ricky's allowance because he keeps forgetting to clean his room. But times have changed dramatically. **Thesis** Being a parent today is much more difficult than it was a generation ago. **Plan of development** Parents nowadays must protect their children from a growing number of distractions, from sexually explicit material, and from life-threatening situations.   1

First supporting paragraph — **Topic sentence** Today's parents must try, first of all, to control all the new distractions that tempt children away from schoolwork. At home, a child may have a room furnished with a stereo, television, and computer. Not many young people can resist the urge to listen to CDs, go online, play computer games, or watch MTV--especially if it is time to do schoolwork. Outside the home, the distractions are even more alluring. Children no longer "hang out" on a neighborhood corner within earshot of Mom or Dad's reminder to come in and do homework. Instead, they congregate in vast shopping malls, buzzing video arcades, and gleaming fast-food restaurants. Parents and school assignments have obvious difficulty competing with such enticing alternatives.   2

Second
supporting
paragraph

Topic sentence
with link to
previous
paragraph

Besides dealing with these distractions, parents have to   3
shield their children from a flood of sexually explicit materials.
Today, children can find sex magazines and pornographic
paperbacks in the same corner store that once offered only
comics and candy. Children will not see the fuzzily
photographed nudes that a previous generation did but will
encounter the hard-core raunchiness of <u>Playboy</u> or <u>Penthouse</u>.
Moreover, the movies young people attend often focus on
highly sexual situations. It is difficult to teach children
traditional values when films show teachers seducing
students and young people treating sex as a casual sport.
Unfortunately, television, with its often heavily sexual content,
is no better. With just a flick of the dial, children can see soap-
opera stars cavorting in bed or watch cable programs where
nudity is common. But the sexually graphic content of TV
shows is nothing compared to the seamy material on the
Internet. Many parents report that their children, sometimes
without intending to, access pornographic chat rooms and
websites that haunt the youngsters for months afterward.

Third supporting
paragraph

Topic sentence
with emphasis
signal

Most disturbing to parents today, however, is the   4
increase in life-threatening dangers that face young people.
When children are small, parents fear that their youngsters
may be victims of violence. Every news program seems to
carry a report about a mass murderer who preys on young
girls, a deviant who has buried six boys in his cellar, or an
organized child pornography ring that molests preschoolers.
When children are older, parents begin to worry about their
kids' use of drugs. Peer pressure to experiment with drugs is
often stronger than parents' warnings. This pressure to
experiment can be fatal. Finally, even if young people escape
the hazards associated with drugs, they must still resist the
pressure to drink. Although alcohol has always held an
attraction for teenagers, reports indicate that they are drinking
more than ever before. As many parents know, the
consequences of this attraction can be deadly--especially
when drinking is combined with driving.

Conclusion

Within one generation, the world as a place to raise   5
children has changed dramatically. One wonders how
yesterday's parents would have dealt with today's problems.

References to
TV shows recall
introduction

Could the Andersons have kept Bud away from MTV? Could
the Nelsons have shielded little Ricky from sexually explicit
material on the Internet? Could the Cleavers have protected
Beaver from drugs and alcohol? Parents must be aware of all
these distractions and dangers yet be willing to give their
children the freedom they need to become responsible adults.
This is not an easy task.

COMMENTARY

 Introduction and thesis.   The opening paragraph attracts readers' interest by recalling several vintage television shows that have almost become part of our cultural heritage. Harriet begins with these examples from the past because they offer such a sharp contrast to the present, thus underscoring the idea expressed in her *thesis:* "Being a parent today is much more difficult than it was a generation ago." Opening in this way, with material that serves as a striking contrast to what follows, is a common and effective strategy. Note, too, that Harriet's thesis states the paper's subject (being a parent) as well as her attitude toward the subject (the job is more demanding than it was years ago).

Plan of development.   Harriet follows her thesis with a *plan of development* that anticipates the three major points to be covered in the essay's supporting paragraphs. When revising her first draft, Harriet followed peer reviewer Frank Tejada's recommendation (page 63) to put her thesis and plan of development in separate sentences. Unfortunately, though, her plan of development ends up being somewhat mechanical, with the major points being trotted past the reader in one long, awkward sentence. To deal with the problem, Harriet could have rewritten the sentence or eliminated the plan of development altogether, ending the introduction with her thesis.

Patterns of development.   Although Harriet develops her thesis primarily through *examples,* she also draws on two other patterns of development. The whole paper implies a *contrast* between the way life and parenting are now and the way they used to be. The essay also contains an element of *causal analysis* since all the factors that Harriet cites affect children and the way they are raised.

Purpose, audience, and tone.   Given the essay's *purpose* and *audience,* Harriet adopts a serious *tone,* providing no-nonsense evidence to support her thesis. But assume she had been asked by her daughters' school newspaper to write a humorous column about the trials and tribulations that parents face raising children. Aiming for a different tone, purpose, and audience, Harriet would have taken another approach. Drawing on her experience as a mother of two teenage daughters, she might have confessed how she survives MTV's flash and dazzle, as well as the din of stereos blasting rock music at all hours: she stuffs her ears with cotton, hides her daughters' CDs, and cuts off the electricity. This material—with its personalized perspective, exaggeration, and light tone—would be appropriate.

Organization.   Structuring the essay around a series of *relevant* and *specific examples,* Harriet uses *emphatic order* to sequence the paper's three main points: that a growing number of distractions, sexually explicit materials, and life-threatening situations make parenting difficult nowadays. The third supporting paragraph begins with the words "Most disturbing to parents today . . . ," signaling that Harriet feels particular concern about the physical dangers children face. Moreover, she uses basic organizational strategies to sequence the supporting examples within each paragraph. The details in the first supporting paragraph are organized *spatially*, starting with distractions at home and moving to those outside the home. The second supporting paragraph arranges examples *emphatically*. Harriet starts with sexually explicit publications and ends with the "seamy material on the Internet," which is even more disturbing than TV's "heavily sexual content." Note that Harriet followed Frank's peer review advice (page 63) about omitting her first-draft observation that kids don't get enough homework—or that they get too much busywork. The third and final supporting paragraph is organized *chronologically*; it begins by discussing dangers to small children and concludes by talking about teenagers. Again, Frank's advice—to use a clearer time sequence in this paragraph (page 63)—was invaluable when Harriet was revising.

The essay also displays Harriet's familiarity with other kinds of organizational strategies. Each supporting paragraph opens with a *topic sentence*. Further, *signal devices* are used throughout the paper to show how ideas are related to one another: *transitions* ("Instead, they congregate in vast shopping malls"; "Moreover, the movies young people attend often focus on highly sexual situations"); *repetition* ("sexual situations" and "sexual content"); *synonyms* ("distractions . . . enticing alternatives" and "life-threatening . . . fatal"); *pronouns* ("young people . . . they"); and *bridging sentences* ("Besides dealing with these distractions, parents have to shield their children from a flood of sexually explicit material").

Two minor problems.   Harriet's efforts to write a well-organized essay result in a somewhat predictable structure. It might have been better had she rewritten one of the paragraphs, perhaps embedding the topic sentence in the middle of the paragraph or saving it for the end. Similarly, Harriet's signal devices are a little heavy-handed. Even so, an essay with a sharp focus and clear signals is preferable to one with a confusing or inaccessible structure. As she gains more experience, Harriet can work on making the structure of her essays more subtle.

Conclusion.   Following Frank's suggestion, Harriet dropped from the final paragraph the first draft's problematic reference to Holden Caulfield (page 63). Having done that, she's able to bring the essay to a satisfying *close* by reminding readers of the paper's central idea and three main points. The final paragraph also extends the essay's scope by introducing a new but related issue: that parents have to strike a balance between their need to provide limitations and their children's need for freedom. Besides eliminating the distracting reference to Holden Caulfield, she replaced the shopworn opening sentence ("Most adults love their children . . . ") with three interesting and rhythmical questions ("Could the Andersons . . . ? Could the Nelsons . . . ? Could the Cleavers . . . ?"). Because these questions recall the essay's main points and echo the introduction's reference to vintage television shows, they help unify Harriet's paper and bring it to a rounded close.

These are just a few of the changes Harriet made when reworking her essay. Realizing that writing is a process, she left herself enough time to revise—and to carefully consider Frank Tejada's comments. Early in her composition course, Harriet learned that attention to the various stages in the writing process yields satisfying results, for writer and reader alike.

Activity: Revise the Essay

Return to the draft you wrote in response to either activity 1 or activity 2 on page 60. Also look at any written feedback you received on the draft. To identify any further problems in the draft, get together with several people (classmates, friends, or family members) and request that one of them read the draft aloud to you. Then ask your audience focused questions about the areas you sense need work, or use the checklist on the inside front cover to focus the feedback. In either case, summarize and rank the comments on a feedback chart or in marginal annotations. Then, using the comments as a guide, go ahead and revise the draft. Either type a new version or do your revising by hand, perhaps on a photocopy of the draft. Don't forget to proofread closely before submitting the paper to your instructor.

DESCRIPTION

WHAT IS DESCRIPTION?

All of us respond in a strong way to sensory stimulation. The sweet perfume of a candy shop takes us back to childhood; the blank white walls of the campus infirmary remind us of long vigils at a hospital where a grandmother lay dying; the screech of a subway car sets our nerves on edge.

Without any sensory stimulation, we sink into a less-than-human state. Neglected babies, left alone with no human touch, no colors, no lullabies, become withdrawn and unresponsive. And prisoners dread solitary confinement, knowing that the sensory deprivation can be unbearable, even to the point of madness.

Because sensory impressions are so potent, descriptive writing has a unique power and appeal. *Description* can be defined as the expression, in vivid language, of what the five senses experience. A richly rendered description freezes a subject in time, evoking sights, smells, sounds, textures, and tastes in such a way that readers become one with the writer's world.

HOW DESCRIPTION FITS YOUR
PURPOSE AND AUDIENCE

Description can be a supportive technique that develops part of an essay, or it can be the dominant technique used throughout an essay. Here are some examples of the way description can help you meet the objective of an essay developed chiefly through another pattern of development:

71

- In a *causal analysis* showing the *consequences* of pet overpopulation, you might describe the desperate appearance of a pack of starving stray dogs.
- In an *argumentation-persuasion* essay urging more rigorous handgun control, you might start with a description of a violent family confrontation that ended in murder.
- In a *process analysis* explaining the pleasure of making ice cream at home, you might describe the beauty of an old-fashioned, hand-cranked ice-cream maker.
- In a *narrative essay* recounting a day in the life of a street musician, you might describe the musician's energy and the joyous appreciation of passersby.

In each case, the essay's overall purpose would affect the amount of description needed.

Your readers also influence how much description to include. As you write, ask yourself, "What do my particular readers need to know to understand and experience keenly what I'm describing? What descriptive details will they enjoy most?" Your answers to these and similar questions will help you tailor your description to specific readers. Consider an article intended for professional horticulturists; its purpose is to explain a new technique for controlling spider mites. Because of readers' expertise, there would be little need for a lengthy description of the insects. Written for a college newspaper, however, the article would probably provide a detailed description of the mites so student gardeners could distinguish between the pesky parasites and flecks of dust.

While your purpose and audience define *how much* to describe, you have great freedom deciding *what* to describe. Description is especially suited to objects (your car or desk, for example), but you can also describe a person, an animal, a place, a time, and a phenomenon or concept. You might write an effective description of a friend who runs marathons (person), a pair of ducks that return each year to a neighbor's pond (animals), the kitchen of a fast-food restaurant (place), a period when you were unemployed (time), the "fight or flight" response to danger (phenomenon or concept).

Description can be divided into two types: *objective* and *subjective*. In an objective description, you describe the subject in a straightforward and literal way, without revealing your attitude or feelings. Reporters, as well as technical and scientific writers, specialize in objective description; their jobs depend on their ability to detail experiences without emotional bias. For example, a reporter may write an unemotional account of a township meeting that ended in a fistfight. Or a marine biologist may write a factual report describing the way sea mammals are killed by the plastic refuse (sandwich wrappings, straws, fishing lines) that humans throw into the ocean.

In contrast, when writing a subjective description, you convey a highly personal view of your subject and seek to elicit a strong emotional response from your readers. Such subjective descriptions often take the form of reflective pieces or character studies. For example, in an essay describing the rich plant life in an inner-city garden, you might reflect on people's longing to connect with the soil and express admiration for the gardeners' hard work—an admiration you'd like readers to share. Or, in a character study of your grandfather, you might describe his stern appearance and gentle behavior, hoping that the contradiction will move readers as much as it moves you.

The *tone* of a subjective description is determined by your purpose, your attitude toward the subject, and the reader response you wish to evoke. Consider an essay about a dynamic woman who runs a center for disturbed children. If you want readers to admire the woman, your tone will be serious and appreciative. But if you want to criticize her high-pressure tactics and management style, your tone will be disapproving and severe.

The language of a descriptive piece also depends, to a great extent, on whether your purpose is primarily objective or subjective. If the description is objective, the language is straightforward, precise, and factual. Such *denotative* language consists of neutral dictionary meanings. To describe as dispassionately as possible fans' violent behavior at a football game, you might write about the "large crowd" and its "mass movement onto the field." But for a subjective piece that inspires outrage in readers, you might write about the "swelling mob" and its "rowdy stampede onto the field." In the latter case, the language you used would be *connotative* and emotionally charged so that readers would share your feelings.

Subjective and objective descriptions often overlap. Sometimes a single sentence contains both objective and subjective elements: "Although his hands were large and misshapen by arthritis, they were gentle to the touch, inspiring confidence and trust." Other times, part of an essay may provide a factual description (the physical appearance of a summer cabin your family rented), while another part of the essay may be highly subjective (how you felt in the cabin, sitting in front of a fire on a rainy day).

At this point, you have a good sense of the way writers use description to achieve their purpose and to connect with their readers. Now take a moment to look closely at the photograph at the beginning of this chapter. Imagine you're writing a column, accompanied by the photo, for the local newspaper. Your purpose is to encourage businesspeople to support the city's mural arts program. Jot down some phrases you might use to *describe* the mural and its impact on the community.

SUGGESTIONS FOR USING DESCRIPTION IN AN ESSAY

The following suggestions will be helpful whether you use description as a dominant or a supportive pattern of development.

1. Focus a descriptive essay around a dominant impression.   Like other kinds of writing, a descriptive essay must have a thesis, or main point. In a descriptive essay with a subjective slant, the thesis usually centers on the *dominant impression* you have about your subject. Suppose you decide to write an essay on your ninth-grade history teacher, Ms. Hazzard. You want the paper to convey how unconventional and flamboyant she was. The essay could, of course, focus on a different dominant impression—how insensitive she could be to students, for example. What's important is that you establish—early in the paper—the dominant impression you intend to convey. Although descriptive essays often imply, rather than explicitly state, the dominant impression, that impression should be unmistakable.

2. Select the details to include.   The power of description hinges on your ability to select from all possible details only those that support the dominant impression. All others, no matter how vivid or interesting, must be left out. If you're describing how flamboyant Ms. Hazzard could be, the details in the following paragraph would be appropriate.

> A large-boned woman, Ms. Hazzard wore her bright red hair piled on top of her head, where it perched precariously. By the end of class, wayward strands of hair tumbled down and fell into eyes fringed by spiky false eyelashes. Ms. Hazzard's nails, filed into crisp points, were painted either bloody burgundy or neon pink. Plastic bangle bracelets, also either burgundy or pink, clattered up and down her ample arms as she scrawled on the board the historical dates that had, she claimed, "changed the world."

Such details—the heavy eye makeup, stiletto nails, gaudy bracelets—contribute to the impression of a flamboyant, unusual person. Even if you remembered times that Ms. Hazzard seemed perfectly conventional and understated, most likely you wouldn't describe those times since they contradict the dominant impression.

You must also be selective in the *number of details* you include. Having a dominant impression helps you eliminate many details gathered during prewriting, but there still will be choices to make. For example, it would be inappropriate to describe in exhaustive detail everything in a messy room:

> The brown desk, made of a grained plastic laminate, is directly under a small window covered by a torn yellow-and-gold plaid curtain. In the left corner of the desk are four crumbled balls of blue-lined yellow paper, three red markers,

two fine-point blue pens, an ink eraser, and four letters, two bearing special wildlife stamps. A green down-filled vest and a red cable-knit sweater are thrown over the back of the bright blue metal bridge chair pushed under the desk. Under the chair is an oval braided rug, its once brilliant blues and greens spotted by old coffee stains.

Readers will be reluctant to wade through such undifferentiated specifics. Even more important, such excessive detailing dilutes the focus of the essay. You end up with a seemingly endless list of specifics rather than with a carefully crafted picture in words. In this regard, sculptors and writers are similar—what they take away is as important as what they leave in.

Perhaps you're wondering how to generate the details that support your dominant impression. As you can imagine, you have to develop heightened powers of observation and recall. To sharpen these key faculties, it can be helpful to make up a chart with separate columns for each of the five senses. If you can observe your subject directly, enter in the appropriate columns what you see, hear, taste, and so on. If you're attempting to remember something from the past, try to recollect details under each of these sense headings. Ask yourself questions ("How did it smell? What did I hear?") and list each memory recaptured. You'll be surprised how this simple technique can tune you in to your experiences and help uncover the specific details needed to develop your dominant impression.

3. Organize the descriptive details.   Select the organizational pattern (or combination of patterns) that best supports your dominant impression. The paragraphs in a descriptive essay are usually sequenced *spatially* (from top to bottom, interior to exterior, near to far) or *chronologically* (as the subject is experienced in time). But the paragraphs can also be ordered *emphatically* (ending with your subject's most striking elements) or by *sensory impression* (first smell, then taste, then touch, and so on).

You might, for instance, use a *spatial* pattern to organize a description of a large city as you viewed it from the air, a taxi, and a subway car. A description of your first day on a new job might move *chronologically*, starting with how you felt the first hour on the job and proceeding through the rest of the day. In a paper describing a bout with the flu, you might arrange details *emphatically*, beginning with a description of your low-level aches and pains and concluding with an account of your raging fever. An essay about a neighborhood garbage dump, euphemistically called an "ecology landfill" by its owners, could be organized by *sensory impressions:* the sights of the dump, its smells, its sounds. Regardless of the organizational pattern you use, provide enough *signal devices* (for example, *about, next, worst of all*) so that readers can follow the description easily.

Finally, although descriptive essays don't always have conventional topic sentences, each descriptive paragraph should have a clear focus. Often this focus is indicated by a sentence early in the paragraph that names the scene, object, or individual to be described. Such a sentence functions as a kind of *informal topic sentence;* the paragraph's descriptive details then develop that topic sentence.

4. Use vivid sensory language and varied sentence structure.   The connotative language typical of subjective description should be richly evocative. The words you select must etch in readers' minds the same picture that you have in yours. For this reason, rather than relying on vague generalities, you must use language that involves readers' senses. Consider the difference between the following paired descriptions.

Vague	Vivid
The food was unappetizing.	The stew congealed into an oval pool of milky-brown fat.
The toothpaste was refreshing.	The toothpaste, tasting minty sweet, felt good against slippery teeth, free finally from braces.
Filled with passengers and baggage, the car moved slowly down the road.	Burdened with its load of clamoring children and well-worn suitcases, the car labored down down the interstate on bald tires and worn shocks, emitting puffs of blue exhaust and an occasional backfire.

Unlike the *concrete, sensory-packed* sentences on the right, the sentences on the left fail to create vivid word pictures that engage readers. While all good writing blends abstract and concrete language, descriptive writing demands an abundance of specific sensory language.

Keep in mind, too, that *verbs pack more of a wallop* than adverbs. The following sentence has to rely on adverbs (italicized) because its verbs are so weak: "She walked *casually* into the room and *deliberately* tried not to pay much attention to their stares." Rewritten, so that verbs (italicized), not adverbs, do the bulk of the work, the sentence becomes more powerful: "She *strolled* into the room and *ignored* their stares."

Figures of speech—nonliteral, imaginative comparisons between two basically dissimilar things—are another way to enliven descriptive writing. *Similes* use the words *like* or *as* when comparing; *metaphors* state or imply that two things being compared are alike; and *personification* attributes human characteristics to inanimate things.

The examples that follow show how effective figurative language can be in descriptive writing.

Moving as jerkily as a marionette on strings, the old man picked himself up off the sidewalk and staggered down the street. (*simile*)

Stalking their prey, the hall monitors remained hidden in the corridors, motionless and ready to spring on any unsuspecting student who dared to sneak into class late. (*metaphor*)

The scoop of vanilla ice cream, plain and unadorned, cried out for hot-fudge sauce and a sprinkling of sliced pecans. (*personification*)

Finally, when writing descriptive passages, you need to *vary sentence structure*. Don't use the same subject-verb pattern in all sentences. The second example above, for instance, could have been written as follows: "The hall monitors stalked their prey. They hid in the corridors. They remained motionless and ready to spring on any unsuspecting student who tried to sneak into class late." But the sentence is richer and more interesting when the descriptive elements are embedded, eliminating what would otherwise have been a clipped and predictable subject-verb pattern.

REVISION STRATEGIES

Once you have a draft of the essay, you're ready to revise. The following checklist will help you and those giving you feedback apply to description some of the revision techniques discussed on pages 60–62.

☑ DESCRIPTION: A REVISION/PEER REVIEW CHECKLIST

Revise Overall Meaning and Structure

❏ What dominant impression does the essay convey? Is the dominant impression stated or implied? Where? Should it be made more obvious or more subtle?

❏ Is the essay primarily objective or subjective? Should the essay be more emotionally charged or less so?

❏ Which descriptive details don't support the dominant impression? Should they be deleted, or should the dominant impression be adjusted to encompass the details?

Revise Paragraph Development

❏ How are the essay's descriptive paragraphs organized—spatially, chronologically, emphatically, or by sensory impression? Would another organizational pattern be more effective? Which one(s)?

❏ Which paragraphs lack a distinctive focus?

❏ Which descriptive paragraphs are mere lists of sensory impressions?

- ❏ Which descriptive paragraphs fail to engage the reader's senses? How could they be made more concrete?

Revise Sentences and Words

- ❏ What signal devices guide readers through the description? Are there enough signals? Too many?
- ❏ Where should sentence structure be varied to make it less predictable?
- ❏ Which sentences should include more sensory images?
- ❏ Which flat verbs should be replaced with vigorous verbs?
- ❏ Where should there be more or fewer adjectives?
- ❏ Do any figures of speech seem contrived or trite? Which ones?

STUDENT ESSAY

The following student essay was written by Marie Martinez in response to this assignment:

> The essay "Once More to the Lake" is an evocative piece about a spot that had special meaning in E. B. White's life. Write an essay about a place that holds rich significance for you, centering the description on a dominant impression.

While reading Marie's paper, try to determine how well it applies the principles of description. The annotations on Marie's paper and the commentary following it will help you look at the essay more closely.

Salt Marsh
by Marie Martinez

Introduction

In one of his journals, Thoreau told of the difficulty he had escaping the obligations and cares of society: "It sometimes happens that I cannot easily shake off the village. The thought of some work will run in my head and I am not where my body is--I am out of my senses. In my walks I . . . return to my senses." All of us feel out of our senses at times. Overwhelmed

Dominant impression (thesis)

by problems or everyday annoyances, we lose touch with sensory pleasures as we spend our days in noisy cities and stuffy classrooms. Just as Thoreau walked in the woods to return to his senses, I have a special place where I return to

Informal topic sentence:
Definition paragraph

mine: the salt marsh behind my grandparents' house.

My grandparents live on the East Coast, a mile or so inland from the sea. Between the ocean and the mainland is a

1

2

wide fringe of salt marsh. A salt marsh is not a swamp, but an expanse of dark, spongy soil threaded with saltwater creeks and clothed in a kind of grass called salt meadow hay. All the water in the marsh rises and falls daily with the ocean tides, an endless cycle that changes the look of the marsh--partly flooded or mostly dry--as the day progresses.

Informal topic sentence: First paragraph in a four-part spatial sequence → Heading out to the marsh from my grandparents' house, I   3
follow a short path through the woods. As I walk along, a sharp smell of salt mixed with the rich aroma of peaty soil fills my nostrils. I am always amazed by the way the path changes with the seasons. Sometimes I walk in the brilliant green of spring, sometimes in the tawny gold of autumn, sometimes in the grayish tan of winter. No matter the season, the grass flanking the trail is often flattened into swirls, **Simile** → like thick Van Gogh brush strokes that curve and recurve in circular patterns. No people come here. The peacefulness heals me like a soothing drug.

Informal topic sentence: Second paragraph in the spatial sequence → After a few minutes, the trail suddenly opens up to a view   4
that calms me no matter how upset or discouraged I might be: a line of tall waving reeds bordering and nearly hiding the salt marsh creek. To get to the creek, I part the reeds.

Informal topic sentence: Third paragraph in the spatial sequence → The creek is a narrow body of water no more than fifteen   5
feet wide, and it ebbs and flows as the ocean currents sweep toward the land or rush back toward the sea. The creek winds in a sinuous pattern so that I cannot see its beginning or end, the places where it trickles into the marsh or spills into the open ocean. Little brown birds dip in and out of the reeds on the far shore of the creek, making a special "tweep-tweep" sound peculiar to the marsh. When I stand at low tide on the shore of the creek, I am on a miniature cliff, for the bank of the creek falls abruptly and steeply into the water. Below me, green grasses wave and shimmer under the water while tiny minnows flash their silvery sides as they dart through the underwater tangles.

Informal topic sentence: Last paragraph in the spatial sequence → The creek water is often much warmer than the ocean, so   6
I can swim there in three seasons. Sitting on the edge of the creek, I scoop some water into my hand, rub my face and neck, then ease into the water. Where the creek is shallow, my feet sink into a foot of muck that feels **Simile** → like mashed potatoes mixed with motor oil. But once I become accustomed to it, I enjoy squishing the slimy mud through my toes. Sometimes I feel brushing past my legs the blue crabs that live in the creek. Other times, I hear the splash of a turtle or an otter as it slips from the shore into the water. Otherwise, it is silent. The salty water is buoyant and lifts my spirits as I stroke through it to reach the middle of the creek. There in the center, I float weightlessly, surrounded by tall reeds that reduce the world to water and sky. I am at peace.

Conclusion   The salt marsh is not the kind of dramatic landscape found   7
                  on picture postcards. There are no soaring mountains, sandy
                  beaches, or lush valleys. The marsh is a flat world that some
                  consider dull and uninviting. I am glad most people do not
                  respond to the marsh's subtle beauty because that means I can
Echo of idea in   be alone there. Just as the rising tide sweeps over the marsh,
introduction   floating debris out to the ocean, the marsh washes away my
                  concerns and restores me to my senses.

COMMENTARY

The dominant impression.   Marie responded to the assignment by writing a moving tribute to a place having special meaning for her—the salt
marsh near her grandparents' home. Like most descriptive pieces, Marie's
essay is organized around a *dominant impression:* the marsh's peaceful soli-
tude and gentle, natural beauty. The essay's introduction provides a context
for the dominant impression by comparing the pleasure Marie experiences in
the marsh to the happiness Thoreau felt in his walks around Walden Pond.

Combining patterns of development.   Before developing the essay's
dominant impression, Marie uses the second paragraph to *define* a salt marsh.
An *objective description*, the definition clarifies that a salt marsh—with its
spongy soil, haylike grass, and ebbing tides—is not to be confused with a
swamp. Because Marie offers such a factual definition, readers have the background needed to enjoy the personalized view that follows.

Besides the definition paragraph and the comparison in the opening
paragraph, the essay contains a strong element of *causal analysis:* Throughout, Marie describes the marsh's effect on her.

Sensory language.   At times, Marie develops the essay's dominant impression explicitly, as when she writes "No people come here" (paragraph 3) and
"I am at peace" (6). But Marie generally uses the more subtle techniques characteristic of *subjective description* to convey the dominant impression. First of
all, she fills the essay with strong *connotative language,* rich with *sensory images.*
The third paragraph describes what she smells (the "sharp smell of salt mixed
with the rich aroma of peaty soil") and what she sees ("brilliant green," "tawny
gold," and "grayish tan"). In the fifth paragraph, she tells us that she hears the
chirping sounds of small birds. And the sixth paragraph includes vigorous
descriptions of how the marsh feels to Marie's touch. She splashes water on her
face and neck; she digs her toes into the mud at the bottom of the creek; she
delights in the delicate brushing of crabs against her legs.

Figurative language, vigorous verbs, and varied sentence structure.   You
might also have noted that *figurative language, energetic verbs,* and *varied
sentence patterns* contribute to the essay's descriptive power. Marie develops a

simile in the third paragraph when she compares the flattened swirls of swamp grass to the brush strokes in a painting by Van Gogh. Later she uses another simile when she writes that the creek's thick mud feels "like mashed potatoes mixed with motor oil." Moreover, throughout the essay, she uses lively verbs ("shimmer," "flash") to capture the marsh's magical quality. Similarly, Marie enhances descriptive passages by varying the length of her sentences. Long, fairly elaborate sentences are interspersed with short, dramatic statements. In the third paragraph, for example, the long sentence describing the circular swirls of swamp grass is followed by the brief statement "No people come here." And the sixth paragraph uses two short sentences ("Otherwise, it is silent" and "I am at peace") to punctuate the paragraph's longer sentences.

Organization. We can follow Marie's journey through the marsh because she uses an easy-to-follow combination of *spatial, chronological,* and *emphatic* patterns to sequence her experience. The essay relies primarily on a spatial arrangement since the four body paragraphs focus on the different spots that Marie reaches: first, the path behind her grandparents' house (paragraph 3); then the area bordering the creek (4); next, her view of the creek (5); last, the creek itself (6). Each stage of her walk is signaled by an *informal topic sentence* near the start of each paragraph. Furthermore, *signal devices* (marked by italics here) indicate not only her location but also the chronological passage of time: "*As* I walk along, a sharp smell . . . fills my nostrils" (3); "*After* a few minutes, the trail suddenly opens up . . ." (4); "*Below* me, green grasses wave . . ." (5). And to call attention to the creek's serene beauty, Marie saves for last the description of the peace she feels while floating in the creek.

An inappropriate figure of speech. Although the four body paragraphs focus on the distinctive qualities of each location, Marie runs into a minor problem in the third paragraph. Take a moment to reread that paragraph's last sentence. Comparing the peace of the marsh to the effect of a "soothing drug" is jarring. The effectiveness of Marie's essay hinges on her ability to create a picture of a pure, natural world. A reference to drugs is inappropriate. Now, reread the paragraph aloud, stopping after "No people come here." Note how much more in keeping with the essay's dominant impression the paragraph is when the reference to drugs is omitted.

Conclusion. The concluding paragraph brings the essay to a graceful close. The powerful *simile* found in the last sentence contains an implied reference to Thoreau and to Marie's earlier statement about the joy to be found in special places having restorative powers. Such an allusion echoes, with good effect, the paper's opening comments.

Revising the first draft. When Marie met with some classmates during a peer review session, the students agreed that Marie's first draft was strong and moving. But they also said that they had difficulty following her route through the marsh; they found her third paragraph especially confusing. Marie kept track of her classmates' comments on a separate piece of paper and then entered them, numbered in order of importance, in the margin of her first draft. Reprinted here is the original version of Marie's third paragraph.

Original Version of the Third Paragraph

As I head out to the marsh from the house, I follow a short trail through the woods. A smell of salt mixed with the aroma of soil fills my nostrils. The end of the trail suddenly opens up to a view that calms me no matter how upset or discouraged I might be: a line of tall waving reeds bordering the salt marsh creek. Civilization seems far away as I walk the path of flattened grass and finally reach my goal, the salt marsh creek hidden behind the tall waving reeds. The path changes with the seasons; sometimes I walk in the brilliant green of spring, sometimes in the tawny gold of autumn, sometimes in the quiet grayish tan of winter. In some areas, the grass is flattened into swirls that make the marsh resemble one of those paintings by Van Gogh. No people come here. The peacefulness heals me like a soothing drug. The path stops at the line of tall waving reeds, standing upright at the border of the creek. I part the reeds to get to the creek.

When Marie looked more carefully at the paragraph, she agreed it was confusing. For one thing, the paragraph's third and fourth sentences indicated that she had come to the path's end and had reached the reeds bordering the creek. In the following sentences, however, she was on the path again. Then, at the end, she was back at the creek, as if she had just arrived there. Marie resolved this confusion by breaking the single paragraph into two separate ones—the first describing the walk along the path, the second describing her arrival at the creek. This restructuring, especially when combined with clearer transitions, eliminated the confusion.

While revising her essay, Marie also intensified the sensory images in her original paragraph. She changed the "smell of salt and soil" to the "sharp smell of salt mixed with the rich aroma of peaty soil." And when she added the phrase "thick Van Gogh brush strokes that curve and recurve in circular patterns," she made the comparison between the marsh grass and a Van Gogh painting more vivid.

These are just some of the changes Marie made while rewriting her paper. Her skillful revisions provided the polish needed to make an already strong essay even more evocative.

Activities: Description

Prewriting Activities

1. Imagine you're writing two essays: One explains the *process* by which students get "burned out"; the other *argues* that being a spendthrift is better (or worse) than being frugal. Jot down ways you might use description in each essay.

2. Go to a place on campus where students congregate. In preparation for an *objective* description of this place, make notes of various sights, sounds, smells, and textures, as well as the overall "feel" of the place. Then, in preparation for a *subjective* description, observe and take notes on another sheet of paper. Compare the two sets of material. What differences do you see in word choice and selection of details?

Revising Activities

3. Revise each of the following sentence sets twice. The first time, create an unmistakable mood; the second time, create a sharply contrasting mood. To convey atmosphere, vary sentence structure, use vigorous verbs, provide rich sensory details, and pay special attention to words' connotations.

   a. The card players sat around the table. The table was old. The players were, too.
   b. A long line formed outside the movie theater. People didn't want to miss the show. The movie had received a lot of attention recently.
   c. A girl walked down the street in her first pair of high heels. This was a new experience for her.

4. The following descriptive paragraph is from the first draft of an essay showing that personal growth may result when romanticized notions and reality collide. How effective is the paragraph in illustrating the essay's thesis? Which details are powerful? Which could be more concrete? Which should be deleted? Where should sentence structure be more varied? How could the description be made more coherent? Revise the paragraph, correcting any problems you discover and adding whatever sensory details are needed to enliven the description. Feel free to break the paragraph into two or more separate ones.

   As a child, I was intrigued by stories about the farm in Harrison County, Maine, where my father spent his teens. Being raised on a farm seemed more interesting than growing up in the suburbs. So about a year ago, I decided to see for myself what the farm was like. I got there by driving on Route 334, a surprisingly easy-to-drive, four-lane highway that had recently been built with matching state and federal funds. I turned into the dirt road leading to the farm and got out of my car. It had been washed and waxed for the occasion. Then I headed for a dirt-colored barn. Its roof was full of huge, rotted holes. As I rounded the bushes, I saw the house. It too was dirt-colored. Its paint must have worn off decades ago. A couple of dead-looking old cars were sprawled in front of the barn. They were dented and windowless. Also by the barn was an ancient refrigerator, crushed like a discarded accordion. The porch steps to the house were slanted and wobbly. Through the open windows came a stale smell and the sound of television. Looking in the front door screen, I could see two chickens jumping around inside. Everything looked dirty both inside and out. Secretly grateful that no one answered my knock, I bolted down the stairs, got into my clean, shiny car, and drove away.

Gordon Parks

The son of deeply religious tenant farmers, Gordon Parks (1912–2006) grew up in Kansas knowing both the comforts of familial love and the torments of poverty and racism. Sent as a teenager to live with his sister in Minnesota after his mother's death, Parks was thrown out on his own in a frigid winter by his brother-in-law. To support himself, Parks worked as a janitor in a flophouse and as a piano player in a bordello. These and other odd jobs gave Parks the means to buy his first camera. Fascinated by photographic images, Parks studied the masters and eventually developed his own powers as a photographer. So evocative were his photographic studies that both *Life* and *Vogue* brought him on staff, the first Black photographer to be hired by the two magazines. Parks's prodigious creativity has found expression in filmmaking (*Shaft* in 1971), musical composition (both classical and jazz), fiction, nonfiction, and poetry (titles include *The Learning Tree, A Choice of Weapons, To Smile in Autumn, Arias in Silence, Glimpses Toward Infinity, A Star for Noon,* and *The Sun Stalker,* published, respectively, in 1986, 1987, 1988, 1994, 1996, 2000, and 2003.). But it is Parks's photographic essays, covering five decades of American life, that brought him the most acclaim. In the following essay, taken from his 1990 autobiography, *Voices in the Mirror,* Parks tells the story behind one of his most memorable photographic works—that of a twelve-year-old boy and his family, living in the slums of Rio de Janeiro.

Pre-Reading Journal Entry

The problem of poverty has provoked a wide array of proposed solutions. One controversial proposal argues that the government should pay poor women financial incentives to use birth control. What do you think of this proposal? Why is such a policy controversial? Use your journal to explore your thinking on this issue.

Flavio's Home

I've never lost my fierce grudge against poverty. It is the most savage of   1
all human afflictions, claiming victims who can't mobilize their efforts against it, who often lack strength to digest what little food they scrounge up to survive. It keeps growing, multiplying, spreading like a cancer. In my wanderings I attack it wherever I can—in barrios, slums and favelas.

Catacumba was the name of the favela[1] where I found Flavio da Silva. It   2
was wickedly hot. The noon sun baked the mud-rot of the wet mountain-

[1]Slums on the outskirts of Rio de Janeiro, Brazil, inhabited by seven hundred thousand people (editors' note).

side. Garbage and human excrement clogged the open sewers snaking down the slopes. José Gallo, a *Life* reporter, and I rested in the shade of a jacaranda tree halfway up Rio de Janeiro's most infamous deathtrap. Below and above us were a maze of shacks, but in the distance alongside the beach stood the gleaming white homes of the rich.

Breathing hard, balancing a tin of water on his head, a small boy climbed   3
toward us. He was miserably thin, naked but for filthy denim shorts. His legs resembled sticks covered with skin and screwed into his feet. Death was all over him, in his sunken eyes, cheeks and jaundiced coloring. He stopped for breath, coughing, his chest heaving as water slopped over his bony shoulders. Then jerking sideways like a mechanical toy, he smiled a smile I will never forget. Turning, he went on up the mountainside.

The detailed *Life* assignment in my back pocket was to find an impover-   4
ished father with a family, to examine his earnings, political leanings, religion, friends, dreams and frustrations. I had been sent to do an essay on poverty. This frail boy bent under his load said more to me about poverty than a dozen poor fathers. I touched Gallo, and we got up and followed the boy to where he entered a shack near the top of the mountainside. It was a leaning crumpled place of old plankings with a rusted tin roof. From inside we heard the babblings of several children. José knocked. The door opened and the boy stood smiling with a bawling naked baby in his arms.

Still smiling, he whacked the baby's rump, invited us in and offered us a   5
box to sit on. The only other recognizable furniture was a sagging bed and a broken baby's crib. Flavio was twelve, and with Gallo acting as interpreter, he introduced his younger brothers and sisters: "Mario, the bad one; Baptista, the good one; Albia, Isabel and the baby Zacarias." Two other girls burst into the shack, screaming and pounding on one another. Flavio jumped in and parted them. "Shut up, you two." He pointed at the older girl. "That's Maria, the nasty one." She spit in his face. He smacked her and pointed to the smaller sister. "That's Luzia. She thinks she's pretty."

Having finished the introductions, he went to build a fire under the   6
stove—a rusted, bent top of an old gas range resting on several bricks. Beneath it was a piece of tin that caught the hot coals. The shack was about six by ten feet. Its grimy walls were a patchwork of misshapen boards with large gaps between them, revealing other shacks below stilted against the slopes. The floor, rotting under layers of grease and dirt, caught shafts of light slanting down through spaces in the roof. A large hole in the far corner served as a toilet. Beneath that hole was the sloping mountainside. Pockets of poverty in New York's Harlem, on Chicago's south side, in Puerto Rico's infamous El Fungito seemed pale by comparison. None of them had prepared me for this one in the favela of Catacumba.

Flavio washed rice in a large dishpan, then washed Zacarias's feet in the   7
same water. But even that dirty water wasn't to be wasted. He tossed in a chunk of lye soap and ordered each child to wash up. When they were

finished he splashed the water over the dirty floor, and, dropping to his knees, he scrubbed the planks until the black suds sank in. Just before sundown he put beans on the stove to warm, then left, saying he would be back shortly. "Don't let them burn," he cautioned Maria. "If they do and Poppa beats me, you'll get it later." Maria, happy to get at the licking spoon, switched over and began to stir the beans. Then slyly she dipped out a spoonful and swallowed them. Luzia eyed her. "I see you. I'm going to tell on you for stealing our supper."

Maria's eyes flashed anger. "You do and I'll beat you, you little bitch." Luzia threw a stick at Maria and fled out the door. Zacarias dropped off to sleep. Mario, the bad one, slouched in a corner and sucked his thumb. Isabel and Albia sat on the floor clinging to each other with a strange tenderness. Isabel held onto Albia's hair and Albia clutched at Isabel's neck. They appeared frozen in an act of quiet violence.

Flavio returned with wood, dumped it beside the stove and sat down to rest for a few minutes, then went down the mountain for more water. It was dark when he finally came back, his body sagging from exhaustion. No longer smiling, he suddenly had the look of an old man and by now we could see that he kept the family going. In the closed torment of that pitiful shack, he was waging a hopeless battle against starvation. The da Silva children were living in a coffin.

When at last the parents came in, Gallo and I seemed to be part of the family. Flavio had already told them we were there. "Gordunn Americano!" Luzia said, pointing at me. José, the father, viewed us with skepticism. Nair, his pregnant wife, seemed tired beyond speaking. Hardly acknowledging our presence, she picked up Zacarias, placed him on her shoulder and gently patted his behind. Flavio scurried about like a frightened rat, his silence plainly expressing the fear he held of his father. Impatiently, José da Silva waited for Flavio to serve dinner. He sat in the center of the bed with his legs crossed beneath him, frowning, waiting. There were only three tin plates. Flavio filled them with black beans and rice, then placed them before his father. José da Silva tasted them, chewed for several moments, then nodded his approval for the others to start. Only he and Nair had spoons; the children ate with their fingers. Flavio ate off the top of a coffee can. Afraid to offer us food, he edged his rice and beans toward us, gesturing for us to take some. We refused. He smiled, knowing we understood.

Later, when we got down to the difficult business of obtaining permission from José da Silva to photograph his family, he hemmed and hawed, wallowing in the pleasant authority of the decision maker. He finally gave in, but his manner told us that he expected something in return. As we were saying good night Flavio began to cough violently. For a few moments his lungs seemed to be tearing apart. I wanted to get away as quickly as possible. It was cowardly of me, but the bluish cast of his skin beneath the sweat, the choking and spitting were suddenly unbearable.

Gallo and I moved cautiously down through the darkness trying not to 12 appear as strangers. The Catacumba was no place for strangers after sundown. Desperate criminals hid out there. To hunt them out, the police came in packs, but only in daylight. Gallo cautioned me. "If you get caught up here after dark it's best to stay at the da Silvas' until morning." As we drove toward the city the large white buildings of the rich loomed up. The world behind us seemed like a bad dream. I had already decided to get the boy Flavio to a doctor, and as quickly as possible.

The plush lobby of my hotel on the Copacabana waterfront was 13 crammed with people in formal attire. With the stink of the favela in my clothes, I hurried to the elevator hoping no passengers would be aboard. But as the door was closing a beautiful girl in a white lace gown stepped in. I moved as far away as possible. Her escort entered behind her, swept her into his arms and they indulged in a kiss that lasted until they exited on the next floor. Neither of them seemed to realize that I was there. The room I returned to seemed to be oversized; the da Silva shack would have fit into one corner of it. The steak dinner I had would have fed the da Silvas for three days.

Billowing clouds blanketed Mount Corcovado as we approached the 14 favela the following morning. Suddenly the sun burst through, silhouetting Cristo Redentor, the towering sculpture of Christ with arms extended, its back turned against the slopes of Catacumba. The square at the entrance to the favela bustled with hundreds of favelados. Long lines waited at the sole water spigot. Others waited at the only toilet on the entire mountainside. Women, unable to pay for soap, beat dirt from their wash at laundry tubs. Men, burdened with lumber, picks and shovels and tools important to their existence threaded their way through the noisy throngs. Dogs snarled, barked and fought. Woodsmoke mixed with the stench of rotting things. In the mist curling over the higher paths, columns of favelados climbed like ants with wood and water cans on their heads.

We came upon Nair bent over her tub of wash. She wiped away sweat 15 with her apron and managed a smile. We asked for her husband and she pointed to a tiny shack off to her right. This was José's store, where he sold kerosene and bleach. He was sitting on a box, dozing. Sensing our presence, he awoke and commenced complaining about his back. "It kills me. The doctors don't help because I have no money. Always talk and a little pink pill that does no good. Ah, what is to become of me?" A woman came to buy bleach. He filled her bottle. She dropped a few coins and as she walked away his eyes stayed on her backside until she was out of sight. Then he was complaining about his back again.

"How much do you earn a day?" Gallo asked. 16

"Seventy-five cents. On a good day maybe a dollar." 17

"Why aren't the kids in school?" 18

"I don't have money for the clothes they need to go to school."   19

"Has Flavio seen a doctor?"   20

He pointed to a one-story wooden building. "That's the clinic right   21
there. They're mad because I built my store in front of their place. I won't
tear it down so they won't help my kids. Talk, talk, talk and pink pills." We
bid him good-bye and started climbing, following mud trails, jutting rock,
slime-filled holes and shack after shack propped against the slopes on shaky
pilings. We sidestepped a dead cat covered with maggots. I held my breath
for an instant, only to inhale the stench of human excrement and garbage.
Bare feet and legs with open sores climbed above us—evils of the terrible soil
they trod every day, and there were seven hundred thousand or more afflicted people in favelas around Rio alone. Touching me, Gallo pointed to Flavio
climbing ahead of us carrying firewood. He stopped to glance at a man
descending with a small coffin on his shoulder. A woman and a small child
followed him. When I lifted my camera, grumbling erupted from a group of
men sharing beer beneath a tree.

"They're threatening," Gallo said. "Keep moving. They fear cameras.   2:
Think they're evil eyes bringing bad luck." Turning to watch the funeral procession, Flavio caught sight of us and waited. When we took the wood from
him he protested, saying he was used to carrying it. He gave in when I hung
my camera around his neck. Then, beaming, he climbed on ahead of us.

The fog had lifted and in the crisp morning light the shack looked more   2
squalid. Inside the kids seemed even noisier. Flavio smiled and spoke above
their racket. "Someday I want to live in a real house on a real street with
good pots and pans and a bed with sheets." He lit the fire to warm leftovers
from the night before. Stale rice and beans—for breakfast and supper. No
lunch; midday eating was out of the question. Smoke rose and curled up
through the ceiling's cracks. An air current forced it back, filling the place
and Flavio's lungs with fumes. A coughing spasm doubled him up, turned
his skin blue under viscous sweat. I handed him a cup of water, but he waved
it away. His stomach tightened as he dropped to his knees. His veins
throbbed as if they would burst. Frustrated, we could only watch; there was
nothing we could do to help. Strangely, none of his brothers or sisters
appeared to notice. None of them stopped doing whatever they were doing.
Perhaps they had seen it too often. After five interminable minutes it was
over, and he got to his feet, smiling as though it had all been a joke. "Maria,
it's time for Zacarias to be washed!"

"But there's rice in the pan!"   2

"Dump it in another pan—and don't spill water!"   2

Maria picked up Zacarias, who screamed, not wanting to be washed.   2
Irritated, Maria gave him a solid smack on his bare bottom. Flavio stepped
over and gave her the same, then a free-for-all started with Flavio, Maria and
Mario slinging fists at one another. Mario got one in the eye and fled the
shack calling Flavio a dirty son-of-a-bitch. Zacarias wound up on the floor

sucking his thumb and escaping his washing. The black bean and rice breakfast helped to get things back to normal. Now it was time to get Flavio to the doctor.

The clinic was crowded with patients—mothers and children covered with open sores, a paralytic teenager, a man with an ear in a state of decay, an aged blind couple holding hands in doubled darkness. Throughout the place came wailings of hunger and hurt. Flavio sat nervously between Gallo and me. "What will the doctor do to me?" he kept asking. 27

"We'll see. We'll wait and see." 28

In all, there were over fifty people. Finally, after two hours, it was Flavio's turn and he broke out in a sweat, though he smiled at the nurse as he passed through the door to the doctor's office. The nurse ignored it; in this place of misery, smiles were unexpected. 29

The doctor, a large, beady-eyed man with a crew cut, had an air of impatience. Hardly acknowledging our presence, he began to examine the frightened Flavio. "Open your mouth. Say 'Ah.' Jump up and down. Breathe out. Take off those pants. Bend over. Stand up. Cough. Cough louder. Louder." He did it all with such cold efficiency. Then he spoke to us in English so Flavio wouldn't understand. "This little chap has just about had it." My heart sank. Flavio was smiling, happy to be over with the examination. He was handed a bottle of cough medicine and a small box of pink pills, then asked to step outside and wait. 30

"This the da Silva kid?" 31

"Yes." 32

"What's your interest in him?" 33

"We want to help in some way." 34

"I'm afraid you're too late. He's wasted with bronchial asthma, malnutrition and, I suspect, tuberculosis. His heart, lungs and teeth are all bad." He paused and wearily rubbed his forehead. "All that at the ripe old age of twelve. And these hills are packed with other kids just as bad off. Last year ten thousand died from dysentery alone. But what can we do? You saw what's waiting outside. It's like this every day. There's hardly enough money to buy aspirin. A few wealthy people who care help keep us going." He was quiet for a moment. "Maybe the right climate, the right diet, and constant medical care might . . ." He stopped and shook his head. "Naw. That poor lad's finished. He might last another year—maybe not." We thanked him and left. 35

"What did he say?" Flavio asked as we scaled the hill. 36

"Everything's going to be all right, Flav. There's nothing to worry about." 37

It had clouded over again by the time we reached the top. The rain swept in, clearing the mountain of Corcovado. The huge Christ figure loomed up again with clouds swirling around it. And to it I said a quick prayer for the boy walking beside us. He smiled as if he had read my thoughts. "Papa says 'El Cristo' has turned his back on the favela." 38

"You're going to be all right, Flavio."   39

"I'm not scared of death. It's my brothers and sisters I worry about.   40
What would they do?"

"You'll be all right, Flavio."[2]   41

---

[2]Parks's photo-essay on Flavio generated an unprecedented response from *Life* readers. Indeed, they sent so much money to the da Silvas that the family was able to leave the *favela* for better living conditions. Parks brought Flavio to the United States for medical treatment, and the boy's health was restored. However, Flavio's story didn't have an unqualifiedly happy ending. Although he overcame his illness and later married and had a family, Flavio continuously fantasized about returning to the United States, convinced that only by returning to America could he improve his life. His obsession eventually eroded the promise of his life in Brazil (editors' note).

Questions for Close Reading

1. What is the selection's thesis (or dominant impression)? Locate the sentence(s) in which Parks states his main idea. If he doesn't state the thesis explicitly, express it in your own words.
2. What is Flavio's family like? Why does Flavio have so much responsibility in the household?
3. What are some of the distinctive characteristics of Flavio's neighborhood and home?
4. What seems to be the basis of Flavio's fear of giving food to Parks and Gallo? What did Parks and Gallo understand that led them to refuse?
5. Refer to your dictionary as needed to define the following words used in the selection: *barrios* (paragraph 1), *jacaranda* (2), *jaundiced* (3), and *spigot* (14).

Questions About the Writer's Craft

1. **The pattern.** Without stating it explicitly, Parks conveys a dominant impression about Flavio. What is that impression? What details create it?
2. **Other patterns.** When relating how Flavio performs numerous household tasks, Parks describes several *processes*. How do these step-by-step explanations reinforce Parks's dominant impression of Flavio?
3. Parks provides numerous sensory specifics to depict Flavio's home. Look closely, for example, at the description in paragraph 6. Which words and phrases convey strong sensory images? How does Parks use transitions to help the reader move from one sensory image to another?
4. Paragraph 13 includes a scene that occurs in Parks's hotel. What's the effect of this scene? What does it contribute to the essay that the most detailed description of the *favela* could not?

Writing Assignments Using Description
as a Pattern of Development

∞ 1. Parks paints a wrenching portrait of a person who remains vibrant and hopeful even though he is suffering greatly—from physical illness, poverty, overwork, and worry. Write a description about someone you know who has shown courage or other positive qualities during a time of personal trouble. Include, as Parks does, plentiful details about the person's appearance and behavior so that you don't have to state directly what you admire about the person. Maya Angelou's "Sister Flowers" (page 100) shows how one writer conveys the special quality of an admirable individual.

2. Parks presents an unforgettable description of the *favela* and the living conditions there. Write an essay about a region, city, neighborhood, or building that also projects an overwhelming negative feeling. Include only those details that convey your dominant impression, and provide—as Parks does—vivid sensory language to convey your attitude toward your subject.

Writing Assignments Combining Patterns of Development

3. The doctor reports that a few wealthy people contribute to the clinic, but the reader can tell from the scene in Parks's hotel that most people are insensitive to those less fortunate. Write an essay *describing* a specific situation that you feel reflects people's tendency to ignore the difficulties of others. Analyze why people distance themselves from the problem; then present specific *steps* that could be taken to sensitize them to the situation. Charmie Gholson's "Charity Display?" (page 151), John M. Darley and Bibb Latané's "Why People Don't Help in a Crisis" (page 417), and Mark Twain's "The Damned Human Race" (page 527) will provide some perspective on the way people harden themselves to the pain of others.

4. Although Parks celebrates Flavio's generosity of spirit, the writer also *illustrates* the brutalizing effect of an impoverished environment. Prepare an essay in which you also show that setting, architecture, even furnishings can influence mood and behavior. You may, as Parks does, focus on the corrosive effect of a negative environment, or you may write about the nurturing effect of a positive environment. Either way, provide vivid *descriptive* details of the environment you're considering. Possible subjects include a park in the middle of a city, a bus terminal, and a college library.

Writing Assignment Using a Journal Entry as a Starting Point

5. Write an essay explaining why you think impoverished women should—or should not—be paid financial incentives to practice birth control. To help define your position, review your pre-reading journal entry, and interview classmates, friends, and family members to get their opinions. Consider supplementing this informal research with material gathered in the library and/or on the Internet. Weigh all the evidence carefully before formulating your position.

David Helvarg

David Helvarg is a journalist and environmental activist. Born in 1951, he started his career as a freelance journalist and then became a war correspondent. Today he writes primarily about politics, AIDS, and marine life. Helvarg is also the founder and president of Blue Frontier Campaign, a marine conservation lobbying group that was inspired by his book about the world's oceans, *Blue Frontier.* Helvarg's lobbying on environmental issues grows out of his experiences covering war, political conflict, and marine biology. This article is excerpted from the September/October 2005 issue of *Multinational Monitor,* a magazine that examines multinational corporations and also covers issues relating to the environment and development.

Pre-Reading Journal Entry

Although humans have shaped the environment in many ways, we are still at the mercy of nature at times. Recall a hurricane, tornado, thunderstorm, windstorm, mudslide, earthquake, volcanic eruption, tsunami, drought, flood, or other natural event that affected you and your community. What was the event? What was the experience like? Use your journal to answer these questions.

The Storm This Time
Urban Floodplain

I arrive in Baton Rouge with a planeload of relief workers, FEMA functionaries and crew cut contractors, all working their cell phones and BlackBerries. After renting a car and making my way through the daily traffic jam (Baton Rouge's population has exploded since the storm) I head south on Interstate 10, tuning into the United Radio Broadcasters of New Orleans, a consortium of local stations playing 24/7 information and call-in reports on Katrina's aftermath.

A police spokesperson assures listeners there are still 20 to 30 roadblocks around New Orleans and 11,000 guardsmen in the city. The mayor wants to open the city back up to residents but the approach of Hurricane Rita has forced him to postpone his plan.

Around the New Orleans airport in Jefferson Parish, I begin to see box stores, warehouses and motels with their roofs ripped off or caved in, downed trees and broken street signs, house roofs covered in blue tarps and high-rises with glass windows popped out like broken eyes. I hit a traffic jam and follow an SUV across the median strip to an exit where I stop to take a picture of a small office complex with its second story front and roof gone. Rain-soaked cardboard boxes fill the exposed floor above a CPA's office. I talk to a carpet-store owner removing samples. He helps me locate where we are on a map. I get a call from a contact at the New Orleans Aquarium. They lost most of their fish when the pumps failed but managed to evacuate the penguins and sea otters to Monterey. I get on a wide boulevard that leads to a roadblock where a police officer checks my press identification. "This is only for emergency vehicles, but go ahead," she says.

I drive into Lakeview, one of the large sections of the city that sat under-   4
water for two weeks and will likely have to be bulldozed. It reminds me of war zones I've been in after heavy street fighting. There are trees and power poles down, electric lines hanging, metal sheets and street signs on mud-caked pavement, smashed cars, boats on sidewalks and torn-open houses, all colored in sepia tones of gray and brown. Unable to drive far in the debris chocked streets, I get out of my car, half expecting the sweet, rotting smell of death. Instead, I'm confronted with an equally noxious odor. It's what I'll come to think of as the smell of a dead city, like dried cow pies and mold with a stinging chemical aftertaste. Fine yellow dust starts rising up from under my boots and infiltrating the car. I retreat. The I-10 exit is barricaded, forcing me north again. I do a U-turn at a major roadblock and get chased down by some angry cops. I explain that I'm just following another cop's helpful directions and soon find myself speeding along a near-empty freeway bridge approaching downtown.

The rusted ruined roof of the Superdome inspires me to choose an exit   5
and, after getting turned around at a friendly National Guard checkpoint, I'm soon in the deserted streets of the central business district, checking out the rubble piles and empty highrises. A big wind-damaged 'Doubletree' hotel sign reads D UL EE. The French Quarter is still intact with even a few bars open for soldiers, FBI agents and fire fighters. On Canal Street, it looks like a Woodstock for first responders with Red Cross and media satellite trucks, tents and RVs pulled up on the central streetcar median by the Sheraton. Red-bereted troops from the 82nd Airborne cruise by in open-sided trucks, M-4s at the ready in case the undead should appear at sunset. Uptown, some boats lie in the middle of the street, along with cars crushed by a falling wall and a pharmacy trashed by looters. Further on are the smashed homes and muddied boulevards and still-flooded underpasses and cemeteries, abandoned cars and broken levees of an eerily hollow city.

In the coming days. I'll travel across this new urban landscape, tracing   6
the brown floodwater line that marks tens of thousands of homes, schools, offices, banks, churches, grocery stores and other ruined structures, includ-ing the main sewage plant. I'll cross paths with animal rescue crews, military patrols, utility crews from New York and Pennsylvania, and body recovery search teams with K-9 dogs using orange spray paint to mark the doors of

New Orleans house showing flood line and searcher's graffiti. The zero indicates that no bodies were found in the house. (©*David Helvarg*)

still unexamined buildings, writing the date and adding a zero for no bodies or numbers where bodies have been found. . . .

Life After Katrina

I put up with an AP colleague in the less damaged Algiers Point section   7 of the city just across the Mississippi from where the helicopter assault ship Iwo Jima and Carnival Cruise Line ship Ecstasy are being used to house city employees and relief workers. Blackhawk helicopters fly overhead at sunset while a Red Cross truck down the street offers hot food to the handful of residents still here.

Back in Lakeview, I encounter Bob Chick. Bob snuck past the checkpoints   8 to see if he can salvage anything from his green Cajun Cottage near where the 17th Street floodwall breached.

He hasn't had much luck, "just some tools that might be OK," he says.   9 "I left all my photos on top of a chest of drawers thinking the water wouldn't get that high. They say if you have more than five inches of water in your house for five days it's a loss. We had eight feet for two weeks." He's found one of his cats dead but thinks the other two might have escaped. He invites me to look inside. From the door it's a jumble of furniture, including a sofa, table, twisted carpet, lamps and wooden pieces all covered in black and gray gunk, reeking of mold and rotted cat food. I try not to breathe too deeply. "I had a collection of Jazz Fest T shirts going back to '79 but they're gone." He's wearing a mask, rubber boots and gloves, but still manages to give an expressive shrug of resignation when I take his picture. "I lived in this house 16 years. We'd have been fine if the levee hadn't broke. We'd be moving back right now." . . .

Bob Chick examines his flood-ruined house in the Lakeview section of New Orleans. (©*David Helvarg*)

A Disappeared Town

I catch a ride along the west bank of the Mississippi in Plaquemines Parish south of New Orleans with deputy Sheriff Ken Harvey. This is where towns of several thousand, like Empire and Buras, got washed away and some oil tank farms ruptured. Where the road's cut by water, we drive up on the eroded levee and keep going. There are boats on the land, and houses in the water or washed onto the road or turned into woodpiles. At one point where the levee broke and the water poured through, there's nothing but a field where Diamond, an unincorporated town of about 300 including many trailer-park residents, stood. Those folks never seem to catch a break.   10

I take a picture of an antebellum white mansion in the water along with a floating pickup, a larger truck hanging off a tree, a semi-trailer cab under the bottom of an uplifted house, a speedboat through a picture window, the Buras water tower collapsed next to a wrecked store, shrimp boats on the levee, on the road and in the bushes with military patrols passing by. We stop and stare in awe at a 200-foot barge tossed atop the levee like a bath toy on a tub rim.   11

Approaching the Empire Bridge, I note the white church facing north towards us is still intact and suggest that's a hopeful sign. "It used to face the road," Ken points out. . . .   12

Unfortunately, as I drive east through Mississippi and Alabama I find most of [the] coastal trees and wetlands festooned with plastic like Tibetan prayer flags (as if monks were praying over dead turtles and seabirds). In Biloxi, along with smashed casinos, historic homes and neighborhoods, I find miles of beachfront covered in plastic buckets and insulation, mattresses, furniture, chunks of drywall and Styrofoam pellets that the seabirds are eyeing   13 as potential snack food. I wave down a truck marked "Department of Natural Resources," but the guys inside are from Indiana.

I feel like an eco-geek being more concerned about the gulls and wetlands than the lost revenue from the casinos that everyone else seems to be obsessing on. The waterside wing of the new Hard Rock Casino is now a smashed tangle of twisted girders and concrete. I pull over by an 8,000 ton, 600-foot-long casino barge that was pushed half a mile by the storm, landing on Beach Drive. Somewhere underneath its barnacle-encrusted black hull is a historic mansion. Nearby, the Grand Casino barge has taken out much of the stately facade of the six story yellow brick Biloxi Yacht Club before grounding next to it. Another barge landed on the Holiday Inn, where more than 25 people may have been trying to ride out the hurricane. No one's been able to do a body-recovery there yet.

Because Southern Baptist and other religious conservatives objected to 'land-based' gambling in Mississippi, much of Biloxi's wetlands were torn up to make way for these floating casinos.

I talk with Phil Sturgeon, a Harrah's security agent hanging out with some cops from Winter Park, Florida. He's in jeans and a gray shirt with a toothbrush and pen sticking out the pocket. He tells me the storm surge crested at about 35 feet, at least five feet higher than Camille in '69.

In Waveland, I drive over twisted railroad tracks where the eye of Katrina passed into neighborhoods of jagged wooden debris. A middle-aged couple is trying to clear the drive to the lot where their home once stood. A surfboard leans up against one of the live oaks that seem to have fared better then the houses in between them.

"Are you an adjuster," the woman asks.

"No, a reporter."

"Good, because we don't like adjusters. Nationwide was not on our side." Apparently they've been offered $1,700 on their $422,000 home.

"At least you've got your surfboard," I tell John, her husband, "Oh, that's not my surfboard," he grins, pointing around. "And that's not my boat, and that's not my Corvette (buried to its hood in the rubble), and that's not our roof. We think it might belong to the house at the end of the street." . . .

Starting Again

I'm back in New Orleans on Canal Street, where the Salvation Army offers me cold water, a baloney sandwich (I decline) and a fruit cocktail. It's been a long day with the Army Corps of Engineers, who've leased helicopters that are dropping 3,000 and 7,000 pound sandbags on the latest breach in the Industrial Canal which has reflooded the Lower Ninth Ward. I enter the Sheraton after getting cleared by muscular Blackwater Security guys in tan and khaki tee shirts and shorts with Glocks on their hips. Another one sits by the elevators checking room IDs. I wonder if being a professional mercenary is good training for concierge duty. I sit by the Pelican bar in the lobby looking out the big three-story glass window at the media RVs and SUVs on the street—feeling as if I've been in this hotel before in various war zones and Third World capitals like Managua, Tegucigalpa, and Suva.

The Gulf region is now very much like a war zone, only with fewer deaths   24
(about 1,200 bodies recovered at the time of my visit) and far more extensive damage. It also offers many of the same ironies and bizarre moments. Unity Radio announces that if you're going to tonight's Louisiana State University football game in Baton Rouge you can return after curfew provided you show your game stubs to the deputies at the roadblocks.

Three years ago I made a decision. I'd lost a key person in my life and was   25
trying to decide what to do next. I was considering either going back to war reporting, as George Bush was clearly planning a pre-emptive invasion of Iraq, or turning from journalism to ocean advocacy. . . . Finally, I decided that while we'll probably always have wars, we may not always have living reefs, wild fish or protective coastal wetlands.

What we know we are going to have are more environmental disasters   26
like the Hurricane Season of '05 linked to fossil-fuel-fired climate change and bad coastal policies driven by saltwater special interests.

Still, destruction on a biblical scale also offers Noah-like opportunities   27
for restoration after the flood. There are practical solutions to the dangers we confront, along with models of how to live safely by the sea. Things can be done right in terms of building wisely along the coasts, and advancing social and environmental equity. But it will take a new wave of citizen activism to avoid repetition of old mistakes, with even more dire consequences.

Questions for Close Reading

1. What is the selection's thesis? Locate the sentence(s) in which Helvarg states his main idea. If he doesn't state his thesis explicitly, express it in your own words.
2. Helvarg uses headings to divide his essay into sections. What is the subject of the section entitled "Urban Floodplain"? How does this section frame the remainder of the essay?
3. Most of the details in Helvarg's essay focus on the destruction caused by the hurricane and the recovery effort. However, he does give a description of an activity that shows life going on as normal. What is it? Why does Helvarg include this description?
4. Some words are so new they are not yet in dictionaries. Helvarg uses such a word when he describes himself as an "eco-geek" in paragraph 14. Given the context, and the meanings of the root *eco* and the word *geek*, how would you define this word?
5. Refer to your dictionary as needed to define the following words used in the selection: *consortium* (paragraph 1), *infiltrating* (4), *Woodstock* (5), *salvage* (8), *ruptured* (10), *antebellum* (11), *festooned* (13), *storm surge* (16), *adjuster* (18), and *mercenary* (23).

Questions About the Writer's Craft

1. **The pattern.** How does Helvarg organize his points in this essay? What transitional words and phrases does he use to keep the reader oriented as his essay progresses?
2. Most of the description in this essay focuses on visual details, but Helvarg also describes some other sensations. Find the passages in which Helvarg describes something other than the sights of the post-Katrina landscape, and evaluate their vividness. What do these passages contribute to the essay?
3. In paragraphs 4 and 24, to what does Helvarg compare the post-Katrina Gulf Coast? How does this analogy help the reader envision the destruction? How does it help express the dominant impression of the essay?
4. Helvarg took the photographs that accompany this essay. Compare the photograph of the marked door on page 94 with the author's description of it in paragraph 6. Does this photograph add to the description in the essay, or is the author's description so vivid that the photograph is unnecessary? Now compare the photograph of Bob Chick on page 95 with the author's description of him in paragraph 9. Does this photograph add to the description of Bob in the essay, or is the author's description so vivid that the photograph is unnecessary? If you were writing this essay, would you include the photographs? If so, how would they affect the way you wrote the essay?

Writing Assignments Using Description as a Pattern of Development

1. One reason Helvarg's essay has such an impact is that destruction of the normal Gulf Coast environment was sudden as well as devastating. Not all environmental destruction is so dramatic, however. Find something in your own environment— your home, neighborhood, city, or region—that has been damaged or destroyed by gradual overuse or neglect. For example, your home may have a shabby room, or part of your yard may be overgrown. Or your neighborhood may have a run-down playground or park, or roads full of potholes, or an abandoned building. Select a location that has been neglected or overused, and write an essay in which you describe this damaged environment.
2. Although severe weather, like Hurricane Katrina, provides good subject matter for description, so does more common, less destructive weather. Think of a day on which the weather was important to you but turned out badly. For example, you might have planned an outdoor event and it rained, or you might have scheduled a trip and it snowed, or you might have worn great new clothes and been too hot or too cold. Write an essay in which you describe this uncooperative weather. Use sensory details and figures of speech to convey your feelings about this day.

Writing Assignments Combining Patterns of Development

3. In "The Storm This Time," the environmental devastation was caused by a natural event. However, much destruction of the environment is caused by people rather than by weather or other natural disasters. Select a place you know that has changed

for the worse through human use. For example, you might choose an industrial site, a polluted river or lake, or a park. *Compare* and *contrast* the place as it once was and as it is now. Provide vivid *descriptions* of how the place has changed. Before you start, you can read about a place that humans have polluted in Rachel Carson's "A Fable for Tomorrow" on page 350.

4. The Gulf Coast has a lot of experience with hurricanes; Katrina was just the most destructive one in recent years. Other areas are prone to other types of natural disasters. Research the destructive weather and other natural events that your area typically experiences. Good places to start are the websites of the Federal Emergency Management Agency (www.fema.gov) and the National Atmospheric and Oceanic Administration (www.noaa.gov). Then write an essay in which you *classify* the natural disasters that occur in your area and *describe* each type, giving specific *examples* where possible.

Writing Assignment Using a Journal
Entry as a Starting Point

5. Review your pre-reading journal entry about the natural disaster or event that you experienced. Write an essay in which you *describe* its aftermath. How did it *affect* you and others in your community? How did the event change your attitude toward nature? How did it *affect* the way you prepare for future natural emergencies? You might first read Joan Didion's "The Santa Ana" (page 601), an essay about a recurring hot wind that affects southern California.

Maya Angelou

Born Marguerite Johnson in 1928, Maya Angelou spent her childhood in Stamps, Arkansas, with her brother, Bailey, and her grandmother, "Momma." Although her youth was difficult—she was raped at age eight and became a mother at sixteen—Angelou somehow managed to thrive. Multi-talented, she later worked as a professional dancer, starred in an off-Broadway play, appeared in the television miniseries *Roots,* served as a coordinator for the Southern Christian Leadership Conference, and wrote several well-received volumes of poetry—among them *Oh Pray My Wings Are Gonna Fit Me Well* (1975) and *And Still I Rise* (1996). She has also written essay collections, such as *Even the Stars Look Lonesome* (1997), and children's books, including *My Painted House, My Friendly Chicken, and Me* (1994), and *Kofi and His Magic* (1996). A professor at Wake Forest University since 1991, Angelou delivered at the 1993 presidential inauguration a stirring poem written for the occasion. The recipient of numerous honorary doctorates, Angelou is best known for her series of six autobiographical books, starting with *I Know Why the Caged Bird Sings* (1970) and concluding with *A Song Flung Up to Heaven* (2002). The following essay is taken from *I Know Why the Caged Bird Sings.*

Pre-Reading Journal Entry

Growing up isn't easy. In your journal, list several challenges you've had to face in your life. In each case, was there someone who served as a "lifeline," providing you with crucial guidance and support? Who was that individual? How did this person steer you through the difficulty?

Sister Flowers

1   For nearly a year [after I was raped], I sopped around the house, the Store, the school and the church, like an old biscuit, dirty and inedible. Then I met, or rather got to know, the lady who threw me my first life line.

2   Mrs. Bertha Flowers was the aristocrat of Black Stamps. She had the grace of control to appear warm in the coldest weather, and on the Arkansas summer days it seemed she had a private breeze which swirled around, cooling her. She was thin without the taut look of wiry people, and her printed voile dresses and flowered hats were as right for her as denim overalls for a farmer. She was our side's answer to the richest white woman in town.

3   Her skin was a rich black that would have peeled like a plum if snagged, but then no one would have thought of getting close enough to Mrs. Flowers

to ruffle her dress, let alone snag her skin. She didn't encourage familiarity. She wore gloves too.

I don't think I ever saw Mrs. Flowers laugh, but she smiled often. A slow 4 widening of her thin black lips to show even, small white teeth, then the slow effortless closing. When she chose to smile on me, I always wanted to thank her. The action was so graceful and inclusively benign.

She was one of the few gentlewomen I have ever known, and has 5 remained throughout my life the measure of what a human being can be.

Momma had a strange relationship with her. Most often when she passed 6 on the road in front of the Store, she spoke to Momma in that soft yet carrying voice, "Good day, Mrs. Henderson." Momma responded with "How you, Sister Flowers?"

Mrs. Flowers didn't belong to our church, nor was she Momma's famil-7 iar. Why on earth did she insist on calling her Sister Flowers? Shame made me want to hide my face. Mrs. Flowers deserved better than to be called Sister. Then, Momma left out the verb. Why not ask, "How *are* you, *Mrs.* Flowers?" With the unbalanced passion of the young, I hated her for showing her ignorance to Mrs. Flowers. It didn't occur to me for many years that they were as alike as sisters, separated only by formal education.

Although I was upset, neither of the women was in the least shaken by 8 what I thought an unceremonious greeting. Mrs. Flowers would continue her easy gait up the hill to her little bungalow, and Momma kept on shelling peas or doing whatever had brought her to the front porch.

Occasionally, though, Mrs. Flowers would drift off the road and down 9 to the Store and Momma would say to me, "Sister, you go on and play." As she left I would hear the beginning of an intimate conversation. Momma persistently using the wrong verb, or none at all.

"Brother and Sister Wilcox is sho'ly the meanest—" "Is," Momma? 10 "Is"? Oh, please, not "is," Momma, for two or more. But they talked, and from the side of the building where I waited for the ground to open up and swallow me, I heard the soft-voiced Mrs. Flowers and the textured voice of my grandmother merging and melting. They were interrupted from time to time by giggles that must have come from Mrs. Flowers (Momma never giggled in her life). Then she was gone.

She appealed to me because she was like people I had never met person-11 ally. Like women in English novels who walked the moors (whatever they were) with their loyal dogs racing at a respectful distance. Like the women who sat in front of roaring fireplaces, drinking tea incessantly from silver trays full of scones and crumpets. Women who walked over the "heath" and read morocco-bound books and had two last names divided by a hyphen. It would be safe to say that she made me proud to be Negro, just by being herself.

She acted just as refined as whitefolks in the movies and books and she 12 was more beautiful, for none of them could have come near that warm color without looking gray by comparison.

It was fortunate that I never saw her in the company of powhitefolks. 13
For since they tend to think of their whiteness as an evenizer, I'm certain that
I would have had to hear her spoken to commonly as Bertha, and my image
of her would have been shattered like the unmendable Humpty-Dumpty.

One summer afternoon, sweet-milk fresh in my memory, she stopped 14
at the Store to buy provisions. Another Negro woman of her health and
age would have been expected to carry the paper sacks home in one hand,
but Momma said, "Sister Flowers, I'll send Bailey up to your house with
these things."

She smiled that slow dragging smile, "Thank you, Mrs. Henderson. I'd 1?
prefer Marguerite, though." My name was beautiful when she said it. "I've
been meaning to talk to her, anyway." They gave each other age-group looks.

Momma said, "Well, that's all right then. Sister, go and change your 16
dress. You going to Sister Flowers's."

The chifforobe was a maze. What on earth did one put on to go to 1?
Mrs. Flowers's house? I knew I shouldn't put on a Sunday dress. It might be
sacrilegious. Certainly not a house dress, since I was already wearing a fresh
one. I chose a school dress, naturally. It was formal without suggesting that
going to Mrs. Flowers's house was equivalent to attending church.

I trusted myself back into the Store. 18

"Now, don't you look nice." I had chosen the right thing, for once. . . . 19

There was a little path beside the rocky road, and Mrs. Flowers walked 20
in front swinging her arms and picking her way over the stones.

She said, without turning her head, to me, "I hear you're doing very 2
good school work, Marguerite, but that it's all written. The teachers report
that they have trouble getting you to talk in class." We passed the triangular
farm on our left and the path widened to allow us to walk together. I hung
back in the separate unasked and unanswerable questions.

"Come and walk along with me, Marguerite." I couldn't have refused 2
even if I wanted to. She pronounced my name so nicely. Or more correctly,
she spoke each word with such clarity that I was certain a foreigner who
didn't understand English could have understood her.

"Now no one is going to make you talk—possibly no one can. But bear 2
in mind, language is man's way of communicating with his fellow man and
it is language alone which separates him from the lower animals." That was
a totally new idea to me, and I would need time to think about it.

"Your grandmother says you read a lot. Every chance you get. That's good, 2
but not good enough. Words mean more than what is set down on paper. It
takes the human voice to infuse them with the shades of deeper meaning."

I memorized the part about the human voice infusing words. It seemed 2
so valid and poetic.

She said she was going to give me some books and that I not only must 2
read them, I must read them aloud. She suggested that I try to make a sentence sound in as many different ways as possible.

"I'll accept no excuse if you return a book to me that has been badly 27
handled." My imagination boggled at the punishment I would deserve if in
fact I did abuse a book of Mrs. Flowers's. Death would be too kind and brief.

The odors in the house surprised me. Somehow I had never connected 28
Mrs. Flowers with food or eating or any other common experience of common people. There must have been an outhouse, too, but my mind never
recorded it.

The sweet scent of vanilla had met us as she opened the door. 29

"I made tea cookies this morning. You see, I had planned to invite you 30
for cookies and lemonade so we could have this little chat. The lemonade is
in the icebox."

It followed that Mrs. Flowers would have ice on an ordinary day, when 31
most families in our town bought ice late on Saturdays only a few times during the summer to be used in the wooden ice-cream freezers.

She took the bags from me and disappeared through the kitchen door. 32
I looked around the room that I had never in my wildest fantasies imagined
I would see. Browned photographs leered or threatened from the walls and
the white, freshly done curtains pushed against themselves and against the
wind. I wanted to gobble up the room entire and take it to Bailey, who
would help me analyze and enjoy it.

"Have a seat, Marguerite. Over there by the table." She carried a platter 33
covered with a tea towel. Although she warned that she hadn't tried her
hand at baking sweets for some time, I was certain that like everything else
about her the cookies would be perfect.

They were flat round wafers, slightly browned on the edges and butter- 34
yellow in the center. With the cold lemonade they were sufficient for childhood's lifelong diet. Remembering my manners, I took nice little lady-like
bites off the edges. She said she had made them expressly for me and that
she had a few in the kitchen that I could take home to my brother. So I
jammed one whole cake in my mouth and the rough crumbs scratched the
insides of my jaws, and if I hadn't had to swallow, it would have been a
dream come true.

As I ate she began the first of what we later called "my lessons in living." 35
She said that I must always be intolerant of ignorance but understanding of
illiteracy. That some people, unable to go to school, were more educated and
even more intelligent than college professors. She encouraged me to listen
carefully to what country people called mother wit. That in those homely
sayings was couched the collective wisdom of generations.

When I finished the cookies she brushed off the table and brought a 36
thick, small book from the bookcase. I had read *A Tale of Two Cities* and
found it up to my standards as a romantic novel. She opened the first page
and I heard poetry for the first time in my life.

"It was the best of times and the worst of times . . ." Her voice slid in 37
and curved down through and over the words. She was nearly singing. I

wanted to look at the pages. Were they the same that I had read? Or were there notes, music, lined on the pages, as in a hymn book? Her sounds began cascading gently. I knew from listening to a thousand preachers that she was nearing the end of her reading, and I hadn't really heard, heard to understand, a single word.

"How do you like that?"   38

It occurred to me that she expected a response. The sweet vanilla flavor   39 was still on my tongue and her reading was a wonder in my ears. I had to speak.

I said, "Yes, ma'am." It was the least I could do, but it was the most also.   40

"There's one more thing. Take this book of poems and memorize one   41 for me. Next time you pay me a visit, I want you to recite."

I have tried often to search behind the sophistication of years for the   42 enchantment I so easily found in those gifts. The essence escapes but its aura remains. To be allowed, no, invited, into the private lives of strangers, and to share their joys and fears, was a chance to exchange the Southern bitter wormwood for a cup of mead with Beowulf[1] or a hot cup of tea and milk with Oliver Twist.[2] When I said aloud, "It is a far, far better thing that I do, than I have ever done . . ."[3] tears of love filled my eyes at my selflessness.

On that first day, I ran down the hill and into the road (few cars ever   43 came along it) and had the good sense to stop running before I reached the Store.

I was liked, and what a difference it made. I was respected not as   44 Mrs. Henderson's grandchild or Bailey's sister but for just being Marguerite Johnson.

Childhood's logic never asks to be proved (all conclusions are absolute).   45 I didn't question why Mrs. Flowers had singled me out for attention, nor did it occur to me that Momma might have asked her to give me a little talking to. All I cared about was that she had made tea cookies for *me* and read to *me* from her favorite book. It was enough to prove that she liked me.

---

[1]The hero of an Old English epic poem dating from the eighth century (editors' note).
[2]The main character in Charles Dickens's novel *Oliver Twist* (1837) (editors' note).
[3]The last words of Sydney Carton, the selfless hero of Charles Dickens's novel *A Tale of Two Cities* (1859) (editors' note).

Questions for Close Reading

1. What is the selection's thesis (or dominant impression)? Locate the sentence(s) in which Angelou states her main idea. If she doesn't state the thesis explicitly, express it in your own words.
2. Angelou states that Mrs. Flowers "has remained throughout my life the measure of what a human being can be" (paragraph 5). What does Angelou admire about Mrs. Flowers?

3. Why is young Angelou so ashamed of Momma when Mrs. Flowers is around? How do Momma and Mrs. Flowers behave with each other?

4. What are the "lessons in living" that Angelou receives from Mrs. Flowers during their first visit? How do you think these lessons might have subsequently influenced Angelou?

5. Refer to your dictionary as needed to define the following words used in the selection: *taut* (paragraph 2), *voile* (2), *benign* (4), *unceremonious* (8), *gait* (8), *moors* (11), *incessantly* (11), *scones* (11), *crumpets* (11), *heath* (11), *chifforobe* (17), *sacrilegious* (17), *infuse* (24), *couched* (35), and *aura* (42).

Questions About the Writer's Craft

1. **The pattern.** Reread the essay, focusing on the descriptive passages first of Mrs. Flowers and then of Angelou's visit to Mrs. Flowers's house. To what senses does Angelou appeal in these passages? What method of organization (see pages 40–42) does she use to order these sensory details?

2. To enrich the description of her eventful encounter with Mrs. Flowers, Angelou draws upon figures of speech (see page 76). Consider, for example, the similes in paragraphs 1 and 11. How do these figures of speech contribute to the essay's dominant impression?

3. **Other patterns.** Because Angelou's description has a strong *narrative* component, it isn't surprising that there's a considerable amount of dialogue in the selection. For example, in paragraphs 7 and 10, Angelou quotes Momma's incorrect grammar. She then provides an imagined conversation in which the young Angelou scolds Momma and corrects her speech. What do these imagined scoldings of Momma reveal about young Angelou? How do they relate to Mrs. Flowers's subsequent "lessons in life"?

4. Although it's not the focus of this selection, the issue of race remains in the background of Angelou's portrait of Mrs. Flowers. Where in the selection does Angelou imply that race was a fact of life in her town? How does this specter of racism help Angelou underscore the significance of her encounter with Mrs. Flowers?

Writing Assignments Using Description as a Pattern of Development

1. At one time or another, just about all of us have met someone who taught us to see ourselves more clearly and helped us understand what we wanted from life. Write an essay describing such a person. Focus on the individual's personal qualities, as a way of depicting the role he or she played in your life. Be sure not to limit yourself to an objective description. Subjective description, filled with lively language and figures of speech, will serve you well as you provide a portrait of this special person.

2. Thrilled by the spectacle of Mrs. Flowers's interesting home, Angelou says she wanted to "gobble up the room entire" and share it with her brother. Write an essay describing in detail a place that vividly survives in your memory. You may describe a setting that you visited only once or a familiar setting that holds a special place in your heart. Before you write, list the qualities and sensory impressions you associate with this special place; then refine the list so that all details support

your dominant impression. You may want to read E. B. White's "Once More to the Lake" (page 107) to see how a professional writer evokes the qualities of a special place in his life.

Writing Assignments Combining Patterns of Development

3. When the young Angelou discovers, thanks to Mrs. Flowers, the thrill of acceptance, she experiences a kind of *epiphany*—a moment of enlightenment. Write an essay about an event in your life that represented a kind of epiphany. You might write about a positive discovery, such as when you realized you had a special talent for something, or about a negative discovery, such as when you realized that a beloved family member had a serious flaw. To make the point that the moment was a turning point in your life, start by *describing* what kind of person you were before the discovery. Then *narrate* the actual incident, using vivid details and dialogue to make the event come alive. End by discussing the importance of this epiphany in your life. For additional accounts of personal epiphanies, you might read Audre Lorde's "The Fourth of July" (page 137), Langston Hughes's "Salvation" (page 155), and Beth Johnson's "Bombs Bursting in Air" (page 209).

4. Think of an activity that engages you completely, one that provides—as reading does for Angelou—an opportunity for growth and expansion. Possibilities include reading, writing, playing an instrument, doing crafts, dancing, hiking, playing a sport, cooking, or traveling. Write an essay in which you *argue* the merits of your chosen pastime. Assume that some of your readers are highly skeptical. To win them over, you'll need to provide convincing *examples* that demonstrate the pleasure and benefits you have discovered in the activity.

Writing Assignment Using a Journal Entry as a Starting Point

5. Write an essay about a time when someone threw you a much-needed "lifeline" at a challenging time. Review your pre-reading journal entry, selecting *one* time when a person's encouragement and support made a great difference in your life. Be sure to describe the challenge you faced before recounting the specific details of the person's help. Dialogue and descriptive details will help you recreate the power of the experience. You should consider reading "Beauty: When the Other Dancer Is the Self" (page 408), in which Alice Walker shows how loving guidance made a world of difference in her life.

E. B. White

Elwyn Brooks White (1899–1985) is considered one of America's finest essayists. For many years, White was a member of the *New Yorker* magazine staff and wrote the magazine's popular column "The Talk of the Town." He also wrote children's books, including the classic *Charlotte's Web* (1952), and was the coauthor with William Strunk, Jr., of the renowned guide for writers, *The Elements of Style* (1959). But most memorable are the essays White produced during his life—gems of clarity, wit, and heartfelt expression. White's contribution to literature earned him many awards, including the Presidential Medal of Freedom and the National Medal for Literature. The classic essay reprinted here is taken from *The Essays of E. B. White* (1977).

Pre-Reading Journal Entry

In your journal, list at least two occasions—either serious or humorous—that made you keenly aware that you were growing older. What was it about each situation that forced this realization upon you? How did the realization affect you? Did it please or distress you? Jot down as many details about each instance as you can.

Once More to the Lake

One summer, along about 1904, my father rented a camp on a lake in Maine and took us all there for the month of August. We all got ringworm from some kittens and had to rub Pond's Extract on our arms and legs night and morning, and my father rolled over in a canoe with all his clothes on; but outside of that the vacation was a success and from then on none of us ever thought there was any place in the world like that lake in Maine. We returned summer after summer—always on August 1 for one month. I have since become a salt-water man, but sometimes in summer there are days when the restlessness of the tides and the fearful cold of the sea water and the incessant wind that blows across the afternoon and into the evening make me wish for the placidity of a lake in the woods. A few weeks ago this feeling got so strong I bought myself a couple of bass hooks and a spinner and returned to the lake where we used to go, for a week's fishing and to revisit old haunts.

I took along my son, who had never had any fresh water up his nose and who had seen lily pads only from train windows. On the journey over to the lake I began to wonder what it would be like. I wondered how time would have marred this unique, this holy spot—the coves and streams, the hills that the sun set behind, the camps and the paths behind the camps. I was sure that the tarred road would have found it out, and I wondered in what other ways it would be desolated. It is strange how much you can remember about places like that once you allow your mind to return into the grooves that lead back. You remember one thing, and that suddenly reminds you of another thing. I guess I remembered clearest of all the early mornings, when the lake was cool and motionless, remembered how the bedroom smelled of the lumber it was made of and of the wet woods whose scent entered through the screen. The partitions in the camp were thin and did not extend clear to the top of the rooms, and as I was always the first up I would dress softly so as not to wake the others, and sneak out into the sweet outdoors and start out in the canoe, keeping close along the shore in the long shadows of the pines. I remembered being very careful never to rub my paddle against the gunwale for fear of disturbing the stillness of the cathedral.

The lake had never been what you would call a wild lake. There were   3
cottages sprinkled around the shores, and it was in farming country although the shores of the lake were quite heavily wooded. Some of the cottages were owned by nearby farmers, and you would live at the shore and eat your meals at the farmhouse. That's what our family did. But although it wasn't wild, it was a fairly large and undisturbed lake and there were places in it that, to a child at least, seemed infinitely remote and primeval.

I was right about the tar: it led to within half a mile of the shore. But when   4
I got back there, with my boy, and we settled into a camp near a farmhouse and into the kind of summertime I had known, I could tell that it was going to be pretty much the same as it had been before—I knew it, lying in bed the first morning, smelling the bedroom and hearing the boy sneak quietly out and go off along the shore in a boat. I began to sustain the illusion that he was I, and therefore, by simple transposition, that I was my father. This sensation persisted, kept cropping up all the time we were there. It was not an entirely new feeling, but in this setting it grew much stronger. I seemed to be living a dual existence. I would be in the middle of some simple act, I would be picking up a bait box or laying down a table fork, or I would be saying something, and suddenly it would be not I but my father who was saying the words or making the gesture. It gave me a creepy sensation.

We went fishing the first morning. I felt the same damp moss covering the   5
worms in the bait can, and saw the dragonfly alight on the tip of my rod as it hovered a few inches from the surface of the water. It was the arrival of this fly that convinced me beyond any doubt that everything was as it always had been, that the years were a mirage and that there had been no years. The small waves were the same, chucking the rowboat under the chin as we fished at anchor, and the boat was the same boat, the same color green and the ribs broken in the same places, and under the floorboards the same fresh-water leavings and débris—the dead helgramite, the wisps of moss, the rusty discarded

fishhook, the dried blood from yesterday's catch. We stared silently at the tips of our rods, at the dragonflies that came and went. I lowered the tip of mine into the water, tentatively, pensively dislodging the fly, which darted two feet away, poised, darted two feet back, and came to rest again a little farther up the rod. There had been no years between the ducking of this dragonfly and the other one—the one that was part of memory. I looked at the boy, who was silently watching his fly, and it was my hands that held his rod, my eyes watching. I felt dizzy and didn't know which rod I was at the end of.

We caught two bass, hauling them in briskly as though they were mack-   6
erel, pulling them over the side of the boat in a businesslike manner without any landing net, and stunning them with a blow on the back of the head. When we got back for a swim before lunch, the lake was exactly where we had left it, the same number of inches from the dock, and there was only the merest suggestion of a breeze. This seemed an utterly enchanted sea, this lake you could leave to its own devices for a few hours and come back to, and find that it had not stirred, this constant and trustworthy body of water. In the shallows, the dark, water-soaked sticks and twigs, smooth and old, were undulating in clusters on the bottom against the clean ribbed sand, and the track of the mussel was plain. A school of minnows swam by, each minnow with its small individual shadow, doubling the attendance, so clear and sharp in the sunlight. Some of the other campers were in swimming, along the shore, one of them with a cake of soap, and the water felt thin and clear and unsubstantial. Over the years there had been this person with the cake of soap, this cultist, and here he was. There had been no years.

Up to the farmhouse to dinner through the teeming, dusty field, the   7
road under our sneakers was only a two-track road. The middle track was missing, the one with the marks of the hooves and the splotches of dried, flaky manure. There had always been three tracks to choose from in choosing which track to walk in; now the choice was narrowed down to two. For a moment I missed terribly the middle alternative. But the way led past the tennis court, and something about the way it lay there in the sun reassured me; the tape had loosened along the backline, the alleys were green with plantains and other weeds, and the net (installed in June and removed in September) sagged in the dry noon, and the whole place steamed with midday heat and hunger and emptiness. There was a choice of pie for dessert, and one was blueberry and one was apple, and the waitresses were the same country girls, there having been no passage of time, only the illusion of it as in a dropped curtain—the waitresses were still fifteen; their hair had been washed, that was the only difference—they had been to the movies and seen the pretty girls with the clean hair.

Summertime, oh, summertime, pattern of life indelible, the fade-proof   8
lake, the woods unshatterable, the pasture with the sweetfern and the juniper forever and ever, summer without end; this was the background, and the life along the shore was the design, the cottagers with their innocent and

tranquil design, their tiny docks with the flagpole and the American flag floating against the white clouds in the blue sky, the little paths over the roots of the trees leading from camp to camp and the paths leading back to the outhouses and the can of lime for sprinkling, and at the souvenir counters at the store the miniature birch-bark canoes and the postcards that showed things looking a little better than they looked. This was the American family at play, escaping the city heat, wondering whether the newcomers in the camp at the head of the cove were "common" or "nice," wondering whether it was true that the people who drove up for Sunday dinner at the farmhouse were turned away because there wasn't enough chicken.

It seemed to me, as I kept remembering all this, that those times and those summers had been infinitely precious and worth saving. There had been jollity and peace and goodness. The arriving (at the beginning of August) had been so big a business in itself, at the railway station the farm wagon drawn up, the first smell of the pine-laden air, the first glimpse of the smiling farmer, and the great importance of the trunks and your father's enormous authority in such matters, and the feel of the wagon under you for the long ten-mile haul, and at the top of the last long hill catching the first view of the lake after eleven months of not seeing this cherished body of water. The shouts and cries of the other campers when they saw you, and the trunks to be unpacked, to give up their rich burden. (Arriving was less exciting nowadays, when you sneaked up in your car and parked it under a tree near the camp and took out the bags and in five minutes it was all over, no fuss, no loud wonderful fuss about trunks.)

Peace and goodness and jollity. The only thing that was wrong now, really, was the sound of the place, an unfamiliar nervous sound of the outboard motors. This was the note that jarred, the one thing that would sometimes break the illusion and set the years moving. In those other summertimes all motors were inboard; and when they were at a little distance, the noise they made was a sedative, an ingredient of summer sleep. They were one-cylinder and two-cylinder engines, and some were make-and-break and some were jump-spark, but they all made a sleepy sound across the lake. The one-lungers throbbed and fluttered, and the twin-cylinder ones purred and purred, and that was a quiet sound, too. But now the campers all had outboards. In the daytime, in the hot mornings, these motors made a petulant, irritable sound; at night, in the still evening when the afterglow lit the water, they whined about one's ears like mosquitoes. My boy loved our rented outboard, and his great desire was to achieve single-handed mastery over it, and authority, and he soon learned the trick of choking it a little (but not too much), and the adjustment of the needle valve. Watching him I would remember the things you could do with the old one-cylinder engine with the heavy flywheel, how you could have it eating out of your hand if you got really close to it spiritually. Motorboats in those days didn't have clutches, and you would make a landing by shutting off the motor at the proper time and coasting in with a dead rudder. But there was a way of reversing them, if you learned the trick, by cutting the switch and putting it on again exactly on the final dying revolution of the flywheel, so that it would kick back against compression and begin reversing. Approaching a dock in a strong following breeze, it was difficult to slow up sufficiently by the ordinary coasting method, and if a boy felt he had complete mastery over his motor, he was tempted to keep it running beyond its time and then reverse it a few feet from the dock. It took a cool nerve, because if you threw the switch a twentieth of a second too soon you would catch the flywheel when it still had speed enough to go up past center, and the boat would leap ahead, charging bullfashion at the dock.

We had a good week at the camp. The bass were biting well and the sun shone endlessly, day after day. We would be tired at night and lie down in the accumulated heat of the little bedrooms after the long hot day and the breeze would stir almost imperceptibly outside and the smell of the swamp drift in through the rusty screens. Sleep would come easily and in the morning the red squirrel would be on the roof, tapping out his gay routine. I kept remembering everything, lying in bed in the mornings—the small steamboat that had a long rounded stern like the lip of a Ubangi, and how quietly she ran on the moonlight sails, when the older boys played their mandolins and the girls sang and we ate doughnuts dipped in sugar, and how sweet the music was on the water in the shining night, and what it had felt like to think about girls then. After breakfast we would go up to the store and the things were in the same place—the minnows in a bottle, the plugs and spinners disarranged and pawed over by the youngsters from the boys' camp, the Fig Newtons and the Beeman's gum. Outside, the road was tarred and cars stood in front of the store. Inside, all was just as it had always been, except there was more Coca-Cola and not so much Moxie and root beer and birch beer and sarsaparilla. We would walk out with the bottle of pop apiece and sometimes the pop would backfire up our noses and hurt. We explored the streams, quietly, where the turtles slid off the sunny logs and dug their way into the soft bottom; and we lay on the town wharf and fed worms to the tame bass. Everywhere we went I had trouble making out which was I, the one walking at my side, the one walking in my pants.

One afternoon while we were there at the lake a thunderstorm came up. It was like the revival of an old melodrama that I had seen long ago with childish awe. The second-act climax of the drama of the electrical disturbance over a lake in America had not changed in any important respect. This was the big scene, still the big scene. The whole thing was so familiar, the first feeling of oppression and heat and a general air around camp of not wanting to go very far away. In midafternoon (it was all the same) a curious darkening of the sky, and a lull in everything that had made life tick; and then the way the boats suddenly swung the other way at their moorings with the coming of a breeze out of the new quarter, and premonitory rumble. Then the kettle drum, then the snare, then the bass drum and cymbals, then cackling light against the dark, and the gods grinning and licking their chops in the hills. Afterward the calm, the rain steadily rustling in the calm lake, the return of light and hope and spirits, and the campers running out in joy and relief to go swimming in the rain, their bright cries perpetuating the deathless joke about how they were getting simply drenched, and the children screaming with delight at the new sensation of bathing in the rain, and the joke about getting drenched linking the generations in a strong indestructible chain. And the comedian who waded in carrying an umbrella.

When the others went swimming, my son said he was going in, too. He   13
pulled his dripping trunks from the line where they had hung all through the shower and wrung them out. Languidly, and with no thought of going in, I watched him, his hard little body, skinny and bare, saw him wince slightly as he pulled up around his vitals the small, soggy, icy garment. As he buckled the swollen belt, suddenly my groin felt the chill of death.

Questions for Close Reading

1. What is the selection's thesis (or dominant impression)? Locate the sentence(s) in which White states his main idea. If he doesn't state the thesis explicitly, express it in your own words.
2. Why does White return to the lake in Maine he had visited as a child? Why do you think he has waited to revisit it until he has a young son to bring along?
3. Several times in the essay, White notes that he felt as if he were his own father— and that his son became his childhood self. What event first prompts this sensation? What actions and thoughts cause it to recur?
4. How is the latest visit to the lake similar to White's childhood summers? What differences does White notice? What effects do the differences have on him?
5. Refer to your dictionary as needed to define the following words used in the selection: *incessant* (paragraph 1), *placidity* (1), *primeval* (3), *transposition* (4), *undulating* (6), *indelible* (8), *petulant* (10), and *languidly* (13).

Questions About the Writer's Craft

1. **The pattern.** Through vivid language, descriptive writing evokes sensory experiences. In "Once More to the Lake," White overlays two sets of sensory details: those of the present-day lake and those of the lake as it was in his boyhood. Which set of details is more objective? Which seems sharper and more powerful? Why?
2. To describe the lake, White chooses many words and phrases with religious connotations. Give some examples. What might have been his purpose in using such language?
3. **Other patterns.** In paragraph 12, White uses a metaphor to describe a thunderstorm. To what does he *compare* a thunderstorm? Why does he make this comparison?

4. White refers to "the chill of death" in the final paragraph. What brings on this feeling? Why does he feel it "in his groin"? Where has this idea been hinted at previously in the essay?

Writing Assignments Using Description as a Pattern of Development

1. Write an essay describing a special place in your life. The place need not be a natural setting like White's lake; it could be a city or building that has meant a great deal to you. Use sensory details and figurative language, as White does, to enliven your description and convey the place's significance for you. Before writing, read Maya Angelou's "Sister Flowers" (page 100) to see how a professional writer conveys the special qualities of a memorable childhood place.

2. White was fortunate that his lake had remained virtually unchanged. But many other special spots have been destroyed or are threatened with destruction. Write an essay describing a place (a park, a school, an old-fashioned ice-cream parlor) that is "infinitely precious and worth saving." For your dominant theme, show which aspects of your subject make it worthy of being preserved for future generations. Before writing your essay, you might want to read Rachel Carson's "A Fable for Tomorrow" (page 350), an essay that laments the loss of a special place, and David Helvarg's "The Storm This Time" (page 92), which describes the devastation of the Gulf Coast by Hurricane Katrina.

Writing Assignments Combining Patterns of Development

3. Sometimes, we, like White, are suddenly reminded of the nearness of death: a crushed animal lies in the road, a politician is assassinated, a classmate is killed in a car crash. Write an essay about a time you were forced to think about mortality. *Narrate* what happened and *describe* your thoughts and feelings afterwards.

4. Have your older relatives attempted to share with you some special experiences of their younger years? Have you done the same thing with your own children, nephews, or nieces? You may have taken loved ones to a special place, as White did, or listened to stories or looked at photographs. Write an essay *recounting* such an experience. Explain the motivations of the older generation and the *effects* on the younger one. Judith Ortiz Cofer's "A Partial Remembrance of a Puerto Rican Childhood" (page 114) will spark some thoughts about special family times.

Writing Assignment Using a Journal Entry as a Starting Point

5. Write an essay narrating an incident that reminded you that you weren't as young as you used to be. Review your pre-reading journal entry, selecting the *one* occasion you would most enjoy writing about. Draw upon the specifics in your journal, providing additional details about both external circumstances and your internal state of mind. End your essay by discussing how your realization affected your subsequent thoughts and actions.

Judith Ortiz Cofer

Born in Puerto Rico, raised both on her native island and in the United States, and educated in sites that included Oxford University in England, Judith Ortiz Cofer (1952–) knows what it is to move between cultures, absorbing from each while keeping mindful of her own heritage. Cofer earned a master's degree in English from the University of Florida before spending a year in graduate study at Oxford. Following a stint as a bilingual teacher, Cofer taught English at several colleges and universities and currently teaches Creative Writing at the University of Georgia. She has published collections of poetry, including *Peregrine* (1986), *Terms of Survival* (1995), *Reaching for the Mainland and Selected New Poems* (1995), and *A Love Story Beginning in Spanish* (2005); novels, *The Line of the Sun* (1989), *The Meaning of Consuelo* (2003), and *Call Me Maria* (2004); and four books of essays, *Silent Dancing: A Partial Remembrance of a Puerto Rican Childhood* (1990), *The Latin Deli: Telling the Lives of Barrio Women* (1993), *An Island Like You: Stories of the Barrio* (1995), and *Woman in Front of the Sun* (2000). The following essay is taken from *Silent Dancing*.

Pre-Reading Journal Entry

Everyone loves a good story. But stories do more than merely entertain us. Use your journal to reflect on two or more stories that adults told you in your childhood as a way to teach an important lesson about life. In addition to sketching out the stories themselves, outline the circumstances of hearing the stories: who told them, where you were when you heard the stories, why the stories were recounted.

A Partial Remembrance of a Puerto Rican Childhood

At three or four o'clock in the afternoon, the hour of *café con leche*,[1] the women of my family gathered in Mamá's living room to speak of important things and retell familiar stories meant to be overheard by us young girls, their daughters. In Mamá's house (everyone called my grandmother Mamá) was a large parlor built by my grandfather to his wife's exact specifications so that it was always cool, facing away from the sun. The doorway was on the side of the house so no one could walk directly into her living room. First they had to take a little stroll through and around her beautiful garden where

1

[1]Spanish for "coffee with milk" (editors' note).

prize-winning orchids grew in the trunk of an ancient tree she had hollowed out for that purpose. This room was furnished with several mahogany rocking chairs, acquired at the births of her children, and one intricately carved rocker that had passed down to Mamá at the death of her own mother.

It was on these rockers that my mother, her sisters, and my grandmother sat on these afternoons of my childhood to tell their stories, teaching each other, and my cousin and me, what it was like to be a woman, more specifically, a Puerto Rican woman. They talked about life on the island, and life in *Los Nueva Yores,* their way of referring to the United States from New York City to California: the other place, not home, all the same. They told real-life stories though, as I later learned, always embellishing them with a little or a lot of dramatic detail. And they told *cuentos,* the morality and cautionary tales told by the women in our family for generations: stories that became a part of my subconscious as I grew up in two worlds, the tropical island and the cold city, and that would later surface in my dreams and in my poetry.

One of these tales was about the woman who was left at the altar. Mamá liked to tell that one with histrionic intensity. I remember the rise and fall of her voice, the sighs, and her constantly gesturing hands, like two birds swooping through her words. This particular story usually would come up in a conversation as a result of someone mentioning a forthcoming engagement or wedding. The first time I remember hearing it, I was sitting on the floor at Mamá's feet, pretending to read a comic book. I may have been eleven or twelve years old, at that difficult age when a girl was no longer a child who could be ordered to leave the room if the women wanted freedom to take their talk into forbidden zones, nor really old enough to be considered a part of their conclave. I could only sit quietly, pretending to be in another world, while absorbing it all in a sort of unspoken agreement of my status as silent auditor. On this day, Mamá had taken my long, tangled mane of hair into her ever-busy hands. Without looking down at me and with no interruption of her flow of words, she began braiding my hair, working at it with the quickness and determination that characterized all her actions. My mother was watching us impassively from her rocker across the room. On her lips played a little ironic smile. I would never sit still for *her* ministrations, but even then, I instinctively knew that she did not possess Mamá's matriarchal power to command and keep everyone's attention. This was never more evident than in the spell she cast when telling a story.

"It is not like it used to be when I was a girl," Mamá announced. "Then, a man could leave a girl standing at the church altar with a bouquet of fresh flowers in her hands and disappear off the face of the earth. No way to track him down if he was from another town. He could be a married man, with maybe even two or three families all over the island. There was no way to know. And there were men who did this. *Hombres*[2] with the devil in their

2

3

4

---

[2]Spanish for "men" (editors' note).

flesh who would come to a *pueblo*,[3] like this one, take a job at one of the *haciendas*,[4] never meaning to stay, only to have a good time and to seduce the women."

The whole time she was speaking, Mamá would be weaving my hair into   5 a flat plait that required pulling apart the two sections of hair with little jerks that made my eyes water; but knowing how grandmother detested whining and *boba* (sissy) tears, as she called them, I just sat up as straight and stiff as I did at La Escuela San Jose, where the nuns enforced good posture with a flexible plastic ruler they bounced off of slumped shoulders and heads. As Mamá's story progressed, I noticed how my young Aunt Laura lowered her eyes, refusing to meet Mamá's meaningful gaze. Laura was seventeen, in her last year of high school, and already engaged to a boy from another town who had staked his claim with a tiny diamond ring, then left for Los Nueva Yores to make his fortune. They were planning to get married in a year. Mamá had expressed serious doubts that the wedding would ever take place. In Mamá's eyes, a man set free without a legal contract was a man lost. She believed that marriage was not something men desired, but simply the price they had to pay for the privilege of children and, of course, for what no decent (synonymous with "smart") woman would give away for free.

"María La Loca was only seventeen when *it* happened to her." I listened   6 closely at the mention of this name. María was a town character, a fat middle-aged woman who lived with her old mother on the outskirts of town. She was to be seen around the pueblo delivering the meat pies the two women made for a living. The most peculiar thing about María, in my eyes, was that she walked and moved like a little girl though she had the thick body and wrinkled face of an old woman. She would swing her hips in an exaggerated, clownish way, and sometimes even hop and skip up to someone's house. She spoke to no one. Even if you asked her a question, she would just look at you and smile, showing her yellow teeth. But I had heard that if you got close enough, you could hear her humming a tune without words. The kids yelled out nasty things at her, calling her *La Loca*,[5] and the men who hung out at the *bodega*[6] playing dominoes sometimes whistled mockingly as she passed by with her funny, outlandish walk. But María seemed impervious to it all, carrying her basket of *pasteles*[7] like a grotesque Little Red Riding Hood through the forest.

María La Loca interested me, as did all the eccentrics and crazies of our   7 pueblo. Their weirdness was a measuring stick I used in my serious quest for

---

[3]Spanish for "community" (editors' note).
[4]Spanish for "large estate" or "ranch" (editors' note).
[5]Spanish for "crazy one" (editors' note).
[6]Spanish for a neighborhood grocery store (editors' note).
[7]Spanish for "pastries" (editors' note).

a definition of normal. As a Navy brat shuttling between New Jersey and the pueblo, I was constantly made to feel like an oddball by my peers, who made fun of my two-way accent: a Spanish accent when I spoke English, and when I spoke Spanish I was told that I sounded like a *Gringa*.[8] Being the outsider had already turned my brother and me into cultural chameleons. We developed early on the ability to blend into a crowd, to sit and read quietly in a fifth story apartment building for days and days when it was too bitterly cold to play outside, or, set free, to run wild in Mamá's realm, where she took charge of our lives, releasing Mother for a while from the intense fear for our safety that our father's absences instilled in her. In order to keep us from harm when Father was away, Mother kept us under strict surveillance. She even walked us to and from Public School No. 11, which we attended during the months we lived in Paterson, New Jersey, our home base in the States. Mamá freed all three of us like pigeons from a cage. I saw her as my liberator and my model. Her stories were parables from which to glean the *Truth*.

"María La Loca was once a beautiful girl. Everyone thought she would   8
marry the Méndez boy." As everyone knew, Rogelio Méndez was the richest man in town. "But," Mamá continued, knitting my hair with the same intensity she was putting into her story, "this *macho* made a fool out of her and ruined her life." She paused for the effect of her use of the word "macho," which at that time had not yet become a popular epithet for an unliberated man. This word had for us the crude and comical connotation of "male of the species," stud; a *macho* was what you put in a pen to increase your stock.

I peeked over my comic book at my mother. She too was under Mamá's   9
spell, smiling conspiratorially at this little swipe at men. She was safe from Mamá's contempt in this area. Married at an early age, an unspotted lamb, she had been accepted by a good family of strict Spaniards whose name was old and respected, though their fortune had been lost long before my birth. In a rocker Papá had painted sky blue sat Mamá's oldest child, Aunt Nena. Mother of three children, stepmother of two more, she was a quiet woman who liked books but had married an ignorant and abusive widower whose main interest in life was accumulating wealth. He too was in the mainland working on his dream of returning home rich and triumphant to buy the *finca*[9] of his dreams. She was waiting for him to send for her. She would leave her children with Mamá for several years while the two of them slaved away in factories. He would one day be a rich man, and she a sadder woman. Even now her life-light was dimming. She spoke little, an aberration in Mamá's house, and she read avidly, as if storing up spiritual food for the long winters that awaited her in Los Nueva Yores without her family. But even Aunt Nena came alive to Mamá's words, rocking gently, her hands over a thick book in her lap.

[8]A negatively charged Latin American slang expression for a female foreigner (editors' note).
[9]Spanish for "farm" or "ranch" (editors' note).

Her daughter, my cousin Sara, played jacks by herself on the tile porch out-   10
side the room where we sat. She was a year older than I. We shared a bed and
all our family's secrets. Collaborators in search of answers, Sara and I discussed
everything we heard the women say, trying to fit it all together like a puzzle
that, once assembled, would reveal life's mysteries to us. Though she and I
still enjoyed taking part in boys' games—chase, volleyball, and even *vaque-
ros,* the island version of cowboys and Indians involving cap-gun battles and
violent shoot-outs under the mango tree in Mamá's backyard—we loved best
the quiet hours in the afternoon when the men were still at work, and the
boys had gone to play serious baseball at the park. Then Mamá's house
belonged only to us women. The aroma of coffee perking in the kitchen, the
mesmerizing creaks and groans of the rockers, and the women telling their
lives in *cuentos* are forever woven into the fabric of my imagination, braided
like my hair that day I felt my grandmother's hands teaching me about
strength, her voice convincing me of the power of storytelling.

That day Mamá told how the beautiful María had fallen prey to a man   11
whose name was never the same in subsequent versions of the story; it was
Juan one time, José, Rafael, Diego, another. We understood that neither the
name or any of the *facts* were important, only that a woman had allowed love
to defeat her. Mamá put each of us in María's place by describing her wedding dress in loving detail: how she looked like a princess in her lace as she
waited at the altar. Then, as Mamá approached the tragic denouement of her
story, I was distracted by the sound of my Aunt Laura's violent rocking. She
seemed on the verge of tears. She knew the fable was intended for her. That
week she was going to have her wedding gown fitted, though no firm date
had been set for the marriage. Mamá ignored Laura's obvious discomfort,
digging out a ribbon from the sewing basket she kept by her rocker while
describing María's long illness, "a fever that would not break for days." She
spoke of a mother's despair: "that woman climbed the church steps on her
knees every morning, wore only black as a *promesa* to the Holy Virgin in
exchange for her daughter's health." By the time María returned from her
honeymoon with death, she was ravished, no longer young or sane. "As you
can see, she is almost as old as her mother already," Mamá lamented while
tying the ribbon to the ends of my hair, pulling it back with such force that
I just knew I would never be able to close my eyes completely again.

"That María's getting crazier every day." Mamá's voice would take a   1
lighter tone now, expressing satisfaction, either for the perfection of my
braid, or for a story well told—it was hard to tell. "You know that tune María
is always humming?" Carried away by her enthusiasm, I tried to nod, but
Mamá still had me pinned between her knees.

"Well, that's the wedding march." Surprising us all, Mamá sang out,   1
"Da, da, dara . . . da, da, dara." Then lifting me off the floor by my skinny
shoulders, she would lead me around the room in an impromptu waltz—

another session ending with the laughter of women, all of us caught up in the infectious joke of our lives.

Questions for Close Reading

1. What is the selection's thesis (or dominant impression)? Locate the sentence(s) in which Cofer states her main idea. If she doesn't state the thesis explicitly, express it in your own words.
2. Who are the women who participate in the storytelling sessions? Why is Cofer allowed to join them? Why aren't men or boys part of the group?
3. What lessons about men and women does Mamá intend the story of María La Loca to teach?
4. What information does Cofer provide about her aunts and her mother? What similarities and/or differences are there between each of their lives and the story of María La Loca?
5. Refer to your dictionary as needed to define the following words used in the selection: *intricately* (paragraph 1), *embellishing* (2), *cautionary* (2), *histrionic* (3), *conclave* (3), *auditor* (3), *impassively* (3), *ministrations* (3), *matriarchal* (3), *quest* (7), *chameleons* (7), *surveillance* (7), *conspiratorially* (9), *aberration* (9), *mesmerizing* (10), *denouement* (11), *ravished* (11), and *impromptu* (13).

Questions About the Writer's Craft

1. **The pattern.** Of all the women mentioned in the essay, only María La Loca is described in detail. What descriptive details does Cofer offer about her? Why do you suppose Cofer provides so much description about this particular woman?
2. In paragraph 7, Cofer provides some specifics about her childhood as a "Navy brat." What would have been lost if Cofer hadn't included this material?
3. **Other patterns.** Reread paragraphs 4, 6, 8, and 11–13, where Cofer *recounts* her grandmother's story. Why do you think Cofer doesn't tell the story straight through, without interruptions? What purpose do the interruptions serve? How does Cofer signal when she is moving away from the story or back to it?
4. Why might Cofer have mentioned in several spots the braiding of her hair, which goes on the whole time Mamá tells María's story? What similarities are there between the braiding and the storytelling session? What similarities are there between the braiding and Cofer's descriptive style (consider especially the last sentence of paragraph 10)?

Writing Assignments Using Description as a Pattern of Development

1. Cofer paints a vivid picture of a childhood ritual: the telling of stories among the women in her family. Think of a specific scene, event, or ritual from your own childhood or youth that has special meaning for you. Then write a descriptive essay conveying the distinctive flavor of that occasion. Draw upon vivid sensory language to capture your dominant impression of that time. Consider using dialogue, as Cofer does, to texturize your description and to reveal character.

2. To Cofer, Mamá was a "liberator" and a "model." Think of a person in your life who served as a role model or opened doors for you, and write an essay describing that person. Like Cofer, place the person in a characteristic setting and supply vigorous details about the person's actions, speech, looks, and so forth. Make sure that all the descriptive details reinforce your dominant impression of the individual. You may want to read Maya Angelou's "Sister Flowers" (page 100) to see how one especially skilled writer describes a powerful, influential person.

Writing Assignments Combining Patterns of Development

3. Cofer's family is close-knit, but family life nowadays is more likely to be fragmented, with everyone going separate ways. Write an essay explaining what *steps* families could take to offset this tendency toward fragmentation. You might want to focus on a particular area of family life, such as mealtimes, after-supper hours, or vacations. Be sure to spend some time discussing the expected *outcomes* of the steps you propose. You might benefit from conducting research in the library and/or on the Internet into how to increase the quality and quantity of family time.

4. The stories Cofer heard taught her "what it was like to be a woman." What information and experiences shaped your understanding of your gender? Write an essay showing how your perception of your gender identity was *influenced* by what you heard, witnessed, and experienced as a child. Along the way, you might briefly *narrate* one or more of these gender-shaping interactions. Before writing your paper, you may wish to read some of the following essays, each of which provides insight into gender expectations: Charmie Gholson's "Charity Display?" (page 151), Barbara Ehrenreich's "What I've Learned From Men" (page 215), Dave Barry's "The Ugly Truth About Beauty" (page 368), Camille Paglia's "Rape: A Bigger Danger Than Feminists Know" (page 541), and Susan Jacoby's "Common Decency" (page 547).

Writing Assignment Using a Journal Entry as a Starting Point

5. Write an essay narrating an experience that put to the test the moral of a story you were told when you were young. Select from your pre-reading journal entry the *one* story whose "truth" was most memorably validated *or* discredited by an experience later in your life. Your tone might be serious or humorous. In either case, be sure to make clear how you felt about the truth of the story after it was "tested" by experience.

Additional Writing Topics

DESCRIPTION

General Assignments

Write an essay using description to develop any of the following topics. Remember that an effective description focuses on a dominant impression and arranges details in a way that best supports that impression. Your details—vivid and appealing to the senses—should be carefully chosen so that the essay isn't overburdened with material of secondary importance. When writing, keep in mind that varied sentence structure and imaginative figures of speech are ways to make a descriptive piece compelling.

1. A favorite item of clothing
2. A school as a young child might see it
3. A hospital room you visited or stayed in
4. An individualist's appearance
5. A coffee shop, a bus shelter, a newsstand, or some other small place
6. A parade or victory celebration
7. A banana, a squash, or another fruit or vegetable
8. A particular drawer in a desk or bureau
9. A houseplant
10. A "media event"
11. A dorm room
12. An elderly person
13. An attractive man or woman
14. A prosthetic device or wheelchair
15. A TV, film, or music celebrity
16. A student lounge
17. A once-in-a-lifetime event
18. The inside of something, such as a cave, boat, car, shed, or machine
19. A friend, a roommate, or another person you know well
20. An essential gadget or a useless gadget

Assignments With a Specific Purpose, Audience, and Point of View

On Campus

1. For an audience of incoming first-year students, prepare a speech describing registration day at your college. Use specific details to help prepare students for the actual event. Choose an adjective that represents your dominant impression of the experience, and keep that word in mind as you write.
2. Your college has decided to replace an old campus structure (for example, a dorm or dining hall) with a new version. Write the administration a letter of protest

describing the place so vividly and appealingly that its value and need for preservation are unquestionable.

3. As a staff member of the campus newspaper, you have been asked to write a weekly column of social news and gossip. For your first column, you plan to describe a recent campus event—a dance, party, or concert, or other social activity. With a straightforward or tongue-in-cheek tone, describe where the event was held, the appearance of the people who attended, and so on.

At Home or in the Community

4. As a subscriber to a community-wide dating service, you've been asked to submit a description of the kind of person you'd like to meet. Describe your ideal date. Focus on specifics about physical appearance, personal habits, character traits, and interests.

5. As a resident of a particular town, you're angered by the appearance of a certain spot and by the activities that take place there. Write the town council a letter describing in detail the undesirable nature of this place (a video arcade, an adult bookstore, a bar, a bus station, a neglected park or beach). End with some suggestions about ways to improve the situation.

On the Job

6. You've noticed a recurring problem in your workplace, and you want to bring it to the attention of your boss, who is typically inattentive. Write a letter to your boss describing the problem. Your goal is not to provide solutions, but rather, to provide vivid description—complete with sensory details—so that your boss can no longer deny the problem.

NARRATION

WHAT IS NARRATION?

Human beings are instinctively storytellers. In prehistoric times, our ancestors huddled around campfires to hear tales of hunting and magic. In ancient times, warriors gathered in halls to listen to bards praise in song the exploits of epic heroes. Things are no different today. Boisterous children invariably settle down to listen when their parents read to them; millions of people tune in day after day to the ongoing drama of their favorite soap operas; vacationers sit motionless on the beach, caught up in the latest best-sellers; and all of us enjoy saying, "Just listen to what happened to me today." Our hunger for storytelling is a basic part of us.

Narration means telling a single story or several related stories. The story can be a means to an end, a way to support a main idea or thesis. For instance, to demonstrate that television has become the constant companion of many children, you might narrate a typical child's day in front of the television—starting with frantic cartoons in the morning and ending with dizzy situation comedies at night. Or to support the point that the college registration process should be reformed, you could tell the tale of a chaotic morning spent trying to enroll in classes.

Narration is powerful. Every public speaker, from politician to classroom teacher, knows that stories capture the attention of listeners as nothing else can. Narration speaks to us strongly because it is about us; we want to know what happened to others, not simply because we're curious, but because their experiences shed light on the nature of our own lives. Narration lends force to opinions, triggers the flow of memory, and evokes places and times in ways that are compelling and affecting.

HOW NARRATION FITS YOUR PURPOSE AND AUDIENCE

Because narratives tell a story, you may think they are found only in novels or short stories. But narration can also appear in essays, sometimes as a supplemental pattern of development. For example, if your purpose in a paper is to *persuade* apathetic readers that airport security regulations must be followed strictly, you might lead off with a brief account of a friend who inadvertently boarded a plane with a pocket knife in his backpack. In a paper *defining* good teaching, you might keep readers engaged by including satirical anecdotes about one hapless instructor, the antithesis of an effective teacher. An essay on the *effects* of an overburdened judicial system might provide—in an attempt to involve readers—a dramatic account of the way one clearly guilty murderer plea-bargained his way to freedom.

In addition to providing effective support in one section of your paper, narration can also serve as an essay's dominant pattern of development. In fact, most of this chapter shows you how to use a single extended narrative to convey a central point and share with readers your view of what happened. You might choose to narrate the events of a day spent with your three-year-old nephew as a way of revealing how you rediscovered the importance of family life. Or you might relate the story of your roommate's mugging, evoking the powerlessness and terror of being a victim. Any story can form the basis for a narrative essay as long as you convey the essence of the experience and evoke its meaning.

At this point, you have a good sense of the way writers use narration to achieve their purpose and to connect with their readers. Now take a moment to look closely at the photograph at the beginning of this chapter. Imagine you're writing a "Recent Events" update, accompanied by the photo, for the website of an organization that supports (*or* opposes) the war in Iraq. Your purpose is to recount what happened at the protest in such a way that your account supports the website's 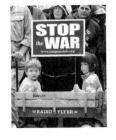 position on the conflict. Jot down some phrases you might use when *narrating* the events of the day.

SUGGESTIONS FOR USING NARRATION IN AN ESSAY

The following suggestions will be helpful whether you use narration as a dominant or a supportive pattern of development.

1. Identify the conflict in the event.   The power of many narratives is rooted in a special kind of tension that "hooks" readers and makes them want to follow the story to its end. This narrative tension is often a by-product of some form of *conflict* within the story. Many narratives revolve around an internal dilemma experienced by a key person in the story. Or the conflict may be between people in the story or between a pivotal character and some social institution or natural phenomenon.

2. Identify the point of the narrative.   In *The Adventures of Huckleberry Finn*, Mark Twain warned: "Persons attempting to find a motive in this narrative will be prosecuted; persons attempting to find a moral in it will be banished; persons attempting to find a plot in it will be shot." Twain was, of course, being ironic; his novel's richness lies in its "motives" and "morals." Similarly, when you recount a narrative, it's your responsibility to convey the event's *significance* or *meaning*. In other words, be sure readers are clear about your *narrative point*, or thesis.

Suppose you decide to write about the time you got locked in a mall late at night. Your narrative might focus on the way the mall looked after hours and the way you struggled with mounting terror. But you would also use the narrative to make a point. Perhaps you want to emphasize that fear can be instructive. Or your point might be that malls have a disturbing, surreal underside. You could state this thesis explicitly. ("After hours, the mall shed its cheerful daytime demeanor and took on a more sinister quality.") Or you could refrain from stating the thesis directly, relying on your details and language to convey the point of the narrative: "The mannequins stared at me with glazed eyes and frozen smiles" and "The steel grates pulled over each store's entrance glinted in the cold light, making each shop look like a prison cell."

3. Develop only those details that advance the narrative point.   You know from experience that nothing is more boring than a storyteller who gets sidetracked and drags out a story with nonessential details. If a friend started to tell about the time his car broke down in the middle of an expressway—but interrupted his story to complain at length about the slipshod work done by his auto repair shop—you might clench your teeth in annoyance, wishing your friend would hurry up and get back to the interesting part of the story.

Brainstorming ("What happened? When? Where? Who was involved? Why did it happen?") can be valuable for helping you amass narrative details. Then, after generating the specifics, you cull out the nonessential and devote your energies to the key specifics needed to advance your narrative point. When telling a story, you maintain an effective narrative pace by focusing on that point and eliminating details that don't support it. A good narrative depends not only on what is included, but also on what has been left out.

But how do you determine which specifics to omit, which to treat briefly, and which to emphasize? Having a clear sense of your narrative point and knowing your audience are crucial. Assume you're writing a narrative about a disastrous get-acquainted dance sponsored by your college the first week of the academic year. In addition to telling what happened, you want to make a point; perhaps you want to emphasize that, despite the college's good intentions, such official events actually make it difficult to meet people. With this purpose in mind, you might write about how stiff and unnatural students seemed, all dressed up in their best clothes; you might narrate snatches of strained conversation you overheard; you might describe the way males gathered on one side of the room, females on the other—reverting to behaviors supposedly abandoned in fifth grade. All these details would support your narrative point.

Because you don't want to get waylaid by detours that lead away from that point, you would leave out details about the topnotch band and the appetizing refreshments at the dance. The music and food may have been surprisingly good, but since these details don't advance the point you want to make, they should be omitted.

You also need to keep your audience in mind when selecting narrative details. If the audience consists of your instructor and other students—all of them familiar with the new student center where the dance was held—specific details about the center probably wouldn't have to be provided. But imagine that the essay is going to appear in the quarterly magazine published by the college's community relations office. Many of the magazine's readers are former graduates who haven't been on campus for several years. They may need some additional specifics about the student center: its location, how many people it holds, how it is furnished.

As you write, keep asking yourself, "Is this detail or character or snippet of conversation essential? Does my audience need this detail to understand the conflict in the situation? Does this detail advance or intensify the narrative action?" Summarize details that have some importance but do not deserve lengthy treatment ("Two hours went by . . ."). And try to limit *narrative commentary*—statements that tell rather than show what happened—since such remarks interrupt the narrative flow. Focus instead on the specifics that propel action forward in a vigorous way.

Sometimes, especially if the narrative re-creates an event from the past, you won't be able to remember what happened detail for detail. In such a case, you should take advantage of what is called *dramatic license*. Using as a guide your powers of recall as well as the perspective you now have of that particular time, feel free to reshape events to suit your narrative point.

4. Organize the narrative sequence.   All of us know the traditional beginning of fairy tales: "Once upon a time. . . ." Every narrative begins somewhere, presents a span of time, and ends at a certain point. Frequently, you'll want to use a straightforward time order, following the event *chronologically* from beginning to end: first this happened, next this happened, finally this happened.

But sometimes a strict chronological recounting may not be effective—especially if the high point of the narrative gets lost somewhere in the middle of the time sequence. To avoid that possibility, you may want to disrupt chronology, plunge the reader into the middle of the story, and then return in a *flashback* to the beginning of the tale. You're probably familiar with the way flashback is used on television and in film. You see someone appealing to the main character for financial help, then return to an earlier time when both were students in the same class, before learning how the rest of the story unfolds. Narratives can also use *flashforward*. You give readers a glimpse of the future (the main character being jailed) before the story continues in the present (the events leading to the arrest). These techniques shift the story onto several planes and keep it from becoming a step-by-step, predictable account. Reserve flashforwards and flashbacks, however, for crucial incidents only, since breaking out of chronological order acts as emphasis. Here are examples of how flashback and flashforward can be used in narrative writing:

Flashback

Standing behind the wooden counter, Greg wielded his knife expertly as he shucked clams--one every ten seconds--with practiced ease. The scene contrasted sharply with his first day on the job, when his hands broke out in blisters and when splitting each shell was like prying open a safe.

Flashforward

Rushing to move my car from the no-parking zone, I waved a quick goodbye to Karen as she climbed the steps to the bus. I didn't know then that by the time I picked her up at the bus station later that day, she had made a decision that would affect both our lives.

Whether or not you choose to include flashbacks or flashforwards in an essay, remember to limit the time span covered by the narrative. Otherwise, you will have trouble generating the details needed to give the story depth and meaning. Also, regardless of the time sequence you select, organize the tale so that it drives toward a strong finish. Be careful that your story doesn't trail off into minor, anticlimactic details.

5. Make the narrative easy to follow.   Describing each distinct action in a separate paragraph helps readers grasp the flow of events. Although narrative essays don't always have conventional topic sentences, each narrative paragraph should have a clear focus. Often this focus is indicated by a sentence early in the paragraph that directs attention to the action taking place. Such a sentence functions as a kind of *informal topic sentence;* the rest of the paragraph then develops that topic sentence. You should also be sure to use time signals when narrating a story. Words like *now, then, next, after,* and *later* ensure that your reader won't get lost as the story progresses.

6. Make the narrative vigorous and immediate.   A compelling narrative provides an abundance of specific details, making readers feel as if they're experiencing the story being told. Readers must be able to see, hear, touch, smell, and taste the event you're narrating. *Vivid sensory description* is, therefore, an essential part of an effective narrative. Not only do specific sensory details make writing a pleasure to read—we all enjoy learning the particulars about people, places, and things—but they also give the narrative the stamp of reality. The specifics convince the reader that the event being described actually did, or could, occur.

Compare the following excerpts from a narrative essay. The first version is lifeless and dull; the revised version, packed with sensory images, grabs readers with its sense of foreboding:

> That eventful day started out like every other summer day. My sister Tricia and I made several elaborate mud pies, which we decorated with care. A little later on, as we were spraying each other with the garden hose, we heard my father walk up the path.

> That sad summer day started out uneventfully enough. My sister Tricia and I spent a few hours mixing and decorating mud pies. Our hands caked with dry mud, we sprinkled each lopsided pie with alternating rows of dandelion and clover petals. Later when the sun got hotter, we tossed our white T-shirts over the red picket fence--forgetting my grandmother's frequent warnings to be more ladylike. Our sweaty backs bared to the sun, we doused each other with icy sprays from the garden hose. Caught up in the primitive pleasure of it all, we barely heard my father as he walked up the garden path, the gravel crunching under his heavy work boots.

A caution: Sensory language enlivens narration, but it also slows the pace. Be sure that the slower pace suits your purpose. For example, a lengthy description fits an account of a leisurely summer vacation but is inappropriate in a tale about a frantic search for a misplaced wallet.

Another way to create an aura of narrative immediacy is to use *dialogue* while telling a story. Our sense of other people comes, in part, from what they say and from the way they sound. Conversational exchanges allow the reader to experience characters directly. Compare the following fragments of a narrative, one with dialogue and one without, noting how much more energetic the second version is.

> When I finally found my way back to the campsite, the trail guide commented on my disheveled appearance.

> When I finally found my way back to the campsite, the trail guide took one look at me and drawled, "What on earth happened to you, Daniel Boone? You look as though you've been dragged through a haystack backwards."
> "I'd look a lot worse if I hadn't run back here. When a bullet whizzes by me, I don't stick around to see who's doing the shooting."

Note that, when using dialogue, you generally begin a new paragraph to indicate a shift from one person's speech to another's (as in the second example above).

Using *varied sentence structure* is another strategy for making narratives lively and vigorous. Sentences that plod along predictably (subject-verb, subject-verb) put readers to sleep. Experiment with your sentences by juggling length and sentence type; mix long and short sentences, simple and complex. Compare the following original and revised versions to get an idea of how effective varied sentence rhythm can be in narrative writing.

Original

The store manager went to the walk-in refrigerator every day. The heavy metal door clanged shut behind her. I had visions of her freezing to death among the hanging carcasses. The shiny door finally swung open. She waddled out.

Revised

Each time the store manager went to the walk-in refrigerator, the heavy metal door clanged shut behind her. Visions of her freezing to death among the hanging carcasses crept into my mind until the shiny door finally swung open and she waddled out.

Original

The yellow-and-blue-striped fish struggled on the line. Its scales shimmered in the sunlight. Its tail waved frantically. I saw its desire to live. I decided to let it go.

Revised

Scales shimmering in the sunlight, tail waving frantically, the yellow-and-blue-striped fish struggled on the line. Seeing its desire to live, I let it go.

Finally, *vigorous verbs* lend energy to narratives. Use active verb forms ("The boss *yelled at* him") rather than passive ones ("He *was yelled at* by the boss"), and try to replace anemic *to be* verbs ("She *was* a good basketball player") with more dynamic constructions ("She *played* basketball well").

7. Keep your point of view and verb tense consistent.   All stories have a *narrator*, the person who tells the story. If you, as narrator, tell a story as you experienced it, the story is written in the *first-person point of view* ("*I* saw the dog pull loose"). But if you observed the event (or heard about it from others) and want to tell how someone else experienced the incident, you would use the *third-person point of view* ("*Anne* saw the dog pull loose"). Each point of view has advantages and limitations. First person allows you to express ordinarily private thoughts and to re-create an event as you actually experienced it. This point of view is limited, though, in its ability to depict the inner thoughts of other people involved in the event. By way of contrast, third person makes it easier to provide insight into the thoughts of all the participants. However, its objective, broad perspective may undercut some of the subjective immediacy typical of the "I was there" point of view. No matter which point of view you select, stay with that vantage point throughout the entire narrative.

Knowing whether to use the *past* or *present tense* ("I *strolled* into the room" as opposed to "I *stroll* into the room") is important. In most narrations, the past tense predominates, enabling the writer to span a considerable period of time. Although more rarely used, the present tense can be powerful for events of short duration—a wrestling match or a medical emergency, for instance. A narrative in the present tense prolongs each moment, intensifying the reader's sense of participation. Be careful, though; unless the event is intense and fast-paced, the present tense can seem contrived. Whichever tense you choose, avoid shifting midstream—starting, let's say, in the past tense ("she skated") and switching to the present ("she runs").

REVISION STRATEGIES

Once you have a draft of the essay, you're ready to revise. The following checklist will help you and those giving you feedback apply to narration some of the revision techniques discussed on pages 60–62.

☑ NARRATION: A REVISION/PEER REVIEW CHECKLIST

Revise Overall Meaning and Structure

❑ What is the essay's main point? Is it stated explicitly or is it implied? Where? Could the point be conveyed more clearly? How?

❑ What is the narrative's conflict? Is it stated explicitly or is it implied? Where? Could the conflict be made more dramatic? How?

❑ From what point of view is the narrative told? Is it the most effective point of view for this essay? Why or why not?

Revise Paragraph Development

❑ Which paragraphs fail to advance the action, reveal character, or contribute to the story's mood? Should these sections be condensed or eliminated?

❑ Where should the narrative pace be slowed down or quickened?

❑ Where is it difficult to follow the chronology of events? Should the order of paragraphs be changed? How? Where would additional time signals help?

❑ How could flashback or flashforward paragraphs be used to highlight key events?

❑ Would dramatic dialogue or mood-setting description help make the essay's opening paragraph more compelling?

❑ What could be done to make the essay's closing paragraph more effective? Should the essay end earlier? Should it close by echoing an idea or image from the opening?

Revise Sentences and Words

❑ Where is sentence structure monotonous? Where would combining sentences, mixing sentence types, and alternating sentence length help?

❑ Where could dialogue replace commentary to convey character and propel the story forward?

❑ Which sentences and words are inconsistent with the essay's tone?

❑ Where do vigorous verbs convey action? Where could active verbs replace passive ones? Where could dull *to be* verbs be converted to more dynamic forms?

❑ Where are there inappropriate shifts in point of view or verb tense?

STUDENT ESSAY

The following student essay was written by Paul Monahan in response to this assignment.

In "Shooting an Elephant," George Orwell tells about an incident that forced him to act in a manner that ran counter to his better

instincts. Write a narrative about a time when you faced a disturbing conflict and ended up doing something you later regretted.

While reading Paul's paper, try to determine how well it applies the principles of narration. The annotations on Paul's paper and the commentary following it will help you look at the essay more closely.

If Only
by Paul Monahan

Introduction

1   Having worked at a 7-Eleven store for two years, I
thought I had become successful at what our manager calls
"customer relations." I firmly believed that a friendly smile
and an automatic "sir," "ma'am," and "thank you" would see
me through any situation that might arise, from soothing
impatient or unpleasant people to apologizing for giving out

Narrative point
(thesis)

the wrong change. But the other night an old woman
shattered my belief that a glib response could smooth over
the rough spots of dealing with other human beings.

Informal topic
sentence

2   The moment she entered, the woman presented a sharp
contrast to our shiny store with its bright lighting and neatly
arranged shelves. Walking as if each step were painful, she
slowly pushed open the glass door and hobbled down the
nearest aisle. She coughed dryly, wheezing with each breath.

Sensory details

On a forty-degree night, she was wearing only a faded print
dress, a thin, light beige sweater too small to button, and
black vinyl slippers with the backs cut out to expose
calloused heels. There were no stockings or socks on her
splotchy, blue-veined legs.

3   After strolling around the store for several minutes, the
old woman stopped in front of the rows of canned vegetables.
She picked up some corn niblets and stared with a strange
intensity at the label. At that point, I decided to be a good,

Informal topic
sentence

courteous employee and asked her if she needed help. As I
stood close to her, my smile became harder to maintain; her

Sensory details

red-rimmed eyes were partially closed by yellowish crusts;
her hands were covered with layer upon layer of grime; and
the stale smell of sweat rose in a thick vaporous cloud from
her clothes.

Start of dialogue

4   "I need some food," she muttered in reply to my bright
"Can I help you?"

5   "Are you looking for corn, ma'am?"

6   "I need some food," she repeated. "Any kind."

7   "Well, the corn is ninety-five cents," I said in my most
helpful voice. "Or, if you like, we have a special on bologna
today."

| | "I can't pay," she said. | 8 |

Conflict established → For a second, I was tempted to say, "Take the corn." But the employee rules flooded into my mind: Remain polite, but do not let customers get the best of you. Let them know that you are in control. For a moment, I even entertained the idea that this was some sort of test, and that this woman was someone from the head office, testing my loyalty. I responded dutifully, "I'm sorry, ma'am, but I can't give away anything free." **9**

Informal topic sentence → The old woman's face collapsed a bit more, if that were possible, and her hands trembled as she put the can back on the shelf. She shuffled past me toward the door, her torn and dirty clothing barely covering her bent back. **10**

Conclusion

Echoing of narrative point in the introduction → Moments after she left, I rushed out the door with the can of corn, but she was nowhere in sight. For the rest of my shift, the image of the woman haunted me. I had been young, healthy, and smug. She had been old, sick, and desperate. Wishing with all my heart that I had acted like a human being rather than a robot, I was saddened to realize how fragile a hold we have on our better instincts. **11**

COMMENTARY

Point of view, tense, and conflict.   Paul chose to write "If Only" from the *first-person point of view*, a logical choice because he appears as a main character in his own story. Using the *past tense*, Paul recounts an incident filled with *conflicts*—between him and the woman and between his fear of breaking the rules and his human instinct to help someone in need.

Narrative point.   It isn't always necessary to state the *narrative point* of an essay; it can be implied. But Paul decided to express the controlling idea of his narrative in two places—in the introduction ("But the other night an old woman shattered my belief that a glib response could smooth over the rough spots of dealing with other human beings") and again in the conclusion, where he expands his idea about rote responses overriding impulses of independent judgment and compassion. All of the essay's *narrative details* contribute to the point of the piece; Paul does not include any extraneous information that would detract from the central idea he wants to convey.

Organization.   The narrative is *organized chronologically*, from the moment the woman enters the store to Paul's reaction after she leaves. Paul limits the narrative's time span. The entire incident probably occurs in under ten minutes, yet the introduction serves as a kind of *flashback* by providing some necessary background about Paul's past experiences. To help the reader follow the course of the narrative, Paul uses *time signals: "The moment* she entered, the woman presented a sharp contrast" (paragraph 2); "*At that point,* I decided to be a good, courteous employee" (3); "*For the rest of my shift,* the image of the woman haunted me" (11).

The paragraphs (except for those consisting solely of dialogue) also contain *informal topic sentences* that direct attention to the specific stage of action being narrated. Indeed, each paragraph focuses on a distinct event: the elderly woman's actions when she first enters the store, the encounter between Paul and the woman, Paul's resulting inner conflict, the woman's subsequent response, and Paul's delayed reaction.

Combining patterns of development.   This chronological chain of events, with one action leading to another, illustrates that the *cause-effect* pattern underlies the basic structure of Paul's essay. And by means of another pattern—*description*—Paul gives dramatic immediacy to the events being recounted. Throughout, he provides rich sensory details to engage the reader's interest. For instance, the sentence "her red-rimmed eyes were partially closed by yellowish crusts" (3) vividly re-creates the woman's appearance while also suggesting Paul's inner reaction to the woman.

Dialogue and sentence structure.   Paul uses other techniques to add energy and interest to his narrative. For one thing, he dramatizes his conflict with the woman through *dialogue* that crackles with tension. And he achieves a vigorous narrative pace by *varying the length and structure of his sentences.* In the second paragraph, a short sentence ("There were no stockings or socks on her splotchy, blue-veined legs") alternates with a longer one ("On a forty-degree night, she was wearing only a faded print dress, a thin, light beige sweater too small to button, and black vinyl slippers with the backs cut out to expose calloused heels"). Some sentences in the essay open with a subject and verb ("She coughed dryly"), while others start with dependent clauses or participial phrases ("As I stood close to her, my smile became harder to maintain"; "Walking as if each step were painful, she slowly pushed open the glass door") or with a prepositional phrase ("For a second, I was tempted").

Revising the first draft.   Comparing the final version of the essay's third paragraph, shown above, with the preliminary version reprinted below reveals some of the changes Paul made while revising the essay.

Original Version of the Third Paragraph

After sneezing and hacking her way around the store, the old woman stopped in front of the vegetable shelves. She picked up a can of corn and stared at the label. She stayed like this for several minutes. Then I walked over to her and asked if I could be of help.

After putting the original draft aside for a while, Paul reread his paper aloud and realized the third paragraph especially lacked power. So he decided to add compelling descriptive details about the woman ("the stale smell of sweat," for example). When revising, he also worked to reduce the paragraph's choppiness. By expanding and combining sentences, he gave the paragraph an easier, more graceful rhythm. Much of the time, revision involves paring down excess material. In this case, though, Paul made the right decision to elaborate his sentences. Furthermore, he added the following comment to the third paragraph: "I decided to be a good, courteous employee." These few words introduce an appropriate note of irony and serve to echo the essay's controlling idea.

Finally, Paul decided to omit the words "sneezing and hacking" because he realized they were too comic or light for his subject. Still, the first sentence in the revised paragraph is somewhat jarring. The word *strolling* isn't quite appropriate since it implies a leisurely grace inconsistent with the impression he wants to convey. Replacing *strolling* with, say, *shuffling* would bring the image more into line with the essay's overall mood.

Despite this slight problem, Paul's revisions are right on the mark. The changes he made strengthened his essay, turning it into a more evocative, more polished piece of narrative writing.

Activities: Narration

Prewriting Activities

1. Imagine you're writing two essays: One analyzes the *effect* of insensitive teachers on young children; the other *argues* the importance of family traditions. With the help of your journal or freewriting, identify different narratives you could use to open each essay.

2. For each of the situations below, identify two different conflicts that would make a story worth relating. Then prepare six to ten lines of natural-sounding dialogue for each potential conflict in *one* of the situations.
   a. Going to the supermarket with a friend
   b. Telling your parents which college you've decided to attend
   c. Participating in a demonstration
   d. Preparing for an exam in a difficult course

Revising Activities

3. Revise each of the following narrative sentence groups twice: once with words that carry negative connotations, and again with words that carry positive connotations. Use varied sentence structure, sensory details, and vigorous verbs to convey mood.

a. The bell rang. It rang loudly. Students knew the last day of class was over.
b. Last weekend, our neighbors burned leaves in their yard. We went over to speak with them.
c. The sun shone in through my bedroom window. It made me sit up in bed. Daylight was finally here, I told myself.

4. The following paragraph is the introduction from the first draft of an essay proposing harsher penalties for drunk drivers. Revise this narrative paragraph to make it more effective. How can you make sentence structure less predictable? Which details should you delete? As you revise, provide language that conveys the event's sights, smells, and sounds. Also, clarify the chronological sequence.

As I drove down the street in my bright blue sports car, I saw a car coming rapidly around the curve. The car didn't slow down as it headed toward the traffic light. The light turned yellow and then red. A young couple, dressed like models, started crossing the street. When the woman saw the car, she called out to her husband. He jumped onto the shoulder. The man wasn't hurt but, seconds later, it was clear the woman was. I ran to a nearby emergency phone and called the police. The ambulance arrived, but the woman was already dead. The driver, who looked terrible, failed the sobriety test, and the police found out that he had two previous offenses. It's apparent that better ways have to be found for getting drunk drivers off the road.

Audre Lorde

Named poet laureate of the state of New York in 1991, Audre Lorde (1934–92) was a New Yorker born of African-Caribbean parents. After earning degrees at Hunter College and Columbia University, Lorde held numerous teaching positions throughout the New York City area. She later toured the world as a lecturer, forming women's rights coalitions in the Caribbean, Africa, and Europe. Best known as a feminist theorist, Lorde combined social criticism and personal revelation in her writing on such topics as race, gender relations, and sexuality. Her numerous poems and non-fiction pieces were published in a variety of magazines and literary journals. Her books include *The Black Unicorn: Poems* (1978), *Sister Outsider: Essays and Speeches* (1984), and *A Burst of Light* (1988). The following selection is an excerpt from her autobiography, *Zami: A New Spelling of My Name* (1982).

Pre-Reading Journal Entry

When you were a child, what beliefs about the United States did you have? List these beliefs. For each, indicate whether subsequent experience maintained or shattered your childhood understanding of these beliefs. Take a little time to explore these issues in your journal.

The Fourth of July

The first time I went to Washington, D.C., was on the edge of the summer when I was supposed to stop being a child. At least that's what they said to us all at graduation from the eighth grade. My sister Phyllis graduated at the same time from high school. I don't know what she was supposed to stop being. But as graduation presents for us both, the whole family took a Fourth of July trip to Washington, D.C., the fabled and famous capital of our country. 1

It was the first time I'd ever been on a railroad train during the day. When I was little, and we used to go to the Connecticut shore, we always went at night on the milk train, because it was cheaper. 2

Preparations were in the air around our house before school was even over. We packed for a week. There were two very large suitcases that my father carried, and a box filled with food. In fact, my first trip to Washington was a mobile feast; I started eating as soon as we were comfortably ensconced in our seats, and did not stop until somewhere after Philadelphia. 3

I remember it was Philadelphia because I was disappointed not to have passed by the Liberty Bell.

My mother had roasted two chickens and cut them up into dainty bite-size pieces. She packed slices of brown bread and butter and green pepper and carrot sticks. There were little violently yellow iced cakes with scalloped edges called "marigolds," that came from Cushman's Bakery. There was a spice bun and rock-cakes from Newton's, the West Indian bakery across Lenox Avenue from St. Mark's School, and iced tea in a wrapped mayonnaise jar. There were sweet pickles for us and dill pickles for my father, and peaches with the fuzz still on them, individually wrapped to keep them from bruising. And, for neatness, there were piles of napkins and a little tin box with a washcloth dampened with rosewater and glycerine for wiping sticky mouths.

I wanted to eat in the dining car because I had read all about them, but my mother reminded me for the umpteenth time that dining car food always costs too much money and besides, you never could tell whose hands had been playing all over that food, nor where those same hands had been just before. My mother never mentioned that Black people were not allowed into railroad dining cars headed south in 1947. As usual, whatever my mother did not like and could not change, she ignored. Perhaps it would go away, deprived of her attention.

I learned later that Phyllis's high school senior class trip had been to Washington, but the nuns had given her back her deposit in private, explaining to her that the class, all of whom were white, except Phyllis, would be staying in a hotel where Phyllis "would not be happy," meaning, Daddy explained to her, also in private, that they did not rent rooms to Negroes. "We will take you to Washington, ourselves," my father had avowed, "and not just for an overnight in some measly fleabag hotel."

American racism was a new and crushing reality that my parents had to deal with every day of their lives once they came to this country. They handled it as a private woe. My mother and father believed that they could best protect their children from the realities of race in america and the fact of american racism by never giving them name, much less discussing their nature. We were told we must never trust white people, but *why* was never explained, nor the nature of their ill will. Like so many other vital pieces of information in my childhood, I was supposed to know without being told. It always seemed like a very strange injunction coming from my mother, who looked so much like one of those people we were never supposed to trust. But something always warned me not to ask my mother why she wasn't white, and why Auntie Lillah and Auntie Etta weren't, even though they were all that same problematic color so different from my father and me, even from my sisters, who were somewhere in-between.

In Washington, D.C., we had one large room with two double beds and an extra cot for me. It was a back-street hotel that belonged to a friend of my father's who was in real estate, and I spent the whole next day after Mass squinting up at the Lincoln Memorial where Marian Anderson[1] had sung after the D.A.R.[2] refused to allow her to sing in their auditorium because she was Black. Or because she was "Colored," my father said as he told us the story. Except that what he probably said was "Negro," because for his time, my father was quite progressive.

I was squinting because I was in that silent agony that characterized all 9 of my childhood summers, from the time school let out in June to the end of July, brought about by my dilated and vulnerable eyes exposed to the summer brightness.

I viewed Julys through an agonizing corolla of dazzling whiteness and I 10 always hated the Fourth of July, even before I came to realize the travesty such a celebration was for Black people in this country.

My parents did not approve of sunglasses, nor of their expense. 11

I spent the afternoon squinting up at monuments to freedom and past 12 presidencies and democracy, and wondering why the light and heat were both so much stronger in Washington, D.C., than back home in New York City. Even the pavement on the streets was a shade lighter in color than back home.

Late that Washington afternoon my family and I walked back down 13 Pennsylvania Avenue. We were a proper caravan, mother bright and father brown, the three of us girls step-standards in-between. Moved by our historical surroundings and the heat of the early evening, my father decreed yet another treat. He had a great sense of history, a flair for the quietly dramatic and the sense of specialness of an occasion and a trip.

"Shall we stop and have a little something to cool off, Lin?" 14

Two blocks away from our hotel, the family stopped for a dish of vanil- 15 la ice cream at a Breyer's ice cream and soda fountain. Indoors, the soda fountain was dim and fan-cooled, deliciously relieving to my scorched eyes.

Corded and crisp and pinafored, the five of us seated ourselves one by 16 one at the counter. There was I between my mother and father, and my two sisters on the other side of my mother. We settled ourselves along the white mottled marble counter, and when the waitress spoke at first no one understood what she was saying, and so the five of us just sat there.

The waitress moved along the line of us closer to my father and spoke 17 again. "I said I kin give you to take out, but you can't eat here. Sorry." Then she dropped her eyes looking very embarrassed, and suddenly we heard what it was she was saying all at the same time, loud and clear.

---

[1]Acclaimed African-American opera singer (1902–93), famed for her renderings of Black spirituals (editors' note).
[2]Daughters of the American Revolution. A society, founded in 1890, for women who can prove direct lineage to soldiers or others who aided in winning American independence from Great Britain during the Revolutionary War (1775–83) (editors' note).

Straight-backed and indignant, one by one, my family and I got down   18
from the counter stools and turned around and marched out of the store,
quiet and outraged, as if we had never been Black before. No one would
answer my emphatic questions with anything other than a guilty silence.
"But we hadn't done anything!" This wasn't right or fair! Hadn't I written
poems about Bataan and freedom and democracy for all?

My parents wouldn't speak of this injustice, not because they had con-   19
tributed to it, but because they felt they should have anticipated it and avoided it. This made me even angrier. My fury was not going to be acknowledged
by a like fury. Even my two sisters copied my parents' pretense that nothing
unusual and anti-american had occurred. I was left to write my angry letter
to the president of the united states all by myself, although my father did
promise I could type it out on the office typewriter next week, after I showed
it to him in my copybook diary.

The waitress was white, and the counter was white, and the ice cream I   20
never ate in Washington, D.C., that summer I left childhood was white, and
the white heat and the white pavement and the white stone monuments of
my first Washington summer made me sick to my stomach for the whole rest
of that trip and it wasn't much of a graduation present after all.

Questions for Close Reading

1. What is the selection's thesis (or narrative point)? Locate the sentence(s) in which
   Lorde states her main idea. If she doesn't state the thesis explicitly, express it in
   your own words.
2. In paragraph 4, Lorde describes the elaborate picnic her mother prepared for the
   trip to Washington, D.C. Why did Lorde's mother make such elaborate preparations? What do these preparations tell us about Lorde's mother?
3. Why does Lorde have trouble understanding her parents' dictate that she "never
   trust white people" (paragraph 7)?
4. In general, how do Lorde's parents handle racism? How does the family as a whole
   deal with the racism they encounter in the ice-cream parlor? How does the family's reaction to the ice-cream parlor incident make Lorde feel?
5. Refer to your dictionary as needed to define the following words used in the selection: *fabled* (paragraph 1), *injunction* (7), *progressive* (8), *dilated* (9), *vulnerable*
   (9), *travesty* (10), *decreed* (13), and *pretense* (19).

Questions About the Writer's Craft

1. **The pattern.** What techniques does Lorde use to help readers follow the unfold-
   ing of the story as it occurs in both time and space?
2. When telling a story, skilled writers limit narrative commentary—statements that
   tell rather than show what happened—because such commentary tends to interrupt
   the narrative flow. Lorde, however, provides narrative commentary in several spots.
   Find these instances. How is the information she provides in these places essential
   to her narrative?

3. In paragraphs 7 and 19, Lorde uses all lowercase letters for *America, American,* and *President of the United States.* Why do you suppose she doesn't follow the rules of capitalization? In what ways does her rejection of these rules reinforce what she is trying to convey through the essay's title?

4. What key word does Lorde repeat in paragraph 20? What effect do you think she hopes the repetition will have on readers?

Writing Assignments Using Narration as a Pattern of Development

1. Lorde recounts an incident during which she was treated unfairly. Write a narrative about a time when either you were treated unjustly or you treated someone else in an unfair manner. Like Lorde, use vivid details to make the incident come alive and to convey how it affected you. Essays including George Orwell's "Shooting an Elephant" (page 143) and Charmie Gholson's "Charity Display?" (page 151) will prompt some ideas worth exploring.

2. Write a narrative about an experience that dramatically changed your view of the world. The experience might have been jarring and painful, or it may have been positive and uplifting. In either case, recount the incident with compelling narrative details. To illustrate the shift in your perspective, begin with a brief statement of the way you viewed the world before the experience. The following essays provide insight into the way a single experience can alter one's understanding of the world: Maya Angelou's "Sister Flowers" (page 100), Langston Hughes's "Salvation" (page 155), and Alice Walker's "Beauty: When the Other Dancer Is the Self" (page 408).

Writing Assignments Combining Patterns of Development

3. Lorde suggests that her parents use the coping mechanism of denial to deal with life's harsh realities. For example, she writes that whatever her mother "did not like and could not change, she ignored." Refer to a psychology textbook to learn more about denial as a coping mechanism. When is it productive? When is it counterproductive? Drawing upon your own experiences as well as those of friends, family, and classmates, write an essay *contrasting* effective and ineffective uses of denial. Near the end of the paper, present brief *guidelines* that will help readers identify when denial may be detrimental.

4. In her essay, Lorde decries and by implication takes a strong stance against racial discrimination. Brainstorm with friends, family members, and classmates to identify other injustices in American society. To prompt discussion, you might begin by considering attitudes toward the elderly, the overweight, the physically disabled; the funding of schools in poor and affluent neighborhoods; the portrayal of a specific ethnic group on television; and so on. Focusing on *one* such injustice, write an essay *arguing* that such an injustice indeed exists. To document the nature and extent of the injustice, use the library and/or Internet research. You should also consider *recounting* your own and other people's experiences. Acknowledge and, when you can, dismantle the views of those who think there isn't a problem.

Writing Assignment Using a Journal
Entry as a Starting Point

∞ **5.** Write an essay comparing and/or contrasting the beliefs you had about the United States as a child with those you have as an adult. Review your pre-reading journal entry, and select *one* American belief to focus on. Provide strong, dramatic examples that show why your childhood belief in this concept has been strengthened or weakened. Before writing, you should consider reading Yuh Ji-Yeon's "Let's Tell the Story of All America's Cultures" (page 517), a powerful account of personal disillusionment with American ideals, and Stanley Fish's "Free-Speech Follies" (page 534), a strongly argued examination of rights covered by the First Amendment of the Constitution. Jonathan Alter's "Time to Think About Torture" (page 552) and Henry Porter's "Now the Talk Is About Bringing Back Torture" (page 557) also address the painful clash of high national ideals with harsh realities.

George Orwell

Born Eric Blair in the former British colony of India, George Orwell (1903–50) is probably best known for his two novels, *Animal Farm* (1946) and *1984* (1949), both searing depictions of totalitarian societies. Orwell was also the author of numerous books and essays, many based on his diverse life experiences. He served with the Indian imperial police in Burma, worked at various jobs in London and Paris, and fought in the Spanish Civil War. His experiences in Burma provide the basis for the following essay, which is taken from his collection, *Shooting an Elephant and Other Essays* (1950).

Pre-Reading Journal Entry

Think of times when you were keenly aware of institutional injustice—an action, law, or regulation that was legally in the right but that you felt was wrong. In your journal, record several such examples. Why do you consider them wrong? Have you always felt that way? If not, what changed your opinion?

Shooting an Elephant

In Moulmein, in Lower Burma, I was hated by large numbers of people— the only time in my life that I have been important enough for this to happen to me. I was sub-divisional police officer of the town, and in an aimless, petty kind of way anti-European feeling was very bitter. No one had the guts to raise a riot, but if a European woman went through the bazaars alone somebody would probably spit betel juice over her dress. As a police officer I was an obvious target and was baited whenever it seemed safe to do so. When a nimble Burman tripped me up on the football field and the referee (another Burman) looked the other way, the crowd yelled with hideous laughter. This happened more than once. In the end the sneering yellow faces of young men that met me everywhere, the insults hooted after me when I was at a safe distance, got badly on my nerves. The young Buddhist priests were the worst of all. There were several thousand of them in the town and none of them seemed to have anything to do except stand on street corners and jeer at Europeans.

All this was perplexing and upsetting. For at that time I had already made up my mind that imperialism was an evil thing and the sooner I chucked up my job and got out of it the better. Theoretically—and secretly, of course—I was all for the Burmese and all against their oppressors, the

1

2

British. As for the job I was doing, I hated it more bitterly than I can perhaps make clear. In a job like that you see the dirty work of Empire at close quarters. The wretched prisoners huddling in the stinking cages of the lock-ups, the grey, cowed faces of the long-term convicts, the scarred buttocks of the men who had been flogged with bamboos—all these oppressed me with an intolerable sense of guilt. But I could get nothing into perspective. I was young and ill-educated and I had had to think out my problems in the utter silence that is imposed on every Englishman in the East. I did not even know that the British Empire is dying, still less did I know that it is a great deal better than the younger empires that are going to supplant it. All I knew was that I was stuck between my hatred of the empire I served and my rage against the evil-spirited little beasts who tried to make my job impossible. With one part of my mind I thought of the British Raj as an unbreakable tyranny, as something clamped down, in *saecula saeculorum*,[1] upon the will of prostrate peoples; with another part I thought that the greatest joy in the world would be to drive a bayonet into a Buddhist priest's guts. Feelings like these are the normal by-products of imperialism; ask any Anglo-Indian official, if you can catch him off duty.

One day something happened which in a roundabout way was enlight-   3
ening. It was a tiny incident in itself, but it gave me a better glimpse than I had had before of the real nature of imperialism—the real motives for which despotic governments act. Early one morning the sub-inspector at a police station at the other end of the town rang me up on the 'phone and said that an elephant was ravaging the bazaar. Would I please come and do something about it? I did not know what I could do, but I wanted to see what was happening and I got onto a pony and started out. I took my rifle, an old .44 Winchester and much too small to kill an elephant, but I thought the noise might be useful *in terrorem*.[2] Various Burmans stopped me on the way and told me about the elephant's doings. It was not, of course, a wild elephant, but a tame one which had gone "must." It had been chained up, as tame elephants always are when their attack of "must" is due, but on the previous night it had broken its chain and escaped. Its mahout, the only person who could manage it when it was in that state, had set out in pursuit, but had taken the wrong direction and was now twelve hours' journey away, and in the morning the elephant had suddenly reappeared in the town. The Burmese population had no weapons and were quite helpless against it. It had already destroyed somebody's bamboo hut, killed a cow and raided some fruit-stalls and devoured the stock; also it had met the municipal rubbish van and, when the driver jumped out and took to his heels, had turned the van over and inflicted violence upon it.

[1] For ever and ever (editors' note).
[2] As a warning (editors' note).

The Burmese sub-inspector and some Indian constables were waiting   4
for me in the quarter where the elephant had been seen. It was a very poor
quarter, a labyrinth of squalid bamboo huts, thatched with palm-leaf, winding all over a steep hillside. I remember that it was a cloudy, stuffy morning
at the beginning of the rains. We began questioning the people as to where
the elephant had gone and, as usual, failed to get any definite information.
That is invariably the case in the East; a story always sounds clear enough at
a distance, but the nearer you get to the scene of events the vaguer it
becomes. Some of the people said that the elephant had gone in one direction, some said that he had gone in another, some professed not even to have
heard of any elephant. I had almost made up my mind that the whole story
was a pack of lies, when we heard yells a little distance away. There was a loud,
scandalized cry of "Go away, child! Go away this instant!" and an old woman
with a switch in her hand came round the corner of a hut, violently shooing
away a crowd of naked children. Some more women followed, clicking their
tongues and exclaiming; evidently there was something that the children
ought not to have seen. I rounded the hut and saw a man's dead body sprawling in the mud. He was an Indian, a black Dravidian coolie, almost naked, and
he could not have been dead many minutes. The people said that the elephant
had come suddenly upon him round the corner of the hut, caught him with
its trunk, put its foot on his back and ground him into the earth. This was the
rainy season and the ground was soft, and his face had scored a trench a foot
deep and a couple of yards long. He was lying on his belly with arms cruci-
fied and head sharply twisted to one side. His face was coated with mud, the
eyes wide open, the teeth bared and grinning with an expression of unen-
durable agony. (Never tell me, by the way, that the dead look peaceful. Most
of the corpses I have seen looked devilish.) The friction of the great beast's
foot had stripped the skin from his back as neatly as one skins a rabbit. As soon
as I saw the dead man I sent an orderly to a friend's house nearby to borrow
an elephant rifle. I had already sent back the pony, not wanting it to go mad
with fright and throw me if it smelt the elephant.

The orderly came back in a few minutes with a rifle and five cartridges,   5
and meanwhile some Burmans had arrived and told us that the elephant was
in the paddy fields below, only a few hundred yards away. As I started forward practically the whole population of the quarter flocked out of the houses and followed me. They had seen the rifle and were all shouting excitedly
that I was going to shoot the elephant. They had not shown much interest
in the elephant when he was merely ravaging their homes, but it was different now that he was going to be shot. It was a bit of fun to them, as it would
be to an English crowd; besides they wanted the meat. It made me vaguely
uneasy. I had no intention of shooting the elephant—I had merely sent for
the rifle to defend myself if necessary—and it is always unnerving to have a
crowd following you. I marched down the hill, looking and feeling a fool,

with the rifle over my shoulder and an ever-growing army of people jostling at my heels. At the bottom, when you got away from the huts, there was a metalled road and beyond that a miry waste of paddy fields a thousand yards across, not yet ploughed but soggy from the first rains and dotted with coarse grass. The elephant was standing eight yards from the road, his left side towards us. He took not the slightest notice of the crowd's approach. He was tearing up bunches of grass, beating them against his knees to clean them and stuffing them into his mouth.

I had halted on the road. As soon as I saw the elephant I knew with per-   6
fect certainty that I ought not to shoot him. It is a serious matter to shoot a working elephant—it is comparable to destroying a huge and costly piece of machinery—and obviously one ought not to do it if it can possibly be avoided. And at that distance, peacefully eating, the elephant looked no more dangerous than a cow. I thought then and I think now that his attack of "must" was already passing off; in which case he would merely wander harmlessly about until the mahout came back and caught him. Moreover, I did not in the least want to shoot him. I decided that I would watch him for a little while to make sure that he did not turn savage again, and then go home.

But at that moment I glanced round at the crowd that had followed me.   7
It was an immense crowd, two thousand at the least and growing every minute. It blocked the road for a long distance on either side. I looked at the sea of yellow faces above the garish clothes—faces all happy and excited over this bit of fun, all certain that the elephant was going to be shot. They were watching me as they would watch a conjurer about to perform a trick. They did not like me, but with the magical rifle in my hands I was momentarily worth watching. And suddenly I realized that I should have to shoot the elephant after all. The people expected it of me and I had got to do it; I could feel their two thousand wills pressing me forward, irresistibly. And it was at this moment, as I stood there with the rifle in my hands, that I first grasped the hollowness, the futility of the white man's dominion in the East. Here was I, the white man with his gun, standing in front of the unarmed native crowd— seemingly the leading actor of the piece; but in reality I was only an absurd puppet pushed to and fro by the will of those yellow faces behind. I perceived in this moment that when the white man turns tyrant it is his own freedom that he destroys. He becomes a sort of hollow, posing dummy, the conventionalized figure of a sahib. For it is the condition of his rule that he shall spend his life in trying to impress the "natives," and so in every crisis he has got to do what the "natives" expect of him. He wears a mask, and his face grows to fit it. I had got to shoot the elephant. I had committed myself to doing it when I sent for the rifle. A sahib has got to act like a sahib; he has got to appear resolute, to know his own mind and do definite things. To come all that way, rifle in hand, with two thousand people marching at my heels, and then to trail feebly away, having done nothing—no, that was impossible. The crowd would

laugh at me. And my whole life, every white man's life in the East, was one long struggle not to be laughed at.

But I did not want to shoot the elephant. I watched him beating his 8 bunch of grass against his knees, with that preoccupied grandmotherly air that elephants have. It seemed to me that it would be murder to shoot him. At that age I was not squeamish about killing animals, but I had never shot an elephant and never wanted to. (Somehow it always seems worse to kill a *large* animal.) Besides, there was the beast's owner to be considered. Alive, the elephant was worth at least a hundred pounds; dead, he would only be worth the value of his tusks, five pounds, possibly. But I had got to act quickly. I turned to some experienced-looking Burmans who had been there when we arrived, and asked them how the elephant had been behaving. They all said the same thing: he took no notice of you if you left him alone, but he might charge if you went too close to him.

It was perfectly clear to me what I ought to do. I ought to walk up to 9 within, say, twenty-five yards of the elephant and test his behavior. If he charged, I could shoot; if he took no notice of me, it would be safe to leave him until the mahout came back. But also I knew that I was going to do no such thing. I was a poor shot with a rifle and the ground was soft mud into which one would sink at every step. If the elephant charged and I missed him, I should have about as much chance as a toad under a steam-roller. But even then I was not thinking particularly of my own skin, only of the watchful yellow faces behind. For at that moment, with the crowd watching me, I was not afraid in the ordinary sense, as I would have been if I had been alone. A white man mustn't be frightened in front of "natives"; and so, in general, he isn't frightened. The sole thought in my mind was that if anything went wrong those two thousand Burmans would see me pursued, caught, trampled on and reduced to a grinning corpse like that Indian up the hill. And if that happened it was quite probable that some of them would laugh. That would never do. There was only one alternative. I shoved the cartridges into the magazine and lay down on the road to get a better aim.

The crowd grew very still, and a deep, low, happy sigh, as of people who 10 see the theatre curtain go up at last, breathed from innumerable throats. They were going to have their bit of fun after all. The rifle was a beautiful German thing with cross-hair sights. I did not then know that in shooting an elephant one would shoot to cut an imaginary bar running from ear-hole to ear-hole. I ought, therefore, as the elephant was sideway on, to have aimed straight at his ear-hole; actually I aimed several inches in front of this, thinking the brain would be further forward.

When I pulled the trigger I did not hear the bang or feel the kick—one 11 never does when a shot goes home—but I heard the devilish roar of glee that went up from the crowd. In that instant, in too short a time, one would have thought, even for the bullet to get there, a mysterious, terrible change had come over the elephant. He neither stirred nor fell, but every line of his body had altered. He looked suddenly stricken, shrunken, immensely old, as though the frightful impact of the bullet had paralyzed him without knocking him down. At last, after what seemed a long time—it might have been five seconds, I dare say—he sagged flabbily to his knees. His mouth slobbered. An enormous senility seemed to have settled upon him. One could have imagined him thousands of years old. I fired again into the same spot. At the second shot he did not collapse but climbed with desperate slowness to his feet and stood weakly upright, with legs sagging and head drooping. I fired a third time. That was the shot that did for him. You could see the agony of it jolt his whole body and knock the last remnant of strength from his legs. But in falling he seemed for a moment to rise, for as his hind legs collapsed beneath him he seemed to tower upward like a huge rock toppling, his trunk reaching skywards like a tree. He trumpeted, for the first and only time. And then down he came, his belly towards me, with a crash that seemed to shake the ground even where I lay.

I got up. The Burmans were already racing past me across the mud. It was obvious that the elephant would never rise again, but he was not dead. He was breathing very rhythmically with long rattling gasps, his great mound of a side painfully rising and falling. His mouth was wide open—I could see far down into caverns of pale pink throat. I waited a long time for him to die, but his breathing did not weaken. Finally I fired my two remaining shots into the spot where I thought his heart must be. The thick blood welled out of him like red velvet, but still he did not die. His body did not even jerk when the shots hit him, the tortured breathing continued without a pause. He was dying, very slowly and in great agony, but in some world remote from me where not even a bullet could damage him further. I felt that I had got to put an end to that dreadful noise. It seemed dreadful to see the great beast lying there, powerless to move and yet powerless to die, and not even to be able to finish him. I sent back for my small rifle and poured shot after shot into his heart and down his throat. They seemed to make no impression. The tortured gasps continued as steadily as the ticking of a clock.

In the end I could not stand it any longer and went away. I heard later that it took him half an hour to die. Burmans were bringing dahs and baskets even before I left, and I was told they had stripped the body almost to the bones by the afternoon.

Afterwards, of course, there were endless discussions about the shooting of the elephant. The owner was furious, but he was only an Indian and could do nothing. Besides, legally I had done the right thing, for a mad elephant has to be killed, like a mad dog, if its owner fails to control it. Among the Europeans opinion was divided. The older men said I was right, the younger men said it was a damn shame to shoot an elephant for killing a coolie, because an elephant was worth more than any damn Coringhee coolie. And afterwards I was very glad that the coolie had been killed; it put me legally in the right and it gave me a sufficient pretext for shooting the elephant. I often wondered whether any of the others grasped that I had done it solely to avoid looking a fool.

Questions for Close Reading

1. What is the selection's thesis (or narrative point)? Locate the sentence(s) in which Orwell states his main idea. If he doesn't state the thesis explicitly, express it in your own words.
2. How does Orwell feel about the Burmans? What words does he use to describe them?
3. What reasons does Orwell give for shooting the elephant?
4. In paragraph 3, Orwell says that the elephant incident gave him a better understanding of "the real motives for which despotic governments act." What do you think he means? Before you answer, reread paragraph 7 carefully.
5. Refer to your dictionary as needed to define the following words used in the selection: *imperialism* (paragraph 2), *prostrate* (2), *despotic* (3), *mahout* (3), *miry* (5), *conjurer* (7), *futility* (7), and *sahib* (7).

Questions About the Writer's Craft

1. **The pattern.** Most effective narratives encompass a restricted time span. How much time elapses from the moment Orwell gets his gun to the death of the elephant? What time signals does Orwell provide to help the reader follow the sequence of events in this limited time span?
2. Orwell doesn't actually begin his narrative until the third paragraph. What purposes do the first two paragraphs serve?
3. **Other patterns.** In paragraph 6, Orwell says that shooting a working elephant "is comparable to destroying a huge and costly piece of machinery." This kind of *comparison* is called an *analogy*—describing something unfamiliar, often abstract, in terms of something more familiar and concrete. Find at least three additional analogies in Orwell's essay. What effect do they have?
4. **Other patterns.** Much of the power of Orwell's narrative comes from his ability to convey sensory impressions—what he saw, heard, smelled. Orwell's *description* becomes most vivid when he writes about the death of the elephant in paragraphs 11 and 12. Find some evocative words and phrases that give the description its power.

Writing Assignments Using Narration as a Pattern of Development

1. Orwell recounts a time he acted under great pressure. Write a narrative about an action you once took simply because you felt pressured. Perhaps you were attempting to avoid ridicule or to fulfill someone else's expectations. Like Orwell, use vivid details to bring the incident to life and to convey its effect on you. Langston Hughes's "Salvation" (page 155) may lead you to some insights about the way stress influences behavior.
2. Write a narrative essay about an experience that gave you, like Orwell, a deeper insight into your own nature. You may have discovered, for instance, that you can

be surprisingly naive, compassionate, petty, brave, rebellious, or good at something. Consider first reading David Helvarg's "The Storm This Time" (page 92) and Adam Mayblum's "The Price We Pay" (page 159), essays showing how the authors' responses to a challenge revealed much about their character.

Writing Assignments Combining Patterns of Development

3. Was Orwell justified in shooting the elephant? Write an essay *arguing* that Orwell was either justified *or* not justified. To develop your thesis, cite several specific reasons, each supported by *examples* drawn from the essay. Here are some points you might consider: the legality of Orwell's act, the elephant's temperament, the crowd's presence, the aftermath of the elephant's death, the death itself.

4. Orwell's essay concerns, in part, the tendency to conceal indecision and confusion behind a facade of authority. Focusing on one or two groups of people (parents, teachers, doctors, politicians, and so on), write an essay *arguing* that people in authority sometimes *pretend* to know what they're doing so that subordinates won't suspect their insecurity or incompetence. Part of your essay should focus on the *consequences* of such behaviors.

Writing Assignment Using a Journal Entry as a Starting Point

5. Review your pre-reading journal entry, and select *one* action, law, or regulation that you consider indefensible. Interview friends, family, and classmates in an effort to gather views on all sides of the issue. Also consider supplementing this informal research with information gathered in the library and/or on the Internet. After weighing all your material, formulate a thesis; then write an essay convincing readers of the validity of your position.

Charmie Gholson

Born in 1962, Charmie Gholson has had a varied career. She has been a waitress, a birthing coach, a radio producer, and a nutrition counselor. Today she writes features and reviews for the *Ann Arbor Observer* and a cooking column for *Current Magazine*. She also hosts a local public affairs radio show called *Renegade Solutions*. The mother of three sons, Gholson lives in Ann Arbor, Michigan. This article was published in *The New York Times Magazine* on January 2, 2005.

Pre-Reading Journal Entry

Americans usually respond generously to others in times of need, either by volunteering their time and labor in community service or by donating money. Reflect on an occasion in which you made a donation to a charitable cause. What caused you to give? Did you give time, money, or both? What effect, if any, did your actions have? How did volunteering or donating make you feel? Use your journal to respond to these questions.

Charity Display?

I didn't recognize the cellphone on caller ID but answered anyway. A man started talking about a local charity. "Look," I interrupted, "I don't have any money to give you. My husband left me. I've got two little kids, and I'm behind on the rent." 1

He quickly clarified that he wasn't calling for a donation but to help. He said he was a doctor and a volunteer for an organization called Warm the Children, and I had signed up for help at my son's school. He offered to give me $80 for each of my children to buy clothes. All I had to do was meet him at Meijer—a local, family-owned superstore—to do the shopping. I was shoving pants onto my son Gabriel, who never wants to get dressed, so it took a minute to comprehend: Could it be true? 2

The doctor mentioned filling out forms. While I imagined letting a stranger pay for our clothes, Gabriel took off his pants and ran away. Did I really want a handout? Should I endure a bit of humiliation to provide some essentials for my kids? I felt as if I had no choice. Sammy, my 7-year-old, had outgrown his shoes. 3

The night before we were to meet, the kids were with their dad, so I went to the store to shop, making sure to stay within the allotted amount. 4

Then, I found a manager. We put a note on the clothes and left it behind the customer-service counter. I was hoping this would expedite the process and minimize my contact with the doctor: here we go, hey, thanks, goodbye.

In the morning I dressed the kids in clean clothes. (There, I thought, we don't look poor.) On the way to Meijer, the boys jumped in puddles, soaking themselves to the waist. With mud.

The lady behind the service counter couldn't find my basket but had a good idea where it went. "There's an Asian woman who doesn't speak English," she said. "I bet she put it all back." I ran around the store grabbing snow boots, dress shirts and socks I chose the night before.

While we waited by the entrance, my littlest guy climbed out of the cart and started hopping up and down while watching himself on a security monitor. I knew this dance; it meant I had about 10 minutes before he had a meltdown. I thought about leaving; maybe my father would give me more money. But then I saw Sammy, who never complains, just sitting bleary-eyed in the cart, tolerating his boredom.

When the doctor arrived, he looked as kind and reassuring as he sounded on the phone. He greeted me and introduced a lanky teenager: "This is my son, Jack." He didn't tell Jack my name or introduce my kids. I shook Jack's hand before he retreated a safe distance behind his father, eyeballing my kids and me. I could not imagine why the doctor brought him along.

Once we were in line, I tried to keep the kids quiet; the doctor smiled and blinked at me. I talked nonstop, peppering Jack with polite questions: "What school do you go to? Do you play sports?" He gazed at the ground in my general direction. Occasionally he spat out a one-word answer. This stage of growing up is so awkward. I wondered who had it worse that morning, Jack or I.

The doctor showed me the forms we had to fill out. By mistake, he also handed me a set of instructions for how to facilitate this "encounter." At the top, it said: "DO NOT OFFER TRANSPORTATION TO THE CLIENTS." I looked at him in disbelief and repeated it aloud. *Do not offer transportation to the clients?* The doctor just shrugged. I couldn't tell if he was as embarrassed as I was, or if he had any idea how hard it was to accept charity.

Our cashier didn't know how to process my forms. After the manager showed her how, I realized I'd overshot my limit, so the cashier called the manager back for an override. The line behind us had grown long with frustrated shoppers, all of whom I assumed intended to pay for their purchases. Everyone stood in an uncomfortable silence—except my boys, who pestered me for some water and got way too close to the doctor. I fantasized about adopting a hillbilly accent and shouting, "Now you kids shut up er Santa ain't coming!" Finally we were done. Gabriel was clinging to me and chanting, "I want a drink." The doctor and his son said goodbye and hightailed it out of there.

Back at home, a friend called. I couldn't shake the feeling that the doctor used me as an example. "For what?" she asked when I told her. "I'm not even sure," I said. To make his son grateful? To put a face on poverty? Realistically, the doctor could have just been on his way to drop his son somewhere, but now I was angry. At my soon-to-be ex-husband. At the polarized society we live in where the working poor voted themselves into deeper poverty while the rich still coast. Despite the doctor's best intentions, I felt scrutinized—especially with his son there to witness my inability to buy my own kids their damn socks.

"You are under an incredible amount of stress," my friend insisted. "I hardly remember most of my divorce."

With luck, neither will I.

Questions for Close Reading

1. What is the selection's thesis? Locate the sentence(s) in which Gholson states her main idea. If she doesn't state her thesis explicitly, express it in your own words.
2. What is the internal conflict that Gholson experiences in her encounters with the doctor?
3. In paragraph 10, the author sees one of the instructions the doctor has been given: "Do not offer transportation to the clients." Why does she react to this warning "in disbelief"?
4. What does the title of the essay mean? Why does Gholson use a question mark?
5. Refer to your dictionary as needed to define the following words used in the selection: *humiliation* (paragraph 3), *expedite* (4), *lanky* (8), *facilitate* (10), *polarized* (12), and *scrutinized* (12).

Questions About the Writer's Craft

1. **The pattern.** How does Gholson organize the events in this essay? What transitional words and phrases does she use to keep the reader oriented as her story progresses?
2. **Other patterns.** In some passages, Gholson *describes* the behavior of her sons. What do these descriptions contribute to the narrative?
3. In paragraphs 3, 4, 5, and elsewhere, Gholson tells us her thoughts. What effect do these sections have on the pace of the narrative? How do they affect our understanding of what is happening?
4. There are several places in this essay in which Gholson uses dialogue. Find one of these places, and explain why the use of dialogue is (or is not) effective. What function does the dialogue have?

Writing Assignments Using Narration as a Pattern of Development

1. All of us have experienced humiliation at some point, and for Gholson, being the object of charity was such an experience. Think of an experience from your own life that made you feel humiliated. It might have been an important experience,

like completely flubbing a performance in front of a hundred people, or a minor experience, like having an assignment criticized by an instructor. Write a narrative of this experience. Be sure to discuss your thoughts and feelings as well as the actions involved in the story.

2. Write a narrative about a time in your life in which you needed help from others, and explain how this made you feel. The experience might have been painful, like Gholson's, or empowering, or somewhere in between. Use either flashback or flashforward to emphasize an event in your narrative. To read an essay that uses flashback, see "Once More to the Lake" by E. B. White (page 107).

Writing Assignments Combining Patterns of Development

3. In paragraph 9, Gholson describes how she tried to keep up a conversation with Jack as they waited in line to pay for her purchases. The conversation lacked any real content or exchange of information, but for Gholson it had other functions. Write an essay in which you describe the *causes* and *effects* of Gholson's effort to carry on a polite conversation. Why did Gholson try to engage Jack even though he was uncommunicative? What were the *results* of her attempts at conversation? *Compare* and *contrast* Gholson's approach to this interaction with Jack's. Are the differences between them related to gender? To age? To the social situation? To gain another perspective on this type of communication, read "What I've Learned From Men" by Barbara Ehrenreich (page 215).

4. Warm the Children, the charitable group helping Gholson's sons, is an organization dedicated to providing clothes to needy children. Research this organization or another charitable organization on the Internet, and write an essay analyzing the *process* involved in participating in it and *persuading* others to join it.

Writing Assignment Using a Journal Entry as a Starting Point

5. Review your pre-reading journal entry, in which you *recounted* a time that you either volunteered your time or donated money to a cause. *Compare* your story to that of the doctor in Gholson's essay. How did your experience differ from his? How was it similar? If you were to give time or money again, would you do so the same way, or would you do it differently? Why?

Langston Hughes

One of the foremost members of the 1920s literary movement known as the Harlem Renaissance, Langston Hughes (1902–67) committed himself to portraying the richness of Black life in the United States. A poet and a writer of short stories, Hughes was greatly influenced by the rhythms of blues and jazz. In his later years, he published two autobiographical works, *The Big Sea* (1940) and *I Wonder as I Wander* (1956), and he wrote a history of the National Association for the Advancement of Colored People (NAACP). The following selection is from *The Big Sea*.

Pre-Reading Journal Entry

Young people often feel pressured by family and community to adopt certain values, beliefs, or traditions. In your journal, reflect on some of the pressures that you've experienced. What was your response to these pressures? What have been the consequences of your response? Do you think your experience with these family or community pressures was unique or fairly common?

Salvation

I was saved from sin when I was going on thirteen. But not really saved. 1
It happened like this. There was a big revival at my Auntie Reed's church. Every night for weeks there had been much preaching, singing, praying, and shouting, and some very hardened sinners had been brought to Christ, and the membership of the church had grown by leaps and bounds. Then just before the revival ended, they held a special meeting for children, "to bring the young lambs to the fold." My aunt spoke of it for days ahead. That night I was escorted to the front row and placed on the mourners' bench with all the other young sinners, who had not yet been brought to Jesus.

My aunt told me that when you were saved you saw a light, and some- 2
thing happened to you inside! And Jesus came into your life! And God was with you from then on! She said you could see and hear and feel Jesus in your soul. I believed her. I had heard a great many old people say the same thing and it seemed to me they ought to know. So I sat there calmly in the hot, crowded church, waiting for Jesus to come to me.

The preacher preached a wonderful rhythmical sermon, all moans and 3
shouts and lonely cries and dire pictures of hell, and then he sang a song about the ninety and nine safe in the fold, but one little lamb was left out in

the cold. Then he said: "Won't you come? Won't you come to Jesus? Young lambs, won't you come?" And he held out his arms to all us young sinners there on the mourners' bench. And the little girls cried. And some of them jumped up and went to Jesus right away. But most of us just sat there.

A great many older people came and knelt around us and prayed, old women with jet-black faces and braided hair, old men with work-gnarled hands. And the church sang a song about the lower lights are burning, some poor sinners to be saved. And the whole building rocked with prayer and song.

Still I kept waiting to *see* Jesus.

Finally all the young people had gone to the altar and were saved, but one boy and me. He was a rounder's son named Westley. Westley and I were surrounded by sisters and deacons praying. It was very hot in the church, and getting late now. Finally Westley said to me in a whisper: "God damn! I'm tired o' sitting here. Let's get up and be saved." So he got up and was saved.

Then I was left all alone on the mourners' bench. My aunt came and knelt at my knees and cried, while prayers and songs swirled all around me in the little church. The whole congregation prayed for me alone, in a mighty wail of moans and voices. And I kept waiting serenely for Jesus, waiting, waiting—but he didn't come. I wanted to see him, but nothing happened to me. Nothing! I wanted something to happen to me, but nothing happened.

I heard the songs and the minister saying: "Why don't you come? My dear child, why don't you come to Jesus? Jesus is waiting for you. He wants you. Why don't you come? Sister Reed, what is this child's name?"

"Langston," my aunt sobbed.

"Langston, why don't you come? Why don't you come and be saved? Oh, Lamb of God! Why don't you come?"

Now it was really getting late. I began to be ashamed of myself, holding everything up so long. I began to wonder what God thought about Westley, who certainly hadn't seen Jesus either, but who was now sitting proudly on the platform, swinging his knickerbockered legs and grinning down at me, surrounded by deacons and old women on their knees praying. God had not struck Westley dead for taking his name in vain or for lying in the temple. So I decided that maybe to save further trouble, I'd better lie, too, and say that Jesus had come, and get up and be saved.

So I got up.

Suddenly the whole room broke into a sea of shouting, as they saw me rise. Waves of rejoicing swept the place. Women leaped in the air. My aunt threw her arms around me. The minister took me by the hand and led me to the platform.

When things quieted down, in a hushed silence, punctuated by a few ecstatic "Amens," all the new young lambs were blessed in the name of God. Then joyous singing filled the room.

That night, for the last time in my life but one—for I was a big boy 15 twelve years old—I cried. I cried, in bed alone, and couldn't stop. I buried my head under the quilts, but my aunt heard me. She woke up and told my uncle I was crying because the Holy Ghost had come into my life, and because I had seen Jesus. But I was really crying because I couldn't bear to tell her that I had lied, that I had deceived everybody in the church, and I hadn't seen Jesus, and that now I didn't believe there was a Jesus any more, since he didn't come to help me.

Questions for Close Reading

1. What is the selection's thesis (or narrative point)? Locate the sentence(s) in which Hughes states his main idea. If Hughes doesn't state the thesis explicitly, express it in your own words.
2. During the revival meeting, what pressures are put on the young Langston to get up and be saved?
3. How does Westley's attitude differ from Hughes's?
4. Does the narrator's Auntie Reed really understand him? Why can't he tell her the truth about his experience in the church?
5. Refer to your dictionary as needed to define the following words used in the selection: *revival* (paragraph 1), *knickerbockered* (11), *punctuated* (14), and *ecstatic* (14).

Questions About the Writer's Craft

1. **The pattern.** A narrative's power can often be traced to a conflict within the event being recounted. What conflict does the narrator of "Salvation" experience? How does Hughes create tension about this conflict?
2. What key role does Westley serve in the resolution of the narrator's dilemma? How does Hughes's inclusion of Westley in the story help us to understand the narrator better?
3. **Other patterns.** The thirteenth paragraph presents a *metaphor* of the church as an ocean. What images develop this metaphor? What does the metaphor tell us about Hughes's feelings and those of the church people?
4. The singing of hymns is a major part of this religious service. Why do you think Hughes has the narrator reveal the subjects and even the lyrics of some of the hymns?

Writing Assignments Using Narration as a Pattern of Development

1. Like Hughes, we sometimes believe that deception is our best alternative. Write a narrative about a time you felt deception was the best way either to protect those you care about or to maintain the respect of those important to you.
2. Write a narrative essay about a chain of events that caused you to become disillusioned about a person or institution you had previously regarded highly. Begin as Hughes does by presenting your initial beliefs. Relate the sequence of events

that changed your evaluation of the person or organization. In the conclusion, explain the short- and long-term effects of the incident. For more accounts of childhood disillusionment, read Audre Lorde's "The Fourth of July" (page 137) and Beth Johnson's "Bombs Bursting in Air" (page 209).

Writing Assignments Combining Patterns of Development

3. Hughes writes, "My aunt told me that when you were saved, you saw a light, and something happened to you inside! And Jesus came into your life!" What *causes* people to change their beliefs? Do such changes come from waiting calmly, as Hughes tried to do in church, or must they come from a more active process? Write an essay explaining your viewpoint. You may use *process analysis, causal analysis,* or some other organizational pattern to develop your thesis. Be sure to include specific examples to support your understanding of the way beliefs change.

4. Write a *persuasive* essay *arguing* either that lying is sometimes right or that lying is always wrong. Apply your thesis to particular situations and show how lying is or is not the right course of action. Be sure to keep your *narration* of these situations brief and focused on your point. Remember to acknowledge the opposing viewpoint. Stephanie Ericsson's "The Ways We Lie" (page 240) and William Lutz's "Doublespeak" (page 263) may help you define your position. You might even mention these authors' perspectives in your essay.

Writing Assignment Using a Journal Entry as a Starting Point

5. Review your pre-reading journal entry, and select *one* family or community pressure with which you've had to contend. Then write an essay examining the effect that this pressure has had on you. Refer to your journal as you prepare to explain the values, beliefs, or traditions that you were expected to adopt. Discuss your response to this pressure and how your reaction has affected you.

Adam Mayblum

On September 11, 2001, as thirty-five-year-old Adam Mayblum worked in his investment firm's office on the eighty-seventh floor of the World Trade Center's North Tower, a terrorist-hijacked plane crashed into the building. His presence of mind—and a great deal of good fortune—allowed him to escape from the tower before it collapsed. The day after the attacks, he sent an e-mail to friends and family describing his experiences. The e-mail, later titled "The Price We Pay," was soon being forwarded around the world and reprinted in newspapers and magazines and on websites. (Mayblum's account appears below in much the same form as when he sent it; it has not been corrected for grammar or mechanics.) Today, Mayblum works at a new firm located just a few blocks from the site of the former World Trade Center. He lives with his wife and two children in New Rochelle, New York.

Pre-Reading Journal Entry

The terrorist attacks against the United States on September 11, 2001, had a profound impact on people the world over. Where were you the morning of that fateful day? What was your reaction when you learned of the attacks? What was the reaction of those around you? How did your feelings change over time? How, if at all, did the event alter your perspectives about larger issues? Explore these questions in your pre-reading journal.

The Price We Pay

My name is Adam Mayblum. I am alive today. I am committing this to "paper" so I never forget. SO WE NEVER FORGET. I am sure that this is one of thousands of stories that will emerge over the next several days and weeks. 1

I arrived as usual a little before 8am. My office was on the 87th floor of 1World Trade Center, AKA: Tower 1, AKA: the North Tower. Most of my associates were in by 8:30am. We were standing around, joking around, eating breakfast, checking emails, and getting set for the day when the first plane hit just a few stories above us. I must stress that we did not know that it was a plane. The building lurched violently and shook as if it were an earthquake. People screamed. I watched out my window as the building seemed to move 10 to 20 feet in each direction. It rumbled and shook long enough for me to get my wits about myself and grab a co-worker and seek shelter 2 under a doorway. Light fixtures and parts of the ceiling collapsed. The kitchen was destroyed. We were certain that it was a bomb. We looked out the windows. Reams of paper were flying everywhere, like a ticker tape parade. I looked down at the street. I could see people in Battery Park City looking up. Smoke started billowing in through the holes in the ceiling. I believe that there were 13 of us.

We did not panic. I can only assume that we thought that the worst was   3
over. The building was standing and we were shaken but alive. We checked the halls. The smoke was thick and white and did not smell like I imagined smoke should smell. Not like your BBQ or your fireplace or even a bonfire. The phones were working. My wife had taken our 9 month old for his check up. I called my nanny at home and told her to page my wife, tell her that a bomb went off, I was ok, and on my way out. I grabbed my laptop. Took off my tee shirt and ripped it into 3 pieces. Soaked it in water. Gave 2 pieces to my friends. Tied my piece around my face to act as an air filter. And we all started moving to the staircase. One of my dearest friends said that he was staying until the police or firemen came to get him. In the halls there were tiny fires and sparks. The ceiling had collapsed in the men's bathroom. It was gone along with anyone who may have been in there. We did not go in to look. We missed the staircase on the first run and had to double back. Once in the staircase we picked up fire extinguishers just in case. On the 85th floor a brave associate of mine and I headed back up to our office to drag out my partner who stayed behind. There was no air, just white smoke. We made the rounds through the office calling his name. No response. He must have succumbed to the smoke. We left defeated in our efforts and made our way back to the stairwell. We proceeded to the 78th floor where we had to change over to a different stairwell. 78 is the main junction to switch to the upper floors. I expected to see more people. There were some 50 to 60 more. Not enough. Wires and fires all over the place. Smoke too. A brave man was fighting a fire with the emergency hose. I stopped with two friends to make sure that everyone from our office was accounted for. We ushered them and confused people into the stairwell. In retrospect, I recall seeing Harry, my head trader, doing the same several yards behind me. I am only 35. I have known him for over 14 years. I headed into the stairwell with 2 friends.

We were moving down very orderly in Stair Case A. very slowly. No   4
panic. At least not overt panic. My legs could not stop shaking. My heart was pounding. Some nervous jokes and laughter. I made a crack about ruining a brand new pair of Merrells.[1] Even still, they were right, my feet felt great. We all laughed. We checked our cell phones. Surprisingly, there was a very good signal, but the Sprint network was jammed. I heard that the Blackberry 2-way email devices worked perfectly. On the phones, 1 out of 20 dial attempts got through. I knew I could not reach my wife so I called my parents. I told

---

[1] A brand of men's shoes (editors' note).

them what happened and that we were all okay and on the way down. Soon, my sister in law reached me. I told her we were fine and moving down. I believe that was about the 65th floor. We were bored and nervous. I called my friend Angel in San Francisco. I knew he would be watching. He was amazed I was on the phone. He told me to get out that there was another plane on its way. I did not know what he was talking about. By now the second plane had struck Tower 2. We were so deep into the middle of our building that we did not hear or feel anything. We had no idea what was really going on. We kept making way for wounded to go down ahead of us. Not many of them, just a few. No one seemed seriously wounded. Just some cuts and scrapes. Everyone cooperated.

Everyone was a hero yesterday. No questions asked. I had co-workers in another office on the 77th floor. I tried dozens of times to get them on their cell phones or office lines. It was futile. Later I found that they were alive. One of the many miracles on a day of tragedy.

On the 53rd floor we came across a very heavyset man sitting on the stairs. I asked if he needed help or was he just resting. He needed help. I knew I would have trouble carrying him because I have a very bad back. But my friend and I offered anyway. We told him he could lean on us. He hesitated, I don't know why. I said do you want to come or do you want us to send help for you. He chose for help. I told him he was on the 53rd floor in Stairwell A and that's what I would tell the rescue workers. He said okay and we left.

On the 44th floor my phone rang again. It was my parents. They were hysterical. I said relax, I'm fine. My father said get out, there is third plane coming. I still did not understand. I was kind of angry. What did my parents think? Like I needed some other reason to get going? I couldn't move the thousand people in front of me any faster. I know they love me, but no one inside understood what the situation really was. My parents did. Starting around this floor the firemen, policemen, WTC K-9 units without the dogs, anyone with a badge, started coming up as we were heading down. I stopped a lot of them and told them about the man on 53 and my friend on 87. I later felt terrible about this. They headed up to find those people and met death instead.

On the 33rd floor I spoke with a man who somehow knew most of the details. He said 2 small planes hit the building. Now we all started talking about which terrorist group it was. Was it an internal organization or an external one? The overwhelming but uninformed opinion was Islamic Fanatics. Regardless, we now knew that it was not a bomb and there were potentially more planes coming. We understood.

On the 3rd floor the lights went out and we heard & felt this rumbling coming towards us from above. I thought the staircase was collapsing upon itself. It was 10am now and that was Tower 2 collapsing next door. We did not know that. Someone had a flashlight. We passed it forward and left the stairwell and headed down a dark and cramped corridor to an exit. We could not see at all. I recommended that everyone place a hand on the shoulder of the person in front of them and call out if they hit an obstacle so others would know to avoid it. They did. It worked perfectly. We reached another stairwell and saw a female officer emerge soaking wet and covered in soot. She said we could not go that way it was blocked. Go up to 4 and use the other exit. Just as we started up she said it was ok to go down instead. There was water everywhere. I called out for hands on shoulders again and she said that was a great idea. She stayed behind instructing people to do that. I do not know what happened to her.

We emerged into an enormous room. It was light but filled with smoke. I commented to a friend that it must be under construction. Then we realized where we were. It was the second floor. The one that overlooks the lobby. We were ushered out into the courtyard, the one where the fountain used to be. My first thought was of a TV movie I saw once about nuclear winter and fallout. I could not understand where all of the debris came from. There was at least five inches of this gray pasty dusty drywall soot on the ground as well as a thickness of it in the air. Twisted steel and wires. I heard there were bodies and body parts as well, but I did not look. It was bad enough. We hid under the remaining overhangs and moved out to the street. We were told to keep walking towards Houston Street. The odd thing is that there were very few rescue workers around. Less than five. They all must have been trapped under the debris when Tower 2 fell. We did not know that and could not understand where all of that debris came from. It was just my friend Kern and I now. We were hugging but sad. We felt certain that most of our friends ahead of us died and we knew no one behind us.

We came upon a post office several blocks away. We stopped and looked up. Our building, exactly where our office is (was), was engulfed in flame and smoke. A postal worker said that Tower 2 had fallen down. I looked again and sure enough it was gone. My heart was racing. We kept trying to call our families. I could not get in touch with my wife. Finally I got through to my parents. Relieved is not the word to explain their feelings. They got through to my wife, thank God and let her know I was alive. We sat down. A girl on a bike offered us some water. Just as she took the cap off her bottle we heard a rumble. We looked up and our building, Tower 1 collapsed. I did not note the time but I am told it was 10:30am. We had been out less than 15 minutes.

We were mourning our lost friends, particularly the one who stayed in the office as we were now sure that he had perished. We started walking towards Union Square. I was going to Beth Israel Medical Center to be looked at. We stopped to hear the President speaking on the radio. My phone rang. It was my wife. I think I fell to my knees crying when I heard her voice. Then she told me the most incredible thing. My partner who had stayed behind called her. He was alive and well. I guess we just lost him in the commotion. We started jumping and hugging and shouting. I told my wife that my brother had arranged for a hotel in midtown. He can be very resourceful in that way. I told her I would call her from there. My brother and I managed to get a gypsy cab to take us home to Westchester instead. I cried on my son and held my wife until I fell asleep.

As it turns out my partner, the one who I thought had stayed behind was behind us with Harry Ramos, our head trader. This is now second-hand information. They came upon Victor, the heavyset man on the 53rd floor. They helped him. He could barely move. My partner bravely/stupidly tested the elevator on the 52nd floor. He rode it down to the sky lobby on 44. The doors opened, it was fine. He rode it back up and got Harry and Victor. I don't yet know if anyone else joined them. Once on 44 they made their way back into the stairwell. Someplace around the 39th to 36th floors they felt the same rumble I felt on the 3rd floor. It was 10am and Tower 2 was coming down. They had about 30 minutes to get out. Victor said he could no longer move. They offered to have him lean on them. He said he couldn't do it. My partner hollered at him to sit on his butt and scooch down the steps. He said he was not capable of doing it. Harry told my partner to go ahead of them. Harry had once had a heart attack and was worried about this mans heart. It was his nature to be this way. He was/is one of the kindest people I know. He would not leave a man behind. My partner went ahead and made it out. He said he was out maybe 10 minutes before the building came down. This means that Harry had maybe 25 minutes to move Victor 36 floors. I guess they moved 1 floor every 1.5 minutes. Just a guess. This means Harry was around the 20th floor when the building collapsed. As of now 12 of 13 people are accounted for. As of 6pm yesterday his wife had not heard from him. I fear that Harry is lost. However, a short while ago I heard that he may be alive. Apparently there is a website with survivor names on it and his name appears there. Unfortunately, Ramos is not an uncommon name in New York. Pray for him and all those like him.[2]

With regards to the firemen heading upstairs, I realize that they were going up anyway. But, it hurts to know that I may have made them move quicker to find my friend. Rationally, I know this is not true and that I am not the responsible one. The responsible ones are in hiding somewhere on this planet and damn them for making me feel like this. But they should know that they failed in terrorizing us. We were calm. Those men and women that went up were heroes in the face of it all. They must have known what was going on and they did their jobs. Ordinary people were heroes too. Today the images that people around the world equate with power and democracy are gone but "America" is not an image it is a concept. That concept is only

[2]Sadly, it later was confirmed that Harry Ramos did not survive the collapse of the towers that day (editors' note).

strengthened by our pulling together as a team. If you want to kill us, leave us alone because we will do it by ourselves. If you want to make us stronger, attack and we unite. This is the ultimate failure of terrorism against The United States and the ultimate price we pay to be free, to decide where we want to work, what we want to eat, and when & where we want to go on vacation. The very moment the first plane was hijacked, democracy won.

Questions for Close Reading

1. What is the selection's thesis (or narrative point)? Locate the sentence(s) in which Mayblum states his main idea. If he doesn't state the thesis explicitly, express it in your own words.
2. Strong narrative involves conflict (see page 125). What is the main conflict in "The Price We Pay"?
3. What reason does Mayblum give for writing his account? What additional reasons might he have?
4. In Mayblum's view, the World Trade Center attacks were part of "the price we pay." What is it that he believes Americans paid for on September 11, 2001? Do you agree? Why or why not?
5. Refer to your dictionary as needed to define the following terms used in the selection: *aka* (2), *lurched* (2), *reams* (2), *ticker tape* (2), *succumbed* (3), *junction* (3), *ushered* (3), *retrospect* (3), *nuclear winter* (10), *fallout* (10), *debris* (10), *engulfed* (11), *commotion* (12), and *gypsy cab* (12).

Questions About the Writer's Craft

1. **The pattern.** As is common in narration, Mayblum tells his story primarily in past tense. However, he occasionally interjects present tense into his account. Identify some instances where he uses present tense. What effect does his use of present tense have on the narrative?
2. Mayblum's essay is marked by two clear stylistic characteristics: First, he uses many sentence fragments and short sentences, and second, he omits quotation marks around people's exact words. How do these choices affect the narrative?
3. Many of Mayblum's sentences begin with *We*—for example, "We did not panic" (3), "We all laughed" (4), and "We understood" (7). How does the prevalent use of *we* and *our* fit with Mayblum's theme?
4. Mayblum illustrates American freedom with three examples: the freedom to "decide where we want to work, what we want to eat, and when & where we want to go on vacation" (14). Do you find these examples effective and appropriate? Why or why not?

Writing Assignments Using Narration as a Pattern of Development

∞ 1. Mayblum tells a story of courage, compassion, and quick thinking in the face of horror. Think back on your own life and take a few moments to freewrite about a situation in which you experienced terror or alarm. Maybe you were snowbound in a blizzard, got lost in the woods, or witnessed a crime. Write an essay in which you recount your frightening situation. What exactly took place? How did you react? How did others react? What did you learn from the experience? Be sure to provide vivid details to recreate the sights, sounds, and feelings surrounding the event. For additional accounts of weathering a harrowing situation, read David Helvarg's "The Storm This Time" (page 92), George Orwell's "Shooting an Elephant" (page 143), Beth Johnson's "Bombs Bursting in Air" (page 209), and Alice Walker's "Beauty: When the Other Dancer Is the Self" (page 408).

2. Americans cherish their personal liberties. Recall a time when, in your view, you were wrongly deprived of some freedom. Perhaps you were punished for expressing your opinion or ordered not to associate with particular people. Write an essay that narrates the unjust incident, focusing on the main conflict. What were the circumstances? Who was involved? Discuss your treatment and why you felt it was unjust. In addition, provide some thoughts on whether now, in retrospect, you have a different perspective on the event than you did at the time. Consider also reading Audre Lorde's "The Fourth of July" (page 137), an essay exploring the personal impact of unfair discrimination, and Stanley Fish's "Free-Speech Follies" (page 534), about First Amendment rights.

Writing Assignments Combining Patterns of Development

3. In an emergency, some people stay calm; others panic. Think of the person you would most want to be with in a crisis. Next, think of the person you would *least* want to be with. Freewrite thoughts about each of these people in your journal. Then, in a serious or humorous piece, *contrast* these two people's personalities, revealing why one would probably be a reliable partner in a crisis whereas the other would probably be a disastrous one. Be sure to provide *examples* of these people's behavior to *illustrate* why you regard each of them as you do.

4. After lengthy delay, new structures are being erected on the site of the destroyed World Trade Center towers. Several groups continue to have an interest in how the site is developed. The commercial developer wants to ensure that there are profitable office buildings to replace the destroyed office space. The city and state governments, as well as local residents and businesses, want any development to revitalize the surrounding area. And families of September 11th victims want to make sure that those who died are properly memorialized and that their story is adequately told. Write an essay in which you *describe* the current development plans for the World Trade Center site and *argue* whether the development of the site is meeting the needs of these various interest groups. Research the development progress and plans in the library and/or on the Internet, making sure to consult reputable sources.

Writing Assignment Using a Journal Entry as a Starting Point

5. It is clear from Mayblum's account that the events of September 11, 2001, had a profound impact on his life. But a person need not have been actively involved in

the events to have felt their repercussions. Review the thoughts you recorded in your pre-reading journal. Then write an essay about how the events of that day have *affected* you. You might organize the essay by first considering your immediate response to the events, perhaps as part of a *narrative* of when and how you found out. What kinds of emotions and thoughts did you experience at the time? Then you might proceed by discussing longer-term effects on your thoughts or feelings. For instance, has the attack made you feel any closer to your family and friends? Has it left you feeling unsafe or depressed? Has it changed your view of America or the rest of the world?

Additional Writing Topics

NARRATION

General Assignments

Prepare an essay on any of the following topics, using narration as the paper's dominant method of development. Be sure to select details that advance the essay's narrative purpose; you may even want to experiment with flashback or flashforward. In any case, keep the sequence of events clear by using transitional cues. Within the limited time span covered, use vigorous details and varied sentence structure to enliven the narrative. Tell the story from a consistent point of view.

1. An emergency that brought out the best or worst in you
2. The hazards of taking children out to eat
3. An incident that made you believe in fate
4. Your best or worst day at school or work
5. A major decision
6. An encounter with a machine
7. An important learning experience
8. A narrow escape
9. Your first date, first day on the job, or first anything
10. A memorable childhood experience
11. A fairy tale the way you would like to hear it told
12. A painful moment
13. An incredible but true story
14. A significant family event
15. An experience in which a certain emotion (pride, anger, regret, or some other) was dominant
16. A surprising coincidence
17. An act of heroism
18. An unpleasant confrontation
19. A cherished family story
20. An imagined meeting with an admired celebrity or historical figure

Assignments With a Specific Purpose, Audience, and Point of View

On Campus

1. Write an article for your old high school newspaper. The article will be read primarily by seniors who are planning to go away to college next year. In the article, narrate a story that points to some truth about the "breaking away" stage of life.
2. A friend of yours has seen someone cheat on a test, plagiarize an entire paper, or seriously violate some other academic policy. In a letter, convince this friend to

inform the instructor or a campus administrator by narrating an incident in which a witness did (or did not) speak up in such a situation. Tell what happened as a result.

At Home or in the Community

3. You have had a disturbing encounter with one of the people who seems to have "fallen through the cracks" of society—a street person, an unwanted child, or anyone else who is alone and abandoned. Write a letter to the local newspaper describing this encounter. Your purpose is to arouse people's indignation and compassion and to get help for such unfortunates.

4. Your younger brother, sister, relative, or neighborhood friend can't wait to be your age. Write a letter in which you narrate a dramatic story that shows the young person that your age isn't as wonderful as he or she thinks. Be sure to select a story that the person can understand and appreciate.

On the Job

5. As fund-raiser for a particular organization (for example, the Red Cross, the SPCA, Big Brothers/Big Sisters), you're sending a newsletter to contributors. Support your cause by telling the story of a time when your organization made all the difference—the blood donation that saved a life, the animal that was rescued from abuse, and so on.

6. A customer has written a letter to you (or your boss) telling about a bad experience that he or she had with someone in your workplace. On the basis of that single experience, the customer now regards your company and its employees with great suspicion. It's your responsibility to respond to this complaint. Write a letter to the customer balancing his or her negative picture by narrating a story that shows the "flip side" of your company and its employees.

EXEMPLIFICATION

WHAT IS EXEMPLIFICATION?

If someone asked you, "Have you been to any good restaurants lately?" you probably wouldn't answer "Yes" and then immediately change the subject. Most likely, you would go on to illustrate with *examples*. Perhaps you'd give the names of restaurants you've enjoyed and talk briefly about the specific things you liked: the attractive prices, the tasty main courses, the pleasant service, the tempting desserts. Such examples and details are needed to convince others that your opinion—in this or any matter—is valid. Similarly, when you talk about larger and more important issues, people won't pay much attention to your opinion if all you do is string together vague generalizations: "We have to do something about acid rain. It's had disastrous consequences for the environment. Its negative effects increase every year. Action must be taken to control the problem." To be taken seriously and to convince others that your point is well-founded, you must provide specific supporting examples: "The forests in the Adirondacks are dying"; "Yesterday's rainfall was fifty times more acidic than normal"; "Pine Lake, in the northern part of the state, was once a great fishing spot but now has no fish population."

Examples are equally important when you write an essay. It's not fuzzy generalities and highfalutin abstractions that make writing impressive. Just the opposite is true. Facts, anecdotes, statistics, details, opinions, and observations are at the heart of effective writing, giving your work substance and solidity.

HOW EXEMPLIFICATION FITS YOUR PURPOSE AND AUDIENCE

The wording of assignments and essay exam questions may signal the need for specific examples:

Soap operas, whether shown during the day or in the evening, are among the most popular television programs. Why do you think this is so? Provide specific examples to support your position.

Some observers claim that college students are less interested in learning than in getting ahead in their careers. Cite evidence to support or refute this claim.

A growing number of people feel that parents should not allow young children to participate in highly competitive team sports. Basing your conclusion on your own experiences and observations, indicate whether you think this point of view is reasonable.

Such phrases as "Provide specific examples," "Cite evidence," and "Basing your conclusion on your own experiences and observations" signal that each essay should be developed through examples.

Usually, though, you won't be told so explicitly to provide examples. Instead, as you think about the best way to achieve your essay's purpose, you'll see the need for illustrative details—no matter which patterns of development you use. For instance, to *persuade* skeptical readers that the country needs a national health system, you might mention specific cases to dramatize the inadequacy of our current health-care system: a family bankrupted by medical bills; an uninsured accident victim turned away by a hospital; a chronically ill person rapidly deteriorating because he didn't have enough money to visit a doctor. Or imagine a lightly satiric piece that pokes fun at cat lovers. Insisting that "cat people" are pretty strange creatures, you might make your point—and make readers chuckle—with a series of examples *contrasting* cat lovers and dog lovers: the qualities admired by each group (loyalty in dogs versus independence in cats) and the different expectations each group has for its pets (dog lovers want Fido to be obedient and lovable, whereas cat lovers are satisfied with Felix's occasional spurts of docility and affection). Similarly, you would supply examples in a *causal analysis* speculating on the likely impact of a proposed tuition hike at your college. To convince the college administration of the probable negative effects of such a hike, you might cite the following examples: articles reporting a nationwide upswing in student transfers to less expensive schools; statistics indicating a significant drop in grades among already employed students forced to work more hours to pay increased tuition costs; interviews with students too financially strapped to continue their college education.

Whether you use examples as the primary or a supplemental method of development, they serve a number of important purposes. For one thing, examples make writing *interesting*. Assume you're writing an essay showing that television commercials are biased against women. Your essay would be lifeless and boring if all it did was repeat, in a general way, that commercials present stereotyped views of women.

> An anti-female bias is rampant in television commercials. It is very much alive, yet most viewers seem to take it all in stride. Few people protest the obviously sexist characters and statements in such commercials. Surely, these commercials misrepresent the way most of us live.

Without interesting particulars, readers may respond, "Who cares?" But if you provide specific examples, you'll attract your readers' attention:

> Sexism is rampant in television commercials. Although millions of women hold responsible jobs outside the home, commercials continue to portray women as simple creatures who spend most of their time thinking about wax buildup, cottony-soft bathroom tissue, and static-free clothes. Men, apparently, have better things to do than fret over such mundane household matters. How many commercials can you recall that depict men proclaiming the virtues of squeaky-clean dishes or sparkling bathrooms? Not many.

Examples also make writing *persuasive.* Most writing conveys a point, but many readers are reluctant to accept someone else's point of view unless evidence demonstrates its validity. Imagine you're writing an essay showing that latchkey children are more self-sufficient and emotionally secure than children who return from school to a home where a parent awaits them. Your thesis is obviously controversial. Without specific examples—from your own experience, personal observations, or research studies—your readers would undoubtedly question your position's validity.

Further, examples *help explain* difficult, abstract, or unusual ideas. Suppose you're assigned an essay on a complex subject such as inflation, zero population growth, or radiation exposure. As a writer, you have a responsibility to your readers to make these difficult concepts concrete and understandable. If writing an essay on radiation exposure in everyday life, you might start by providing specific examples of home appliances that emit radiation—color televisions, computers, and microwave ovens—and tell exactly how much radiation we absorb in a typical day from such equipment. To illustrate further the extent of our radiation exposure, you could also provide specifics about unavoidable sources of natural radiation (the sun, for instance) and details about the widespread use of radiation in medicine (X rays, radiation therapy). These examples would ground your discussion, making it immediate and concrete, preventing it from flying off into the vague and theoretical.

Finally, examples *help prevent unintended ambiguity.* All of us have experienced the frustration of having someone misinterpret what we say. In face-to-face communication, we can provide on-the-spot clarification. In writing, however, instantaneous feedback isn't available, so it's crucial that meaning be as unambiguous as possible. Examples will help.

Assume you're writing an essay asserting that ineffective teaching is on the rise in today's high schools. To clarify what you mean by "ineffective," you provide examples: the instructor who spends so much time disciplining unruly students that he never gets around to teaching; the moonlighting teacher who is so tired in class that she regularly takes naps during tests; and the teacher who accepts obviously plagiarized reports because he's grateful that students hand in something. Without such concrete examples, your readers will supply their own ideas—and these may not be what you had in mind. Readers might imagine "ineffective" to mean harsh and punitive, whereas your concrete examples would show that you intend it to mean out of control and irresponsible. Such specifics help prevent misunderstanding.

At this point, you have a good sense of the way writers use exemplification to achieve their purposes and to connect with their readers. Now take a moment to look closely at the advertisement at the beginning of this chapter. Imagine you're taking part in a "focus group" assembled by the advertiser of this product. Your task is to rate the ad on a scale of 1 (negative) to 10 (positive) on the basis of the images it promotes. To support your rating, jot down some phrases that express the values that you believe are *illustrated* by the ad.

SUGGESTIONS FOR USING EXEMPLIFICATION IN AN ESSAY

The following suggestions will be helpful whether you use examples as a dominant or a supportive pattern of development.

1. Generate examples.   Where do you get the examples to develop your essay? The first batch of examples is generated during the prewriting stage. With your purpose and thesis in mind, you make a broad sweep for examples, using brainstorming, freewriting, the mapping technique—whichever prewriting technique you prefer. During this preliminary search for examples, you may also read through your journal for relevant specifics, interview other people, or conduct library research.

Examples can take several forms, including specific names (of people, places, products, and so on), anecdotes, personal observations, expert opinion, as well as facts, statistics, and case studies gathered through research. While prewriting, try to generate more examples than you think you'll need. Starting with abundance—and then picking out the strongest examples—will give you a firm base on which to build the essay. If you have a great deal of trouble finding examples to support your thesis, you may need to revise the thesis; you may be trying to support an idea that has little validity. On the other hand, while prewriting, you may unearth numerous examples but find that many of them contradict the point you started out to support. If that happens, don't hesitate to recast your central point, always remembering that your thesis and examples must fit.

2. Select the examples to include.   Once you've used prewriting to generate as many examples as possible, you're ready to limit your examples to the strongest ones. Keeping your purpose, thesis, and audience in mind, ask yourself several key questions: "Which examples support my thesis? Which do not? Which are most convincing? Which are most likely to interest readers and clarify meaning?"

You may include several brief examples within a single sentence:

The French people's fascination with some American literary figures, such as Poe and Hawthorne, is understandable, but their great respect for "artists" like comedian Jerry Lewis is a mystery.

Or you may develop a paragraph with a number of "for instances":

A uniquely American style of movie-acting reached its peak in the 1950s. Certain charismatic actors completely abandoned the stage techniques and tradition that had been the foundation of acting up to that time. Instead of articulating their lines clearly, the actors mumbled; instead of making firm eye contact with their colleagues, they hung their heads, shifted their eyes, even talked with their eyes closed. Marlon Brando, Montgomery Clift, and James Dean were three actors who exemplified this new trend.

As the preceding paragraph shows, *several examples* are usually needed to make a point. An essay with the thesis "Rock videos are dangerously violent" wouldn't be convincing if you gave only one example of a violent rock video. Several strong examples would be needed for readers to feel you had illustrated your point sufficiently.

As a general rule, you should strive for variety in the kinds of examples you include. For instance, you might choose a *personal-experience example* drawn from your own life or from the life of someone you know. Such examples pack the wallop of personal authority and lend drama to writing. Or you might include a *typical-case example,* an actual event or situation that did occur—but not to you or to anyone you know. (Perhaps you learned about the event through a magazine article, newspaper account, or television report.) The objective nature of such cases makes them especially convincing. You might also include a speculative or *hypothetical example* ("Imagine how difficult it must be for an elderly person to carry bags of groceries from the market to a bus stop several blocks away"). You'll find that hypothetical cases are effective for clarifying and dramatizing key points, but be sure to acknowledge that the example is indeed invented (*"Suppose* that . . ." or "Let's for a moment *assume* that . . ."). Make certain, too, that the invented situation is easily imagined and could conceivably happen. Finally, you might create a *generalized example*— one that is a composite of the typical or usual. Such generalized examples are often signaled by words that involve the reader (*"All of us,* at one time or another, have been driven to distraction by a trivial annoyance like the buzzing of a fly or the sting of a paper cut"), or they may refer to humanity in general ("When *most people* get a compliment, they perk up, preen, and think the praise-giver is blessed with astute powers of observation").

Occasionally, *one extended example,* fully developed with many details, can support an essay. It might be possible, for instance, to support the thesis "Federal legislation should raise the legal drinking age to twenty-one" with a single compelling, highly detailed example of the effects of one teenager's drunken-driving spree.

The examples you choose must also be *relevant;* that is, they must have direct bearing on the point you want to make. You would have a hard time convincing readers that Americans have callous attitudes toward the elderly if you described the wide range of new programs, all staffed by volunteers, at a well-financed center for senior citizens. Because these examples *contradict,* rather than support, your thesis, readers are apt to dismiss what you have to say.

Make certain, too, that your examples are *accurate.* Exercise special caution when using statistics. An old saying warns that there are lies, damned lies, and statistics—meaning that statistics can be misleading. A commercial may claim, "In a taste test, 80 percent of those questioned indicated that they preferred Fizzy Cola." Impressed? Don't be—at least, not until you find out how the test was conducted. Perhaps the subjects had to choose between Fizzy Cola and battery acid, or perhaps there were only five subjects, all Fizzy Cola vice presidents.

Finally, select *representative* examples. Picking the oddball, one-in-a-million example to support a point—and passing it off as typical—is dishonest. Consider an essay with the thesis "Part-time jobs contribute to academic success." Citing only one example of a student who works at a job twenty-five hours a week while earning straight As isn't playing fair. Why not? You've made a *hasty generalization* based on only one case. To be convincing, you need to show how holding down a job affects *most* students' academic performance. (For more on hasty generalizations, see page 491.)

3. Develop your examples sufficiently.   To ensure that you get your ideas across, your examples must be *specific*. An essay on the types of heroes in American movies wouldn't succeed if you simply strung together a series of undeveloped examples in paragraphs like this one:

> Heroes in American movies usually fall into types. One kind of hero is the tight-lipped loner, men like Clint Eastwood and Humphrey Bogart. Another movie hero is the quiet, shy, or fumbling type who has appeared in movies since the beginning. The main characteristic of this hero is lovableness, as seen in actors like Jimmy Stewart. Perhaps the most one-dimensional and predictable hero is the superman who battles tough odds. This kind of hero is best illustrated by Sylvester Stallone as Rocky and Rambo.

If you developed the essay in this way—if you moved from one undeveloped example to another—you would be doing little more than making a list. To be effective, key examples must be expanded in sufficient detail. The examples in the preceding paragraph could be developed in paragraphs of their own. You could, for instance, develop the first example this way:

> Heroes can be tight-lipped loners who appear out of nowhere, form no permanent attachments, and walk, drive, or ride off into the sunset. In many of his Westerns, from the low-budget "spaghetti Westerns" of the 1960s to Unforgiven in 1992, Clint Eastwood personifies this kind of hero. He is remote, mysterious, and not talkative. Yet he guns down an evil sheriff, runs other villains out of town, and helps a handicapped girl--acts that cement his heroic status. The loner might also be Sam Spade as played by Humphrey Bogart. Spade solves the crime and sends the guilty off to jail, yet he holds his emotions in check and has no permanent ties beyond his faithful secretary and shabby office. One gets the feeling that he could walk away from these, too, if necessary. Even in The Right Stuff, an account of the United States's early astronauts, the scriptwriters mold Chuck Yeager, the man who broke the sound barrier, into a classic loner. Yeager, portrayed by the aloof Sam Shepard, has a wife, but he is nevertheless insular. Taking mute pride in his ability to distance himself from politicians, bureaucrats, even colleagues, he soars into space, dignified and detached.

(For hints on ways to make writing specific, see pages 34–36.)

4. Organize the examples.   If, as is usually the case, several examples support your point, be sure that you present the examples in an *organized* manner. Often you'll find that other patterns of development (cause-effect, comparison-contrast, definition, and so on) suggest ways to sequence examples. Let's say you're writing an essay showing that stay-at-home vacations offer numerous opportunities to relax. You might begin the essay with examples that *contrast* stay-at-home and get-away vacations. Then you might move to a *process analysis* that illustrates different techniques for unwinding at home. The essay might end with examples showing the *effect* of such leisurely at-home breaks.

Finally, you need to select an *organizational approach consistent* with your *purpose* and *thesis*. Imagine you're writing an essay about students' adjustment during the first months of college. The supporting examples could be arranged *chronologically*. You might start by illustrating the ambivalence many students feel the first day of college when their parents leave for home; you might then offer an anecdote or two about students' frequent calls to Mom and Dad during the opening weeks of the semester; the essay might close with an account of students' reluctance to leave campus at the midyear break.

Similarly, an essay demonstrating that a room often reflects the character of its occupant might be organized *spatially:* from the empty soda cans on the floor to the spitballs on the ceiling. In an essay illustrating the kinds of skills taught in a composition course, you might move from *simple* to *complex* examples: starting with relatively matter-of-fact skills such as spelling and punctuation and ending with more conceptually difficult skills such as formulating a thesis and organizing an essay. Last, the *emphatic sequence*—in which you lead from your first example to your final, most significant one— is another effective way to organize an essay with many examples. A paper about Americans' characteristic impatience might progress from minor examples (dependence on fast food, obsession with ever faster mail delivery) to more disturbing manifestations of impatience (using drugs as quick solutions to problems, advocating simple answers to complex international problems: "Bomb them!").

5. Choose a point of view.   Many essays developed by illustration place the subject in the foreground and the writer in the background. Such an approach calls for the *third-person point of view*. For example, even if you draw examples from your own personal experience, you can present them without using the *first-person* "I." You might convert such personal material into generalized examples (see page 173), or you might describe the personal experience as if it happened to someone else. Of course, you may use the first person if the use of "I" will make the example more believable and dramatic. But remember: Just because an event happened to you personally doesn't mean you have to use the first-person point of view.

REVISION STRATEGIES

Once you have a draft of the essay, you're ready to revise. The following checklist will help you and those giving you feedback apply to exemplification some of the revision techniques discussed on pages 60–62.

> ☑ EXEMPLIFICATION: A REVISION/PEER REVIEW CHECKLIST
>
> *Revise Overall Meaning and Structure*
>
> ❏ What thesis is being advanced? Which examples don't support the thesis? Should these examples be deleted, or should the thesis be reshaped to fit the examples? Why?
>
> ❏ Which patterns of development and methods of organization (chronological, spatial, simple-to-complex, emphatic) provide the essay's framework? Would other ordering principles be more effective? If so, which ones?
>
> *Revise Paragraph Development*
>
> ❏ Which paragraphs contain too many or too few examples? Which contain examples that are too brief or too extended? Which include insufficiently or overly detailed examples?
>
> ❏ Which paragraphs contain examples that could be made more compelling?
>
> ❏ Which paragraphs include examples that are atypical or incorrect?
>
> *Revise Sentences and Words*
>
> ❏ What signal devices introduce examples and clarify the line of thought? Where are there too many or too few of these devices?
>
> ❏ Where would more varied sentence structure heighten the essay's illustrations?
>
> ❏ Where would more concrete and specific words make the examples more effective?

STUDENT ESSAY

The following student essay was written by Michael Pagano in response to this assignment:

> One implication in Beth Johnson's "Bombs Bursting in Air" is that, given life's unanticipated tragedies, people need to focus on what's really important rather than on trivial complications and distractions. Observe closely the way you and others conduct your daily lives. Use your observations for an essay that supports or refutes Johnson's point of view.

While reading Michael's paper, try to determine how effectively it applies the principles of exemplification. The annotations on Michael's paper and the commentary following it will help you look at the essay more closely.

Pursuit of Possessions
by Michael Pagano

Introduction

In the essay "Bombs Bursting in Air," Beth Johnson   1
develops the extended metaphor of bombs exploding
unexpectedly to represent the tragedies that occur without
warning in our daily lives. Herself a survivor of innumerable
life bombs, Johnson suggests that in light of life's fragility, we
need to remember and appreciate what's really important to
us. But very often, we lose sight of what truly matters in our
lives, instead occupying ourselves with trivial distractions. In

Thesis ——————— particular, many of us choose to spend our lives in pursuit of
material possessions. Much of our time goes into buying new

Plan of
development ———— things, dealing with the complications they create, and
working madly to buy more things or pay for the things we
already have.

Topic sentence ——————→ We devote a great deal of our lives to acquiring the   2
material goods we imagine are essential to our well-being.
Hours are spent planning and thinking about our future

The first of three   purchases. We window-shop for designer jogging shoes; we
paragraphs in a   leaf through magazines looking at ads for elaborate stereo
chronological   equipment; we research back issues of Consumer Reports to
sequence   find out about recent developments in exercise equipment.
Moreover, once we find what we are looking for, more time is
taken up when we decide to actually buy the items. How do
we find this time? That's easy. We turn evenings, weekends,
and holidays--time that used to be set aside for family and
friends--into shopping expeditions. No wonder family life is
deteriorating and children spend so much time in front of
television sets. Their parents are seldom around.

Topic sentence ——————→ As soon as we take our new purchases home, they begin   3
to complicate our lives. A sleek new sports car has to be

The second   washed, waxed, and vacuumed. A fashionable pair of
paragraph in the   overpriced dress pants can't be thrown in the washing
chronological   machine but has to be taken to the dry cleaner. New stereo
sequence   equipment has to be connected with a tangled network of
cables to the TV, radio, and cassette deck. Eventually, of

A paragraph   course, the inevitable happens. Our indispensable possessions
with many   break down and need to be repaired. The home computer
specific   starts to lose data, the microwave has to have its temperature
examples   controls adjusted, and the DVD player has to be serviced when
a disc becomes jammed in the machine.

Topic sentence ——————→ After more time has gone by, we sometimes discover that   4
our purchases don't suit us anymore, and so we decide to

The third   replace them. Before making our replacement purchases,
paragraph in the   though, we have to find ways to get rid of the old items. If we
chronological   want to replace our "small" 19-inch television set with a
sequence

35-inch one, we have to find time to put an ad in the classified section of the paper. Then we have to handle phone calls and set up times people can come to look at the TV. We could store the set in the basement--if we are lucky enough to find a spot that isn't already filled with other discarded purchases.

Topic sentence ⟶ with emphasis signal

Worst of all, this mania for possessions often influences 5 our approach to work. It is not unusual for people to take a second or even a third job to pay off the debt they fall into because they have overbought. After paying for food, clothing, and shelter, many people see the rest of their paycheck go to Visa, MasterCard, department store charge accounts, and time payments. Panic sets in when they realize there simply is not enough money to cover all their expenses. Just to stay afloat, people may have to work overtime or take on additional jobs.

Conclusion

It is clear that many of us have allowed the pursuit of 6 possessions to dominate our lives. We are so busy buying, maintaining, and paying for our worldly goods that we do not have much time to think about what is really important. We should try to step back from our compulsive need for more of everything and get in touch with the basic values that are the real point of our lives.

COMMENTARY

Thesis, combining patterns of development, and plan of development. In "Pursuit of Possessions," Michael analyzes the mania for acquiring material goods that permeates our society. He begins by addressing an implication conveyed in Beth Johnson's "Bombs Bursting in Air"—that life's fragility dictates that we need to focus on what really matters in our lives. This reference to Johnson gives Michael a chance to *contrast* the reflective way she suggests we should live with the acquisitive and frenzied way many people lead their lives. This contrast leads to the essay's *thesis:* "[M]any of us choose to spend our lives in pursuit of material possessions."

Besides introducing the basic contrast at the heart of the essay, Michael's opening paragraph helps readers see that the essay contains an element of *causal analysis.* The final sentence of the introductory paragraph lays out the effects of our possession obsession. This sentence also serves as the essay's *plan of development* and reveals that Michael feels the pursuit of possessions negatively affects our lives in three key ways.

Essays of this length often don't need a plan of development. But since Michael's paper is filled with many *examples,* the plan of development helps readers see how all the details relate to the essay's central point.

Evidence.   Support for the thesis consists of numerous examples presented in the *first-person-plural point of view* ("*We* choose to clutter our lives . . . ,"

"*We* devote a great deal of our lives . . . ," and so on). Many of these examples seem drawn from Michael's, his friends', or his family's experiences; however, to emphasize the events' universality, Michael converts these essentially personal examples into generalized ones that "we" all experience.

These examples, in turn, are organized around the three major points signaled by the plan of development. Michael uses one paragraph to develop his first and third points and two paragraphs to develop his second point. Each of the four supporting paragraphs is focused by a *topic sentence* that appears at the start of the paragraph. The transitional phrase "Worst of all" (paragraph 5) signals that Michael has sequenced his major points *emphatically*, saving for last the issue he considers most significant: how the "mania for possessions . . . influences our approach to work."

Organizational strategies. Emphatic order isn't Michael's only organizational technique. When reading the paper, you probably felt that there was an easy flow from one supporting paragraph to the next. How does Michael achieve such *coherence between paragraphs*? For one thing, he sequences paragraphs 2–4 *chronologically:* what happens before a purchase is made; what happens afterward. Secondly, topic sentences in paragraphs 3 and 4 include *signal devices* that indicate this passage of time. The topic sentences also strengthen coherence by *linking back* to the preceding paragraph: "*As soon as we take our new purchases home,* they . . . complicate our lives" and "*After more time has gone by,* we . . . discover that our purchases don't suit us anymore."

The same organizing strategies are used *within paragraphs* to make the essay coherent. Details in paragraphs 2 through 4 are sequenced chronologically, and to help readers follow the chronology, Michael uses *signal devices:* "*Moreover, once* we find what we are looking for, more time is taken up . . ." (2); "*Eventually,* of course, the inevitable happens" (3); "*Then* we have to handle phone calls . . ." (4).

Problems with paragraph development. You probably recall that an essay developed primarily through exemplification must include examples that are *relevant, interesting, convincing, representative, accurate,* and *specific*. On the whole, Michael's examples meet these requirements. The third and fourth paragraphs, especially, include vigorous details that show how our mania for buying things can govern our lives. We may even laugh with self-recognition when reading about "overpriced dress pants [that] can't be thrown in the washing machine" or a basement "filled with other discarded purchases."

The fifth paragraph, however, is underdeveloped. We know that this paragraph presents what Michael considers his most significant point, but the paragraph's examples are rather *flat* and *unconvincing*. To make this final section more compelling, Michael could mention specific people who overspend, revealing how much they are in debt and how much they have to work to become solvent again. Or he could cite a television documentary or magazine article dealing with the issue of consumer debt. Such specifics would give the paragraph the solidity it now lacks.

Shift in tone.   The fifth paragraph has a second, more subtle problem; *a shift in tone*. Although Michael has, up to this point, been critical of our possession-mad culture, he has poked fun at our obsession and kept his tone conversational and gently satiric. In this paragraph, though, he adopts a serious tone and, in the next paragraph, his tone becomes even weightier, almost preachy. It is, of course, legitimate to have a serious message in a lightly satiric piece. In fact, most satiric writing has such an additional layer of meaning. But because Michael has trouble blending these two moods, there's a jarring shift in the essay.

Shift in focus.   The second paragraph shows another kind of shift—in *focus*. The paragraph's controlling idea is that too much time is spent acquiring possessions. However, starting with "No wonder family life is deteriorating," Michael includes two sentences that introduce a complex issue beyond the scope of the essay. Since these last two sentences disrupt the paragraph's unity, they should be deleted.

Revising the first draft.   Although the final version of the essay needs work in spots, it's much stronger than Michael's first draft. To see how Michael went about revising the draft, compare his paper's second and third supporting paragraphs with his draft version reprinted here.

Original Version of the Second Paragraph

Our lives are spent not only buying things but in dealing with the inevitable complications that are created by our newly acquired possessions. First, we have to find places to put all the objects we bring home. More clothes demand more closets; a second car demands more garage space; a home entertainment center requires elaborate shelving. We shouldn't be surprised that the average American family moves once every three years. A good many families move simply because they need more space to store all the things they buy. In addition, our possessions demand maintenance time. A person who gets a new car will spend hours washing it, waxing it, and vacuuming it. A new pair of pants has to go to the dry cleaners. New stereo systems have to be connected to already existing equipment. Eventually, of course, the inevitable happens. Our new items need to be repaired. Or we get sick of them and decide to replace them. Before making our replacement purchases, though, we have to get rid of the old items. That can be a real inconvenience.

When Michael looked more closely at this paragraph, he realized it rambled and lacked energy. He started to revise the paragraph by tightening the first sentence, making it more focused and less awkward. Certainly, the revised sentence ("As soon as we take our new purchases home, they begin to complicate our lives") is crisper than the original. Next, he decided to omit the discussion about finding places to put new possessions; these sentences about inadequate closet, garage, and shelf space were so exaggerated that they undercut the valid point he wanted to make. He also chose to eliminate the sentences about the mobility of American families. This was, he felt, an interesting point, but it introduced an issue too complex to be included in the paragraph.

Michael strengthened the rest of the paragraph by making his examples more specific. A "new car" became a "sleek new sports car," and a "pair of pants" became a "fashionable pair of overpriced dress pants." Michael also realized he had to do more than merely write, "Eventually, . . . our new items need to be repaired." This point had to be dramatized by sharp, convincing details. Therefore, Michael added lively examples to describe how high-tech possessions—microwaves, home computers, DVD players—break down. Similarly, Michael realized it wasn't enough simply to say, as he had in the original, that we run into problems when we try to replace out-of-favor purchases. Vigorous details were again needed to illustrate the point. Michael thus used a typical "replaceable" (a "small" 19-inch TV set) as his key example and showed the annoyance involved in handling phone calls and setting up appointments so people could see the TV.

After adding these specifics, Michael realized he had enough material to devote a separate paragraph to the problems associated with replacing old purchases. By dividing his original paragraph, Michael ended up with two well-focused paragraphs, neither of which has the rambling quality found in the original.

In short, Michael strengthened his essay through substantial revision. Another round of rewriting would have made the essay stronger still. Even without this additional work, Michael's essay provides an interesting perspective on an American preoccupation.

ACTIVITIES: EXEMPLIFICATION

Prewriting Activities

1. Imagine you're writing two essays: One is a serious paper analyzing the factors that *cause* large numbers of public school teachers to leave the profession each year; the other is a light essay *defining* "preppie," "head banger," or some other slang term used to describe a kind of person. Jot down ways you might use examples in each essay.

2. Use mapping or another prewriting technique to gather examples illustrating the truth of *one* of the following familiar sayings. Then, using the same or a

different prewriting technique, accumulate examples that counter the saying. Weigh both sets of examples to determine the saying's validity. After developing an appropriate thesis, decide which examples you would elaborate in an essay.

a. Haste makes waste.
b. There's no use crying over spilled milk.
c. A bird in the hand is worth two in the bush.

Revising Activities

3. The following paragraph is from the first draft of an essay about the decline of small-town shopping districts. The paragraph is meant to show what small towns can do to revitalize business. Revise the paragraph, strengthening it with specific and convincing examples.

> A small town can compete with a large new mall for shoppers. But merchants must work together, modernizing the stores and making the town's main street pleasant, even fun to walk. They should also copy the malls' example by including attention-getting events as often as possible.

4. Reprinted here is a paragraph from the first draft of a light-spirited essay showing that Americans' pursuit of change for change's sake has drawbacks. The paragraph is meant to illustrate that infatuation with newness costs consumers money yet leads to no improvement in product quality. How effective is the paragraph? Which examples are specific and convincing? Which are not? Do any seem nonrepresentative, offensive, or sexist? How could the paragraph's organization be improved? Consider these questions as you rewrite the paragraph. Add specific examples where needed. Depending on the way you revise, you may want to break this one paragraph into several.

> We end up paying for our passion for the new and improved. Trendy clothing styles convince us that last year's outfits are outdated, even though our old clothes are fine. Women are especially vulnerable in this regard. What, though, about items that have to be replaced periodically, like shampoo? Even slight changes lead to new formulations requiring retooling of the production process. That means increased manufacturing costs per item--all of which get passed on to us, the consumer. Then there are those items that tout new, trendsetting features that make earlier versions supposedly obsolete. Some manufacturers, for example, boast that their stereo or CD systems transmit an expanded-frequency range. The problem is that humans can't even hear such frequencies. But the high-tech feature dazzles men who are too naive to realize they're being hoodwinked.

Charles Sykes

A journalist whose work has appeared in the *The New York Times, The Wall Street Journal,* and other leading newspapers, Charles Sykes (1954–) usually writes about education issues. His books include *ProfScam: Professors and the Demise of Higher Education* (1988), *The Hollow Men: Politics and Corruption in Higher Education* (1990), *A Nation of Victims: The Decay of the American Character* (1992), and *The End of Privacy* (1999). A senior fellow at the Wisconsin Policy Research Institute and host of a popular Milwaukee radio show, Sykes lectures widely on topics having to do with what he sees as the collapse of standards in American culture. The following excerpt is from Sykes's 1995 book, *Dumbing Down Our Kids: Why America's Children Feel Good About Themselves But Can't Read, Write, or Add.*

Pre-Reading Journal Entry

Studies reveal that sexual misbehavior, drug use, shoplifting, and cheating are common among some young people. In your journal, explore your thinking about young people's misconduct in two of these (or other) areas. Why do you think young people engage in such risky behavior?

The "Values" Wasteland

Eric Richardson was a seventeen-year-old member of the Spur Posse, a group of boys accused of raping girls as young as ten years old. After their arrests, the posse members reportedly returned to school as heroes, applauded for their exploits by their fellow students. In talk show appearances and media interviews, the boys were unrepentant. "They pass out condoms, teach sex education and pregnancy this and pregnancy that," Eric said after polishing off a Nacho Supreme and necking with his girlfriend in a booth at the Taco Bell. "But they don't teach us any rules."[1] His response was too glib and too convenient; it wasn't our fault, he was saying, you taught us to be like this. No school, however misguided, can ever be blamed for a piece of work like Eric Richardson. Even so, the evidence suggests that his ethical compass is not an isolated aberration.

[1]Jane Gross, "Where 'Boys will be Boys,' And Adults Are Bewildered," *New York Times,* 29 March 1993.

A 1988 study of more than 2,000 Rhode Island students in grades six 2 through nine found that two-thirds of the boys and half of the girls thought that "it was acceptable for a man to force sex on a woman" if they had been dating six months or more.[2] A write-in survey of 126,000 teenagers found that 25 to 40 percent of teens see nothing wrong with cheating on exams, stealing from employers, or keeping money that wasn't theirs. A seventeen-year-old high school senior explained: "A lot of it is a gray area. It's every-body doing their own thing."[3]

A 1992 survey by the Josephson Institute for Ethics of nearly 7,000 high 3 school and college students, most of them from middle- and upper middle-class backgrounds, found the equivalent of a "hole in the moral ozone" among American youth.

- A third of high school students and 16 percent of college students said they have shoplifted in the last year. Nearly the same number (33 percent of high school students and 11 percent of college students) said they have stolen from their parents or relatives at least once.[4]
- One in eight college students admitted to committing an act of fraud, including borrowing money they did not intend to repay, and lying on financial aid or insurance forms.
- A third of high school and college students said they would lie to get a job. One in six said they have already done so at least once.
- More than 60 percent of high school students said they had cheated at least once on an exam.
- Forty percent of the high school students who participated in this survey admitted that they "were not completely honest" on at least one or two questions—meaning that they may have lied on a survey about lying.[5]

"I think it's very easy to get through high school and college these days 4 and hardly ever hear, 'That's wrong,'" commented Patrick McCarthy of Pasadena's Jefferson Center for Character Education. Michael Josephson, the president of the Josephson Institute of Ethics, describes a large and growing population as the "I-Deserve-Its," or IDIs. "Their IDI-ology is exceptionally and dangerously self-centered, preoccupied with personal needs, wants, don't-wants and rights." In pursuit of success, or comfort, or self-gratification, the IDIs are blithely willing to jettison traditional ethical restraints, and as a result "IDIs are more likely to lie, cheat and engage in irresponsible behavior when it suits their purposes. IDIs act as if they need

[2] J. Kikuchi, "Rhode Island Develops Successful Intervention Program for Adolescents," *National Coalition Against Sexual Assault Newsletter*, Fall 1988.
[3] *USA Weekend*, 21–22 August 1992.
[4] Gary Abrams, "Youth Gets Bad Marks in Morality," *Los Angeles Times*, 12 November 1992.
[5] Ibid.

whatever they want and deserve whatever they need. . . ."[6] American youth's culture of entitlement cannot, of course, be laid solely at the feet of the schools. If there has been an ethical meltdown among young Americans we need to look first to their parents, communities, the media, and even the churches for explanations. Society's shift from a culture of self-control to one of self-gratification, self-actualization, and self-realization, and its changing norms regarding personal responsibility and character, was not restricted to the arena of public education. Even so, the ethical state of America's young people may, at least in part, have something to do with the way our schools teach them about right and wrong.

At one time, American students used to study historical role models like   5 Benjamin Franklin, Florence Nightingale, Thomas Edison, Madame Curie, Abraham Lincoln, and George Washington—whose stories were used to provide object lessons in inventiveness, character, compassion, curiosity, and truthfulness. Following Aristotle, ethicists recognized that humanity does not become virtuous simply by precept, but by "nature, habit, rational principle." "We become just by the practice of just actions," Aristotle observed, "self-controlled by exercising self-control." This process was most effectively begun by placing examples of such virtues in front of young people for them to emulate. But while Asian children continue to read about stories of perseverance, hard work, loyalty, duty, prudence, heroism, and honesty, [educational researcher] Harold Stevenson finds that "For the most part, such cultural models have been displaced in the United States today."[7] In its place, we provide children a jumbled smorgasbord of moral choices.

How Do You *Feel* About Cheating?

The course is officially about "citizenship," but the subject is values.[8]   6 Specially prepared for students in the fourth to sixth grades, the class is designed to help students clarify and discover their own values on issues like lying and cheating. As a group or by secret ballot, the fourth, fifth, and sixth graders are asked: "How many of you . . .

Think children should have to work for their allowances?
Think most rules are dumb?
Think that there are times when cheating is ok?
Wish you didn't have grades in school?
Think prizes should be awarded for everything?"

[6]Michael Josephson, "Young America Is Looking Out for No. 1," *Los Angeles Times*, 16 October 1990.
[7]Harold W. Stevenson and James W. Stigler, *The Learning Gap* (New York: Summit Books, 1992), pp. 85–86.
[8]"Citizenship: 4th–6th Grade," xeroxed worksheets, undated. Several copies were provided to me by parents whose children had been given the assignment during class.

The section on cheating asks students: "What are your attitudes toward cheating?" They are asked to complete the following statements:

Tests are _____
Grades are _____
The bad thing about cheating is _____
The good thing about cheating is _____
If there were no such things as grades, would your attitude toward cheating change?
Is school the only place cheating takes place? Where else does cheating take place?
Is it ever OK to cheat? When?

It is not clear whether there are ever any right and wrong answers to   7
these questions. The class takes a similar approach to lying. Students are asked, "Lying, What's Your View?". . . Children in the class are . . . presented with a series of ethical problems. They are not asked to define right and wrong or moral or immoral. Instead, they are asked to say which actions are "acceptable . . . and . . . which are . . . unacceptable. Do any of the situations involve lying?"

A factory worker oversleeps and is late for work. He tells his supervisor that he was involved in a minor traffic accident.
Janine just can't face a big history exam for which she hasn't studied. She convinces her mother that she has a terrible sore throat and must stay home.
Bill runs into a friend he hasn't seen in months. The friend asks how he is. Bill smiles and answers "great!" even though his dog just died, he's flunking English, and he just broke up with his girlfriend. . . .

Such nonjudgmentalism is a feature of the approach known as "values   8
clarification," in which, as [journalist] William Kirk Kilpatrick writes, classroom discussions are turned into "'bull sessions' where opinions go back and forth but conclusions are never reached." . . . Many of these classes seem to be based on the rather fantastic notion that since none of the civilizations anywhere in the world throughout the entire sweep of human history has been able to work out a moral code of conduct worthy of being passed on, we should therefore leave it to fourth graders to work out questions of right and wrong on their own.

The Values Clarifiers

The developers of Values Clarification and other nonjudgmental   9
approaches to moral decision making often claimed to be value-free, but

their agenda was quite specific. Their bête noir was "moralizing" in any form. "Moralizing," the authors of *Values Clarification: A Handbook of Practical Strategies for Teachers and Students* wrote in 1978, "is the direct, although sometimes subtle inculcation of the adults' values upon the young."[9] For the authors of the new curriculum, this was not merely authoritarian and stifling, but also dangerous to the ethical health of children. By passing on a set of moral values, they argued, parents were hampering the ability of children to come up with their own values. "Young people brought up by moralizing adults are not prepared to make their own responsible choices," they warned.[10] In any case, moralizing was no longer practical. Children were bombarded with so many different sets of values and parents were only some of the many voices they heard. In the end, they argue, every child had to make his own choices. That, of course, is true—making choices is the essence of free will. But where values clarification departed from older moral philosophies was in its contention that children do not need to be grounded in value systems or provided with moral road maps before they are asked to make such choices. Values clarifiers also did not care what values the child chose to follow. Specifically, values clarification did not concern itself with inculcating values such as self-control, honesty, responsibility, loyalty, prudence, duty, or justice. In its purest form, values clarification did not even argue that these virtues were superior or preferable to their opposites and had little to say about concepts of right and wrong. The goal of values clarification was not to create a virtuous young person, or young adult with character or probity; its goal was empowering youngsters to make their own decisions, *whatever those decisions were. . . .*

The assumption behind such programs was that children had the capacity to develop character on their own; that students as young as third grade had the knowledge, insight, and cognitive abilities to wrestle through difficult dilemmas and thorny moral paradoxes without the benefit of a moral compass, either from parents or teachers. . . .

At the heart of the values clarification program was the effort to have students develop an individual identity. One exercise was "Are You Someone Who . . ." followed by a long list of options, including: "is likely to marry someone of another religion?"; "is likely to grow a beard?"; "would consider joining the John Birch Society?"; "is apt to go out of your way to have a black (white) neighbor?"; "will subscribe to *Playboy* magazine?"; will change your religion?"; "will be likely to win a Nobel Peace Prize?"; "is apt to experiment with pot?"; "would get therapy on your own initiative?"; "will make a faithless husband? wife?"

---

[9] Sidney B. Simon, Leland W. Howe, and Howard Kirschenbaum, *Values Clarification: A Handbook of Practical Strategies for Teachers and Students* (New York: Hart Publishing, 1972), p. 15.
[10] Ibid., p. 16.

The authors explain that such questions will cause students "to consider more thoughtfully what they value, what they want out of life and what type of persons they want to become."[11] But the questions send another message as well by treating the various options simply as different choices of apparently equal weight, like choices on a personality buffet line: Will you win the Nobel Prize or experiment with pot? Subscribe to *Playboy* or change your religion? There is no suggestion that growing a beard or cheating on your wife might be decisions that carry rather different moral weights.

12

Ultimately, the values clarification approach reduces moral choice to a matter of personal taste with no more basis in objective reality than a preference for a red car rather than a blue one. There is no right or wrong answer and no real ground to regard your own choice either as better or more valid than any other.

13

But is this really a process of working out moral values or is it simply a process of rationalization? Humans rationalize because it is convenient and it suits our interests. If we choose, we can shape morality to meet our inclinations and impulses, rather than try to shape our inclinations to accord with moral law. Moral reasoning, in contrast, involves asking whether an act is good, whether it is made with right intent, and examining the act's circumstances. To make such judgments requires an understanding of what the moral law might be, not simply how we feel about the act. But to take the subjective state of mind and make it the sole test of morality is to rationalize and call it moral reasoning. Checking one's inclinations is not the same as examining one's conscience, precisely because the conscience needs to be educated.

14

One would never get that idea from watching a values clarification "simulation" of a moral choice. In one popular exercise, students have to imagine that their class has been trapped in a cave-in. In the exercise, students are asked to imagine that they have to form a single line to work their way out of the cave. At any moment, another rock slide may close the way out. Those at the head of the line are therefore the most likely to survive. In the class exercise, each member of the class must give the reason he or she should be at the head of the line. The teacher tells them: "Your reasons can be of two kinds. You can tell us what you want to live for or what you have yet to get out of life that is important to you. Or you can talk about what you have to contribute to others in the world that would justify your being near the front of the line." After hearing all of the pleas, the class then decides the order in which they will file out of the cave.[12]

15

Like other values clarification chestnuts, youngsters are asked to make life-and-death decisions. But what are the practical implications? Do students emerge from the class more empathetic? More willing to sacrifice for others?

16

[11]Ibid., p. 366.
[12]Ibid., p. 288.

Are they likely to treat their peers with more respect? Show more self-restraint in the presence of their parents? Or are they likely to have a keener sense of their own egos? . . .

Other exercises ask students to choose who should be allowed to stay in a fallout shelter (and who should be left to die) during a nuclear attack; to decide whether it is morally permissible for a poor man to steal a drug that his desperately ill wife needs; to work through the dilemma of trapped settlers who must decide whether to turn to cannibalism or starve to death; to put themselves in the place of a mother who must choose which of her two children she will save; and consider the ethical dilemma of a doctor who must decide to operate on an injured child despite the religious objections of the parents. "Like a roller-coaster ride," William Kilpatrick writes, "the dilemma approach can leave its passengers a bit breathless. That is one of its attractions. But like a roller-coaster ride, it may also leave them a bit disoriented— or more than a bit."[13] As entertaining as such problems may be, they are hardly a guide for developing a moral code; morality is more than solving a complex and perhaps even unsolvable puzzle. Take the case of the man whose wife is dying of an incurable illness and who needs a rare and expensive drug. Kilpatrick wonders whether youngsters who spend a diverting and lively class period debating whether stealing is right or wrong in this case would be less likely to steal themselves? Or lie? Or cheat? Or will they come to the conclusion that moral questions are inevitably so complicated, so fraught with doubt, that no one answer is necessarily ever any better than any other and that all moral questions come down in the end simply to a matter of opinion? Or will they get the idea that it is less important whether one steals or not than that one has developed a system of "valuing" with which one is comfortable?

One of the striking things about spending time with high school students is the near universality of this notion that values are something they work out on their own. One frequent speaker on ethical issues recounts his experience with high school students in which he presents them with a typical values clarification dilemma. They must imagine that they are on a lifeboat with another person and their family dog; the students can save only one, so they must choose either the human being, who is a complete stranger, or the beloved and cherished family dog. Typically, some of the students choose to save the dog and allow the man to die; most students choose to save the human being. But then the speaker asks them what they thought of their classmates who had opted for the dog over the man. Almost never, says the speaker, do students say that those choices were "wrong" or morally objectionable.[14] Even for those who made the correct moral choice, it was

[13]William Kirk Kilpatrick, *Why Johnny Can't Tell Right From Wrong* (New York: Simon & Schuster, 1992), p. 84.
[14]Dennis Prager, conversation with author.

merely a matter of personal opinion, and they refuse to be judgmental toward those who put the dog's life ahead of the human being's. The concept that there might be universal and objective moral principles at stake is completely alien to these youngsters.

Questions for Close Reading

1. What is the selection's thesis? Locate the sentence(s) in which Sykes states his main idea. If he doesn't state it directly, express it in your own words.
2. What, according to Sykes, is the difference between contemporary American education and American education in the past?
3. What group of people does Sykes blame for the erosion of morality in American education? What justification do these people provide for their approach?
4. Reread paragraphs 15 and 18. In each, Sykes describes a classroom exercise in "values clarification." What is the educational intent of the two exercises? How are they similar? How do they differ? What is Sykes's opinion of the two exercises?
5. Refer to your dictionary as needed to define the following words used in the selection: *unrepentant* (paragraph 1), *self-actualization* (4), *precept* (5), *emulate* (5), *perseverance* (5), *smorgasbord* (5), *bête noir* (9), *moralizing* (9), *cognitive* (10), *rationalization* (14), and *fraught* (17).

Questions About the Writer's Craft

1. **The pattern.** In the first three paragraphs of his essay, Sykes provides numerous examples to illustrate what he considers the moral looseness of young people. Why do you think he starts with the example of the seventeen-year-old rapist? In what ways is this example different from the examples he provides in paragraphs 2 and 3?
2. Why do you suppose Sykes entitles his essay "The 'Values' Wasteland"? Consider what each word means. Why do you think he puts quotation marks around the word "Values"?
3. In paragraphs 2 and 3, Sykes makes heavy use of statistics. Why do you suppose he cites statistics only in the beginning of the essay?
4. **Other patterns.** How would you characterize Sykes's tone? How does this tone reinforce his *argument*?

Writing Assignments Using Exemplification as a Pattern of Development

1. Sykes contends that modern education fails to teach morality. Do you agree? Write an essay illustrating the point that contemporary schooling blunts *or* enhances young people's moral sense. In either case, offer convincing examples from your own and other people's schooling to support your point of view. Consider opening your essay, as Sykes does, with a highly dramatic example.
2. Sykes believes that the moral fiber of young people has deteriorated. Interview classmates, friends, and family members of varying ages to see if they think that young people today are less moral than they were in earlier times. Ask each person to supply at least one example to illustrate his or her opinion. Review the examples, and decide whether you agree with or reject Sykes's position. Then

write an essay in which you support your opinion, using the most compelling examples from your interviews as well as your own experiences and observations.

Writing Assignments Combining
Patterns of Development

 3. Sykes believes that there are "universal and objective moral principles." Write an essay *narrating* a time when you faced a moral dilemma but knew deep down that there was only one moral way to act—even though such an action might have been to your personal disadvantage. *Describe* the situation, the conflict you experienced, and how you resolved the conflict. You might also conclude by briefly reflecting on the *results* of your actions. Before writing, read one or more of the following essays for insight into humans' moral impulse: George Orwell's "Shooting an Elephant" (page 143), Langston Hughes's "Salvation" (page 155), and Stephanie Ericsson's "The Ways We Lie" (page 240).

4. Sykes writes that "we need to look first to . . . parents, communities, the media, and even the churches" to explain the "ethical meltdown" in young people. Focus on *one* of these forces, and write an essay analyzing the positive and negative *effects* it can have on young people's moral sense. To support your analysis, draw upon *examples* from your own observations as well as those of friends, classmates, and family members. Reading Kay S. Hymowitz's "Tweens: Ten Going on Sixteen" (page 202) and Buzz Bissinger's "Innocents Afield" (page 424) might give you further perspective on how social influences can have a detrimental impact on children.

Writing Assignment Using a Journal
Entry as a Starting Point

5. Reread your pre-reading journal entry, and decide which *one* type of misconduct you think is most prevalent among young people nowadays. Then write an essay in which you illustrate the extent of the impropriety, using several persuasive examples to make your point. One section of the essay should explore causes of the misbehavior; another should discuss consequences. Brainstorming with others will help you identify examples, causes, and effects of the misbehavior. At the end of your essay, you might suggest steps that could be taken to set young people in the right direction. Also, consider supplementing your observations with information about your topic gathered in the library and/or on the Internet.

Leslie Savan

Leslie Savan is a critic and writer whose work has appeared in *The Village Voice, Time, The New Yorker, The New York Times,* and *Salon.* Born in 1951, she has been a finalist for the Pulitzer Prize and a commentator on National Public Radio. In 1994 she published her first book, *The Sponsored Life: Ads, TV, and American Culture.* For several years, Savan wrote a column on advertising for *The Village Voice,* and she began to notice that certain popular words and phrases kept reoccurring in ads. She paid attention to the "pop" language of advertising and other media and eventually wrote a book about it. This essay is excerpted from *Slam Dunks and No-Brainers: Language in Your Life, the Media, Business, Politics, and Like, Whatever,* which was published in 2005.

Pre-Reading Journal Entry

Different groups of people have special words and phrases—often slang—that they frequently use among themselves. Think about the slang words and phrases that are in common use among your friends. In your journal, list some of these words and phrases. What do they mean?

Black Talk and Pop Culture

African-American vernacular, black English, black talk, Ebonics, hip-hop 1
slang—whatever you want to call it, black-inspired language is all over mainstream pop talk like white on rice.

The talk may be everywhere, but, oddly enough, even during the rabid 2
debate over Ebonics in the late 1990s rarely was there any mention of black English's deep imprint on American English. Yet linguists and other language experts know that America's language wouldn't be what it is—and certainly wouldn't pop as much—without black English.

"In the past, White society has resisted the idea," wrote Robert McCrum, 3
William Cran, and Robert MacNeil in *The Story of English,* "but there is now no escaping the fact that [Blacks' influence] has been one of the most profound contributions to the English language."

"First, one cannot help but be struck by the powerful influence of African- 4
American vernacular on the slang of all 20th-century American youth," Tom Dalzell wrote in *Flappers 2 Rappers.* "There were other influences, to be sure,

on the slang of America's young, but none as powerful as that of the streets of Harlem and Chicago."

The linguist Connie Eble, author of *Slang and Sociability* and a college and youth slang expert at the University of North Carolina, Chapel Hill, calls the black influence on the American language "overwhelming."

White people (and not just the young) draw from a black lexicon every day, sometimes unaware of the words' origins, sometimes using them because of their origins. Here are just some of the words and phrases—born in different decades and now residing at various levels of popdom—that African Americans either coined or popularized, and, in either case, that they created the catchiest meaning of: *all that, back in the day, bling bling, blues, bogus, boogie, bootie, bro, chick, chill, come again, cook, cool, dawg, dig, dis, do your own thing, don't go there, freak, funky, get-go, get it on, get over, gig, give it up, groovy, heavy, hip, homeboy, hot, in your face, kick back, lame, living large, man, my bad, Micky D's, old school, nitty gritty, player, riff, righteous, rip off, rock 'n' roll, soul, tell it like it is, 24/7, uptight, wannabe, whack, Whassup?/sup?, Whassup with that?, when the shit hits the fan, you know what I'm saying?*

You know what I'm saying. Most of us talk, and all of us hear in the media, some of that talk every day. Some phrases are said with an implicit nod to their source (*street cred, chill, You the man,* as well as a fist pound or high five), while others have been so widely adopted that they're beginning to feel sourceless (*24/7, lame, in your face*). *It's a black thang* has become everybody's thing, from *It's a dick thing* to (most offensively, considering who pushed it) "Virginia Slims: It's a Woman Thing."

But black vernacular didn't just add more lively, "colorful" words to the pop vocabulary. Much as marketing has influenced pop language, so black English has changed the American language in more fundamental ways. And that's what we're talking here—not about black talk per se, but about what happens when black talk meets, and transforms, the wider, whiter pop.

First and foremost, this language of outsiders has given us *cool:* the word itself—the preeminent pop word of all time—and quite a sizable chunk of the cool stance that underlies pop culture itself. Pop culture's desire for cool is second only to its desire for money—the two, in fact, are inextricably linked. (Cool may be first and foremost, but more on why it rules later.)

A second way African-American vernacular has affected the broader pop is that black talk has operated as a template for what it means to talk pop in the first place. As an often playful, ironic alternative to the official tongue, black slang has prefigured pop language in much the same way that black music has prefigured, and has often become, pop music. While there are important differences, some of the dynamics underlying black talk and pop talk are similar: Like black English, pop language sparks with wordplays and code games; it assumes that certain, often previously unacknowledged experiences deserve their own verbal expression; and it broadcasts the sense that only those who share the experiences can really get the words. For instance, black talk's running commentary on social exclusion is a model for pop talk's running commentary on media experiences.

Why do I say that pop is modeled on black and not the other way   11
around? It's not just because black talk did these things earlier and still does them more intensely than pop, but as the original flipside to the voice of the Man, as the official unofficial speech of America, black talk is the object of pop talk's crush on everything "alternative" and "outsider."

There's an attitude in pop language that it is somehow undermining the   12
stale old ways and sending a wake-up call to anyone who just doesn't get it. You can feel the attitude in everything from advertising's furious but phony rebelliousness to the faintly up-yours, tough-talking phrases like *Get a life* and *Don't even* think *about it*. It's not that these particular phrases are black or black-inspired, or that white people aren't perfectly capable of rebelliousness, anger at authority, and clever put-downs on their own. But the black experience, publicized more widely than ever now through hip-hop and its celebrities, has encouraged everyone else to more vigorously adopt the style of fighting the power—at least with the occasional catchphrase.

It may seem twisted, given American history, that general pop language   13
draws from the experience of black exclusion at all. But white attempts to *yo* here and *dis* there are an important piece of identity-and-image building for individuals and corporations alike. Today, the language of an excluded people is repeated by the nonexcluded in order to make themselves sound more included. As the mainstream plays the titillating notes of marginalization, we are collectively creating that ideal mass personality mentioned earlier: We can be part black (the part presumed to be cool and soulful, real and down, jazzy or hip-hop, choose your sound) and be part white (the privileged part, the part that has the luxury to easily reference other parts).

Related to all this imitation and referencing is the most noticeable way   14
that pop talk is affected by black talk: Black talk has openly joined the sales force. At white society's major intersection with black language—that is, in entertainment—white society has gone from mocking black talk, as in minstrel shows, to marketing it, as in hip-hop. In the more than a hundred years between these two forms of entertainment, black language has by and large entered white usage as if it were a sourceless slang or perhaps the latest lingo of some particularly hep white cats, like the fast-talking disc jockeys of the 1950s and 1960s who purveyed black jive to white teenagers. Black language may have been the single most important factor in shaping generations of American slang, primarily through blues, jazz, and rock 'n' roll. But only relatively recently has black talk been used openly, knowingly, and not mockingly to sell products.

This would have been unthinkable once. Even fifteen or twenty years   15
ago, car makers were loath to show black people in commercials for fear that their product would be tainted as inferior or, worse, as "a black car." Although many car companies are still skittish, by 2001 Buick was actually

ending its commercials with the rap-popularized phrase "It's all good." (And by 2004, a BMW ad was featuring an interracial couple.) The phrase went from M. C. Hammer's 1994 song "It's All Good" to replacing "I love this game" as the official slogan of the National Basketball Association in 2001. Both Buick and the NBA have since dropped *It's all good*, but with their help the phrase massified, at least for a while. "It's huge" among white "sorority sisters and stoners alike," a twenty-seven-year-old white friend in Chicago told me in 2003.

So it's not all bad, this commercialization of black talk, especially if it can get the auto industry to move from shunning to quoting African Americans. But it comes laden with price tags. To read them, look at MTV, which has to be *the* major force in the sea change from whites-only to black's-da-bomb.

It may be difficult to believe now, but for years MTV wouldn't touch black music videos. The channel relented only under pressure, with videos by Prince and Michael Jackson. Black just wouldn't appeal to its white suburban teen audience, MTV explained. In 1989 with the appearance of the successful *Yo! MTV Raps*, that rationale was turned inside out, and—ka-ching!— black videos began to appear regularly. Since so much of MTV is advertising posing as entertainment (the videos are record company promotions, the parties and other bashes that appear are often visibly sponsored events), MTV has contributed significantly to two marketing trends: To the young, advertising has become an acceptable—nay, desirable—part of the cool life they aspire to; and a black, hip-hop-ish vernacular has become a crucial cog in the youth market machinery.

The outsider style is not solely black or hip-hop, but, at least in the marketing mind, a black package can be the most efficient buy to achieve that style. For corporate purposes, hip-hop in particular is a lucrative formula. Not only does the hip-hop black man represent the ultimate outsider who simultaneously stands at the nexus of cool, but much of hip-hop, created by the kind of people gated communities were meant to exclude, sings the praises of acquiring capitalism's toys. These paradoxes of racism are commercial-ready. . . .

When Sprite realized that teenagers no longer believed its TV commercials telling them that "Image Is Nothing" and that they shouldn't trust commercials or celebrity endorsements (said only half tongue-in-cheek by celebrities like NBA star Grant Hill), the soft drink's marketing department decided to up the ante. So, when you need outsider verisimilitude, who ya gonna call? Why, black rappers, of course, preferably on the hardcore side. Get *them* to testify to the soft drink's beyond-the-bounds, can't-be-bought spirit at Sprite.com launch parties (to be run later on MTV). Or get real kids, looking and sounding ghetto, to rap their own lyrics in TV spots about, say, "a situation that is not too sweet, which is an attribute of Sprite," as a Sprite publicist said. How else to get kids, usually white kids, to understand that you understand that they're sick of commercials telling them what's cool?

And so, while Sprite had long used rappers in its overall "Obey Your 20
Thirst" campaign, now it pumped up the volume. Only by obeying the first
commandment that image is everything can you become, as Sprite did by the
late nineties, the fastest-growing soft-drink brand in the world. . . .

When whites talk black—or, just as commonly, when major corporations 21
do it for them—it makes you wanna shout, *Whassup with that?!*

Terms and Props

Before I address wannabe black talk and other points where black lan- 22
guage crosses over into pop, a few words about what "black language" and
"black words" are.

I've been using the terms "black English," "black slang," "black talk," 23
and "African-American vernacular" rather interchangeably, which, in plain
English, seems OK. Yet, at the same time, each term is a bit off the mark.

No one phrase is the perfect vehicle to explain how a people speak, 24
because "a people" don't all speak (or do anything) one way. That's one of
the problems with the terms "black English" and "black dialect." "Black
English" was more or less booted out of formal linguistic circles, because, as
linguist Peter Trudgill wrote in the 1995 revised edition of his book *Socio-
linguistics,* "it suggested that all Blacks speak this one variety of English—
which is not the case." The newer scholarly term, African American Vernacular English (AAVE), has pros and cons: It "distinguishes those Blacks who do
not speak standard American English from those who do," wrote Trudgill,
"although it still suggests that only one nonstandard variety, homogeneous
through the whole of the USA, is involved, which is hardly likely." The word
Ebonics was created in 1973 by African-American scholars to "define black
language from a black perspective," writes Geneva Smitherman, director of
the African American Language and Literacy Program at Michigan State University. But the 1997 Ebonics controversy loaded the word with so much baggage . . . that, outside of some hip-hop use, it has become nearly immobile.

"Black slang" can't describe black language, because clearly most black 25
language is composed of standard English. However, when referring to actual slang that blacks created (*my bad, dis*), "black slang" is the right term. Personally, I like "black talk" (which is also the title of one of Smitherman's
books). Although, like any phrase starting with the adjective "black," it might
suggest that all black people talk this way all the time, "black talk" (like "pop
talk") is colloquial and flexible, encompassing vocabulary and then some. . . .

Origins tend to get lost in the roaring mainstream. Some words that seem 26
white are black, and vice versa. For instance, until I looked into *24/7,* I would
have guessed its roots were cyber or maybe something out of the conve-
nience-store industry. But *24/7* arose from a hip-hop fondness for number
phrases. Rapdict.org lists some sixty number phrases, many of which are too

obscure or gangsta to cross over; *411* is one of the few others that has gone pop. (A recent Mercedes-Benz magazine ad advised, "Get the 411.")

Bogus, which sounds so surfer, dude, dates back at least as far as 1798, when a glossary defined it as a "spurious coin," write David Barnhart and Allan Metcalf in *America in So Many Words.* "Its origins are obscure, but one guess that is as good as any is that it is from *boko,* meaning 'deceit' or 'fake' in the Hausa language of west central Africa. The word then would have been brought over by Africans sold into slavery here." In addition, some nuances that no one doubts are African American may run deeper in black history than most people, black or white, imagine. When *bad* is used to mean good, the meaning (though obviously not the word itself) is derived, Smitherman writes,[1] from a phrase in the Mandinka language in West Africa, "*a ka nyi ko-jugu,* which means, literally, 'it is good badly,' that is, it is very good, or it is so good that it's bad!"

Meanwhile, some words that most people would identify as black, and that black people did indeed popularize, originated among others. Southern phrases in particular jumped races, "from black to white in the case of *bubba* and *big daddy,* from white to black in the case of *grits* and *chitlins,*" write the Rickfords.[2] *Cat,* meaning a hip guy, is a dated piece of slang (though often on the verge of a comeback) that most people attribute to black jazz musicians; Ken Burns's television series *Jazz* states that Louis Armstrong was the first person to have said it. But, as Tom Dalzell writes, in "the late 19th century and early 20th century, *cat* in the slang and jargon of hobos meant an itinerant worker . . . possibly because the migratory worker slunk about like a 'homeless cat.'" However, it did take Armstrong, and then other jazz musicians in the 1920s, to introduce the word into broader usage. That old rap word *fly* (stylish, good-looking, smooth) was flying long before rap. "The most well-established slang meaning of *fly* was in the argot of thieves, where *fly* meant sly, cunning, wide-awake, knowing, or smart," writes Dalzell, who notes those uses of *fly* as early as 1724 and in *Bleak House* by Dickens in 1853. But again, *fly* didn't really buzz until black musicians picked up on it, beginning around 1900, well before *Superfly* in the 1970s and rap in the 1980s.

Wannabe Nation

Whether black-born or black-raised, black words are the ones that many white people are wearing like backwards baseball caps. That brings us to a particularly telling term that went from black to pop. *Wannabe* originally referred to people who wanted to be something they weren't; it was often said of a black person who wanted to be white. In Spike Lee's 1988 film

---

[1]In her book, *Black Talk: Words and Phrases from the Hood to the Amen Corner* (editors' note).
[2]In *Spoken Soul: The Story of Black English,* by John R. Rickford and Russell J. Rickford (editors' note).

School Daze, the conflict was between the dark-skinned, activist "Jigaboos" and the light-skinned sorority sister "Wannabes." Beginning around the time of that movie, *wannabe* was used by just about everybody to mean anybody who wanted to be somebody he or she wasn't—there have been surfer wannabes, Madonna wannabes, and dot.com start-up wannabes. But *wannabe* is not just a blast from decades past. More recently, "podcaster wannabes" have developed, and in just one week on TV and radio in late 2004, I heard of "artist wannabes," "geek wannabes," and "wannabe homeland security chief" Bernard Kerik.

Racially speaking, *wannabe* has reversed field. Since at least the early   30
nineties, with hip-hop an entrenched, virtually mainstream hit, *wannabe* has been far more likely to refer to whites, especially teenagers, who want to be black or do the style. Sometimes called *wiggers* or *wiggas* (*white* plus *nigger/ nigga*), black wannabes try to dance the dance and talk the talk. Even whites who would hate to be black will maintain the right to add the occasional black flourish. Some whites flash a black word or gesture like an honorary badge of cool, to show they're down with black people on certain occasions, usually involving sports or entertainment. Or maybe they do it because some of their best friends and some of the best commercials are flashing it, too. Or maybe they just need to know that black people like them. Take "Johnny and Sally," the fictitious white couple on the very funny Web site BlackPeople LoveUs.com, which is full of "testimonials" to their racial bigheartedness. As one unnamed black man attested, "Johnny always alters his given name and refers to himself in the third person—for example, 'J-Dog don't play that' or 'J-Dog wants to know wusssaappp.' It comforts me to know that my parlance has such broad appeal."

African Americans aren't the only people whose parlance has broad   31
appeal. Non-Latino blacks dabble in Spanish, Catholics in Yiddish, adults in teenage talk. Cultural skin is always permeable, absorbing any word that has reached a critical mass of usefulness or fun. The human species can't help but borrow—after all, that's how languages develop.

But whether we call it wannabe talk or the less derogatory crossover talk,   32
something about white society's sampling of black speech is more loaded than the usual borrowing. Black vernacular's contributions to English are larger in number and run deeper linguistically and psychologically than do any other ethnic group's. And black English, born in slavery, resounds with our society's senses of guilt, fear, identity, and style.

Black-to-white crossover talk, which also began during slavery, is hardly   33
new. But, like most pop talk today, it radiates a new gloss, a veneer in which you can catch the reflection of its increased market value. Black talk comes from something real—"serious as a heart attack," Smitherman says—but, whoop, there it is, sparking out of TV commercials, out of white politicians, out of anyone who has something to promote, spin, or get over.

Questions for Close Reading

1. What is the selection's thesis? Locate the sentence(s) in which Savan states her main idea. If she doesn't state her thesis explicitly, express it in your own words.
2. What does Savan mean by "pop language" and "pop talk"? What are some examples of these?
3. Why does Savan characterize the word *cool* as the most important pop word of all time?
4. In the section "Wannabe Nation," Savan describes the appeal of being Black to white Americans. According to Savan, what is troubling about the white mainstream culture's appropriation of Black words and phrases?
5. Refer to your dictionary as needed to define the following words used in the selection: *vernacular* (paragraph 1), *lexicon* (6), *per se* (8), *preeminent* (9), *template* (10), *catchphrase* (12), *minstrel shows* (14), *loath* (15), *lucrative* (18), *nexus* (18), *verisimilitude* (19), *colloquial* (25), *spurious* (27), and *argot* (28).

Questions About the Writer's Craft

1. **The pattern.** Why does Savan use so many examples of Black talk to illustrate its role in modern American English? Why does she use several lengthy examples as well? What are some of these extended examples?
2. **The pattern.** In paragraphs 16 through 21, Savan discusses the use of Black talk in marketing products. How does she organize the examples in this section of the essay? What is the purpose of this organization?
3. **Other patterns.** In the section entitled "Terms and Props," Savan discusses the *definitions* of the terms she has been using for Black talk. Why does she stop the flow of the essay to delve deeper into these terms? Why does she prefer the term "black talk" over the terms "black English," "black dialect," and "African American Vernacular English"? How effective is this section of the essay?
4. To support her thesis, Savan uses evidence from advertising, MTV, and the Internet. Find one example of a use of Black talk in each of these media. Why do you think Savan chose each example? How does each example support the essay's thesis? Would the essay have been as effective without these examples?

Writing Assignments Using Exemplification as a Pattern of Development

1. Savan discusses the role hip-hop artists play in modern marketing. Select a current hip-hop artist who markets products and do research on him or her. Write an essay about the role of marketing and advertising in this artist's career, providing examples to support your thesis.
2. Savan's essay focuses on Black talk, but there are many other subgroups of American English. For example, there is "Spanglish," a blend of Spanish and English occasionally spoken by Hispanic Americans; jargon, which includes words such as *debug* associated with a specific field like computer science; place names that have their origin in Native American languages; and regional dialects that have their own special words and phrases. Select one type of specialized American English words

with which you are familiar and write an essay that *exemplifies* it. Include specific examples of words and phrases and their use to make your essay interesting.

Writing Assignments Combining Patterns of Development

3. Savan discusses how marketers use Black language and culture to sell products. Select two TV commercials or print ads for the same type of product and *describe* them using vivid, sensory language. Then analyze each commercial or ad, *dividing* your analysis into the various techniques it uses to persuade you, the consumer, to buy the product. *Compare* and *contrast* the effectiveness of the two ads. For another perspective on advertising, you may want to read "Propaganda Techniques in Today's Advertising" by Ann McClintock (page 270).

4. Most of the examples in Savan's essay are of the use of Black talk in spoken popular language. In contrast, written language is usually more formal. Write an essay in which you *compare* and *contrast* the language you use when speaking with the language you use when writing. Give examples of both spoken and written language to support your thesis.

Writing Assignment Using a Journal Entry as a Starting Point

5. Review your pre-reading journal entry, and select two or three of the words and phrases that you and your friends use among yourselves. Then write an essay giving examples of situations in which these words are used. Explain why you choose to use them rather than using conventional phrases from standard English. What function do these words and phrases have in the psychology of the group?

Kay S. Hymowitz

A senior fellow at the Manhattan Institute and a contributing editor of the urban-policy magazine *City Journal*, Kay S. Hymowitz (1948–) writes on education and childhood in America. A native of Philadelphia, Hymowitz received an undergraduate English degree from Brandeis University and graduate degrees from Tufts University and Columbia University. She has taught English literature and composition at Brooklyn College and at Parsons School of Design. Hymowitz is the author of *Ready or Not: Why Treating Our Children as Small Adults Endangers Their Future and Ours* (1999) and is a principal contributor to *Modern Sex: Liberation and Its Discontents* (2001). In 2003, she published *Liberation's Children: Parents and Kids in a Postmodern Age*, a collection of her *City Journal* essays. Her work has appeared in publications including *The New York Times, The Washington Post,* and *The New Republic*. Hymowitz lives in Brooklyn with her husband and three children. The following essay appeared in the Autumn 1998 issue of *City Journal*.

Pre-Reading Journal Entry

Think back on your childhood. What were some possessions and activities that you cherished and enjoyed? Freewrite for a few moments in your pre-reading journal about these beloved objects and/or pastimes. What exactly were they? Why did you enjoy them so much? Did your feelings about them change as you matured into adolescence?

Tweens: Ten Going on Sixteen

During the past year my youngest morphed from child to teenager. Down   1
came the posters of adorable puppies and the drawings from art class; up went
the airbrushed faces of Leonardo di Caprio and Kate Winslet. CDs of Le Ann
Rimes and Paula Cole appeared mysteriously, along with teen fan magazines
featuring glowering movie and rock-and-roll hunks. . . . She started reading
the newspaper—or at least the movie ads—with all the intensity of a Talmudic
scholar, scanning for glimpses of her beloved Leo or, failing that, Matt Damon.
As spring approached and younger children skipped past our house on their
way to the park, she swigged from a designer water bottle, wearing the oblig-
atory tank top and denim shorts as she whispered on the phone to friends
about games of Truth or Dare. The last rites for her childhood came when,
embarrassed at reminders of her foolish past, she pulled a sheet over her years-
in-the-making American Girl doll collection, now dead to the world.

So what's new in this dog-bites-man story? Well, as all this was going on,   2
my daughter was ten years old and in the fourth grade.

Those who remember their own teenybopper infatuation with Elvis or   3
the Beatles might be inclined to shrug their shoulders as if to say, "It was ever
thus." But this is different. Across class lines and throughout the country,
elementary and middle-school principals and teachers, child psychologists
and psychiatrists, marketing and demographic researchers all confirm the
pronouncement of Henry Trevor, middle-school director of the Berkeley
Carroll School in Brooklyn, New York: "There is no such thing as pre-
adolescence anymore. Kids are teenagers at ten."

Marketers have a term for this new social animal, kids between eight   4
and 12: they call them "tweens." The name captures the ambiguous reality:
though chronologically midway between early childhood and adolescence,
this group is leaning more and more toward teen styles, teen attitudes, and,
sadly, teen behavior at its most troubling.

The tween phenomenon grows out of a complicated mixture of biology,   5
demography, and the predictable assortment of Bad Ideas. But putting aside
its causes for a moment, the emergence of tweendom carries risks for both
young people and society. Eight- to 12-year-olds have an even more wobbly
sense of themselves than adolescents; they rely more heavily on others to tell
them how to understand the world and how to place themselves in it. Now,
for both pragmatic and ideological reasons, they are being increasingly
"empowered" to do this on their own, which leaves them highly vulnerable
both to a vulgar and sensation-driven marketplace and to the crass authority
of their immature peers. In tweens, we can see the future of our society taking shape, and it's not at all clear how it's going to work.

Perhaps the most striking evidence for the tweening of children comes   6
from market researchers. "There's no question there's a deep trend, not a
passing fad, toward kids getting older younger," says research psychologist
Michael Cohen of Arc Consulting, a public policy, education, and marketing
research firm in New York. "This is not just on the coasts. There are no real
differences geographically." It seems my daughter's last rites for her American Girl dolls were a perfect symbol not just for her own childhood but for
childhood, period. The Toy Manufacturers of America Factbook states that,
where once the industry could count on kids between birth and 14 as their
target market, today it is only birth to ten. "In the last ten years we've seen
a rapid development of upper-age children," says Bruce Friend, vice president of worldwide research and planning for Nickelodeon, a cable channel
aimed at kids. "The 12- to 14-year-olds of yesterday are the ten to 12s of
today." The rise of the preteen teen is "the biggest trend we've seen."

Scorning any symbols of their immaturity, tweens now cultivate a self-   7
image that emphasizes sophistication. The Nickelodeon-Yankelovich Youth
Monitor found that by the time they are 12, children describe themselves as
"flirtatious, sexy, trendy, athletic, cool." Nickelodeon's Bruce Friend reports

that by 11, children in focus groups say they no longer even think of themselves as children.

They're very concerned with their "look," Friend says, even more so   8
than older teens. Sprouting up everywhere are clothing stores like the chain Limited Too and the catalog company Delia, geared toward tween girls who scorn old-fashioned, little-girl flowers, ruffles, white socks, and Mary Janes[1] in favor of the cool—black mini-dresses and platform shoes. . . . Teachers complain of ten- or 11-year-old girls arriving at school looking like madams, in full cosmetic regalia, with streaked hair, platform shoes, and midriff-revealing shirts. Barbara Kapetanakes, a psychologist at a conservative Jewish day school in New York, describes her students' skirts as being about "the size of a belt." Kapetanakes says she was told to dress respectfully on Fridays, the eve of the Jewish Sabbath, which she did by donning a long skirt and a modest blouse. Her students, on the other hand, showed their respect by looking "like they should be hanging around the West Side Highway," where prostitutes ply their trade.

Lottie Sims, a computer teacher in a Miami middle school, says that the   9
hooker look for tweens is fanning strong support for uniforms in her district. But uniforms and tank-top bans won't solve the problem of painted young ladies. "You can count on one hand the girls not wearing makeup," Sims says. "Their parents don't even know. They arrive at school with huge bags of lipstick and hair spray, and head straight to the girls' room."

Though the tweening of youth affects girls more visibly than boys, espe-   10
cially since boys mature more slowly, boys are by no means immune to these obsessions. Once upon a time, about ten years ago, fifth- and sixth-grade boys were about as fashion-conscious as their pet hamsters. But a growing minority have begun trading in their baseball cards for hair mousse and baggy jeans. In some places, $200 jackets, emblazoned with sports logos like the warm-up gear of professional athletes, are *de rigueur;* in others, the preppy look is popular among the majority, while the more daring go for the hipper style of pierced ears, fade haircuts, or ponytails. Often these tween peacocks strut through their middle-school hallways taunting those who have yet to catch on to the cool look. . . .

Those who seek comfort in the idea that the tweening of childhood is   11
merely a matter of fashion—who maybe even find their lip-synching, hip-swaying little boy or girl kind of cute—might want to think twice. There are disturbing signs that tweens are not only eschewing the goody-goody childhood image but its substance as well. . . .

The clearest evidence of tweendom's darker side concerns crime.   12
Although children under 15 still represent a minority of juvenile arrests, their numbers grew disproportionately in the past 20 years. According to a report

[1]Trademark name of patent-leather shoes for girls, usually having a low heel and a strap that fastens at the side (editors' note).

by the Office of Juvenile Justice and Delinquency Prevention, "offenders under age 15 represent the leading edge of the juvenile crime problem, and their numbers are growing." Moreover, the crimes committed by younger teens and preteens are growing in severity. "Person offenses,[2] which once constituted 16 percent of the total court cases for this age group," continues the report, "now constitute 25 percent." Headline grabbers—like Nathaniel Abraham of Pontiac, Michigan, an 11-year-old who stole a rifle from a neighbor's garage and went on a shooting spree in October 1997, randomly killing a teenager coming out of a store; and 11-year-old Andrew Golden, who, with his 13-year-old partner, killed four children and one teacher at his middle school in Jonesboro, Arkansas—are extreme, exceptional cases, but alas, they are part of a growing trend toward preteen violent crime. . . .

The evidence on tween sex presents a troubling picture, too. Despite a 13 decrease among older teens for the first time since records have been kept, sexual activity among tweens increased during that period. It seems that kids who are having sex are doing so at earlier ages. Between 1988 and 1995, the proportion of girls saying they began sex before 15 rose from 11 percent to 19 percent. (For boys, the number remained stable, at 21 percent.) This means that approximately one in five middle-school kids is sexually active. Christie Hogan, a middle-school counselor for 20 years in Louisville, Kentucky, says: "We're beginning to see a few pregnant sixth-graders." Many of the principals and counselors I spoke with reported a small but striking minority of sexually active seventh-graders. . . .

Certainly the days of the tentative and giggly preadolescent seem to be 14 passing. Middle-school principals report having to deal with miniskirted 12-year-olds "draping themselves over boys" or patting their behinds in the hallways, while 11-year-old boys taunt girls about their breasts and rumors about their own and even their parents' sexual proclivities. Tweens have even given new connotations to the word "playground": one fifth-grade teacher from southwestern Ohio told me of two youngsters discovered in the bushes during recess.

Drugs and alcohol are also seeping into tween culture. The past six years 15 have seen more than a doubling of the number of eighth-graders who smoke marijuana (10 percent today) and those who no longer see it as dangerous. "The stigma isn't there the way it was ten years ago," says Dan Kindlon, assistant professor of psychiatry at Harvard Medical School and co-author with Michael Thompson of *Raising Cain*. "Then it was the fringe group smoking pot. You were looked at strangely. Now the fringe group is using LSD."

Aside from sex, drugs, and rock and roll, another teen problem—eating 16 disorders—is also beginning to affect younger kids. This behavior grows out of premature fashion-consciousness, which has an even more pernicious effect on tweens than on teens, because, by definition, younger kids have a more

[2]Crimes against a person. They include assault, robbery, rape, and homicide (editors' note).

vulnerable and insecure self-image. Therapists say they are seeing a growing number of anorexics and obsessive dieters even among late-elementary-school girls. "You go on Internet chat rooms and find ten- and 11-year-olds who know every [fashion] model and every statistic about them," says Nancy Kolodny, a Connecticut-based therapist and author of *When Food's a Foe: How You Can Confront and Conquer Your Eating Disorder.* "Kate Moss is their god. They can tell if she's lost a few pounds or gained a few. If a powerful kid is talking about this stuff at school, it has a big effect."

What change in our social ecology has led to the emergence of tweens? 1 Many note that kids are reaching puberty at earlier ages, but while earlier physical maturation may play a small role in defining adolescence down, its importance tends to be overstated. True, the average age at which girls begin to menstruate has fallen from 13 to between 11 and 12½ today, but the very gradualness of this change means that 12-year-olds have been living inside near-adult bodies for many decades without feeling impelled to build up a cosmetics arsenal or head for the bushes at recess. In fact, some experts believe that the very years that have witnessed the rise of the tween have also seen the age of first menstruation stabilize. Further, teachers and principals on the front lines see no clear correlation between physical and social matu-ration. Plenty of budding girls and bulking boys have not put away childish things, while an abundance of girls with flat chests and boys with squeaky voices ape the body language and fashions of their older siblings. . . .

Of course, the causes are complex, and most people working with tweens 1 know it. In my conversations with educators and child psychologists who work primarily with middle-class kids nationwide, two major and fairly predictable themes emerged: a sexualized and glitzy media-driven marketplace and absen-tee parents. What has been less commonly recognized is that at this age, the two causes combine to augment the authority of the peer group, which in turn both weakens the influence of parents and reinforces the power of the media. Taken together, parental absence, the market, and the peer group form a vicious circle that works to distort the development of youngsters. . . .

Questions for Close Reading

1. What is the selection's thesis? Locate the sentence(s) in which Hymowitz states her main idea. If she doesn't state the thesis explicitly, express it in your own words.
2. According to Hymowitz, what self-image do tweens cultivate? How do they pro-ject this image to others?
3. What physically dangerous behavioral trends does Hymowitz link to the tween phenomenon?
4. According to Hymowitz, what are the primary causes of the tween phenomenon?
5. Refer to your dictionary as needed to define the following words used in the selection: *glowering* (1), *Talmudic* (1), *rites* (1), *demographic* (3), *pragmatic* (5),

ideological (5), *regalia* (8), *donning* (8), *ply* (8), *emblazoned* (10), *de rigueur* (10), *eschewing* (11), *tentative* (14), *proclivities* (14), *connotations* (14), *stigma* (15), *pernicious* (16), *correlation* (17), and *augment* (18).

Questions About the Writer's Craft

1. **The pattern.** Hymowitz opens her essay with an anecdotal example of tween-hood—her daughter's. What does this example add to her essay?
2. **The pattern.** What types of examples does Hymowitz provide in her essay? (See pages 173–174 for a discussion of the various forms that examples can take.) Cite at least one example of each type. How does each type of example contribute to her thesis?
3. How would you characterize Hymowitz's tone in the selection? Cite vocabulary that conveys this tone.
4. **Other patterns.** In paragraph 8, Hymowitz uses clothing as a means of presenting an important *contrast*. What does she contrast in these paragraphs? How does this contribute to her thesis?

Writing Assignments Using Exemplification as a Pattern of Development

1. Hymowitz is troubled and perplexed by her daughter's behavior. Think about an older person, such as a parent or another relative, who finds *your* behavior troubling and perplexing. Write an essay in which you illustrate why your behavior distresses this person. (Or, conversely, think of an elder whose behavior *you* find problematic, and write an essay illustrating why that person evokes this response in you.) You might structure your essay by picking the two or three most irksome characteristics or habits and developing supporting paragraphs around each of them. However you choose to organize your essay, be sure to provide abundant examples throughout.

2. The cultivation of a sophisticated self-image is, according to Hymowitz, a hallmark of tweenhood. Think back to when you were around that age. What was your self-image at that time? Did you think of yourself as worldly or inexperienced? Cool or awkward? Attractive or unappealing? In your journal, freewrite about the traits that you would have identified in yourself as either a tween or an adolescent. Write an essay in which you illustrate your self-image at that age, focusing on two to three dominant characteristics you associated with yourself. It's important that you illustrate each trait with examples of when and how you displayed it. For example, if you saw yourself as "dorky," you might recall an embarrassing time when you tripped and fell in the middle of your school lunchroom. Conclude your essay by reflecting on whether the way you saw yourself at the time was accurate, and whether your feelings about yourself have changed since then. You'd also benefit from reading any of the following authors' musings on their childhood self-perceptions: Maya Angelou's "Sister Flowers" (page 100), Judith Ortiz Cofer's "A Partial Remembrance of a Puerto Rican Childhood" (page 114), Audre Lorde's "The Fourth of July" (page 137), Langston Hughes's "Salvation" (page 155), Beth Johnson's "Bombs Bursting in Air" (page 209), and Alice Walker's "Beauty: When the Other Dancer Is the Self" (page 408).

Writing Assignments Combining Patterns of Development

3. Hymowitz advances a powerful argument about the alarming contemporary trend of tweenhood. But many would disagree with her entirely pessimistic analysis. Write an essay in which you *argue,* contrary to Hymowitz, that tweens today actually exhibit several *positive* characteristics. You might say, for example, that tweens today are more independent or more socially conscious than kids in the past. In order to develop your argument, you'll need to show how each characteristic you're discussing *contrasts* favorably with that characteristic in a previous generation of kids. Be sure, too, to acknowledge opposing arguments as you proceed. Research conducted in the library and/or on the Internet might help you develop your pro-tween argument.

4. Though she doesn't use the term explicitly, Hymowitz points to peer pressure as a significant factor in tweens' premature maturity. In your journal, take a few moments to reflect on your own experiences with peer pressure, whether as a preteen or teen, or even into adulthood. What are some incidents that stand out in your memory? Write an essay *narrating* a particularly memorable incident of peer pressure in which you were involved. You may have been the object of the pressure, or even perhaps the source. What were the circumstances? Who was involved? How did you respond at the time? How did the episode *affect* you? In retrospect, how do you feel about the incident today? Be sure to use dialogue as well as *descriptive* language in order to make the episode come alive.

Writing Assignment Using a Journal Entry as a Starting Point

5. As a way of illustrating her daughter's evolving tween tastes, Hymowitz cites the "years-in-the-making American Girl doll collection" over which her disaffected daughter has now drawn a sheet. Reviewing what you wrote in your pre-reading journal entry, identify some once-loved childhood items or activities that you distanced yourself from as you got older. Write an essay in which you exemplify your growth into adolescence by identifying two or three childhood possessions or activities that you cast off. You might, for example, discuss building up a beloved rock collection or playing with action figures. As you introduce these items, be sure to describe them and to explain the significance they once held for you, as well as your reasons for leaving them behind. Conclude your essay by offering some reflections on whether you currently regard the childhood items with the same distaste or disinterest you felt as a teen.

Beth Johnson

Beth Johnson (1956–) is a writer, occasional college teacher, and freelance editor. A graduate of Goshen College and Syracuse University, Johnson is the author of several college texts, including *Everyday Heroes* (1996) and *Reading Changed My Life* (2003). Containing profiles of men and women who have triumphed over obstacles to achieve personal and academic success, the books have provided a motivational boost to college students nationwide. She is also the coauthor of the textbook *Voices and Values: A Reader for Writers* (2002). She lives with her husband and three children in Lederach, Pennsylvania. The following piece is one of several that Johnson has written about the complexities and wonders of life.

Pre-Reading Journal Entry

When you were young, did adults acknowledge the existence of life's tragedies, or did they deny such harsh truths? In your journal, list several difficult events that you observed or experienced firsthand as a child. How did the adults in your life explain these hardships? In each case, do you think the adults acted appropriately? If not, how should they have responded?

Bombs Bursting in Air

It's Friday night and we're at the Olympics, the Junior Olympics, that is. My son is on a relay-race team competing against fourth-graders from all over the school district. His little sister and I sit high in the stands, trying to pick Isaac out from the crowd of figures milling around on the field during these moments of pre-game confusion. The public address system sputters to life and summons our attention. "And now," the tinny voice rings out, "please join together in the singing of our national anthem." 1

"Oh saaay can you seeeeee," we begin. My arm rests around Maddie's shoulders. I am touching her a lot today, and she notices. "Mom, you're *squishing* me," she chides, wriggling from my grip. I content myself with stroking her hair. News that reached me today makes me need to feel her near. We pipe along, squeaking out the impossibly high note of "land of the freeeeeeeee." Maddie clowns, half-singing, half-shouting the lyrics, hitting the "b's" explosively on "bombs bursting in air." 2

Bombs indeed, I think, replaying the sound of my friend's voice over the phone that afternoon: "Bumped her head sledding. Took her in for an x-ray, 3

just to make sure. There was something strange, so they did more tests . . .
a brain tumor . . . Children's Hospital in Boston Tuesday . . . surgery, yes,
right away. . . ." Maddie's playmate Shannon, only five years old. We'd last
seen her at Halloween, dressed in her blue princess costume, and we'd talked
of Furby and Scooby-Doo and Tootsie Rolls. Now her parents were hurriedly learning a new vocabulary—CAT scans, glioma, pediatric neurosurgery, and frontal lobe.[1] A bomb had exploded in their midst, and, like
troops under attack, they were rallying in response.

The games over, the children and I edge our way out of the school park-   4
ing lot, bumper to bumper with other parents ferrying their families home. I
tell the kids as casually as I can about Shannon. "She'll have to have an operation. It's lucky, really, that they found it by accident this way while it's small."

"I want to send her a present," Maddie announces. "That'd be nice," I   5
say, glad to keep the conversation on a positive note.

But my older son is with us now. Sam, who is thirteen, says, "She'll be   6
OK, though, right?" It's not a question, really; it's a statement that I must
either agree with or contradict. I want to say yes. I want to say of course
she'll be all right. I want them to inhabit a world where five-year-olds do not
develop silent, mysterious growths in their brains, where "malignancy" and
"seizure" are words for *New York Times* crossword puzzles, not for little
girls. They would accept my assurance; they would believe me and sleep well
tonight. But I can't; the bomb that exploded in Shannon's home has sent
splinters of shrapnel into ours as well, and they cannot be ignored or lied
away. "We hope she'll be just fine," I finally say. "She has very good doctors.
She has wonderful parents who are doing everything they can. The tumor is
small. Shannon's strong and healthy."

"*She'll* be OK," says Maddie matter-of-factly. "In school we read about   7
a little boy who had something wrong with his leg and he had an operation
and got better. Can we go to Dairy Queen?"

Bombs on the horizon don't faze Maddie. Not yet. I can just barely   8
remember from my own childhood the sense that still surrounds her, that
feeling of being cocooned within reassuring walls of security and order. Back
then, Monday meant gym, Tuesday was pizza in the cafeteria, Wednesday
brought clarinet lessons. Teachers stood in their familiar spots in the classrooms, telling us with reassuring simplicity that World War II happened
because Hitler, a very bad man, invaded Poland. Midterms and report cards,
summer vacations and new notebooks in September gave a steady rhythm to
the world. It wasn't all necessarily happy—through the years there were poor
grades, grouchy teachers, exclusion from the desired social group, dateless
weekends when it seemed the rest of the world was paired off—but it was

---

[1]A CAT scan is a computerized cross-sectional image of an internal body structure; a glioma is a
tumor in the brain or spinal cord; pediatric neurosurgery is surgery performed on the nerves,
brain, or spinal cord of a child; the frontal lobe is the largest section of the brain (editors' note).

familiar territory where we felt walled off from the really bad things that happened to other people.

There were hints of them, though, even then. Looking back, I recall the 9 tiny shock waves, the tremors from far-off explosions that occasionally rattled our shelter. There was the little girl who was absent for a week and when she returned wasn't living with her mother and stepfather anymore. There was a big girl who threw up in the bathroom every morning and then disappeared from school. A playful, friendly custodian was suddenly fired, and it had something to do with an angry parent. A teacher's husband had a heart attack and died. These were interesting tidbits to report to our families over dinner, mostly out of morbid interest in seeing our parents bite their lips and exchange glances.

As we got older, the bombs dropped closer. A friend's sister was arrest- 10 ed for selling drugs; we saw her mother in tears at church that Sunday. A boy I thought I knew, a school clown with a sweet crooked grin, shot himself in the woods behind his house. A car full of senior boys, going home from a dance where I'd been sent into ecstasy when the cutest of them all greeted me by name, rounded a curve too fast and crashed, killing them. We wept and hugged each other in the halls. Our teachers listened to us grieve and tried to comfort us, but their words came out impatient and almost angry. I realize now that what sounded like anger was a helplessness to teach us lessons we were still too young or too ignorant to learn. For although our sorrow was real, we still had some sense of a protective curtain between us and the bombs. If only, we said. If only she hadn't used drugs. If only he'd told someone how depressed he was. If only they'd been more careful. *We* weren't like them; we were careful. Like magical incantations, we recited the things that we would or wouldn't do in order to protect ourselves from such sad, unnecessary fates.

And then my best friend, a beautiful girl of sixteen, went to sleep one 11 January night and never woke up. I found myself shaken to the core of my being. My grief at the loss of my vibrant, laughing friend was great. But what really tilted my universe was the nakedness of my realization that there was no "if only." There were no drugs, no careless action, no crime, no accident, nothing I could focus on to explain away what had happened. She had simply died. Which could only mean that there was no magic barrier separating me and my loved ones from the bombs. We were as vulnerable as everyone else. For months the shock stayed with me. I sat in class watching my teachers draw diagrams of Saturn, talk about Watergate,[2] multiply fractions, and wondered at their apparent cheer and normalcy. Didn't they *know* we were

[2]In June 1972, supporters of Republican President Richard Nixon were caught breaking into the Democratic campaign headquarters in the Watergate office complex in Washington, D.C. The resulting investigation of the White House connection to the break-in led to President Nixon's eventual resignation in August 1974 (editors' note).

all doomed? Didn't they know it was only a matter of time until one of us took a direct hit? What was the point of anything?

But time moved on, and I moved with it. College came and went, graduate school, adulthood, middle age. My heightened sense of vulnerability began to subside, though I could never again slip fully into the soothing security of my younger days. I became more aware of the intertwining threads of joy, pain, and occasional tragedy that weave through all our lives. College was stimulating, exciting, full of friendship and challenge. I fell in love for the first time, reveled in its sweetness, then learned the painful lesson that love comes with no guarantee. A beloved professor lost two children to leukemia, but continued with skill and passion to introduce students to the riches of literature. My father grew ill, but the last day of his life, when I sat by his bed holding his hand, remains one of my sweetest memories. The marriage I'd entered into with optimism ended in bitter divorce, but produced three children whose existence is my daily delight. At every step along the way, I've seen that the most rewarding chapters of my life have contained parts that I not only would not have chosen, but would have given much to avoid. But selecting just the good parts is not an option we are given.

The price of allowing ourselves to truly live, to love and be loved, is (and it's the ultimate irony) the knowledge that the greater our investment in life, the larger the target we create. Of course, it is within our power to refuse friendship, shrink from love, live in isolation, and thus create for ourselves a nearly impenetrable bomb shelter. There are those among us who choose such an existence, the price of intimacy being too high. Looking about me, however, I see few such examples. Instead, I am moved by the courage with which most of us, ordinary folks, continue soldiering on. We fall in love, we bring our children into the world, we forge our friendships, we give our hearts, knowing with increasing certainty that we do so at our own risk. Still we move ahead with open arms, saying yes, yes to life.

Shannon's surgery is behind her; the prognosis is good. Her mother reports that the family is returning to its normal routines, laughing again and talking of ordinary things, even while they step more gently, speak more quietly, are more aware of the precious fragility of life and of the blessing of every day that passes without explosion.

Bombs bursting in air. They can blind us, like fireworks at the moment of explosion. If we close our eyes and turn away, all we see is their fiery image. But if we have the courage to keep our eyes open and welcoming, even bombs finally fade against the vastness of the starry sky.

Questions for Close Reading

1. What is the selection's thesis? Locate the sentence(s) in which Johnson states her main idea. If she doesn't state the thesis explicitly, express it in your own words.

2. In paragraph 2, Johnson describes her "need to feel her [daughter] near." What compels her to want to be physically close to her daughter? Why do you think Johnson responds this way?

3. In describing her family's responses to Shannon's illness, Johnson presents three reactions: Maddie's, Sam's, and her own. How do these responses differ? In what ways do Maddie's, Sam's, and Johnson's reactions typify the age groups to which they belong?

4. In paragraph 13, Johnson describes two basic ways people respond to life's inevitable "bombs." What are these ways? Which response does Johnson endorse?

5. Refer to your dictionary as needed to define the following words used in the selection: *ferrying* (paragraph 4), *shrapnel* (6), *faze* (8), *cocooned* (8), *tremors* (9), *incantations* (10), *vulnerable* (11), *intertwining* (12), *impenetrable* (13), *soldiering on* (13), *prognosis* (14), and *fragility* (14).

Questions About the Writer's Craft

1. **The pattern.** Although Johnson provides many examples of life's "bombs," she gives more weight to some examples than to others. Which examples does she emphasize? Which ones receive less attention? Why?

2. **Other patterns.** What important *contrast* does Johnson develop in paragraph 6? How does this contrast reinforce the essay's main idea?

3. Writers generally vary sentence structure in an effort to add interest to their work. But in paragraphs 9 and 10, Johnson employs a repetitive sentence structure. Where is the repetition in these two paragraphs? Why do you think she uses this technique?

4. Johnson develops her essay by means of an extended metaphor (see page 76), using bombs as her central image. Identify all the places where Johnson draws upon language and imagery related to bombs and battles. What do you think Johnson hopes to achieve with this sustained metaphor?

Writing Assignments Using Exemplification as a Pattern of Development

1. In paragraphs 9 and 10, Johnson catalogues a number of events that made her increasingly aware of life's bombs. Write an essay of your own, illustrating how you came to recognize the inevitability of painful life events. Start by listing the difficult events you've encountered. Select the three most compelling occurrences, and do some freewriting to generate details about each. Before writing, decide whether you will order your examples chronologically or emphatically; use whichever illustrates more effectively your dawning realization of life's complexity. End with some conclusions about your ability to cope with difficult times.

2. Johnson describes her evolving understanding of life. In an essay of your own, show the way several events combined to change your understanding of a specific aspect of your life. Perhaps a number of incidents prompted you to reconsider career choices, end a relationship, or appreciate the importance of family. Cite only those events that illustrate your emerging understanding. Your decision to use either chronological or emphatic sequence depends on which illustrates more

dramatically the change in your perception. To see how other writers describe their journeys of self-discovery, read Maya Angelou's "Sister Flowers" (page 100), Richard Rodriguez's "Workers" (page 361), Jacques D'Amboise's "Showing What Is Possible" (page 402), and Alice Walker's "Beauty: When the Other Dancer Is the Self" (page 408).

Writing Assignments Combining Patterns of Development

3. Johnson explores the lasting impact the death of her friend had on her life. Write an essay about the *effect* of a *single* bomb on your life. You might *recount* getting left back in school, losing a loved one, seeing the dark side of someone you admired, and so on. Your causal analysis should make clear how the event affected your life. Perhaps the event had painful short-term consequences but positive long-term repercussions. Langston Hughes's "Salvation" (page 155) and Jacques D'Amboise's "Showing What Is Possible" (page 402) provide helpful models for examining the effects of a life-changing event.

4. In an essay, offer readers a *guide* to surviving a specific life calamity. You might, for instance, explain how to survive a pet's death, a painful breakup, a financial hardship. Consider doing some library and/or Internet research on your subject. Combining your own insights with any material gathered through research, *describe* fully the *steps* readers should take to recover from the devastating events.

Writing Assignment Using a Journal Entry as a Starting Point

5. Johnson asserts that painful truths shouldn't "be ignored or lied away" by adults. Do you agree? Write an essay explaining why you think adults should protect children from harsh realities—or why they should present the whole truth, even when it's painful. Review your pre-reading journal entry, searching for strong examples to support your position. Discussing this topic with others will also help you shape your point of view, as will reading Audre Lorde's "The Fourth of July" (page 137) and Yuh Ji-Yeon's "Let's Tell the Story of All America's Cultures" (page 517).

Barbara Ehrenreich

Barbara Ehrenreich (1941–) has been a college professor, investigative reporter, magazine editor, and social activist. A graduate of Reed College, Ehrenreich received her Ph.D. in biology from Rockefeller University. She has cowritten several books, including *For Her Own Good: 150 Years of the Experts' Advice to Women* (1978), *Remaking Love: The Feminization of Sex* (1986), and *Global Woman* (2003). Her more recent books include *Fear of Falling: The Inner Life of the Middle Class* (1989), *The Worst Years of Our Lives* (1990), *Snarling Citizen: Essays* (1995), *Blood Rites* (1997), *Nickle and Dimed* (2001), and the novel *Kipper's Game* (1993). A regular columnist for *Time, The Guardian,* and *The Nation,* Ehrenreich has published articles in many other magazines, such as *Esquire, Vogue,* and the *New Republic.* "What I've Learned From Men" first appeared in *Ms.* in 1985.

Pre-Reading Journal Entry

Drawing upon childhood experiences and recent observations, reflect in your journal about the way children's gender identity is formed. What traits do parents and society tend to encourage in boys? In girls? How do these gendered characteristics benefit and/or hinder boys and girls later in life?

What I've Learned From Men

For many years I believed that women had only one thing to learn from men: how to get the attention of a waiter by some means short of kicking over the table and shrieking. Never in my life have I gotten the attention of a waiter, unless it was an off-duty waiter whose car I'd accidentally scraped in a parking lot somewhere. Men, however, can summon a maître d' just by thinking the word "coffee," and this is a power women would be well-advised to study. What else would we possibly want to learn from them? How to interrupt someone in mid-sentence as if you were performing an act of conversational euthanasia? How to drop a pair of socks three feet from an open hamper and keep right on walking? How to make those weird guttural gargling sounds in the bathroom?

But now, at mid-life, I am willing to admit that there are some real and useful things to learn from men. Not from all men—in fact, we may have the most to learn from some of the men we like the least. This realization does not mean that my feminist principles have gone soft with age: what I think

215

women could learn from men is how to get *tough*. After more than a decade of consciousness-raising, assertiveness training, and hand-to-hand combat in the battle of the sexes, we're still too ladylike. Let me try that again—we're just too *damn* ladylike.

Here is an example from my own experience, a story that I blush to recount. A few years ago, at an international conference held in an exotic and luxurious setting, a prestigious professor invited me to his room for what he said would be an intellectual discussion on matters of theoretical importance. So far, so good. I showed up promptly. But only minutes into the conversation—held in all-too-adjacent chairs—it emerged that he was interested in something more substantial than a meeting of minds. I was disgusted, but not enough to overcome 30-odd years of programming in ladylikeness. Every time his comments took a lecherous turn, I chattered distractingly; every time his hand found its way to my knee, I returned it as if it were something he had misplaced. This went on for an unconscionable period (as much as 20 minutes); then there was a minor scuffle, a dash for the door, and I was out—with nothing violated but my self-esteem. I, a full-grown feminist, conversant with such matters as rape crisis counseling and sexual harassment at the workplace, had behaved like a ninny—or, as I now understand it, like a lady.

The essence of ladylikeness is a persistent servility masked as "niceness." For example, we (women) tend to assume that it is our responsibility to keep everything "nice" even when the person we are with is rude, aggressive, or emotionally AWOL. (In the above example, I was so busy taking responsibility for preserving the veneer of "niceness" that I almost forgot to take responsibility for myself.) In conversations with men, we do almost all the work: sociologists have observed that in male-female social interactions it's the woman who throws out leading questions and verbal encouragements ("So how did you *feel* about that?" and so on) while the man, typically, says "Hmmmm." Wherever we go, we're perpetually smiling—the on-cue smile, like the now-outmoded curtsy, being one of our culture's little rituals of submission. We're trained to feel embarrassed if we're praised, but if we see a criticism coming at us from miles down the road, we rush to acknowledge it. And when we're feeling aggressive or angry or resentful, we just tighten up our smiles or turn them into rueful little moues. In short, we spend a great deal of time acting like wimps.

For contrast, think of the macho stars we love to watch. Think, for example, of Mel Gibson facing down punk marauders in *The Road Warrior* . . . John Travolta swaggering his way through the early scenes of *Saturday Night Fever* . . . or Marlon Brando shrugging off the local law in *The Wild One*. Would they simper their way through tight spots? Chatter aimlessly to keep the conversation going? Get all clutched up whenever they think they might—just might—have hurt someone's feelings? No, of course not, and therein, I think, lies their fascination for us.

The attraction of the "tough guy" is that he has—or at least seems to
have—what most of us lack, and that is an aura of power and control. In an
article, feminist psychiatrist Jean Baker Miller writes that "a woman's using
self-determined power for herself is equivalent to selfishness [and] destructiveness"—an equation that makes us want to avoid even the appearance of
power. Miller cites cases of women who get depressed just when they're on
the verge of success—and of women who do succeed and then bury their
achievement in self-deprecation. As an example, she describes one company's
periodic meetings to recognize outstanding salespeople: when a woman is
asked to say a few words about her achievement, she tends to say something
like, "Well, I really don't know how it happened. I guess I was just lucky this
time." In contrast, the men will cheerfully own up to the hard work, intelligence, and so on, to which they owe their success. By putting herself down,
a woman avoids feeling brazenly powerful and potentially "selfish"; she also
does the traditional lady's work of trying to make everyone else feel better
("She's not really so smart, after all, just lucky").   6

So we might as well get a little tougher. And a good place to start is
by cutting back on the small acts of deference that we've been programmed
to perform since girlhood. Like unnecessary smiling. For many women—
waitresses, flight attendants, receptionists—smiling is an occupational requirement, but there's no reason for anyone to go around grinning when she's
not being paid for it. I'd suggest that we save our off-duty smiles for when
we truly feel like sharing them, and if you're not sure what to do with your
face in the meantime, study Clint Eastwood's expressions—both of them.   7

Along the same lines, I think women should stop taking responsibility
for every human interaction we engage in. In a social encounter with a
woman, the average man can go 25 minutes saying nothing more than "You
don't say?" "Izzat so?" and, of course, "Hmmmm." Why should we do all
the work? By taking so much responsibility for making conversations go well,
we act as if we had much more at stake in the encounter than the other
party—and that gives him (or her) the power advantage. Every now and
then, we deserve to get more out of a conversation than we put into it: I'd
suggest not offering information you'd rather not share ("I'm really terrified
that my sales plan won't work") and not, out of sheer politeness, soliciting
information you don't really want ("Wherever did you get that lovely tie?").
There will be pauses, but they don't have to be awkward for *you*.   8

It is true that some, perhaps most, men will interpret any decrease in
female deference as a deliberate act of hostility. Omit the free smiles and
perky conversation-boosters and someone is bound to ask, "Well, what's
come over *you* today?" For most of us, the first impulse is to stare at our feet
and make vague references to a terminally ill aunt in Atlanta, but we should
have as much right to be taciturn as the average (male) taxi driver. If you're
taking a vacation from smiles and small talk and some fellow is moved to   9

inquire about what's "bothering" you, just stare back levelly and say, the international debt crisis, the arms race, or the death of God.

There are all kinds of ways to toughen up—and potentially move up— 10 at work, and I leave the details to the purveyors of assertiveness training. But Jean Baker Miller's study underscores a fundamental principle that anyone can master on her own. We can stop acting less capable than we actually are. For example, in the matter of taking credit when credit is due, there's a key difference between saying "I was just lucky" and saying "I had a plan and it worked." If you take the credit you deserve, you're letting people know that you were confident you'd succeed all along, and that you fully intend to do so again.

Finally, we may be able to learn something from men about what to do 11 with anger. As a general rule, women get irritated: men get *mad*. We make tight little smiles of ladylike exasperation; they pound on desks and roar. I wouldn't recommend emulating the full basso profundo male tantrum, but women do need ways of expressing justified anger clearly, colorfully, and, when necessary, crudely. If you're not just irritated, but *pissed off*, it might help to say so.

I, for example, have rerun the scene with the prestigious professor many 12 times in my mind. And in my mind, I play it like Bogart. I start by moving my chair over to where I can look the professor full in the face. I let him do the chattering, and when it becomes evident that he has nothing serious to say, I lean back and cross my arms, just to let him know that he's wasting my time. I do not smile, neither do I nod encouragement. Nor, of course, do I respond to his blandishments with apologetic shrugs and blushes. Then, at the first flicker of lechery, I stand up and announce coolly, "All right, I've had enough of this crap." Then I walk out—slowly, deliberately, confidently. Just like a man.

Or—now that I think of it—just like a woman. 1

Questions for Close Reading

1. What is the selection's thesis? Locate the sentence(s) in which Ehrenreich states her main idea. If she doesn't state the thesis explicitly, express it in your own words.
2. Why did Ehrenreich handle the lecherous professor as she did? In retrospect, how does she wish she had dealt with the situation? How does her current perspective of the way she should have behaved reinforce her thesis in the essay?
3. What does "behaving like a lady" mean, according to Ehrenreich? What is her opinion of "ladylike" behavior?
4. Why, in Ehrenreich's view, do we like "macho stars" (paragraph 5)? What can we learn from them?
5. Refer to your dictionary as needed to define the following words used in the selection: *euthanasia* (paragraph 1), *guttural* (1), *lecherous* (3), *distractingly* (3), *unconscionable* (3), *ninny* (3), *servility* (4), *veneer* (4), *moues* (4), *marauders* (5),

aura (6), *brazenly* (6), *deference* (9), *taciturn* (9), *purveyors* (10), *emulating* (11), *basso profundo* (11), and *blandishments* (12).

Questions About the Writer's Craft

1. **The pattern.** In paragraphs 3 and 12, Ehrenreich uses her own personal experience as a key example. Why do you think she chooses to include this example? Why do you suppose she presents it so early in the essay and then returns to it at the end?

2. **Other patterns.** Locate places in the essay where Ehrenreich uses examples to *contrast* the different responses and behaviors of males and females. How do these contrasts help the writer develop her main idea?

3. Do you think that Ehrenreich is speaking primarily to a male or to a female audience? What in the essay makes you feel this way? Do you think that the author expects her audience to be positive, hostile, or neutral toward her ideas? What in the essay leads you to this conclusion?

4. In her attack on "ladylikeness," Ehrenreich deliberately avoids using a "ladylike" or "nice" tone. Which of her phrases or expressions seem to defy stereotypes about the way "ladies" should express themselves?

Writing Assignments Using Exemplification as a Pattern of Development

1. If, as Ehrenreich suggests, women have much to learn from men, is it also true that men could learn from women? Write an essay illustrating your belief that men would indeed be better off if they acquired some attitudes and behaviors traditionally associated with women. Be sure to provide numerous examples from your own experience and observations. You may take a humorous or serious approach when showing that men should—in some respects—become more like women. Dave Barry's "The Ugly Truth About Beauty" (page 368) may spark some insight into characteristically male and female behavioral patterns.

2. Ehrenreich points to the popularity of several "macho stars": Mel Gibson in *The Road Warrior,* John Travolta in *Saturday Night Fever,* Marlon Brando in *The Wild One,* and Clint Eastwood in anything. Choose several female characters from film or television who you feel provide positive role models for both males and females. Write an essay in which you use these characters as examples of the way that men and women should conduct their lives. Before writing, consider reading Maya Angelou's "Sister Flowers" (page 100), a loving portrait of a memorable female role model.

Writing Assignments Combining Patterns of Development

3. Ehrenreich suggests that some of the problems women experience in relationships and careers are of their own making—they smile too much, are too deferential, and fail to claim their own achievements. Pick one or two areas in which women tend to experience difficulty and write an essay *arguing* either that women sabotage themselves or that they are sabotaged by society's attitudes and

expectations. Brainstorm with others to gather ideas and *examples* for your paper. For other perspectives, you may want to read one or more of the following essays: Dave Barry's "The Ugly Truth About Beauty" (page 368), Camille Paglia's "Rape: A Bigger Danger Than Feminists Know" (page 541), Susan Jacoby's "Common Decency" (page 547), and Virginia Woolf's "Professions for Women" (page 588).

4. Like Ehrenreich, most of us have been subjected at one time or another to the inappropriate or unpleasant behavior of others: slurs on our abilities, interests, or appearance; derision about our sex or sexual preference; taunts about our race, religion, or ethnic background. Focus on *one category* of insult, and brainstorm with others to identify *ways* for dealing with such an affront. Then write an essay describing different *strategies* for coping with the offensive behavior. Reach some conclusions about which approach is most effective. Caroline Rego's "The Fine Art of Complaining" (page 327) may spark some ideas worth exploring.

Writing Assignment Using a Journal Entry as a Starting Point

5. Drawing upon your pre-reading journal entry, write an essay in which you compare and/or contrast the qualities that parents and the culture at large nurture in boys with those they nurture in girls. Brainstorming with others will help you identify telling examples. Reach some conclusions about the long-term effects on children of these parental and societal influences. Consider supplementing your informal research with library and/or Internet information about the formation of children's gender identity.

Additional Writing Topics

EXEMPLIFICATION

General Assignments

Use examples to develop any one of the following topics into a well-organized essay. When writing the paper, choose enough relevant examples to support your thesis. Organize the material into a sequence that most effectively illustrates the thesis, keeping in mind that emphatic order is often the most compelling way to present specifics.

1. Many of today's drivers have dangerous habits.
2. Drug and alcohol abuse is (or is not) a serious problem among many young people.
3. One rule of restaurant dining is "Management often seems oblivious to problems that are perfectly obvious to customers."
4. Children today are not encouraged to use their imaginations.
5. The worst kind of hypocrite is a religious hypocrite.
6. The best things in life are definitely not free.
7. A part-time job is an important experience that every college student should have.
8. The Internet has resulted in a generation of lazy young people.
9. _____ (name someone you know well) is a _____ (use a quality: open-minded, dishonest, compulsive, reliable, gentle, and so on) person.
10. Television commercials stereotype the elderly (or another minority group).
11. Today, salespeople act as if they're doing you a favor by taking your money.
12. Most people behave decently in their daily interactions with each other.
13. Pettiness, jealousy, and selfishness abound in our daily interactions with each other.
14. You can tell a lot about people by observing what they wear and eat.
15. Too many Americans are overly concerned/completely unconcerned with being physically fit.
16. There are several study techniques that will help a student learn more efficiently.
17. Some teachers seem to enjoy turning tests into ordeals.
18. "How to avoid bad eating habits" is one course all college students should take.
19. More needs to be done to eliminate obstacles faced by the physically handicapped.
20. Some of the best presents are those that cost the least.

Assignments With a Specific Purpose, Audience, and Point of View

On Campus

1. Lately, many people at your college have been experiencing stress. As a member of the Student Life Committee, you've been asked to prepare a pamphlet illustrating

221

strategies for reducing different kinds of stress. Decide which stresses to discuss, and explain coping strategies for each, providing helpful examples as you go.

2. A friend of yours will be going away to college in an unfamiliar environment— in a bustling urban setting or in a quiet rural one. To help your friend prepare for this new environment, write a letter giving examples of what life on an urban or a rural campus is like. You might focus on the benefits and dangers with which your friend is unlikely to be familiar.

At Home or in the Community

3. Shopping for a new car, you become annoyed at how many safety features are available only as expensive options. Write a letter of complaint to the auto manufacturer, citing at least three examples of such options. Avoid sounding hostile.

4. A pet food company is having an annual contest to choose a new animal to feature in its advertising. To win the contest, you must convince the company that your pet is personable, playful, and unique. Write an essay giving examples of your pet's special qualities.

On the Job

5. Assume that you're an elementary school principal planning to give a speech in which you'll try to convince parents that television distorts children's perceptions of reality. Write the speech, illustrating your point with vivid examples.

6. The online publication you work for has asked you to write an article on what you consider to be the "three best consumer products of the past twenty-five years." Support your opinion with lively, engaging specifics that are consistent with the website's offbeat and slightly ironic tone.

DIVISION-CLASSIFICATION

WHAT IS DIVISION-CLASSIFICATION?

Imagine what life would be like if this is how an average day unfolded:

You plan to stop at the supermarket for only five items, but your marketing takes over an hour because all the items in the store are jumbled together. Clerks put new shipments anywhere they please; the milk might be with the vegetables on Monday but with laundry detergent on Thursday. Next, you go to the drugstore to pick up some photos you left to be developed. You don't have time, though, to wait while the cashier roots through the large carton into which all the pickup envelopes have been thrown. You return to your car and decide to stop at the town hall to pay a parking ticket. But the town hall baffles you. The offices are unmarked, and there's not even a directory to tell you on which floor the Violations Bureau can be found. Annoyed, you get back into your car and, minutes later, end up colliding with another car, which is driving toward you in your lane. When you wake up in the hospital, you find there are three other patients in your room: a middle-aged man with a heart problem, a young boy ready to have his tonsils removed, and a woman about to go into labor.

Such a muddled world, lacking the most basic forms of organization, would make daily life chaotic. All of us instinctively look for ways to order our environment. Without systems, categories, or sorting mechanisms, we'd be overwhelmed by life's complexity. An organization such as a college or university, for example, is made manageable by being divided into various schools (Liberal Arts, Performing Arts, Engineering, and so on). The schools are then separated into departments (English, History, Political Science), and each department's offerings are grouped into distinct categories—English, for instance, into Literature and Composition—before being further divided into specific courses.

The kind of ordering system we've been discussing is called *division-classification*, a logical way of thinking that allows us to make sense of a complex world. Division and classification, though separate processes, are often used together as complementary techniques. *Division* involves taking a single unit or concept, breaking the unit down into its parts, and then analyzing the connections among the parts and between the parts and the whole. For instance, if we wanted to organize the chaotic hospital described at the start of the chapter, we might think about how the single concept "a hospital" could be broken down into its components. We might come up with the following breakdown: pediatric wing, cardiac wing, maternity wing, and so on.

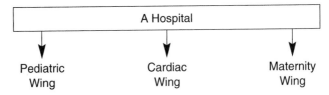

What we have just done involves division: We've taken a single entity (a hospital) and divided it into some of its component parts (wings), each with its own facilities and patients.

In contrast, *classification* brings two or more related items together and categorizes them according to type or kind. If the disorganized supermarket described earlier were to be restructured, the clerks would have to classify the separate items arriving at the loading dock. Cartons of lettuce, tomatoes, cucumbers, butter, yogurt, milk, shampoo, conditioner, and styling gel would be assigned to the appropriate categories:

HOW DIVISION-CLASSIFICATION FITS
YOUR PURPOSE AND AUDIENCE

The reorganized hospital and supermarket show the way division and classification work in everyday life. But division and classification also come into play during the writing process. Because division involves breaking a subject into parts, it can be a helpful strategy during prewriting, especially if you're analyzing a broad, complex subject: the structure of a film; the motivation of a character in a novel; the problem your community has with vandalism; the controversy surrounding school prayer. An editorial examining a recent hostage crisis, for example, might divide the crisis into three areas: how the hostages were treated by (1) their captors, (2) the governments negotiating their release, and (3) the media. The purpose of the editorial might be to show readers that the governments' treatment of the hostages was particularly exploitative.

Classification can be useful for imposing order on the hodgepodge of ideas generated during prewriting. You examine that material to see which of your rough ideas are alike and which are dissimilar, so that you can cluster related items in the same category. Classification would, then, be a helpful strategy in analyzing topics like these: techniques for impressing teachers; comic styles of talk-show hosts; views on abortion; reasons for the current rise in volunteerism. You might, for instance, use classification in a paper showing that Americans are undermining their health through their obsessive pursuit of various diets. Perhaps you begin by brainstorming all the diets that have gained popularity in recent years (Atkins, South Beach, Zone, whatever). Then you categorize the diets according to type: high-fiber, low-protein, high-carbohydrate, and so on. Once the diets are grouped, you can discuss the problems within each category, demonstrating to readers why some of the diets may not be safe or effective.

Division-classification can be crucial when responding to college assignments like the following:

> From your observations, what kinds of appeals do television advertisers use when selling automobiles? In your view, are any of these appeals morally irresponsible?

> Analyze the components that go into being an effective parent. Indicate those you consider most vital for raising confident, well-adjusted children.

> Describe the hierarchy of the typical high school clique, identifying the various parts of the hierarchy. Use your analysis to support or refute the view that adolescence is a period of rigid conformity.

> Many social commentators have observed that discourtesy is on the rise. Indicate whether you think this is a valid observation by characterizing the types of everyday encounters you have with people.

These assignments suggest division-classification through the use of such words as *kinds, components, parts,* and *types.* Generally, though, you won't receive such clear signals to use division-classification. Instead, the broad purpose of the essay—and the point you want to make—will lead you to the analytical thinking characteristic of division-classification.

Sometimes division-classification will be the dominant technique for structuring an essay; other times it will be used as a supplemental pattern in an essay organized primarily according to another pattern of development. Let's look at some examples. Say you want to write a paper *explaining a process* (surviving divorce; creating a hit record; shepherding a bill through Congress; using the Heimlich maneuver on people who are choking). You could *divide* the process into parts or stages, showing, for instance, that the Heimlich maneuver is an easily mastered skill that readers should acquire. Or perhaps you plan to write a light-spirited essay analyzing the *effect* that increased awareness of sexual stereotypes has had on college students' social lives. In such a case, you might use *classification.* To show readers that shifting gender roles make young men and women comically self-conscious, you could categorize the places where students scout each other out: in class, at the library, at parties, in dorms. You could then show how students—not wishing to be macho or coyly feminine—approach each other with laughable tentativeness in these four environments.

Now imagine that you're writing an *argumentation-persuasion* essay urging that the federal government prohibit the use of growth-inducing antibiotics in livestock feed. The paper could begin by *dividing* the antibiotics cycle into stages: the effects of antibiotics on livestock; the short-term effects on humans who consume the animals; the possible long-term effects of consuming antibiotic-tainted meat. To increase readers' understanding of the problem, you might also discuss the antibiotics controversy in terms of an even larger issue: the dangerous ways food is treated before being consumed. In this case, you would consider the various procedures (use of additives, preservatives, artificial colors, and so on), *classifying* these treatments into several types—from least harmful (some additives or artificial colors, perhaps) to most harmful (you might slot the antibiotics here). Such an essay would be developed using both division *and* classification: first, the division of the antibiotics cycle and then the classification of the various food treatments. Frequently, this interdependence will be reversed, and classification will precede rather than follow division.

At this point, you have a good sense of the way writers use division-classification to achieve their purpose and to connect with their readers. Now take a moment to look closely at the photograph at the beginning of this chapter. Imagine you're writing an article, accompanied by the photo, for a parenting magazine. Your purpose is twofold: to alert parents to the danger of pushing young children to achieve, and to help parents foster in chil- dren healthy attitudes toward achievement. Jot down some ideas you might include when *dividing* and/or *classifying* things parents should and shouldn't do to foster a balanced view of accomplishment and success in youngsters.

SUGGESTIONS FOR USING DIVISION-CLASSIFICATION IN AN ESSAY

The following suggestions will be helpful whether you use division-classification as a dominant or a supportive pattern of development.

1. Select a principle of division-classification consistent with your purpose. Most subjects can be divided or classified according to a *number of different principles*. For example, when writing about an ideal vacation, you could divide your subject according to any of these principles: location, cost, recreation available. Similarly, when analyzing students at your college, you could base your classification on a variety of principles: students' majors, their racial or ethnic background, whether they belong to a fraternity or sorority. In all cases, though, the principle of division-classification you select must meet one stringent requirement: It must help you meet your overall purpose and reinforce your central point.

Sometimes a principle of division-classification seems so attractive that you latch on to it without examining whether it's consistent with your pur-pose. Suppose you want to write a paper asserting that several episodes of a new television comedy are destined to become classics. Here's how you might go wrong.

You begin by doing some brainstorming about the episodes. Then, as you start to organize the prewriting material, you hit on a possible principle of classification: grouping the characters in the show according to the frequency with which they appear (main characters appearing in every show, supporting characters appearing in most shows, and guest characters appearing once or twice). You name the characters and explain which characters fit where. But is this principle of classification significant? Has it anything to do with why the shows will become classics? No, it hasn't. Such an essay would be little more than a meaningless exercise in classifying things just to classify them.

In contrast, a significant principle of classification might involve categorizing a number of shows according to the easily recognized human types portrayed: the Pompous Know-It-All, the Boss Who's Out of Control, the Lovable Grouch, the Surprisingly Savvy Innocent. You might illustrate the way certain episodes offer delightful twists on these stock figures, making such shows models of comic plotting and humor.

When you write an essay that uses division-classification as its primary method of development, a *single principle* of division-classification provides the foundation for each major section of the paper. Imagine you're writing an essay showing that the success of contemporary music groups has less to do with musical talent than with the groups' ability to market themselves to a distinct segment of the listening audience. To develop your point, you might categorize several performers according to the age ranges they appeal to (preteens, adolescents, people in their late twenties) and then analyze the marketing strategies the musicians use to gain their fans' support. The essay's logic would be undermined if you switched, in the middle of your analysis, to another principle of classification—say, the influence of earlier groups on today's music scene.

Don't, however, take this caution to mean that essays can never use more than one principle of division-classification as they unfold. They can— as long as the *shift from one principle to another* occurs in *different parts* of the paper. Imagine you want to write about widespread disillusionment with student government leaders at your college. You could develop this point by breaking down the dissatisfaction into the following: disappointment with the students' qualifications for office; disenchantment with their campaign tactics; frustration with their performance once elected. That section of the essay completed, you might move to a second principle of division—how students can get involved in campus government. Perhaps you break the proposed involvement into the following possibilities: serving on nominating committees; helping to run candidates' campaigns; attending open sessions of the student government.

2. Apply the principle of division-classification logically.   In an essay using division-classification, you need to demonstrate to readers that your analysis is the result of careful thought. First of all, your division-classification should be as *complete* as possible. Your analysis should include—within reason—all the parts into which you can divide your subject, or all the types into which you can categorize your subjects. Let's say you're writing an essay showing that where college students live is an important factor in determining how satisfied they are with college life. Keeping your purpose in mind, you classify students according to where they live: with parents, in dorms, in fraternity and sorority houses. But what about all the students who live in rented apartments, houses, or rooms off campus? If these places of residence are ignored, your classification won't be complete; you will lose credibility with your readers because they'll probably realize that you have overlooked several important considerations.

Your division-classification should also be *consistent:* The parts into which you break your subject or the groups into which you place your subjects should be as mutually exclusive as possible. The parts or categories should not be mixed, nor should they overlap. Assume you're writing an essay describing the animals at the zoo in a nearby city. You decide to describe the zoo's mammals, reptiles, birds, and endangered species. But such a classification is inconsistent. You begin by categorizing the animals according to scientific class (mammals, birds, reptiles), then switch to another principle when you classify some animals according to whether they are endangered. Because you drift over to a different principle of classification, your categories are no longer mutually exclusive: Endangered species could overlap with any of the other categories. In which section of the paper, for instance, would you describe an exotic parrot that is obviously a bird but is also nearly extinct? And how would you categorize the zoo's rare mountain gorilla? This impressive creature is a mammal, but it is also an endangered species. Such overlapping categories undercut the logic that gives an essay its integrity.

A helpful tip: A solid outline is invaluable when you use division-classification. The outline encourages you to do the rigorous thinking needed to arrive at divisions and classifications that are logical, complete, and consistent.

3. Prepare an effective thesis.   If your essay uses division-classification as its dominant method of development, it might be helpful to prepare a thesis that does more than signal the paper's subject and suggest your attitude toward that general subject. You might also want the thesis to state the principle of division-classification at the heart of the essay. Furthermore, you might want the thesis to reveal which part or category you regard as most important.

Consider the two thesis statements that follow:

As the observant beachcomber moves from the tidal area to the upper beach to the sandy dunes, rich variations in marine life become apparent.

Although most people focus on the dangers associated with the disposal of toxic waste in the land and ocean, the incineration of toxic matter may pose an even more serious threat to human life.

The first thesis statement makes clear that the writer will organize the paper by classifying forms of marine life according to location. Because the purpose of the essay is to inform as objectively as possible, the thesis doesn't suggest the writer's opinion about which category is most significant.

The second thesis signals that the essay will evolve by dividing the issue of toxic waste according to methods of disposal. Moreover, because the paper takes a stance on a controversial subject, the thesis is worded to reveal which aspect of the topic the writer considers most important. Such a clear statement of the writer's position is an effective strategy in an essay of this kind.

You may have noted that each thesis statement also signals the paper's plan of development. The first essay, for example, will use specific facts, examples, and details to describe the kinds of marine life found in the tidal area, upper beach, and dunes. However, thesis statements in papers developed primarily through division-classification don't have to be so structured. If a paper is well written, your principle of division-classification, your opinion about which part or category is most important, and the essay's plan of development will become apparent as the essay unfolds.

4. Organize the paper logically.   Whether your paper is developed wholly or in part by division-classification, it should have a logical structure. As much as possible, you should try to discuss *comparable points* in each section of the paper. In the essay on seashore life, for example, you might describe life in the tidal area by discussing the mollusks, crustaceans, birds, and amphibians that live or feed there. You would then follow through, as much as you could, with this arrangement in the paper's other sections (upper beach and dune). Forgetting to describe the bird life thriving in the dunes, especially when you had discussed bird life in the tidal and upper-beach areas, would compromise the paper's structure. Of course, perfect parallelism is not always possible—there are no mollusks in the dunes, for instance. You should also use *signal devices* to connect various parts of the paper: "*Another* characteristic of marine life battered by the tides"; "A *final* important trait of both tidal and upper-beach crustaceans"; "*Unlike* the creatures of the tidal area and the upper beach." Such signals clarify the connections among the essay's ideas.

5. State any conclusions or recommendations in the paper's final section.   The analytic thinking that occurs during division-classification often leads to surprising insights. Such insights may be introduced early on, or they may be reserved for the end, where they are stated as conclusions or recommendations. A paper might categorize different kinds of coaches—from inspiring to incompetent—and make the point that athletes learn a great deal about human relations simply by having to get along with their coaches, regardless of the coaches' skills. Such a paper might conclude that participation in a team sport teaches more about human nature than several courses in psychology. Or the essay might end with a proposal: Rookies and seasoned team members should be paired so that novice players can get advice on dealing with coaching eccentricities.

REVISION STRATEGIES

Once you have a draft of the essay, you're ready to revise. The following checklist will help you and those giving you feedback apply to division-classification some of the revision techniques discussed on pages 60–62.

☑ DIVISION-CLASSIFICATION: A REVISION/PEER REVIEW CHECKLIST

Revise Overall Meaning and Structure

❑ What is the principle of division-classification at the heart of the essay? How does this principle contribute to the essay's overall purpose and thesis?

❑ Does the thesis state the essay's principle of division-classification? Should it? Does the thesis signal which part or category is most important? Should it? Does the thesis reveal the essay's plan of development? Should it?

❑ Is the essay organized primarily through division, classification, or a blend of both?

❑ If the essay is organized mainly through division, is the subject sufficiently complex to be broken down into parts? What are the parts?

❑ If the essay is organized mainly through classification, what are the categories? How does this categorizing reveal similarities and/or differences that would otherwise not be apparent?

Revise Paragraph Development

❑ Are comparable points discussed in each of the paper's sections? What are these points?

❑ In which paragraphs does the division-classification seem illogical, incomplete, or inconsistent? In which paragraphs are parts or categories not clearly explained?

❑ Are the subject's different parts or categories discussed in separate paragraphs? Is there any overlap among categories?

Revise Sentences and Words

❑ What signal devices help integrate the paper? Are there enough signals? Too many?

❑ Where should sentences and words be made more specific in order to clarify the parts and categories being discussed?

STUDENT ESSAY

The following student essay was written by Gail Oremland in response to this assignment:

> In "Propaganda Techniques in Today's Advertising," Ann McClintock describes the flaws in many of the persuasive strategies used by advertisers. Choose another group of people whose job is also to communicate—for example, parents, bosses, teachers. Then, in an essay of your own, divide the group into types according to the flaws they make when communicating.

While reading Gail's paper, try to determine how effectively it applies the principles of division-classification. The annotations on Gail's paper and the commentary following it will help you look at the essay more closely.

The Truth About College Teachers
by Gail Oremland

Introduction

A recent TV news story told about a group of college professors from a nearby university who were hired by a local school system to help upgrade the teaching in the community's public schools. The professors were to visit classrooms, analyze teachers' skills, and then conduct workshops to help the teachers become more effective at their jobs. But after the first round of workshops, the superintendent of schools decided to cancel the whole project. He fired the learned professors and sent them back to their ivory tower. Why did the project fall apart? There was a simple reason. The college professors, who were supposedly going to show the public school teachers how to be more effective, were themselves poor teachers. Many college students could have predicted such a disastrous outcome. They know, firsthand, that college teachers are strange. They know that professors

Thesis

often exhibit bizarre behaviors, relating to students in ways that make it difficult for students to stay awake, or--if awake--to learn.

Topic sentence

The first of three paragraphs on the first category of teacher

One type of professor assumes, legitimately enough, that her function is to pass on to students the vast store of knowledge she has acquired. But because the "Knowledgeable One" regards herself as an expert and her students as the ignorant masses, she adopts an elitist approach that sabotages learning. The Knowledgeable One enters a lecture hall with a self-important air, walks to the podium, places her yellowed-with-age notes on the stand, and begins her lecture at the exact second the class is officially scheduled to begin.

1

2

The first paragraph in a three-part chronological sequence: What happens *before* class

There can be a blizzard or hurricane raging outside the lecture hall; students can be running through freezing sleet and howling winds to get to class on time. Will the Knowledgeable One wait for them to arrive before beginning her lecture? Probably not. The Knowledgeable One's time is precious. She's there, set to begin, and that's what matters.

Topic sentence

The second paragraph on the first category of teacher

The second paragraph in the chronological sequence: What happens *during* class

Once the monologue begins, the Knowledgeable One drones on and on. The Knowledgeable One is a fact person. She may be the history prof who knows the death toll of every Civil War battle, the biology prof who can diagram all the common biological molecules, the accounting prof who enumerates every clause of the federal tax form. Oblivious to students' glazed eyes and stifled yawns, the Knowledgeable One delivers her monologue, dispensing one dry fact after another. The only advantage to being on the receiving end of this boring monologue is that students do not have to worry about being called on to question a point or provide an opinion; the Knowledgeable One is not willing to relinquish one minute of her time by giving students a voice. Assume for one improbable moment that a student actually manages to stay awake during the monologue and is brave enough to ask a question. In such a case, the Knowledgeable One will address the questioning student as "Mr." or "Miss." This formality does not, as some students mistakenly suppose, indicate respect for the student as a fledgling member of the academic community. Not at all. This impersonality represents the Knowledgeable One's desire to keep as wide a distance as possible between her and her students.

3

Topic sentence

The third paragraph on the first category of teacher

The final paragraph in the chronological sequence: What happens *after* class

The Knowledgeable One's monologue always comes to a close at the precise second the class is scheduled to end. No sooner has she delivered her last forgettable word than the Knowledgeable One packs up her notes and shoots out the door, heading back to the privacy of her office, where she can pursue her specialized academic interests--free of any possible interruption from students. The Knowledgeable One's hasty departure from the lecture hall makes it clear she has no desire to talk with students. In her eyes, she has met her obligations; she has taken time away from her research to transmit to students what she knows. Any closer contact might mean she would risk contagion from students, that great unwashed mass. Such a danger is to be avoided at all costs.

4

Topic sentence

Unlike the Knowledgeable One, the "Leader of Intellectual Discussion" seems to respect students. Emphasizing class discussion, the Leader encourages students to confront ideas ("What is Twain's view of morality?" "Was our intervention in Iraq justified?" "Should big business be given tax breaks?") and discover their own truths. Then, about three weeks into

5

Paragraph on the second category of teacher

the semester, it becomes clear that the Leader wants students to discover <u>his</u> version of the truth. Behind the Leader's democratic guise lurks a dictator. When a student voices an opinion that the Leader accepts, the student is rewarded by hearty nods of approval and "Good point, good point." But if a student is rash enough to advance a conflicting viewpoint, the Leader responds with killing politeness: "Well, yes, that's an interesting perspective. But don't you think that . . . ?" Grade-conscious students soon learn not to chime in with their viewpoint. They know that when the Leader, with seeming honesty, says, "I'd be interested in hearing what you think. Let's open this up for discussion," they had better figure out what the Leader wants to hear before advancing their own theories. "Me-tooism" rather than independent thinking, they discover, guarantees good grades in the Leader's class.

Topic sentence ———→

Paragraph on the third category of teacher

Then there is the professor who comes across as the students' "Buddy." This kind of professor does not see himself as an imparter of knowledge or a leader of discussion but as a pal, just one in a community of equals. The Buddy may start his course this way. "All of us know that this college stuff--grades, degrees, exams, required reading--is a game. So let's not play it, okay?" Dressed in jeans, sweatshirt, and scuffed sneakers, the Buddy projects a relaxed, casual attitude. He arranges the class seats in a circle (he would never take a position in front of the room) and insists that students call him by his first name. He uses no syllabus and gives few tests, believing that such constraints keep students from directing their own learning. A free spirit, the Buddy often teaches courses like "The Psychology of Interpersonal Relations" or "The Social Dynamics of the Family." If students choose to use class time to discuss the course material, that's fine. If they want to discuss something else, that's fine, too. It's the self-expression, the honest dialogue, that counts. In fact, the Buddy seems especially fond of digressions from academic subjects. By talking about his political views, his marital problems, his tendency to drink one too many beers, the Buddy lets students see that he is a regular guy--just like them. At first, students look forward to classes with the Buddy. They enjoy the informality, the chitchat, the lack of pressure. But after a while, they wonder why they are paying for a course where they learn nothing. They might as well stay home and watch the soaps.

6

Conclusion

Echoes opening anecdote

Obviously, some college professors are excellent. They are learned, hardworking, and imaginative; they enjoy their work and like being with students. On the whole, though, college professors are a strange lot. Despite their advanced degrees and their own exposure to many different kinds of teachers, they do not seem to understand how to relate to students.

7

Rather than being hired as consultants to help others upgrade their teaching skills, college professors should themselves hire consultants to tell them what they are doing wrong and how they can improve. Who should these consultants be? That's easy: the people who know them best--their students.

COMMENTARY

Introduction and thesis.   After years of being graded by teachers, Gail took special pleasure in writing an essay that gave her a chance to evaluate her teachers—in this case, her college professors. Even the essay's title, "The Truth About College Teachers," implies that Gail is going to have fun knocking profs down from their ivory towers. To introduce her subject, she uses a timely news story. This brief anecdote leads directly to the essay's *thesis:* "Professors often exhibit bizarre behaviors, relating to students in ways that make it difficult for students to stay awake, or—if awake—to learn." Note that Gail's thesis isn't highly structured; it doesn't, for example, name the specific categories to be discussed. Still, her thesis suggests that the essay is going to *categorize* a range of teaching behaviors, using as a *principle of classification* the strange ways that college profs relate to students.

Purpose.   As with all good papers developed through division-classification, Gail's essay doesn't use classification as an end in itself. Gail uses classification because it helps her achieve a broader *purpose*. She wants to *convince* readers—without moralizing or abandoning her humorous tone—that such teaching styles inhibit learning. In other words, there's a serious underside to her essay. This additional layer of meaning is characteristic of satiric writing.

Categories and topic sentences.   The essay's body, consisting of five paragraphs, presents the three categories that make up Gail's analysis. According to Gail, college teachers can be categorized as the Knowledgeable One (paragraphs 2–4), the Leader of Intellectual Discussion (5), or the Buddy (6). Obviously, there are other ways professors might be classified. But given Gail's purpose, audience, tone, and point of view, her categories are appropriate; they are reasonably *complete, consistent,* and *mutually exclusive.* Note, too, that Gail uses *topic sentences* near the beginning of each category to help readers see which professorial type she's discussing.

Overall organization and paragraph structure.   Gail is able to shift smoothly and easily from one category to the next. How does she achieve such graceful transitions? Take a moment to reread the sentences that introduce her second and third categories (paragraphs 5 and 6). Look at the way each sentence's beginning (in italics here) links back to the preceding category or categories: "*Unlike the Knowledgeable One*, the 'Leader of Intellectual Discussion' seems to respect students"; and "[the Buddy] . . . *does not see himself as an imparter of knowledge or a leader of discussion* but as a pal. . . ."

Gail is equally careful about providing an easy-to-follow structure within each section. She uses a *chronological sequence* to organize her three-paragraph discussion of the Knowledgeable One. The first paragraph deals with the beginning of the Knowledgeable One's lecture; the second, with the lecture itself; the third, with the end of the lecture. And the paragraphs' *topic sentences* clearly indicate this passage of time. Similarly, *transitions* are used in the paragraphs on the Leader of Intellectual Discussion and the Buddy to ensure a logical progression of points: "*Then,* about three weeks into the semester, it becomes clear that the Leader wants students to discover *his* version of the truth" (5) and "*At first,* students look forward to classes with the Buddy. . . . But *after a while,* they wonder why they are paying for a course where they learn nothing" (6).

Tone.   The essay's unity can also be traced to Gail's skill in sustaining her satiric tone. Throughout the essay, Gail selects details that fit her gently mocking attitude. She depicts the Knowledgeable One lecturing from "yellowed-with-age notes . . . , oblivious to students' glazed eyes and stifled yawns," unwilling to wait for students who "run . . . through freezing sleet and howling winds to get to class on time." Then she presents another tongue-in-cheek description, this one focusing on the way the Leader of Intellectual Discussion conducts class: "Good point, good point. . . . Well, yes, that's an interesting perspective. But don't you think that . . . ?" Finally, with similar killing accuracy, Gail portrays the Buddy, democratically garbed in "jeans, sweatshirt, and scuffed sneakers."

Combining patterns of development.   Gail's satiric depiction of her three professorial types employs a number of techniques associated with *narrative* and *descriptive writing*: vigorous images, highly connotative language, and dialogue. *Definition, exemplification, causal analysis,* and *comparison-contrast* also come into play. Gail defines the characteristics of each type of professor; she provides numerous examples to support her categories; she explains the effects of the different teaching styles on students; and, in her description of the Leader of Intellectual Discussion, she contrasts the appearance of democracy with the dictatorial reality.

Unequal development of categories.   Although Gail's essay is unified, organized, and well-developed, you may have felt that the first category outweighs the other two. There is, of course, no need to balance the categories exactly. But Gail's extended treatment of the first category sets up an expectation that the others will be treated as fully. One way to remedy this problem would be to delete some material from the discussion of the Knowledgeable

One. Gail might, for instance, omit the last five sentences in the third paragraph (about the professor's habit of addressing students as "Mr." or "Miss"). Such a change could be made without taking the bite out of her portrayal. Even better, Gail could simply switch the order of her sections, putting the portrait of the Knowledgeable One at the essay's end. Here, the extended discussion wouldn't seem out of proportion. Instead, the sections would appear in *emphatic order*, with the most detailed category saved for last.

Revising the first draft.   It's apparent that an essay as engaging as Gail's must have undergone a good deal of revising. That was in fact the case. Gail made many changes in the body of the essay, but it's particularly interesting to review what happened to the introduction as she revised the paper. Reprinted here is Gail's original introduction.

Original Version of the Introduction

Despite their high IQs, advanced degrees, and published papers, some college professors just don't know how to teach. Found in almost any department, in tenured and untenured positions, they prompt student apathy. They fail to convey ideas effectively and to challenge or inspire students. Students thus finish their courses having learned very little. Contrary to popular opinion, these professors' ineptitude is not simply a matter of delivering boring lectures or not caring about students. Many of them care a great deal. Their failure actually stems from their unrealistic perceptions of what a teacher should be. Specifically, they adopt teaching styles or roles that alienate students and undermine learning. Three of the most common ones are "The Knowledgeable One," "The Leader of Intellectual Discussion," and "The Buddy."

When Gail showed the first draft of the essay to her composition instructor, he laughed—and occasionally squirmed—as he read what she had prepared. He was enthusiastic about the paper but felt that there was a problem with the introduction's tone; it was too serious when compared to the playful, lightly satiric mood of the rest of the essay. When Gail reread the paragraph, she agreed, but she was uncertain about the best way to remedy the problem. After revising other sections of the essay, she decided to let the paper sit for a while before going back to rewrite the introduction.

In the meantime, Gail switched on the TV. The timing couldn't have been better; she tuned into a news story about several supposedly learned professors who had been fired from a consulting job because they had turned out to know so little about teaching. This was exactly the kind of item Gail needed to start her essay. Now she was able to prepare a completely new introduction, making it consistent in spirit with the rest of the paper.

With this stronger introduction and the rest of the essay well in hand, Gail was ready to write a conclusion. Now, as she worked on the concluding paragraph, she deliberately shaped it to recall the story about the fired consultants. By echoing the opening anecdote in her conclusion, Gail was able to end the paper with another poke at professors—a perfect way to close her clever and insightful essay.

ACTIVITIES: DIVISION-CLASSIFICATION

Prewriting Activities

1. Imagine you're writing two essays: One is a humorous paper outlining a *process* for impressing college instructors; the other is a serious essay examining the *causes* of the recent rise in volunteerism. What about the topics might you divide and/or classify?

2. Use group brainstorming to identify three principles of division for *one* of the topics in Set A below. Focusing on one of the principles, decide what your thesis might be if you were writing an essay. That done, use group brainstorming to identify three principles of classification that might provide the structure for *one* of the topics in Set B. Focusing on one of the principles, decide what your thesis might be if you were writing an essay.

Set A
- Rock music
- A shopping mall
- A good horror movie

Set B
- Why people get addicted to computers
- How fast-food restaurants affect family life
- Why long-term relationships break up

Revising Activities

3. Following is a scratch outline for an essay developed through division-classification. On what principle of division-classification is the essay based? What problem do you see in the way the principle is applied? How could the problem be remedied?

Thesis: The same experience often teaches opposite things to different people.

- What working as a fast-food cook teaches: Some learn responsibility; others learn to take a "quick and dirty" approach.
- What a negative experience teaches optimists: Some learn from their mistakes; others continue to maintain a positive outlook.
- What a difficult course teaches: Some learn to study hard; others learn to avoid demanding courses.
- What the breakup of a close relationship teaches: Some learn how to negotiate differences; others learn to avoid intimacy.

4. Following is a paragraph from the first draft of an essay urging that day care centers adopt play programs tailored to children's developmental needs. What principle of division-classification focuses the paragraph? Is the principle applied consistently and logically? Are parts/categories developed sufficiently? Revise

the paragraph, eliminating any problems you discover and adding specific details where needed.

Within a few years, preschool children move from self-absorbed to interactive play. Babies and toddlers engage in solitary play. Although they sometimes prefer being near other children, they focus primarily on their own actions. This is very different from the highly interactive play of the elementary school years. Sometime in children's second year, solitary play is replaced by parallel play, during which children engage in similar activities near one another. However, they interact only occasionally. By age three, most children show at least some cooperative play, a form that involves interaction and cooperative role-taking. Such role-taking can be found in the "pretend" games that children play to explore adult relationships (games of "Mommy and Daddy") and anatomy (games of "Doctor"). Additional signs of youngsters' growing awareness of peers can be seen at about age four. At this age, many children begin showing a special devotion to one other child and may want to play only with that child. During this time, children also begin to take special delight in physical activities such as running and jumping, often going off by themselves to expend their abundant physical energy.

Stephanie Ericsson

Stephanie Ericsson (1953–) is a writer, screenwriter, and ad copywriter who often uses her own life experiences as starting points for her deeply personal work. She wrote *Companion Through the Darkness: Inner Dialogues on Grief* (1993) in response to her husband's sudden death while she was pregnant, and she chronicled her struggles with substance abuse in both *Shamefaced* (1985) and *Women of AA: Recovering Together* (1986). Ericsson's latest book is *Companion into the Dawn: Inner Dialogues on Loving* (1994). A frequent speaker on the subject of loss, she lives in Minneapolis, Minnesota. "The Ways We Lie" was originally published in the *Utne Reader* in 1992.

Pre-Reading Journal Entry

Something that everyone is guilty of, but may not want to admit to, is lying. Think for a moment about times when you told a lie. In your pre-reading journal, begin by listing any episodes of lying you can recall. Then go back and freewrite to a greater extent about these incidents. In each case, why did you tell the lie—what were the circumstances? What was the outcome? Do you now regret having lied, or are you thankful you did it?

The Ways We Lie

The bank called today and I told them my deposit was in the mail, even though I hadn't written a check yet. It'd been a rough day. The baby I'm pregnant with decided to do aerobics on my lungs for two hours, our three-year-old daughter painted the living room couch with lipstick, the IRS put me on hold for an hour, and I was late to a business meeting because I was tired. 1

I told my client that traffic had been bad. When my partner came home, his haggard face told me his day hadn't gone any better than mine, so when he asked, "How was your day?" I said, "Oh, fine," knowing that one more straw might break his back. A friend called and wanted to take me to lunch. I said I was busy. Four lies in the course of a day, none of which I felt the least bit guilty about. 2

We lie. We all do. We exaggerate, we minimize, we avoid confrontation, we spare people's feelings, we conveniently forget, we keep secrets, we justify lying to the big-guy institutions. Like most people, I indulge in small falsehoods and still think of myself as an honest person. Sure I lie, but it doesn't hurt anything. Or does it? 3

240

I once tried going a whole week without telling a lie, and it was paralyz-   4
ing. I discovered that telling the truth all the time is nearly impossible. It means
living with some serious consequences: The bank charges me $60 in overdraft
fees, my partner keels over when I tell him about my travails, my client fires me
for telling her I didn't feel like being on time, and my friend takes it personally when I say I'm not hungry. There must be some merit to lying.

But if I justify lying, what makes me any different from slick politicians   5
or the corporate robbers who raided the S&L industry?[1] Saying it's okay to
lie one way and not another is hedging. I cannot seem to escape the voice
deep inside me that tells me: When someone lies, someone loses.

What far-reaching consequences will I, or others, pay as a result of my   6
lie? Will someone's trust be destroyed? Will someone else pay *my* penance
because I ducked out? We must consider the *meaning of our actions*. Deception, lies, capital crimes, and misdemeanors all carry meanings. *Webster's* definition of *lie* is specific:

> 1: a false statement or action especially made with the intent to
> deceive; 2: anything that gives or is meant to give a false impression.

A definition like this implies that there are many, many ways to tell a lie.   7
Here are just a few.

The White Lie

A man who won't lie to a woman has very little consideration for her feelings.

—Bergen Evans

The white lie assumes that the truth will cause more damage than a   8
simple, harmless untruth. Telling a friend he looks great when he looks like
hell can be based on a decision that the friend needs a compliment more than
a frank opinion. But, in effect, it is the liar deciding what is best for the lied
to. Ultimately, it is a vote of no confidence. It is an act of subtle arrogance
for anyone to decide what is best for someone else.

Yet not all circumstances are quite so cut-and-dried. Take, for instance,   9
the sergeant in Vietnam who knew one of his men was killed in action but
listed him as missing so that the man's family would receive indefinite com-
pensation instead of the lump-sum pittance the military gives widows and
children. His intent was honorable. Yet for twenty years this family kept their
hopes alive, unable to move on to a new life.

---

[1]Reference to the savings and loan scandal of the 1980s, in which corrupt owners of bank-like
institutions defrauded the federal government of vast amounts of money (editors' note).

Façades

Et tu, Brute?

—Caesar

We all put up façades to one degree or another. When I put on a suit to   1(
go to see a client, I feel as though I am putting on another face, obeying the
expectation that serious businesspeople wear suits rather than sweatpants. But
I'm a writer. Normally, I get up, get the kid off to school, and sit at my computer in my pajamas until four in the afternoon. When I answer the phone,
the caller thinks I'm wearing a suit (though the UPS man knows better).

But façades can be destructive because they are used to seduce others   1)
into an illusion. For instance, I recently realized that a former friend was a
liar. He presented himself with all the right looks and the right words and
offered lots of new consciousness theories, fabulous books to read, and fascinating insights. Then I did some business with him, and the time came for
him to pay me. He turned out to be all talk and no walk. I heard a plethora
of reasonable excuses, including in-depth descriptions of the big break
around the corner. In six months of work, I saw less than a hundred bucks.
When I confronted him, he raised both eyebrows and tried to convince me
that I'd heard him wrong, that he'd made no commitment to me. A simple
investigation into his past revealed a crowded graveyard of disenchanted former friends.

Ignoring the Plain Facts

Well, you must understand that Father Porter is only human. . . .

—A Massachusetts priest

In the '60s, the Catholic Church in Massachusetts began hearing com-   1.
plaints that Father James Porter was sexually molesting children. Rather than
relieving him of his duties, the ecclesiastical authorities simply moved him
from one parish to another between 1960 and 1967, actually providing him
with a fresh supply of unsuspecting families and innocent children to abuse.
After treatment in 1967 for pedophilia, he went back to work, this time in
Minnesota. The new diocese was aware of Father Porter's obsession with children, but they needed priests and recklessly believed treatment had cured
him. More children were abused until he was relieved of his duties a year later.
By his own admission, Porter may have abused as many as a hundred children.

Ignoring the facts may not in and of itself be a form of lying, but con-   1
sider the context of this situation. If a lie is *a false action done with the intent
to deceive,* then the Catholic Church's conscious covering for Porter created
irreparable consequences. The church became a co-perpetrator with Porter.

Deflecting

When you have no basis for an argument, abuse the plaintiff.

—Cicero

I've discovered that I can keep anyone from seeing the true me by being   14
selectively blatant. I set a precedent of being up-front about intimate issues,
but I never bring up the things I truly want to hide; I just let people assume
I'm revealing everything. It's an effective way of hiding.

Any good liar knows that the way to perpetuate an untruth is to deflect   15
attention from it. When Clarence Thomas[2] exploded with accusations that the
Senate hearings were a "high-tech lynching," he simple switched the focus
from a highly charged subject to a radioactive subject. Rather than defending
himself, he took the offensive and accused the country of racism. It was a brilliant maneuver. Racism is now politically incorrect in official circles—unlike
sexual harassment, which still rewards those who can get away with it.

Some of the most skillful deflectors are passive-aggressive[3] people who,   16
when accused of inappropriate behavior, refuse to respond to the accusations. This you-don't-exist stance infuriates the accuser, who, understandably, screams something obscene out of frustration. The trap is sprung and
the act of deflection successful, because now the passive-aggressive person
can indignantly say, "Who can talk to someone as unreasonable as you?" The
real issue is forgotten and the sins of the original victim become the focus.
Feeling guilty of namecalling, the victim is fully tamed and crawls into a hole,
ashamed. I have watched this fighting technique work thousands of times in
disputes between men and women, and what I've learned is that the real cul-
prit is not necessarily the one who swears the loudest.

Omission

The cruelest lies are often told in silence.

—R. L. Stevenson

Omission involves telling most of the truth minus one or two key facts   17
whose absence changes the story completely. You break a pair of glasses that
are guaranteed under normal use and get a new pair, without mentioning
that the first pair broke during a rowdy game of basketball. Who hasn't tried

---

[2]Nominated to the Supreme Court in 1993, Clarence Thomas, an African American jurist, was
accused by former colleague Anita Hill of sexual harassment. Much of Thomas's confirmation
hearing, televised nationwide, focused on this issue (editors' note).
[3]A psychological pattern in which hostility is expressed through an infuriating detachment and
nonresponsiveness (editors' note).

something like that? But what about omission of information that could make a difference in how a person lives his or her life?

For instance, one day I found out that rabbinical legends tell of another woman in the Garden of Eden before Eve. I was stunned. The omission of the Sumerian goddess Lilith from Genesis—as well as her demonization by ancient misogynists as an embodiment of female evil—felt like spiritual robbery. I felt like I'd just found out my mother was really my stepmother. To take seriously the tradition that Adam was created out of the same mud as his equal counterpart, Lilith, redefines all of Judeo-Christian history.

Some renegade Catholic feminists introduced me to a view of Lilith that had been suppressed during many centuries when this strong goddess was seen only as a spirit of evil. Lilith was a proud goddess who defied Adam's need to control her, attempted negotiations, and when this failed, said adios and left the Garden of Eden.

This omission of Lilith from the Bible was a patriarchal strategy to keep women weak. Omitting the strong-woman archetype of Lilith from Western religions and starting the story with Eve the Rib has helped keep Christian and Jewish women believing they were the lesser sex for thousands of years.

Stereotypes and Clichés

Where opinion does not exist, the status quo becomes stereotyped and all originality is discouraged.

—Bertrand Russell

Stereotype and cliché serve a purpose as a form of shorthand. Our need for vast amounts of information in nanoseconds has made the stereotype vital to modern communication. Unfortunately, it often shuts down original thinking, giving those hungry for the truth a candy bar of misinformation instead of a balanced meal. The stereotype explains a situation with just enough truth to seem unquestionable.

All the "isms"—racism, sexism, ageism, et al.—are founded on and fueled by the stereotype and the cliché, which are lies of exaggeration, omission, and ignorance. They are always dangerous. They take a single tree and make it a landscape. They destroy curiosity. They close minds and separate people. The single mother on welfare is assumed to be cheating. Any black male could tell you how much of his identity is obliterated daily by stereotypes. Fat people, ugly people, beautiful people, old people, large-breasted women, short men, the mentally ill, and the homeless all could tell you how much more they are like us than we want to think. I once admitted to a group of people that I had a mouth like a truck driver. Much to my surprise, a man stood up and said, "I'm a truck driver, and I never cuss." Needless to say, I was humbled.

Groupthink

Who is more foolish, the child afraid of the dark, or the man afraid of the flight?

—Maurice Freehill

Irving Janis, in *Victims of Group Think*, defines this sort of lie as a psy- 23
chological phenomenon within decision-making groups in which loyalty to
the group has become more important than any other value, with the result
that dissent and the appraisal of alternatives are suppressed. If you've ever
worked on a committee or in a corporation, you've encountered groupthink.
It requires a combination of other forms of lying—ignoring facts, selective
memory, omission, and denial, to name a few.

The textbook example of groupthink came on December 7, 1941. From 24
as early as the fall of 1941, the warnings came in, one after another, that Japan
was preparing for a massive military operation. The Navy command in Hawaii
assumed Pearl Harbor was invulnerable—the Japanese weren't stupid enough
to attack the United States' most important base. On the other hand, racist
stereotypes said the Japanese weren't smart enough to invent a torpedo effective in less than 60 feet of water (the fleet was docked in 30 feet); after all,
U.S. technology hadn't been able to do it.

On Friday, December 5, normal weekend leave was granted to all the 25
commanders at Pearl Harbor, even though the Japanese consulate in Hawaii
was busy burning papers. Within the tight, good-ole-boy cohesiveness of the
U.S. command in Hawaii, the myth of invulnerability stayed well entrenched.
No one in the group considered the alternatives. The rest is history.

Out-and-Out Lies

The only form of lying that is beyond reproach is lying for its own sake.

—Oscar Wilde

Of all the ways to lie, I like this one the best, probably because I get tired 26
of trying to figure out the real meanings behind things. At least I can trust
the bald-faced lie. I once asked my five-year-old nephew, "Who broke the
fence?" (I had seen him do it.) He answered, "The murderers." Who could
argue?

At least when this sort of lie is told it can be easily confronted. As the 27
person who is lied to, I know where I stand. The bald-faced lie doesn't toy
with my perceptions—it argues with them. It doesn't try to refashion reality, it tries to refute it. *Read my lips* . . . No sleight of hand.[4] No guessing. If

[4]A phrase used by presidential candidate George H. W. Bush during the 1988 campaign (and
often parodied thereafter): "Read my lips. . . . No new taxes" (editors' note).

this were the only form of lying, there would be no such things as floating anxiety[5] or the adult, children-of-alcoholics movement.

Dismissal

Pay no attention to that man behind the curtain! I am the Great Oz!

—The Wizard of Oz

Dismissal is perhaps the slipperiest of all lies. Dismissing feelings, perceptions, or even the raw facts of a situation ranks as a kind of lie that can do as much damage to a person as any other kind of lie.

The roots of many mental disorders can be traced back to the dismissal of reality. Imagine that a person is told from the time she is a tot that her perceptions are inaccurate. *"Mommy, I'm scared."* "No you're not, darling." *"I don't like that man next door, he makes me feel icky."* "Johnny, that's a terrible thing to say, of course you like him. You go over there right now and be nice to him."

I've often mused over the idea that madness is actually a sane reaction to an insane world. Psychologist R. D. Laing supports this hypothesis in *Sanity, Madness and the Family,* an account of his investigations into the families of schizophrenics. The common thread that ran through all of the families he studied was a deliberate, staunch dismissal of the patient's perceptions from a very early age. Each of the patients started out with an accurate grasp of reality, which, through meticulous and methodical dismissal, was demolished until the only reality the patient could trust was catatonia.

Dismissal runs the gamut. Mild dismissal can be quite handy for forgiving the foibles of others in our day-to-day lives. Toddlers who have just learned to manipulate their parents' attention sometimes are dismissed out of necessity. Absolute attention from the parents would require so much energy that no one would get to eat dinner. But we must be careful and attentive about how far we take our "necessary" dismissals. Dismissal is a dangerous tool, because it's nothing less than a lie.

Delusion

We lie loudest when we lie to ourselves.

—Eric Hoffer

I could write the book on this one. Delusion, a cousin of dismissal, is the tendency to see excuses as facts. It's a powerful lying tool because it filters

---

[5]A psychological condition in which a person feels generalized anxiety for no specific reason (editor's note).

out information that contradicts what we want to believe. Alcoholics who believe that the problems in their lives are legitimate reasons for drinking rather than results of the drinking offer the classic example of deluded thinking. Delusion uses the mind's ability to see things in myriad ways to support what it wants to be the truth.

But delusion is also a survival mechanism we all use. If we were to fully 33 contemplate the consequences of our stockpiles of nuclear weapons or global warming, we could hardly function on a day-to-day level. We don't want to incorporate that much reality into our lives because to do so would be paralyzing.

Delusion acts as an adhesive to keep the status quo intact. It shamelessly 34 employs dismissal, omission, and amnesia, among other sorts of lies. Its most cunning defense is that it cannot see itself.

● ● ●

The liar's punishment . . . is that he cannot believe anyone else.

—George Bernard Shaw

These are only a few of the ways we lie. Or are lied to. As I said earlier, 35 it's not easy to entirely eliminate lies from our lives. No matter how pious we may try to be, we will still embellish, hedge, and omit to lubricate the daily machinery of living. But there is a world of difference between telling functional lies and living a lie. Martin Buber[6] once said, "The lie is the spirit committing treason against itself." Our acceptance of lies becomes a cultural cancer that eventually shrouds and reorders reality until moral garbage becomes as invisible to us as water is to a fish.

How much do we tolerate before we become sick and tired of being sick 36 and tired? When will we stand up and declare our *right* to trust? When do we stop accepting that the real truth is in the fine print? Whose lips do we read this year when we vote for president? When will we stop being so reticent about making judgments? When do we stop turning over our personal power and responsibility to liars?

Maybe if I don't tell the bank the check's in the mail I'll be less tolerant 37 of the lies told me every day. A country song I once heard said it all for me: "You've got to stand for something or you'll fall for anything."

───────────────

[6]A German Jewish scholar and philosopher (1878–1965) (editors' note).

Questions for Close Reading

1. What is the selection's thesis? Locate the sentence(s) in which Ericsson states her main idea. If she doesn't state the thesis explicitly, express it in your own words.

2. What did Ericsson discover when she tried to go a whole week without lying?

3. Ericsson classifies as "lies" some behaviors not always considered dishonest. How can "ignoring the plain facts," "deflecting," and "omission" be types of lies? How do "stereotypes and clichés" and "groupthink" qualify as lies?

4. Why doesn't Ericsson easily accept the fact that lies are a necessary part of her life and that of most people?

5. Refer to your dictionary as needed to define the following words used in the selection: *travails* (paragraph 4), *hedging* (5), *penance* (4), *pittance* (9), *façades* (10), *plethora* (11), *disenchanted* (11), *ecclesiastical* (12), *pedophilia* (12), *irreparable* (13), *blatant* (14), *demonization* (18), *misogynists* (18), *embodiment* (18), *archetype* (20), *obliterated* (22), *dissent* (23), *cohesiveness* (25), *invulnerability* (25), *entrenched* (25), *catatonia* (30), and *gamut* (31).

Questions About the Writer's Craft

1. **The pattern.** In paragraph 6, Ericsson asserts that we "must consider the *meaning of our actions*" when deciding whether or not we have lied. How does this principle of classification help her show that each category of behavior discussed is a type of lying?

2. **Other patterns.** In the body of her essay, Ericsson draws upon both personal experience and third-person material to make her point. Her introduction, though, includes only a first-person *narrative*. Why do you suppose Ericsson decided to open the essay with this brief first-person account?

3. Despite the seriousness of her subject, Ericsson's overall tone is informal—almost conversational. Identify at least five instances of this informality. Why do you suppose Ericsson adopted such a tone?

4. **Other patterns.** In her concluding paragraphs (35–37), Ericsson *contrasts* two broad types of lies, saying that "there is a world of difference between telling functional lies and living a lie." How does this contrast help her sum up the essay?

Writing Assignments Using Division-Classification as a Pattern of Development

1. Ericsson takes an often used, seemingly simple word and, by categorizing its various manifestations, shows that it represents a complex phenomenon. Choose another frequently used word—such as *loyalty, excellence, arrogance,* or *hypocrisy*—and show its complexity by categorizing its different types. Before presenting your categories, offer a definition, either yours or the dictionary's, of the word; then provide dramatic examples to illustrate the various categories.

2. In paragraph 23, Ericsson cites Irving Janus's definition of "groupthink." Using this definition as a starting point, analyze several situations involving groupthink that you have observed or heard about. Classify the kinds of groupthink that are revealed in these situations, illustrating each type with at least one vivid example. To deepen your understanding of groupthink, read the following essays before writing your paper: George Orwell's "Shooting an Elephant" (page 143), Langston Hughes's "Salvation" (page 155), and John M. Darley and Bibb Latané's "Why People Don't Help in a Crisis" (page 417).

Writing Assignments Combining Patterns of Development

3. Stereotypes, Ericsson writes, "explain a situation with just enough truth to seem unquestionable." Write a *narrative* about a specific time that you or someone you know either falsely stereotyped a person or reacted stereotypically to a situation. Include only those details and *examples* that dramatize your narrative point. Before writing, you'll find it helpful to read one of the following essays, which show how pervasive and corrosive stereotypes can be: Audre Lorde's "The Fourth of July" (page 137), Joseph H. Suina's "And Then I Went to School" (page 354), or William Raspberry's "The Handicap of Definition" (page 471).

4. Many social commentators call attention, as Ericsson does in paragraph 15, to the growing tendency of individuals to absolve themselves from responsibility for something they've done by claiming that *they* are actually the victims. Gain some background on the issue of victimization by brainstorming with others and locating relevant material in the library and/or on the Internet. (You might find articles and books by Charles Sykes and William Raspberry especially helpful.) Then write an essay *arguing* that we are or are not becoming a nation of victims and crybabies. Discredit the opposing viewpoint as much as possible by drawing upon your own and other people's experiences, as well as the outside sources you've read. And, in the course of your essay, speculate about the *causes* of the behavior you have identified.

Writing Assignment Using a Journal Entry as a Starting Point

5. At the beginning of her essay, Ericsson says that "there are many, many ways to tell a lie." Refer to your pre-reading journal entry, and select *one* memorable incident in which you lied, making sure the incident you select is substantial enough to support an entire essay. Then review Ericsson's ten categories of lying and determine which one best applies to the lie in question. Write an essay in which you *narrate* your episode of lying as a way of *illustrating* that particular category. Be sure, at the beginning of your essay, to briefly cite Ericsson's explanation of the category. As you narrate the incident involving your lie, point out the ways in which it illustrates that category. In addition, you should conclude with some commentary on whether lying was justified in the circumstances. You might benefit, too, from reading Langston Hughes's "Salvation" (page 155), a compelling account of telling a childhood, but not a *childish*, lie.

William Zinsser

Currently on the faculty of the Columbia University Graduate School of Journalism, William Zinsser has written news journalism, drama criticism, magazine columns, and several books on U.S. culture. Born in 1922 in New York, Zinsser attended Princeton University and worked for the *New York Herald Tribune, Life,* and *Look.* In 1970, Zinsser designed a course in nonfiction writing for Yale University. Based on what he learned at Yale about the way college students approach the writing process, Zinsser wrote the popular guide *On Writing Well* (1976). His other books include *The City Dwellers* (1962), *Pop Goes America* (1966), *The Lunacy Boom* (1970), *Writing with a Word Processor* (1982), *American Places: A Writer's Pilgrimage to 15 of This Country's Most Visited and Cherished Sites* (1992), and *Speaking of Journalism* (1994). He also co-edited *Inventing the Truth: The Art & Craft of Memoir* (1995). The following essay first appeared in the magazine *Country Journal* in 1979.

Pre-Reading Journal Entry

Many students feel pressured by college graduation requirements. Do you? What courses are you required to take that you wouldn't ordinarily choose? What courses would you like to take but don't have time for? Should colleges require students to take courses that aren't part of their majors? Why or why not? Use your journal to respond to these questions.

College Pressures

Dear Carlos: I desperately need a dean's excuse for my chem midterm which will begin in about 1 hour. All I can say is that I totally blew it this week. I've fallen incredibly, inconceivably behind.

Carlos: Help! I'm anxious to hear from you. I'll be in my room and won't leave it until I hear from you. Tomorrow is the last day for . . .

Carlos: I left town because I started bugging out again. I stayed up all night to finish a take-home make-up exam & am typing it to hand in on the 10th. It was due on the 5th. P.S. I'm going to the dentist. Pain is pretty bad.

Carlos: Probably by Friday I'll be able to get back to my studies. Right now I'm going to take a long walk. This whole thing has taken a lot out of me.

Carlos: I'm really up the proverbial creek. The problem is I really *bombed* the history final. Since I need that course for my major I . . .

Carlos: Here follows a tale of woe. I went home this weekend, had to help my Mom, & caught a fever so didn't have much time to study. My professor . . .

Carlos: Aargh! Trouble. Nothing original but everything's piling up at once. To be brief, my job interview . . .

Hey Carlos, good news! I've got mononucleosis.

Who are these wretched supplicants, scribbling notes so laden with anx- 1
iety, seeking such miracles of postponement and balm? They are men and women who belong to Branford College, one of the twelve residential colleges at Yale University, and the messages are just a few of the hundreds that they left for their dean, Carlos Hortas—often slipped under his door at 4 A.M.—last year.

But students like the ones who wrote those notes can also be found on 2
campuses from coast to coast—especially in New England and at many other private colleges across the country that have high academic standards and highly motivated students. Nobody could doubt that the notes are real. In their urgency and their gallows humor they are authentic voices of a generation that is panicky to succeed.

My own connection with the message writers is that I am master of 3
Branford College. I live in its Gothic quadrangle and know the students well. (We have 485 of them.) I am privy to their hopes and fears—and also to their stereo music and their piercing cries in the dead of the night ("Does anybody *ca-a-are?*"). If they went to Carlos to ask how to get through tomorrow, they come to me to ask how to get through the rest of their lives.

Mainly I try to remind them that the road ahead is a long one and that 4
it will have more unexpected turns than they think. There will be plenty of time to change jobs, change careers, change whole attitudes and approaches. They don't want to hear such liberating news. They want a map—right now—that they can follow unswervingly to career security, financial security, Social Security and, presumably, a prepaid grave.

What I wish for all students is some release from the clammy grip of the 5
future. I wish them a chance to savor each segment of their education as an experience in itself and not as a grim preparation for the next step. I wish them the right to experiment, to trip and fall, to learn that defeat is as instructive as victory and is not the end of the world.

My wish, of course, is naïve. One of the few rights that America does not proclaim is the right to fail. Achievement is the national god, venerated in our media—the million-dollar athlete, the wealthy executive—and glorified in our praise of possessions. In the presence of such a potent state religion, the young are growing up old.

I see four kinds of pressure working on college students today: economic pressure, parental pressure, peer pressure, and self-induced pressure. It is easy to look around for villains—to blame the colleges for charging too much money, the professors for assigning too much work, the parents for pushing their children too far, the students for driving themselves too hard. But there are no villains; only victims.

"In the late 1960s," one dean told me, "the typical question that I got from students was 'Why is there so much suffering in the world?' or 'How can I make a contribution?' Today it's 'Do you think it would look better for getting into law school if I did a double major in history and political science, or just majored in one of them?'" Many other deans confirmed this pattern. One said: "They're trying to find an edge—the intangible something that will look better on paper if two students are about equal."

Note the emphasis on looking better. The transcript has become a sacred document, the passport to security. How one appears on paper is more important than how one appears in person. *A* is for Admirable and *B* is for Borderline, even though, in Yale's official system of grading, *A* means "excellent" and *B* means "very good." Today, looking very good is no longer good enough, especially for students who hope to go on to law school or medical school. They know that entrance into the better schools will be an entrance into the better law firms and better medical practices where they will make a lot of money. They also know that the odds are harsh. Yale Law School, for instance, matriculates 170 students from an applicant pool of 3,700; Harvard enrolls 550 from a pool of 7,000.

It's all very well for those of us who write letters of recommendation for our students to stress the qualities of humanity that will make them good lawyers or doctors. And it's nice to think that admission officers are really reading our letters and looking for the extra dimension of commitment or concern. Still, it would be hard for a student not to visualize these officers shuffling so many transcripts studded with *A*s that they regard a *B* as positively shameful.

The pressure is almost as heavy on students who just want to graduate and get a job. Long gone are the days of the "gentleman's *C*," when students journeyed through college with a certain relaxation, sampling a wide variety of courses—music, art, philosophy, classics, anthropology, poetry, religion—that would send them out as liberally educated men and women. If I were an employer I would rather employ graduates who have this range and curiosity than those who narrowly pursued safe subjects and high grades. I know countless students whose inquiring minds exhilarate me. I like to hear the play of their ideas. I don't know if they are getting *A*s or *C*s, and I don't care. I also like them as people. The country needs them, and they will find satisfying jobs. I tell them to relax. They can't.

Nor can I blame them. They live in a brutal economy. Tuition, room, and board at most private colleges now comes to at least $7,000 [in 1979], not counting books and fees. This might seem to suggest that the colleges are getting rich. But they are equally battered by inflation. Tuition covers only 60 percent of what it costs to educate a student, and ordinarily the remainder comes from what colleges receive in endowments, grants, and gifts. Now the remainder keeps being swallowed by the cruel costs—higher every year—of just opening the doors. Heating oil is up. Insurance is up. Postage is up. Health-premium costs are up. Everything is up. Deficits are up. We are witnessing in America the creation of a brotherhood of paupers—colleges, parents, and students, joined by the common bond of debt.   12

Today it is not unusual for a student, even if he works part time at college and full time during the summer, to accrue $5,000 in loans after four years—loans that he must start to repay within one year after graduation. Exhorted at commencement to go forth into the world, he is already behind as he goes forth. How could he not feel under pressure throughout college to prepare for this day of reckoning? I have used "he," incidentally, only for brevity. Women at Yale are under no less pressure to justify their expensive education to themselves, their parents, and society. In fact, they are probably under more pressure. For although they leave college superbly equipped to bring fresh leadership to traditionally male jobs, society hasn't yet caught up with this fact.   13

Along with economic pressure goes parental pressure. Inevitably, the two are deeply intertwined.   14

I see many students taking pre-medical courses with joyless tenacity. They go off to their labs as if they were going to the dentist. It saddens me because I know them in other corners of their life as cheerful people.   15

"Do you want to go to medical school?" I ask them.   16

"I guess so," they say, without conviction, or "Not really."   17

"Then why are you going?"   18

"Well, my parents want me to be a doctor. They're paying all this money and . . ."   19

Poor students, poor parents. They are caught in one of the oldest webs of love and duty and guilt. The parents mean well; they are trying to steer their sons and daughters toward a secure future. But the sons and daughters want to major in history or classics or philosophy—subjects with no "practical" value. Where's the payoff on the humanities? It's not easy to persuade   20 such loving parents that the humanities do indeed pay off. The intellectual faculties developed by studying subjects like history and classics—an ability to synthesize and relate, to weigh cause and effect, to see events in perspective—are just the faculties that make creative leaders in business or almost any general field. Still, many fathers would rather put their money on courses that point toward a specific profession—courses that are pre-law, pre-medical, pre-business, or, as I sometimes heard it put, "pre-rich."

But the pressure on students is severe. They are truly torn. One part of them feels obligated to fulfill their parents' expectations; after all, their parents are older and presumably wiser. Another part tells them that the expectations that are right for their parents are not right for them.

I know a student who wants to be an artist. She is very obviously an artist and will be a good one—she has already had several modest local exhibits. Meanwhile she is growing as a well-rounded person and taking humanistic subjects that will enrich the inner resources out of which her art will grow. But her father is strongly opposed. He thinks that an artist is a "dumb" thing to be. The student vacillates and tries to please everybody. She keeps up with her art somewhat furtively and takes some of the "dumb" courses her father wants her to take—at least they are dumb courses for her. She is a free spirit on a campus of tense students—no small achievement in itself—and she deserves to follow her muse.

Peer pressure and self-induced pressure are also intertwined, and they begin almost at the beginning of freshman year.

"I had a freshman student I'll call Linda," one dean told me, "who came in and said she was under terrible pressure because her roommate, Barbara, was much brighter and studied all the time. I couldn't tell her that Barbara had come in two hours earlier to say the same thing about Linda."

The story is almost funny—except that it's not. It's symptomatic of all the pressures put together. When every student thinks every other student is working harder and doing better, the only solution is to study harder still. I see students going off to the library every night after dinner and coming back when it closes at midnight. I wish they would sometimes forget about their peers and go to a movie. I hear the clacking of typewriters in the hours before dawn. I see the tension in their eyes when exams are approaching and papers are due: *Will I get everything done?*

Probably they won't. They will get sick. They will get "blocked." They will sleep. They will oversleep. They will bug out. *Hey, Carlos, help!*

Part of the problem is that they do more than they are expected to do. A professor will assign five-page papers. Several students will start writing ten-page papers to impress him. Then more students will write ten-page papers, and a few will raise the ante to fifteen. Pity the poor student who is still just doing the assignment.

"Once you have twenty or thirty percent of the student population deliberately overexerting," one dean points out, "it's bad for everybody.

When a teacher gets more and more effort from his class, the student who is doing normal work can be perceived as not doing well. The tactic works, psychologically."

Why can't the professor just cut back and not accept longer papers? He 29 can, and he probably will. But by then the term will be half over and the damage done. Grade fever is highly contagious and not easily reversed. Besides, the professor's main concern is with his course. He knows his students only in relation to the course and doesn't know that they are also overexerting in their other courses. Nor is it really his business. He didn't sign up for dealing with the student as a whole person and with all the emotional baggage the student brought along from home. That's what deans, masters, chaplains, and psychiatrists are for.

To some extent this is nothing new: a certain number of professors have 30 always been self-contained islands of scholarship and shyness, more comfortable with books than with people. But the new pauperism has widened the gap still further, for professors who actually like to spend time with students don't have as much time to spend. They are also overexerting. If they are young, they are busy trying to publish in order not to perish, hanging by their fingernails onto a shrinking profession. If they are old and tenured, they are buried under the duties of administering departments—as departmental chairmen or members of committees—that have been thinned out by the budgetary axe.

Ultimately it will be the students' own business to break the circles in 31 which they are trapped. They are too young to be prisoners of their parents' dreams and their classmates' fears. They must be jolted into believing in themselves as unique men and women who have the power to shape their own future.

"Violence is being done to the undergraduate experience," says Carlos 32 Hortas. "College should be open-ended: at the end it should open many, many roads. Instead, students are choosing their goal in advance, and their choices narrow as they go along. It's almost as if they think that the country has been codified in the type of jobs that exist—that they've got to fit into certain slots. Therefore, fit into the best-paying slot.

"They ought to take chances. Not taking chances will lead to a life of 33 colorless mediocrity. They'll be comfortable. But something in the spirit will be missing."

I have painted too drab a portrait of today's students, making them seem 34 a solemn lot. That is only half of their story; if they were so dreary I wouldn't so thoroughly enjoy their company. The other half is that they are easy to like. They are quick to laugh and to offer friendship. They are not introverts. They are unusually kind and are more considerate of one another than any student generation I have known.

Nor are they so obsessed with their studies that they avoid sports and 35 extracurricular activities. On the contrary, they juggle their crowded hours to play on a variety of teams, perform with musical and dramatic groups, and write for campus publications. But this in turn is one more cause of anxiety. There are too many choices. Academically, they have 1,300 courses to select from; outside class they have to decide how much spare time they can spare and how to spend it.

This means that they engage in fewer extracurricular pursuits than their predecessors did. If they want to row on the crew and play in the symphony they will eliminate one; in the '60s they would have done both. They also tend to choose activities that are self-limiting. Drama, for instance, is flourishing in all twelve of Yale's residential colleges as it never has before. Students hurl themselves into these productions—as actors, directors, carpenters, and technicians—with a dedication to create the best possible play, knowing that the day will come when the run will end and they can get back to their studies.

They also can't afford to be the willing slave of organizations like the *Yale Daily News*. . . . At the one-hundredth anniversary banquet of that paper—whose past chairmen include such once and future kings as Potter Stewart, Kingman Brewster, and William F. Buckley, Jr.—much was made of the fact that the editorial staff used to be small and totally committed and that "newsies" routinely worked fifty hours a week. In effect they belonged to a club; Newsies is how they defined themselves at Yale. Today's student will write one or two articles a week, when he can, and he defines himself as a student. I've never heard the word Newsie except at the banquet.

If I have described the modern undergraduate primarily as a driven creature who is largely ignoring the blithe spirit inside who keeps trying to come out and play, it's because that's where the crunch is, not only at Yale but throughout American education. It's why I think we should all be worried about the values that are nurturing a generation so fearful of risk and so goal-obsessed at such an early age.

I tell students that there is no one "right" way to get ahead—that each of them is a different person, starting from a different point and bound for a different destination. I tell them that change is a tonic and that all the slots are not codified nor the frontiers closed. One of my ways of telling them is to invite men and women who have achieved success outside the academic world to come and talk informally with my students during the year. They are heads of companies or ad agencies, editors of magazines, politicians, public officials, television magnates, labor leaders, business executives, Broadway producers, artists, writers, economists, photographers, scientists, historians— a mixed bag of achievers.

I ask them to say a few words about how they got started. The students assume that they started in their present profession and knew all along that it was what they wanted to do. Luckily for me, most of them got into their field by a circuitous route, to their surprise, after many detours. The students are startled. They can hardly conceive of a career that was not pre-planned. They can hardly imagine allowing the hand of God or chance to nudge them down some unforeseen trail.

Questions for Close Reading

1. What is the selection's thesis? Locate the sentence(s) in which Zinsser states his main idea. If he doesn't state the thesis explicitly, express it in your own words.
2. According to Zinsser, why are the pressures on college students so harmful?
3. Zinsser says that some of the pressures are "intertwined." What does he mean? Give examples from the essay.
4. What actions or attitudes on the part of students can help free them from the pressures that Zinsser describes?
5. Refer to your dictionary as needed to define the following words used in the selection: *privy* (paragraph 3), *venerated* (6), *exhorted* (13), *tenacity* (15), *vacillates* (22), *furtively* (22), and *circuitous* (40).

Questions About the Writer's Craft

1. **The pattern.** When analyzing a subject, writers usually try to identify divisions and classifications that are—within reason—mutually exclusive. But Zinsser acknowledges that the four pressures he discusses can be seen as two distinct pairs, with each pair consisting of two "deeply intertwined" pressures. How does this overlapping of categories help Zinsser make his point?
2. **Other patterns.** In addition to using classification in this essay, what other pattern of development does Zinsser use? How does this additional pattern help him make his point?
3. Why do you suppose Zinsser uses the notes to Carlos as his essay's introduction? What profile of college students does the reader get from these notes?
4. In paragraph 4, the author writes that students want a map "they can follow unswervingly to career security, financial security, Social Security and, presumably, a prepaid grave." What tone is Zinsser using here? Where else does he use this tone?

Writing Assignments Using Division-Classification as a Pattern of Development

1. Zinsser writes as if all students are the same—panicky, overwrought, and materialistic. Take a position counter to his, and write an essay explaining that campuses contain many students different from those Zinsser writes about. To support your point, categorize students into types, giving examples of what each type is like. Be sure that the categories you identify refute Zinsser's analysis of the typical student. The tone of your essay may be serious or playful. You might first consider reading James Barszcz's "Can You Be Educated From a Distance?" (page 522), which explores how students can approach their education.
2. Is economic security the only kind of satisfaction that college students should pursue? Write an essay classifying the various kinds of satisfactions that students could aim for. At the end of the paper, include brief recommendations about ways that students could best spend their time preparing for these different kinds of

satisfactions. James Barszcz's "Can You Be Educated from a Distance?" (page 522) might offer you further perspective on what constitutes a satisfying education.

Writing Assignments Combining Patterns of Development

 3. Using Zinsser's analysis of the pressures on college students, write an essay explaining how these pressures can be reduced or eliminated. Give *practical suggestions* showing how students can avoid or get around the pressures. Also, indicate what society, parents, and college staff can do to help ease students' anxieties. You might benefit from gathering *examples* of and information on this topic in the library and/or on the Internet before writing.

4. Zinsser's essay indicates that today's students are "slotting" themselves into preordained careers and not leaving themselves open to later opportunities. Write an essay *arguing* that this tendency to specialize early in college is either beneficial *or* disastrous for students. Consider such issues as individual freedom, career confusion, changing job markets, changes in society, and the like. In making your argument, consider the *effects* on students of earlier specialization.

Writing Assignment Using a Journal Entry as a Starting Point

5. Write an essay arguing in favor of *or* against the policy of requiring college students to take courses outside their major field. Take the ideas in your pre-reading journal entry and shape them into a convincing argument, remembering to cite the opposing point of view. To gain insight into the complexity of this issue, interview a variety of people having a broad range of viewpoints.

David Brooks

David Brooks is a syndicated columnist whose work appears in newspapers through-out the nation. He was born in 1961 and graduated from the University of Chicago with a degree in history in 1983. Brooks began his journalism career as a police reporter for the City News Bureau in Chicago and then spent nine years at *The Wall Street Journal* as a critic, foreign correspondent, and op-ed page editor. In 1995 he joined *The Weekly Standard* at its inception, and in 2003 he began to write a regular column for *The New York Times*. Brooks is interested in cultural as well as political issues, and he often is on National Public Radio, including *The Diane Rehm Show*, as an analyst. He has written two books, *Bobos in Paradise: The New Upper Class and How They Got There* and *How We Live Now (and Always Have) in the Future Tense*. He is editor of the anthology *Backward and Upward: The New Conservative Writing*. This column was published in *The New York Times* on November 13, 2005.

Pre-Reading Journal Entry

When you are a student, it's natural to think of success and failure simply in terms of grades. However, academic accomplishment is not the only measure of success in one's life. What are your own strengths and successes in life, beyond what you may have achieved in school? Who or what has inspired you to undertake each of these pursuits? Take a few minutes to respond to these questions in your journal.

Psst! "Human Capital"

Help! I'm turning into the "plastics" guy from *The Graduate*.[1] I'm pull-ing people aside at parties and whispering that if they want to understand the future, it's just two words: "Human Capital." 1

If we want to keep up with the Chinese and the Indians, we've got to develop our Human Capital. If we want to remain a just, fluid society: Human Capital. If we want to head off underclass riots: Human Capital. 2

---

[1]Refers to an oft-cited scene in the 1967 film, *The Graduate*. The main character, Benjamin Braddock, has just graduated college and feels adrift about the future. At a family party, the character of Mr. McGuire cryptically "tips off" Benjamin about the plastics industry. He says, "There's a great future in plastics. Think about it. Will you think about it? . . . Shh! Enough said." (editors' note).

As people drift away from me at these parties by pretending to recognize long-lost friends across the room, I'm convinced that they don't really understand what human capital is.

Most people think of human capital the way economists and policy makers do—as the skills and knowledge people need to get jobs and thrive in a modern economy. When President [George W.] Bush proposed his big education reform, he insisted on tests to measure skills and knowledge. When commissions issue reports, they call for longer school years, revamped curriculums and more funds so teachers can transmit skills and knowledge.

But skills and knowledge—the stuff you can measure with tests—is only the most superficial component of human capital. U.S. education reforms have generally failed because they try to improve the skills of students without addressing the underlying components of human capital.

These underlying components are hard to measure and uncomfortable to talk about, but they are the foundation of everything that follows.

There's cultural capital: the habits, assumptions, emotional dispositions and linguistic capacities we unconsciously pick up from families, neighbors and ethnic groups—usually by age 3. In a classic study, James S. Coleman found that what happens in the family shapes a child's educational achievement more than what happens in school. In more recent research, James Heckman and Pedro Carneiro found that "most of the gaps in college attendance and delay are determined by early family factors."

There's social capital: the knowledge of how to behave in groups and within institutions. This can mean, for example, knowing what to do if your community college loses your transcript. Or it can mean knowing the basic rules of politeness. The University of North Carolina now offers seminars to poorer students so they'll know how to behave in restaurants.

There's moral capital: the ability to be trustworthy. Students who drop out of high school, but take the G.E.D. exam, tend to be smarter than high school dropouts. But their lifetime wages tend to be no higher than they are for those with no high school diplomas. That's because many people who pass the G.E.D. are less organized and less dependable than their less educated peers—as employers soon discover. Brains and skills don't matter if you don't show up on time.

There's cognitive capital. This can mean pure, inherited brainpower. But important cognitive skills are not measured by IQ tests and are not fixed. Some people know how to evaluate themselves and their abilities, while others with higher IQ's are clueless. Some low-IQ people can sense what others are feeling, while brainier peers cannot. Such skills can be improved over a lifetime.

Then there's aspirational capital: the fire-in-the-belly ambition to achieve. In his book *The Millionaire Mind,* Thomas J. Stanley reports that the average millionaire had a B-minus collegiate G.P.A.—not very good. But millionaires often had this experience: People told them they were too stupid to achieve something, so they set out to prove the naysayers wrong.

Over the past quarter-century, researchers have done a lot of work trying   12
to understand the different parts of human capital. Their work has been almost
completely ignored by policy makers, who continue to treat human capital as
just skills and knowledge. The result? A series of expensive policy failures.

We now spend more per capita on education than just about any other   13
country on earth, and the results are mediocre. No Child Left Behind treats
students as skill-acquiring cogs in an economic wheel, and the results have
been disappointing. We pour money into Title 1 and Head Start, but the
long-term gains are insignificant.

These programs are not designed for the way people really are. The only   14
things that work are local, human-to-human immersions that transform the
students down to their very beings. Extraordinary schools, which create
intense cultures of achievement, work. Extraordinary teachers, who inspire
students to transform their lives, work. The programs that work touch all the
components of human capital.

There's a great future in Human Capital, buddy. Enough said.   15

Questions for Close Reading

1. What is the selection's thesis? Locate the sentence(s) in which Brooks states his
   main idea. If he doesn't state his thesis explicitly, express it in your own words.
2. According to Brooks, why do policies that focus on teaching children skills and
   knowledge ultimately fail to develop human capital? What policies does he use as
   examples of such failure?
3. In Brooks's view, what role does the family play in the development of human
   capital?
4. What type of human capital do many millionaires possess, and how did they
   acquire it?
5. Refer to your dictionary as needed to define the following words used in the selection: *capital* (paragraph 1), *revamped* (4), *cognitive* (10), *aspirational* (11), *naysayers* (11), *per capita* (13), and *immersions* (14).

Questions About the Writer's Craft

1. Brooks opens this essay by comparing himself to a character in the 1967 movie
   The Graduate. What are the benefits and risks of using such a reference to frame
   the contents of an essay? In your opinion, is this a successful opening? Why or
   why not?
2. **The pattern.** How does Brooks organize his explanation of what human capital
   really consists of? What cues guide the reader in following Brooks's discussion?
3. **Other patterns.** In paragraphs 7 through 11, Brooks develops his ideas about the
   components of human capital. What patterns does he use in each of these paragraphs?
4. This essay was published as a newspaper op-ed column, a type of writing that is
   relatively short—about 750 words. How does the limited length of the piece
   affect the development of Brooks's ideas and evidence? If the piece were longer,
   how could Brooks strengthen its argument?

Writing Assignments Using Division-Classification as a Pattern of Development

1. Choose one of the elements of human capital that Brooks describes, and write an essay in which you analyze it further into its component parts. For example, if you choose cognitive capital, you can write about specific cognitive skills such as memorizing, learning, problem solving, and creativity.

 2. According to economists, capital is any human-made resource used to produce goods and services. For example, capital includes buildings, factories, machinery, equipment, parts, tools, roads, and railroads. Do some research on the concept of capital as used by economists, and write an essay explaining how economists categorize various types of capital, including the human capital Brooks discusses in his essay.

Writing Assignments Combining Patterns of Development

 3. Brooks indicates that the results of the government programs No Child Left Behind, Title I, and Head Start fail to improve human capital. Select one of these programs, and do some research on it at the library or on the Internet. Write an essay that *explains* how aspects of the program are designed to solve specific problems. *Compare* and *contrast* the goals of the program with its actual *effects*.

4. Brooks's concept of moral capital is closely tied to the moral values that society holds important and that children learn from their families and others with whom they interact. Write an essay in which you *narrate* the story of a moral issue you have faced, *comparing* and *contrasting* the choices you had. Explain the *process* you went through to resolve the problem.

Writing Assignment Using a Journal Entry as a Starting Point

 5. Review your pre-reading journal entry about your successes and strengths beyond what you may have achieved in school. Select the two or three most significant ones, and write an essay in which you divide and classify these achievements. Are these achievements athletic, artistic, or service- or family-oriented—or do they belong to some other category? As you write about each achievement, consider who or what has *caused* or inspired you to strive for that accomplishment. To see how two writers address the issue of how children's character can be influenced, read Ellen Goodman's "Family Counterculture" (page 6) and Gordon Parks's "Flavio's Home" (page 84).

William Lutz

With a dash of humor, William Lutz (1941–), professor of English at Rutgers University and former editor of the *Quarterly Review of Doublespeak,* writes about a subject he takes very seriously: doublespeak—the use of language to evade, deceive, and mislead. An expert on language, Lutz has appeared on many national television programs, among them the *Today Show, Larry King Live,* and the *MacNeil-Lehrer News Hour.* Lutz, who has both a doctorate in English and a Doctor of Law degree, has written over two dozen articles and is the author or coauthor of fourteen books, including the best-selling *Doublespeak: From Revenue Enhancement to Terminal Living* (1989) as well as its sequels, *Why No One Knows What Anyone's Saying Anymore* (1996) and *Doublespeak Defined: Cut Through the Bull★★★★ and Get to the Point* (1999). He is also the coauthor of *Firestorm at Peshtigo* (2002) about the devastating 1871 fire in a Wisconsin mining town. The following piece is from *Doublespeak.*

Pre-Reading Journal Entry

At one time or another, everyone twists language in order to avoid telling the full truth. In your journal, list several instances which demonstrate that indirect, partially true language ("doublespeak") is sometimes desirable, even necessary. In each case, why was this evasive language used?

Doublespeak

There are no potholes in the streets of Tucson, Arizona, just "pavement 1
deficiencies." The Reagan Administration didn't propose any new taxes, just
"revenue enhancement" through new "user's fees." Those aren't bums on
the street, just "non-goal oriented members of society." There are no more
poor people, just "fiscal underachievers." There was no robbery of an automatic teller machine, just an "unauthorized withdrawal." The patient didn't
die because of medical malpractice, it was just a "diagnostic misadventure of
a high magnitude." The U.S. Army doesn't kill the enemy anymore, it just
"services the target." And the doublespeak goes on.

Doublespeak is language that pretends to communicate but really doesn't. 2
It is language that makes the bad seem good, the negative appear positive,
the unpleasant appear attractive or at least tolerable. Doublespeak is language
that avoids or shifts responsibility, language that is at variance with its real or

purported meaning. It is language that conceals or prevents thought; rather than extending thought, doublespeak limits it. . . .

How to Spot Doublespeak

How can you spot doublespeak? Most of the time you will recognize   3
doublespeak when you see or hear it. But, if you have any doubts, you can identify doublespeak just by answering these questions: Who is saying what to whom, under what conditions and circumstances, with what intent, and with what results? Answering these questions will usually help you identify as doublespeak language that appears to be legitimate or that at first glance doesn't even appear to be doublespeak.

First Kind of Doublespeak

There are at least four kinds of doublespeak. The first is the euphemism,   4
an inoffensive or positive word or phrase used to avoid a harsh, unpleasant, or distasteful reality. But a euphemism can also be a tactful word or phrase which avoids directly mentioning a painful reality, or it can be an expression used out of concern for the feelings of someone else, or to avoid directly discussing a topic subject to a social or cultural taboo.

When you use a euphemism because of your sensitivity for someone's   5
feelings or out of concern for a recognized social or cultural taboo, it is not doublespeak. For example, you express your condolences that someone has "passed away" because you do not want to say to a grieving person, "I'm sorry your father is dead." When you use the euphemism "passed away," no one is misled. Moreover, the euphemism functions here not just to protect the feelings of another person, but to communicate also your concern for that person's feelings during a period of mourning. When you excuse yourself to go to the "restroom," or you mention that someone is "sleeping with" or "involved with" someone else, you do not mislead anyone about your meaning, but you do respect the social taboos about discussing bodily functions and sex in direct terms. You also indicate your sensitivity to the feelings of your audience, which is usually considered a mark of courtesy and good manners.

However, when a euphemism is used to mislead or deceive, it becomes   6
doublespeak. For example, in 1984 the U.S. State Department announced that it would no longer use the word "killing" in its annual report on the status of human rights in countries around the world. Instead, it would use the phrase "unlawful or arbitrary deprivation of life," which the department claimed was more accurate. Its real purpose for using this phrase was simply to avoid discussing the embarrassing situation of government-sanctioned killings in countries that are supported by the United States and have been certified by the United States as respecting the human rights of their citizens.

This use of a euphemism constitutes doublespeak, since it is designed to mislead, to cover up the unpleasant. Its real intent is at variance with its apparent intent. It is language designed to alter our perception of reality.

The Pentagon, too, avoids discussing unpleasant realities when it refers   7
to bombs and artillery shells that fall on civilian targets as "incontinent ordnance." And in 1977 the Pentagon tried to slip funding for the neutron bomb unnoticed into an appropriations bill by calling it a "radiation enhancement device."

Second Kind of Doublespeak

A second kind of doublespeak is jargon, the specialized language of a   8
trade, profession, or similar group, such as that used by doctors, lawyers, engineers, educators, or car mechanics. Jargon can serve an important and useful function. Within a group, jargon functions as a kind of verbal shorthand that allows members of the group to communicate with each other clearly, efficiently, and quickly. Indeed, it is a mark of membership in the group to be able to use and understand the group's jargon.

But jargon, like the euphemism, can also be doublespeak. It can be—and   9
often is—pretentious, obscure, and esoteric terminology used to give an air of profundity, authority, and prestige to speakers and their subject matter. Jargon as doublespeak often makes the simple appear complex, the ordinary profound, the obvious insightful. In this sense it is used not to express but impress. With such doublespeak, the act of smelling something becomes "organoleptic analysis," glass becomes "fused silicate," a crack in a metal support beam becomes a "discontinuity," conservative economic policies become "distributionally conservative notions."

Lawyers, for example, speak of an "involuntary conversion" of property   10
when discussing the loss or destruction of property through theft, accident, or condemnation. If your house burns down or if your car is stolen, you have suffered an involuntary conversion of your property. When used by lawyers in a legal situation, such jargon is a legitimate use of language, since lawyers can be expected to understand the term.

However, when a member of a specialized group uses its jargon to com-   11
municate with a person outside the group, and uses it knowing that the nonmember does not understand such language, then there is doublespeak. For example, on May 9, 1978, a National Airlines 727 airplane crashed while attempting to land at the Pensacola, Florida airport. Three of the fifty-two passengers aboard the airplane were killed. As a result of the crash, National made an after-tax insurance benefit of $1.7 million, or an extra 18¢ a share dividend for its stockholders. Now National Airlines had two problems: It did not want to talk about one of its airplanes crashing, and it had to account for the $1.7 million when it issued its annual report to its stockholders.

National solved the problem by inserting a footnote in its annual report which explained that the $1.7 million income was due to "the involuntary conversion of a 727." National thus acknowledged the crash of its airplane and the subsequent profit it made from the crash, without once mentioning the accident or the deaths. However, because airline officials knew that most stockholders in the company, and indeed most of the general public, were not familiar with legal jargon, the use of such jargon constituted doublespeak.

Third Kind of Doublespeak

A third kind of doublespeak is gobbledygook or bureaucratese. Basically, such doublespeak is simply a matter of piling on words, of overwhelming the audience with words, the bigger the words and the longer the sentences the better. Alan Greenspan, then chair of President Nixon's Council of Economic Advisors, was quoted in *The Philadelphia Inquirer* in 1974 as having testified before a Senate committee that "It is a tricky problem to find the particular calibration in timing that would be appropriate to stem the acceleration in risk premiums created by falling incomes without prematurely aborting the decline in the inflation-generated risk premiums."

Nor has Mr. Greenspan's language changed since then. Speaking to the meeting of the Economic Club of New York in 1988, Mr. Greenspan, now Federal Reserve chair,[1] said, "I guess I should warn you, if I turn out to be particularly clear, you've probably misunderstood what I've said." Mr. Greenspan's doublespeak doesn't seem to have held back his career.

Sometimes gobbledygook may sound impressive, but when the quote is later examined in print it doesn't even make sense. During the 1988 presidential campaign, vice-presidential candidate Senator Dan Quayle explained the need for a strategic-defense initiative by saying, "Why wouldn't an enhanced deterrent, a more stable peace, a better prospect to denying the ones who enter conflict in the first place to have a reduction of offensive systems and an introduction to defense capability? I believe this is the route the country will eventually go."

The investigation into the Challenger disaster in 1986 revealed the doublespeak of gobbledygook and bureaucratese used by too many involved in the shuttle program. When Jesse Moore, NASA's associate administrator, was asked if the performance of the shuttle program had improved with each launch or if it had remained the same, he answered, "I think our performance in terms of the liftoff performance and in terms of the orbital performance, we knew more about the envelope we were operating under, and we have been pretty accurately staying in that. And so I would say the performance has not by design drastically improved. I think we have been

---

[1]Alan Greenspan resigned as chair of the Federal Reserve on January 31, 2006 (editors' note).

able to characterize the performance more as a function of our launch experience as opposed to it improving as a function of time." While this language may appear to be jargon, a close look will reveal that it is really just gobbledygook laced with jargon. But you really have to wonder if Mr. Moore had any idea what he was saying.

Fourth Kind of Doublespeak

The fourth kind of doublespeak is inflated language that is designed to make the ordinary seem extraordinary; to make everyday things seem impressive; to give an air of importance to people, situations, or things that would not normally be considered important; to make the simple seem complex. Often this kind of doublespeak isn't hard to spot, and it is usually pretty funny. While car mechanics may be called "automotive internists," elevator operators members of the "vertical transportation corps," used cars "preowned" or "experienced cars," and black-and-white television sets described as having "non-multicolor capability," you really aren't misled all that much by such language.   16

However, you may have trouble figuring out that, when Chrysler "initiates a career alternative enhancement program," it is really laying off five thousand workers; or that "negative patient care outcome" means the patient died; or that "rapid oxidation" means a fire in a nuclear power plant.   17

The doublespeak of inflated language can have serious consequences. In Pentagon doublespeak, "pre-emptive counterattack" means that American forces attacked first; "engaged the enemy on all sides" means American troops were ambushed; "backloading of augmentation personnel" means a retreat by American troops. In the doublespeak of the military, the 1983 invasion of Grenada was conducted not by the U.S. Army, Navy, Air Force, and Marines, but by the "Caribbean Peace Keeping Forces." But then, according to the Pentagon, it wasn't an invasion, it was a "predawn vertical insertion." . . .   18

The Dangers of Doublespeak

These . . . examples of doublespeak should make it clear that doublespeak is not the product of carelessness or sloppy thinking. Indeed, most doublespeak is the product of clear thinking and is carefully designed and constructed to appear to communicate when in fact it doesn't. It is language designed not to lead but mislead. It is language designed to distort reality and corrupt thought. . . . When a fire in a nuclear reactor building is called "rapid oxidation," an explosion in a nuclear power plant is called an "energetic disassembly," the illegal overthrow of a legitimate government is termed "destabilizing a government," and lies are seen as "inoperative statements," we are hearing doublespeak that attempts to avoid responsibility and   19 make the bad seem good, the negative appear positive, something unpleasant appear attractive; and which seems to communicate but doesn't. It is language designed to alter our perception of reality and corrupt our thinking. Such language does not provide us with the tools we need to develop, advance, and preserve our culture and our civilization. Such language breeds suspicion, cynicism, distrust, and, ultimately, hostility.

Questions for Close Reading

1. What is the selection's thesis? Locate the sentence(s) in which Lutz states his main idea. If he doesn't state the thesis explicitly, express it in your own words.
2. According to Lutz, four questions help people "spot" doublespeak. What are the questions? How do they help people distinguish between legitimate language and doublespeak?
3. Lutz's headings indicate simply "First Kind of Doublespeak," "Second Kind of Doublespeak," and so on. What terms does Lutz use to identify the four kinds of doublespeak? Cite one example of each kind.
4. What, according to Lutz, are the dangers of doublespeak?
5. Refer to your dictionary as needed to define the following words used in the selection: *variance* (paragraph 6), *esoteric* (9), *profundity* (9), *dividend* (11), and *initiative* (14).

Questions About the Writer's Craft

1. **The pattern.** Does Lutz make his four categories of doublespeak mutually exclusive, or does he let them overlap? Cite specific examples to support your answer. Why do you think Lutz took the approach he did?
2. **Other patterns.** What other patterns, besides division-classification, does Lutz use in this selection? Cite examples of at least two other patterns. Explain how each pattern reinforces Lutz's thesis.
3. Lutz quotes Alan Greenspan twice: first in paragraph 12 and again in paragraph 13. What is surprising about Greenspan's second comment (paragraph 13)? Why might Lutz have included this second quotation?
4. How would you characterize Lutz's tone in the essay? What key words indicate his attitude toward the material he discusses? Why do you suppose he chose this particular tone?

Writing Assignments Using Division-Classification as a Pattern of Development

∞ 1. According to Lutz, doublespeak "is language designed to alter our perception of reality." Using two of Lutz's categories (or any others you devise), analyze an advertisement or commercial that you think deliberately uses doublespeak to mislead consumers. Before writing your paper, read Ann McClintock's "Propaganda Techniques in Today's Advertising" (page 270). Feel free to include any of McClintock's interpretations in your paper.

2. Select *one* area of life that you know well. Possibilities include life in a college dormitory, the parent-child relationship, the dating scene, and sibling conflicts. Focus on a specific type of speech (for example, gossip, reprimands, flirtation, or criticism) that occurs in this area. Then identify the component parts of that type of speech. You might, for example, analyze dormitory gossip about individual students, couples, and professors. Reach some conclusions about the kinds of speech you discuss. Do you consider them funny, pathetic, or troubling? Your tone should be consistent with the conclusions you reach.

Writing Assignments Combining Patterns of Development

3. Find a spoken or written *example* of doublespeak that disturbs you. Possibilities include a political advertisement, television commercial, newspaper article, or legal document. Write a letter of complaint to the appropriate person or office, using convincing examples to point out what is misleading about the communication. Pointing out negative impressions or *consequences* resulting from the doublespeak will enhance your position. Caroline Rego's "The Fine Art of Complaining" (page 327) offers guidelines for writing effective letters of complaint.

4. In his essay, Lutz examines the relationship between language and perception. Identify two closely related terms, and *contrast* the different perceptions of reality represented by each term. For example, you might contrast "African American" and "Negro," "Ms." and "Miss," "gay" and "homosexual," "dolls" and "action figures," or "pro-life" and "anti-abortion." Interviewing family, friends, and classmates will help you identify ideas and *examples* to explore in the essay. For a discussion of the connection between language and perception, read at least one of the following: Leslie Savan's "Black Talk and Pop Culture" (page 193), Ann McClintock's "Propaganda Techniques in Today's Advertising" (page 270), David Shipley's "Talk About Editing" (page 296), and Stanley Fish's "Free-Speech Follies" (page 534).

Writing Assignment Using a Journal Entry as a Starting Point

5. Select from your pre-reading journal entry two or three compelling instances of *beneficial* doublespeak. Use these examples in an essay arguing that doublespeak isn't always harmful. For each example cited, contrast the positive effects of doublespeak with the potentially negative consequences of *not* using it. Brainstorming with others will help you generate convincing examples. Before you begin writing, consider reading one of the following essays, all of which illustrate varying instances of doublespeak: Audre Lorde's "The Fourth of July" (page 137) and Beth Johnson's "Bombs Bursting in Air" (page 209).

Ann McClintock

Ann McClintock (1946–) was educated at Temple University in Philadelphia and later earned an advanced degree from the University of Pennsylvania. Formerly director of occupational therapy at Ancora State Hospital in New Jersey, she has also worked as a freelance editor and writer. A frequent speaker before community groups, McClintock is especially interested in the effects of advertising on American life. The following selection, revised for this text, is part of a work in progress on the way propaganda techniques are used to sell products and political candidates.

Pre-Reading Journal Entry

How susceptible are you to ads and commercials? Do you consider yourself an easy target, or are you a "hard sell"? Have you purchased any products simply because you were won over by effective advertising strategies? What products have you not purchased because you deliberately didn't let yourself be swayed by advertisers' tactics? In your journal, reflect on these questions.

Propaganda Techniques in Today's Advertising

Americans, adults and children alike, are being seduced. They are being brainwashed. And few of us protest. Why? Because the seducers and the brainwashers are the advertisers we willingly invite into our homes. We are victims, content—even eager—to be victimized. We read advertisers' propaganda messages in newspapers and magazines; we watch their alluring images on television. We absorb their messages and images into our subconscious. We all do it—even those of us who claim to see through advertisers' tricks and therefore feel immune to advertising's charm. Advertisers lean heavily on propaganda to sell products, whether the "products" are a brand of toothpaste, a candidate for office, or a particular political viewpoint.

Propaganda is a systematic effort to influence people's opinions, to win them over to a certain view or side. Propaganda is not necessarily concerned with what is true or false, good or bad. Propagandists simply want people to believe the messages being sent. Often, propagandists will use outright lies or more subtle deceptions to sway people's opinions. In a propaganda war, any tactic is considered fair.

When we hear the word "propaganda," we usually think of a foreign   3
menace: anti-American radio programs broadcast by a totalitarian regime or
brainwashing tactics practiced on hostages. Although propaganda may seem
relevant only in the political arena, the concept can be applied fruitfully to
the way products and ideas are sold in advertising. Indeed, the vast majority
of us are targets in advertisers' propaganda war. Every day, we are bombarded with slogans, print and Internet pop-up ads, commercials, packaging
claims, billboards, trademarks, logos, and designer brands—all forms of propaganda. One study reports that each of us, during an average day, is exposed
to over *five hundred* advertising claims of various types. This saturation may
even increase in the future since current trends include ads on movie screens,
shopping carts, videocassettes, even public television.

What kind of propaganda techniques do advertisers use? There are seven   4
basic types:

1. *Name Calling*   Name calling is a propaganda tactic in which nega-   5
tively charged names are hurled against the opposing side or competitor. By
using such names, propagandists try to arouse feelings of mistrust, fear, and
hate in their audiences. For example, a political advertisement may label an
opposing candidate a "loser," "fence-sitter," or "warmonger." Depending
on the advertiser's target market, labels such as "a friend of big business" or
"a dues-paying member of the party in power" can be the epithets that damage an opponent. Ads for products may also use name calling. An American
manufacturer may refer, for instance, to a "foreign car" in its commercial—
not an "imported" one. The label of foreignness will have unpleasant connotations in many people's minds. A childhood rhyme claims that "names
can never hurt me," but name calling is an effective way to damage the opposition, whether it is another car maker or a congressional candidate.

2. *Glittering Generalities*   Using glittering generalities is the opposite   6
of name calling. In this case, advertisers surround their products with attractive—and slippery—words and phrases. They use vague terms that are difficult to define and that may have different meanings to different people:
freedom, democratic, all-American, progressive, Christian, and *justice.* Many
such words have strong, affirmative overtones. This kind of language stirs
positive feelings in people, feelings that may spill over to the product or idea
being pitched. As with name calling, the emotional response may over-
whelm logic. Target audiences accept the product without thinking very
much about what the glittering generalities mean—or whether they even
apply to the product. After all, how can anyone oppose "truth, justice, and
the American way"?

The ads for politicians and political causes often use glittering generali-   7
ties because such "buzz words" can influence votes. Election slogans include
high-sounding but basically empty phrases like the following:

"He cares about people." (That's nice, but is he a better candidate than
   his opponent?)
"Vote for progress." (Progress by *whose* standards?)
"They'll make this country great again." (What does "great" mean?
   Does "great" mean the same thing to others as it does to me?)
"Vote for the future." (What kind of future?)
"If you love America, vote for Phyllis Smith." (If I don't vote for Smith,
   does that mean I don't love America?)

Ads for consumer goods are also sprinkled with glittering generalities.
Product names, for instance, are supposed to evoke good feelings: *Luvs* diapers, *Stayfree* feminine hygiene products, *Joy* liquid detergent, *Loving Care*
hair color, *Almost Home* cookies, *Yankee Doodle* pastries. Product slogans
lean heavily on vague but comforting phrases: Sears is "Good life. Great
price," General Electric "brings good things to life," and Dow Chemical
"lets you do great things." Chevrolet, we are told, is the "heartbeat of America," and Chrysler boasts cars that are "built by Americans for Americans."

   3. *Transfer*   In transfer, advertisers try to improve the image of a product by associating it with a symbol most people respect, like the American flag
or Uncle Sam. The advertisers hope that the prestige attached to the symbol
will carry over to the product. Many companies use transfer devices to identify their products: Lincoln Insurance shows a profile of the president; Conti-
nental Insurance portrays a Revolutionary War minuteman; Amtrak's logo is
red, white, and blue; Liberty Mutual's corporate symbol is the Statue of Liberty; Allstate's name is cradled by a pair of protective, fatherly hands.
   Corporations also use the transfer technique when they sponsor prestigious shows on radio and television. These shows function as symbols of
dignity and class. Kraft Corporation, for instance, sponsored a "Leonard
Bernstein Conducts Beethoven" concert, while Gulf Oil is the sponsor of
National Geographic specials and Mobil supports public television's *Master-
piece Theater.* In this way, corporations can reach an educated, influential
audience and, perhaps, improve their public image by associating themselves
with quality programming.
   Political ads, of course, practically wrap themselves in the flag. Ads for a
political candidate often show either the Washington Monument, a Fourth
of July parade, the Stars and Stripes, a bald eagle soaring over the mountains,
or a white-steepled church on the village green. The national anthem or
"America the Beautiful" may play softly in the background. Such appeals to
Americans' love of country can surround the candidate with an aura of patriotism and integrity.

   4. *Testimonial*   The testimonial is one of advertisers' most-loved and most-
used propaganda techniques. Similar to the transfer device, the testimonial

capitalizes on the admiration people have for a celebrity to make the product shine more brightly—even though the celebrity is not an expert on the product being sold.

Print and television ads offer a nonstop parade of testimonials: here's 13
William Shatner for Priceline.com; here's basketball star Michael Jordan eating Wheaties; a slew of well-known people (including pop star Madonna) advertise clothing from the Gap; and Jerry Seinfeld assures us he never goes anywhere without his American Express card. Testimonials can sell movies, too; newspaper ads for films often feature favorable comments by well-known reviewers. And, in recent years, testimonials have played an important role in pitching books; the backs of paperbacks frequently list complimentary blurbs by celebrities.

Political candidates, as well as their ad agencies, know the value of testi- 14
monials. Barbra Streisand lent her star appeal to the presidential campaign of Bill Clinton, while Arnold Schwarzenegger endorsed George H. W. Bush. Even controversial social issues are debated by celebrities. The nuclear-freeze debate, for instance, starred Paul Newman for the pro side and Charlton Heston for the con.

As illogical as testimonials sometimes are (Pepsi's Michael Jackson, for 15
instance, is a health-food adherent who does not drink soft drinks), they are effective propaganda. We like the *person* so much that we like the *product* too.

5. *Plain Folks*   The plain folks approach says, in effect, "Buy me or vote 16
for me. I'm just like you." Regular folks will surely like Bob Evans's Down on the Farm Country Sausage or good old-fashioned Countrytime Lemonade. Some ads emphasize the idea that "we're all in the same boat." We see people making long-distance calls for just the reasons we do—to put the baby on the phone to Grandma or to tell Mom we love her. And how do these folksy, warmhearted (usually saccharine) scenes affect us? They're supposed to make us feel that AT&T—the multinational corporate giant—has the same values we do. Similarly, we are introduced to the little people at Ford, the ordinary folks who work on the assembly line, not to bigwigs in their executive offices. What's the purpose of such an approach? To encourage us to buy a car built by these honest, hardworking "everyday Joes" who care about quality as much as we do.

Political advertisements make almost as much use of the "plain folks" 17
appeal as they do of transfer devices. Candidates wear hard hats, farmers' caps, and assembly-line coveralls. They jog around the block and carry their own luggage through the airport. The idea is to convince voters that the candidates are average people, not the elite—not wealthy lawyers or executives but common citizens.

6. *Card Stacking*   When people say that "the cards were stacked 18
against me," they mean that they were never given a fair chance. Applied to

propaganda, card stacking means that one side may suppress or distort evidence, tell half-truths, oversimplify the facts, or set up a "straw man"—a false target—to divert attention from the issue at hand. Card stacking is a difficult form of propaganda both to detect and to combat. When a candidate claims that an opponent has "changed his mind five times on this important issue," we tend to accept the claim without investigating whether the candidate had good reasons for changing his mind. Many people are simply swayed by the distorted claim that the candidate is "waffling" on the issue.

Advertisers often stack the cards in favor of the products they are pushing. They may, for instance, use what are called "weasel words." These are small words that usually slip right past us, but that make the difference between reality and illusion. The weasel words are underlined in the following claims:

> "Helps control dandruff symptoms." (The audience usually interprets this as *stops* dandruff.)
>
> "Most dentists surveyed recommend sugarless gum for their patients who chew gum." (We hear the "most dentists" and "for their patients," but we don't think about how many were surveyed or whether the dentists first recommended that the patients not chew gum at all.)
>
> "Sticker price $1,000 lower than most comparable cars." (How many is "most"? What car does the advertiser consider "comparable"?)

Advertisers also use a card stacking trick when they make an unfinished claim. For example, they will say that their product has "twice as much pain reliever." We are left with a favorable impression. We don't usually ask, "Twice as much pain reliever as what?" Or advertisers may make extremely vague claims that sound alluring but have no substance: Toyota's "Oh, what a feeling!"; Vantage cigarettes' "The taste of success"; "The spirit of Marlboro"; Coke's "the real thing." Another way to stack the cards in favor of a certain product is to use scientific-sounding claims that are not supported by sound research. When Ford claimed that its LTD model was "400% quieter," many people assumed that the LTD must be quieter than all other cars. When taken to court, however, Ford admitted that the phrase referred to the difference between the noise level inside and outside the LTD. Other scientific-sounding claims use mysterious ingredients that are never explained as selling points: "Retsyn," "special whitening agents," "the ingredient doctors recommend."

7. *Bandwagon* In the bandwagon technique, advertisers pressure, "Everyone's doing it. Why don't you?" This kind of propaganda often succeeds because many people have a deep desire not to be different. Political

ads tell us to vote for the "winning candidate." Advertisers know we tend to feel comfortable doing what others do; we want to be on the winning team. Or ads show a series of people proclaiming, "I'm voting for the Senator. I don't know why anyone wouldn't." Again, the audience feels under pressure to conform.

In the marketplace, the bandwagon approach lures buyers. Ads tell us   22
that "nobody doesn't like Sara Lee" (the message is that you must be weird if you don't). They tell us that "most people prefer Brand X two to one over other leading brands" (to be like the majority, we should buy Brand X). If we don't drink Pepsi, we're left out of "the Pepsi generation." To take part in "America's favorite health kick," the National Dairy Council asks us, "Got Milk?" And Honda motorcycle ads, praising the virtues of being a follower, tell us, "Follow the leader. He's on a Honda."

Why do these propaganda techniques work? Why do so many of us buy   23
the products, viewpoints, and candidates urged on us by propaganda messages? They work because they appeal to our emotions, not to our minds. Often, in fact, they capitalize on our prejudices and biases. For example, if we are convinced that environmentalists are radicals who want to destroy America's record of industrial growth and progress, then we will applaud the candidate who refers to them as "treehuggers." Clear thinking requires hard work: analyzing a claim, researching the facts, examining both sides of an issue, using logic to see the flaws in an argument. Many of us would rather let the propagandists do our thinking for us.

Because propaganda is so effective, it is important to detect it and under-   24
stand how it is used. We may conclude, after close examination, that some propaganda sends a truthful, worthwhile message. Some advertising, for instance, urges us not to drive drunk, to become volunteers, to contribute to charity. Even so, we must be aware that propaganda is being used. Otherwise, we have consented to handing over to others our independence of thought and action.

Questions for Close Reading

1. What is the selection's thesis? Locate the sentence(s) in which McClintock states her main idea. If she doesn't state the thesis explicitly, express it in your own words.
2. What is *propaganda?* What mistaken associations do people often have with this term?
3. What are "weasel words"? How do they trick listeners?
4. Why does McClintock believe we should be better informed about propaganda techniques?
5. Refer to your dictionary as needed to define the following words used in the selection: *seduced* (paragraph 1), *warmonger* (5), and *elite* (17).

Questions About the Writer's Craft

1. **The pattern and other patterns.** Before explaining the categories into which propaganda techniques can be grouped, McClintock provides a *definition* of propaganda. Is the definition purely informative, or does it have a larger objective? If you think the latter, what is the definition's broader purpose?
2. In her introduction, McClintock uses loaded words such as *seduced* and *brainwashed*. What effect do these words have on the reader?
3. Locate places in the essay where McClintock uses questions. Which are rhetorical and which are genuine queries?
4. What kind of conclusion does McClintock provide for the essay?

Writing Assignments Using Division-Classification as a Pattern of Development

∞ 1. McClintock cautions us to be sensitive to propaganda in advertising. Young children, however, aren't capable of this kind of awareness. With pen or pencil in hand, watch some commercials aimed at children, such as those for toys, cereals, and fast food. Then analyze the use of propaganda techniques in these commercials. Using division-classification, write an essay describing the main propaganda techniques you observed. Support your analysis with examples drawn from the commercials. Remember to provide a thesis that indicates your opinion of the advertising techniques. For additional insight into this issue, read Ellen Goodman's "Family Counterculture" (page 6) and Kay S. Hymowitz's "Tweens: Ten Going on Sixteen" (page 202).
2. Like advertising techniques, television shows can be classified. Avoiding the obvious system of classifying according to game shows, detective shows, and situation comedies, come up with your own original division-classification principle. Possibilities include how family life is depicted, the way work is presented, how male-female relationships are portrayed. Using one such principle, write an essay in which you categorize popular TV shows into three types. Refer to specific shows to support your classification system. Your attitude toward the shows being discussed should be made clear.

Writing Assignments Combining Patterns of Development

∞ 3. McClintock says that card stacking "distort[s] evidence, tell[s] half-truths, oversimpli[fies] the facts" (paragraph 18). Focusing on an extended *example* such as an editorial, a political campaign, a print ad, or a television commercial, analyze the extent to which card stacking is used as a *persuasive* strategy. Reading William Lutz's "Doublespeak" (page 263) will deepen your understanding of the extent to which the truth can be distorted.
4. To increase further your sensitivity to the moral dimensions of propaganda, write a proposal outlining an ad campaign for a real or imaginary product or elected official. The introduction to your proposal should identify who or what is to be promoted, and the thesis or plan of development should indicate the specific

propaganda techniques you suggest. In the paper's supporting paragraphs, explain the *process* by which these techniques would be used to promote your product or candidate and what their desired *effects* would be.

Writing Assignment Using a Journal Entry as a Starting Point

5. Write an essay showing that, on the whole, you are fairly susceptible to *or* are fairly immune to advertising ploys. Drawing upon your pre-reading journal entry, illustrate your position with lively details of advertising campaigns that won you over—or that failed to sway you. Draw upon some of McClintock's terminology when describing advertisers' techniques. Your essay may have a serious or a playful tone.

Additional Writing Topics

DIVISION-CLASSIFICATION

General Assignments

Choose one of the following subjects and write an essay developed wholly or in part through division-classification. Start by determining the purpose of the essay. Do you want to inform, compare and contrast, or persuade? Apply a single, significant principle of division or classification to your subject. Don't switch the principle midway through your analysis. Also, be sure that the types or categories you create are as complete and mutually exclusive as possible.

Division

1. A shopping mall
2. A video and/or stereo system
3. A fruit, such as a pineapple, an orange, or a banana
4. A tax dollar
5. A particular kind of team
6. A word-processing system
7. A human hand
8. A meal
9. A meeting
10. A favorite poem, story, or play
11. A favorite restaurant
12. A school library
13. A basement
14. A playground, gym, or other recreational area
15. A church service
16. A wedding or funeral
17. An eventful week in your life
18. A college campus
19. A television show or movie
20. A homecoming or other special weekend

Classification

1. People in a waiting room
2. Holidays
3. Closets
4. Roommates
5. Salad bars
6. Divorces
7. Beds
8. Students in a class
9. Shoes

10. Summer movies
11. Teachers
12. Neighbors
13. College courses
14. Bosses
15. Computer/Internet users
16. Mothers or fathers
17. Commercials
18. Vacations
19. Trash
20. Relatives

Assignments With a Specific Purpose, Audience, and Point of View

On Campus

1. You're a dorm counselor. During orientation week, you'll be talking to students on your floor about the different kinds of problems they may have with roommates. Write your talk, describing each kind of problem and explaining how to cope with it.

2. As your college newspaper's TV critic, you plan to write a review of the fall shows, most of which—in your opinion—lack originality. To show how stereotypical the programs are, select one type (for example, situation comedies or crime dramas). Then use a specific division-classification principle to illustrate that the same stale formulas are trotted out from show to show.

3. Asked to write an editorial for the campus paper, you decide to do a half-serious piece on taking "mental health" days off from classes. Structure your essay around three kinds of occasions when "playing hooky" is essential for maintaining sanity.

At Home or in the Community

4. Your favorite magazine runs an editorial asking readers to send in what they think are the main challenges facing their particular gender group. Write a letter to the editor in which you identify at least three categories of problems that your sex faces. Be sure to provide lively, specific examples to illustrate each category. In your letter, you may adopt a serious or lighthearted tone, depending on your overall subject matter.

On the Job

5. As a driving instructor, you decide to prepare a lecture on the types of drivers that your students are likely to encounter on the road. In your lecture, categorize drivers according to a specific principle and show the behaviors of each type.

6. A seasoned camp counselor, you've been asked to prepare, for new counselors, an informational sheet on children's emotional needs. Categorizing those needs into types, explain what counselors can do to nurture youngsters emotionally.

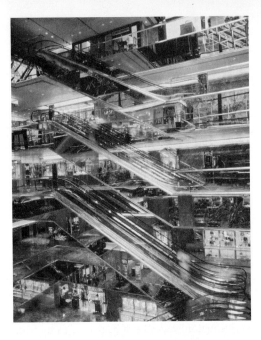

PROCESS ANALYSIS

WHAT IS PROCESS ANALYSIS?

Perhaps you've noticed the dogged determination of small children when they learn how to do something new. Whether trying to tie their shoelaces or tell time, little children struggle along, creating knotted tangles, confusing the hour with the minute hand. But they don't give up. Mastering such basic skills makes them feel less dependent on the adults of the world—all of whom seem to know how to do everything. Actually, none of us is born knowing how to do very much. We spend a good deal of our lives learning— everything from speaking our first word to balancing our first bank statement. Indeed, the milestones in our lives are often linked to the processes we have mastered: how to cross the street alone; how to drive a car; how to make a speech without being paralyzed by fear.

Process analysis, a technique that explains the steps or sequence involved in doing something, satisfies our need to learn as well as our curiosity about how the world works. All the self-help books flooding the market today (*Managing Stress, How to Make a Million in Real Estate, Ten Days to a Perfect Body*) are examples of process analysis. The instructions on the federal tax form and the recipes in a cookbook are also process analyses. Several television shows also capitalize on our desire to learn how things happen: *The Wild Kingdom* shows how animals survive in faraway lands, and *CSI: Crime Scene Investigation* details how investigators gather evidence and use crime lab techniques to catch criminals. Process analysis can be more than merely interesting or entertaining, though; it can be of critical importance. Consider a waiter hurriedly skimming

280

the "Choking Aid" instructions posted on a restaurant wall or an air-traffic controller following emergency procedures in an effort to prevent a midair collision. In these last examples, the consequences could be fatal if the process analyses were slipshod, inaccurate, or confusing.

Undoubtedly, all of us have experienced less dramatic effects of poorly written process analyses. Perhaps you've tried to assemble a bicycle and spent hours sorting through a stack of parts, only to end up with one or two extra pieces never mentioned in the instructions. Or maybe you were baffled when putting up a set of wall shelves because the instructions used unfamiliar terms such as *mitered cleat, wing nut,* and *dowel pin.* No wonder many people stay clear of anything that actually admits "assembly required."

HOW PROCESS ANALYSIS FITS YOUR PURPOSE AND AUDIENCE

You will use process analysis in two types of writing situations: (1) when you want to give step-by-step instructions to readers showing how they can do something, or (2) when you want readers to understand how something happens even though they won't actually follow the steps outlined. The first kind of process analysis is *directional;* the second is *informational.*

When you look at the cooking instructions on a package of frozen vegetables or follow guidelines for completing a job application, you're reading directional process analysis. A serious essay explaining how to select a college and a humorous essay telling readers how to get on the good side of a professor are also examples of directional process analysis. Using a variety of tones, informational process analyses can range over equally diverse subjects; they can describe mechanical, scientific, historical, sociological, artistic, or psychological processes: for example, how the core of a nuclear reactor melts down; how television became so important in political campaigns; how abstract painters use color; how to survive a blind date.

Process analysis, both directional and informational, is often appropriate in *problem-solving situations.* In such cases, you say, "Here's the problem and here's what should be done to solve the problem." Indeed, college assignments frequently take the form of problem-solving process analyses. Consider these examples:

> Community officials have been accused of mismanaging recent unrest over the public housing ordinance. Describe the steps the officials took, indicating why you think their strategy was unwise. Then explain how you think the situation should have been handled.

> Over the years, there have been many reports citing the abuse of small children in day care centers. What can parents do to guard against the mistreatment of their children?

Because many colleges have changed the eligibility requirements for financial aid, fewer students can depend on loans or scholarships. How can students cope with the rising costs of higher education?

Note that the first assignment asks students to explain what's wrong with the current approach before they present their own step-by-step solution. Problem-solving process analyses are often organized in this way. You may also have noted that none of the assignments explicitly requires an essay response using process analysis. However, the wording of the assignments—"*Describe* the steps," "*What* can parents *do*," "*How* can students *cope*,"—suggests that process analysis would be an appropriate strategy for developing the responses.

Assignments don't always signal the use of process analysis so clearly. But during the prewriting stage, you'll often realize that you can best achieve your purpose by developing the essay using process analysis. Sometimes process analysis will be the primary strategy for organizing an essay; other times it will help make a point in an essay organized according to another pattern of development. Let's look at process analysis as a supporting strategy.

Assume that you're writing a *causal analysis* examining the impact of television commercials on people's buying behavior. To help readers see that commercials create a need where none existed before, you might describe the various stages of an advertising campaign to pitch a new, completely frivolous product. In an essay *defining* a good boss, you could convey the point that effective managers must be skilled at settling disputes by explaining the steps your boss took to resolve a heated disagreement between two employees. If you write an *argumentation-persuasion* paper urging the funding of programs to ease the plight of the homeless, to dramatize the tragedy of these people's lives, you could explain how the typical street person goes about the desperate jobs of finding a place to sleep and getting food to eat.

At this point, you have a good sense of the way writers use process analysis to achieve their purpose and to connect with their readers. Now take a moment to look closely at the photograph of the brand-new mall at the beginning of this chapter. Imagine you're writing an article, accompanied by the photo, for a local newspaper. Your purpose is to suggest to local store owners, who are losing business to the new mall, ways they might attract more customers to the area's downtown shopping district. Jot down some ideas you might include in a *process analysis* explaining the steps the business owners should take.

SUGGESTIONS FOR USING PROCESS ANALYSIS IN AN ESSAY

The suggestions that follow will be helpful whether you use process analysis as a dominant or a supportive pattern of development.

1. Identify the desired outcome of the process analysis.   Many papers developed primarily through process analysis have a clear-cut purpose—simply to *inform* readers as objectively as possible about a process: "Here's a way of making french fries at home that will surpass the best served in your favorite fast-food restaurant." But a process analysis essay may also have a *persuasive* edge, with the writer advocating a point of view about the process, perhaps even urging a course of action: "If you don't want your arguments to deteriorate into ugly battles, you should follow a series of foolproof steps for having disagreements that leave friendships intact." Before starting to write, you need to decide if the essay is to be purely factual or if it will include this kind of persuasive dimension.

2. Formulate a thesis that clarifies your attitude toward the process. Like the thesis in any other paper, the thesis in a process analysis should do more than announce your subject. ("Here's how the college's work-study program operates.") It should also state or imply your attitude toward the process: "Enrolling in the college's work-study program has become unnecessarily complicated. The procedure could be simplified if the college adopted the helpful guidelines prepared by the Student Senate."

3. Keep your audience in mind.   Only when you gauge how much your readers already know (or don't know) about the process can you determine how much explanation you'll have to provide. Suppose you've been asked to write an article informing students of the best way to use the university computer center. The article will be published in a newsletter for computer science majors. You would seriously misjudge your audience—and probably put them to sleep—if you explained in detail how to transfer material from disk to disk or how to delete information from a file. However, an article on the same topic prepared for a general audience—your composition class, for instance—would probably require such detailed instructions.

To determine how much explanation is needed, put yourself in your readers' shoes. Don't assume readers will know something just because you do. Ask questions such as these about your audience: "Will my readers need some background about the process before I describe it in depth?" "Are there technical terms I should define?" "If my essay is directional, should I specify near the beginning the ingredients, materials, and equipment needed to perform the process?" (For more help in analyzing your audience, see the checklist on page 17.)

4. Use prewriting to identify the steps in the process.   To explain a sequence to your readers, you need to think through the process thoroughly, identifying its major parts and subparts, locating possible missteps or trouble spots. With your purpose, thesis, and audience in mind, use the appropriate prewriting techniques (brainstorming and mapping should be especially helpful) to break down the process into its component parts. In prewriting, it's a good idea to start by generating more material than you expect to use. Then the raw material can be shaped and pruned to fit your purpose and the needs of your audience. The amount of work done during the prewriting stage will have a direct bearing on the clarity of your presentation.

5. Identify the directional and informational aspects of the process analysis.   Directional and informational process analyses are not always distinct. In fact, they may be complementary. Your prewriting may reveal that you'll need to provide background information about a process before outlining its steps. For example, in a paper describing a step-by-step approach for losing weight, you might first need to explain how the body burns calories. Or, in a paper on gardening, you could provide some theory about the way organic fertilizers work before detailing a plan for growing vegetables. Although both approaches may be appropriate in a paper, one generally predominates.

The kind of process analysis chosen has implications for the way you will relate to your reader. When the process analysis is *directional,* the reader is addressed in the *second person:* "You should first rinse the residue from the radiator by . . . ," or "Wrap the injured person in a blanket and then. . . ." (In the second example, the pronoun *you* is implied.)

If the process analysis has an *informational* purpose, you won't address the reader directly but will choose from a number of other options. For example, you might use the *first-person* point of view. In a humorous essay explaining how not to prepare for finals, you could cite your own disastrous study habits: "Filled with good intentions, I sit on my bed, pick up a pencil, open my notebook, and promptly fall asleep." The *third-person singular or plural* can also be used in informational process essays: "The door-to-door salesperson walks up the front walk, heart pounding, more than a bit nervous, but also challenged by the prospect of striking a deal," or "The new recruits next underwent a series of important balance tests in what was called the 'horror chamber.'" Whether you use the first, second, or third person, avoid shifting point of view midstream.

You might have noticed that in the third-person examples, the present tense ("walks up") is used in one sentence, the past tense ("underwent") in the other. The past tense is appropriate for events already completed, whereas the present tense is used for habitual or ongoing actions. ("A dominant male goose usually flies at the head of the V-wedge during migration.") The present tense is also effective when you want to lend a sense of dramatic immediacy to a process, even if the steps were performed in the past. ("The surgeon gently separates the facial skin and muscle from the underlying bony skull.") As with point of view, be on guard against changing tenses in the middle of your explanation.

6. Explain the process, one step at a time.   Prewriting helped you identify key stages and sort out the directional and informational aspects of the process. Now you're ready to organize your raw material into an easy-to-follow sequence. At times your purpose will be to explain a process with a *fairly fixed chronological sequence:* how to make pizza, how to pot a plant, how to change a tire. In such cases, you should include all necessary steps, in the correct chronological order. However, if a strict chronological ordering of steps means that a particularly important part of the sequence gets buried in the middle, the sequence probably should be juggled so that the crucial step receives the attention it deserves.

Other times your goal will be to describe a process having *no commonly accepted sequence.* For example, in an essay explaining how to discipline a child or how to pull yourself out of a blue mood, you will have to come up with your own definition of the key steps and then arrange those steps in some logical order. You may also use process analyses to *reject* or *reformulate* a traditional sequence. In this case, you would propose a more logical series of steps: "Our system for electing congressional representatives is inefficient and undemocratic; it should be reformed in the following ways."

Whether the essay describes a generally agreed-on process or one that is not commonly accepted, you must provide all the details needed to explain the process. Your readers should be able to understand, even visualize, the process. There should be no fuzzy patches or confusing cuts from one step to another. Don't, however, go into obsessive detail about minor stages or steps. If you dwell for several hundred words on how to butter the pan, your readers will never stay with you long enough to learn how to make the omelet.

It's not unusual, especially in less defined sequences, for some steps in a process to occur simultaneously and overlap. When this happens, you should present the steps in the most logical order, being sure to tell your readers that several steps are not perfectly distinct and may merge. For example, in an essay explaining how a species becomes extinct, you would have to indicate that overpopulation of hardy strains and destruction of endangered breeds are often simultaneous events. You would also need to clarify that the depletion of food sources both precedes and follows the demise of a species.

7. Provide readers with the help they need to follow the sequence.   As you move through the steps of a process analysis, don't forget to *warn readers about difficulties* they might encounter. For example, when writing a paper on the artistry involved in butterflying a shrimp, you might say something like this:

> Next, make a shallow cut with your sharpened knife along the convex curve of the shrimp's intestinal tract. The tract, usually a thin black line along the outside curve of the shrimp, is faintly visible beneath the translucent flesh. But some shrimp have a thick orange, blue, or gray line instead of a thin black one. In all cases, be careful not to slice too deeply, or you will end up with two shrimp halves instead of one butterflied shrimp.

You have told readers what to look for, citing the exceptions, and have warned them against making too deep a cut. Anticipating spots where communication might break down is a key part of writing an effective process analysis.

Transitional words and phrases are also critical in helping readers understand the order of the steps being described. Time signals such as *first, next, now, while, after, before,* and *finally* provide readers with a clear sense of the sequence. Entire sentences can also be used to link parts of the process, reminding your audience of what has already been discussed and indicating what will now be explained: "Once the panel of experts finishes its evaluation of the exam questions, randomly selected items are field-tested in schools throughout the country."

8. Maintain an appropriate tone.   When writing a process analysis essay, be sure your tone is consistent with your purpose, your attitude toward your subject, and the effect you want to have on the reader. When explaining how fraternities and sororities recruit new members, do you want to use an objective, nonjudgmental tone? To decide, take into account readers' attitudes toward your subject. Does your audience have a financial or emotional investment in the process being described? Does your own interest in the process coincide or conflict with that of your audience? Awareness of your readers' stance can be crucial. Consider another example: Assume you're writing a letter to the director of the student health center proposing a new system to replace the currently chaotic one. You'd do well to be tactful in your criticisms. Offend your reader, and your cause is lost. If, however, the letter is slated for the college newspaper and directed primarily to other students, you could adopt a more pointed, even sarcastic tone. Readers, you would assume, will probably share your view and favor change.

Once you settle on the essay's tone, maintain it throughout. If you're writing a light piece on the way computers are taking over our lives, you wouldn't include a grim step-by-step analysis of the way confidential computerized medical records may become public.

9. Open and close the process analysis effectively.   A paper developed primarily through process analysis should have a strong beginning. The introduction should state the process to be described and imply whether the essay has an informational or directional intent.

If you suspect readers are indifferent to your subject, use the introduction to motivate them, telling them how important the subject is:

> Do you enjoy the salad bars found in many restaurants? If you do, you probably have noticed that the vegetables are always crisp and fresh--no matter how many hours they have been exposed to the air. What are the restaurants doing to make the vegetables look so inviting? There's a simple answer. Many restaurants spray the vegetables with, or dip them into, potent chemicals to make them appetizing.

If you think your audience may be intimidated by your subject (perhaps because it's complex or relatively obscure), the introduction is the perfect spot to reassure them that the process being described is not beyond their grasp:

> Studies show that many people willingly accept a defective product just so they won't have to deal with the uncomfortable process of making a complaint. But once a few easy-to-learn basics are mastered, anyone can register a complaint that gets results.

Most process analysis essays don't end as soon as the last step in the sequence is explained. Instead, they usually include some brief final comments that round out the piece and bring it to a satisfying close. This final section of the essay may summarize the main steps in the process—not by repeating the steps verbatim but by rephrasing and condensing them in several concise sentences. The conclusion can also be an effective spot to underscore the significance of the process, recalling what may have been said in the introduction about the subject's importance. Or the essay can end by echoing the note of reassurance that may have been included at the start.

REVISION STRATEGIES

Once you have a draft of the essay, you're ready to revise. The following checklist will help you and those giving you feedback apply to process analysis some of the revision techniques discussed on pages 60–62.

☑ PROCESS ANALYSIS: A REVISION/PEER
REVIEW CHECKLIST

Revise Overall Meaning and Structure

❏ What purpose does the process analysis serve—to inform, to persuade, or to do both?

❏ Is the process analysis primarily *directional* or *informational*? How can you tell?

❏ Where does the process seem confusing? Where have steps been left out? Which steps need simplifying?

❏ What is the essay's tone? Is the tone appropriate for the essay's purpose and readers? Where are there distracting shifts in tone?

Revise Paragraph Development

❏ Does the introduction specify the process to be described? Does it provide an overview? Should it?

❏ Which paragraphs are difficult to follow? Have any steps or materials been omitted or explained in too much or too little detail? Which paragraphs should warn readers about potential trouble spots or overlapping steps?

❏ Where are additional time signals needed to clarify the sequence within and between paragraphs? Where does overreliance on time signals make the sequence awkward and mechanical?

❏ Which paragraph describes the most crucial step in the sequence? How has the step been highlighted?

❏ How could the conclusion be more effective?

Revise Sentences and Words

❏ What technical or specialized terms appear in the essay? Have they been sufficiently explained? Where could simpler, less technical language be used?

❏ Are there any places where the essay's point of view awkwardly shifts? How could this problem be corrected?

❏ Does the essay use correct verb tenses—the past tense for completed events, the present tense for habitual or ongoing actions?

❏ Where does the essay use the passive voice ("The hole is dug")? Would the active voice ("You dig the hole") be more effective?

STUDENT ESSAY

The following student essay was written by Robert Barry in response to this assignment:

> In "How to Say Nothing in 500 Words," Paul Roberts makes fun of college students' addiction to an inflated, padded writing style. By observing people, identify another example of an obsessive behavior that borders on the addictive. Then write a light-spirited

essay explaining the various stages in the addiction. Since your essay is humorous in tone, be sure to describe an addiction that doesn't have serious consequences.

While reading Robert's paper, try to determine how effectively it applies the principles of process analysis. The annotations on Robert's paper and the commentary following it will help you look at the essay more closely.

Becoming a Videoholic
by Robert Barry

Introduction	Videocassette recorders (VCRs) have been around for quite a few years. At last count, three out of four U.S. households owned at least one VCR. As a technological breakthrough, the VCR has been an enormous success—almost as popular as television itself. You can buy a VCR just about anywhere, and very affordably. No consumer warning labels are attached to these rapidly multiplying VCRs, but there should be. VCRs can be dangerous. Barely aware of what is happening, a person can turn into a compulsive videotaper. The descent from innocent hobby to full-blown addiction takes place in several stages.	1

Start of two-
sentence thesis

Topic sentence

First stage in
process (VCR
addiction)

In the first innocent stage, the unsuspecting person buys a VCR for occasional use. I was at this stage when I asked my parents if they would buy me a VCR as a birthday gift. With the VCR, I could tape reruns of Seinfeld and new episodes of The Simpsons, shows that I would otherwise miss on nights I was at work. The VCR was perfect. I hooked it up to the old TV in my bedroom, recorded the antics of Jerry, Elaine, George, and Kramer and the adventures of my favorite cartoon family, and then watched the tape the next day. Occasionally, I taped a movie, which my friends and I watched over the weekend. I had just one cassette, but that was all I needed since I watched every show I recorded and simply taped over the preceding show when I recorded another. In these early days, my use of the VCR was the equivalent of light social drinking. 2

Beginning
of analogy
to alcoholism

Topic sentence

Second stage
in process

In the second phase on the road to videoholism, an individual uses the VCR more frequently and begins to stockpile tapes rather than watch them. My troubles began in July when my family and I went to the shore for a week's vacation. I programmed the VCR to tape all five episodes of Seinfeld while I was at the beach perfecting my tan. Since I used the VCR's long-play mode, I could get all five Seinfelds on one cassette. But that ended up creating a problem. Even I, an avid Jerry Seinfeld fan, didn't want to watch five shows in one sitting. I viewed two shows, but the three unwatched shows tied up my tape, making it impossible to record other shows. 3

How did I resolve this problem? Very easily. I went out and bought several more blank cassettes. Once I had these additional tapes, I was free to record as many <u>Seinfelds</u> as I wanted, plus I could tape reruns of classics like <u>Law & Order</u> and <u>Buffy the Vampire Slayer</u>. Very quickly, I accumulated six <u>Seinfelds</u>, four <u>Law & Orders</u>, and three <u>Buffys</u>. Then a friend—who shall go nameless—told me that only 144 episodes of <u>Buffy</u> existed. Only 144! Excited by the thought that I could acquire as impressive a collection of tapes as a Hollywood executive, I continued recording <u>Buffy</u>, even taping shows while I watched them. Clearly, my once innocent hobby was getting out of control. I was now using the VCR on a regular basis—the equivalent of several stiff drinks a day.

Continuation of analogy

Topic sentence → In the third stage of videoholism, the amount of taping   4 increases significantly, which leads to an even more irrational stockpiling of cassettes. The catalyst that propelled me into this third stage was my parents' decision to get satellite TV. Selfless guy that I am, I volunteered to move my VCR and hook it up to the living room TV, where the satellite connection was located. Now I could tape all the most recent movies and specials. With that delightful possibility in mind, I went out and bought two six-packs of blank tapes. Then, in addition to my regular lineup, I began to record a couple of additional shows every day. I also went movie-crazy and taped <u>Gangs of New York</u>, <u>Barbershop</u>, and <u>The Godfather I</u>, <u>II</u>, and <u>III</u>. I taped an HBO comedy special with Chris Rock, and an MTV concert featuring Radiohead. Where did I get time to watch all these tapes? I didn't. Taping at this point was more satisfying than watching. Reason and common sense were abandoned. Getting things on tape had become an obsession, and I was taping all the time.

Third stage in process

Continuation of analogy

Topic sentence → In the fourth stage, videoholism creeps into other parts of   5 the addict's life, influencing behavior in strange ways. Secrecy becomes commonplace. One day, my mother came into my room and saw my bookcase filled with tapes--rather than with the paperbacks that used to be there. "Robert," she exclaimed, "isn't this getting a bit out of hand?" I assured her it was just a hobby, but I started hiding my tapes, putting them in a suitcase stored in my closet. I also taped at night, slipping downstairs to turn on the VCR after my parents had gone to bed and getting down first thing in the morning to turn off the VCR and remove the cassette before my parents noticed. Also, denial is not unusual during this stage of VCR addiction. At the dinner table, when my younger sister commented, "Robert tapes all the time," I laughingly told everyone--including myself--that the taping was no big deal. I was getting bored with it and was going to stop any day, I assured my family.

Fourth stage in process

Continuation of analogy

Obsessive behavior also characterizes the fourth stage of videoholism. Each week, I pulled out the TV magazine from the Sunday paper and went through it carefully, circling in red all the shows I wanted to tape. Another sign of addiction was my compulsive organization of all the tapes I had stockpiled. Working more diligently than I ever had for any term paper, I typed up labels and attached them to each cassette. I also created an elaborate list that showed my tapes broken down into categories such as police dramas, horror movies, and comedies.

Topic sentence ——→ In the final stage of an addiction, the individual either 6
Continuation of analogy —— succumbs completely to the addiction or is able to break away from the habit. I broke my addiction, and I broke it cold turkey.
Final stage in process This total withdrawal occurred when I went off to college. There was no point in taking my VCR to school because TVs were not allowed in the freshman dorms. Even though there were many things to occupy my time during the school week, cold sweats overcame me whenever I thought about everything on TV I was not taping. I even considered calling home and asking members of my family to tape things for me, but I knew they would think I was crazy. At the beginning of the semester, I also had to resist the overwhelming desire to travel the three hours home every weekend so I could get my fix. But after a while, the urgent need to tape subsided. Now, months later, as I write this, I feel detached and sober.

Conclusion I have no illusions, though. I know that once a videoholic, 7 always a videoholic. Soon I will return home for the holidays, which, as everyone knows, can be a time for excess eating--
Final references to analogy —— and taping. But I will cope with the pressure. I will take each day one at a time. I will ask my little sister to hide my blank tapes from me. And if I feel myself succumbing to the temptations of taping, I will pick up the telephone and dial the videoholics' hot line: 1-800-VCR-TAPE. I will win the battle.

COMMENTARY

Purpose, thesis, and tone. Robert's essay is an example of *informational process analysis;* his purpose is to describe—rather than teach—the process of becoming a "videoholic." The title, with its coined term *videoholic,* tips us off that the essay is going to be entertaining. And the introductory paragraph clearly establishes the essay's playful, mock-serious tone. The tone established, Robert briefly defines the term *videoholic* as a "compulsive videotaper" and then moves to the essay's *thesis:* "Barely aware of what is happening, a person can turn into a compulsive videotaper. The descent from innocent hobby to full-blown addiction takes place in several stages."

Throughout the essay, Robert sustains the introduction's humor by mocking his own motivations and poking fun at his quirks: "Selfless guy that I am, I volunteered to move my VCR" (paragraph 4), and "Working more diligently than I ever had for any term paper, I typed up labels" (5). Robert probably uses a bit of *dramatic license* when reporting some of his obsessive behavior, and we, as readers, understand that he's exaggerating for comic effect. Most likely he didn't break out in a cold sweat at the thought of the TV shows he was unable to tape, and he probably didn't hide his tapes in a suitcase. Nevertheless, this tinkering with the truth is legitimate because it allows Robert to create material that fits the essay's lightly satiric tone.

Organization and topic sentences.   To meet the requirements of the assignment, Robert needed to provide a *step-by-step* explanation of a process. And because he invented the term *videoholism,* Robert also needed to invent the stages in the progression of his addiction. During his prewriting, Robert discovered five stages in his videoholism: Presented *chronologically,* these stages provide the organizing focus for his paper. Specifically, each supporting paragraph is devoted to one stage, with the *topic sentence* for each paragraph indicating the stage's distinctive characteristics.

Transitions.   Although Robert's essay is playful, it is nonetheless a process analysis and so must have an easy-to-follow structure. Keeping this in mind, Robert wisely includes *transitions* to signal what happened at each stage of his videoholism: "*Once* I had these additional tapes, I was free to record" (paragraph 3); "*Then,* in addition to my regular lineup, I began to record" (4); "*One day,* my mother came into my room" (5); and "*But after a while,* the urgent need to tape subsided" (6). In addition to such transitions, Robert also uses crisp questions to move from idea to idea within a paragraph: "How did I resolve this problem? Very easily. I . . . bought several more blank cassettes" (3), and "Where did I get time to watch all these tapes? I didn't" (4).

Combining patterns of development.   Even though Robert's essay is a process analysis, it contains elements of other patterns of development. For example, his paper is unified by an *analogy*—a sustained *comparison* between Robert's video addiction and the obviously more serious addiction to alcohol. Handled incorrectly, the analogy could have been offensive, but Robert makes the comparison work to his advantage. The analogy is stated specifically in several spots: "In these early days, my use of the VCR was the equivalent of light social drinking" (paragraph 2); "I was now using the VCR on a regular basis—the equivalent of several stiff drinks a day" (3). Another place where Robert touches wittily on the analogy occurs in the middle of the fourth paragraph: "I went out and bought two six-packs of blank tapes." To illustrate his progression toward videoholism, Robert depicts the *effects* of his addiction. Finally, he generates numerous lively details or *examples* to illustrate the different stages in his addiction.

Two unnecessary sentences.   Perhaps you noticed that Robert runs into a minor problem at the end of the fourth paragraph. Starting with the sentence "Reason and common sense were abandoned," he begins to ramble and repeat himself. The paragraph's last two sentences fail to add anything substantial. Take a moment to read paragraph 4 aloud, omitting the last two sentences. Note how much sharper the new conclusion is: "Where did I get time to watch all these tapes? I didn't. Taping at this point was more satisfying than watching." This new ending says all that needs to be said.

Revising the first draft.   When it was time to revise, Robert—in spite of his apprehension—showed his paper to his roommate and asked him to read it out loud. Robert knew this strategy would provide a more objective point of view on his work. His roommate, at first an unwilling recruit, nonetheless laughed as he read the essay aloud. That was just the response Robert wanted. But when his roommate got to the conclusion, Robert heard that the closing paragraph was flat and anticlimactic. Here is Robert's original conclusion.

Original Version of the Conclusion

I have no illusions, though, that I am over my videoholism. Soon I will be returning home for the holidays, which can be a time for excess taping. All I can do is ask my little sister to hide my blank tapes. After that, I will hope for the best.

Robert and his roommate brainstormed ways to make the conclusion livelier and more in spirit with the rest of the essay. They decided that the best approach would be to continue the playful, mock-serious tone that characterized earlier parts of the essay. Robert thus made three major changes in the conclusion. First, he tightened the first sentence of the paragraph ("I have no illusions, though, that I am over my videoholism"), making it crisper and more dramatic: "I have no illusions, though." Second, he added a few sentences to sustain the light, self-deprecating tone he had used earlier: "I know that once a videoholic, always a videoholic"; "But I will cope with the pressure"; "I will win the battle." Third, and perhaps most important, he returned to the alcoholism analogy: "I will take each day one at a time. . . . And if I feel myself succumbing to the temptations of taping, I will pick up the telephone and dial the videoholics' hotline. . . ."

These weren't the only changes Robert made while reworking his paper, but they give you some sense of how sensitive he was to the effect he wanted to achieve. Certainly, the recasting of the conclusion was critical to the overall success of this amusing essay.

ACTIVITIES: PROCESS ANALYSIS

Prewriting Activities

1. Imagine you're writing two essays: One *defines* the term "comparison shopping"; the other *contrasts* two different teaching styles. Jot down ways you might use process analysis in each essay.

2. Select *one* of the essay topics that follow and determine what your purpose, tone, and point of view would be for each audience indicated in parentheses. Then use brainstorming, questioning, mapping, or another prewriting technique to identify the points you'd cover for each audience. Finally, organize the raw material, noting the differences in emphasis and sequence for each group of readers.

   a. How to buy a car (*young people who have just gotten a driver's license; established professionals*)
   b. How children acquire their values (*first-time parents; elementary school teachers*)
   c. How to manage money (*grade school children; college students*)
   d. How loans or scholarships are awarded to incoming students on your campus (*high school graduates applying for financial aid; high school guidance counselors*)
   e. How arguments can strengthen relationships (*preteen children; young adults*)
   f. How to relax (*college students; parents with young children*)

Revising Activities

3. Below is the brainstorming for a brief essay that describes the steps involved in making a telephone sales call. The paper has the following thesis: "Establishing rapport with customers is the most challenging and the most important part of phone sales." Revise the brainstormed material by deleting anything that undermines the paper's unity and organizing the steps in a logical sequence.

   * Keep customers on the phone as long as possible to learn what they need
   * The more you know about customers' needs, the better
   * The tone of the opening comments is very important
   * Gently introduce the product
   * Use a friendly tone in opening comments
   * End on a friendly tone, too
   * Don't introduce the product right away
   * Growing rudeness in society. Some people hang up right away. Very upsetting.
   * Try in a friendly way to keep the person on the phone
   * Many people are so lonely they don't mind staying on the phone so they can talk to someone--anyone

- How sad that there's so much loneliness in the world
- Describe the product's advantages--price, convenience, installment plan
- If person is not interested, try in a friendly way to find out why
- Don't tell people that their reasons for not being interested are silly
- Don't push people if they're not interested
- Encourage credit card payment--the product will arrive earlier
- Explain payment--check, money order, or credit card payment

4. Reprinted here is a paragraph from the first draft of a humorous essay advising shy college students how to get through a typical day. Written as a process analysis, the paragraph outlines techniques for surviving class. Revise the paragraph, deleting digressions that disrupt the paragraph's unity, eliminating unnecessary repetition, and sequencing the steps in the proper order. Also correct inappropriate shifts in person and add transitions where needed. Feel free to add any telling details.

Simply attending class can be stressful for shy people. Several strategies, though, can lessen the trauma. Shy students should time their arrival to coincide with that of most other class members--about two minutes before the class is scheduled to begin. If you arrive too early, you may be seen sitting alone, or, even worse, may actually be forced to talk with another early arrival. If you arrive late, all eyes will be upon you. Before heading to class, the shy student should dress in the least conspicuous manner possible--say, in the blue jeans, sweatshirt, and sneakers that 99.9 percent of your classmates wear. That way you won't stand out from everyone else. Take a seat near the back of the room. Don't, however, sit at the very back since professors often take sadistic pleasure in calling on students back there, assuming they chose those seats because they didn't want to be called on. A friend of mine who is far from shy uses just the opposite ploy. In an attempt to get in good with her professors, she sits in the front row and, incredibly enough, volunteers to participate. However, since shy people don't want to call attention to themselves, they should stifle any urge to sneeze or cough. You run the risk of having people look at you or offer you a tissue or cough drop. And of course, never, ever volunteer to answer. Such a display of intelligence is sure to focus all eyes on you. In other words, make yourself as inconspicuous as possible. How, you might wonder, can you be inconspicuous if you're blessed (or cursed) with great looks? Well, . . . have you ever considered earning your degree through the mail?

David Shipley

David Shipley, a journalist, is the editor of *The New York Times*'s op-ed page, on which opinion pieces by *New York Times* columnists and other journalists, as well as private citizens, are published. He was born in Portland, Oregon, in 1963 and graduated with a degree in English from Williams College in 1985. Shipley won a Thomas J. Watson Fellowship for 1985–1986, which allowed him to spend a year traveling to do independent study. From 1993 to 1995 he was executive editor of *The New Republic*, and from 1995 to 1997 he was a special assistant and senior speechwriter for President Bill Clinton. Shipley joined *The New York Times* in 1998 and was deputy editor of the Sunday *New York Times Magazine*'s millennium issues, senior editor of the magazine, and enterprise editor of the national desk before moving to his present position as op-ed editor. With coauthor Will Schwalbe, Shipley is writing a book about e-mail entitled *Send*. This essay, originally entitled "What We Talk About When We Talk About Editing," appeared in *The New York Times* on July 31, 2005.

Pre-Reading Journal Entry

People often seek advice and help from others to help them do a job or improve their performance. For example, if you were writing your résumé, you might ask a friend to edit and proofread it. Or if you were trying out for a sports team, you might ask a coach for feedback and advice. Think of some occasions in the past when you asked others for help with your work or gave help to someone else when asked. What was the task? What was your goal in helping or being helped? Did the assistance actually improve the end product, or was it useless? Use your journal to answer these questions.

Talk About Editing

. . . Not surprisingly, readers have lots of questions about the editing that goes on [on the *New York Times* op-ed page]. What kind of changes do we suggest—and why? What kind of changes do we insist on—and why? When do we stay out of the way? And the hardy perennial: do we edit articles to make them adhere to a particular point of view? I thought I'd try to provide a few answers. 1

Just like Times news articles and editorials, Op-Ed essays are edited. Before something appears in our pages, you can bet that questions have been asked, arguments have been clarified, cuts have been suggested—as have 2 additions—and factual, typographical and grammatical errors have been caught. (We hope.)

Our most important rule, however, is that nothing is published on the Op-Ed page unless it has been approved by its author. Articles go to press only after the person under whose name the article appears has explicitly O.K.'d the editing.   3

While it's important to know that we edit, it's also important to know how we edit. The best way to explain this is to take a walk through the process.   4

Say you send us an article by regular mail, e-mail, fax or, this summer at least, owl post[1]—and it's accepted. You'll be told that we'll contact you once your article is scheduled for publication. That could be days, weeks or even months away.   5

When your article does move into the on-deck circle, you'll be sent a contract, and one of the several editors here will get to work.   6

Here are the clear-cut things the editor will do: 7

- Correct grammatical and typographical errors.   8
- Make sure that the article conforms to *The New York Times Manual of Style and Usage*. Courtesy titles, for example, will miraculously appear if they weren't there before; expletives will be deleted; some words will be capitalized, others lowercased.   9
- See to it that the article fits our allotted space. With staff columnists, advertisements and illustrations, there's a limit to the number of words we can squeeze onto the page.   10
- Fact-check the article. While it is the author's responsibility to ensure that everything written for us is accurate, we still check facts—names, dates, places, quotations.   11

We also check assertions. If news articles—from The Times and other publications—are at odds with a point or an example in an essay, we need to resolve whatever discrepancy exists.   12

For instance, an Op-Ed article critical of newly aggressive police tactics in Town X can't flatly say the police have no reason to change their strategy if there have been news reports that violence in the town is rising. This doesn't mean the writer can't still argue that there are other ways to deal with Town X's crime problem—he just can't say that the force's decision to change came out of the blue.   13

How would we resolve the Town X issue? Well, we'd discuss it with the writer—generally by telephone or e-mail—and we'd try to find a solution that preserves the writer's argument while also adhering to the facts.   14

[1]In J. K. Rowling's Harry Potter books, mail is delivered each morning to Hogwarts, Harry's school, by owls (editors' note).

Now to some people, this may sound surprising, as if we're putting words in people's mouths. But there's a crucial distinction to be made between changing a writer's argument—and suggesting language that will help a writer make his point more effectively.

Besides grammar and accuracy, we're also concerned about readability. Our editors try to approach articles as average readers who know nothing about the subject. They may ask if a point is clear, if a writer needs transitional language to bridge the gap between two seemingly separate points, if a leap of logic has been made without sufficient explanation.

To make a piece as clear and accessible as possible, the editor may add a transition, cut a section that goes off point or move a paragraph. If a description is highly technical, the editor may suggest language that lay readers will understand. If it isn't clear what a writer is trying to say, the editor may take a guess, based on what he knows from the author, and suggest more precise language. (There are also times when we do precious little.)

The editor will then send the edited version of the article to the writer. The changes will often be highlighted to make it easy for the author to see what's been done. (I tend to mark edits I've made with an //ok?//.) If a proposed revision is significant, the editor will often write a few sentences to describe the reasoning behind the suggestion.

Every change is a suggestion, not a demand. If a solution offered by an editor doesn't work for a writer, the two work together to find an answer to the problem. Editing is not bullying.

Of course, it's not always warm and cuddly, either. The people who write for Op-Ed have a responsibility to be forthright and specific in their arguments. There's no room on the page for articles that are opaque or written in code.

What our editors expressly do not do is change a point of view. If you've written an article on why New York's street fairs should be abolished, we will not ask you to change your mind and endorse them. We're going to help you make the best case you can. If you followed this page carefully in the run-up to the Iraq war, for example, you saw arguments both for and against the invasion—all made with equal force.

Editing is a human enterprise. Like writing, it is by nature subjective. Sometimes an editor will think a writer is saying something that she isn't. But our editing process gives writer and editor plenty of time to sort out any misunderstandings before the article goes to press. And if a mistake gets through, we do our best to correct it as quickly as possible.

The Op-Ed page is a venue for people with a wide range of perspectives, experiences and talents. Some of the people who appear in this space have written a lot; others haven't. If we published only people who needed no editing, we'd wind up relying on only a very narrow range of professional writers, and the page would be much the worse for it.

So what's the agenda? A lively page of clashing opinions, one where as   24
many people as possible have the opportunity to make the best arguments
they can.

And just so you know, this article has been edited. Changes have been   25
suggested—and gratefully accepted. Well, most of them.

Questions for Close Reading

1. What is the selection's thesis? Locate the sentence(s) in which Shipley states his main idea. If he doesn't state his thesis explicitly, express it in your own words.
2. What tasks are involved in editing an op-ed piece for *The New York Times*? Of these, which does Shipley seem to think need the most explanation?
3. In paragraphs 18 through 22, Shipley describes the relationship between the editor and writer of an op-ed piece. What is the nature of this relationship?
4. In paragraph 22, Shipley says that "Editing is a human enterprise." What does he mean by this?
5. Refer to your dictionary as needed to define the following words used in the selection: *hardy* (paragraph 1), *perennial* (1), *on-deck circle* (6), *expletives* (9), *assertions* (12), *adhering* (14), *readability* (16), and *venue* (23).

Questions About the Writer's Craft

1. **The pattern.** Who is the audience for Shipley's essay? Why would this audience be interested in this topic? What type of process analysis does Shipley use?
2. **Other patterns.** Shipley *divides* the editing process into three main types of tasks and covers each type in its own section. Identify the main editing tasks and the paragraph(s) that introduce each type. Why does he break down the process this way rather than deal with the editing process as a whole?
3. In paragraphs 13 and 14, Shipley uses an example to clarify what he means by checking "assertions." Why does he provide an example here? Is the example effective?
4. Shipley concludes this essay with some mild humor. What is the joke? What does this use of humor contribute to the point he has been making in his essay?

Writing Assignments Using Process Analysis as a Pattern of Development

1. Shipley describes the process involved in editing opinion pieces, or arguments, that appear in a newspaper with national circulation. However, many other types of works are edited. For example, news articles, news broadcasts, documentaries, movies, commercials, advertisements, novels, and comic strips are all edited. Select one of these media and do research on the tasks involved in editing it. Write an essay in which you analyze the editing process and explain why it is important.
2. Before a piece can be edited, it must be written. Examine the process involved in producing an essay from the writer's rather than the editor's point of view. What process do you use when you write an essay in your English course? Write an essay

in which you analyze your own writing process. For inspiration, you might want to read "How to Say Nothing in 500 Words" by Paul Roberts (page 314).

Writing Assignments Combining Patterns of Development

3. Op-ed pieces are usually arguments about current issues; in contrast, news articles are more objective, describing or narrating events. From *The New York Times* or your local newspaper, select one op-ed page essay and one news article on a related topic, if possible. *Compare* and *contrast* the two pieces, analyzing their purpose and content. What patterns of development are used in each piece? Give *examples* to support your analysis.

4. A process analysis essay describes a general procedure, such as how to make chili, whereas a narrative presents a specific story, for example, a story about the time you dropped a pot of chili right before your guests arrived for dinner. Write an essay in which you blend a *process analysis* with a *specific narrative*. You can emphasize either the process analysis or the narrative, whichever seems more effective. Your essay can be humorous, serious, fantastical, or ironic.

Writing Assignment Using a Journal Entry as a Starting Point

5. Review your pre-reading journal entry and select one of the occasions on which you helped someone or were helped to perform a task. First, identify the steps in the process and any missteps or problems. Second, decide whether the process lends itself to an informative or a directional process analysis, or some combination of the two. Finally, write an essay in which you describe the process. To add interest to your essay, you might want to use humor, describe interpersonal conflicts, give examples, or focus on problem areas. Be sure—perhaps in your conclusion—to indicate whether the assistance you gave or received was effective in getting the task done.

Jessica Mitford

Dubbed "Queen of the Muckrakers" by *Time*, English-born Jessica Mitford (1917–96) came to the United States in 1939 at the age of twenty-one. Mitford worked as a bartender and salesperson before becoming an investigator for the Office of Price Administration in Washington. She didn't begin her writing career until the age of thirty-eight. Her books include two autobiographies, *Daughters and Rebels* (1960) and *A Fine Old Conflict* (1976); an examination of the American penal system, *Kind and Usual Punishment* (1974); a collection of essays, *Poison Penmanship* (1979); a critique of the birthing business, *The American Way of Birth* (1993); and a novel about celebrities and the media, *Grace Had an English Heart* (1989). The following selection is from the book *The American Way of Death* (1963), which earned Mitford a national reputation as an investigative writer. A scathing attack on the U.S. funeral industry, this book shocked readers and enraged morticians.

Pre-Reading Journal Entry

If you've ever attended a funeral, you know that efforts are made to avoid the appearance or even the mention of death. Many significant life experiences are also accompanied by elaborate rituals that obscure the real meaning of the events. List several such life events in your journal. For each, describe briefly the rituals that typically mark the event.

The American Way of Death

Embalming is indeed a most extraordinary procedure, and one must 1
wonder at the docility of Americans who each year pay hundreds of millions of dollars for its perpetuation, blissfully ignorant of what it is all about, what is done, how it is done. Not one in ten thousand has any idea of what actually takes place. Books on the subject are extremely hard to come by. They are not to be found in most libraries or bookshops.

In an era when huge television audiences watch surgical operations in 2
the comfort of their living rooms, when, thanks to the animated cartoon, the geography of the digestive system has become familiar territory even to the nursery school set, in a land where the satisfaction of curiosity about almost all matters is a national pastime, the secrecy surrounding embalming can, surely, hardly be attributed to the inherent gruesomeness of the subject. Custom in this regard has within this century suffered a complete reversal. In the

early days of American embalming, when it was performed in the home of the deceased, it was almost mandatory for some relative to stay by the embalmer's side and witness the procedure. Today, family members who might wish to be in attendance would certainly be dissuaded by the funeral director. All others, except apprentices, are excluded by law from the preparation room.

A close look at what does actually take place may explain in large measure   3
the undertaker's intractable reticence concerning a procedure that has become his major *raison d'être*. Is it possible he fears that public information about embalming might lead patrons to wonder if they really want this service? If the funeral men are loath to discuss the subject outside the trade, the reader may, understandably, be equally loath to go on reading at this point. For those who have the stomach for it, let us part the formaldehyde curtain. . . .

The body is first laid out in the undertaker's morgue—or rather,   4
Mr. Jones is reposing in the preparation room—to be readied to bid the world farewell.

The preparation room in any of the better funeral establishments has the   5
tiled and sterile look of a surgery, and indeed the embalmer-restorative artist who does his chores there is beginning to adopt the term "dermasurgeon" (appropriately corrupted by some mortician-writers as "demisurgeon") to describe his calling. His equipment, consisting of scalpels, scissors, augers, forceps, clamps, needles, pumps, tubes, bowls and basins, is crudely imitative of the surgeon's, as is his technique, acquired in a nine- or twelve-month post-high-school course in an embalming school. He is supplied by an advanced chemical industry with a bewildering array of fluids, sprays, pastes, oils, powders, creams, to fix or soften tissue, shrink or distend it as needed, dry it here, restore the moisture there. There are cosmetics, waxes and paints to fill and cover features, even plaster of Paris to replace entire limbs. There are ingenious aids to prop and stabilize the cadaver: a Vari-Pose Head Rest, the Edwards Arm and Hand Positioner, the Repose Block (to support the shoulders during the embalming), and the Throop Foot Positioner, which resembles an old-fashioned stocks.

Mr. John H. Eckles, president of the Eckles College of Mortuary Science,   6
thus describes the first part of the embalming procedure: "In the hands of a skilled practitioner, this work may be done in a comparatively short time and without mutilating the body other than by slight incision—so slight that it scarcely would cause serious inconvenience if made upon a living person. It is necessary to remove the blood, and doing this not only helps in the disinfecting, but removes the principal cause of disfigurements due to discoloration."

Another textbook discusses the all-important time element: "The earlier   7
this is done, the better, for every hour that elapses between death and embalming will add to the problems and complications encountered. . . ." Just how soon should one get going on the embalming? The author tells us, "On the basis of such scanty information made available to this profession

through its rudimentary and haphazard system of technical research, we must conclude that the best results are to be obtained if the subject is embalmed before life is completely extinct—that is, before cellular death has occurred. In the average case, this would mean within an hour after somatic death." For those who feel that there is something a little rudimentary, not to say haphazard, about this advice, a comforting thought is offered by another writer. Speaking of fears entertained in early days of premature burial, he points out, "One of the effects of embalming by chemical injection, however, has been to dispel fears of live burial." How true; once the blood is removed, chances of live burial are indeed remote.

To return to Mr. Jones, the blood is drained out through the veins and replaced by embalming fluid pumped in through the arteries. As noted in *The Principles and Practices of Embalming,* "every operator has a favorite injection and drainage point—a fact which becomes a handicap only if he fails or refuses to forsake his favorites when conditions demand it." Typical favorites are the carotid artery, femoral artery, jugular vein, subclavian vein. There are various choices of embalming fluid. If Flextone is used, it will produce a "mild, flexible rigidity. The skin retains a velvety softness, the tissues are rubbery and pliable. Ideal for women and children." It may be blended with B. and G. Products Company's Lyf-Lyk tint, which is guaranteed to reproduce "nature's own skin texture . . . the velvety appearance of living tissue." Suntone comes in three separate tints: Suntan; Special Cosmetic Tint, a pink shade "especially indicated for young female subjects"; and Regular Cosmetic Tint, moderately pink.   8

About three to six gallons of a dyed and perfumed solution of formaldehyde, glycerin, borax, phenol, alcohol, and water is soon circulating through Mr. Jones, whose mouth has been sewn together with a "needle directed upward between the upper lip and gum and brought out through the left nostril," with the corners raised slightly "for a more pleasant expression." If he should be bucktoothed, his teeth are cleaned with Bon Ami and coated with colorless nail polish. His eyes, meanwhile, are closed with flesh-tinted eye caps and eye cement.   9

The next step is to have at Mr. Jones with a thing called a trocar. This is a long, hollow needle attached to a tube. It is jabbed into the abdomen, poked around the entrails and chest cavity, the contents of which are pumped out and replaced with "cavity fluid." This done, and the hole in the abdomen sewn up, Mr. Jones's face is heavily creamed (to protect the skin from burns which may be caused by leakage of the chemicals), and he is covered with a sheet and left unmolested for a while. But not for long—there is more, much more, in store for him. He has been embalmed, but not yet restored, and the best time to start the restorative work is eight to ten hours after embalming, when the tissues have become firm and dry.   10

The object of all this attention to the corpse, it must be remembered, is to make it presentable for viewing in an attitude of healthy repose. "Our customs   11 require the presentation of our dead in the semblance of normality . . . unmarred by the ravages of illness, disease or mutilation," says Mr. J. Sheridan Mayer in his *Restorative Art*. This is rather a large order since few people die in the full bloom of health, unravaged by illness and unmarked by some disfigurement. The funeral industry is equal to the challenge: "In some cases the gruesome appearance of a mutilated or disease-ridden subject may be quite discouraging. The task of restoration may seem impossible and shake the confidence of the embalmer. This is the time for intestinal fortitude and determination. Once the formative work is begun and affected tissues are cleaned or removed, all doubts of success vanish. It is surprising and gratifying to discover the results which may be obtained."

The embalmer, having allowed an appropriate interval to elapse, returns to the attack, but now he brings into play the skill and equipment of sculptor and cosmetician. Is a hand missing? Casting one in plaster of Paris is a simple matter. "For replacement purposes, only a cast of the back of the hand is necessary; this is within the ability of the average operator and is quite adequate." If a lip or two, a nose or an ear should be missing, the embalmer has at hand a variety of restorative waxes with which to model replacements. Pores and skin texture are simulated by stippling with a little brush, and over this cosmetics are laid on. Head off? Decapitation cases are rather routinely handled. Ragged edges are trimmed, and head joined to torso with a series of splints, wires and sutures. It is a good idea to have a little something at the neck—a scarf or high collar—when time for viewing comes. Swollen mouth? Cut out tissue as needed from inside the lips. If too much is removed, the surface contour can easily be restored by padding with cotton. Swollen necks and cheeks are reduced by removing tissue through vertical incisions made down each side of the neck. "When the deceased is casketed, the pillow will hide the suture incisions . . . as an extra precaution against leakage, the suture may be painted with liquid sealer."

The opposite condition is more likely to present itself—that of emaciation. His hypodermic syringe now loaded with massage cream, the embalmer seeks out and fills the hollowed and sunken areas by injection. In this procedure the backs of the hands and fingers and the under-chin area should not be neglected.

Positioning the lips is a problem that recurrently challenges the ingenuity of the embalmer. Closed too tightly they tend to give a stern, even disapproving expression. Ideally, embalmers feel, the lips should give the impression of being ever so slightly parted, the upper lip protruding slightly for a more youthful appearance. This takes some engineering, however, as the lips tend to drift apart. Lip drift can sometimes be remedied by pushing one or two straight pins through the inner margin of the lower lip and then inserting them between the two front upper teeth. If Mr. Jones happens to have no teeth, the pins can just as easily be anchored in his Armstrong Face Former and Denture Replacer. Another method to maintain lip closure is to dislocate the lower jaw, which is then held in its new position by a wire run through holes which have been drilled through the upper and lower jaws at the midline. As the French are fond of saying, *il faut souffrir pour être belle.*[1]

If Mr. Jones has died of jaundice, the embalming fluid will very likely turn   15
him green. Does this deter the embalmer? Not if he has intestinal fortitude. Masking pastes and cosmetics are heavily laid on, burial garments and casket interiors are color-correlated with particular care, and Jones is displayed beneath rose-colored lights. Friends will say, "How *well* he looks." Death by carbon monoxide, on the other hand, can be rather a good thing from the embalmer's viewpoint: "One advantage is the fact that this type of discoloration is an exaggerated form of a natural pink coloration." This is nice because the healthy glow is already present and needs but little attention.

The patching and filling completed, Mr. Jones is now shaved, washed and   16
dressed. Cream-based cosmetic, available in pink, flesh, suntan, brunette, and blond, is applied to his hands and face, his hair is shampooed and combed (and, in the case of Mrs. Jones, set), his hands manicured. For the horny-handed son of toil special care must be taken; cream should be applied to remove ingrained grime, and the nails cleaned. "If he were not in the habit of having them manicured in life, trimming and shaping is advised for better appearance—never questioned by kin."

Jones is now ready for casketing (this is the present participle of the verb   17
"to casket"). In this operation his right shoulder should be depressed slightly "to turn the body a bit to the right and soften the appearance of lying flat on the back." Positioning the hands is a matter of importance, and special rubber positioning blocks may be used. The hands should be cupped slightly for a more lifelike, relaxed appearance. Proper placement of the body requires a delicate sense of balance. It should lie as high as possible in the casket, yet not so high that the lid, when lowered, will hit the nose. On the other hand, we are cautioned, placing the body too low "creates the impression that the body is in a box."

Jones is next wheeled into the appointed slumber room where a few last   18
touches may be added—his favorite pipe placed in his hand or, if he was a great reader, a book propped into position. (In the case of little Master Jones a Teddy bear may be clutched.) Here he will hold open house for a few days, visiting hours 10 A.M. to 9 P.M.

---

[1]One has to suffer to be beautiful (editors' note).

Questions for Close Reading

1. What is the selection's thesis? Locate the sentence(s) in which Mitford states her main idea. If she doesn't state the thesis explicitly, express it in your own words.

2. Why, according to Mitford, do Americans know so little about the embalming process?

3. Mitford quotes from a textbook on embalming practices (paragraph 11). What does the passage reveal about the goals of mortuary science?

4. In what ways is the body made to look even better than it did when alive?

5. Refer to your dictionary as needed to define the following words used in the selection: *docility* (paragraph 1), *intractable* (3), *raison d'être* (3), *augers* (5), *distend* (5), *stippling* (12), and *jaundice* (15).

Questions About the Writer's Craft

1. **The pattern.** What are the main stages of the mortician's craft? What happens in each step? What words and phrases does Mitford use to indicate that she's moving from one step to the next?

2. Why does Mitford refer to the body being embalmed as Mr. Jones? What effect does this naming have on the reader?

3. Mitford interweaves her description of the embalming and restoring process with many quotations from mortuary science texts. Why do you suppose she does this? What do you notice about the writing style of the authors of these texts?

4. What is Mitford's tone in this essay? Do you feel she is being objective in her description of the funeral industry? Explain.

Writing Assignments Using Process Analysis as a Pattern of Development

∞ 1. Many important events in our lives are marked by celebrations or rituals. Often, the basic outlines of these rituals are established by tradition, but we can always personalize these traditions in one way or another. Select an important event that you will celebrate in the future and explain how you would like to experience the event. Your choice could include any of the following: your marriage, the birth of a child, your graduation, your parent's retirement, or some other notable occurrence. Before writing, you may find it helpful to read Judith Ortiz Cofer's "A Partial Remembrance of a Puerto Rican Childhood" (page 114), an essay about a shared family ritual.

2. Write a paper telling your survivors how you wish to be treated after death. Explain how they should conduct your funeral, whether they should embalm you, where they should put your remains, and, most important, what you would like said in your eulogy. Be as specific as possible as you outline the steps to be taken.

Writing Assignments Combining Patterns of Development

3. Write an essay *describing* a funeral or viewing that you attended. Focus on what seems to you the most important scene. Your thesis should express a dominant feeling about the scene and its *effect* on you: depression, grief, discomfort, fear, relief, or some other emotion. Alternatively, write an essay describing any other ceremony or ritual you have experienced (for example, a wedding, a bar or bat mitzvah, or a graduation). Your dominant feeling may be positive or negative.

∞ 4. Write an essay *arguing* that Americans often pretend that death doesn't exist or isn't really happening. Give *examples* drawn from your own life, your family's life, or public events. You might consider the following: the expressions we use with children ("Grandpa's gone away"; "Kitty is sleeping"); the euphemistic language we have for death ("passed away"; "no longer with us"); our obsession with looking young and keeping fit; our beliefs about "eternal life"; people's resistance to making a will. William Lutz's "Doublespeak" (page 263) will deepen your understanding of the way language can be used to hide uncomfortable truths.

Writing Assignment Using a Journal Entry as a Starting Point

5. Review your pre-reading journal entry, and select *one* major life event whose genuine significance is somehow masked by its accompanying rituals. Then write an essay describing this event and its rituals. If you need to supplement the material in your journal, interview others about their experiences and observations. Your essay may have a serious or a lighthearted tone.

Clifford Stoll

Clifford Stoll, born in 1950, is an astronomer, lecturer, commentator on MSNBC, and occasional visiting teacher of astronomy in elementary, middle, and high schools. He is the best-selling author of *The Cuckoo's Egg: Tracking a Spy Through the Maze of Computer Espionage* (1990) and *Silicon Snake Oil: Second Thoughts on the Information Superhighway* (1995), both of which address the complications of the computer age. As he reveals in the preface of *High-Tech Heretic: Reflections of a Computer Contrarian* (1999), despite having programmed and used computers since the mid-sixties, Stoll seeks to inject "a few notes of skepticism into the utopian dreams of a digital wonderland." According to his website, he is a "stay-at-home daddy" who lives with his family in the San Francisco Bay Area. The following essay appears as a chapter in *High-Tech Heretic*.

Pre-Reading Journal Entry

Over the past several years, the Internet has become increasingly popular as an educational resource. What do you think are the merits and the drawbacks of including the Internet as part of school assignments? Is your response affected by the age of the students in question? Record in your journal the pros and cons of requiring students—at the elementary, high school, and college levels, respectively—to access the Net as part of their studies.

Cyberschool

Welcome to the classroom of the future! Complete with electronic links to the world, it'll revolutionize education. Students will interact with information infrastructures and knowledge processors to learn group work and telework, whatever that means. You'll be enriched, empowered, and enabled by the digital classroom; immersed in an optimal learning environment. Yee-ha! 1

Worried that things rarely turn out as promised? Well, let me present a pessimal[1] view of the schoolroom of the future. 2

Suppose you're a harried school board member. Voters complain about high taxes. Teachers' unions strike for higher wages and smaller classes. Parents worry about plummeting scores on standardized tests. Newspapers criticize backward teaching methods, outdated textbooks, and security problems. Unruly students cut classes and rarely pay attention. Instructors teach topics 3

---

[1]The opposite of optimal?

which aren't in the curriculum or, worse, inject their own opinions into subject matter.

Sound like a tough call? Naw—it's easy to solve all these problems, placate the taxpayers, and get re-elected. High technology! 4

First, the school district buys a computer for every student. Sure, this'll 5 set back the budget—maybe a few hundred dollars per student. Quantity discounts and corporate support should keep the price down, and classroom savings will more than offset the cost of the equipment.

Next buy a pile of CD-ROMs for the students, each preprogrammed 6 with fun edutainment[2] programs. The educational games will exactly cover the curriculum . . . for every paragraph in the syllabus, the game will have an interactive aspect. As students climb to more advanced levels, the game naturally becomes more challenging and rewarding. But always fun.

Every student will work at her own pace. The youngest will watch happy 7 cartoon characters and exciting animations. The kid that likes horses will listen to messages from a chatty pony; the child that dreams of fire engines will hear from Fred the Firefighter. High schoolers get multimedia images of film stars and rock and roll celebrities. With access to interactive video sessions, chat rooms, and e-mail, students can collaborate with each other. It's the ultimate in individualized, child-centered instruction.

Naturally, the edu-games will be programmed so that students become 8 adept at standardized tests. No reason to teach anything that's not on the ACT, PSAT, or SAT exams. And the students will have fun because all this information will be built into games like Myst, Dungeon, or Doom. They'll master the games, and automatically learn the material.

Meanwhile, the computers will keep score, like pinball machines. They'll 9 send e-mail to parents and administrators . . . scores that will become part of each kid's permanent record. No more subjectivity in grading: The principal will know instantly how each child's doing. And if a student gets confused or falls behind, automated help will be just a mouse click away.

We'll update crowded classrooms, too. Replace desks with individual 10 cubicles, comfortable chairs, and multimedia monitors. With no outside interruptions, kids' attention will be directed into the approved creative learning experiences, built into the software. Well compartmentalized, students will hardly ever see other . . . neatly ending classroom discipline problems.

Naturally, teachers are an unnecessary appendix at this cyberschool. No 11 need for 'em when there's a fun, multimedia system at each student's fingertips. Should students have a question, they can turn to the latest on-line encyclopedia, enter an electronic chat room, or send e-mail to a professional educator. Those laid-off teachers can be retrained as data entry clerks.

As librarians and teachers become irrelevant, they'll be replaced by a 12 cadre of instructional specialists, consultants, and professional hall monitors.

---

[2]A term, coined by Stoll, combining the words *education* and *entertainment* (editors' note).

Any discipline problems could be handled by trained security guards, who'd monitor the cubicles via remote video links.

Effect? With no more wasted time on student-teacher interactions or off-topic discussions, education will become more efficient. Since the computers' content would be directed at maximizing test performance, standardized test scores will zoom.

Eliminating teachers and luxuries such as art lessons and field trips will save enough to recoup the cost of those fancy computers. With little effort, this electronic education could even become a profit center. Merely sell advertising space in the edutainment programs. Corporate sponsors, eager to market their messages to impressionable minds, would pay school systems to plug their products within the coursework.

Concerned that such a system might be dehumanizing? Not to worry. Interactive chat sessions will encourage a sense of community and enhance kids' social skills. Should a student have questions, the Internet will put her in instant touch with a trained support mentor. When necessary, real-time instructors will appear on the distance learning displays, available to interact via two-way video.

The Cyberschool will showcase technology and train students for the upcoming electronic workplace. As local employment prospects change, the school board will issue updates to the curriculum over its interactive website. And the school board will monitor what each student learns—without idiosyncratic teachers to raise unpopular topics or challenge accepted beliefs.

Advanced students can sign up for on-line extracurricular activities—perhaps joining the Virtual Compassion Corps. There, students will be paired up across racial, gender, and class lines. Our children would offer foreigners advice and even arrange interviews with prospective employers. In this way, students will perform community service and mentor others, while displaying their cultural awareness over the network. All without ever having to shake hands with a real person, travel to a distant country, or (gasp!) face the real problems of another culture.[3] Simple, safe, and sterile.

Should parents worry about Johnny's progress, they need only log in over the Internet to see their son's latest test scores. In addition, they'll receive e-mailed reports summarizing their child's work. And at any time, they can click on an icon to see live images of their young scholar, automatically uploaded by a school video camera.

Yep, just sign up for the future: the parent-pleasin', tax-savin', teacher-firin', interactive-educatin', child-centerin' Cyberschool. No stuffy classrooms. No more teacher strikes. No outdated textbooks. No expensive

---

[3]An actual proposal from the director of MIT's Laboratory for Computer Science, Michael Dertouzos.

clarinet lessons. No boring homework. No learning. Coming soon to a school district near you.[4]

---

[4]Idea for a computer game: Cyberschool Superintendent. Players score by saving money. They could eliminate teachers, close libraries, or blow up music studios. Competitors advance by wiring schools, adding computers, and plugging in multimedia systems. Evil monsters might appear in the form of teachers, scholars, and librarians who insist that you read a book. Bonus points, labeled Pilot Project Grants, would be awarded for writing vapid press releases.

Questions for Close Reading

1. What is the selection's thesis? Locate the sentence(s) in which Stoll states his main idea. If he doesn't state the thesis explicitly, express it in your own words.
2. What process does Stoll describe in the essay? What are the basic steps of this process? What is Stoll's underlying attitude toward these measures?
3. What specific group of people does Stoll imagine as being especially in favor of the "cyberschool"? According to Stoll, how do these individuals justify using computers to teach children?
4. What role does Stoll indicate teachers will play in the "cyberschool"? What attitude does he convey about this role? Explain.
5. Refer to your dictionary as needed to define the following words used in the selection: *infrastructures* (paragraph 1), *optimal* (1), *harried* (3), *placate* (4), *adept* (8), *standardized* (8), *cubicles* (10), *compartmentalized* (10), *cadre* (12), *recoup* (14), and *idiosyncratic* (16).

Questions About the Writer's Craft

1. **The pattern.** Is Stoll's process analysis primarily directional or primarily informational? Explain. To what extent does Stoll try to persuade readers that the process he describes should be followed?
2. Focusing on his word choices, how would you characterize Stoll's tone in his essay? In your opinion, does his tone enhance or detract from the point he's trying to make? Explain.
3. **Other patterns.** Underlying Stoll's process analysis is an *argument* against a particular form of education. To write an effective argument, writers need to establish their own credibility. Based on what you learned about Stoll in his biography (page 308), what makes him appear qualified to write about his subject?
4. **Other patterns.** In his persona of pro-cyberschool spokesman, Stoll addresses opposition to idea of the cyberschool in paragraph 15. How does Stoll represent and rebut the *arguments* against the cyberschool? Are his arguments effective, in your opinion?

Writing Assignments Using Process Analysis as a Pattern of Development

1. In his essay, Stoll offers a cynical recipe for creating an "optimal learning environment." Write an essay in which you present a process analysis of concrete ways the

school you currently attend or one you have attended in the past could realistically be improved. You might, for instance, discuss physical improvements such as updating the equipment in the computer lab, or less tangible measures such as cultivating a more interactive classroom environment. Brainstorm on your own or with others to generate specific ideas to include in your process.

2. In his essay, Stoll ironically suggests a course of action that he implies should not be taken in order to improve children's education. Taking a similarly ironic stance, write an essay *mis*guiding readers on how to "improve" some other significant institution or serious condition. For instance, you might discuss ways to increase the efficiency of a particular government agency, how to even out inequities between classes or races of people, how to protect the environment, and so on—all the while presenting steps that would work to the contrary. Like Stoll, you should ultimately reveal your true position in the concluding paragraph, preferably in a subtle way. You should consider reading Paul Roberts's "How to Say Nothing in 500 Words" (page 314) to see how another writer recommends a course of action that is antithetical to what he initially seems to advocate.

Writing Assignments Combining Patterns of Development

3. According to Stoll, computers serve as a distraction to students rather than a legitimate learning tool. What are other kinds of distractions students face? Write an essay in which you *classify* the different types of distractions that can make learning difficult. You may adopt a serious tone and address categories such as, for example, problems at home and pressure from peers. Or you might adopt a humorous tone and discuss distractions that include interest in the opposite sex and the temptation of computer games. Provide vivid *examples* to illustrate each of the categories you create. For additional viewpoints about the pressures to which students are subject, read Mary Sherry's "In Praise of the 'F' Word" (page 512) and Buzz Bissinger's "Innocents Afield" (page 424).

4. With the increasing popularity of the Internet, the future of traditional printed materials—such as books, magazines, and newspapers—has come into question. Write an essay in which you *compare* and *contrast* using printed materials with using the Internet in order to perform research. Be sure to provide at least one extended example or a few briefer examples to *illustrate* the differences and/or similarities you're pointing out. Your best source of information might be a "hands-on" approach: to research a topic using both methods in order to see for yourself what the differences are. By the end of your essay, make clear to your reader which of the two methods you find preferable, and why.

Writing Assignment Using a Journal Entry as a Starting Point

5. In an indirect way, Stoll argues against the wholesale computerization of the classroom. Write an essay in which you argue that the Internet specifically should *or* should not play a significant role in the education of *one* particular age group of

students (elementary, high school, or college). In formulating your argument, refer to the material you generated in your pre-reading journal entry. For additional perspectives on this issue, you might consider doing some research on this topic in the library and/or on the Internet. In writing your essay, you should acknowledge and rebut opposing points of view.

Paul Roberts

Paul Roberts (1917–67) was a scholar of linguistics and a respected teacher whose textbooks helped scores of high school and college students become better writers. Roberts's works include *English Syntax* (1954) and *Patterns of English* (1956). The following selection is from his best-known book, *Understanding English* (1958).

Pre-Reading Journal Entry

Many educators argue that first-year college students write bland essays because their high school English classes didn't teach them how to think clearly and creatively. Do you agree? Take some time to reflect in your journal about your best and worst high school English classes. For each class, focus on teaching style, classroom atmosphere, assignments, activities, and so on.

How to Say Nothing in 500 Words

Nothing About Something

It's Friday afternoon, and you have almost survived another week of classes. You are just looking forward dreamily to the weekend when the English instructor says: "For Monday you will turn in a five-hundred-word composition on college football."

Well, that puts a good big hole in the weekend. You don't have any strong views on college football one way or the other. You get rather excited during the season and go to all the home games and find it rather more fun than not. On the other hand, the class has been reading Robert Hutchins in the anthology and perhaps Shaw's "Eighty-Yard Run," and from the class discussion you have got the idea that the instructor thinks college football is for the birds. You are no fool, you. You can figure out what side to take.

After dinner you get out the portable typewriter that you got for high school graduation. You might as well get it over with and enjoy Saturday and Sunday. Five hundred words is about two double-spaced pages with normal margins. You put in a sheet of paper, think up a title, and you're off:

Why College Football Should Be Abolished

College football should be abolished because it's bad for the   4
school and also bad for the players. The players are so busy practicing that they don't have any time for their studies.

This, you feel, is a mighty good start. The only trouble is that it's only   5
thirty-two words. You still have four hundred and sixty-eight to go, and
you've pretty well exhausted the subject. It comes to you that you do your
best thinking in the morning, so you put away the typewriter and go to the
movies. But the next morning you have to do your washing and some math
problems, and in the afternoon you go to the game. The English instructor
turns up too, and you wonder if you've taken the right side after all. Saturday night you have a date, and Sunday morning you have to go to church.
(You shouldn't let English assignments interfere with your religion.) What
with one thing and another, it's ten o'clock Sunday night before you get out
the typewriter again. You make a pot of coffee and start to fill out your views
on college football. Put a little meat on the bones.

Why College Football Should Be Abolished

In my opinion, it seems to me that college football should be   6
abolished. The reason why I think this to be true is because I feel that
football is bad for the colleges in nearly every respect. As Robert
Hutchins says in his article in our anthology in which he discusses
college football, it would be better if the colleges had race horses and
had races with one another, because then the horses would not have
to attend classes. I firmly agree with Mr. Hutchins on this point, and
I am sure that many other students would agree too.

One reason why it seems to me that college football is bad is   7
that it has become too commercial. In the olden times when people played football just for the fun of it, maybe college football was
all right, but they do not play football just for the fun of it now as
they used to in the old days. Nowadays college football is what
you might call a big business. Maybe this is not true at all schools,
and I don't think it is especially true here at State, but certainly
this is the case at most colleges and universities in America nowadays, as Mr. Hutchins points out in his very interesting article.
Actually the coaches and alumni go around to the high schools
and offer the high school stars large salaries to come to their colleges and play football for them. There was one case where a high
school star was offered a convertible if he would play football for
a certain college.

Another reason for abolishing college football is that it is bad for the players. They do not have time to get a college education, because they are so busy playing football. A football player has to practice every afternoon from three to six, and then he is so tired that he can't concentrate on his studies. He just feels like dropping off to sleep after dinner, and then the next day he goes to his classes without having studied and maybe he fails the test.

(Good ripe stuff so far, but you're still a hundred and fifty-one words from home. One more push.)

Also I think college football is bad for the colleges and the universities because not very many students get to participate in it. Out of a college of ten thousand students only seventy-five or a hundred play football, if that many. Football is what you might call a spectator sport. That means that most people go to watch it but do not play it themselves.

(Four hundred and fifteen. Well, you still have the conclusion, and when you retype it, you can make the margins a little wider.)

These are the reasons why I agree with Mr. Hutchins that college football should be abolished in American colleges and universities.

On Monday you turn it in, moderately hopeful, and on Friday it comes back marked "weak in content" and sporting a big "D."

This essay is exaggerated a little, not much. The English instructor will recognize it as reasonably typical of what an assignment on college football will bring in. He knows that nearly half of the class will contrive in five hundred words to say that college football is too commercial and bad for the players. Most of the other half will inform him that college football builds character and prepares one for life and brings prestige to the school. As he reads paper after paper all saying the same thing in almost the same words, all bloodless, five hundred words dripping out of nothing, he wonders how he allowed himself to get trapped into teaching English when he might have had a happy and interesting life as an electrician or a confidence man.

Well, you may ask, what can you do about it? The subject is one on which you have few convictions and little information. Can you be expected to make a dull subject interesting? As a matter of fact, this is precisely what you are expected to do. This is the writer's essential task. All subjects, except sex, are dull until somebody makes them interesting. The writer's job is to find the argument, the approach, the angle, the wording that will take the reader with him. This is seldom easy, and it is particularly hard in subjects that have been much discussed: College Football, Fraternities, Popular Music, Is

Chivalry Dead?, and the like. You will feel that there is nothing you can do with such subjects except repeat the old bromides. But there are some things you can do which will make your papers, if not throbbingly alive, at least less insufferably tedious than they might otherwise be.

Avoid the Obvious Content

Say the assignment is college football. Say that you've decided to be 14 against it. Begin by putting down the arguments that come to your mind: it is too commercial, it takes the students' minds off their studies, it is hard on the players, it makes the university a kind of circus instead of an intellectual center, for most schools it is financially ruinous. Can you think of any more arguments just off hand? All right. Now when you write your paper, *make sure that you don't use any of the material on this list.* If these are the points that leap to your mind, they will leap to everyone else's too, and whether you get a "C" or a "D" may depend on whether the instructor reads your paper early when he is fresh and tolerant or late, when the sentence "In my opinion, college football has become too commercial," inexorably repeated, has brought him to the brink of lunacy.

Be against college football for some reason or reasons of your own. If 15 they are keen and perceptive ones, that's splendid. But even if they are trivial or foolish or indefensible, you are still ahead so long as they are not everybody else's reasons too. Be against it because the colleges don't spend enough money on it to make it worth while, because it is bad for the characters of the spectators, because the players are forced to attend classes, because the football stars hog all the beautiful women, because it competes with baseball and is therefore un-American and possibly Communist inspired. There are lots of more or less unused reasons for being against college football.

Sometimes it is a good idea to sum up and dispose of the trite and con- 16 ventional points before going on to your own. This has the advantage of indicating to the reader that you are going to be neither trite nor conventional. Something like this:

> We are often told that college football should be abolished 17
> because it has become too commercial or because it is bad for the
> players. These arguments are no doubt very cogent, but they don't
> really go to the heart of the matter.

Then you go to the heart of the matter.

Take the Less Usual Side

One rather simple way of getting interest into your paper is to take the 18 side of the argument that most of the citizens will want to avoid. If the assignment is an essay on dogs, you can, if you choose, explain that dogs are faithful and lovable companions, intelligent, useful as guardians of the house and protectors of children, indispensable in police work—in short, when all is said and done, man's best friends. Or you can suggest that those big brown eyes conceal, more often than not, a vacuity of mind and an inconstancy of purpose; that the dogs you have known most intimately have been mangy, ill-tempered brutes, incapable of instruction; and that only your nobility of mind and fear of arrest prevent you from kicking the flea-ridden animals when you pass them on the street.

Naturally, personal convictions will sometimes dictate your approach. If the assigned subject is "Is Methodism Rewarding to the Individual?" and you are a pious Methodist, you have really no choice. But few assigned subjects, if any, will fall in this category. Most of them will lie in broad areas of discussion with much to be said on both sides. They are intellectual exercises and it is legitimate to argue now one way and now another, as debaters do in similar circumstances. Always take the side that looks to you hardest, least defensible. It will almost always turn out to be easier to write interestingly on that side.

This general advice applies where you have a choice of subjects. If you are to choose among "The Value of Fraternities" and "My Favorite High School Teacher" and "What I Think About Beetles," by all means plump for the beetles. By the time the instructor gets to your paper, he will be up to his ears in tedious tales about the French teacher at Bloombury High and assertions about how fraternities build character and prepare one for life. Your views on beetles, whatever they are, are bound to be a refreshing change.

Don't worry too much about figuring out what the instructor thinks about the subject so that you can cuddle up with him. Chances are his views are no stronger than yours. If he does have convictions and you oppose them, his problem is to keep from grading you higher than you deserve in order to show he is not biased. This doesn't mean that you should always cantankerously dissent from what the instructor says; that gets tiresome too. And if the subject assigned is "My Pet Peeve," do not begin, "My pet peeve is the English instructor who assigns papers on 'my pet peeve.'" This was still funny during the War of 1812, but it has sort of lost its edge since then. It is in general good manners to avoid personalities.

Slip Out of Abstraction

If you will study the essay on college football . . . you will perceive that one reason for its appalling dullness is that it never gets down to particulars. It is just a series of not very glittering generalities: "football is bad for the colleges," "it has become too commercial," "football is a big business," "it is bad for the players," and so on. Such round phrases thudding against the reader's brain are unlikely to convince him, though they may well render him unconscious.

If you want the reader to believe that college football is bad for the play-   23
ers, you have to do more than say so. You have to display the evil. Take your
roommate, Alfred Simkins, the second-string center. Picture poor old Alfy
coming home from football practice every evening, bruised and aching, ago-
nizingly tired, scarcely able to shovel the mashed potatoes into his mouth.
Let us see him staggering up to the room, getting out his econ textbook,
peering desperately at it with his good eye, falling asleep and failing the test
in the morning. Let us share his unbearable tension as Saturday draws near.
Will he fail, be demoted, lose his monthly allowance, be forced to return to
the coal mines? And if he succeeds, what will be his reward? Perhaps a slight
ripple of applause when the third-string center replaces him, a moment of
elation in the locker room if the team wins, of despair if it loses. What will
he look back on when he graduates from college? Toil and torn ligaments.
And what will be his future? He is not good enough for pro football, and he
is too obscure and weak in econ to succeed in stocks and bonds. College
football is tearing the heart from Alfy Simkins and, when it finishes with him,
will callously toss aside the shattered hulk.

This is no doubt a weak enough argument for the abolition of college   24
football, but it is a sight better than saying, in three or four variations, that
college football (in your opinion) is bad for the players.

Look at the work of any professional writer and notice how constantly   25
he is moving from the generality, the abstract statement, to the concrete
example, the facts and figures, the illustration. If he is writing on juvenile
delinquency, he does not just tell you that juveniles are (it seems to him)
delinquent and that (in his opinion) something should be done about it. He
shows you juveniles being delinquent, tearing up movie theatres in Buffalo,
stabbing high school principals in Dallas, smoking marijuana in Palo Alto.
And more than likely he is moving toward some specific remedy, not just a
general wringing of the hands.

It is no doubt possible to be *too* concrete, too illustrative or anecdotal,   26
but few inexperienced writers err this way. For most the soundest advice is
to be seeking always for the picture, to be always turning general remarks
into seeable examples. Don't say, "Sororities teach girls the social graces."
Say "Sorority life teaches a girl how to carry on a conversation while pouring tea, without sloshing the tea into the saucer." Don't say, "I like certain
kinds of popular music very much." Say, "Whenever I hear Gerber Spinklit-
tle play 'Mississippi Man' on the trombone, my socks creep up my ankles."

Get Rid of Obvious Padding

The student toiling away at his weekly English theme is too often tor-   27
mented by a figure: five hundred words. How, he asks himself, is he to
achieve this staggering total? Obviously by never using one word when he
can somehow work in ten.

He is therefore seldom content with a plain statement like "Fast driving   2&
is dangerous." This has only four words in it. He takes thought, and the sentence becomes:

> In my opinion, fast driving is dangerous.

Better, but he can do better still:

> In my opinion, fast driving would seem to be rather dangerous.

If he is really adept, it may come out:

> In my humble opinion, though I do not claim to be an expert
> on this complicated subject, fast driving, in most circumstances,
> would seem to be rather dangerous in many respects, or at least so
> it would seem to me.

Thus four words have been turned into forty, and not an iota of content has been added.

Now this is a way to go about reaching five hundred words, and if you   2&
are content with a "D" grade, it is as good a way as any. But if you aim higher, you must work differently. Instead of stuffing your sentences with straw, you must try steadily to get rid of the padding, to make your sentences lean and tough. If you are really working at it, your first draft will greatly exceed the required total, and then you will work it down, thus:

> It is thought in some quarters that fraternities do not contribute as much as might be expected to campus life.
> Some people think that fraternities contribute little to campus life.

> The average doctor who practices in small towns or in the country must toil night and day to heal the sick.
> Most country doctors work long hours.

> When I was a little girl, I suffered from shyness and embarrassment in the presence of others.
> I was a shy little girl.

> It is absolutely necessary for the person employed as a marine fireman to give the matter of steam pressure his undivided attention at all times.
> The fireman has to keep his eye on the steam gauge.

You may ask how you can arrive at five hundred words at this rate. Sim-   30
ply. You dig up more real content. Instead of taking a couple of obvious
points off the surface of the topic and then circling warily around them for six
paragraphs, you work in and explore, figure out the details. You illustrate. You
say that fast driving is dangerous, and then you prove it. How long does it
take to stop a car at forty and at eighty? How far can you see at night? What
happens when a tire blows? What happens in a head-on collision at fifty miles
an hour? Pretty soon your paper will be full of broken glass and blood and
headless torsos, and reaching five hundred words will not really be a problem.

Call a Fool a Fool

Some of the padding in freshman themes is to be blamed not on anxiety   31
about the word minimum but on excessive timidity. The student writes, "In
my opinion, the principal of my high school acted in ways that I believe every
unbiased person would have to call foolish." This isn't exactly what he means.
What he means is, "My high school principal was a fool." If he was a fool, call
him a fool. Hedging the thing about with "in-my-opinion's" and "it-seems-
to-me's" and "as-I-see-it's" and "at-least-from-my-point-of-view's" gains you
nothing. Delete these phrases whenever they creep into your paper.

The student's tendency to hedge stems from a modesty that in other cir-   32
cumstances would be commendable. He is, he realizes, young and inexperienced, and he half suspects that he is dopey and fuzzy-minded beyond the
average. Probably only too true. But it doesn't help to announce your
incompetence six times in every paragraph. Decide what you want to say and
say it as vigorously as possible, without apology and in plain words.

Linguistic diffidence can take various forms. One is what we call   33
euphemism. This is the tendency to call a spade "a certain garden implement"
or women's underwear "unmentionables." It is stronger in some eras than
others and in some people than others but it always operates more or less in
subjects that are touchy or taboo: death, sex, madness, and so on. Thus we
shrink from saying "He died last night" but say instead "passed away," "left
us," "joined his Maker," "went to his reward." Or we try to take off the tension with a lighter cliché: "kicked the bucket," "cashed in his chips," "handed
in his dinner pail." We have found all sorts of ways to avoid saying *mad:* "mentally ill," "touched," "not quite right upstairs," "feeble-minded," "innocent,"
"simple," "off his trolley," "not in his right mind." Even such a now plain
word as *insane* began as a euphemism with the meaning "not healthy."

Modern science, particularly psychology, contributes many polysyllables   34
in which we can wrap our thoughts and blunt their force. To many writers
there is no such thing as a bad schoolboy. Schoolboys are maladjusted or
unoriented or misunderstood or in need of guidance or lacking in continued
success toward satisfactory integration of the personality as a social unit, but

they are never bad. Psychology no doubt makes us better men or women, more sympathetic and tolerant, but it doesn't make writing any easier. Had Shakespeare been confronted with psychology, "To be or not to be" might have come out, "To continue as a social unit or not to do so. That is the personality problem. Whether 'tis a better sign of integration at the conscious level to display a psychic tolerance toward the maladjustments and repressions induced by one's lack of orientation in one's environment or—" But Hamlet would never have finished the soliloquy.

Writing in the modern world, you cannot altogether avoid modern jargon. Nor, in an effort to get away from euphemism, should you salt your paper with four-letter words. But you can do much if you will mount guard against those roundabout phrases, those echoing polysyllables that tend to slip into your writing to rob it of its crispness and force.

Beware of the Pat Expression

Other things being equal, avoid phrases like "other things being equal." Those sentences that come to you whole, or in two or three doughy lumps, are sure to be bad sentences. They are no creation of yours but pieces of common thought floating in the community soup.

Pat expressions are hard, often impossible, to avoid, because they come too easily to be noticed and seem too necessary to be dispensed with. No writer avoids them altogether, but good writers avoid them more often than poor writers.

By "pat expressions" we mean such tags as "to all practical intents and purposes," "the pure and simple truth," "from where I sit," "the time of his life," "to the ends of the earth," "in the twinkling of an eye," "as sure as you're born," "over my dead body," "under cover of darkness," "took the easy way out," "when all is said and done," "told him time and time again," "parted the best of friends," "stand up and be counted," "gave him the best years of her life," "worked her fingers to the bone." Like other clichés, these expressions were once forceful. Now we should use them only when we can't possibly think of anything else.

Some pat expressions stand like a wall between the writer and thought. Such a one is "the American way of life." Many student writers feel that when they have said that something accords with the American way of life or does not they have exhausted the subject. Actually, they have stopped at the highest level of abstraction. The American way of life is the complicated set of bonds between a hundred and eighty million ways. All of us know this when we think about it, but the tag phrase too often keeps us from thinking about it.

So with many another phrase dear to the politician: "this great land of ours," "the man in the street," "our national heritage." These may prove our patriotism or give a clue to our political beliefs, but otherwise they add nothing to the paper except words.

Colorful Words

The writer builds with words, and no builder uses a raw material more   41
slippery and elusive and treacherous. A writer's work is a constant struggle
to get the right word in the right place, to find that particular word that will
convey his meaning exactly, that will persuade the reader or soothe him or
startle or amuse him. He never succeeds altogether—sometimes he feels that
he scarcely succeeds at all—but such successes as he has are what make the
thing worth doing.

There is no book of rules for this game. One progresses through ever-   42
lasting experiment on the basis of ever-widening experience. There are few
useful generalizations that one can make about words as words, but there are
perhaps a few.

Some words are what we call "colorful." By this we mean that they are   43
calculated to produce a picture or induce an emotion. They are dressy
instead of plain, specific instead of general, loud instead of soft. Thus, in
place of "Her heart beat," we may write "Her heart *pounded, throbbed, fluttered, danced.*" Instead of "He sat in his chair," we may say, "He *lounged, sprawled, coiled.*" Instead of "It was hot," we may say, "It was *blistering, sultry, muggy, suffocating, steamy, wilting.*"

However, it should not be supposed that the fancy word is always bet-   44
ter. Often it is as well to write "Her heart beat" or "It was hot" if that is all
it did or all it was. Ages differ in how they like their prose. The nineteenth
century liked it rich and smoky. The twentieth has usually preferred it lean
and cool. The twentieth-century writer, like all writers, is forever seeking the
exact word, but he is wary of sounding feverish. He tends to pitch it low, to
understate it, to throw it away. He knows that if he gets too colorful, the
audience is likely to giggle.

See how this strikes you: "As the rich, golden glow of the sunset died   45
away along the eternal western hills, Angela's limpid blue eyes looked softly
and trustingly into Montague's flashing brown ones, and her heart pounded
like a drum in time with the joyous song surging in her soul." Some people
like that sort of thing, but most modern readers would say, "Good grief,"
and turn on the television.

Colored Words

Some words we would call not so much colorful as colored—that is,   46
loaded with associations, good or bad. All words—except perhaps structure
words—have associations of some sort. We have said that the meaning of a

word is the sum of the contexts in which it occurs. When we hear a word, we hear with it an echo of all the situations in which we have heard it before.

In some words, these echoes are obvious and discussable. The word *mother,* for example, has, for most people, agreeable associations. When you hear *mother* you probably think of home, safety, love, food, and various other pleasant things. If one writes, "She was like a mother to me," he gets an effect which he would not get in "She was like an aunt to me." The advertiser makes use of the associations of *mother* by working it in when he talks about his product. The politician works it in when he talks about himself.

So also with such words as *home, liberty, fireside, contentment, patriot, tenderness, sacrifice, childlike, manly, bluff, limpid.* All of these words are loaded with favorable associations that would be rather hard to indicate in a straightforward definition. There is more than a literal difference between "They sat around the fireside" and "They sat around the stove." They might have been equally warm and happy around the stove, but *fireside* suggests leisure, grace, quiet tradition, congenial company, and *stove* does not.

Conversely, some words have bad associations. *Mother* suggests pleasant things, but *mother-in-law* does not. Many mothers-in-law are heroically lovable and some mothers drink gin all day and beat their children insensible, but these facts of life are beside the point. The thing is that *mother* sounds good and *mother-in-law* does not.

Or consider the word *intellectual.* This would seem to be a complimentary term, but in point of fact it is not, for it has picked up associations of impracticality and ineffectuality and general dopiness. So also with such words as *liberal, reactionary, Communist, socialist, capitalist, radical, schoolteacher, truck driver, undertaker, operator, salesman, huckster, speculator.* These convey meanings on the literal level, but beyond that—sometimes, in some places—they convey contempt on the part of the speaker.

The question of whether to use loaded words or not depends on what is being written. The scientist, the scholar, try to avoid them; for the poet, the advertising writer, the public speaker, they are standard equipment. But every writer should take care that they do not substitute for thought. If you write, "Anyone who thinks that is nothing but a Socialist (or Communist or capitalist)," you have said nothing except that you don't like people who think that, and such remarks are effective only with the most naïve readers. It is always a bad mistake to think your readers more naïve than they really are.

Colorless Words

But probably most student writers come to grief not with words that are colorful or those that are colored but with those that have no color at all. A pet example is *nice,* a word we would find it hard to dispense with in casual conversation but which is no longer capable of adding much to a description. Colorless words are those of such general meaning that in a particular sentence they mean nothing. Slang adjectives, like *cool* ("That's real cool") tend to explode all over the language. They are applied to everything, lose their original force, and quickly die.

Beware also of nouns of very general meaning, like *circumstances, cases,* 53 *instances, aspects, factors, relationships, attitudes, eventualities,* etc. In most circumstances you will find that those cases of writing which contain too many instances of words like these will in this and other aspects have factors leading to unsatisfactory relationships with the reader resulting in unfavorable attitudes on his part and perhaps other eventualities, like a grade of "D." Notice also what "etc." means. It means "I'd like to make this list longer, but I can't think of any more examples."

Questions for Close Reading

1. What is the selection's thesis? Locate the sentence(s) in which Roberts states his main idea. If he doesn't state the thesis explicitly, express it in your own words.
2. According to Roberts, what do students assume they have to do to get a good grade on an English composition?
3. How do "colorful words," "colored words," and "colorless words" differ? Which should be used in essay writing? Why?
4. What are Roberts's most important pieces of advice for the student writer?
5. Refer to the dictionary as needed to define the following words used in the selection: *bromides* (paragraph 13), *insufferably* (13), *inexorably* (14), *dissent* (21), *abolition* (24), *adept* (28), *euphemism* (33), and *insensible* (49).

Questions About the Writer's Craft

1. **The pattern.** What two processes does Roberts analyze in this essay? Is each process informational, directional, or a combination of the two?
2. Why do you think Roberts uses the second person "you" throughout the essay? How does this choice of point of view affect your response to the essay?
3. What is Roberts's tone in the essay? Find some typical examples of his tone. How does Roberts achieve this tone? Considering the author's intended audience, is this tone a good choice? Explain.
4. Does Roberts "practice what he preaches" about writing? Review the section headings of the essay and find examples of each piece of advice in the essay.

Writing Assignments Using Process Analysis as a Pattern of Development

1. Write a humorous essay showing how to avoid doing schoolwork, household chores, or anything else most people tend to put off. You may use the second person as Roberts does. Or you may use the first person and describe your typical method of avoidance. Before writing, read Clifford Stoll's "Cyberschool" (page 308), a humorous model for a how-*not*-to guide.
2. Borrowing some of Roberts's lively techniques, make a routine, predictable process interesting to read about. You might choose an activity such as how to

register to vote, apply for a driver's license, sign up for college courses, take care of laundry, play a simple game, study for an exam, or execute some other familiar process. Caroline Rego's "The Fine Art of Complaining" (page 327) may give you some ideas on how to explain a process in a helpful yet entertaining way.

Writing Assignments Combining Patterns of Development

3. Should a composition course be required of all first-year college students? Write an essay *arguing* the value—or lack of value—of such a course. Follow Roberts's advice for writing a lively composition: avoid obvious padding, choose unusual points and *examples*, avoid abstractions, go to the heart of the matter, use colorful words.
4. Write a paper detailing your experiences as a student in English classes—from elementary school up to now. Using several *examples, describe* how successfully or unsuccessfully English has been taught, and recommend any specific reforms or changes you feel are needed.

Writing Assignment Using a Journal Entry as a Starting Point

5. Write an essay describing an ideal high school English class. What kind of teacher would be at the helm? What kind of learning atmosphere would prevail? What sorts of skills would be covered? How? To formulate your position, review your pre-reading journal entry, drawing upon your experiences as a guide. End the essay by briefly discussing the factors that might prevent English classes from being like the ideal one you've described. To broaden your perspective on the issues involved, consider discussing the topic with friends and classmates.

Caroline Rego

Caroline Rego was born in 1950 in Edmond, Oklahoma. A graduate of the University of Oklahoma, she began her journalistic career as a police reporter for a daily newspaper in Montana. Later, while filling in for a vacationing colleague in the features section of another newspaper, she found her true calling: writing consumer-affairs articles that teach readers how to protect themselves against shoddy service, dangerous products, and inefficiency. A sought-after public speaker, Rego talks frequently to students and community groups on strategies for becoming an informed consumer. The following selection is part of a work in progress on consumer empowerment.

Pre-Reading Journal Entry

When you're disappointed with someone or something, how do you typically react—passively, assertively, or in some other way? In your journal, list a few disappointments you've experienced. How did you respond on each occasion? In retrospect, are you happy with your responses? Why or why not?

The Fine Art of Complaining

You waited forty-five minutes for your dinner, and when it came it was 1
cold—and not what you ordered in the first place. You washed your supposedly machine-washable, preshrunk T-shirt (the one the catalogue claimed was "indestructible"), and now it's the size of a napkin. Your new car broke down a month after you bought it, and the dealer says the warranty doesn't apply.

Life's annoyances descend on all of us—some pattering down like gen- 2
tle raindrops, others striking with the bruising force of hailstones. We dodge the ones we can, but inevitably, plenty of them make contact. And when they do, we react fairly predictably. Many of us—most of us, probably—grumble to ourselves and take it. We scowl at our unappetizing food but choke it down. We stash the shrunken T-shirt in a drawer, vowing never again to order from a catalogue. We glare fiercely at our checkbooks as we pay for repairs that should have been free.

A few of us go to the other extreme. Taking our cue from the crazed 3
newscaster in the 1976 movie *Network,* we go through life mad as hell and unwilling to take it anymore. In offices, we shout at hapless receptionists when we're kept waiting for appointments. In restaurants, we make scenes that have fellow patrons craning their necks to get a look at us. In stores, we

argue with salespeople for not waiting on us. We may notice after a while that our friends seem reluctant to venture into public with us, but hey—we're just standing up for our rights. Being a patsy doesn't get you anywhere in life.

It's true—milquetoasts live unsatisfying lives. However, people who go   4
through the day in an eye-popping, vein-throbbing state of apoplectic rage don't win any prizes either. What persons at both ends of the scale need— what could empower the silent sufferer and civilize the Neanderthal—is a course in the gentle art of *effective* complaining.

Effective complaining is not apologetic and half-hearted. It's not mak-   5
ing one awkward attempt at protest—"Uh, excuse me, I don't think I ordered the squid and onions"—and then slinking away in defeat. But nei- ther is it roaring away indiscriminately, attempting to get satisfaction through the sheer volume of our complaint.

Effective complainers are people who act businesslike and important.   6
Acting important doesn't mean puffing up your chest and saying, "Do you know who I am?"—an approach that would tempt anyone to take you down a peg or two. It doesn't mean shouting and threatening—techniques that will only antagonize the person whose help you need. It *does* mean making it clear that you know your request is reasonable and that you are confident it will be taken care of. People are generally treated the way they expect to be treated. If you act like someone making a fair request, chances are that request will be granted. Don't beg, don't explain. Just state your name, the problem, and what you expect to have done. Remain polite. But be firm. "My car has been in your garage for three days, and a mechanic hasn't even looked at it yet," you might say. "I want to know when it is going to be worked on." Period. Now it is up to them to give you a satisfactory response. Don't say, "Sorry to bother you about this, but . . ." or "I, uh, was sort of expecting. . . ." You're only asking people to remedy a problem, after all; that is not grounds for apology.

If your problem requires an immediate response, try to make your   7
complaint in person; a real, live, in-the-flesh individual has to be dealt with in some way. Complaining over the telephone, by contrast, is much less effective. When you speak to a disembodied voice, when the person at the other end of the line doesn't have to face you, you're more likely to get a runaround.

Most importantly, complain to the right person. One of the greatest   8
frustrations in complaining is talking to a clerk or receptionist who cannot solve your problem and whose only purpose seems to be to drive you crazy. Getting mad doesn't help; the person you're mad at probably had nothing to do with your actual problem. And you'll have to repeat everything you've said to the clerk once you're passed along to the appropriate person. So make sure from the start that you're talking to someone who can help—a manag- er or supervisor.

If your problem doesn't require an immediate response, complaining by 9
letter is probably the most effective way to get what you want. A letter of
complaint should be brief, businesslike, and to the point. If you have a new
vacuum cleaner that doesn't work, don't spend a paragraph describing how
your Uncle Joe tried to fix the problem and couldn't. As when complaining
in person, be sure you address someone in a position of real authority. Here's
an example of an effective letter of complaint.

Ms. Anne Lublin   10
Manager
Mitchell Appliances
80 Front Street
Newton, MA 02159

Dear Ms. Lublin: 11

First section: Explain the problem. Include facts to back up your story.   12

On August 6, I purchased a new Perma-Kool freezer from your store (a copy of 13
my sales receipt is enclosed). In the two weeks I have owned the freezer, I have
had to call your repair department three times in an attempt to get it running
properly. The freezer ran normally when it was installed, but since then it has
repeatedly turned off, causing the food inside to spoil. My calls to your repair
department have not been responded to promptly. After I called the first time, on
August 10, I waited two days for the repair person to show up. It took three days
to get a repair person here after my second call, on August 15. The freezer
stopped yet again on August 20. I called to discuss this recent problem, but no
one has responded to my call.

Second section: Tell how you trust the company and are confident that your 14
reader will fix the problem. This is to "soften up" the reader a bit.

I am surprised to receive such unprofessional service and poor quality from Mitchell 15
Appliances since I have been one of your satisfied customers for fifteen years. In
the past, I have purchased a television, air conditioner, and washing machine
from your company. I know that you value good relations with your customers,
and I'm sure you want to see me pleased with my most recent purchase.

Third section: Explain exactly what you want to be done—repair, replacement, 16
refund, etc.

Although your repair department initially thought that the freezer needed only 17
some minor adjustments, the fact that no one has been able to permanently fix
the problem convinces me that the freezer has some serious defect. I am
understandably unwilling to spend any more time having repairs made.
Therefore, I expect you to exchange the freezer for an identical model by the end

of this week (August 30). Please call me to arrange for the removal of the defective freezer and the delivery of the new one.

Sincerely,   1£

Janice Becker

P.S. (Readers always notice a P.S.) State again when you expect the problem to   1ⁱ
be taken care of, and what you will do if it isn't.

P.S. I am confident that we can resolve this problem by August 30. If the   2(
defective freezer is not replaced by then, however, I will report this incident to
the Better Business Bureau.

Notice that the P.S. says what you'll do if your problem isn't solved. In other   2ⁱ
words, you make a threat—a polite threat. Your threat must be reasonable
and believable. A threat to burn down the store if your purchase price isn't
refunded is neither reasonable nor believable—or if it *were* believed, you
could end up in jail. A threat to report the store to a consumer-protection
agency, such as the Better Business Bureau, however, is credible.

Don't be too quick to make one of the most common—and commonly   2ⁱ
empty—threats: "I'll sue!" A full-blown lawsuit is more trouble, and more
expensive, than most problems are worth. On the other hand, most areas
have a small-claims court where suits involving modest amounts of money
are heard. These courts don't use complex legal language or procedures, and
you don't need a lawyer to use them. A store or company will often settle
with you—if your claim is fair—rather than go to small-claims court.

Whether you complain over the phone, in person, or by letter, be persis-   2
tent. One complaint may not get results. In that case, keep on complaining,
and make sure you keep complaining to the same person. Chances are he or
she will get worn out and take care of the situation, if only to be rid of you.

Someday, perhaps, the world will be free of the petty annoyances that   2ⁱ
plague us all from time to time. Until then, however, toasters will break
down, stores will refuse to honor rainchecks, and bills will include items that
were never purchased. You can depend upon it—there will be grounds for
complaint. You might as well learn to be good at it.

Questions for Close Reading

1. What is the selection's thesis? Locate the sentence(s) in which Rego states her
   main idea. If she doesn't state the thesis explicitly, express it in your own words.
2. In Rego's opinion, what types of actions and statements are *not* helpful when making a complaint?
3. What should be included in a letter of complaint? What should be omitted?
4. What does Rego suggest doing if a complaint is ignored?

5. Refer to your dictionary as needed to define the following words used in the selection: *hapless* (paragraph 3), *venture* (3), *patsy* (3), *milquetoasts* (4), *apoplectic* (4), *Neanderthal* (4), *indiscriminately* (5), *disembodied* (7), and *credible* (21).

Questions About the Writer's Craft

1. **The pattern.** Is Rego's process analysis primarily directional or primarily informational? Explain. To what extent does Rego try to persuade readers to follow her process?

2. **Other patterns.** Where does Rego include *narrative* elements in her essay? What do these brief narratives add to the piece?

3. **Other patterns.** Numerous oppositions occur throughout the essay. How do these *contrasts* enliven the essay and help Rego persuade readers to adopt her suggestions?

4. Reread the essay, noting where Rego shifts point of view. Where does she use the second-person (*you*), the first-person-plural (*we*), and the third-person-plural (*they*) points of view? How does her use of multiple points of view add to the essay's effectiveness?

Writing Assignments Using Process Analysis as a Pattern of Development

1. Write an essay explaining to college students how to register—with someone in a position of authority—an effective complaint about a campus problem. You could show, for example, how to complain to a professor about a course's grading policy, to the bookstore manager about the markup on textbooks, to security about the poorly maintained college parking lots. Feel free to adapt some of Rego's recommendations, but be sure to invent several strategies of your own. In either case, provide—as Rego does—lively examples to illustrate the step-by-step procedure for registering an effective complaint with a specific authority figure on campus.

2. Rego argues that "people who go through the day in an eye-popping, vein-throbbing state of apoplectic rage don't win any prizes." But sometimes, getting mad can be appropriate—even productive. Write an essay explaining the best process for expressing anger effectively. Explain how to vent emotion safely, communicate the complaint in a nonthreatening way, encourage more honest interaction, and prompt change for the better. Illustrate the process by drawing upon your own experiences and observations. Consider reading Barbara Ehrenreich's "What I've Learned From Men" (page 215), which provides some insight into the dynamics of anger and resentment, and James Gleick's "Life As Type A" (page 450), which addresses the origins of high-intensity behavior.

Writing Assignments Combining Patterns of Development

3. Think about a service or product that failed to live up to your expectations. Perhaps you were disgruntled about your mechanic's car repair, a store's return policy, or a hotel's accommodations. Using Rego's suggestions, write a letter of complaint

in which you *describe* the problem, convey confidence in the reader's ability to resolve the problem, and state your request for specific action. Remember that a firm but cordial tone will *persuade* your reader that you have legitimate grounds for seeking the resolution you propose.

∞ 4. Rego shows that events often don't turn out as we had hoped. In an essay, *contrast* how you thought a specific situation would be with the way it actually turned out. Was the unexpected outcome better or worse than what you had expected? Did you have trouble adjusting, or did you adapt with surprising ease? Provide vivid *specifics* about the unforeseen turn of events and your *reaction* to it. Before writing, you might read Audre Lorde's "The Fourth of July" (page 137) and Charmie Gholson's "Charity Display?" (page 151), two professional writers' accounts of experiences that dramatically departed from their expectations.

Writing Assignment Using a Journal Entry as a Starting Point

∞ 5. Write an essay contrasting the way you reacted to a specific disappointment with the way you wish you had reacted. Reread your pre-reading journal entry, and select *one* incident that illustrates this discrepancy most dramatically. Use vigorous narrative details to make the contrast vivid and real. In your conclusion, indicate what you've learned in hindsight. Before writing, consider reading three other essays that document personal reactions to life's minor—and major—calamities: Langston Hughes's "Salvation" (page 155), Adam Mayblum's "The Price We Pay" (page 159), and Beth Johnson's "Bombs Bursting in Air" (page 209).

Additional Writing Topics

PROCESS ANALYSIS

General Assignments

Develop one of the following topics through process analysis. Explain the process one step at a time, organizing the steps chronologically. If there's no agreed-on sequence, design your own series of steps. Use transitions to ease the audience through the steps in the process. You may use any tone you wish, from serious to light.

Directional: How to Do Something

1. How to improve a course you have taken
2. How to drive defensively
3. How to get away with _____
4. How to succeed at a job interview
5. How to relax
6. How to show appreciation to others
7. How to get through school despite personal problems
8. How to be a responsible pet owner
9. How to conduct a garage or yard sale
10. How to look fashionable on a limited budget
11. How to protect a home from burglars
12. How to meet more people
13. How to improve the place where you work
14. How to gain or lose weight
15. How to get over a disappointment

Informational: How Something Happens

1. How a student becomes burned out
2. How a library's card catalog or computerized catalog organizes books
3. How a dead thing decays (or how some other natural process works)
4. How the college registration process works
5. How *Homo sapiens* choose a mate
6. How a DVD player (or some other machine) works
7. How a bad habit develops
8. How people fall into debt
9. How someone becomes an Internet addict/junkie
10. How a child develops a love of reading

Assignments With a Specific Purpose, Audience, and Point of View

On Campus

1. As an experienced campus tour guide for prospective students, you've been asked by your school's Admissions Office to write a pamphlet explaining to new tour

guides how to conduct a tour of your school's campus. When explaining the process, keep in mind that tour guides need to portray the school in its best light.

2. You write an "advice to the lovelorn" column for the campus newspaper. A correspondent writes saying that he or she wants to break up with a steady girlfriend/boyfriend but doesn't know how to do this without hurting the person. Give the writer guidance on how to end a meaningful relationship with a minimal amount of pain.

At Home or in the Community

3. To help a sixteen-year-old friend learn how to drive, explain a specific driving maneuver one step at a time. You might, for example, describe how to make a three-point turn, parallel park, or handle a skid. Remember, your friend lacks self-confidence and experience.

4. Your best friend plans to move into his or her own apartment but doesn't know the first thing about how to choose one. Explain the process of selecting an apartment—where to look, what to investigate, what questions to ask before signing a lease.

On the Job

5. As a staff writer for a consumer magazine, you've been asked to write an article on how to shop for a certain product. Give specific steps explaining how to save money, buy a quality product, and the like.

6. An author of books for elementary school children, you want to show children how to do something—take care of a pet, get along with siblings, keep a room clean. Explain the process in terms a child would understand yet not find condescending.

Isn't it time you bought a **Bendix Washer?**

8

COMPARISON-CONTRAST

WHAT IS COMPARISON-CONTRAST?

We frequently try to make sense of the world by finding similarities and differences in our experiences. Seeing how things are alike (comparing) and seeing how they are different (contrasting) helps us impose meaning on experiences that otherwise might remain fragmented and disconnected. Barely aware of the fact that we're comparing and contrasting, we may think to ourselves, "I woke up in a great mood this morning, but now I feel uneasy and anxious. I wonder why I feel so different." This inner questioning, which often occurs in a flash, is just one example of the way we use comparison and contrast to understand ourselves and our world.

Comparing and contrasting also helps us make choices. We compare and contrast everything—from two brands of soap we might buy to two colleges we might attend. We listen to a favorite radio station, watch a preferred nightly news show, select a particular dessert from a menu—all because we have done some degree of comparing and contrasting. We often weigh these alternatives in an unstudied, casual manner, as when we flip from one radio station to another. But when we have to make important decisions, we tend to think rigorously about how things are alike or different: Should I live in a dorm or rent an apartment? Should I accept the higher-paying job or the lower-paying one that offers more challenges? Such a deliberate approach to comparison-contrast may also provide us with needed insight into complex contemporary issues: Is television's coverage of political campaigns more or less objective than it used to be? What are the merits of the various positions on abortion?

HOW COMPARISON-CONTRAST FITS YOUR PURPOSE AND AUDIENCE

When is it appropriate in writing to use the comparison-contrast method of development? Comparison-contrast works well if you want to demonstrate any of the following: (1) that one thing is better than another (the first example below); (2) that things which seem different are actually alike (the second example below); (3) that things which seem alike are actually different (the third example below).

Compare and contrast the way male and female relationships are depicted in *Cosmopolitan, Ms., Playboy,* and *Esquire.* Which publication has the most limited view of men and women? Which has the broadest perspective?

Football, basketball, and baseball differ in the ways they appeal to fans. Describe the unique drawing power of each sport, but also reach some conclusions about the appeals the three sports have in common.

Studies show that both college students and their parents feel that post-secondary education should equip young people to succeed in the marketplace. Yet the same studies report that the two groups have a very different understanding of what it means to succeed. What differences do you think the studies identify?

Other assignments will, in less obvious ways, lend themselves to comparison-contrast. For instance, although terms like *compare, contrast, differ,* and *have in common* don't appear in the following assignments, essay responses to the assignments could be organized around the comparison-contrast format:

The emergence of the two-career family is one of the major phenomena of our culture. Discuss the advantages and disadvantages of having both parents work, showing how you feel about such two-career households.

Some people believe that the 1950s, often called the golden age of television, produced several never-to-be-equaled comedy classics. Do you agree that such shows as *I Love Lucy* and *The Honeymooners* are superior to the situation comedies aired on television today?

There has been considerable criticism recently of the news coverage by the city's two leading newspapers, the *Herald* and the *Beacon*. Indicate whether you think the criticism is valid by discussing the similarities and differences in the two papers' news coverage.

Note: The last assignment shows that a comparison-contrast essay may cover similarities *and* differences, not just one or the other.

As you have seen, comparison-contrast can be the key strategy for achieving an essay's purpose. But comparison-contrast can also be a supplemental method used to help make a point in an essay organized chiefly around another pattern of development. A serious, informative essay intended for lay-people might *define* clinical depression by contrasting that state of mind with ordinary run-of-the-mill blues. Writing humorously about the exhausting *effects* of trying to get in shape, you might dramatize your plight for readers by contrasting the leisurely way you used to spend your day with your current rigidly compulsive exercise regimen. Or, in an urgent *argumentation-persuasion* essay on the need for stricter controls over drug abuse in the workplace, you might provide readers with background by comparing several companies' approaches to the problem.

At this point, you have a good sense of the way writers use comparison-contrast to achieve their purpose and to connect with their readers. Now take a moment to look closely at the advertisement at the beginning of this chapter. Imagine you're preparing an ad for another product that's revolutionized everyday life. Jot down some phrases you might use when *comparing* and/or *contrasting* life before and after the introduction of the product.

SUGGESTIONS FOR USING COMPARISON-CONTRAST IN AN ESSAY

The following suggestions will be helpful whether you use comparison-contrast as a dominant or a supportive pattern of development.

1. Be sure your subjects are at least somewhat alike.   Unless you plan to develop an *analogy* (see below), the subjects you choose to compare or contrast should share some obvious characteristics or qualities. It makes sense to compare different parts of the country, two comedians, or several college teachers. But a reasonable paper wouldn't result from, let's say, a comparison of a television game show with a soap opera. Your subjects must belong to the same general group so that your comparison-contrast stays within good logical bounds and doesn't veer off into pointlessness.

2. Stay focused on your purpose.   When writing, remember that comparison-contrast isn't an end in itself. That is, your objective isn't to turn an essay into a mechanical list of "how A differs from B" or "how A is like B." Like the other patterns of development discussed in this book, comparison-contrast is a strategy for making a point or meeting a larger purpose.

Consider the assignment on page 337 about the two newspapers. Your purpose here might be simply to *inform*, to present information as objectively as possible: "This is what the *Herald*'s news coverage is like. This is what the *Beacon*'s news coverage is like."

More frequently, though, you'll use comparison-contrast to *evaluate* your subjects' pros and cons, your goal being to reach a conclusion or make a judgment: "Both the *Herald* and the *Beacon* spend too much time reporting local news," or "The *Herald*'s analysis of the recent hostage crisis was more insightful than the *Beacon*'s." Comparison-contrast can also be used to *persuade* readers to take action: "People interested in thorough coverage of international events should read the *Herald* rather than the *Beacon*." Persuasive essays may also propose a change, contrasting what now exists with a more ideal situation: "For the *Beacon* to compete with the *Herald*, it must assign more reporters to international stories."

Yet another purpose you might have in writing a comparison-contrast essay is to *clear up misconceptions* by revealing previously hidden similarities or differences. For example, perhaps your town's two newspapers are thought to be sharply different. However, a comparison-contrast analysis might reveal that—although one paper specializes in sensationalized stories while the other adopts a more muted approach—both resort to biased, emotionally charged analyses of local politics. Or the essay might illustrate that the tabloid's treatment of the local arts scene is surprisingly more comprehensive than that of its competitor.

Comparing and contrasting also make it possible to *draw an analogy* between two seemingly unrelated subjects. An analogy is an imaginative comparison that delves beneath the surface differences of subjects in order to expose their significant and often unsuspected similarities or differences. Your purpose may be to show that singles bars and zoos share a number of striking similarities. Or you may want to illustrate that wolves and humans raise their young in much the same way, but that wolves go about the process in a more civilized manner. The analogical approach can make a complex subject easier to understand—as when the national deficit is compared to a household budget gone awry. Analogies are often dramatic and instructive, challenging you and your audience to consider subjects in a new light. But analogies don't speak for themselves. You must make clear to the reader how the analogy demonstrates your purpose.

3. Formulate a strong thesis. An essay developed primarily through comparison-contrast should be focused by a solid thesis. Besides revealing your attitude, the thesis will often do the following:

- Name the subjects being compared and contrasted.
- Indicate whether the essay focuses on the subjects' similarities, differences, or both.
- State the essay's main point of comparison or contrast.

Not all comparison-contrast essays need thesis statements as structured as those that follow. Even so, these examples can serve as models of clarity. Note that the first thesis statement signals similarities, the second differences, and the last both similarities and differences:

Middle-aged parents are often in a good position to empathize with adolescent children because the emotional upheavals experienced by the two age groups are much the same.

The priorities of most retired people are more conducive to health and happiness than the priorities of most young professionals.

College students in their thirties and forties face many of the same pressures as younger students, but they are better equipped to withstand these pressures.

4. Select the points to be discussed. Once you have identified the essay's subjects, purpose, and thesis, you need to decide which aspects of the subjects to compare or contrast. College professors, for instance, could be compared and contrasted on the basis of their testing methods, ability to motivate students, confidence in front of a classroom, personalities, level of enthusiasm, and so forth.

Brainstorming, freewriting, and mapping are valuable for gathering possible points to cover. Whichever prewriting technique you use, try to produce more raw material than you'll need, so that you have the luxury of narrowing the material down to the most significant points.

When selecting points to cover, be sure to consider your audience. Ask yourself: "Will my readers be familiar with this item? Will I need it to get my message across? Will my audience find this item interesting or convincing?" What your readers know, what they don't know, and what you can predict about their reactions should influence your choices. And, of course, you need to select points that support your thesis. If your essay explains the differences between healthy, sensible diets and dangerous crash diets, it wouldn't be appropriate to talk about aerobic exercise. Similarly, imagine you want to write an essay making the point that, despite their differences, hard rock of the 1960s and punk rock of the 1970s both reflected young people's disillusionment with society. It wouldn't make much sense to contrast the long, uncombed hairstyle of the 1960s with the short, spikey cuts of the 1970s. But contrasting song lyrics (protest versus nihilistic messages) would help support your thesis and lead to interesting insights.

5. Organize the points to be discussed.   After deciding which points to include, you should use a systematic, logical plan for presenting those ideas. If the points aren't organized, your essay will be little more than a confusing jumble of ideas. There are two common ways to organize an essay developed wholly or in part by comparison-contrast: the one-side-at-a-time method and the point-by-point method. Although both strategies may be used in a paper, one method usually predominates.

In the *one-side-at-a-time method* of organization, you discuss everything relevant about one subject before moving to another subject. For example, responding to the earlier assignment that asked you to analyze the news coverage in two local papers, you might first talk about the *Herald's* coverage of international, national, and local news; then you would discuss the *Beacon's* coverage of the same categories. Note that the areas discussed should be the same for both newspapers. It wouldn't be logical to review the *Herald's* coverage of international, national, and local news and then to detail the *Beacon's* magazine supplements, modern living section, and comics page. Moreover, the areas compared and contrasted should be presented in the same order.

This is how you would organize the essay using the one-side-at-a-time method.

Everything about A	*Herald's* news coverage
	• International
	• National
	• Local
Everything about B	*Beacon's* news coverage
	• International
	• National
	• Local

In the *point-by-point method* of organization, you alternate from one aspect of the first subject to the same aspect of your other subject(s). For example, to use this method when comparing or contrasting the *Herald* and the *Beacon,* you would first discuss the *Herald's* international coverage, then the *Beacon's* international coverage; next the *Herald's* national coverage, then the *Beacon's*; and finally, the *Herald's* local coverage, then the *Beacon's*.

Using the point-by-point method, this is how the essay would be organized.

First aspect of A and B   *Herald:* International coverage
                               Beacon: International coverage

Second aspect of A and B   *Herald:* National coverage
                               Beacon: National coverage

Third aspect of A and B   *Herald:* Local coverage
                               Beacon: Local coverage

Deciding which of these two methods of organization to use is largely a personal choice, though there are several factors to consider. The one-side-at-a-time method tends to convey a more unified feeling because it highlights broad similarities and differences. It is, therefore, an effective approach for subjects that are fairly uncomplicated. This strategy also works well when essays are brief; the reader won't find it difficult to remember what has been said about subject A when reading about subject B.

Because the point-by-point method permits more extensive coverage of similarities and differences, it is often a wise choice when subjects are complex. This pattern is also useful for lengthy essays since readers would probably find it difficult to remember, let's say, ten pages of information about subject A while reading the next ten pages about subject B. The point-by-point approach, however, may cause readers to lose sight of the broader picture, so remember to keep them focused on your central point.

6. Supply the reader with clear transitions.   Although a well-organized comparison-contrast format is important, it doesn't guarantee that readers will be able to follow your line of thought easily. *Transitions*—especially those signaling similarities or differences—are needed to show readers where they have been and where they are going. Such cues are essential in all writing, but they're especially crucial in a paper using comparison-contrast. By indicating clearly when subjects are being compared or contrasted, the transitions help weave the discussion into a coherent whole.

The transitions (in boldface) in the following examples could be used to *signal similarities* in an essay discussing the news coverage in the *Herald* and the *Beacon:*

- The *Beacon* **also** allots only a small portion of the front page to global news.
- **In the same way**, the *Herald* tries to include at least three local stories on the first page.
- **Likewise**, the *Beacon* emphasizes the importance of up-to-date reporting of town meetings.

- The *Herald* is **similarly** committed to extensive coverage of high school and college sports.

The transitions (in boldface) in the following examples could be used to *signal differences:*

- **By way of contrast**, the *Herald's* editorial page deals with national matters on the average of three times a week.
- **On the other hand**, the *Beacon* does not share the *Herald's* enthusiasm for interviews with national figures.
- The *Beacon*, **however**, does not encourage its reporters to tackle national stories the way the *Herald* does.
- **But** the *Herald's* coverage of the Washington scene is much more comprehensive than its competitor's.

REVISION STRATEGIES

Once you have a draft of the essay, you're ready to revise. The following checklist will help you and those giving you feedback apply to comparison-contrast some of the revision techniques discussed on pages 60–62.

☑ COMPARISON-CONTRAST: A REVISION/PEER
REVIEW CHECKLIST

Revise Overall Meaning and Structure

❑ Are the subjects sufficiently alike for the comparison-contrast to be logical and meaningful?

❑ What purpose does the essay serve—to inform, to evaluate, to persuade readers to accept a viewpoint, to eliminate misconceptions, or to draw a surprising analogy?

❑ What is the essay's thesis? How could the thesis be stated more effectively?

❑ Is the overall essay organized primarily by the one-side-at-a-time method or by the point-by-point method? Why is that the best strategy for this essay?

❑ Are the same features discussed for each subject? Are they discussed in the same order?

❑ Which points of comparison and/or contrast need further development? Which points should be deleted? Where do significant points seem to be missing? How has the most important similarity or difference been emphasized?

Revise Paragraph Development

❏ If the essay uses the one-side-at-a-time method, which paragraph marks the switch from one subject to another?

❏ If the essay uses the point-by-point method, do paragraphs consistently alternate between subjects? If this alternation becomes too elaborate or predictable, what could be done to eliminate the problem?

❏ If the essay uses both methods, which paragraph marks the switch from one method to the other? If the switch is confusing, how could it be made less so?

❏ Where would signal devices make it easier to see similarities and differences between the subjects being discussed?

Revise Sentences and Words

❏ Where do too many signal devices make sentences awkward and mechanical?

❏ Which sentences and words fail to convey the intended tone?

STUDENT ESSAY

The following student essay was written by Carol Siskin in response to this assignment:

> In "The Ugly Truth About Beauty," Dave Barry humorously contrasts two attitudes toward personal appearance, finding merit in the one normally considered less praiseworthy. In an essay of your own, contrast two personality types, lifestyles, or stages of life, showing that the one most people consider inferior is actually superior.

While reading Carol's paper, try to determine how well it applies the principles of comparison-contrast. The annotations on Carol's paper and the commentary following it will help you look at the essay more closely.

The Virtues of Growing Older
by Carol Siskin

The first of a two-paragraph introduction ──→ Our society worships youth. Advertisements convince us to buy Grecian Formula and Oil of Olay so we can hide the gray in our hair and smooth the lines on our face. Television shows feature attractive young stars with firm bodies, perfect complexions, and thick manes of hair. Middle-aged folks work out in gyms and jog down the street, trying to delay the effects of age.   1

The second introductory paragraph **Thesis**	→ Wouldn't any person over thirty gladly sign with the devil 2 just to be young again? Isn't aging an experience to be dreaded? Perhaps it is un-American to say so, but I believe the answer is "No." Being young is often pleasant, but being older has distinct advantages.
First half of topic sentence for point 1: Appearance **Start of what it's like being young**	→ When young, you are apt to be obsessed with your 3 appearance. When my brother Dave and I were teens, we worked feverishly to perfect the bodies we had. Dave lifted weights, took megadoses of vitamins, and drank a half-dozen milkshakes a day in order to turn his wiry adolescent frame into some muscular ideal. And as a teenager, I dieted constantly. No matter what I weighed, though, I was never satisfied with the way I looked. My legs were too heavy, my shoulders too broad, my waist too big. When Dave and I were young, we begged and pleaded for the "right" clothes. If our parents didn't get them for us, we felt our world would fall apart. How could we go to school wearing loose-fitting overcoats when everyone else would be wearing fitted leather jackets? We would be considered freaks. I often wonder how
Second half of topic sentence for point 1	my parents, and parents in general, manage to tolerate their children during the adolescent years. Now, however, Dave and I are beyond such adolescent agonies. My rounded figure
Start of what it's like being older	seems fine, and I don't deny myself a slice of pecan pie if I feel in the mood. Dave still works out, but he has actually become fond of his tall, lanky frame. The two of us enjoy wearing fashionable clothes, but we are no longer slaves to style. And women, I'm embarrassed to admit, even more than men, have always seemed to be at the mercy of fashion. Now my
First half of topic sentence for point 2: Life choices	clothes--and my brother's--are attractive yet easy to wear. We no longer feel anxious about what others will think. As long as we feel good about how we look, we are happy.
Start of what it's like being older	Being older is preferable to being younger in another way. 4 Obviously, I still have important choices to make about my life, → but I have already made many of the critical decisions that confront those just starting out. I chose the man I wanted to
Second half of topic sentence for point 2	marry. I decided to have children. I elected to return to college to complete my education. But, when you are young, major decisions await you at every turn. "What college should I
Start of what it's like being younger	attend? What career should I pursue? Should I get married? Should I have children?" These are just a few of the issues facing young people. It's no wonder that, despite their carefree facade, they are often confused, uncertain, and troubled by all
Topic sentence for point 3: Self-concept	the unknowns in their future. But the greatest benefit of being forty is knowing who I 5 am. The most unsettling aspect of youth is the uncertainty you
Start of what it's like being younger	feel about your values, goals, and dreams. Being young means wondering what is worth working for. Being young means feeling happy with yourself one day and wishing you were

never born the next. It means trying on new selves by taking up with different crowds. It means resenting your parents and their way of life one minute and then feeling you will never be as good or as accomplished as they are. By way of contrast,

Start of what it's like being older ─

forty is sanity. I have a surer self-concept now. I don't laugh at jokes I don't think are funny. I can make a speech in front of a town meeting or complain in a store because I am no longer terrified that people will laugh at me; I am no longer anxious that everyone must like me. I no longer blame my parents for my every personality quirk or keep a running score of everything they did wrong raising me. Life has taught me that I, not they, am responsible for who I am. We are all human beings--neither saints nor devils.

Conclusion

Most Americans blindly accept the idea that newer is automatically better. But a human life contradicts this premise. There is a great deal of happiness to be found as we grow older. My own parents, now in their sixties, recently told me that they are happier now than they have ever been. They would not want to be my age. Did this surprise me? At first, yes. Then it gladdened me. Their contentment holds out great promise for me as I move into the next--perhaps even better-- phase of my life.

6

COMMENTARY

Purpose and thesis.   In her essay, Carol disproves the widespread belief that being young is preferable to being old. The *comparison-contrast* pattern allows her to analyze the drawbacks of one and the merits of the other, thus providing the essay with an *evaluative purpose*. Using the title to indicate her point of view, Carol places the *thesis* at the end of her two-paragraph introduction: "Being young is often pleasant, but being older has distinct advantages." Note that the thesis accomplishes several things. It names the two subjects to be discussed and clarifies Carol's point of view about her subjects. The thesis also implies that the essay will focus on the contrasts between these two periods of life.

Points of support and overall organization.   To support her assertion that older is better, Carol supplies examples from her own life and organizes the examples around three main points: attitudes about appearance, decisions about life choices, and questions of self-concept. Using the *point-by-point method* to organize the overall essay, she explores each of these key ideas in a separate paragraph. Each paragraph is further focused by one or two sentences that serve as a topic sentence.

Sequence of points, organizational cues, and paragraph development. Let's look more closely at the way Carol presents her three central points in the essay. She obviously considers appearance the least important of a person's worries, life choices more important, and self-concept the most critical. So she uses *emphatic order* to sequence the supporting paragraphs, with the phrase "But the greatest benefit" signaling the special significance of the last issue. Carol is also careful to use *transitions* to help readers follow her line of thinking: "*Now, however,* Dave and I are beyond such adolescent agonies" (paragraph 3); "*But* when you are young, major decisions await you at every turn" (4); and "*By way of contrast,* forty is sanity" (5).

Although Carol has worked hard to write a well-organized paper—and has on the whole been successful—she doesn't feel compelled to make the paper fit a rigid format. As you've seen, the essay as a whole uses the point-by-point method, but each supporting paragraph uses the *one-side-at-a-time* method—that is, everything about one age group is discussed before there is a shift to the other age group. Notice too that the third and fifth paragraphs start with young people and then move to adults, whereas the fourth paragraph reverses the sequence by starting with older people.

Combining patterns of development.   Carol uses the comparison-contrast format to organize her ideas, but other patterns of development also come into play. To illustrate her points, she makes extensive use of *exemplification,* and her discussion also contains elements typical of *causal analysis.* Throughout the essay, for instance, she traces the effect of being a certain age on her brother, herself, and her parents.

A problem with unity.   As you read the third paragraph, you might have noted that Carol's essay runs into a problem. Two sentences in the paragraph disrupt the *unity* of Carol's discussion: "I often wonder how my parents, and parents in general, manage to tolerate their children during the adolescent years," and "women, I'm embarrassed to admit . . . have always seemed to be at the mercy of fashion." These sentences should be deleted because they don't develop the idea that adolescents are overly concerned with appearance.

Conclusion.   Carol's final paragraph brings the essay to a pleasing and interesting close. The conclusion recalls the point made in the introduction: Americans overvalue youth. Carol also uses the conclusion to broaden the scope of her discussion. Rather than continuing to focus on herself, she briefly mentions her parents and the pleasure they take in life. By bringing her parents into the essay, Carol is able to make a gently philosophical observation about the promise that awaits her as she grows older. The implication is that a similarly positive future awaits us, too.

Revising the first draft.   To help guide her revision, Carol asked her husband to read her first draft aloud. As he did, Carol took notes on what she sensed were the paper's strengths and weaknesses. She then jotted down her observations, as well as her husband's, on the draft. Keeping these comments in mind, Carol made a number of changes in her paper. You'll get a good sense of how she proceeded if you compare the original introduction reprinted here with the final version in the full essay.

Original Version of the Introduction

America is a land filled with people who worship youth. We admire dynamic young achievers; our middle-aged citizens work out in gyms; all of us wear tight tops and colorful sneakers--clothes that look fine on the young but ridiculous on aging bodies. Television shows revolve around perfect-looking young stars, while commercials entice us with products that will keep us young.

Wouldn't every older person want to be young again? Isn't aging to be avoided? It may be slightly unpatriotic to say so, but I believe the answer is "No." Being young may be pleasant at times, but I would rather be my forty-year-old self. I no longer have to agonize about my physical appearance, I have already made many of my crucial life decisions, and I am much less confused about who I am.

After hearing her original two-paragraph introduction read aloud, Carol was dissatisfied with what she had written. Although she wasn't quite sure how to proceed, she knew that the paragraphs were flat and that they failed to open the essay on a strong note. She decided to start by whittling down the opening sentence, making it crisper and more powerful: "Our society worships youth." That done, she eliminated two bland statements ("We admire dynamic young achievers" and "all of us wear tight tops and colorful sneakers") and made several vague references more concrete and interesting. For example, "Commercials entice us with products that will keep us young" became "Grecian Formula and Oil of Olay . . . hide the gray in our hair and smooth the lines on our face"; "perfect-looking young stars" became "attractive young stars with firm bodies, perfect complexions, and thick manes of hair." With the addition of these specifics, the first paragraph became more vigorous and interesting.

Carol next made some subtle changes in the two questions that opened the second paragraph of the original introduction. She replaced "Wouldn't every older person want to be young again?" and "Isn't aging to be avoided?" with two more emphatic questions: "Wouldn't any person over thirty gladly sign with the devil just to be young again?" and "Isn't aging an experience to be dreaded?" Carol also made some changes at the end of the original second paragraph. Because the paper is relatively short and the subject matter easy to understand, she decided to omit her somewhat awkward *plan of development* ("I no longer have to agonize about my physical appearance, I have already made many of my crucial life decisions, and I am much less confused about who I am"). This deletion made it possible to end the introduction with a clear statement of the essay's thesis.

Once these revisions were made, Carol was confident that her essay got off to a stronger start. Feeling reassured, she moved ahead and made changes in other sections of her paper. Such work enabled her to prepare a solid piece of writing that offers food for thought.

ACTIVITIES: COMPARISON-CONTRAST

Prewriting Activities

1. Imagine you're writing two essays: One explores the *effects* of holding a job while in college; the other explains a *process* for budgeting money wisely. Jot down ways you might use comparison-contrast in each essay.

2. Using your journal or freewriting, jot down the advantages and disadvantages of two ways of doing something (for example, watching movies in the theater versus watching them on a DVD player at home; following trends versus ignoring them; dating one person versus playing the field; and so on). Reread your prewriting and determine what your thesis, purpose, audience, tone, and point of view might be if you were to write an essay. Make a scratch list of the main ideas you would cover. Would a point-by-point or a one-side-at-a-time method of organization work more effectively?

Revising Activities

3. Of the statements that follow, which would *not* make effective thesis statements for comparison-contrast essays? Identify the problem(s) in the faulty statements and revise them accordingly.

   a. Although their classroom duties often overlap, teacher aides are not as equipped as teachers to handle disciplinary problems.
   b. This college provides more assistance to its students than most schools.
   c. During the state's last congressional election, both candidates relied heavily on television to communicate their messages.
   d. There are many differences between American and foreign cars.

4. The following paragraph is from the draft of an essay detailing the qualities of a skillful manager. How effective is this comparison-contrast paragraph? What revisions would help focus the paragraph on the point made in the topic sentence? Where should details be added or deleted? Rewrite the paragraph, providing necessary transitions and details.

   A manager encourages creativity and treats employees courteously, while a boss discourages staff resourcefulness and views it as a threat. At the hardware store where I work, I got my boss's approval to develop a system for organizing excess stock in the storeroom. I shelved items in roughly the same order as they were displayed in the store. The system was helpful to all the salespeople, not just to me, since everyone was stymied by the boss's helter-skelter system. What he did was store overstocked items according to each wholesaler, even though most of us weren't there long enough to know which items came from which wholesaler. His supposed system created chaos. When he saw what I had done, he was furious and insisted that we continue to follow the old slapdash system. I had assumed he would welcome my ideas the way my manager did last summer when I worked in a drugstore. But he didn't and I had to scrap my work and go back to his eccentric system. He certainly could learn something about employee relations from the drugstore manager.

Rachel Carson

Once accused of being a fearmonger, biologist Rachel Carson (1907–64) is now recognized as one of the country's first environmentalists. She was the author of three popular books about the marine world: *The Sea Around Us* (1951), *Under the Sea Wind* (1952), and *The Edge of the Sea* (1955). But it was the publication of *Silent Spring* (1962), Carson's alarming study of the use of pesticides and herbicides, that brought her special attention and established her reputation as a passionate advocate for a clean environment. The following selection is taken from *Silent Spring*.

Pre-Reading Journal Entry

Take a few minutes to record in your journal your impressions of a place that has special meaning for you—but that is being threatened in one way or another. Jot down sensory details about the place, focusing on those specifics that capture its unique qualities.

A Fable for Tomorrow

There was once a town in the heart of America where all life seemed to 1 live in harmony with its surroundings. The town lay in the midst of a checkerboard of prosperous farms, with fields of grain and hillsides of orchards where, in spring, white clouds of bloom drifted above the green fields. In autumn, oak and maple and birch set up a blaze of color that flamed and flickered across a backdrop of pines. Then foxes barked in the hills and deer silently crossed the fields, half hidden in the mists of the fall mornings.

Along the roads, laurel, viburnum and alder, great ferns and wildflowers 2 delighted the traveler's eye through much of the year. Even in winter the roadsides were places of beauty, where countless birds came to feed on the berries and on the seed heads of the dried weeds rising above the snow. The countryside was, in fact, famous for the abundance and variety of its bird life, and when the flood of migrants was pouring through in spring and fall people traveled from great distances to observe them. Others came to fish the streams, which flowed clear and cold out of the hills and contained shady pools where trout lay. So it had been from the days many years ago when the first settlers raised their houses, sank their wells, and built their barns.

Then a strange blight crept over the area and everything began to 3 change. Some evil spell had settled on the community: mysterious maladies swept the flocks of chickens; the cattle and sheep sickened and died. Everywhere was a shadow of death. The farmers spoke of much illness among their families. In the town the doctors had become more and more puzzled by new kinds of sickness appearing among their patients. There had been several sudden and unexplained deaths, not only among adults but even among children, who would be stricken suddenly while at play and die within a few hours.

There was a strange stillness. The birds, for example—where had they   4
gone? Many people spoke of them, puzzled and disturbed. The feeding stations in the backyards were deserted. The few birds seen anywhere were moribund; they trembled violently and could not fly. It was a spring without voices. On the mornings that had once throbbed with the dawn chorus of robins, catbirds, doves, jays, wrens, and scores of other bird voices there was now no sound; only silence lay over the fields and woods and marsh.

On the farms the hens brooded, but no chicks hatched. The farmers   5
complained that they were unable to raise any pigs—the litters were small and the young survived only a few days. The apple trees were coming into bloom but no bees droned among the blossoms, so there was no pollination and there would be no fruit.

The roadsides, once so attractive, were now lined with browned and   6
withered vegetation as though swept by fire. These, too, were silent, deserted by all living things. Even the streams were now lifeless. Anglers no longer visited them, for all the fish had died.

In the gutters under the eaves and between the shingles of the roofs, a   7
white granular powder still showed a few patches; some weeks before it had fallen like snow upon the roofs and the lawns, the fields and streams.

No witchcraft, no enemy action had silenced the rebirth of new life in   8
this stricken world. The people had done it themselves.

This town does not actually exist, but it might easily have a thousand   9
counterparts in America or elsewhere in the world. I know of no community that has experienced all the misfortunes I describe. Yet every one of these disasters has actually happened somewhere, and many real communities have already suffered a substantial number of them. A grim specter has crept upon us almost unnoticed, and this imagined tragedy may easily become a stark reality we all shall know.

Questions for Close Reading

1. What is the selection's thesis? Locate the sentence(s) in which Carson states her main idea. If she doesn't state the thesis explicitly, express it in your own words.
2. What are some of the delights of Carson's beautiful, healthy countryside?
3. When Carson writes of "a strange blight," an "evil spell" (paragraph 3), whose point of view is she adopting?
4. What are the effects of the blight?

5. Refer to your dictionary as needed to define the following words used in the selection: *viburnum* (paragraph 2), *alder* (2), *moribund* (4), and *specter* (9).

Questions About the Writer's Craft

1. **The pattern.** To develop her essay, Carson uses the one-side-at-a-time method of comparison-contrast. What does this method enable her to do that the point-by-point approach would not?
2. **Other patterns.** Throughout the essay, Carson appeals to the reader's senses of sight and hearing. Which paragraphs are developed primarily through visual or auditory *description*? How do the sensory images in these paragraphs reinforce Carson's thesis?
3. Carson's diction (word choice) and sentence rhythm often resemble those of the Bible. For example, we read, "So it had been from the days many years ago" (paragraph 2), "a strange blight crept over the area" (3), and "Everywhere was a shadow of death" (3). Why do you suppose Carson chose to echo the Bible in this way?
4. How does Carson's approach to her subject change in the last paragraph? What is the effect of this change?

Writing Assignments Using Comparison-Contrast as a Pattern of Development

1. Carson imagines a fictional town that has changed for the worse. Consider a place you know well that has changed for the *better.* You might focus on a renovated school, a rehabilitated neighborhood, a newly preserved park. Write an essay contrasting the place before and after the change. At the end of your essay, describe briefly the effects of the change.
2. In her essay, Carson provides descriptive details unique to particular seasons. For example, she writes that "in autumn, oak and maple and birch set up a blaze of color that flamed and flickered across a backdrop of pines" (paragraph 1). Choosing a place you know well, contrast its sights, sounds, and smells during one season with those you've noticed during another time of year. Use rich sensory details to convey the differences between the two seasons. Consider first reading Joan Didion's "The Santa Ana" (page 601), which recounts, in vivid detail, a specific natural phenomenon and its impact on regional inhabitants.

Writing Assignments Combining Patterns of Development

3. Carson cites "white granular powder" (paragraph 7) as the cause of the blight. Write an essay about a time you noticed a visible environmental problem—say, smog blurring a city skyline, soot coating a window, or medical syringes discarded on the beach. Use vivid *narrative details* to capture the effect of the experience on you.
4. Carson graphically shows the effects of herbicides and pesticides on the environment. Focus on some other less global environmental problem: graffiti on a public building; vandalized trees and shrubs; beer cans thrown in a neighborhood park, for example. Discuss the *effects* of this situation on the physical environment and

on people's attitudes and actions. Conclude with suggestions about possible *strategies* for remedying the problem. Gordon Parks's "Flavio's Home" (page 84) and David Helvarg's "The Storm This Time" (page 92) will help you appreciate the interaction between the environment and human behavior.

Writing Assignment Using a Journal Entry as a Starting Point

5. Write an essay describing an endangered place that is very important to you. Describe the potential threat either at the beginning or at the end of the essay, and paint such a vivid picture of the place in the rest of the essay that readers understand why the potential threat is so unfortunate. Select from your pre-reading journal entry only those details that convey the special qualities of the place, adding more texture and specifics where needed.

Joseph H. Suina

Still living on the Cochiti Pueblo Reservation in New Mexico where he grew up, former U.S. Marine Joseph H. Suina (1944–) teaches in the Multicultural Teacher Education Program at the University of New Mexico. Suina's work as an educator led to his coauthoring a book for teachers, *The Learning Environment: An Instructional Strategy* (1982). The following selection first appeared in *Linguistic and Cultural Influences on Learning Mathematics,* edited by Rodney Cocking and Jose Mestre (1988).

Pre-Reading Journal Entry

Bilingualism—instruction in a student's native language as well as in English—remains an important educational issue in many parts of the country. Do you think non-English-speaking students should be forced to speak only English when they start school, or should they for a time be taught in their native tongue as well? Use your journal to reflect on your beliefs about this question.

And Then I Went to School

I lived with my grandmother from the ages of five through nine. It was the early 1950s when electricity had not yet invaded the homes of the Cochiti Indians. The village day school and health clinic were first to have it and to the unsuspecting Cochitis this was the approach of a new era in their uncomplicated lives.

Transportation was simple then. Two good horses and a sturdy wagon met most needs of a villager. Only five or six individuals possessed an automobile in the Pueblo of 300. A flatbed truck fixed with wooden rails and a canvas top made a regular Saturday trip to Santa Fe. It was always loaded beyond capacity with Cochitis taking their wares to town for a few staples. With an escort of a dozen barking dogs, the straining truck made a noisy exit, northbound from the village.

During those years, Grandmother and I lived beside the plaza in a one-room house. It consisted of a traditional fireplace, a makeshift cabinet for our few tin cups and dishes, and a wooden crate that held our two buckets of all-purpose water. At the far end of the room were two rolls of bedding we used as comfortable sitting "couches." Consisting of thick quilts, sheepskin, and assorted blankets, these bed rolls were undone each night. A wooden pole the length of one side of the room was suspended about 10 inches from the ceiling beams. A modest collection of colorful shawls, blankets, and sashes was draped over the pole making this part of the room most interesting. In one corner was a bulky metal trunk for our ceremonial wear and a few valuables. A dresser, which was traded for some of my grandmother's well-known pottery, held the few articles of clothing we owned and the "goody bag." Grandmother always had a flour sack filled with candy, store bought cookies, and Fig Newtons. These were saturated with a sharp odor of moth balls. Nevertheless, they made a fine snack with coffee before we turned in for the night. Tucked securely in my blankets, I listened to one of her stories or accounts of how it was when she was a little girl. These accounts seemed so old fashioned compared to the way we lived. Sometimes she softly sang a song from a ceremony. In this way I fell asleep each night.

Earlier in the evening we would make our way to a relative's house if   4
someone had not already come to visit us. I would play with the children while the adults caught up on all the latest. Ten-cent comic books were finding their way into the Pueblo homes. For us children, these were the first link to the world beyond the Pueblo. We enjoyed looking at them and role playing as one of the heroes rounding up the villains. Everyone preferred being a cowboy rather than an Indian because cowboys were always victorious. Sometimes, stories were related to both children and adults. These get-togethers were highlighted by refreshments of coffee and sweet bread or fruit pies baked in the outdoor oven. Winter months would most likely include roasted pinon nuts or dried deer meat for all to share. These evening gatherings and sense of closeness diminished as the radios and televisions increased over the following years. It was never to be the same again.

The winter months are among my fondest recollections. A warm fire   5
crackled and danced brightly in the fireplace and the aroma of delicious stew filled our one-room house. To me the house was just right. The thick adobe walls wrapped around the two of us protectingly during the long freezing nights. Grandmother's affection completed the warmth and security I will always remember.

Being the only child at Grandmother's, I had lots of attention and plen-   6
ty of reasons to feel good about myself. As a pre-schooler, I already had the chores of chopping firewood and hauling in fresh water each day. After "heavy work," I would run to her and flex what I was certain were my gigantic biceps. Grandmother would state that at the rate I was going I would soon attain the status of a man like the adult males in the village. Her shower of praises made me feel like the Indian Superman of all times. At age five, I suppose I was as close to that concept of myself as anyone.

In spite of her many years, Grandmother was still active in the village   7
ceremonial setting. She was a member of an important women's society and

attended all the functions, taking me along to many of them. I would wear one of my colorful shirts she handmade for just such occasions. Grandmother taught me the appropriate behavior at these events. Through modeling she taught me to pray properly. Barefooted, I would greet the sun each morning with a handful of cornmeal. At night I would look to the stars in wonderment and let a prayer slip through my lips. I learned to appreciate cooperation in nature and my fellowmen early in life. About food and material things, Grandmother would say, "There is enough for everyone to share and it all comes from above, my child." I felt very much a part of the world and our way of life. I knew I had a place in it and I felt good about me.

At age six, like the rest of the Cochiti six-year-olds that year, I had to begin my schooling. It was a new and bewildering experience. One I will not forget. The strange surroundings, new concepts about time and expectations, and a foreign tongue were overwhelming to us beginners. It took some effort to return the second day and many times thereafter.

To begin with, unlike my grandmother, the teacher did not have pretty brown skin and a colorful dress. She was not plump and friendly. Her clothes were one color and drab. Her pale and skinny form made me worry that she was very ill. I thought that explained why she did not have time just for me and the disappointed looks and orders she seemed to always direct my way. I didn't think she was so smart because she couldn't understand my language. "Surely that was why we had to leave our 'Indian' at home." But then I did not feel so bright either. All I could say in her language was "yes teacher," "my name is Joseph Henry," and "when is lunch time." The teacher's odor took some getting used to also. In fact, many times it made me sick right before lunch. Later, I learned from the girls that this odor was something she wore called perfume.

The classroom too had its odd characteristics. It was terribly huge and smelled of medicine like the village clinic I feared so much. The walls and ceiling were artificial and uncaring. They were too far from me and I felt naked. The fluorescent light tubes were eerie and blinked suspiciously above me. This was quite a contrast to the fire and sunlight that my eyes were accustomed to. I thought maybe the lighting did not seem right because it was man-made, and it was not natural. Our confinement to rows of desks was another unnatural demand from our active little bodies. We had to sit at these hard things for what seemed like forever before relief (recess) came midway through the morning and afternoon. Running carefree in the village and fields was but a sweet memory of days gone by. We all went home for lunch because we lived within walking distance of the school. It took coaxing and sometimes bribing to get me to return and complete the remainder of the school day.

School was a painful experience during those early years. The English language and the new set of values caused me much anxiety and embarrassment.

I could not comprehend everything that was happening but yet I could understand very well when I messed up or was not doing so well. The negative aspect was communicated too effectively and I became unsure of myself more and more. How I wished I could understand other things just as well in school.

The value conflict was not only in school performance but in other areas   12
of my life as well. For example, many of us students had a problem with head lice due to "the lack of sanitary conditions in our homes." Consequently, we received a severe shampooing that was rough on both the scalp and the ego. Cleanliness was crucial and a washing of this type indicated to the class how filthy a home setting we came from. I recall that after one such treatment I was humiliated before my peers with a statement that I had "She'na" (lice) so tough that I must have been born with them. Needless to say, my Super Indian self-image was no longer intact.

My language, too, was questionable from the beginning of my school   13
career. "Leave your Indian (language) at home" was like a trademark of school. Speaking it accidentally or otherwise was a sure reprimand in the form of a dirty look or a whack with a ruler. This punishment was for speaking the language of my people which meant so much to me. It was the language of my grandmother and I spoke it well. With it, I sang beautiful songs and prayed from my heart. At that young and tender age, comprehending why I had to part with it was most difficult for me. And yet at home I was encouraged to attend school so that I might have a better life in the future. I knew I had a good village life already but this was communicated less and less each day I was in school. . . .

I had to leave my beloved village of Cochiti for my education beyond   14
Grade 6. I left to attend a Bureau of Indian Affairs boarding school 30 miles from home. Shined shoes and pressed shirt and pants were the order of the day. I managed to adjust to this just as I had to most of the things the school shoved at me or took away from me. Adjusting to leaving home and the village was tough indeed. It seemed the older I got, the further away I became from the ways I was so much a part of. Because my parents did not own an automobile, I saw them only once a month when they came up in the community truck. They never failed to come supplied with "eats" for me. I enjoyed the outdoor oven bread, dried meat, and tamales they usually brought. It took a while to get accustomed to the diet of the school. I longed for my grandmother and my younger brothers and sisters. I longed for my house. I longed to take part in a Buffalo Dance. I longed to be free.

I came home for the four-day Thanksgiving break. At first, home did not   15
feel right anymore. It was much too small and stuffy. The lack of running water and bathroom facilities were too inconvenient. Everything got dusty so quickly and hardly anyone spoke English. I did not realize I was beginning to take on the white man's ways, the ways that belittled my own. However, it did

not take long to "get back with it." Once I established my relationships with family, relatives, and friends I knew I was where I came from and where I belonged.

Leaving for the boarding school the following Sunday evening was one 10 of the saddest events in my entire life. Although I enjoyed myself immensely the last few days, I realized then that life would never be the same again. I could not turn back the time just as I could not do away with school and the ways of the white man. They were here to stay and would creep more and more into my life. The effort to make sense of both worlds together was painful and I had no choice but to do so. The schools, television, automobiles, and other white man's ways and values had chipped away at the simple cooperative life I grew up in. The people of Cochiti were changing. The winter evening gatherings, exchanging of stories, and even the performing of certain ceremonies were already only a memory that someone commented about now and then. Still the demands of both worlds were there. The white man's was flashy, less personal, but comfortable. The Indian was both attracted and pushed toward these new ways that he had little to say about. There was no choice left but to compete with the white man on his terms for survival. For that I knew I had to give up a part of my life.

Determined not to cry, I left for school that dreadfully lonely night. My 11 right hand clutched tightly the mound of cornmeal Grandmother placed there and my left hand brushed away a tear as I made my way back to school.

Questions for Close Reading

1. What is the selection's thesis? Locate the sentence(s) in which Suina states his main idea. If he doesn't state the thesis explicitly, express it in your own words.
2. How did the Cochiti instill their values and native culture in their children? How was the Cochiti approach different from the teaching methods used in the white school Suina attended?
3. What non-native influences appear in Suina's town and life before he starts attending school?
4. Why is Suina forced to attend a white school and learn about the whites' lifestyle and language? What does he find confusing about school? How does school change him?
5. Refer to your dictionary as needed to define the following words used in the selection: *adobe* (paragraph 5), *ego* (12), and *belittled* (15).

Questions About the Writer's Craft

1. **The pattern.** Comparison-contrast essays organize material according to the point-by-point or one-side-at-a-time method. Which method predominates in this essay? Why do you think Suina uses this method? Locate places where Suina uses the other method of organization.
2. **Other patterns.** Suina uses *description* to evoke the simple, emotional warmth of the Native American lifestyle as well as the sterile, stark coldness of the white

school. Locate places in the essay where Suina provides sensory details to help readers understand the differences between the two cultures.

3. Consider Suina's word choice in the opening paragraph. How do the words *invade* and *unsuspecting* help establish the essay's overall tone? What do these terms reveal about Suina's attitude toward the transformation of Native American culture?

4. Where in paragraph 14 does Suina use repetition? What is the effect of the repetition?

Writing Assignments Using Comparison-Contrast as a Pattern of Development

1. As a Native American, Suina is made to feel like an outsider in the white school. But cultural differences aren't the only factors that cause children to feel uncomfortable in school. For example, they may have trouble fitting in because they have a learning disability, are shy, are extroverted, or need more (or less) structure than the school provides. Focusing on *one* such problem, write an essay comparing and contrasting present-day education with the way it should be. For some ideas about how education can be different, read Yuh Ji-Yeon's "Let's Tell the Story of All America's Cultures" (page 517).

2. After attending boarding school for a few months, Suina reappraises his home and earlier lifestyle. In a similar way, separation can cause the rest of us to view our home, our school, another institution, or an individual in a more positive or a more negative light. Write an essay comparing and contrasting the feelings you had for a person, place, or institution with your attitude after being separated for a while. Provide vigorous details to show why your attitude changed.

Writing Assignments Combining Patterns of Development

3. Suina reports that his grandmother showered him with praise and made him feel like a "Superman." However, once he entered school, the constant scoldings, dirty looks, and ruler slaps eroded his self-esteem. Write an essay *illustrating* how a person *affected* your view of yourself, either by praising or by criticizing your efforts. Provide several dramatic examples or a single, richly detailed example to show how this person affected you. Before writing, read Maya Angelou's "Sister Flowers" (page 100), an essay that illustrates the influence of a powerful individual.

4. Everyone, at some level of his or her education, has felt anxious about the first day of school. Write an essay in which you explain *steps* that a student can take to reduce the nervousness associated with beginning his or her first semester in college. Where appropriate, *illustrate* the steps with vivid examples. You may adopt a serious or a lighthearted tone in your essay.

Writing Assignment Using a Journal Entry as a Starting Point

5. In school, Suina is pressured to abandon his native language and to speak only English. Refer to your pre-reading journal essay, and conduct some research in the library and/or on the Internet on the subject of bilingualism in education. Then write an essay arguing that schools either should *or* should not teach non-English-speaking students in their own language until they become sufficiently proficient in English to join regular classes. At some point, you should acknowledge and perhaps refute opposing views.

Richard Rodriguez

In his autobiographical work *Hunger of Memory* (1981), from which the following selection is taken, Richard Rodriguez describes his experiences growing up in America as a first-generation Mexican-American. Born in 1944 in San Francisco, Rodriguez spoke only Spanish for the first six years of his life. After winning a scholarship to a private high school, Rodriguez attended Stanford, Columbia, and the University of California at Berkeley, where he earned a doctorate in English literature. Rodriguez now writes for a variety of publications (*The Wall Street Journal* and *Time*, to name just two), serves as an editor at Pacific News Service in San Francisco, and regularly appears on PBS's *NewsHour*. In 1997, he won the Peabody Award for achievement in broadcasting. His books include *Mexico's Children* (1991), *Movements* (1996), and *Brown* (2002), about what it means to be Hispanic in America. The critically acclaimed *Days of Obligation: An Argument With My Mexican Father* (1992) is Rodriguez's second autobiographical book.

Pre-Reading Journal Entry

Young people often find themselves being lectured by adults claiming that kids nowadays want it easy and aren't willing to do unglamorous "real work." Do you agree with these claims? Why or why not? Drawing upon your experiences and observations, respond to these questions in your journal.

Workers

It was at Stanford, one day near the end of my senior year, that a friend told me about a summer construction job he knew was available. I was quickly alert. Desire uncoiled within me. My friend said that he knew I had been looking for summer employment. He knew I needed some money. Almost apologetically he explained: It was something I probably wouldn't be interested in, but a friend of his, a contractor, needed someone for the summer to do menial jobs. There would be lots of shoveling and raking and sweeping. Nothing too hard. But nothing more interesting either. Still, the pay would be good. Did I want it? Or did I know someone who did? 1

I did. Yes, I said, surprised to hear myself say it. 2

In the weeks following, friends cautioned that I had no idea how hard physical labor really is. ("You only *think* you know what it is like to shovel 3 for eight hours straight.") Their objections seemed to me challenges. They resolved the issue. I became happy with my plan. I decided, however, not to tell my parents. I wouldn't tell my mother because I could guess her worried reaction. I would tell my father only after the summer was over, when I could announce that, after all, I did know what "real work" is like.

The day I met the contractor (a Princeton graduate, it turned out), he   4 asked me whether I had done any physical labor before. "In high school, during the summer," I lied. And although he seemed to regard me with skepticism, he decided to give me a try. Several days later, expectant, I arrived at my first construction site. I would take off my shirt to the sun. And at last grasp desired sensation. No longer afraid. At last become like a *bracero*. "We need those tree stumps out of here by tomorrow," the contractor said. I started to work.

I labored with excitement that first morning—and all the days after.   5 The work was harder than I could have expected. But it was never as tedious as my friends had warned me it would be. There was too much physical pleasure in the labor. Especially early in the day, I would be most alert to the sensations of movement and straining. Beginning around seven each morning (when the air was still damp but the scent of weeds and dry earth anticipated the heat of the sun), I would feel my body resist the first thrusts of the shovel. My arms, tightened by sleep, would gradually loosen; after only several minutes, sweat would gather in beads on my forehead and then—a short while later—I would feel my chest silky with sweat in the breeze. I would return to my work. A nervous spark of pain would fly up my arm and settle to burn like an ember in the thick of my shoulder. An hour, two passed. Three. My whole body would assume regular movements; my shoveling would be described by identical, even movements. Even later in the day, my enthusiasm for primitive sensation would survive the heat and the dust and the insects pricking my back. I would strain wildly for sensation as the day came to a close. At three-thirty, quitting time, I would stand upright and slowly let my head fall back, luxuriating in the feeling of tightness relieved.

Some of the men working nearby would watch me and laugh. Two or   6 three of the older men took the trouble to teach me the right way to use a pick, the correct way to shovel. "You're doing it wrong, too fucking hard," one man scolded. Then proceeded to show me—what persons who work with their bodies all their lives quickly learn—the most economical way to use one's body in labor.

"Don't make your back do so much work," he instructed. I stood impa-   7 tiently listening, half listening, vaguely watching, then noticed his work-thickened fingers clutching the shovel. I was annoyed. I wanted to tell him that I enjoyed shoveling the wrong way. And I didn't want to learn the right way. I wasn't afraid of back pain. I liked the way my body felt sore at the end of the day.

I was about to, but, as it turned out, I didn't say a thing. Rather it was at that moment I realized that I was fooling myself if I expected a few weeks of labor to gain me admission to the world of the laborer. I would not learn in three months what my father had meant by "real work." I was not bound to this job; I could imagine its rapid conclusion. For me the sensations were to be feared. Fatigue took a different toll on their bodies—and minds. **8**

It was, I know, a simple insight. But it was with this realization that I took my first step that summer toward realizing something even more important about the "worker." In the company of carpenters, electricians, plumbers, and painters at lunch, I would often sit quietly, observant. I was not shy in such company. I felt easy, pleased by the knowledge that I was casually accepted, my presence taken for granted by men (exotics) who worked with their hands. Some days the younger men would talk and talk about sex, and they would howl at women who drove by in cars. Other days the talk at lunchtime was subdued; men gathered in separate groups. It depended on who was around. There were rough, good-natured workers. Others were quiet. The more I remember that summer, the more I realize that there was no single *type* of worker. I am embarrassed to say I had not expected such diversity. I certainly had not expected to meet, for example, a plumber who was an abstract painter in his off hours and admired the work of Mark Rothko. Nor did I expect to meet so many workers with college diplomas. (They were the ones who were not surprised that I intended to enter graduate school in the fall.) I suppose what I really want to say here is painfully obvious, but I must say it nevertheless: The men of that summer were middle-class Americans. They certainly didn't constitute an oppressed society. Carefully completing their work sheets; talking about the fortunes of local football teams; planning Las Vegas vacations; comparing the gas mileage of various makes of campers—they were not *los pobres* my mother had spoken about. **9**

On two occasions, the contractor hired a group of Mexican aliens. They were employed to cut down some trees and haul off debris. In all, there were six men of varying age. The youngest in his late twenties; the oldest (his father?) perhaps sixty years old. They came and they left in a single old truck. Anonymous men. They were never introduced to the other men at the site. Immediately upon their arrival, they would follow the contractor's directions, start working—rarely resting—seemingly driven by a fatalistic sense that work which had to be done was best done as quickly as possible. **10**

I watched them sometimes. Perhaps they watched me. The only time I saw them pay me much notice was one day at lunchtime when I was laughing with the other men. The Mexicans sat apart when they ate, just as they worked by themselves. Quiet. I rarely heard them say much to each other. All I could hear were their voices calling out sharply to one another, giving directions. Otherwise, when they stood briefly resting, they talked among themselves in voices too hard to overhear. **11**

The contractor knew enough Spanish, and the Mexicans—or at least the oldest of them, their spokesman—seemed to know enough English to communicate. But because I was around, the contractor decided one day to make me his translator. (He assumed I could speak Spanish.) I did what I was told. Shyly I went over to tell the Mexicans that the *patrón* wanted them to do something else before they left for the day. As I started to speak, I was afraid with my old fear that I would be unable to pronounce the Spanish words. But it was a simple instruction I had to convey. I could say it in phrases.

The dark sweating faces turned toward me as I spoke. They stopped their work to hear me. Each nodded in response. I stood there. I wanted to say something more. But what could I say in Spanish, even if I could have pronounced the words right? Perhaps I just wanted to engage them in small talk, to be assured of their confidence, our familiarity. I thought for a moment to ask them where in Mexico they were from. Something like that. And maybe I wanted to tell them (a lie, if need be) that my parents were from the same part of Mexico.

I stood there.

Their faces watched me. The eyes of the man directly in front of me moved slowly over my shoulder, and I turned to follow his glance toward *el patrón* some distance away. For a moment I felt swept up by that glance into the Mexicans' company. But then I heard one of them returning to work. And then the others went back to work. I left them without saying anything more.

When they had finished, the contractor went over to pay them in cash. (He later told me that he paid them collectively—"for the job," though he wouldn't tell me their wages. He said something quickly about the good rate of exchange "in their own country.") I can still hear the loudly confident voice he used with the Mexicans. It was the sound of the *gringo* I had heard as a very young boy. And I can still hear the quiet, indistinct sounds of the Mexican, the oldest, who replied. At hearing that voice I was sad for the Mexicans. Depressed by their vulnerability. Angry at myself. The adventure of the summer seemed suddenly ludicrous. I would not shorten the distance I felt from *los pobres* with a few weeks of physical labor. I would not become like them. They were different from me.

After that summer, a great deal—and not very much really—changed in my life. The curse of physical shame was broken by the sun; I was no longer ashamed of my body. No longer would I deny myself the pleasing sensations of my maleness. During those years when middle-class black Americans began to assert with pride, "Black is beautiful," I was able to regard my complexion without shame. I am today darker than I ever was as a boy. I have taken up the middle-class sport of long-distance running. Nearly every day now I run ten or fifteen miles, barely clothed, my skin exposed to the California winter rain and wind or the summer sun of late afternoon. The torso, the soccer player's calves and thighs, the arms of the twenty-year-old I never was, I possess now in my thirties. I study the youthful parody shape in the mirror: the stomach lipped tight by muscle; the shoulders rounded by chin-ups; the arms veined strong. This man. A man. I meet him. He laughs to see me, what I have become.

The dandy. I wear double-breasted Italian suits and custom-made Eng-   18
lish shoes. I resemble no one so much as my father—the man pictured in those honeymoon photos. At that point in life when he abandoned the dandy's posture, I assume it. At the point when my parents would not consider going on vacation, I register at the Hotel Carlyle in New York and the Plaza Athenée in Paris. I am as taken by the symbols of leisure and wealth as they were. For my parents, however, those symbols became taunts, reminders of all they could not achieve in one lifetime. For me those same symbols are reassuring reminders of public success. I tempt vulgarity to be reassured. I am filled with the gaudy delight, the monstrous grace of the nouveau riche.

In recent years I have had occasion to lecture in ghetto high schools.   19
There I see students of remarkable style and physical grace. (One can see more dandies in such schools than one ever will find in middle-class high schools.) There is not the look of casual assurance I saw students at Stanford display. Ghetto girls mimic high-fashion models. Their dresses are of bold, forceful color; their figures elegant, long; the stance theatrical. Boys wear shirts that grip at their overdeveloped muscular bodies. (Against a powerless future, they engage images of strength.) Bad nutrition does not yet tell. Great disappointment, fatal to youth, awaits them still. For the moment, movements in school hallways are dancelike, a procession of postures in a sexual masque. Watching them, I feel a kind of envy. I wonder how different my adolescence would have been had I been free. . . . But no, it is my parents I see—their optimism during those years when they were entertained by Italian grand opera.

The registration clerk in London wonders if I have just been to Swit-   20
zerland. And the man who carries my luggage in New York guesses the Caribbean. My complexion becomes a mark of my leisure. Yet no one would regard my complexion the same way if I entered such hotels through the service entrance. That is only to say that my complexion assumes its significance from the context of my life. My skin, in itself, means nothing. I stress the point because I know there are people who would label me "disadvantaged" because of my color. They make the same mistake I made as a boy, when I thought a disadvantaged life was circumscribed by particular occupations. That summer I worked in the sun may have made me physically indistinguishable from the Mexicans working nearby. (My skin was actually darker because, unlike them, I worked without wearing a shirt. By late August my hands were probably as tough as theirs.) But I was not one of *los pobres*. What made me different from them was an attitude of *mind*, my imagination of myself.

I do not blame my mother for warning me away from the sun when I was   2
young. In a world where her brother had become an old man in his twenties
because he was dark, my complexion was something to worry about. "Don't
run in the sun," she warns me today. I run. In the end, my father was right—
though perhaps he did not know how right or why—to say that I would never
know what real work is. I will never know what he felt at his last factory job.
If tomorrow I worked at some kind of factory, it would go differently for me.
My long education would favor me. I could act as a public person—able to
defend my interests, to unionize, to petition, to speak up—to challenge and
demand. (I will never know what real work is.) I will never know what the
Mexicans knew, gathering their shovels and ladders and saws.

Their silence stays with me now. The wages those Mexicans received for   2
their labor were only a measure of their disadvantaged condition. Their silence
is more telling. They lack a public identity. They remain profoundly alien.
Persons apart. People lacking a union obviously, people without grounds.
They depend upon the relative good will or fairness of their employers each
day. For such people, lacking a better alternative, it is not such an unreasonable risk.

Their silence stays with me. I have taken these many words to describe   2
its impact. Only: the quiet. Something uncanny about it. Its compliance.
Vulnerability. Pathos. As I heard their truck rumbling away, I shuddered, my
face mirrored with sweat. I had finally come face to face with *los pobres*.

Questions for Close Reading

1. What is the selection's thesis? Locate the sentence(s) in which Rodriguez states his
   main idea. If he doesn't state the thesis explicitly, express it in your own words.
2. What does Rodriguez find appealing about the construction job when his friend
   first offers it to him?
3. Once on the job, how long does it take Rodriguez to realize he will never be a
   "laborer"? Why does he feel this way?
4. According to Rodriguez, what makes him different from *los pobres*? Is poverty the
   only thing that makes them distinctive?
5. Refer to your dictionary as needed to define the following words used in the selection: *menial* (paragraph 1), *skepticism* (4), *luxuriating* (5), *diversity* (9), *ludicrous*
   (16), *nouveau riche* (18), and *pathos* (23).

Questions About the Writer's Craft

1. **The pattern.** One way Rodriguez develops his essay is by comparing and contrasting himself to the two groups of workers. Which group is he more like? What
   specifics does Rodriguez provide to show his similarity to this group and his dis-
   similarity to the other?
2. **Other patterns.** Rodriguez uses narration to develop his comparison-contrast of
   the two groups of workers. How many *narrative* segments appear in the essay?
   Why do you think Rodriguez puts the story about the Mexican workers last?

3. **Other patterns.** Rodriguez uses especially vivid language to *describe* the sun, his sweat, and the sensation of digging. Locate some examples of these descriptions. Which ones particularly stand out? Why?

4. Why does Rodriguez include some Spanish words in his essay? How is the use of these words related to the essay's overall theme?

Writing Assignments Using Comparison-Contrast as a Pattern of Development

1. Write an essay comparing and/or contrasting a part-time or summer job you've had with your (or someone else's) full-time or "real" job. Use examples, description, anecdotes, and illustrations to clarify the points of comparison or contrast.

2. Write an essay in which you compare and/or contrast the job you hope to have after graduation with a job you now have or have had in the past. Your analysis should reach conclusions about your interests, skills, and values. Reading Alexandra Robbins and Abby Wilner's "What Is the Quarterlife Crisis?" (page 463) might help you as you consider your post-graduation aspirations and priorities.

Writing Assignments Combining Patterns of Development

3. In an essay, *define* what you mean by the term *real work*. Support your definition by citing *examples* of experiences you have had and/or have heard about. Jacques D'Amboise's "Showing What Is Possible" (page 402) and Virginia Woolf's "Professions for Women" (page 588) should prompt some interesting thoughts about work.

4. Former talk-show host Phil Donahue once did a show on people who had "terrible jobs." The guests included a garbage man, a toll collector, a car repossessor, an IRS auditor, and a diaper-service truck driver. Write an essay *illustrating* what would be terrible work for you. It might be one or more of the jobs held by Donahue's guests or some other type of job. Provide abundant reasons why you would never want to do such work, including detailed *descriptions* where necessary. You might wrap up your essay by reaching some conclusions about your priorities.

Writing Assignment Using a Journal Entry as a Starting Point

5. Write an essay comparing and/or contrasting the work habits of earlier generations with those of the current generation. Consider kinds of work, working conditions, benefits, hours on the job, and so on. In addition to drawing upon ideas from your pre-reading journal entry, interview an equal number of people of both generations to get their opinions. Where appropriate, include their views in your essay. Begin or end the essay with a statement indicating which generation's work habits you respect more. For additional insight into generational differences, read Alexandra Robbins and Abby Wilner's "What Is the Quarterlife Crisis?" (page 463).

Dave Barry

Pulitzer Prize–winning humorist Dave Barry (1947–) began his writing career covering—as he puts it—"incredibly dull municipal meetings" for the *Daily Local News* of West Chester, Pennsylvania. Next came an eight-year stint trying to teach businesspeople not to write sentences like "Enclosed please find the enclosed enclosures." In 1983, Barry joined the staff of the *The Miami Herald,* where his rib-tickling commentary on the absurdities of everyday life quickly brought him a legion of devoted fans. Barry's column is now syndicated in more than 150 newspapers. A popular guest on television and radio, Barry has written dozens of books, including *Dave Barry's Complete Guide to Guys* (1995), *Dave Barry in Cyberspace* (1996), *Big Trouble* (1999), *Dave Barry Hits Below the Beltway* (2001), *Boogers Are My Beat* (2003), and most recently *Dave Barry's Money Secrets* (2006), as well as the comic mystery novel *Tricky Business* (2002). The father of two, he lives in Miami with his wife. The essay below first appeared in *The Miami Herald* in 1998.

Pre-Reading Journal Entry

To what extent would you say our images of personal attractiveness are influenced by TV commercials and magazine advertisements? Think of commercials and ads you've seen recently. What physical traits are typically identified as attractive in women? In men? List as many as you can. What assumptions does each trait suggest? Use your journal to respond to these questions.

The Ugly Truth About Beauty

If you're a man, at some point a woman will ask you how she looks.
"How do I look?" she'll ask.

You must be careful how you answer this question. The best technique is to form an honest yet sensitive opinion, then collapse on the floor with some kind of fatal seizure. Trust me, this is the easiest way out. Because you will never come up with the right answer.

The problem is that women generally do not think of their looks in the same way that men do. Most men form an opinion of how they look in the seventh grade, and they stick to it for the rest of their lives. Some men form the opinion that they are irresistible stud muffins, and they do not change this opinion even when their faces sag and their noses bloat to the size of eggplants and their eyebrows grow together to form what appears to be a giant forehead-dwelling tropical caterpillar.

Most men, I believe, think of themselves as average-looking. Men will think this even if their faces cause heart failure in cattle at a range of 300 yards. Being average does not bother them; average is fine, for men. This is why men never ask anybody how they look. Their primary form of beauty care is to shave themselves, which is essentially the same form of beauty care that they give to their lawns. If, at the end of his four-minute daily beauty regimen, a man has managed to wipe most of the shaving cream out of his hair and is not bleeding too badly, he feels that he has done all he can, so he stops thinking about his appearance and devotes his mind to more critical issues, such as the Super Bowl.

Women do not look at themselves this way. If I had to express, in three words, what I believe most women think about their appearance, those words would be: "not good enough." No matter how attractive a woman may appear to be to others, when she looks at herself in the mirror, she thinks: woof. She thinks that at any moment a municipal animal-control officer is going to throw a net over her and haul her off to the shelter.

Why do women have such low self-esteem? There are many complex psychological and societal reasons, by which I mean Barbie. Girls grow up playing with a doll proportioned such that, if it were human, it would be seven feet tall and weigh 81 pounds, of which 53 pounds would be bosoms. This is a difficult appearance standard to live up to, especially when you contrast it with the standard set for little boys by their dolls . . . excuse me, by their action figures. Most of the action figures that my son played with when he was little were hideous-looking. For example, he was very fond of an action figure (part of the He-Man series) called "Buzz-Off," who was part human, part flying insect. Buzz-Off was not a looker. But he was extremely self-confident. You could not imagine Buzz-Off saying to the other action figures: "Do you think these wings make my hips look big?"

But women grow up thinking they need to look like Barbie, which for most women is impossible, although there is a multibillion-dollar beauty industry devoted to convincing women that they must try. I once saw an Oprah show wherein supermodel Cindy Crawford dispensed makeup tips to the studio audience. Cindy had all these middle-aged women applying beauty products to their faces; she stressed how important it was to apply them in a certain way, using the tips of their fingers. All the women dutifully did this, even though it was obvious to any sane observer that, no matter how carefully they applied these products, they would never look remotely like Cindy Crawford, who is some kind of genetic mutation.

I'm not saying that men are superior. I'm just saying that you're not going to get a group of middle-aged men to sit in a room and apply cosmetics to themselves under the instruction of Brad Pitt, in hopes of looking more like him. Men would realize that this task was pointless and demeaning. They would find some way to bolster their self-esteem that did not require looking like Brad Pitt. They would say to Brad: "Oh YEAH? Well what do you know about LAWN CARE, pretty boy?"

Of course many women will argue that the reason they become obsessed with trying to look like Cindy Crawford is that men, being as shallow as a drop of spit, WANT women to look that way. To which I have two responses:

1. Hey, just because WE'RE idiots, that does not mean YOU have to be; and

2. Men don't even notice 97 percent of the beauty efforts you make anyway. Take fingernails. The average woman spends 5,000 hours per year worrying about her fingernails; I have never once, in more than 40 years of listening to men talk about women, heard a man say, "She has a nice set of fingernails!" Many men would not notice if a woman had upward of four hands.

Anyway, to get back to my original point: If you're a man, and a woman asks you how she looks, you're in big trouble. Obviously, you can't say she looks bad. But you also can't say that she looks great, because she'll think you're lying, because she has spent countless hours, with the help of the multi-billion-dollar beauty industry, obsessing about the differences between herself and Cindy Crawford. Also, she suspects that you're not qualified to judge anybody's appearance. This is because you have shaving cream in your hair.

Questions for Close Reading

1. What is the selection's thesis? Locate the sentence(s) in which Barry states his main idea. If he doesn't state the thesis explicitly, express it in your own words.
2. Barry tells us that most men consider themselves to be "average-looking" (paragraph 5). Why, according to Barry, do men feel this way?
3. When Barry writes that most women think of themselves as "not good enough" (6), what does he mean? What, according to Barry, causes women to develop low opinions of themselves?
4. Barry implies that women could have a more rational response to the "difficult appearance standard" that pervades society (7). What would that response be?
5. Refer to your dictionary as needed to define the following words used in the selection: *regimen* (paragraph 5), *municipal* (6), *societal* (7), *dispensed* (8), *genetic* (8), *mutation* (8), *demeaning* (9), and *bolster* (9).

Questions About the Writer's Craft

1. **The pattern.** Which comparison-contrast method of organization (point-by-point or one-side-at-a-time) does Barry use to develop his essay? Why might he have chosen this pattern?
2. Barry uses exaggeration, a strategy typically associated with humorous writing. Locate instances of exaggeration in the selection. Why do you think he uses this strategy?
3. **Other patterns.** Barry demonstrates a series of *cause-effect* chains in his essay. Locate some of the cause-effect series. How do they help Barry reinforce his thesis?
4. Barry's title involves an *oxymoron*—a contradiction in terms. What does this title imply about Barry's attitude toward his subject?

Writing Assignments Using Comparison-Contrast as a Pattern of Development

1. Examine the pitches made in magazines and on TV for the male and female versions of *one* kind of grooming product. Possibilities include deodorant, hair dye, soap, and so on. Then write an essay contrasting the persuasive appeals that the product makes to men with those it makes to women. (Don't forget to examine the assumptions behind the appeals.) To gain insight into advertising techniques, you'll find it helpful to read Ann McClintock's "Propaganda Techniques in Today's Advertising" (page 270). For useful perspectives on gender issues, consider reading Barbara Ehrenreich's "What I've Learned From Men" (page 215). For more insight into how we judge beauty, read Natalie Angier's "The Cute Factor" (page 456).

2. Barry contrasts women's preoccupation with looking good to men's lack of concern about their appearance. Now consider the flip side—something men care about deeply that women virtually ignore. Write an essay contrasting men's stereotypical fascination with *one* area to women's indifference. You might, for example, examine male and female attitudes toward sports, cars, tools, even lawn care. Following Barry's example, adopt a playful tone in your essay, illustrating the absurdity of the obsession you discuss.

Writing Assignments Combining Patterns of Development

3. Barry implies that most men, unaffected by the "multibillion-dollar beauty industry," are content to "think of themselves as average looking." Do you agree? Conduct your own research into whether or not Barry's assertions about men are true. Begin by interviewing several male friends, family members, and classmates to see how these men feel about their physical appearance. In addition, in the library or online, research magazines such as *People, Gentlemen's Quarterly,* or *Men's Health* for articles describing how everyday men as well as male celebrities view their looks. Then write an essay *refuting* or *defending* the view that being average-looking doesn't bother most men. Start by acknowledging the opposing view; then support your assertion with convincing *examples* and other evidence drawn from your research.

4. Barry blames Barbie dolls for setting up "a difficult appearance standard" for girls to emulate. Many would *argue* that the toys that *boys* play with also teach negative, ultimately damaging values. Write an essay exploring the values that are conveyed to boys through their toys. Brainstorm with others, especially males, about the toys of their youth or the toys that boys have today. Identify two to three key negative values to write about, *illustrating* each with several examples of toys.

Writing Assignment Using a Journal Entry as a Starting Point

5. Review your pre-reading journal entry. Focusing on the characteristics of male *or* female attractiveness conveyed by the mass media, identify two to three assumptions suggested by these standards. Illustrate each assumption with examples from TV commercials and/or magazine advertisements. Be sure to make clear how you feel about these assumptions.

Stephen Chapman

Stephen Chapman was an associate editor for *The New Republic,* the publication for which he wrote "The Prisoner's Dilemma" in 1980. Since then, he has joined the staff of the *Chicago Tribune,* where his twice-weekly syndicated column on national and international affairs originates. Born in Texas in 1954, Chapman graduated *cum laude* from Harvard University in 1976 and did graduate work in business administration at the University of Chicago. He has contributed articles to national magazines including *The Atlantic, Harper's, Reason,* and *The American Spectator.* Chapman lives with his family outside Chicago.

Pre-Reading Journal Entry

Should wrongdoing be punished in public? Why or why not? Use your journal to consider the pros and cons of public punishment for illegal actions. Think of three or four wrongdoings (from lesser offenses like shoplifting to serious crimes like armed robbery). For each offense, list possible forms of public punishment as well as the advantages and disadvantages of each form.

The Prisoner's Dilemma

One of the amusements of life in the modern West is the opportunity to observe the barbaric rituals of countries that are attached to the customs of the dark ages. Take Pakistan, for example. . . . President Zia, in harmony with the Islamic fervor that is sweeping his part of the world, revived the traditional Moslem practice of flogging lawbreakers in public. In Pakistan, this qualified as mass entertainment, and no fewer than 10,000 law-abiding Pakistanis turned out to see justice done to 26 convicts. To Western sensibilities the spectacle seemed barbaric—both in the sense of cruel and in the sense of pre-civilized. In keeping with Islamic custom each of the unfortunates—who had been caught in prostitution raids the previous night and summarily convicted and sentenced—was stripped down to a pair of white shorts, which were painted with a red stripe across the buttocks (the target). Then he was shackled against an easel, with pads thoughtfully placed over the kidneys to prevent injury. The floggers were muscular, fierce-looking sorts—convicted murderers, as it happens—who paraded around the flogging platform in colorful loincloths. When the time for the ceremony began, one of the floggers took a running start and brought a five-foot stave down across the first victim's buttocks, eliciting screams from the convict and murmurs from the audience. Each of the 26 received from five to 15 lashes. One had to be carried from the stage unconscious.

Flogging is one of the punishments stipulated by Koranic law, which has   2
made it a popular penological device in several Moslem countries, including Pakistan, Saudi Arabia, and, most recently, the ayatollah's Iran. Flogging, or *ta'zir,* is the general punishment prescribed for offenses that don't carry an explicit Koranic penalty. Some crimes carry automatic *hadd* punishments— stoning or scourging (a severe whipping) for illicit sex, scourging for drinking alcoholic beverages, amputation of the hands for theft. Other crimes—as varied as murder and abandoning Islam—carry the death penalty (usually carried out in public). Colorful practices like these have given the Islamic world an image in the West, as described by historian G. H. Jansen, "of blood dripping from the stumps of amputated hands and from the striped backs of malefactors, and piles of stones barely concealing the battered bodies of adulterous couples." Jansen, whose book *Militant Islam* is generally effusive in its praise of Islamic practices, grows squeamish when considering devices like flogging, amputation, and stoning. But they are given enthusiastic endorsement by the Koran itself.

Such traditions, we all must agree, are no sign of an advanced civilization.   3
In the West, we have replaced these various punishments (including the death penalty in most cases) with a single device. Our custom is to confine criminals in prison for varying lengths of time. In Illinois, a reasonably typical state, grand theft carries a punishment of three to five years; armed robbery can get you from six to 30. The lowest form of felony theft is punishable by one to three years in prison. Most states impose longer sentences on habitual offenders. In Kentucky, for example, habitual offenders can be sentenced to life in prison. Other states are less brazen, preferring the more genteel sounding "indeterminate sentence," which allows parole boards to keep inmates locked up for as long as life. It was under an indeterminate sentence of one to 14 years that George Jackson served 12 years in California prisons for committing a $70 armed robbery. Under a Texas law imposing an automatic life sentence for a third felony conviction, a man was sent to jail for life last year because of three thefts adding up to less than $300 in property value. Texas also is famous for occasionally imposing extravagantly long sentences, often running into hundreds or thousands of years. This gives Texas a leg up on Maryland, which used to sentence some criminals to life plus a day— a distinctive if superfluous flourish. . . .

What are the advantages of being a convicted criminal in an advanced   4
culture? First there is the overcrowding in prisons. One Tennessee prison, for example, has a capacity of 806, according to accepted space standards, but it houses 2300 inmates. One Louisiana facility has confined four and five prisoners in a single six-foot-by-six-foot cell. Then there is the disease caused by overcrowding, unsanitary conditions, and poor or inadequate medical care.

A federal appeals court noted that the Tennessee prison had suffered frequent outbreaks of infectious diseases like hepatitis and tuberculosis. But the most distinctive element of American prison life is its constant violence. In his book *Criminal Violence, Criminal Justice,* Charles Silberman noted that in one Louisiana prison, there were 211 stabbings in only three years, 11 of them fatal. There were 15 slayings in a prison in Massachusetts between 1972 and 1975. According to a federal court, in Alabama's penitentiaries (as in many others), "robbery, rape, extortion, theft and assault are everyday occurrences."

At least in regard to cruelty, it's not at all clear that the system of punishment that has evolved in the West is less barbaric than the grotesque practices of Islam. Skeptical? Ask yourself: would you rather be subjected to a few minutes of intense pain and considerable public humiliation, or be locked away for two or three years in a prison cell crowded with ill-tempered sociopaths? Would you rather lose a hand or spend 10 years or more in a typical state prison? I have taken my own survey on this matter. I have found no one who does not find the Islamic system hideous. And I have found no one who *given the choices* mentioned above, would not prefer its penalties to our own. . . .

Imprisonment is now the universal method of punishing criminals in the United States. It is thought to perform five functions, each of which has been given a label by criminologists. First, there is simple *retribution:* punishing the lawbreaker to serve society's sense of justice and to satisfy the victims' desire for revenge. Second, there is *specific deterrence:* discouraging the offender from misbehaving in the future. Third, *general deterrence:* using the offender as an example to discourage others from turning to crime. Fourth, *prevention:* at least during the time he is kept off the streets, the criminal cannot victimize other members of society. Finally, and most important, there is *rehabilitation:* reforming the criminal so that when he returns to society he will be inclined to obey the laws and able to make an honest living.

How satisfactorily do American prisons perform by these criteria? Well, of course, they do punish. But on the other scores they don't do so well. Their effect in discouraging future criminality by the prisoner or others is the subject of much debate, but the soaring rates of the last 20 years suggest that prisons are not a dramatically effective deterrent to criminal behavior. Prisons do isolate convicted criminals, but only to divert crime from ordinary citizens to prison guards and fellow inmates. Almost no one contends any more that prisons rehabilitate their inmates. If anything, they probably impede rehabilitation by forcing inmates into prolonged and almost exclusive association with other criminals. And prisons cost a lot of money. Housing a typical prisoner in a typical prison costs far more than a stint at a top university. This cost would be justified if prisons did the job they were intended for. But it is clear to all that prisons fail on the very grounds—humanity and hope of rehabilitation—that caused them to replace earlier, cheaper forms of punishment. . . .

So the debate continues to rage in all the same old ruts. No one, of course, would think of copying the medieval practices of Islamic nations and experimenting with punishments such as flogging and amputation. But let us consider them anyway. How do they compare with our American prison system in achieving the ostensible objectives of punishment? First, do they punish? Obviously they do, and in a uniquely painful and memorable way. Of course any sensible person, given the choice, would prefer suffering these punishments to years of incarceration in a typical American prison. But presumably no Western penologist would criticize Islamic punishments on the grounds that they are not barbaric enough. Do they deter crime? Yes, and probably more effectively than sending convicts off to prison. Now we read about a prison sentence in the newspaper, then think no more about the criminal's payment for his crimes until, perhaps, years later we read a small item reporting his release. By contrast, one can easily imagine the vivid impression it would leave to be wandering through a local shopping center and to stumble onto the scene of some poor wretch being lustily flogged. And the occasional sight of an habitual offender walking around with a bloody stump at the end of his arm no doubt also would serve as a forceful reminder that crime does not pay.   8

Do flogging and amputation discourage recidivism? No one knows whether the scars on his back would dissuade a criminal from risking another crime, but it is hard to imagine that corporal measures could stimulate a higher rate of recidivism than already exists. Islamic forms of punishment do not serve the favorite new right goal of simply isolating criminals from the rest of society, but they may achieve the same purpose of making further crimes impossible. In the movie *Bonnie and Clyde,* Warren Beatty successfully robs a bank with his arm in a sling, but this must be dismissed as artistic license. It must be extraordinarily difficult, at the very least, to perform much violent crime with only one hand.   9

Do these medieval forms of punishment rehabilitate the criminal? Plainly not. But long prison terms do not rehabilitate either. And it is just as plain that typical Islamic punishments are no crueler to the convict than incarceration in the typical American state prison.   10

Of course there are other reasons besides its bizarre forms of punishment that the Islamic system of justice seems uncivilized to the Western mind. One is the absence of due process. Another is the long list of offenses—such as drinking, adultery, blasphemy, "profiteering," and so on—that can bring on conviction and punishment. A third is all the ritualistic mumbo-jumbo in pronouncements of Islamic law. . . . Even in these matters, however, a little cultural modesty is called for. The vast majority of American criminals are convicted and sentenced as a result of plea bargaining, in which due process plays almost no role. It has been only half a century since a wave of religious fundamentalism stirred this country to outlaw the consumption of alcoholic beverages. Most states also still have laws imposing austere constraints on   11 sexual conduct. The *Washington Post* reported that the FBI had spent two and a half years and untold amounts of money to break up a nationwide pornography ring. Flogging the clients of prostitutes, as the Pakistanis did, does seem silly. But only a few months ago Mayor Koch of New York was proposing that clients caught in his own city have their names broadcast by radio stations. We are not so far advanced on such matters as we often like to think. Finally, my lawyer friends assure me that the rules of jurisdiction for American courts contain plenty of petty requirements and bizarre distinctions that would sound silly enough to foreign ears.

Perhaps it sounds barbaric to talk of flogging and amputation, and perhaps it is. But our system of punishment also is barbaric, and probably more so. Only cultural smugness about their system and willful ignorance about our own make it easy to regard the one as cruel and the other as civilized. We inflict our cruelties away from public view, while nations like Pakistan stage them in front of 10,000 onlookers. Their outrages are visible; ours are not. Most Americans can live their lives for years without having their peace of mind disturbed by the knowledge of what goes on in our prisons. To choose imprisonment over flogging and amputation is not to choose human kindness over cruelty, but merely to prefer that our cruelties be kept out of sight, and out of mind.

Public flogging and amputation may be more barbaric forms of punishment than imprisonment, even if they are not more cruel. Society may pay a higher price for them, even if the particular criminal does not. Revulsion against officially sanctioned violence and infliction of pain derives from something deeply ingrained in the Western conscience, and clearly it is something admirable. Grotesque displays of the sort that occur in Islamic countries probably breed a greater tolerance for physical cruelty, for example, which prisons do not do precisely because they conceal their cruelties. In fact it is our admirable intolerance for calculated violence that makes it necessary for us to conceal what we have not been able to do away with. In a way this is a good thing, since it holds out the hope that we may eventually find a way to do away with it. But in another way it is a bad thing, since it permits us to congratulate ourselves on our civilized humanitarianism while violating its norms in this one area of our national life.

Questions for Close Reading

1. What is the selection's thesis? Locate the sentence(s) in which Chapman states his main idea. If he doesn't state the thesis explicitly, express it in your own words.
2. Chapman calls Islamic punishment practices "barbaric." What are some of these practices? Why would they seem barbaric to most Americans?
3. According to our society's philosophy of punishment, what goals is imprisonment supposed to accomplish? How successful, in Chapman's view, are U.S. prisons in meeting these goals?

4. For Chapman, what is the core difference between the U.S. punishment system and that of Islamic nations like Pakistan? Which system does he find preferable? Why?

5. Refer to your dictionary as needed to define the following words used in the selection: *barbaric* (paragraph 1), *stipulated* (2), *penological* (2), *malefactors* (2), *effusive* (2), *brazen* (3), *genteel* (3), *indeterminate* (3), *superfluous* (3), *extortion* (4), *criteria* (7), *ostensible* (8), *recidivism* (9), *corporal* (9), *blasphemy* (11), and *sanctioned* (13).

Questions About the Writer's Craft

1. The pattern. In paragraphs 7 through 10, Chapman contrasts the success of the American and Islamic systems in meeting the five goals of punishment cited in paragraph 6. How does Chapman help readers keep those goals in mind as he develops his contrast?

2. Other patterns. In paragraphs 1, 2, and 6, Chapman provides a number of *definitions*. How do these definitions help him convince readers to accept key points in his argument?

3. Other patterns. Examine the *examples* that Chapman provides in paragraphs 3 and 4. Why do you think he sequences each set of examples as he does?

4. Examine Chapman's tone, especially in paragraphs 3, 4, 5, and 8 to 9. Where does he shift from a fairly neutral tone to a more sarcastic and mocking one? How does this change help Chapman convince readers of the seriousness of the problems in U.S. justice?

Writing Assignments Using Comparison-Contrast as a Pattern of Development

1. Select one situation in which people are, in your opinion, ineffectively punished for violating a law or regulation. For example, you might focus on the punishment typically imposed for driving while intoxicated, plagiarizing a school paper, or habitually coming to work late. Write an essay describing the violation and its customary punishment. Then contrast this punishment with a more effective way of correcting the offending behavior. Whether you choose the one-side-at-a-time or the point-by-point method, be sure to provide clear signals, as Chapman does, to help readers follow your ideas. You might also consider reading Jonathan Alter's "Time to Think About Torture" (page 552) and Henry Porter's "Now the Talk Is About Bringing Back Torture (page 557) for additional perspectives on crime prevention and punishment.

2. Chapman contrasts two cultures' approaches to criminal punishment. Write an essay comparing and/or contrasting two cultures' approaches to another aspect of life. To structure your paper, use either the one-side-at-a-time or point-by-point method of development. The cultures you discuss need not be nationalities or ethnicities. You might, for example, focus on parents' and teenagers' preferences in music, male and female expectations in a relationship, or high school teachers' and college professors' attitudes toward student responsibility. If appropriate, consider using a humorous tone to make fun of both sides—or to convey which side's approach you find preferable.

Writing Assignments Combining
Patterns of Development

3. Chapman states that there is "universal acknowledgment that prisons do not rehabilitate." Conduct research in the library and/or on the Internet on recent developments in criminal rehabilitation. Bibliographic sources like EBSCOhost, the *Social Sciences Index,* and *Criminal Justice Abstracts* will help you locate relevant information. Then write an essay *refuting* or *defending* the common view that the rehabilitation of prisoners is a futile goal. Start by acknowledging the opposing view, and then support your argument with convincing *examples* and other evidence drawn from your research.

4. Chapman describes people in Islamic cultures flocking to gawk at the misfortunes of others. People in our country are also fascinated, even entertained, by others' problems. They slow down to inspect traffic accidents, follow celebrities' troubles in tabloid publications, and glue themselves to the television when a natural disaster strikes. Write an essay in which you account for the *causes* of our fascination with others' misfortunes. Begin with one or two dramatic *examples* of this phenomenon, and then explain why you think people are so attracted to the troubles of others. Consider reading Stephen King's "Why We Crave Horror Movies" (page 397) and Mark Twain's "The Damned Human Race" (page 527) for some helpful insights into this morbid human tendency.

Writing Assignment Using a Journal
Entry as a Starting Point

5. Write an essay arguing that public punishment would *or* would not be appropriate for a specific transgression. From your pre-reading journal entry, select *one* crime and its most realistic form of public punishment. Supplement the material in your journal by interviewing friends, classmates, and family members. Be sure to seek out and acknowledge the views of those who don't agree with the position you take. Jonathan Alter's "Time to Think About Torture" (page 552) and Henry Porter's "Now the Talk Is About Bringing Back Torture" (page 557), which present pro and con perspectives on the issue of crime and punishment, might be useful for you to read before you write.

Additional Writing Topics

COMPARISON-CONTRAST

General Assignments

Using comparison-contrast, write an essay on one of the following topics. Your thesis should indicate whether the two subjects are being compared, contrasted, or both. Organize the paper by arranging the details in a one-side-at-a-time or point-by-point pattern. Remember to use organizational cues to help the audience follow your analysis.

1. Living at home versus living in an apartment or dorm
2. Two-career family versus one-career family
3. Two approaches for dealing with problems
4. Children's pastimes today and yesterday
5. Life before the Internet versus after the Internet
6. Neighborhood stores versus shopping malls
7. Two characters in a novel or other literary work
8. Two attitudes toward money
9. A sports team then and now
10. Watching a movie on television versus viewing it in a theater
11. Two attitudes about a controversial subject
12. Two approaches to parenting
13. A typical fan of one type of music versus another
14. Marriage versus living together
15. The atmosphere in two classes
16. Two approaches to studying
17. The place where you live and the place where you would like to live
18. Two comedians
19. The coverage of an event on television versus the coverage in a newspaper
20. Significant trend versus passing fad
21. Two horror or adventure movies
22. Handwriting a letter versus sending an e-mail message
23. Two candidates for an office
24. Your attitude before and after getting to know someone
25. Two friends with different lifestyles

Assignments With a Specific Purpose, Audience, and Point of View

On Campus

1. You would like to change your campus living arrangements. Perhaps you want to move from a dormitory to an off-campus apartment or from home to a dorm. Before you do, though, you'll have to convince your parents (who are paying

most of your college costs) that the move will be beneficial. Write out what you would say to your parents. Contrast your current situation with your proposed one, explaining why the new arrangement would be better.

2. Write a guide on "Passing Exams" for first-year college students, contrasting the right and wrong ways to prepare for and take exams. Although your purpose is basically serious, write the section on how *not* to approach exams with some humor.

At Home or in the Community

3. As president of your local Neighbors' Association, you're concerned about the way your local government is dealing with a particular situation (for example, an increase in robberies, muggings, graffiti, and so on). Write a letter to your mayor contrasting the way your local government handles the situation with another city or town's approach. In your conclusion, point out the advantages of adopting the other neighborhood's strategy.

4. Your old high school has invited you back to make a speech before an audience of seniors. The topic will be "how to choose the college that is right for you." Write your speech in the form of a comparison-contrast analysis. Focus on the choices available (two-year versus four-year schools, large versus small, local versus faraway, and so on), showing the advantages and/or disadvantages of each.

On the Job

5. As store manager, you decide to write a memo to all sales personnel explaining how to keep customers happy. Compare and/or contrast the needs and shopping habits of several different consumer groups (by age, spending ability, or sex), and show how to make each group comfortable in your store.

6. You work as a volunteer for a mental health hot line. Many people call simply because they feel "stressed out." Do some research on the subject of stress management, and prepare a brochure for these people, recommending a "Type B" approach to stressful situations. Focus the brochure on the contrast between "Type A" and "Type B" personalities: the former is nervous, hard-driving, competitive; the latter is relaxed and noncompetitive. Give specific examples of how each type tends to act in stressful situations.

CAUSE-EFFECT

WHAT IS CAUSE-EFFECT?

Superstition has it that curiosity killed the cat. Maybe so. Yet our science, technology, storytelling, and fascination with the past and future all spring from our determination to know "Why" and "What if." Seeking explanations, young children barrage adults with endless questions: "Why do trees grow tall?" "What would happen if the sun didn't shine?" But children aren't the only ones who wonder in this way. All of us think in terms of cause and effect, sometimes consciously, sometimes unconsciously: "Why did they give me such an odd look?" we wonder, or "How would I do at another college?" we speculate. This exploration of reasons and results is also at the heart of most professions: "What led to our involvement in Vietnam?" historians question; "What will happen if we administer this experimental drug?" scientists ask.

Cause-effect writing, often called *causal analysis,* is rooted in this elemental need to make connections. Because the drive to understand reasons and results is so fundamental, causal analysis is a common kind of writing. An article analyzing the unexpected outcome of an election, a report linking poor nutrition to low academic achievement, an editorial analyzing the impact of a proposed tax cut—all are examples of cause-effect writing.

Done well, cause-effect pieces can uncover the subtle and often surprising connections between events or phenomena. By rooting out causes and projecting effects, causal analysis enables us to make sense of our experiences, revealing a universe that is somewhat less arbitrary and chaotic.

HOW CAUSE-EFFECT FITS YOUR PURPOSE AND AUDIENCE

Many assignments and exam questions in college involve writing essays that analyze causes, effects, or both. Sometimes, as in the following examples, you'll be asked to write an essay developed primarily through the cause-effect pattern:

> Although divorces have leveled off in the last few years, the number of marriages ending in divorce is still greater than it was a generation ago. What do you think are the causes of this phenomenon?

> Political commentators were surprised that so few people voted in the last election. Discuss the probable causes of this weak voter turnout.

> Americans never seem to tire of gossip about the rich and famous. What effect has this fascination with celebrities had on U.S. culture?

> The federal government is expected to pass legislation that will significantly reduce the funding of student loans. Analyze the possible effects of such a cutback.

Other assignments and exam questions may not explicitly ask you to address causes and effects, but they may use words that suggest causal analysis would be appropriate. Consider these examples, paying special attention to the words in boldface:

> In contrast to the socially involved youth of the 1960s, many young people today tend to remove themselves from political issues. What do you think are the **sources** of the political apathy found among 18- to 25-year-olds? (*cause*)

> A number of experts forecast that drug abuse will be the most significant factor affecting U.S. productivity in the coming decade. Evaluate the validity of this observation by discussing the **impact** of drugs in the workplace. (*effect*)

> According to school officials, a predictable percentage of entering students drop out of college at some point during their first year. What **motivates** students to drop out? What **happens** to them once they leave? (*cause and effect*)

In addition to serving as the primary strategy for achieving an essay's purpose, causal analysis can also be a supplemental method used to help make a point in an essay developed chiefly through another pattern of development.

Assume, for example, that you want to write an essay *defining* the term *the homeless*. To help readers see that unfavorable circumstances can result in nearly anyone becoming homeless, you might discuss some of the unavoidable, everyday factors causing people to live on streets and in subway stations. Similarly, in a *persuasive* proposal urging your college administration to institute an honors program, you would probably spend some time analyzing the positive effect of such a program on students and faculty.

At this point, you have a good sense of the way writers use cause-effect to achieve their purpose and to connect with their readers. Now take a moment to look closely at the photograph at the beginning of this chapter. Imagine you're writing a column, accompanied by the photo, for the website of a local environmental organization. Your purpose is to prevent further development of nearby wilderness areas. Jot down ideas you might include when discussing the *effects* of such development.

SUGGESTIONS FOR USING CAUSE-EFFECT IN AN ESSAY

The following suggestions will be helpful whether you use causal analysis as a dominant or a supportive pattern of development.

1. Stay focused on the purpose of your analysis.   When writing a causal analysis, don't lose sight of your overall purpose. Consider, for example, an essay on the causes of widespread child abuse. If you're concerned primarily with explaining the problem of child abuse to your readers, you might take a purely *informative* approach:

> Although parental stress is the immediate cause of child abuse, the more compelling reason for such behavior lies in the way parents were themselves mistreated in their own families.

Or you might want to *persuade* the audience about some point or idea concerning child abuse:

> The tragic consequences of child abuse provide strong support for more aggressive handling of such cases by social workers and judges.

Then again, you could choose a *speculative* approach, your main purpose being to suggest possibilities:

> Psychologists disagree about the potential effect on youngsters of all the media attention to child abuse. Will children exposed to this media coverage grow up assertive, self-confident, and able to protect themselves? Or will they become fearful and distrustful?

These examples illustrate that an essay's causal analysis may have more than one purpose. For instance, although the last example points to a paper with a primarily speculative purpose, the essay would probably start by informing readers of experts' conflicting views. The paper would also have a persuasive slant if it ended by urging readers to complain to the media about their sensationalized treatment of the child-abuse issue.

2. Adapt content and tone to your purpose and readers.   Your purpose and audience determine what supporting material and what tone will be most effective in a cause-effect essay. Assume you want to direct your essay on child abuse to general readers who know little about the subject. To *inform* readers, you might use facts, statistics, and expert opinion to provide an objective discussion of the causes of child abuse. Your analysis might show the following: (1) adults who were themselves mistreated as children tend to abuse their own offspring; (2) marital stress contributes to the mistreatment of children; and (3) certain personality disorders increase the likelihood of child abuse. Sensitive to what your readers would and wouldn't understand, you would stay away from a technical or formal tone. Rather than writing "Pathological preabuse symptomatology predicts adult transference of high aggressivity," you would say "Psychologists can often predict, on the basis of family histories, who will abuse children."

Now imagine that your purpose is to *convince* future social workers that the failure of social service agencies to act authoritatively in child-abuse cases often has tragic consequences. Hoping to encourage more responsible behavior in the prospective social workers, you would adopt a more emotional tone in the essay, perhaps citing wrenching case histories that dramatize what happens when child abuse isn't taken seriously.

3. Think rigorously about causes and effects.   To write a meaningful causal analysis, you should do some careful thinking about the often complex relationship between causes and effects. Children tend to oversimplify causes and effects ("Mommy and Daddy are getting divorced because I was bad the other day"), and adults' arguments can be characterized by hasty, often slipshod thinking ("All these immigrants willing to work cheaply have made us lose our jobs"). But imprecise thinking has no place in essay writing.

You should be willing to dig for causes, to think creatively about effects. You should examine your subject in depth, looking beyond the obvious and superficial.

Brainstorming, freewriting, and mapping will help you explore causes and effects thoroughly. No matter which prewriting technique you use, generate as many explanations as possible by asking yourself questions like these:

Causes: What happened? What are the possible reasons? Which are most likely? Who was involved? Why?

Effects: What happened? Who was involved? What were the observable results? What are some possible future consequences? Which consequences are negative? Which are positive?

If you remain open and look beyond the obvious, you'll discover that a cause may have many effects. Imagine that you're writing a paper on the effects of cigarette smoking. Prewriting would probably generate a number of consequences that could be discussed, some less obvious but perhaps more interesting than others: increased risk of lung cancer and heart disease, harm traced to secondhand smoke, legal battles regarding the rights of smokers and nonsmokers, lower birth weights in babies of mothers who smoke, and developmental problems experienced by such underweight infants.

In the same way, prewriting will help you see that an effect may have multiple causes. An essay analyzing the reasons for world hunger could discuss many causes, again some less evident but perhaps more thought-provoking than others: climatic changes, inefficient use of land, cultural predispositions for large families, and poor management of international relief funds.

Your analysis may also uncover a *causal chain* in which one cause (or effect) brings about another, which, in turn, brings about another, and so on. Here's an example of a causal chain: The Prohibition Amendment to the U.S. Constitution went into effect on January 29, 1920; bootleggers and organized crime stepped in to supply public demand for alcoholic beverages; ordinary citizens began breaking the law by buying illegal alcohol and patronizing speakeasies; disrespect for legal authority became widespread and acceptable. As you can see, a causal chain often leads to interesting points. In this case, the subject of Prohibition leads not just to the obvious (illegal consumption of alcohol) but also to the more complex issue of society's decreasing respect for legal authority.

Don't grapple with so complex a chain, however, that you become hopelessly entangled. If your subject involves multiple causes and effects, limit what you'll discuss. Identify which causes and effects are *primary* and which are *secondary.* How extensively you cover secondary factors will depend on your purpose and audience. In an essay intended to inform a general audience about the harmful effects of pesticides, you would most likely focus on everyday dangers—polluted drinking water, residues in food, and the like. You probably wouldn't include a discussion of more long-range consequences (evolution of resistant insects, disruption of the soil's acid-alkaline balance).

Similarly, decide whether to focus on *immediate,* more obvious causes and effects, or on less obvious, more *remote* ones. Or perhaps you need to focus on both. In an essay about a faculty strike at your college, should you attribute the strike simply to the faculty's failure to receive a salary increase? Or should you also examine other factors: the union's failure to accept a salary package that satisfied most professors; the administration's inability to coordinate its negotiating efforts? It may be more difficult to explore more remote causes and effects, but it can also lead to more original and revealing essays. Thoughtful analyses take these less obvious considerations into account.

When developing a causal analysis, be careful to avoid the *post hoc fallacy.* Named after the Latin phrase *post hoc, ergo propter hoc,* meaning "after this, therefore because of this," this kind of faulty thinking occurs when you assume that simply because one event *followed* another, the first event *caused* the second. For example, if the Republicans win a majority of seats in Congress and, several months later, the economy collapses, can you conclude that the Republicans caused the collapse? A quick assumption of "Yes" fails the test of logic, for the timing of events could be coincidental and not indicative of any cause-effect relationship. The collapse may have been triggered by uncontrolled inflation that began well before the congressional elections. (For more information on the *post hoc* fallacy, see page 497.)

Also, be careful not to mistake *correlation* for *causation.* Two events correlate when they occur at about the same time. Such co-occurrence, however, doesn't guarantee a cause-effect relationship. For instance, while the number of ice cream cones eaten and the instances of heat prostration both increase during the summer months, this doesn't mean that eating ice-cream causes heat prostration! A third factor—in this case, summer heat—is the actual cause. When writing causal analyses, then, use with caution words that imply a causal link (such as *therefore* and *because*). Words that express simply time of occurrence (like *following* and *previously*) are safer and more objective.

Finally, keep in mind that a rigorous causal analysis involves more than loose generalizations about causes and effects. Creating plausible connections may require library research, interviewing, or both. Often you'll need to provide facts, statistics, details, personal observations, or other corroborative material if readers are going to accept the reasoning behind your analysis.

4. Write a thesis that focuses the paper on causes, effects, or both.   The thesis in an essay developed through causal analysis often indicates whether the essay will deal with mostly causes, effects, or both causes and effects. Here, for example, are three thesis statements for causal analyses dealing with the public school system. You'll see that each thesis signals that essay's particular emphasis:

Our school system has been weakened by an overemphasis on trendy electives. *(causes)*

An ineffectual school system has led to crippling teachers' strikes and widespread disrespect for the teaching profession. *(effects)*

Bureaucratic inefficiency has created a school system unresponsive to children's emotional, physical, and intellectual needs. *(causes and effects)*

Note that the thesis statement—in addition to signaling whether the paper will discuss causes or effects or both—may also point to the essay's plan of development. Consider the last thesis statement; it makes clear that the paper will discuss children's emotional needs first, their physical needs second, and their intellectual needs last.

The thesis statement in a causal analysis doesn't have to specify whether the essay will discuss causes, effects, or both. Nor does the thesis have to be worded in such a way that the essay's plan of development is apparent. But when first writing cause-effect essays, you may find that a highly focused thesis will keep your analysis on track.

5. Choose an organizational pattern. There are two basic ways to organize the points in a cause-effect essay: You may use a chronological or an emphatic sequence. If you select a *chronological order*, you discuss causes and effects in the order in which they occur or will occur. Suppose you're writing an essay on the causes for the popularity of imported cars. These causes might be discussed in chronological sequence: American plant workers became frustrated and dissatisfied on the job; some workers got careless while others deliberately sabotaged the production of sound cars; a growing number of defective cars hit the market; consumers grew dissatisfied with American cars and switched to imports.

Chronology might also be used to organize a discussion about effects. Imagine you want to write an essay about the need to guard against disrupting delicate balances in the country's wildlife. You might start the essay by discussing what happened when the starling, a non-native bird, was introduced into the American environment. Because the starling had few natural predators, the starling population soared out of control; starlings took over the food sources and habitats of native species; the bluebird, a native species, declined and is now threatened with extinction.

Although a chronological pattern can be an effective way to organize material, a strict time sequence can present a problem if your primary cause or effect ends up buried in the middle of the sequence. In such a case, you might use *emphatic order,* reserving the most significant cause or effect for the end. For example, time order could be used to present the reasons behind a candidate's unexpected victory: Less than a month after the candidate's earlier defeat, a full-scale fund-raising campaign for the next election was started; the candidate spoke to many crucial power groups early in the campaign; the candidate did exceptionally well in the pre-election debates; good weather and large voter turnout on election day favored the candidate. However, if you believe that the candidate's appearance before influential groups was the key factor in the victory, it would be more effective to emphasize that point by saving it for the end. This is what is meant by emphatic order—saving the most important point for last.

Emphatic order is an especially effective way to sequence cause-effect points when readers hold what, in your opinion, are mistaken or narrow views about a subject. To encourage readers to look more closely at the issues, you present what you consider the erroneous or obvious views first, show why they are unsound or limited, and then present what you feel to be the actual causes and effects. Such a sequence nudges the audience into giving further thought to the causes and effects you have discovered. Here are informal outlines for two causal analyses using this approach.

Subject: The causes of the riot at the rock concert

1. Some commentators blame the excessively hot weather.
2. Others cite drug use among the concertgoers.
3. Still others blame the beer sold at the concessions.
4. But the real cause of the disaster was poor planning by the concert promoters.

Subject: The effects of campus crime

1. Immediate problems
   a. Students feel insecure and fearful.
   b. Many nighttime campus activities have been curtailed.
2. More significant long-term problems
   a. Unfavorable publicity about campus crime will affect future student enrollments.
   b. Hiring faculty will become more difficult.

When using emphatic order in a causal analysis, you might want to word the thesis in such a way that it signals which point your essay will stress. Look at the following thesis statements:

Although many immigrants arrive in this country without marketable skills, their most pressing problem is learning how to make their way in a society whose language they don't know.

The space program has led to dramatic advances in computer technology and medical science. Even more important, though, the program has helped change many people's attitudes toward the planet we live on.

These thesis statements reflect an awareness of the complex nature of cause-effect relationships. While not dismissing secondary issues, the statements establish which points the writer considers most noteworthy. The second thesis, for instance, indicates that the paper will touch on the technological and medical advances made possible by the space program but will emphasize the way the program has changed people's attitudes toward the earth.

Whether you use a chronological or emphatic pattern to organize your essay, you'll need to provide clear *signals* to identify when you're discussing causes and when you're discussing effects. Expressions such as "Another reason" and "A final outcome" help readers follow your line of thought.

6. Use language that hints at the complexity of cause-effect relationships. Because it's difficult—if not impossible—to identify causes and effects with certainty, you should avoid such absolutes as "It must be obvious" and "There is no doubt." Instead, try phrases like "Most likely" or "It's probable that." Using such language is not indecisive; rather, it reflects your understanding of the often tangled nature of causes and effects. Be careful, though, of going to the other extreme and being reluctant to take a stand on the issues. If you've thought carefully about causes and effects, you have a right to state your analysis with conviction. Don't undercut the hard work you've done by writing as if your ideas were unworthy of your reader's attention.

REVISION STRATEGIES

Once you have a draft of the essay, you're ready to revise. The following checklist will help you and those giving you feedback apply to cause-effect some of the revision techniques discussed on pages 60–62.

☑ CAUSE-EFFECT: A REVISION/PEER REVIEW CHECKLIST

Revise Overall Meaning and Structure

❑ Is the essay's purpose informative, persuasive, speculative, or a combination of these?

❑ What is the essay's thesis? Is it stated specifically or implied? Where? Could it be made any clearer? How?

❑ Does the essay focus on causes, effects, or both? How do you know?

❑ Where has correlation been mistaken for causation? Where is the essay weakened by *post hoc* thinking?

❑ Where does the essay distinguish between primary and secondary causes and effects? Do the most critical causes and effects receive special attention?

❑ Where does the essay dwell on the obvious?

Revise Paragraph Development

❏ Are the essay's paragraphs sequenced chronologically or emphatically? Could they be sequenced more effectively? How?

❏ Where would signal devices make it easier to follow the progression
of thought within and between paragraphs?

❏ Which paragraphs would be strengthened by vivid examples (such as
statistics, facts, anecdotes, or personal observations) that support the
causal analysis?

Revise Sentences and Words

❏ Where do expressions like *as a result, because,* and *therefore* mislead
the reader by implying a cause-effect relationship? Would words such
as *following* and *previously* eliminate the problem?

❏ Do any words or phrases convey an arrogant or dogmatic tone (*there
is no question, undoubtedly, always, never*)? What other expressions
(*most likely, probably*) would improve credibility?

STUDENT ESSAY

The following student essay was written by Carl Novack in response to this
assignment:

> In "Innocents Afield," Buzz Bissinger explores the way high school
> sports have changed in the last few years. Think of another aspect of
> everyday life that has changed recently, and discuss those factors that
> you believe are responsible for the change.

While reading Carl's paper, try to determine how well it applies the principles of causal analysis. The annotations on Carl's paper and the commentary following it will help you look at the essay more closely.

Americans and Food
by Carl Novack

Introduction   An offbeat but timely cartoon recently appeared in the
local newspaper. The single panel showed a gravel-pit
operation with piles of raw earth and large cranes. Next to one
of the cranes stood the owner of the gravel pit--a grizzled,
tough-looking character, hammer in hand, pointing proudly to
the new sign he had just tacked up. The sign read, "Fred's Fill
Dirt and Croissants." The cartoon illustrates an interesting
phenomenon: the changing food habits of Americans. Our

meals used to consist of something like home-cooked pot roast, mashed potatoes laced with butter and salt, a thick slice of apple pie topped with a healthy scoop of vanilla ice cream-- plain, heavy meals, cooked from scratch, and eaten leisurely at home. But America has changed, and as it has, so have what we Americans eat and how we eat it.

Thesis

We used to have simple, unsophisticated tastes and looked with suspicion at anything more exotic than hamburger. Admittedly, we did adopt some foods from the various immigrant groups who flocked to our shores. We learned to eat Chinese food, pizza, and bagels. But in the last few years, the international character of our diet has grown tremendously. We can walk into any mall in Middle America and buy pita sandwiches, quiche, and tacos. Such foods are often changed on their journey from exotic imports to ordinary "American" meals (no Pakistani, for example, eats frozen-on-a-stick boysenberry-flavored yogurt), but the imports are still a long way from hamburger on a bun.

Topic sentence: Background paragraph

Topic sentence: Three causes answer the question

First cause

Why have we become more worldly in our tastes? For one thing, television blankets the country with information about new food products and trends. Viewers in rural Montana know that the latest craving in Washington, D.C., is Cajun cooking or that something called tofu is now available in the local supermarket. Another reason for the growing international flavor of our food is that many young Americans have traveled abroad and gotten hooked on new tastes and flavors. Backpacking students and young professionals vacationing in Europe come home with cravings for authentic French bread or German beer. Finally, continuing waves of immigrants settle in the cities where many of us live, causing significant changes in what we eat. Vietnamese, Haitians, and Thais, for instance, bring their native foods and cooking styles with them and eventually open small markets or restaurants. In time, the new food will become Americanized enough to take its place in our national diet.

Second cause

Third cause

Topic sentence: Another cause

Our growing concern with health has also affected the way we eat. For the last few years, the media have warned us about the dangers of our traditional diet, high in salt and fat, low in fiber. The media also began to educate us about the dangers of processed foods pumped full of chemical additives. As a result, consumers began to demand healthier foods, and manufacturers started to change some of their products. Many foods, such as lunch meat, canned vegetables, and soups, were made available in low-fat, low-sodium versions. Whole-grain cereals and higher-fiber breads also began to appear on the grocery shelves. Moreover, the food industry started to produce all-natural products--everything from potato chips to ice cream--without additives and preservatives. Not

Start of a causal chain

2

3

4

surprisingly, the restaurant industry responded to this switch to healthier foods, luring customers with salad bars, broiled fish, and steamed vegetables.

Topic sentence: Another cause ⟶ Our food habits are being affected, too, by the rapid 5 increase in the number of women working outside the home. Sociologists and other experts believe that two important factors triggered this phenomenon: the women's movement and a changing economic climate. Women were assured that it was acceptable, even rewarding, to work outside the home; many women also discovered that they had to work just to keep up with the cost of living. As the traditional role of homemaker changed, so did the way families ate. With Mom working, there wasn't time for her to prepare the traditional three square meals a day. Instead, families began looking for alternatives to provide quick meals. What was the result? For one thing, there was a boom in fast-food restaurants. The suburban or downtown strip that once contained a lone McDonald's now features Wendy's, Roy Rogers, Taco Bell, Burger King, and Pizza Hut. Families also began to depend on frozen foods as another time-saving alternative. Once again, though, demand changed the kind of frozen food available. Frozen foods no longer consist of foil trays divided into greasy fried chicken, watery corn niblets, and lumpy mashed potatoes. Supermarkets now stock a range of supposedly gourmet frozen dinners--from fettucini in cream sauce to braised beef en brochette.

Start of a causal chain

Conclusion   It may not be possible to pick up a ton of fill dirt and a half- 6 dozen croissants at the same place, but America's food habits are definitely changing. If it is true that "you are what you eat," then America's identity is evolving along with its diet.

COMMENTARY

Title and introduction.   Asked to prepare a paper analyzing the reasons behind a change in our lives, Carl decided to write about a shift he had noticed in Americans' eating habits. The title of the essay, "Americans and Food," identifies Carl's subject but could be livelier and more interesting.

Despite his rather uninspired title, Carl starts his *causal analysis* in an engaging way—with the vivid description of a cartoon. He then connects the cartoon to his subject with the following sentence: "The cartoon illustrates an interesting phenomenon: the changing food habits of Americans." To back up his belief that there has been a revolution in our eating habits, Carl uses the first paragraph to summarize the kind of meal that people used to eat. He then moves into his *thesis:* "But America has changed, and as it has, so have what Americans eat and how we eat it." The thesis implies that Carl's paper will focus on both causes and effects.

Purpose.   Carl's *purpose* was to write an *informative* causal analysis. But before he could present the causes of the change in eating habits, he needed to show that such a change had, in fact, taken place. He therefore uses the second paragraph to document one aspect of this change—the internationalization of our eating habits.

Topic sentences.   At the beginning of the third paragraph, Carl uses a question—"Why have we become more worldly in our tastes?"—to signal that his discussion of causes is about to begin. This question also serves as the paragraph's *topic sentence*, indicating that the paragraph will focus on reasons for the increasingly international flavor of our food. The next two paragraphs, also focused by topic sentences, identify two other major reasons for the change in eating habits: "Our growing concern with health has also affected the way we eat" (paragraph 4), and "Our food habits are being affected, too, by the rapid increase in the number of women working outside the home" (5).

Combining patterns of development.   Carl draws on two patterns—comparison-contrast and exemplification—to develop his causal analysis. At the heart of the essay is a basic *contrast* between the way we used to eat and the way we eat now. And throughout his essay, Carl provides convincing *examples* to demonstrate the validity of his points. Consider for a moment the third paragraph. Here Carl asserts that one reason for our new eating habits is our growing exposure to international foods. He then presents concrete evidence to show that we have indeed become more familiar with international cuisine: Television exposes rural Montana to Cajun cooking; students traveling abroad take a liking to French bread; urban dwellers enjoy the exotic fare served by numerous immigrant groups. The fourth and fifth paragraphs use similarly specific evidence (for example, "low-fat, low-sodium versions" of "lunch meat, canned vegetables, and soups") to illustrate the soundness of key ideas.

Causal chains.   Let's look more closely at the evidence in the essay. Not satisfied with obvious explanations, Carl thought through his ideas carefully and even brainstormed with friends to arrive at as comprehensive an analysis as possible. Not surprisingly, much of the evidence Carl uncovered took the form of *causal chains*. In the fourth paragraph, Carl writes, "The media also began to educate us about the dangers of processed foods pumped full of chemical additives. As a result, consumers began to demand healthier foods, and manufacturers started to change some of their products." And the next paragraph shows how the changing role of American women caused families to search for alternative ways of eating. This shift, in turn, caused the restaurant and food industries to respond with a wide range of food alternatives.

Making the paper easy to follow.   Although Carl's analysis digs beneath the surface and reveals complex cause-effect relationships, he wisely limits his pursuit of causal chains to *primary causes and effects*. He doesn't let the complexities distract him from his main purpose: to show why and how the American diet is changing. Carl is also careful to provide his essay with abundant *connecting devices*, making it easy for readers to see the links between points. Consider the use of *transitions* (signaled by italics) in the following sentences: "*Another* reason for the growing international flavor of our food is that many young Americans have traveled abroad" (paragraph 3); "*As a result*, consumers began to demand healthier foods" (4); and "*As* the traditional role of homemaker changed, so did the way families ate" (5).

A problem with the essay's close.   When reading the essay, you probably noticed that Carl's conclusion is a bit weak. Although his reference to the cartoon works well, the rest of the paragraph limps to a tired close. Ending an otherwise vigorous essay with such a slight conclusion undercuts the effectiveness of the whole paper. Carl spent so much energy developing the body of his essay that he ran out of the stamina needed to conclude the piece more forcefully. Careful budgeting of his time would have allowed him to prepare a stronger concluding paragraph.

Revising the first draft.   When Carl was ready to revise, he showed the first draft of his essay to several classmates during a peer review session. Listening carefully to what they said, he jotted down their most helpful comments and eventually transferred them, numbered in order of importance, to his draft. Comparing Carl's original version of his fourth paragraph (shown here) with his final version in the essay will show you how he went about revising.

Original Version of the Fourth Paragraph

A growing concern with health has also affected the way we eat, especially because the media have sent us warnings the last few years about the dangers of salt, sugar, food additives, high-fat and low-fiber diets. We have started to worry that our traditional meals may have been shortening our lives. As a result, consumers demanded healthier foods and manufacturers started taking some of the salt and sugar out of canned foods. "All-natural" became an effective selling point, leading to many preservative-free products. Restaurants, too, adapted their menus, luring customers with light meals. Because we now know about the link between overweight and a variety of health problems, including heart attacks, we are counting calories. In turn, food companies made fortunes on diet beer and diet cola. Sometimes, though, we seem a bit confused about the health issue; we drink soda that is sugar-free but loaded with chemical sweeteners. Still, we believe we are lengthening our lives through changing our diets.

On the advice of his classmates, Carl decided to omit all references to the way our concern with weight has affected our eating habits. It's true, of course, that calorie-counting has changed how we eat. But as soon as Carl started to discuss this point, he got involved in a causal chain that undercut the paragraph's unity. He ended up describing the paradoxical situation in which we find ourselves. In an attempt to eat healthy, we stay away from sugar and use instead artificial sweeteners that probably aren't very good for us. This is an interesting issue, but it detracts from the point Carl wants to make: that our concern with health has affected our eating habits in a *positive* way.

Carl's peer reviewers also pointed out that the fourth paragraph's first sentence contained too much material to be an effective topic sentence. Carl corrected the problem by breaking the overlong sentence into two short ones: "Our growing concern with health has also affected the way we eat. For the last few years, the media have warned us about the dangers of our traditional diet, high in salt and fat, low in fiber." The first of these sentences serves as a crisp topic sentence that focuses the rest of the paragraph.

Finally, Carl agreed with his classmates that the fourth paragraph lacked convincing specifics. When revising, he changed "manufacturers started taking some of the salt and sugar out of canned foods" to the more specific "Many foods, such as lunch meats, canned vegetables, and soups, were made available in low-fat, low-sodium versions." Similarly, generalizations about "light meals" and "all-natural products" gained life through the addition of concrete examples: restaurants lured "customers with salad bars, broiled fish, and steamed vegetables," and the food industry produced "everything from potato chips to ice cream—without additives and preservatives."

Carl did an equally good job revising other sections of his paper. With the exception of the weak spots already discussed, he made the changes needed to craft a well-reasoned essay, one that demonstrates his ability to analyze a complex phenomenon.

ACTIVITIES: CAUSE-EFFECT

Prewriting Activities

1. Imagine you're writing two essays: One *argues* the need for high school courses in personal finance (how to budget money, balance a checkbook, and the like); the other explains a *process* for showing appreciation. Jot down ways you might use cause-effect in each essay.

2. Use mapping, collaborative brainstorming, or another prewriting technique to generate possible causes and/or effects for *one* of the topics below. Be sure to keep in mind the audience indicated in parentheses. Next, devise a thesis and decide whether your purpose would be informative, persuasive, speculative, or

some combination of these. Finally, organize your raw material into a brief outline, with related causes and effects grouped in the same section.

  a. Pressure on students to do well (*high school students*)
  b. Children's access to pornography on the Internet (*parents*)
  c. Being physically fit (*those who are out of shape*)
  d. Spiraling costs of a college education (*college officials*)

Revising Activities

3. Explain how the following statements demonstrate *post hoc* thinking and confuse correlation and cause-effect.

  a. Our city now has many immigrants from Latin American countries. The crime rate in our city has increased. Latin American immigrants are the cause of the crime wave.
  b. The divorce rate has skyrocketed. More women are working outside the home than ever before. Working outside the home destroys marriages.
  c. A high percentage of people in Dixville have developed cancer. The landfill, used by XYZ Industries, has been located in Dixville for twenty years. The XYZ landfill has caused cancer in Dixville residents.

4. The following paragraph is from the first draft of an essay arguing that technological advances can diminish the quality of life. How solid is the paragraph's causal analysis? Which causes and/or effects should be eliminated? Where is the analysis simplistic? Where does the writer make absolute claims even though cause-effect relationships are no more than a possibility? Keeping these questions in mind, revise the paragraph.

> How did the banking industry respond to inflation? It simply introduced a new technology--the automated teller machine (ATM). By making money more available to the average person, the ATM gives people the cash to buy inflated goods--whether or not they can afford them. Not surprisingly, automated teller machines have had a number of negative consequences for the average individual. Since people know they can get cash at any time, they use their lunch hours for something other than going to the bank. How do they spend this newfound time? They go shopping, and machine-vended money means more impulse buying, even more than with a credit card. Also, because people don't need their checkbooks to withdraw money, they can't keep track of their accounts and therefore develop a casual attitude toward financial matters. It's no wonder children don't appreciate the value of money. Another problem is that people who would never dream of robbing a bank try to trick the machine into dispensing money "for free." There's no doubt that this kind of fraud contributes to the immoral climate in the country.

Stephen King

Probably the best-known living horror writer, Stephen King (1947–) is the author of more than thirty books. Before earning fame through his vastly popular books, including *Carrie* (1974), *The Shining* (1977), *Cujo* (1981), and *Tommyknockers* (1987), King worked as a high school English teacher and an industrial laundry worker. Much of King's prolific output has been adapted for the screen; movies based on King's work include *Misery* (1990), *Stand By Me* (1986), and *The Green Mile* (1999). More recent works include *Dreamcatcher* (2001), *Everything's Eventual* (2002), *From a Buick 8* (2002), and Volumes V, VI, and VII in the *Dark Tower* series (published in 2003, 2004, and 2004, respectively). His most recent novel is *Cell* (2006). King's book *On Writing: A Memoir of the Craft* (2000) offers insight into the writing process and examines the role that writing has played in his own life—especially following a near-fatal accident in 1999. King lives with his wife in Bangor, Maine, and has three adult children. The following essay first appeared in *Playboy* in 1982.

Pre-Reading Journal Entry

Several forms of entertainment, besides horror movies, are highly popular despite what many consider a low level of quality. In your journal, list as many "low-brow" forms of entertainment as you can. Possibilities include professional wrestling, aggressive video games, Internet chat rooms, and so on. Review your list, and respond to the following question in your journal: What is it about each form of entertainment that attracts such popularity—and inspires such criticism?

Why We Crave Horror Movies

I think that we're all mentally ill: those of us outside the asylums only 1 hide it a little better—and maybe not all that much better, after all. We've all known people who talk to themselves, people who sometimes squinch their faces into horrible grimaces when they believe no one is watching, people who have some hysterical fear—of snakes, the dark, the tight place, the long drop . . . and, of course, those final worms and grubs that are waiting so patiently underground.

When we pay our four or five bucks and seat ourselves at tenth-row cen- 2 ter in a theater showing a horror movie, we are daring the nightmare.

Why? Some of the reasons are simple and obvious. To show that we 3 can, that we are not afraid, that we can ride this roller coaster. Which is not to say that a really good horror movie may not surprise a scream out of us at some point, the way we may scream when the roller coaster twists through a complete 360 or plows through a lake at the bottom of the drop. And horror movies, like roller coasters, have always been the special province of the young; by the time one turns 40 or 50, one's appetite for double twists or 360-degree loops may be considerably depleted.

We also go to re-establish our feelings of essential normality; the horror movie is innately conservative, even reactionary. Freda Jackson as the horrible melting woman in *Die, Monster, Die!* confirms for us that no matter how far we may be removed from the beauty of a Robert Redford or a Diana Ross, we are still light-years from true ugliness.

And we go to have fun.

Ah, but this is where the ground starts to slope away, isn't it? Because this is a very peculiar sort of fun indeed. The fun comes from seeing others menaced—sometimes killed. One critic has suggested that if pro football has become the voyeur's version of combat, then the horror film has become the modern version of the public lynching.

It is true that the mythic, "fairytale" horror film intends to take away the shades of gray. . . . It urges us to put away our more civilized and adult penchant for analysis and to become children again, seeing things in pure blacks and whites. It may be that horror movies provide psychic relief on this level because this invitation to lapse into simplicity, irrationality and even outright madness is extended so rarely. We are told we may allow our emotions a free rein . . . or no rein at all.

If we are all insane, then sanity becomes a matter of degree. If your insanity leads you to carve up women like Jack the Ripper or the Cleveland Torso Murderer, we clap you away in the funny farm (but neither of those two amateur-night surgeons was ever caught, heh-heh-heh); if, on the other hand your insanity leads you only to talk to yourself when you're under stress or to pick your nose on the morning bus, then you are left alone to go about your business . . . though it is doubtful that you will ever be invited to the best parties.

The potential lyncher is in almost all of us (excluding saints, past and present; but then, most saints have been crazy in their own ways), and every now and then, he has to be let loose to scream and roll around in the grass. Our emotions and our fears form their own body, and we recognize that it demands its own exercise to maintain proper muscle tone. Certain of these emotional muscles are accepted—even exalted—in civilized society; they are, of course, the emotions that tend to maintain the status quo of civilization itself. Love, friendship, loyalty, kindness—these are all the emotions that we applaud, emotions that have been immortalized in the couplets of Hallmark cards. . . .

When we exhibit these emotions, society showers us with positive reinforcement; we learn this even before we get out of diapers. When, as children, we hug our rotten little puke of a sister and give her a kiss, all the aunts and uncles smile and twit and cry, "Isn't he the sweetest little thing?" Such coveted treats as chocolate-covered graham crackers often follow. But if we deliberately slam the rotten little puke of a sister's fingers in the door, sanctions follow—angry remonstrance from parents, aunts and uncles; instead of a chocolate-covered graham cracker, a spanking.

But anticivilization emotions don't go away, and they demand periodic 11 exercise. We have such "sick" jokes as, "What's the difference between a truckload of bowling balls and a truckload of dead babies?" (You can't unload a truckload of bowling balls with a pitchfork . . . a joke, by the way, that I heard originally from a ten-year-old.) Such a joke may surprise a laugh or a grin out of us even as we recoil, a possibility that confirms the thesis: If we share a brotherhood of man, then we also share an insanity of man. None of which is intended as a defense of either the sick joke or insanity but merely as an explanation of why the best horror films, like the best fairy tales, manage to be reactionary, anarchistic, and revolutionary all at the same time.

The mythic horror movie, like the sick joke, has a dirty job to do. It 12 deliberately appeals to all that is worst in us. It is morbidity unchained, our most base instincts let free, our nastiest fantasies realized . . . and it all happens, fittingly enough, in the dark. For those reasons, good liberals often shy away from horror films. For myself, I like to see the most aggressive of them—*Dawn of the Dead,* for instance—as lifting a trap door in the civilized forebrain and throwing a basket of raw meat to the hungry alligators swimming around in that subterranean river beneath.

Why bother? Because it keeps them from getting out, man. It keeps 13 them down there and me up here. It was Lennon and McCartney who said that all you need is love, and I would agree with that.

As long as you keep the gators fed. 14

Questions for Close Reading

1. What is the selection's thesis? Locate the sentence(s) in which King states his main idea. If he doesn't state the thesis explicitly, express it in your own words.
2. In what ways do King's references to "Jack the Ripper" and the "Cleveland Torso Murderer" (paragraph 8) support his thesis?
3. What does King mean in paragraph 4 when he says that horror movies are "innately conservative, even reactionary"? What does he mean in paragraph 11 when he calls them "anarchistic, and revolutionary"?
4. In paragraphs 12 and 14, King refers to "alligators" and "gators." What does the alligator represent? What does King mean when he says that all the world needs is love—"[a]s long as you keep the gators fed"?
5. Refer to your dictionary as needed to define the following words used in the selection: *hysterical* (paragraph 1), *reactionary* (4), *voyeur's* (6), *lynching* (6), *penchant* (7), *immortalized* (9), *anarchistic* (11), and *morbidity* (12).

Questions About the Writer's Craft

1. **The pattern.** Does King's causal analysis have an essentially informative, speculative, or persuasive (see pages 383–384) purpose? What makes you think so? How might King's profession as a horror writer have influenced his purpose?
2. **Other patterns.** King *compares* and *contrasts* horror movies to roller coasters (paragraph 3), public lynchings (6), and sick jokes (11–12). How do these comparisons and contrasts reinforce King's thesis about horror movies?
3. **Other patterns.** Throughout the essay, King uses several *examples* involving children. Identify these instances. How do these examples help King develop his thesis?
4. What is unusual about paragraphs 2, 5, and 14? Why do you think King might have designed these paragraphs in this way?

Writing Assignments Using Cause-Effect as a Pattern of Development

1. King argues that horror movies have "a dirty job to do": they feed the hungry monsters in our psyche. Write an essay in which you put King's thesis to the test. Briefly describe the first horror movie you ever saw; then explain its effect on you. Like King, speculate about the nature of your response—your feelings and fantasies—while watching the movie.

2. Many movie critics claim that horror movies nowadays are more violent and bloody than they used to be. Write an essay about *one* other medium of popular culture that you think has changed for the worse. You might consider action movies, televised coverage of sports, men's or women's magazines, radio talk shows, TV shows, and so on. Briefly describe key differences between the medium's past and present forms. Analyze the reasons for the change, and, at the end of the essay, examine the effects of the change. For reflections on another questionable cultural practice, read Joan Didion's "Marrying Absurd" (page 604).

Writing Assignments Combining Patterns of Development

3. King advocates the horror movie precisely because "[i]t deliberately appeals to all that is worst in us." Write an essay in which you rebut King. *Argue* instead that horror movies should be avoided precisely *because* they satisfy monstrous feelings in us. To refute King, provide strong *examples* drawn from your own and other people's experience. Consider supplementing your informal research with material gathered in the library and/or on the Internet.

4. Write an essay in which you *argue*, contrary to King, that humans are by nature essentially benevolent and kind. Brainstorm with others to generate vivid *examples* in support of your thesis.

Writing Assignment Using a Journal Entry as a Starting Point

5. King believes that horror movies involve "a very peculiar sort of fun." Review your pre-reading journal entry, and select *one* other form of popular entertainment that

you think provides its own strange kind of enjoyment. Like King, write an essay in which you analyze the causes of people's enjoyment of this type of entertainment. Brainstorm with others to identify convincing examples. You may, like King, endorse the phenomenon you examine—or you may condemn it. For discussion of other strange sources of people's enjoyment, read Stephen Chapman's "The Prisoner's Dilemma" (page 372) and Joan Didion's "Marrying Absurd" (page 604).

Jacques D'Amboise

When Jacques D'Amboise (1934–) was growing up in a tough, gang-infested New York City neighborhood, his French-Canadian mother wanted to give her children a glimpse into a world of beauty. She enrolled D'Amboise's sister in a ballet class and, hoping to protect her son from the dangers of street life, insisted that her son take the class, too. It was there that D'Amboise discovered his love of dance. While still in his teens, D'Amboise joined the New York City Ballet and became one of the foremost dancers of his day. He appeared in several films, including *Seven Brides for Seven Brothers* (1954) and *Carousel* (1956). In 1976, he founded the National Dance Institute (NDI), which offers dance classes to public school students, most from underprivileged backgrounds. Through NDI, hundreds of children have experienced the joy and discipline of dance. D'Amboise's NDI experience provided the basis of a book he coauthored, *Teaching the Magic of Dance* (1983), and his contributions to the arts led to his being honored at the Kennedy Center in 1995. The following selection originally appeared in *Parade* magazine in 1989.

Pre-Reading Journal Entry

While you were growing up, to what extent were you exposed to the arts: music, dance, drawing, painting, and so forth? Looking back, do you think that this exposure—or lack of exposure—worked to your advantage or to your disadvantage? Use your journal to respond to these questions.

Showing What Is Possible

When I was 7 years old, I was forced to watch my sister's ballet classes. 1
This was to keep me off the street and away from my pals, who ran with gangs like the ones in *West Side Story.* The class was taught by Madame Seda, a Georgian-Armenian[1] who had a school at 181st Street and St. Nicholas Avenue in New York City. As she taught the little girls, I would sit, fidget and diabolically try to disrupt the class by making irritating little noises.

But she was very wise, Madame Seda. She let me get away with it, ignor- 2
ing me until the end of the class, when everybody did the big jumps, a series of leaps in place, called *changements.*

---

[1]A person from the neighboring republics of Georgia and Armenia, formerly of the Soviet Union (editors' note).

At that point, Madame Seda turned and, stabbing a finger at me, said, "All right, little brother, if you've got so much energy, get up and do these jumps. See if you can jump as high as the girls." So I jumped. And loved it. I felt like I was flying. And she said, "Oh, that was wonderful! From now on, if you are quiet during the class, I'll let you join in the *changements.*" 3

After that, I'd sit quietly in the class and wait for the jumps. A few classes later, she said, "You've got to learn how to jump and not make any noise when you come down. You should learn to do the *pliés* [graceful knee bends] that come at the beginning of the class." So I would do *pliés,* then wait respectfully for the end of class to do the jumps. 4

Finally she said, "You jump high, and you are landing beautifully, but you look awful in the air, flaying your arms about. You've got to take the rest of the class and learn how to do beautiful hands and arms." 5

I was hooked. 6

An exceptional teacher got a bored little kid, me, interested in ballet. How? She challenged me to a test, complimented me on my effort and then immediately gave me a new challenge. She set up an environment for the achievement of excellence and cared enough to invite me to be part of it. And, without realizing it fully at the time, I made an important discovery. 7

Dance is the most immediate and accessible of the arts because it involves your own body. When you learn to move your body on a note of music, it's exciting. You have taken control of your body and, by learning to do that, you discover that you can take control of your life. 8

I took classes with Madame Seda for six months, once a week, but at the end of spring, in June 1942, she called over my mother, my sister and me and did an unbelievably modest and generous thing. She said, "You and your sister are very talented. You should go to a better teacher." She sent us to George Balanchine's school—the School of American Ballet. 9

Within a few years, I was performing children's roles. At 15, I became part of a classical ballet company. What an extraordinary thing for a street boy from Washington Heights, with friends in gangs. Half grew up to become policemen and the other half gangsters—and I became a ballet dancer! 10

I had dreamed of being a doctor or an archaeologist or a priest. But by the time I was 17, I was a principal dancer performing major roles in the ballets, and by the time I was 21, I was doing movies, Broadway shows and choreography. I then married a ballerina from New York City Ballet, Carolyn George, and we were (and still are) blessed with two boys and twin daughters. 11

It was a joyful career that lasted four decades. That's a long time to be dancing and, inevitably, a time came when I realized that there were not many years left for me as a performer. I wasn't sure what to do next, but then I thought about how I had become a dancer, and the teachers who had graced my life. Perhaps I could engage young children, especially boys, in the magic of the arts—in dance in particular. Not necessarily to prepare them to 12 be professional performers, but to create an awareness by giving them a chance to experience the arts. So I started National Dance Institute.

That was 13 years ago. Since then, with the help of fellow teachers and staff at NDI, I have taught dance to thousands of inner-city children. And in each class, I rediscover why teaching dance to children is so important.

Each time I can use dance to help a child discover that he can control the way he moves, I am filled with joy. At a class I recently taught at P.S. 59 in Brooklyn, there was one boy who couldn't get from his right foot to his left. He was terrified. Everyone was watching. And what he had to do was so simple: take a step with his left foot on a note of music. All his classmates could do it, but he couldn't.

He kept trying, but he kept doing it wrong until finally he was frozen, unable to move at all. I put my arm around him and said, "Let's do it together. We'll do it in slow motion." We did it. I stepped back and said, "Now do it alone, and fast." With his face twisted in concentration, he slammed his left foot down correctly on the note. He did it!

The whole class applauded. He was so excited. But I think I was even happier, because I knew what had taken place. He had discovered he could take control of his body, and from that he can learn to take control of his life. If I can open the door to show a child that that is possible, it is wonderful.

Dance is the art to express time and space. That is what our universe is about. We can hardly make a sentence without signifying some expression of distance, place or time: "See you later." "Meet you at the corner in five minutes."

Dance is the art that human beings have developed to express that we live, right now, in a world of movement and varying tempos.

Dance, as an art, has to be taught. However, when teaching, it's important to set up an environment where both the student and teacher can discover together. Never teach something you don't love and believe in. But how to set up that environment?

When I have a new group of young students and I'm starting a class, I use Madame Seda's technique. I say, "Can you do this test? I'm going to give all 100 of you exactly 10 seconds to get off your seats and be standing and spread out all over the stage floor. And do it silently. Go!" And I start a countdown. Naturally, they run, yelling and screaming, and somehow arrive with several seconds to spare. I say, "Freeze. You all failed. You made noise, and you got there too soon. I said 'exactly 10 seconds'—not 6 or 8 or 11. Go back to your seats, and we'll do it again. And if you don't get it, we'll go back and do it again until you do. And if, at the end of the hour, you still haven't gotten it, I'm not going to teach you."

They usually get it the second time. Never have I had to do it more than three.

Demand precision, be clear and absolutely truthful. When they respond— and they will—congratulate them on the extraordinary control they have just exhibited. Why is that important? Because it's the beginning of knowing yourself, knowing that you can manage yourself if you want. And it's the beginning of dance. Once the children see that we are having a class of precision, order and respect, they are relieved, and we have a great class.

I've taught dance to Russian children, Australian children, Indian children, Chinese children, fat children, skinny children, handicapped children, groups of Australian triathletes, New York City police, senior citizens and 3-year-olds. The technique is the same everywhere, although there are cultural differences. 23

For example, when I was in China, I would say to the children, "I want everybody to come close and watch what I am going to do." But in China they have had to deal with following a teacher when there are masses of them. And they discovered that the way to see what the teacher does is not to move close but to move away. So 100 people moved back to watch the one—me. 24

I realized they were right. How did they learn that? Thousands of years of masses of people having to follow one teacher. 25

There are cultural differences and there are differences among people. In any group of dancers, there are some who are ready and excel more than others. There are many reasons—genetic, environment, the teachers they had. People blossom at different times. 26

But whatever the differences, someone admiring you, encouraging you works so much better than the reverse. "You can do it, you are wonderful," works so much better than, "You're no good, the others are better than you, you've got to try harder." That never works. 27

I don't think there are any untalented children. But I think there are those whose talents never get the chance to flower. Perhaps they were never encouraged. Perhaps no one took the time to find out how to teach them. That is a tragedy. 28

However, the single most terrible thing we are doing to our children, I believe, is polluting them. I don't mean just with smog and crack, but by not teaching them the civilizing things we have taken millions of years to develop. But you cannot have a dance class without having good manners, without having respect. Dance can teach those things. 29

I think of each person as a trunk that's up in the attic. What are you going to put in the trunk? Are you going to put in machine guns, loud noises, foul language, dirty books and ignorance? Because if you do, that's what is going to be left after you, that's what your children are going to have, and that will determine the world of the future. Or are you going to fill that trunk with music, dance, poetry, literature, good manners and loving friends? 30

I say, fill your trunk with the best that is available to you from the wealth of human culture. Those things will nourish you and your children. You can clean up your own environment and pass it on to the next generation. That's why I teach dance. 31

Questions for Close Reading

1. What is the selection's thesis? Locate the sentence(s) in which D'Amboise states his main idea. If he doesn't state the thesis explicitly, express it in your own words.
2. In paragraph 2, D'Amboise says that Madame Seda "was very wise." In what ways was she wise?
3. D'Amboise believes that dance has to be taught in a particular kind of environment. What, according to D'Amboise, are the most important qualities of that environment?
4. What does D'Amboise mean in paragraph 29 when he says that we pollute our children? What does D'Amboise consider the possible consequences of such pollution?
5. Refer to your dictionary as needed to define the following words used in the selection: *diabolically* (paragraph 1), *flaying* (5), *accessible* (8), *choreography* (11), *inevitably* (12), and *triathletes* (23).

Questions About the Writer's Craft

1. **The pattern.** Writers often organize cause-effect pieces using either a chronological or an emphatic sequence—or perhaps a combination of the two. Identify the organizational pattern that D'Amboise uses.
2. **Other patterns.** D'Amboise begins his essay with a *narrative* that tells the story of his first experience with Madame Seda. What is the purpose of this opening narrative? How does it prepare readers for what follows?
3. Reread paragraphs 20–21. The two short sentences in paragraph 21 could have concluded paragraph 20. Why do you think D'Amboise placed these two sentences in a separate paragraph?
4. In the last two paragraphs, D'Amboise uses an *analogy* (a comparison between two objects or people that seem to have little in common). Identify the analogy, and explain its relevance to the essay's central idea.

Writing Assignments Using Cause-Effect as a Pattern of Development

1. According to D'Amboise, a good teacher is one who provides a classroom of precision and order. Without structure and clear expectations, D'Amboise suggests, children will not flourish in the classroom. Do you think the same might be said of children in the home? Write a paper analyzing the effect on children of *one* of the following: a parenting style that imposes a reasonable number of boundaries, one that imposes too many limits, one that imposes too few restrictions. When writing, draw upon your own experiences and observations as well as those of friends, classmates, and family members. The following essays provide insight into different parenting styles: E. B. White's "Once More to the Lake" (page 107), Judith Ortiz Cofer's "A Partial Remembrance of a Puerto Rican Childhood" (page 114), Audre Lorde's "The Fourth of July" (page 137), and Joseph H. Suina's "And Then I Went to School" (page 354).
2. D'Amboise asserts that "the single most terrible thing we are doing to our children . . . is polluting them . . . by not teaching them the civilizing things we have

taken millions of years to develop." Among the pollutants he lists are drugs, violence, and pornography. Select one of these negative influences (or another you consider important), and write an essay analyzing how it pollutes children. You might show how this factor affects children's behavior, self-concept, and attitudes toward others. Before preparing your paper, interview classmates, friends, and family members to learn in what ways they think this factor influences children.

Writing Assignments Combining Patterns of Development

3. D'Amboise attributes his love of dance to Madame Seda, whom he calls an "exceptional teacher." Very likely, you too at some point in your life experienced the influence of a special adult—perhaps a teacher, coach, parent, grandparent, neighbor, or religious instructor. Using one extended *example* or a series of shorter examples, write an essay showing how your interaction with this person taught you important lessons that had a larger *impact* on your life. Before you begin writing, consider reading Maya Angelou's "Sister Flowers" (page 100), a loving portrait of a childhood mentor.

4. D'Amboise's opening narrative *illustrates* how he became interested in dance. Consider the career path you have chosen or are thinking about choosing. What experiences pointed you in that direction? Write an essay in which you explain why you are interested in that particular career. *Recount* at least two experiences that helped you feel this work would be interesting and rewarding. Use vivid dialogue to dramatize the intensity of the experiences.

Writing Assignment Using a Journal Entry as a Starting Point

5. Write an essay arguing that it is *or* is not important for schools to expose children to the arts. The material you generated in your pre-reading journal entry will help you develop your position. You'll probably also find it helpful to talk to others about their experiences with the arts. Since the issue of arts-education funding is currently being debated, you should have little trouble researching this topic in the library and/or on the Internet. No matter which position you take, be sure to acknowledge opposing viewpoints, such as the one Clifford Stoll parodies in "Cyberschool" (page 308).

Alice Walker

The eighth child of Georgia sharecroppers, Alice Walker (1944–) has built a reputation as a sensitive chronicler of the Black experience in America. After studying at Spelman College in Atlanta, Walker graduated from Sarah Lawrence College in New York. Soon after that, she worked in the civil rights movement helping to register Black voters and teaching in Mississippi's Head Start program. The recipient of numerous writing fellowships and the founder of her own publishing company, Walker has written extensively: a biography, *Langston Hughes, American Poet* (1973); poetry, *Revolutionary Petunias and Other Poems* (1973); short stories, collected in *In Love & Trouble* (1973) and *You Can't Keep a Good Woman Down* (1981); essays, gathered in *Living by the Word* (1988) and *Alice Walker Banned* (1996); children's fiction, *To Hell With Dying* (1991); and novels for adults, including *Meridian* (1976), *The Color Purple* (1982), *The Temple of My Familiar* (1989), *By the Light of My Father's Smile* (1998), and *The Way Forward Is With a Broken Heart* (2000). *The Color Purple* won both the Pulitzer Prize and the American Book Award and was made into a feature film. The following selection comes from Walker's 1983 collection of essays, *In Search of Our Mothers' Gardens*.

Pre-Reading Journal Entry

It's easy to become discouraged when we're told we can't have—or be—something we want. That's when we most need the support of others. Who are the people in your life who have helped you focus not on your limitations but on your strengths? What specifically did each person do to encourage you? Use your journal to respond to these questions.

Beauty: When the Other Dancer Is the Self

It is a bright summer day in 1947. My father, a fat, funny man with beautiful eyes and a subversive wit, is trying to decide which of his eight children he will take with him to the county fair. My mother, of course, will not go. She is knocked out from getting most of us ready: I hold my neck stiff against the pressure of her knuckles as she hastily completes the braiding and then beribboning of my hair.

My father is the driver for the rich old white lady up the road. Her name is Miss Mey. She owns all the land for miles around, as well as the house

408

in which we live. All I remember about her is that she once offered to pay my mother thirty-five cents for cleaning her house, raking up piles of her magnolia leaves, and washing her family's clothes, and that my mother—she of no money, eight children, and a chronic earache—refused it. But I do not think of this in 1947. I am two and a half years old. I want to go everywhere my daddy goes. I am excited at the prospect of riding in a car. Someone has told me fairs are fun. That there is room in the car for only three of us doesn't faze me at all. Whirling happily in my starchy frock, showing off my biscuit-polished patent-leather shoes and lavender socks, tossing my head in a way that makes my ribbons bounce, I stand, hands on hips, before my father. "Take me, Daddy," I say with assurance; "I'm the prettiest!"

Later, it does not surprise me to find myself in Miss Mey's shiny black   3
car, sharing the back seat with the other lucky ones. Does not surprise me that I thoroughly enjoy the fair. At home that night I tell the unlucky ones all I can remember about the merry-go-round, the man who eats live chickens, and the teddy bears, until they say: that's enough baby Alice. Shut up now, and go to sleep.

It is Easter Sunday, 1950. I am dressed in a green, flocked, scalloped-   4
hem dress (handmade by my adoring sister, Ruth) that has its own smooth satin petticoat and tiny hot-pink roses tucked into each scallop. My shoes, new T-strap patent leather, again highly biscuit-polished. I am six years old and have learned one of the longest Easter speeches to be heard that day, totally unlike the speech I said when I was two: "Easter lilies / pure and white / blossom in / the morning light." When I rise to give my speech I do so on a great wave of love and pride and expectation. People in the church stop rustling their new crinolines. They seem to hold their breath. I can tell they admire my dress, but it is my spirit, bordering on sassiness (womanishness), they secretly applaud.

"That girl's a little *mess*," they whisper to each other, pleased.   5

Naturally I say my speech without stammer or pause, unlike those who   6
stutter, stammer, or, worst of all, forget. This is before the word "beautiful" exists in people's vocabulary, but "Oh, isn't she the *cutest* thing?" frequently floats my way. "And got so much sense!" they gratefully add . . . for which thoughtful addition I thank them to this day.

It was great fun being cute. But then, one day, it ended.   7

I am eight years old and a tomboy. I have a cowboy hat, cowboy boots,   8
checkered shirt and pants, all red. My playmates are my brothers, two and four years older than I. Their colors are black and green, the only difference in the way we are dressed. On Saturday nights we all go to the picture show, even my mother; Westerns are her favorite kind of movie. Back home, "on the ranch," we pretend we are Tom Mix, Hopalong Cassidy, Lash LaRue (we've even named one of our dogs Lash LaRue); we chase each other for hours rustling cattle, being outlaws, delivering damsels from distress. Then

my parents decide to buy my brothers guns. These are not "real" guns. They shoot "BBs," copper pellets my brothers say will kill birds. Because I am a girl, I do not get a gun. Instantly I am relegated to the position of Indian. Now there appears a great distance between us. They shoot and shoot at everything with their new guns. I try to keep up with my bow and arrows.

One day while I am standing on top of our makeshift "garage"—pieces of tin nailed across some poles—holding my bow and arrow and looking out toward the fields, I feel an incredible blow in my right eye. I look down just in time to see my brother lower his gun.

Both brothers rush to my side. My eye stings, and I cover it with my hand. "If you tell," they say, "we will get a whipping. You don't want that to happen, do you?" I do not. "Here is a piece of wire," says the older brother, picking it up from the roof; "say you stepped on one end of it and the other flew up and hit you." The pain is beginning to start. "Yes," I say. "Yes, I will say that is what happened." If I do not say this is what happened, I know my brothers will find ways to make me wish I had. But now I will say anything that gets me to my mother.

Confronted by our parents we stick to the lie agreed upon. They place me on a bench on the porch and I close my left eye while they examine the right. There is a tree growing from underneath the porch that climbs past the railing to the roof. It is the last thing my right eye sees. I watch as its trunk, its branches, and then its leaves are blotted out by the rising blood.

I am in shock. First there is intense fever, which my father tries to break using lily leaves bound around my head. Then there are chills: my mother tries to get me to eat soup. Eventually, I do not know how, my parents learn what has happened. A week after the "accident" they take me to see a doctor. "Why did you wait so long to come?" he asks, looking into my eye and shaking his head. "Eyes are sympathetic," he says. "If one is blind, the other will likely become blind too."

This comment of the doctor's terrifies me. But it is really how I look that bothers me most. Where the BB pellet struck there is a glob of whitish scar tissue, a hideous cataract, on my eye. Now when I stare at people—a favorite pastime, up to now—they will stare back. Not at the "cute" little girl, but at her scar. For six years I do not stare at anyone, because I do not raise my head.

Years later, in the throes of a mid-life crisis, I ask my mother and sister whether I changed after the "accident." "No," they say, puzzled. "What do you mean?"

What do I mean?

I am eight, and, for the first time, doing poorly in school, where I have been something of a whiz since I was four. We have just moved to the place where the "accident" occurred. We do not know any of the people around us because this is a different county. The only time I see the friends I knew is when we go back to our old church. The new school is the former state penitentiary. It is a large stone building, cold and drafty, crammed to over-flowing with boisterous, ill-disciplined children. On the third floor there is a huge circular imprint of some partition that has been torn out.

"What used to be here?" I ask a sullen girl next to me on our way past   17
it to lunch.

"The electric chair," says she.   18

At night I have nightmares about the electric chair; and about all the   19
people reputedly "fried" in it. I am afraid of the school, where all the stu-dents seem to be budding criminals.

"What's the matter with your eye?" they ask, critically.   20

When I don't answer (I cannot decide whether it was an "accident" or   21
not), they shove me, insist on a fight.

My brother, the one who created the story about the wire, comes to my   22
rescue. But then brags so much about "protecting" me, I become sick.

After months of torture at the school, my parents decide to send me   23
back to our old community, to my old school. I live with my grandparents and the teacher they board. But there is no room for Phoebe, my cat. By the time my grandparents decide there *is* room, and I ask for my cat, she cannot be found. Miss Yarborough, the boarding teacher, takes me under her wing, and begins to teach me to play the piano. But soon she marries an African—a "prince," she says—and is whisked away to his continent.

At my old school there is at least one teacher who loves me. She is the   24
teacher who "knew me before I was born" and bought my first baby clothes. It is she who makes life bearable. It is her presence that finally helps me turn on the one child at the school who continually calls me "one-eyed bitch." One day I simply grab him by his coat and beat him until I am satisfied. It is my teacher who tells me my mother is ill.

My mother is lying in bed in the middle of the day, something I have   25
never seen. She is in too much pain to speak. She has an abscess in her ear. I stand looking down on her, knowing that if she dies, I cannot live. She is being treated with warm oils and hot bricks held against her cheeks. Finally a doctor comes. But I must go back to my grandparents' house. The weeks pass but I am hardly aware of it. All I know is that my mother might die, my father is not so jolly, my brothers still have their guns, and I am the one sent away from home.

"You did not change," they say.   26

Did I imagine the anguish of never looking up?   27

I am twelve. When relatives come to visit I hide in my room. My cousin   28
Brenda, just my age, whose father works in the post office and whose moth-er is a nurse, comes to find me. "Hello," she says. And then she asks, looking

at my recent school picture, which I did not want taken, and on which the "glob," as I think of it, is clearly visible, "You still can't see out of that eye?"

"No," I say, and flop back on the bed over my book.

That night, as I do almost every night, I abuse my eye. I rant and rave at it, in front of the mirror. I plead with it to clear up before morning. I tell it I hate and despise it. I do not pray for sight. I pray for beauty.

"You did not change," they say.

I am fourteen and baby-sitting for my brother Bill, who lives in Boston. He is my favorite brother and there is a strong bond between us. Understanding my feelings of shame and ugliness he and his wife take me to a local hospital, where the "glob" is removed by a doctor named O. Henry. There is still a small bluish crater where the scar tissue was, but the ugly white stuff is gone. Almost immediately I become a different person from the girl who does not raise her head. Or so I think. Now that I've raised my head I win the boyfriend of my dreams. Now that I've raised my head I have plenty of friends. Now that I've raised my head classwork comes from my lips as faultlessly as Easter speeches did, and I leave high school as valedictorian, most popular student, and *queen,* hardly believing my luck. Ironically, the girl who was voted most beautiful in our class (and was) was later shot twice through the chest by a male companion, using a "real" gun, while she was pregnant. But that's another story in itself. Or is it?

"You did not change," they say.

It is now thirty years since the "accident." A beautiful journalist comes to visit and to interview me. She is going to write a cover story for her magazine that focuses on my latest book. "Decide how you want to look on the cover," she says. "Glamorous, or whatever."

Never mind "glamorous," it is the "whatever" that I hear. Suddenly all I can think of is whether I will get enough sleep the night before the photography session: if I don't, my eye will be tired and wander, as blind eyes will.

At night in bed with my lover I think up reasons why I should not appear on the cover of a magazine. "My meanest critics will say I've sold out," I say. "My family will now realize I write scandalous books."

"But what's the real reason you don't want to do this?" he asks.

"Because in all probability," I say in a rush, "my eye won't be straight."

"It will be straight enough," he says. Then, "Besides, I thought you'd made your peace with that."

And I suddenly remember that I have.

I remember:

I am talking to my brother Jimmy, asking if he remembers anything unusual about the day I was shot. He does not know I consider that day the last time my father, with his sweet home remedy of cool lily leaves, chose me, and that I suffered and raged inside because of this. "Well," he says, "all I remember is standing by the side of the highway with Daddy, trying to flag

down a car. A white man stopped, but when Daddy said he needed somebody to take his little girl to the doctor, he drove off."

I remember: 43

I am in the desert for the first time. I fall totally in love with it. I am so   44
overwhelmed by its beauty, I confront for the first time, consciously, the
meaning of the doctor's words years ago: "Eyes are sympathetic. If one is
blind, the other will likely become blind too." I realize I have dashed about
the world madly, looking at this, looking at that, storing up images against
the fading of the light. *But I might have missed seeing the desert!* The shock
of that possibility—and gratitude for over twenty-five years of sight—sends
me literally to my knees. Poem after poem comes—which is perhaps how
poets pray.

On Sight   45

> *I am so thankful I have seen*
> *The Desert*
> *And the creatures in the desert*
> *And the desert Itself.*
>
> *The desert has its own moon*
> *Which I have seen*
> *With my own eye.*
> *There is no flag on it.*
>
> *Trees of the desert have arms*
> *All of which are always up*
> *That is because the moon is up*
> *The sun is up*
> *Also the sky*
> *The stars*
> *Clouds*
> *None with flags.*
>
> *If there were flags, I doubt*
> *the trees would point.*
> *Would you?*

But mostly, I remember this: 46

I am twenty-seven, and my baby daughter is almost three. Since her   47
birth I have worried about her discovery that her mother's eyes are different
from other people's. Will she be embarrassed? I think. What will she say?
Every day she watches a television program called "Big Blue Marble." It
begins with a picture of the earth as it appears from the moon. It is bluish, a
little battered-looking, but full of light, with whitish clouds swirling around

it. Every time I see it I weep with love, as if it is a picture of Grandma's house. One day when I am putting Rebecca down for her nap, she suddenly focuses on my eye. Something inside me cringes, gets ready to try to protect myself. All children are cruel about physical differences, I know from experience, and that they don't always mean to be is another matter. I assume Rebecca will be the same.

But no-o-o-o. She studies my face intently as we stand, her inside and me outside the crib. She even holds my face maternally between her dimpled little hands. Then, looking every bit as serious and lawyerlike as her father, she says, as if it may just possibly have slipped my attention: "Mommy, there's a *world* in your eye." (As in, "Don't be alarmed, or do anything crazy.") And then, gently, but with great interest: "Mommy, where did you *get* that world in your eye?"

For the most part, the pain left then. (So what, if my brothers grew up to buy even more powerful pellet guns for their sons and to carry real guns themselves. So what, if a young "Morehouse man" once nearly fell off the steps of Trevor Arnett Library because he thought my eyes were blue.) Crying and laughing I ran to the bathroom, while Rebecca mumbled and sang herself off to sleep. Yes indeed, I realized, looking into the mirror. There *was* a world in my eye. And I saw that it was possible to love it: that in fact, for all it had taught me of shame and anger and inner vision, I *did* love it. Even to see it drifting out of orbit in boredom, or rolling up out of fatigue, not to mention floating back at attention in excitement (bearing witness, a friend has called it), deeply suitable to my personality, and even characteristic of me.

That night I dream I am dancing to Stevie Wonder's song "Always" (the name of the song is really "As," but I hear it as "Always"). As I dance, whirling and joyous, happier than I've ever been in my life, another bright-faced dancer joins me. We dance and kiss each other and hold each other through the night. The other dancer has obviously come through all right, as I have done. She is beautiful, whole and free. And she is also me.

Questions for Close Reading

1. What is the selection's thesis? Locate the sentence(s) in which Walker states her main idea. If she doesn't state the thesis explicitly, express it in your own words.
2. How does Walker's injury affect her ability to express herself and relate to others?
3. What is the connection between the loss of young Alice's cat and her teacher's marriage (paragraph 23)?
4. How do you interpret the essay's title—"Beauty: When the Other Dancer Is the Self"? How does the title reinforce Walker's thesis?
5. Refer to your dictionary as needed to define the following words used in the selection: *subversive* (paragraph 1), *chronic* (2), *flocked* (4), *crinolines* (4), *cataract* (13), and *abscess* (25).

Questions About the Writer's Craft

1. **The pattern.** Walker's essay is structured around a causal chain that shows the interaction between the external and the internal. Explain how Walker develops this chain throughout the essay.
2. **Other patterns.** Although Walker *narrates* incidents occurring from infancy to midlife, she writes in the present tense. Why do you think she does this?
3. How does Walker signal the ages at which she experiences a crisis or some other major event? What technique does she use?
4. The refrain "You did not change" occurs in differing contexts throughout Walker's essay. What is the effect of this repetition?

Writing Assignments Using Cause-Effect as a Pattern of Development

1. An event initially viewed as handicapping can prove, as Walker shows, to be a blessing. Write a paper showing the effect on your life of an experience that at first seemed negative but turned out for the best.
2. Walker expects her daughter to react with revulsion to her eye injury. To her surprise, her daughter's reaction is tender and gentle. Think of a time you expected someone to treat you with kindness, but instead you were treated harshly, or, conversely, you expected severity but were met with generosity. In an essay, trace the causes of your faulty expectation as well as the possible reasons for the other person's unexpected behavior. Draw some conclusions about human nature.

Writing Assignments Combining Patterns of Development

3. Walker writes of an experience in which joyful, exuberant play turned—in an instant—to terror. Write an essay in which you *narrate* a time in your own or in someone else's life when there was a sudden reversal of events—a positive experience that became negative or vice versa. Use vivid images, varied sentence structure, and dialogue to capture what happened. Did the event leave a lasting impression? If so, end by writing briefly about this *effect*. You might begin your exploration by reading Adam Mayblum's "The Price We Pay" (page 159), an account about an ordinary day gone terribly awry.
4. Walker mentions two elementary school teachers who responded to her in a loving, supportive way. Write a letter to beginning grade school teachers outlining the *steps* they should (and should not) take to make their students' school experience a positive one. Be sure to provide vivid *examples* to illustrate your points. For additional views on what truly matters in education, consider reading Clifford Stoll's "Cyberschool" (page 308) and James Barszcz's "Can You Be Educated From a Distance?" (page 522).

Writing Assignment Using a Journal Entry as a Starting Point

5. Review your pre-reading journal entry and select *one* person who encouraged you to believe in yourself. Then write an essay showing how this individual helped you

shift your focus from what you couldn't do to what you could do. Start by describing briefly how you thought and felt before this person influenced you. Then use several dramatic examples to show how this person helped you develop a more optimistic and affirming mind-set. You might first consider reading Maya Angelou's "Sister Flowers" (page 100), a warm, nostalgic portrait of a childhood mentor.

John M. Darley
Bibb Latané

Harvard graduate John M. Darley (1938–) is professor of psychology at Princeton University, where he studies the principles of moral judgment in children and adults. Bibb Latané (1937–), the former director of the Behavioral Sciences Laboratory at Ohio State University, is professor of psychology at Florida Atlantic University. A doctoral graduate of the University of Minnesota, Latané is interested in social impact and group influence theory. Darley and Latané are coauthors of *The Unresponsive Bystander: Why Doesn't He Help* (1970) and *Help in a Crisis: Bystander Response to an Emergency* (1976). Based on their research into the origins of noninvolvement, "Why People Don't Help in a Crisis? (1968) was awarded an essay prize from the American Association for the Advancement of Science.

Pre-Reading Journal Entry

Faced with a challenging or difficult situation, people sometimes choose *not* to get involved—and then later regret this decision. Such situations might include, for example, helping an injured stranger, standing up for someone being bullied, and letting in a stray animal on a cold day. In your journal, write about one or more times when you faced a difficult situation and failed to respond in a way that you now believe you should have.

Why People Don't Help in a Crisis

Kitty Genovese is set upon by a maniac as she returns home from work at 3 A.M. Thirty-eight of her neighbors in Kew Gardens, N.Y., come to their windows when she cries out in terror; not one comes to her assistance, even though her assailant takes half an hour to murder her. No one so much as calls the police. She dies. 1

Andrew Mormille is stabbed in the head and neck as he rides in a New York City subway train. Eleven other riders flee to another car as the 17-year-old boy bleeds to death; not one comes to his assistance, even though his attackers have left the car. He dies. 2

Eleanor Bradley trips and breaks her leg while shopping on New York City's Fifth Avenue. Dazed and in shock, she calls for help, but the hurrying stream of people simply parts and flows past. Finally, after 40 minutes, a taxi driver stops and helps her to a doctor. 3

How can so many people watch another human being in distress and do nothing? Why don't they help?

Since we started research on bystander responses to emergencies, we have heard many explanations for the lack of intervention in such cases. "The megalopolis in which we live makes closeness difficult and leads to the alienation of the individual from the group," says the psychoanalyst. "This sort of disaster," says the sociologist, "shakes the sense of safety and sureness of the individuals involved and causes psychological withdrawal." "Apathy," says others. "Indifference."

All of these analyses share one characteristic: they set the indifferent witness apart from the rest of us. Certainly not one of us who reads about these incidents in horror is apathetic, alienated or depersonalized. Certainly these terrifying cases have no personal implications for us. We needn't feel guilty, or re-examine ourselves, or anything like that. Or should we?

If we look closely at the behavior of witnesses to these incidents, the people involved begin to seem less inhuman and a lot more like the rest of us. They were not indifferent. The 38 witnesses of Kitty Genovese's murder, for example, did not merely look at the scene once and then ignore it. They continued to stare out of their windows, caught, fascinated, distressed, unwilling to act but unable to turn away.

Why, then, didn't they act?

There are three things the bystander must do if he is to intervene in an emergency: *notice* that something is happening; *interpret* that event as an emergency; and decide that he has *personal responsibility* for intervention. As we shall show, the presence of other bystanders may at each stage inhibit his action.

The Unseeing Eye

Suppose that a man has a heart attack. He clutches his chest, staggers to the nearest building and slumps sitting to the sidewalk. Will a passerby come to his assistance? First, the bystander has to notice that something is happening. He must tear himself away from his private thoughts and pay attention. But Americans consider it bad manners to look closely at other people in public. We are taught to respect the privacy of others, and when among strangers we close our ears and avoid staring. In a crowd, then, each person is less likely to notice a potential emergency than when alone.

Experimental evidence corroborates this. We asked college students to an interview about their reactions to urban living. As the students waited to see the interviewer, either by themselves or with two other students, they filled out a questionnaire. Solitary students often glanced idly about while filling out their questionnaires: those in groups kept their eyes on their own papers.

As part of the study, we staged an emergency: smoke was released into the waiting room through a vent. Two thirds of the subjects who were alone noticed the smoke immediately, but only 25 percent of those waiting in groups saw it as quickly. Although eventually all the subjects did become aware of the smoke—when the atmosphere grew so smoky as to make them cough and rub their eyes—this study indicates that the more people present, the slower an individual may be to perceive an emergency and the more likely he is not to see it at all.

Seeing Is Not Necessarily Believing

Once an event is noticed, an onlooker must decide if it is truly an emergency. Emergencies are not always clearly labeled as such; "smoke" pouring into a waiting room may be caused by fire, or it may merely indicate a leak in a steam pipe. Screams in the street may signal an assault or a family quarrel. A man lying in a doorway may be having a coronary—or he may simply be sleeping off a drunk.   13

A person trying to interpret a situation often looks at those around him to see how he should react. If everyone else is calm and indifferent, he will tend to remain so; if everyone else is reacting strongly, he is likely to become aroused. This tendency is not merely slavish conformity; ordinarily we derive much valuable information about new situations from how others around us behave. It's a rare traveler who, in picking a roadside restaurant, chooses to stop at one where no other cars appear in the parking lot.   14

But occasionally the reactions of others provide false information. The studied nonchalance of patients in a dentist's waiting room is a poor indication of their inner anxiety. It is considered embarrassing to "lose your cool" in public. In a potentially acute situation, then, everyone present will appear more unconcerned that he is in fact. A crowd can thus force inaction on its members by implying, through its passivity, that an event is not an emergency. Any individual in such a crowd fears that he may appear a fool if he behaves as though it were.   15

To determine how the presence of other people affects a person's interpretation of an emergency, Latané and Judith Rodin set up another experiment. Subjects were paid $2 to participate in a survey of game and puzzle preferences conducted at Columbia University by the Consumer Testing Bureau. An attractive young market researcher met them at the door and took them to the testing room, where they were given questionnaires to fill out. Before leaving, she told them that she would be working next door in her office, which was separated from the room by a folding room-divider. She then entered her office, where she shuffled papers, opened drawers and made enough noise to remind the subjects of her presence. After four minutes she turned on a high-fidelity tape recorder.   16

On it, the subjects heard the researcher climb up on a chair, perhaps to reach for a stack of papers on the bookcase. They heard a loud crash and a scream as the chair collapsed and she fell, and they heard her moan, "Oh, my   17

foot . . . I . . . I . . . can't move it Oh, I . . . can't get this . . . thing off me."
Her cries gradually got more subdued and controlled.

Twenty-six people were alone in the waiting room when the "accident"   1
occurred. Seventy percent of them offered to help the victim. Many pushed
back the divider to offer their assistance; others called out to offer their help.

Among those waiting in pairs, only 20 percent—8 out of 40—offered to   1
help. The other 32 remained unresponsive. In defining the situation as a
nonemergency, they explained to themselves why the other member of the
pair did not leave the room; they also removed any reason for action themselves. Whatever had happened, it was believed to be not serious. "A mild
sprain," some said. "I didn't want to embarrass her." In a "real" emergency,
they assured us, they would be among the first to help.

The Lonely Crowd

Even if a person defines an event as an emergency, the presence of other   2
bystanders may still make him less likely to intervene. He feels that his
responsibility is diffused and diluted. Thus, if your car breaks down on a busy
highway, hundreds of drivers whiz by without anyone's stopping to help—
but if you are stuck on a nearly deserted country road, whoever passes you
first is likely to stop.

To test this diffusion-of-responsibility theory, we simulated an emer-   2
gency in which people overheard a victim calling for help. Some thought
they were the only person to hear the cries; the rest believed that others
heard them, too. As with the witnesses to Kitty Genovese's murder, the subjects could not *see* one another or know what others were doing. The kind
of direct group inhibition found in the other two studies could not operate.

For the simulation, we recruited 72 students at New York University to   2
participate in what was referred to as a "group discussion" of personal problems in an urban university. Each student was put in an individual room
equipped with a set of headphones and a microphone. It was explained that
this precaution had been taken because participants might feel embarrassed
about discussing their problems publicly. Also, the experimenter said that he
would not listen to the initial discussion, but would only ask for reactions
later. Each person was to talk in turn.

The first to talk reported that he found it difficult to adjust to New York   2
and his studies. Then, hesitantly and with obvious embarrassment, he mentioned that he was prone to nervous seizures when he was under stress.
Other students then talked about their own problems in turn. The number
of people in the "discussion" varied. But whatever the apparent size of the
group—two, three or six people—only the subject was actually present; the
others, as well as the instructions and the speeches of the victim-to-be, were
present only on a pre-recorded tape.

When it was the first person's turn to talk again, he launched into the   24
following performance, becoming louder and having increasing speech difficulties: "I can see a lot of er of er how other people's problems are similar to
mine because er I mean er they're not er e-easy to handle sometimes and er
I er um I think I I need er if if could er er somebody er er er give me give
me a little er give me a little help here because er I er *uh* I've got a a one of
the er seiz-er er things coming *on* and and er uh uh (choking sounds) . . ."

Eighty-five percent of the people who believed themselves to be alone   25
with the victim came out of their room to help. Sixty-two percent of the
people who believed there was *one* other bystander did so. Of those who
believed there were four other bystanders, only 31 percent reported the fit.
The responsibility-diluting effect of other people was so strong that single
individuals were more than twice as likely to report the emergency as those
who thought other people also knew about it.

The Lesson Learned

People who failed to report the emergency showed few signs of the apa-   26
thy and indifference thought to characterize "unresponsive bystanders."
When the experimenter entered the room to end the situation, the subject
often asked if the victim was "all right." Many of them showed physical signs
of nervousness; they often had trembling hands and sweating palms. If anything, they seemed more emotionally aroused than did those who reported
the emergency. Their emotional behavior was a sign of their continuing conflict concerning whether to respond or not.

Thus, the stereotype of the unconcerned, depersonalized *homo urbanus,*   27
blandly watching the misfortunes of others, proves inaccurate. Instead, we
find that a bystander to an emergency is an anguished individual in genuine
doubt, wanting to do the right thing but compelled to make complex decisions under pressure of stress and fear. His reactions are shaped by the
actions of others—all too frequently by their inaction.

And we are that bystander. Caught up by the apparent indifference of   28
others, we may pass by an emergency without helping or even realizing that
help is needed. Once we are aware of the influence of those around us, however, we can resist it. We can choose to see distress and step forward to
relieve it.

Questions for Close Reading

1. What is the selection's thesis? Locate the sentence(s) in which Darley and Latané
   state their main idea. If they don't state the thesis explicitly, express it in your own
   words.
2. According to the authors, what three factors prevent people in a crowd from helping victims during an emergency?

3. Why did Darley and Latané isolate the subjects in separate rooms during the staged emergency described in paragraphs 21–26?

4. What kind of person, according to the authors, would tend to ignore or bypass a person experiencing a problem? What might encourage this person to act more responsibly?

5. Refer to your dictionary as needed to define the following words used in the selection: *megalopolis* (paragraph 5), *apathy* (5), *indifference* (5), *alienated* (6), *depersonalized* (6), *inhibit* (9), *corroborates* (11), *coronary* (13), *slavish* (14), *nonchalance* (15), *diffused* (20), and *blandly* (27).

Questions About the Writer's Craft

1. **The pattern.** What techniques do Darley and Latané use to help readers focus on the causes of people's inaction during an emergency?

2. **Other patterns.** The three brief *narratives* that open the essay depict events that happened well before Darley and Latané wrote their essay. Why might the authors have chosen to recount these events in the present tense rather than in the past tense?

3. Locate places where Darley and Latané describe the experiments investigating bystander behavior. How do the authors show readers the steps—and the implications—of each experiment?

4. What purpose do you think the authors had in mind when writing the selection? How do you know?

Writing Assignments Using Cause-Effect as a Pattern of Development

1. Write an essay showing the "responsibility-diluting effect" that can occur when several people witness a critical event. Brainstorm with others to gather examples of this effect; then select two or three dramatic situations as the basis of your essay. Be sure to acknowledge other factors that may have played a role in inhibiting people's ability to act responsibly.

2. Although Darley and Latané focus on times when individuals fail to act responsibly, people often respond with moral heroism during difficult situations. Brainstorm with others to identify occasions in which people have taken the initiative to avert a crisis. Focusing on two or three compelling instances, write an essay in which you analyze the possible motives for people's responsible behavior. Also show how their actions affected the other individuals involved. To gain additional insight into the psychology of heroism, read Adam Mayblum's "The Price We Pay" (page 159).

Writing Assignments Combining Patterns of Development

3. How could families or schools or communities or religious organizations encourage children to act rather than withdraw when confronted by someone in difficulty? Focusing on *one* of these situations, talk with friends, classmates, and family

members to gather their experiences and recommendations. Then consider doing some research on this subject in the library and/or on the Internet. Select the most provocative ideas, and write an essay explaining the *steps* that this particular institution could take to help develop children's sense of responsibility to others. Develop your points with specific *examples* of what has been done and what could be done.

4. Darley and Latané cite social critics who believe that the United States has become a nation of strangers, alienated and withdrawn from one another. Write an essay *refuting* this claim by presenting several vivid *instances* of small acts of everyday kindness—examples in which people demonstrate their sense of connectedness to those around them. Generate examples by drawing on your own and other people's experiences. Before writing, you might want to read Maya Angelou's "Sister Flowers" (page 100) for a portrait of an individual who shows—in small, quiet ways—that she cares for others.

Writing Assignment Using a Journal Entry as a Starting Point

5. Though the authors don't state so directly, they suggest that unresponsive bystanders often may regret their inaction later on. Reviewing the material you generated in your journal entry, select the most compelling or profound of the incidents you described. Then write an essay in which you narrate *one* situation in which you chose not to get involved but now realize you should have. Be sure to provide dialogue and vivid descriptive details to bring the incident to life for your readers. Conclude your essay with a brief reflection on what you wish you had done and how your failure to respond properly has affected you. You might also begin by reading Gordon Parks's "Flavio's Home" (page 84), which conveys the author's impulse to get involved when he witnesses the desperate circumstances of another.

Buzz Bissinger

H. G. "Buzz" Bissinger (1954–) worked as a newspaper reporter for fifteen years before moving his family from Philadelphia to Odessa, Texas, in order to write a book about high school football. In 1990 he published the best-selling *Friday Night Lights,* which was made into a movie starring Billy Bob Thornton in 2004 and into a television series in 2006. Bissinger is also the author of *A Prayer for the City,* a portrait of Philadelphia, and has written and produced episodes of the TV series *NYPD Blue.* Today he is a contributing editor for *Vanity Fair* and lives in Philadelphia. This essay was published in *The New York Times* on December 16, 2004.

Pre-Reading Journal Entry

Competitive sports play a large role in many high schools. What was your experience of sports in high school? Were you a high school athlete? Did you attend your school's games? How were athletes regarded in your school? How did being an athlete—or not being an athlete—affect your personal experience of high school sports? What memories do you have of your high school's athletes, teams, or coaches? Use your journal to answer these questions.

Innocents Afield

Earlier this month, the high school football season ended around the country. There were the state championships and before that, the annual Thanksgiving Day games. There were the rose-colored images of innocence and valor and healthy competition, attributes that we continue to insist upon from sports in America even though such attributes have become extinct. 1

We are clinging to the supposed virtues of high school athletics with particular zeal. Everybody knows that pro sports is too far gone (take your pick of recent scandals). Everybody knows that college sports is too far gone (take your pick of recent scandals). But still there's high school sports, still the classic battle of one rival against the other in shaggy glory, what James Jones described in *From Here to Eternity*[1] as "the magnificent foolishness of youth as if the whole of life depended on this game." A half-century later, the 2

---

[1] A novel published in 1951 about World War II and its aftermath (editors' note).

depiction of noble sacrifice at the high school level still forms our baseline, gives us hope that something in sports is still unsullied, restores our faith in the family values fad that has overtaken the low-carb diet.

Except that high school sports in America has become an epidemic of win-at-all-costs in too many places, just as corroded as college and the pros; actually more so because none of the ends can possibly justify the means when many of those involved are still too young to vote. No Super Bowl with television ratings through the roof. No Bowl Championship Series games with millions watching. Just millions of dollars spent by certain school districts that cannot possibly begin to explain the millions they are spending. Just booster clubs, like little Mafia families, filling in the gap between what the board of education is willing to cough up and what the athletic department claims that it needs to keep churning out those precious state championships. Just coaches in some places making close to $90,000 a year without teaching a class. Just further social stratification between the athlete and the non-athlete, those who are in and those who are out and feel humiliated and ridiculed with repercussions that can become deadly. Just steroid abuse, including a 17-year-old baseball player in a Dallas suburb who committed suicide because what of his parents believe was depression caused by stopping anabolic steroids.

Maybe I'm overselling the problem. But my point of reference is the late 1980's, when I moved to Odessa, Tex., to do research for my book. When [*Friday Night Lights*] was published in 1990, Permian High School in Odessa became a national symbol of everything that was wrong in high school sports—spending close to $70,000 on chartered jet trips to several away games, building a high school football stadium that seated nearly 20,000 and cost $5.6 million.

Over the past 14 years, I have had hundreds of conversations with parents about high school sports careening out of control. In virtually all of them, the reaction has been the same—approving nods of solidarity, followed by my own queasy sense that they weren't really listening to a word I said, their own private SportsCenter moment reeling in their heads for their sons and daughters. Over those 14 years, the excesses have only gotten worse.

As *USA Today* reported in October, millions upon millions of dollars are being spent on high school football stadiums and related buildings across the country. Texas, of course, leads the arms race with new or pending high school football stadium projects in the Dallas area alone costing close to $180 million. But in Jefferson, Ind., as part of a privately financed $8 million building project, there's a new 6,000-seat high school football stadium with an expensive video scoreboard. In Valdosta, Ga., $7.5 million was spent to renovate its football stadium, including building a museum to the glory of the Valdosta Wildcats. North Hills High, in the Pittsburgh region, spent $10 million to renovate the stadium and build a 13,000-square-foot field house.

The arguments for these sports centers are as familiar as they are wearying as they are transparent: the football programs not only are self-sustaining but also support other sports; these are stadiums the community wants so there's no harm, particularly when they are privately financed.

But no community, at least no community I would want my children to live in, can justify any of these monoliths. In an age where educational resources are dwindling, how can the building of a lavish new stadium or a field house possibly be justified, much less needed? What does it say to the rest of the student body, the giant-sized majority who do not play football, except that they are inferior, a sloppy second to the football stars who shine on Friday night. How can a community brag about its ability to get financing for a multimillion-dollar football stadium when it can't conjure up the money to hire more teachers that would lead to the nirvana of smaller class sizes? If it's the desire of boosters to pour money into sports, and it usually is, then why not use these private funds for a physical education program to reduce obesity among teenagers?

It isn't simply money that has contributed to the professionalism of high school sports. As a reporter for *The Chicago Tribune,* I spent a year uncovering abuses in Illinois as disturbing as anything in Texas—high school coaches recruiting eighth-grade players with glossy pitches and come-ons straight out of the major-college mold, parents getting so many calls from high school recruiters that they simply had their phones turned off, high school basketball coaches siphoning off Chicago's best players just so they wouldn't compete against them. Jump a level down into that emotional hell known as travel team—there isn't a parent of a travel team player who can't recite at least one horror story of another parent going berserk or a coach flipping out in the name of providing 10- and 11- and 12-year-olds with a little extra competition.

In October, the National Association of State Boards of Education issued a report calling for greater oversight of high school athletics because of the alarming trickle-down of virtually every bad college practice. The list of concerns included steroid use, shady shoe agents, mercenary coaches, dubious recruiting tactics and extravagant gifts. Steroid abuse does exist in high schools. As many as 11 percent of the nation's youth have used them, according to a study by the Mayo Clinic. Based on other research, some of the most disturbing users are freshman high school girls, with a rate of abuse at a minimum of 7 percent. "We have a moral obligation to prevent the exploitation of high school students," the national association said.

Those are important words, but I'm afraid they are going to fall on deaf ears.

Sports as an institution is every bit as powerful in this country as corpo-   12
rate America or the Catholic Church. Yet sports are still considered a side-
light, ancillary to our daily experience. It's still too easy to put on those rose-
colored glasses, . . . to get wrapped up in the supposed character-building
elements of it, the false narratives of heroes and come-from-behind glory fed
us by newspapers and television networks and cable networks in their cease-
less search for easy emotional aphrodisiacs.

Which means that high school sports will continue to fester into shame-   13
ful overemphasis in too many places, will continue to emulate the college
sports model that is America's educational shame. Which means that by the
time we completely ruin the institution of sports for our teenagers, it will be
too late to do anything except appoint a national commission to try to figure out how we could have missed so many warning signs.

Questions for Close Reading

1. What is the selection's thesis? Locate the sentence(s) in which Bissinger states his
   main idea. If he doesn't state his thesis explicitly, express it in your own words.
2. In paragraph 2, Bissinger describes the "supposed virtues" of high school sports.
   What are these "supposed virtues"?
3. What is the role of money in high school sports? What is Bissinger's opinion of
   the role of money in high school sports?
4. In paragraph 10, Bissinger describes a way to rein in the excesses of high school
   sports. What solution does he present? How effective does he think it would be?
5. Refer to your dictionary as needed to define the following words used in the selection: *valor* (paragraph 1), *zeal* (2), *unsullied* (2), *social stratification* (3), *repercussions* (3), *careening* (5), *queasy* (5), *monolith* (8), *conjure* (8), *nirvana* (8), *siphoning*
   (9), *ancillary* (12), and *emulate* (13).

Questions About the Writer's Craft

1. **The pattern.** Bissinger deals with both causes and effects in this essay. According
   to Bissinger, what has helped *cause* the professionalization of high school sports in
   recent years? What are the *effects* of this professionalization on athletes? What are
   the *effects* on nonathletes? Cite the paragraphs in which Bissinger discusses causes
   and effects.
2. **Other patterns.** In paragraph 3, Bissinger *contrasts* the imaginary purchases that
   might be made with high school sports money with the actual purchases. What
   words does he use repeatedly to signal the nonexistent and the actual purchases of
   high school sports? How effective is this use of repetition?
3. **Other patterns.** In paragraph 5, Bissinger *argues* that the excesses of high school
   sports have gotten worse since he published *Friday Night Lights* in 1990. What
   evidence does he cite for this claim? Is the evidence convincing?
4. Bissinger concludes his essay with a prediction (paragraph 13). What is his prediction? Why is he so pessimistic about the future of high school sports?

Writing Assignments Using Cause-Effect as a Pattern of Development

1. Bissinger's essay focuses mostly on the role of money in professionalizing high school sports, but he mentions other factors as well. These factors include recruitment practices, travel teams, and steroid abuse. Do research in the library or on the Internet about one of these other factors and write an essay about its *effect* on high school sports.

2. Bissinger's essay focuses on the negative aspects of high school sports, arguing that the worst aspects of professional and college sports have contaminated competition at the high school level. Write an essay in which you present the beneficial *effects* of high school sports on athletes, families, and communities. For example, you might discuss how playing a team sport teaches students about working with others on a school assignment, a family project, or a community event.

Writing Assignments Combining Patterns of Development

3. *Friday Night Lights,* the movie based on Bissinger's book about high school football in Odessa, Texas, shows that the expectations of classmates, coaches, family, and community take a heavy toll on team members. Still, the film has many of the elements of the classic Hollywood underdog sports movie, in which a team battles great odds to make it to the playoffs or win a championship. These movies—such as *Bad News Bears* (baseball), *Hoosiers* (basketball), *Remember the Titans* (football), and *Miracle* (hockey)—are all inspirational in tone. Select a sports movie that you have seen and show how this movie *exemplifies* particular values of sports in American culture. What is the message of the movie? What *causes* such movies to be so popular?

4. Bissinger contrasts James Jones's 1951 description of the nobility of high school athletics with the modern reality, which has been affected by money and fame. This contrast between an earlier, more innocent version of a present-day cultural practice underlies several of the essays in this book. For example, in "Family Counterculture" (page 6), Ellen Goodman contrasts the past influence of ministers, teachers, and societal leaders on children's development with the present influence of TV and advertising. In "Tweens: Ten Going on Sixteen" (page 202), Kay S. Hymowitz describes how today's eight- to twelve-year-olds are more like teenagers than like children. And in "Marrying Absurd" (page 604), Joan Didion describes the excesses of a Las Vegas wedding. Select a present-day cultural phenomenon, and write an essay in which you *compare* and *contrast* present-day practices with those of the past and explain how and why these practices have *affected* people's behavior. For example, you can write an essay comparing teens' social lives before and after the Internet and explain how the Internet has affected social behavior. Or you can contrast spending habits before and after credit cards became common and explain their effect on people's consumer behavior. Or you can compare modern indoor shopping malls to old-time main streets and describe the effect of malls on shopping habits.

Writing Assignment Using a Journal
Entry as a Starting Point

5. Whether you were an athlete or not, sports probably had some effect on your high school experience. Review your pre-reading journal entry about high school sports. Select one of your experiences with high school sports, whether as an athlete, a spectator, or a fan, and write an essay *narrating* the experience. Was your experience good or bad, or both? How did this experience influence your overall experience of high school?

Additional Writing Topics

CAUSE-EFFECT

General Assignments

Write an essay that analyzes the causes and/or effects of one of the following topics. Determine your purpose before beginning to write: Will the essay be informative, persuasive, or speculative? As you prewrite, think rigorously about causes and effects; try to identify causal chains. Provide solid evidence for the thesis and use either chronological or emphatic order to organize your supporting points.

1. Sleep deprivation
2. Having the parents you have
3. Lack of communication in a relationship
4. Overexercising or not exercising
5. A particular TV or rock star's popularity
6. Skill or ineptitude in sports
7. A major life decision
8. Stiffer legal penalties for drunken driving
9. Changing attitudes toward protecting the environment
10. A particular national crisis
11. The mass movement of women into the workforce
12. Choosing to attend this college
13. "Back to basics" movement in schools
14. Headaches
15. An act of violence
16. A natural event: leaves turning, birds migrating, animals hibernating, an eclipse occurring
17. Pesticide use
18. Use of computers in the classroom
19. Banning disposable cans and bottles
20. A bad habit
21. A fear of _____
22. Legalizing drugs
23. Abolishing the F grade
24. Joining a particular organization
25. Owning a pet

Assignments With a Specific Purpose, Audience, and Point of View

On Campus

1. A debate about the prominence of athletics at colleges and universities is going to be broadcast on the local cable station. For this debate, prepare a speech

pointing out either the harmful or the beneficial effects of "big-time" college athletic programs.

2. Why do students "flunk out" of college? Write an article for the campus newspaper outlining the main causes of failure. Your goal is to steer students away from dangerous habits and situations that lead to poor grades or dropping out.

At Home or in the Community

3. Write a letter to the editor of your favorite newspaper analyzing the causes of the country's current "trash crisis." Be sure to mention the nationwide love affair with disposable items and the general disregard of the idea of thrift. Conclude by offering brief suggestions for how people in your community can begin to remedy this problem.

4. Write a letter to the head of your religious congregation or a civic organization that you belong to suggesting ways, such as installing solar panels, that the group can become more energy efficient. Discuss the positive impact that energy conservation can have on efforts to stop global warming.

On the Job

5. As the manager of a store or office, you've noticed that a number of employees have negative workplace habits and/or attitudes. Write a memo for your employees in which you identify these negative behaviors and show how they affect the workplace environment. Be sure to adopt a tone that will sound neither patronizing nor overly harsh.

6. Why do you think teenage suicide is on the rise? You're a respected psychologist. Write a fact sheet for parents of teenagers and for high school guidance counselors describing the factors that could make a young person desperate enough to attempt suicide. At the end, suggest what parents and counselors can do to help confused, unhappy young people.

DEFINITION

WHAT IS DEFINITION?

In Lewis Carroll's wise and whimsical tale *Through the Looking Glass,* Humpty Dumpty proclaims, "When *I* use a word . . . , it means just what I choose it to mean—neither more nor less." If the world were filled with characters like Humpty Dumpty, all of them bending words to their own purposes and accepting no challenges to their personal definitions, communication would be an exercise in frustration. You would say a word, and it would mean one thing to you but perhaps something completely different to a close friend. Without a common understanding, the two of you would talk at cross-purposes, missing each other's meanings as you blundered through a conversation.

For language to communicate, words must have accepted *definitions.* Dictionaries, the sourcebooks for accepted definitions, are compilations of current word meanings, enabling speakers of a language to understand one another. But as you might suspect, things are not as simple as they first appear. We all know that a word like *discipline* has a standard dictionary definition. We also know, though, that parents argue over what constitutes "discipline" and that controversies about the meaning of "discipline" rage within school systems year after year. Moreover, many of the wrenching moral debates of our time also boil down to questions of definition. Much of the controversy over abortion, for instance, centers on what is meant by "life" and when it "begins."

Words can, in short, be slippery. Each of us has unique experiences, attitudes, and values that influence the way we use words and the way we interpret the words of others. Lewis Carroll may have been exaggerating, but Humpty Dumpty's attitude exists—in a very real way—in all of us.

In addition to the idiosyncratic interpretations that may attach to words, some words may shift in meaning over time. The word *pedagogue,* for instance, originally meant "a teacher or leader of children." However, with time, *pedagogue* has come to mean "a dogmatic, pedantic teacher." And, of course, we invent other words (*modem, byte, e-mail*) as the need arises.

Writing a definition, then, is no simple task. Primarily, the writer tries to answer basic questions: "What does _____ mean?" and "What is the special or true nature of _____?" The word to be defined may be an object, a concept, a type of person, a place, or a phenomenon. Potential subjects might be the "user-friendly" computer, animal rights, a model teacher, cabin fever. As you will see, there are various strategies for expanding definitions far beyond the single-word synonyms or brief phrases that dictionaries provide.

HOW DEFINITION FITS YOUR PURPOSE AND AUDIENCE

Many times, short-answer exam questions call for definitions. Consider the following examples:

Define the term *mob psychology.*

What is the difference between a metaphor and a simile?

How would you explain what a religious cult is?

In such cases, a good response might involve a definition of several sentences or several paragraphs.

Other times, definition may be used in an essay organized mainly around another pattern of development. In this situation, all that's needed is a brief formal definition or a short definition given in your own words. For instance, a *process analysis* showing readers how computers have revolutionized the typical business office might start with a textbook definition of the term *artificial intelligence.* In an *argumentation-persuasion* paper urging students to support recent efforts to abolish fraternities and sororities, you could refer to the definitions of *blackballing* and *hazing* found in the university handbook. Or your personal definition of *hero* could be the starting point for a *causal analysis* that explains to readers why there are few real heroes in today's world.

But the most complex use of definition, and the one we are primarily concerned with in this chapter, involves exploring a subject through an *extended definition.* Extended definition allows you to apply a personal interpretation to a word, to make a case for a revisionist view of a commonly accepted meaning, to analyze words representing complex or controversial issues. "Pornography," "gun control," "secular humanism," and "right-to-life" would be excellent subjects for extended definition—each is multifaceted, often misunderstood, and fraught with emotional meaning. "Junk food," "anger," "leadership," "anxiety" could make interesting subjects, especially if the extended definition helped readers develop a new understanding of the word. You might, for example, define "anxiety" not as a negative state to be avoided but as a positive force that propels us to take action.

An extended definition could perhaps run several paragraphs or a few pages. Keep in mind, however, that an extended definition may require a chapter or even an entire book to develop. If this seems unlikely, remember that theologians, philosophers, and pop psychologists have devoted entire texts to such concepts as "evil" and "love."

At this point, you have a good sense of the way writers use definition to achieve their purpose and to connect with their readers. Now take a moment to look closely at the photograph at the beginning of this chapter. Imagine you're writing an essay, accompanied by the photo, for publication in your campus newspaper. Your purpose is to explain what it means to be an American in the twenty-first century. Jot down some ideas you might include in your *definition*.

SUGGESTIONS FOR USING DEFINITION IN AN ESSAY

The following suggestions will be helpful whether you use definition as a dominant or a supportive pattern of development.

1. Stay focused on the essay's purpose, audience, and tone.   Since your purpose for writing an extended definition shapes the entire paper, you need to keep that objective in mind when developing your definition. Suppose you decide to write an essay defining *jazz*. The essay could be purely *informative* and discuss the origins of jazz, its characteristic tonal patterns, and some of the great jazz musicians of the past. Or the essay could move beyond pure information and take on a *persuasive* edge. It might, for example, argue that jazz is the only contemporary form of music worth considering seriously.

Just as your purpose in writing will vary, so will your tone. A strictly informative definition will generally assume a detached, objective tone ("Apathy is an emotional state characterized by listlessness and indifference"). By way of contrast, a definition essay with a persuasive slant might be urgent in tone ("To combat student apathy, we must design programs that engage students in campus life"), or it might take a satiric approach ("An apathetic stance is a wise choice for any thinking student").

As you write, keep thinking about your audience as well. Not only do your readers determine what terms need to be defined (and in how much detail), but they also keep you focused on the essay's purpose and tone. For instance, you probably wouldn't write a serious, informative piece for the college newspaper about the "mystery meat" served in the campus cafeteria. Instead, you would adopt a light tone as you defined the culinary horror and might even make a persuasive pitch about improving the food prepared on campus.

2. Formulate an effective definition.   A definition essay sometimes begins with a brief *formal definition*—the dictionary's, a textbook's, or the writer's—and then expands that initial definition with supporting details. Formal definitions are traditionally worded as three-part statements that consist of the following: the *term*, the *class* to which the term belongs, and the *characteristics* that distinguish the term from other members of its class.

Term	Class	Characteristics
The peregrine falcon,	an endangered bird,	is the world's fastest flyer.
A bodice-ripper	is a paperback book	that deals with highly charged romance in exotic places and faraway times.
Back to basics	is a trend in education	that emphasizes skill mastery through rote learning.

A definition that meets these guidelines will clarify what your subject *is* and what it *is not*. These guidelines also establish the boundaries of your definition, removing unlike items from consideration in your (and your reader's) mind. For example, defining "back to basics" as a trend that emphasizes rote learning signals a certain boundary; it lets readers know that other educational trends, such as those that emphasize children's social or emotional development, will not be part of the essay's definition.

If you decide to include a formal definition, avoid tired openers like "the dictionary says" or "according to Webster." Such weak starts are just plain boring and often herald an unimaginative essay. You should also keep in mind that a strict dictionary definition may actually confuse readers. Suppose you're writing a paper on the way all of us absorb ideas and values from the media. Likening this automatic response to the process of osmosis, you decide to open the paper with a dictionary definition. If you write, "Osmosis is the tendency of a solvent to disperse through a semipermeable membrane into a more concentrated medium," readers are apt to be baffled, even hostile. Remember: The purpose of a definition is to clarify meaning, not obscure it.

You should also stay clear of ungrammatical "is when" definitions: "Blind ambition is when you want to get ahead, no matter how much other people are hurt." Instead, write "Blind ambition is wanting to get ahead, no matter how much other people are hurt." A final pitfall to avoid in writing formal definitions is *circularity*, saying the same thing twice and therefore defining nothing: "A campus tribunal is a tribunal composed of various members of the university community." Circular definitions like this often repeat the term being defined (*tribunal*) or use words having the same meaning (*campus; university community*). In this case, we learn nothing about what a campus tribunal is; the writer says only that "X is X."

3. Develop the extended definition.   You can choose from a variety of patterns when formulating an extended definition. Description, narration, process analysis, and comparison-contrast can be used—alone or in combination. Imagine that you're planning to write an extended definition of "robotics." You might develop the term by providing *examples* of the ways robots are currently being used in scientific research; by *comparing* and *contrasting* human and robot capabilities; or by *classifying* robots, starting with the most basic and moving to the most advanced or futuristic models.

Which patterns of development to use will often become apparent during the prewriting stage. Here is a list of prewriting questions as well as the pattern of development implied by each question.

Question	Pattern of Development
How does X look, taste, smell, feel, and sound?	Description
What does X do? When? Where?	Narration
What are some typical instances of X?	Exemplification
What are X's component parts? What different forms can X take?	Division-classification
How does X work?	Process analysis
What is X like or unlike?	Comparison-contrast
What leads to X? What are X's consequences?	Cause-effect

Those questions yielding the most material often suggest the effective pattern(s) for developing an extended definition.

4. Organize the material that develops the definition.   If you use a single pattern to develop the extended definition, apply the principles of organization suited to that pattern, as described in the appropriate chapter of this book. Assume that you're defining "fad" by means of *process analysis*. You might organize your paragraphs according to the steps in the process: a fad's slow start as something avant-garde or eccentric; its wildfire acceptance by the general public; the fad's demise as it becomes familiar or tiresome. If you want to define "character" by means of a single *narration*, you would probably organize paragraphs chronologically.

In a definition essay using several methods of development, you should devote separate paragraphs to each pattern. A definition of "relaxation," for instance, might start with a paragraph that *narrates* a particularly relaxing day; then it might move to a paragraph that describes several *examples* of people who find it difficult to unwind; finally, it might end with a paragraph that explains a *process* for relaxing the mind and body.

5. Write an effective introduction.   It can be helpful to provide—near the beginning of a definition essay—a brief formal definition of the term you're going to develop in the rest of the paper. Beyond this basic element, the introduction may include a number of other features. You might explain the *origin* of the term being defined: "Acid rock is a term first coined in the 1960s to describe music that was written or listened to under the influence of the drug LSD." Similarly, you could explain the *etymology,* or linguistic origin, of the key word that focuses the paper. "The term *vigilantism* is derived from the Latin word meaning 'to watch and be awake.'"

You may also use the introduction to clarify what the subject is *not*. Such *definition by negation* can be an effective strategy at the beginning of a paper, especially if readers don't share your view of the subject. In such a case, you might write something like this: "The gorilla, far from being the vicious killer of jungle movies and popular imagination, is a sedentary, gentle creature living in a closely knit family group." Such a statement provides the special focus of your essay and signals some of the misconceptions or fallacies soon to be discussed.

In addition, you may include in the introduction a *stipulative definition,* one that puts special restrictions on a term: "Strictly defined, a mall refers to a one- or two-story enclosed building containing a variety of retail shops and at least two large anchor stores. Highway-strip shopping centers or downtown centers cannot be considered true malls." When a term has multiple meanings, or when its meaning has become fuzzy through misuse, a stipulative definition sets the record straight right at the start, so that readers know exactly what is, and is not, being defined.

Finally, the introduction may end with a *plan of development* that indicates how the definition essay will unfold. A student who returned to school after having raised a family decided to write a paper defining the *midlife crisis* that led to her enrollment in college. After providing a brief formal definition of "midlife crisis," the student rounded off her introduction with this sentence: "Such a midlife crisis starts with vague misgivings, turns into depression, and ends with a significant change in lifestyle."

REVISION STRATEGIES

Once you have a draft of the essay, you're ready to revise. The following checklist will help you and those giving you feedback apply to definition some of the revision techniques discussed on pages 60–62.

☑ DEFINITION: A REVISION/PEER REVIEW CHECKLIST

Revise Overall Meaning and Structure

❑ Is the essay's purpose informative, persuasive, or both?

❑ Is the term being defined clearly distinguished from similar terms?

❑ Where does a circular definition cloud meaning? Where are technical, nonstandard, or ambiguous terms a source of confusion?

❑ Where would a word's historical or linguistic origin clarify meaning? Where would a formal definition, stipulative definition, or definition by negation help?

❑ Which patterns of development are used to develop the definition? How do these help the essay achieve its purpose?

❑ If the essay uses only one pattern, is the essay's method of organization suited to that pattern (step-by-step for process analysis, chronological for narration, and so on)?

❑ Where could a dry formal definition be deleted without sacrificing overall clarity?

Revise Paragraph Development

❑ If the essay uses several patterns of development, where would separate paragraphs for different patterns be appropriate?

❑ Which paragraphs are flat or unconvincing? How could they be made more compelling?

Revise Sentences and Words

❑ Which sentences and words are inconsistent with the essay's tone?

❑ Where should overused phrases like "the dictionary says" and "according to Webster's" be replaced by more original wording?

❑ Have "is when" definitions been avoided?

STUDENT ESSAY

The following student essay was written by Laura Chen in response to this assignment:

> In "Entropy," K. C. Cole takes a scientific term from physics and gives it a broader definition and a wider application. Choose another specialized term and define it in such a way that you reveal something significant about contemporary life.

While reading Laura's paper, try to determine how well it applies the principles of definition. The annotations on Laura's paper and the commentary following it will help you look at the essay more closely.

Physics in Everyday Life
by Laura Chen

Introduction

A boulder sits on a mountainside for a thousand years. 1 The boulder will remain there forever unless an outside force intervenes. Suppose a force does affect the boulder--an earthquake, for instance. Once the boulder begins to thunder down the mountain, it will remain in motion and head in one direction only--downhill--until another force interrupts its progress. If the boulder tumbles into a gorge, it will finally come to rest as gravity anchors it to the earth once more. In both *Formal definition* cases, the boulder is exhibiting the physical principle of inertia: the tendency of matter to remain at rest or, if moving, to keep moving in one direction unless affected by an outside force. *Thesis* → Inertia, an important factor in the world of physics, also plays a crucial role in the human world. Inertia affects our individual *Plan of development* lives as well as the direction taken by society as a whole.

Topic sentence → Inertia often influences our value systems and personal 2 growth. Inertia is at work, for example, when people cling to certain behaviors and views. Like the boulder firmly fixed to the mountain, most people are set in their ways. Without thinking, they vote Republican or Democratic because they have always voted that way. They regard with suspicion a couple having no children, simply because everyone else in the neighborhood has a large family. *Start of a series of causes and effects* It is only when an outside force--a jolt of some sort--occurs that people change their views. A white American couple may think little about racial discrimination, for instance, until they adopt an Asian child and must comfort her when classmates tease her because she looks different. Parents may consider promiscuous any unmarried teenage girl who has a baby until their seventeen-year-old honor student confesses that she is pregnant.

Personal jolts like these force people to think, perhaps for the first time, about issues that now affect them directly.

Topic sentence ⟶ To illustrate how inertia governs our lives, it is helpful to 3 compare the world of television with real life. On TV, inertia

Start of a series of contrasts ⎯⎯ does not exist. Television shows and commercials show people making all kinds of drastic changes. They switch brands of coffee or try a new hair color with no hesitation. In one car commercial, an ambitious young accountant abandons her career with a flourish and is seen driving off into the sunset as she heads for a small cabin by the sea to write poetry. In a soap opera, a character may progress from homemaker to hooker to nun in a single year. But in real life, inertia rules. People tend to stay where they are, to keep their jobs, to be loyal to products. A second major difference between television and real life is that, on television, everyone takes prompt and dramatic action to solve problems. The construction worker with a thudding headache is pain-free at the end of the sixty-second commercial; the police catch the murderer within an hour; the family learns to cope with their son's life-threatening drug addiction by the time the made-for-TV movie ends at eleven. But in the real world, inertia persists, so that few problems are solved neatly or quickly. Illnesses drag on, few crimes are solved, and family conflicts last for years.

Topic sentence ⟶ Inertia is, most importantly, a force at work in the life of 4 our nation. Again, inertia is two-sided. It keeps us from moving and, once we move, it keeps us pointed in one direction. We find ourselves mired in a certain path, accepting

Start of a series of examples ⎯⎯ the inferior, even the dangerous. We settle for toys that break, winter coats with no warmth, and rivers clogged with pollution. Inertia also compels our nation to keep moving in one direction--despite the uncomfortable suspicion that it is the wrong direction. We are not sure if manipulating genes is a good idea, yet we continue to fund scientific projects in genetic engineering. More than fifty years ago, we were shaken when we saw the devastation caused by an atomic bomb. But we went on to develop weapons hundreds of times more destructive. Although warned that excessive television viewing may be harmful, we continue to watch hours of television each day.

Conclusion   We have learned to defy gravity, one of the basic laws of 5 physics; we fly high above the earth, even float in outer space. But most of us have not learned to defy inertia. Those special individuals who are able to act when everyone else seems paralyzed are rare. But the fact that such people do exist means that inertia is not all-powerful. If we use our reasoning ability and our creativity, we can conquer inertia, just as we have conquered gravity.

COMMENTARY

Introduction.   As the title of her essay suggests, Laura has taken a scientific term (*inertia*) from a specialized field and drawn on the term to help explain some everyday phenomena. Using the *simple-to-complex* approach to structure the introduction, she opens with a vivid *descriptive* example of inertia. This description is then followed by a *formal definition* of inertia: "the tendency of matter to remain at rest or, if moving, to keep moving in one direction unless affected by an outside force." Laura wisely begins the paper with the easy-to-understand description rather than with the more-difficult-to-grasp scientific definition. Had the order been reversed, the essay would not have gotten off to nearly as effective a start. She then ends her introductory paragraph with a *thesis*, "Inertia, an important factor in the world of physics, also plays a crucial role in the human world," and with a *plan of development*, "Inertia affects our individual lives as well as the direction taken by society as a whole."

Organization.   To support her definition of inertia and her belief that it can rule our lives, Laura generates a number of compelling examples. She organizes these examples by grouping them into three major points, each point signaled by a *topic sentence* that opens each of the essay's three supporting paragraphs (2–4).

A definite organizational strategy determines the sequence of Laura's three central points. The essay moves from the way inertia affects the individual to the way it affects the nation. The phrase "most importantly" at the beginning of the fourth paragraph shows that Laura has arranged her points emphatically, believing that inertia's impact on society is most critical.

A weak example.   When reading the fourth paragraph, you might have noticed that Laura's examples aren't sequenced as effectively as they could be. To show that we, as a nation, tend to keep moving in the same direction, Laura discusses our ongoing uneasiness about genetic engineering, nuclear arms, and excessive television viewing. The point about nuclear weapons is most significant, yet it gets lost because it's sandwiched in the middle. The paragraph would be stronger if it ended with the point about nuclear arms. Moreover, the example about excessive television viewing doesn't belong in this paragraph since, at best, it has limited bearing on the issue being discussed.

Combining patterns of development.   In addition to using numerous *examples* to illustrate her points, Laura draws on several other patterns of development to show that inertia can be a powerful force. In the second and fourth paragraphs, she uses *causal analysis* to explain how inertia can paralyze people and nations. The second paragraph indicates that only "an outside force—a jolt of some sort—" can motivate inert people to change. To support this view, Laura provides two examples of parents who experience such jolts. Similarly, in the fourth paragraph, she contends that inertia causes the persistence of specific national problems: shoddy consumer goods and environmental pollution.

Another pattern, *comparison-contrast,* is used in the third paragraph to highlight the differences between television and real life: on television, people zoom into action, but in everyday life, people tend to stay put and muddle through. The essay also contains a distinct element of *argumentation-persuasion,* since Laura clearly wants readers to accept her definition of inertia and her view that it often governs human behavior.

Conclusion.   Laura's *conclusion* rounds off the essay nicely and brings it to a satisfying close. Laura refers to another law of physics, one with which we are all familiar—gravity. By creating an *analogy* between gravity and inertia, she suggests that our ability to defy gravity should encourage us to defy inertia. The analogy enlarges the scope of the essay; it allows Laura to reach out to her readers by challenging them to action. Such a challenge is, of course, appropriate in a definition essay having a persuasive bent.

Revising the first draft.   When it was time to rework her essay, Laura began by reading her paper aloud. She noted in the margin of her draft the problems she detected, numbering them in order of importance. After reviewing her notes, she started to revise in earnest, paying special attention to her third paragraph. The first draft of that paragraph is reprinted here:

Original Version of the Third Paragraph

The ordinary actions of daily life are, in part, determined by inertia. To understand this, it is helpful to compare the world of television with real life, for, in the TV-land of ads and entertainment, inertia does not exist. For example, on television, people are often shown making all kinds of drastic changes. They switch brands of coffee or try a new hair color with no hesitation. In one car commercial, a young accountant leaves her career and sets off for a cabin by the sea to write poetry. In a soap opera, a character may progress from homemaker to hooker to nun in a single year. In contrast, inertia rules in real life. People tend to stay where they are, to keep their jobs, to be loyal to products (wives get annoyed if a husband brings home the wrong brand or color of bathroom tissue from the market). Middle-aged people wear the hairstyles or makeup that suited them in high school. A second major difference between television and real life is that, on TV, everyone takes prompt and dramatic action to solve problems. A woman finds the solution to dull clothes at the end of a commercial; the police catch the murderer within an hour; the family learns to cope with a son's disturbing lifestyle by the time the movie is over. In contrast, the law of real-life inertia means that few problems are solved neatly or quickly. Things, once started, tend to stay as they are. Few crimes are actually solved. Medical problems are not easily diagnosed. Messy wars in foreign countries seem endless. National problems are identified, but Congress does not pass legislation to solve them.

After rereading what she had written, Laura realized that her third paragraph rambled. To give it more focus, she removed the last two sentences ("Messy wars in foreign countries seem endless" and "National problems are identified, but Congress does not pass legislation. . . .") because they referred to national affairs but were located in a section focusing on the individual. Then, she eliminated two flat, unconvincing examples: wives who get annoyed when their husbands bring home the wrong brand of bathroom tissue and middle-aged people whose hairstyles and makeup are outdated. Condensing the two disjointed sentences that originally opened the paragraph also helped tighten this section of the essay. Note how much crisper the revised sentences are: "To illustrate how inertia rules our lives, it is helpful to compare the world of television with real life. On TV, inertia does not exist."

Laura also worked to make the details and the language in the paragraph more specific and vigorous. The vague sentence "A woman finds the solution to dull clothes at the end of the commercial" is replaced by the more dramatic "The construction worker with a thudding headache is pain-free at the end of the sixty-second commercial." Similarly, Laura changed a "son's disturbing lifestyle" to a "son's life-threatening drug addiction"; "by the time the movie is over" became "by the time the made-for-TV movie ends at eleven"; and "a young accountant leaves her career and sets off for a cabin by the sea to write poetry" was changed to "an ambitious young accountant abandons her career with a flourish and is seen driving off into the sunset as she heads for a small cabin by the sea to write poetry."

After making these changes, Laura decided to round off the paragraph with a powerful summary statement highlighting how real life differs from television: "Illnesses drag on, few crimes are solved, and family conflicts last for years."

These third-paragraph revisions are similar to those that Laura made elsewhere in her first draft. Her astute changes enabled her to turn an already effective paper into an especially thoughtful analysis of human behavior.

ACTIVITIES: DEFINITION

Prewriting Activities

1. Imagine you're writing two essays: one explains the *process* for registering a complaint that gets results; the other *contrasts* the styles of two stand-up comics. Jot down ways you might use definition in each essay.

2. Select a term whose meaning varies from person to person or one for which you have a personal definition. Some possibilities include:

success	femininity	a liberal
patriotism	affirmative action	a housewife
individuality	pornography	intelligence

Brainstorm with others to identify variations in the term's meaning. Then examine your prewriting material. What thesis comes to mind? If you were writing an essay, would your purpose be informative, persuasive, or both? Finally, prepare a scratch list of the points you might cover.

Revising Activities

3. Explain why each of the following is an effective or ineffective definition. Rewrite those you consider ineffective.

   a. *Passive aggression* is when people show their aggression passively.
   b. A *terrorist* tries to terrorize people.
   c. *Being assertive* means knowing how to express your wishes and goals in a positive, noncombative way.
   d. *Pop music* refers to music that is popular.
   e. *Loyalty* is when someone stays by another person during difficult times.

4. The following introductory paragraph is from the first draft of an essay contrasting walking and running as techniques for reducing tension. Although intended to be a definition paragraph, it actually doesn't tell us anything we don't already know. It also relies on the old-hat "*Webster's* says." Rewrite the paragraph so it is more imaginative. You might use a series of anecdotes or one extended example to define *tension* and introduce the essay's thesis more gracefully.

> According to Webster's, tension is "mental or nervous strain, often accompanied by muscular tightness or tautness." Everyone feels tense at one time or another. It may occur when there's a deadline to meet. Or it could be caused by the stress of trying to fulfill academic, athletic, or social goals. Sometimes it comes from criticism by family, bosses, or teachers. Such tension puts wear and tear on our bodies and on our emotional well-being. Although some people run to relieve tension, research has found that walking is a more effective tension reducer.

K. C. Cole

K. C. Cole's writings about science, especially physics, have made a great deal of specialized knowledge available to the general public. A graduate of Barnard College, Cole has contributed numerous articles to such publications as *The New York Times, The Washington Post,* and *Long Island Newsday,* and writes a regular column for *Discover* magazine. Her work with the Exploratorium, a San Francisco science museum, led her to write several books on the exhibits there. In 1985, Cole published a collection of essays, *Sympathetic Vibrations: Reflections on Physics as a Way of Life.* Other books include *What Only a Mother Can Tell You About Having a Baby* (1986), *The Universe and the Teacup* (1998), *First You Build a Cloud* (1999), *The Hole in the Universe* (2000), and *Mind Over Matter* (2003). She is currently a science writer and editor at the *Los Angeles Times.* The following selection was first published as a "Hers" column in *The New York Times* in 1982.

Pre-Reading Journal Entry

Do you consider yourself an orderly or a disorderly person? What about those around you? What are the benefits and the drawbacks of being orderly? Of being disorderly? Use your journal to reflect on these questions.

Entropy

It was about two months ago when I realized that entropy was getting 1 the better of me. On the same day my car broke down (again), my refrigerator conked out and I learned that I needed root-canal work in my right rear tooth. The windows in the bedroom were still leaking every time it rained and my son's baby sitter was still failing to show up every time I really needed her. My hair was turning gray and my typewriter was wearing out. The house needed paint and I needed glasses. My son's sneakers were developing holes and I was developing a deep sense of futility.

After all, what was the point of spending half of Saturday at the Laundro- 2 mat if the clothes were dirty all over again the following Friday?

Disorder, alas, is the natural order of things in the universe. There is 3 even a precise measure of the amount of disorder, called entropy. Unlike almost every other physical property (motion, gravity, energy), entropy does not work both ways. It can only increase. Once it's created it can never be destroyed. The road to disorder is a one-way street.

Because of its unnerving irreversibility, entropy has been called the arrow of time. We all understand this instinctively. Children's rooms, left on their own, tend to get messy, not neat. Wood rots, metal rusts, people wrinkle and flowers wither. Even mountains wear down; even the nuclei of atoms decay. In the city we see entropy in the rundown subways and worn-out sidewalks and torn-down buildings, in the increasing disorder of our lives. We know, without asking, what is old. If we were suddenly to see the paint jump back on an old building, we would know that something was wrong. If we saw an egg unscramble itself and jump back into its shell, we would laugh in the same way we laugh at a movie run backward.

Entropy is no laughing matter, however, because with every increase in entropy energy is wasted and opportunity is lost. Water flowing down a mountainside can be made to do some useful work on its way. But once all the water is at the same level it can work no more. That is entropy. When my refrigerator was working, it kept all the cold air ordered in one part of the kitchen and warmer air in another. Once it broke down the warm and cold mixed into a lukewarm mess that allowed my butter to melt, my milk to rot and my frozen vegetables to decay.

Of course the energy is not really lost, but it has diffused and dissipated into a chaotic caldron of randomness that can do us no possible good. Entropy is chaos. It is loss of purpose.

People are often upset by the entropy they seem to see in the haphazardness of their own lives. Buffeted about like so many molecules in my tepid kitchen, they feel that they have lost their sense of direction, that they are wasting youth and opportunity at every turn. It is easy to see entropy in marriages, when the partners are too preoccupied to patch small things up, almost guaranteeing that they will fall apart. There is much entropy in the state of our country, in the relationships between nations—lost opportunities to stop the avalanche of disorders that seems ready to swallow us all.

Entropy is not inevitable everywhere, however. Crystals and snowflakes and galaxies are islands of incredibly ordered beauty in the midst of random events. If it was not for exceptions to entropy, the sky would be black and we would be able to see where the stars spend their days; it is only because air molecules in the atmosphere cluster in ordered groups that the sky is blue.

The most profound exception to entropy is the creation of life. A seed soaks up some soil and some carbon and some sunshine and some water and arranges it into a rose. A seed in the womb takes some oxygen and pizza and milk and transforms it into a baby.

The catch is that it takes a lot of energy to produce a baby. It also takes energy to make a tree. The road to disorder is all downhill but the road to creation takes work. Though combating entropy is possible, it also has its price. That's why it seems so hard to get ourselves together, so easy to let ourselves fall apart.

Worse, creating order in one corner of the universe always creates more   11
disorder somewhere else. We create ordered energy from oil and coal at the
price of the entropy of smog.

I recently took up playing the flute again after an absence of several   12
months. As the uneven vibrations screeched through the house, my son covered his ears and said, "Mom, what's wrong with your flute?" Nothing was
wrong with my flute, of course. It was my ability to play it that had atrophied, or entropied, as the case may be. The only way to stop that process
was to practice every day, and sure enough my tone improved, though only
at the price of constant work. Like anything else, abilities deteriorate when
we stop applying our energies to them.

That's why entropy is depressing. It seems as if just breaking even is an   13
uphill fight. There's a good reason that this should be so. The mechanics of
entropy are a matter of chance. Take any ice-cold air molecule milling
around my kitchen. The chances that it will wander in the direction of my
refrigerator at any point are exactly 50-50. The chances that it will wander
away from my refrigerator are also 50-50. But take billions of warm and cold
molecules mixed together, and the chances that all the cold ones will wander
toward the refrigerator and all the warm ones will wander away from it are
virtually nil.

Entropy wins not because order is impossible but because there are   14
always so many more paths toward disorder than toward order. There are so
many more different ways to do a sloppy job than a good one, so many more
ways to make a mess than to clean it up. The obstacles and accidents in our
lives almost guarantee that constant collisions will bounce us on to random
paths, get us off the track. Disorder is the path of least resistance, the easy
but not the inevitable road.

Like so many others, I am distressed by the entropy I see around me   15
today. I am afraid of the randomness of international events, of the lack of
common purpose in the world; I am terrified that it will lead into the ultimate entropy of nuclear war. I am upset that I could not in the city where I
live send my child to a public school; that people are unemployed and inflation is out of control; that tensions between sexes and races seem to be
increasing again; that relationships everywhere seem to be falling apart.

Social institutions—like atoms and stars—decay if energy is not added to   16
keep them ordered. Friendships and families and economies all fall apart
unless we constantly make an effort to keep them working and well oiled.
And far too few people, it seems to me, are willing to contribute consistently to those efforts.

Of course, the more complex things are, the harder it is. If there were   17
only a dozen or so air molecules in my kitchen, it would be likely—if I waited a year or so—that at some point the six coldest ones would congregate
inside the freezer. But the more factors in the equation—the more players in

the game—the less likely it is that their paths will coincide in an orderly way. The more pieces in the puzzle, the harder it is to put back together once order is disturbed. "Irreversibility," said a physicist, "is the price we pay for complexity."

Questions for Close Reading

1. What is the selection's thesis? Locate the sentence(s) in which Cole states her main idea. If she doesn't state the thesis explicitly, express it in your own words.
2. How does entropy differ from the other properties of the physical world? Is the image "the arrow of time" helpful in establishing this difference?
3. Why is the creation of life an exception to entropy? What is the relationship between entropy and energy?
4. Why does Cole say that entropy "is no laughing matter"? What is so depressing about the entropy she describes?
5. Refer to your dictionary as needed to define the following words used in the selection: *futility* (paragraph 1), *dissipated* (6), *buffeted* (7), *tepid* (7), and *atrophied* (12).

Questions About the Writer's Craft

1. **The pattern.** What is Cole's underlying purpose in defining the scientific term *entropy?* What gives the essay its persuasive edge?
2. What tone does Cole adopt to make reading about a scientific concept more interesting? Identify places in the essay where her tone is especially prominent.
3. Cole uses such words as *futility, loss,* and *depressing.* How do these words affect you? Why do you suppose she chose such terms? Find similar words in the essay.
4. **Other patterns.** Many of Cole's sentences follow a two-part pattern involving a *contrast:* "The road to disorder is all downhill but the road to creation takes work" (paragraph 10). Find other examples of this pattern in the essay. Why do you think Cole uses it so often?

Writing Assignments Using Definition as a Pattern of Development

1. Write an essay in which you define *order* or *disorder* by applying the term to a system that you know well—for example, your school, dorm, family, or workplace. Develop your definition through any combination of writing patterns: by supplying examples, by showing contrasts, by analyzing the process underlying the system.
2. Choose, as Cole does, a technical term that you think will be unfamiliar to most readers. In a humorous or serious paper, define the term as it is used technically; then show how the term can shed light on some aspect of your life. For example, the concept in astronomy of a *supernova* could be used to explain your sudden emergence as a new star on the athletic field, in your schoolwork, or on the social scene. Here are a few suggested terms:

symbiosis	volatility	resonance
velocity	erosion	catalyst
neutralization	equilibrium	malleability

Writing Assignments Combining
Patterns of Development

3. Can one person make much difference in the amount of entropy—disorder and chaos—in the world? *Argue* your position in an essay. Use *examples* of people who have tried to overcome the tendency of things to "fall apart." Make clear whether you think these people succeeded or failed in their attempts. To inform your perspective before writing, consider reading James Gleick's "Life As Type A" (page 450), an evaluation of the factors that influence people's compulsion for order.

4. Cole claims that we humans are "buffeted about like so many molecules." Write an essay *arguing* that people either do or do not control their own fates. Support your point with a series of specific *examples*. For different perspectives on the issue, you might want to read Maya Angelou's "Sister Flowers" (page 100), Charmie Gholson's "Charity Display?" (page 151), Joseph H. Suina's "And Then I Went to School" (page 354), and Roberto Rodriguez's "The Border on Our Backs" (page 562).

Writing Assignment Using a Journal
Entry as a Starting Point

5. Write an essay arguing that disorder can be liberating *or* that it can be stifling. Review your pre-reading journal entry, and select strong, compelling examples that support your position. Aim to refute as many opposing arguments as possible. Your essay may have a serious or a humorous tone.

James Gleick

After graduating from Harvard College in 1976, James Gleick helped found *Metropolis,* an alternative newspaper in Minneapolis. He then spent ten years as a reporter and editor with *The New York Times,* where he wrote a column about the impact of science and technology on modern life. His earlier books, *Chaos: Making a New Science* (1987) and *Genius: The Life and Science of Richard Feynman* (1992), were both finalists for the National Book Award and Pulitzer Prize. Most recently, he has written *What Just Happened: A Chronicle From the Information Frontier* (2002) and the biography *Isaac Newton* (2003). Formerly McGraw Distinguished Lecturer at Princeton University, Gleick lives with his wife, writer Cynthia Crossen, in New York. The following piece is taken from *Faster: The Acceleration of Just About Everything* (1999).

Pre-Reading Journal Entry

Like many people, you may feel harried and under pressure at least some of the time. Use your journal to reflect on the sources of stress in your everyday life. List several examples. For each, consider the factors leading to this frenzied feeling.

Life As Type A

Everyone knows about Type A. This magnificently bland coinage, put 1 forward by a pair of California cardiologists in 1959, struck a collective nerve and entered the language. It is a token of our confusion: are we victims or perpetrators of the crime of haste? Are we living at high speed with athleticism and vigor, or are we stricken by hurry sickness?

The cardiologists, Meyer Friedman and Ray Rosenman, listed a set of 2 personality traits which, they claimed, tend to go hand in hand with one another and also with heart disease. They described these traits rather unappealingly, as characteristics about and around the theme of impatience. Excessive competitiveness. Aggressiveness. "A harrying sense of time urgency." The Type A idea emerged in technical papers and then formed the basis of a popular book and made its way into dictionaries. The canonical Type A, as these doctors portrayed him, was "Paul":

> A very disproportionate amount of his emotional energy is consumed in struggling against the normal constraints of time. "How

can I move faster, and do more and more things in less and less time?" is the question that never ceases to torment him.

Paul hurries his thinking, his speech and his movements. He also strives to hurry the thinking, speech, and movements of those about him; they must communicate rapidly and relevantly if they wish to avoid creating impatience in him. Planes must arrive and depart precisely on time for Paul, cars ahead of him on the highway must maintain a speed he approves of, and there must never be a queue of persons standing between him and a bank clerk, a restaurant table, or the interior of a theater. In fact, he is infuriated whenever people talk slowly or circuitously, when planes are late, cars dawdle on the highway, and queues form.

Let's think . . . Do we know anyone like "Paul"?

This was the first clear declaration of *hurry sickness*—another coinage of 3 Friedman's. It inspired new businesses: mind-body workshops; videotapes demonstrating deep breathing; anxiety-management retreats; seminars on and even institutes of stress medicine. "I drove all the way in the right-hand lane," a Pacific Gas and Electric Company executive said proudly one morning in 1987 to a group of self-confessed hurriers, led by Friedman himself, by then seventy-six years old. In the battle against Type A jitters, patients tried anything and everything—the slow lane, yoga, meditation, visualization: "Direct your attention to your feet on the floor. . . . Be aware of the air going in your nostrils cool and going out warm. . . . Visualize a place you like to be. . . . Experience it and see the objects there, the forms and shadows. Take another deep breath and experience the sounds, the surf, the wind, leaves, a babbling brook." Some hospital television systems now feature a "relaxation channel," with hour after hour of surf, wind, leaves, and babbling brooks.

We believe in Type A—a triumph for a notion with no particular scien- 4 tific validity. The Friedman-Rosenman claim has turned out to be both obvious and false. Clearly some heart ailments do result from, or at least go along with, stress (itself an ill-defined term), both chronic and acute. Behavior surely affects physiology, at least once in a while. Sudden dashes for the train, laptop computer in one hand and takeout coffee in the other, can accelerate heartbeats and raise blood pressure. That haste makes coronaries was already a kind of folk wisdom—that is, standard medical knowledge untainted by research. "Hurry has a clearly debilitating effect upon the tissues and may in time injure the heart," admonished Dr. Cecil Webb-Johnson in *Nerve Troubles,* an English monograph of the early 1900s. "The great men of the centuries past were never in a hurry," he added sanctimoniously, "and that is why the world will never forget them in a hurry." It might be natural—even appealing—to expect certain less-great people to receive their cardiovascular comeuppance. But in reality, three decades of attention from cardiologists and psychologists have failed to produce any carefully specified and measurable set of character traits that predict heart disease—or to demonstrate that people who change their Type A behavior will actually lower their risk of heart disease.

Indeed, the study that started it all—Friedman and Rosenman's "Association of Specific Overt Behavior Pattern with Blood and Cardiovascular Findings"—appears to have been a wildly flawed piece of research. It used a small sample—eighty-three people (all men) in what was then called "Group A." The selection process was neither random nor blind. White-collar male employees of large businesses were rounded up by acquaintances of Friedman and Rosenman on a subjective basis—they fit the type. The doctors further sorted the subjects by interviewing them personally and observing their appearance and behavior. Did a man gesture rapidly, clench his teeth, or exhibit a "general air of impatience"? If so, he was chosen. It seems never to have occurred to these experienced cardiologists that they might have been consciously or unconsciously selecting people whose physique indicated excess weight or other markers for incipient heart disease. The doctors' own data show that the final Group A drank more, smoked more, and weighed more than Group B. But the authors dismissed these factors, asserting, astonishingly, that there was no association between heart disease and cigarette smoking.

In the years since, researchers have never settled on a reliable method for identifying Type A people, though not for want of trying. Humans are not reliable witnesses to their own impatience. Researchers have employed questionnaires like the Jenkins Activity Survey, and they have used catalogues of grimaces and frowns—Ekman and Friesen's Facial Action Coding System, for example, or the Cook-Medley Hostility Inventory. In the end, nothing conclusive emerges. Some studies have found Type A people to have *lower* blood pressure. The sedentary and obese have cardiac difficulties of their own.

The notion of Type A has expanded, shifted, and flexed to suit the varying needs of different researchers. V.A. Price adds *hypervigilance* to the list of traits. Some doctors lose patience with the inconclusive results and shift their focus to anger and hostility—mere subsets of the original Type A grab-bag. Cynthia Perry finds that Type A people have fewer daydreams. How does she know? She asks them to monitor lines flashing across a computer screen for forty painfully boring minutes and finds that, when interrupted by a beep (1000 hertz at 53 decibels), they are less likely to press a black button to confess that irrelevant thoughts had strayed into their minds. Studies have labeled as Type A not only children (those with a tendency to interrupt and to play competitively at games) but even babies (those who cry more). Meanwhile, researchers interested in pets link the Type A personality to pet-lessness; a National Institutes of Health panel reports: "The description of a 'coronary-prone behavior pattern,' or Type A behavior, and its link to the probability of developing overt disease provided hope that, with careful training, individuals could exercise additional control over somatic illness by altering their lifestyle. . . . Relaxation, meditation, and stress management have become recognized therapies. . . . It therefore seems reasonable that pets, who provide faithful companionship to many people, also might promote greater psychosocial stability for their owners, and thus a measure of protection from heart disease." This is sweet, but it is not science.

Typically a Type A study will begin with researchers who assume that there are some correlations to be found, look for a wide variety of associations, fail to find some and succeed in finding others. For example, a few dozen preschool children are sorted according to their game-playing styles and tested for blood pressure. No correlation is found. Later, however, when performing a certain "memory game," the supposed Type A children rank somewhat higher in, specifically, systolic pressure. Interesting? The authors of various published papers evidently think so, but they are wrong, because if their technique is to keep looking until they find some correlation, somewhere, they are bound to succeed. Such results are meaningless.   8

The categorizations are too variable and the prophecies too self-fulfilling. It is never quite clear which traits *define* Type A and which are fellow travelers. The "free-floating, but well-rationalized form of hostility"? The "deep-seated insecurity"? "Their restlessness, their tense facial muscles, their tics, or their strident-staccato manner of speaking"? If you are hard-driving yet friendly, chafing yet self-assured—if you race for the airport gate and then settle *happily* into your seat—are you Type A or not? If you are driven to walk briskly, briskly, all the time, isn't that good for your heart?   9

Most forget that there is also supposed to be a Type B, defined not by the personality traits its members possess but by the traits they lack. Type B people are the shadowy opposites of Type A people. They are those who are not so very Type A. They do *not* wear out their fingers punching that elevator button. They do *not* allow a slow car in the fast lane to drive their hearts to fatal distraction; in fact, they are at the wheel of that slow car. Type B played no real part in that mass societal gasp of recognition in the 1970's. Type B-ness was just a foil. Doctors Friedman and Rosenman actually claimed to have had trouble finding eighty men in all San Francisco who were not under any time pressure. They finally came up with a few, they wrote solemnly, "in the municipal clerks' and the embalmers' unions."   10

Even more bizarrely, that first Friedman-Rosenman study also included a Group C, comprising forty-six unemployed blind men. Not much haste in Group C. "The primary reason men of Group C exhibited little ambition, drive, or desire to compete," the doctors wrote, "was the presence of total blindness for ten or more years and the lack of occupational deadlines because none was gainfully employed." No wonder they omitted Type C from the subsequent publicity.   11

If the Type A phenomenon made for poor medical research, it stands   12
nonetheless as a triumph of social criticism. Some of us yield more willingly
to impatience than others, but on the whole Type A is who we are—not just
the coronary-prone among us, but all of us, as a society and as an age. No
wonder the concept has proven too rich a cultural totem to be dismissed.

Questions for Close Reading

1. What is the selection's thesis? Locate the sentence(s) in which Gleick states his
   main idea. If he doesn't state the thesis explicitly, express it in your own words.
2. What is Gleick's opinion of the study Friedman and Rosenman conducted? List at
   least two elements of the study that Gleick uses to support his assessment.
3. In paragraph 7, Gleick observes that the concept of Type A has changed since
   Friedman and Rosenman's study first chronicled it. How has it changed? What
   accounts for this change?
4. According to Gleick, how do Friedman and Rosenman define the Type B personality? Why does Gleick find fault with their definition of this personality type?
5. Refer to your dictionary as needed to define the following words used in the selection: *coinage* (paragraph 1), *harrying* (2), *canonical* (2), *circuitously* (2), *sanctimoniously* (4), *overt* (5), *incipient* (5), *sedentary* (6), *hypervigilance* (7), *correlations* (8), *strident* (9), *staccato* (9), *foil* (10), and *totem* (12).

Questions About the Writer's Craft

1. **The pattern and other patterns.** In their work, Friedman and Rosenman use a
   description of Paul to *define* "canonical Type A" behavior (paragraph 2). Why do
   you suppose that Gleick, who criticizes Friedman and Rosenman's research,
   quotes their portrait of Paul at such length?
2. **The pattern.** Gleick uses a sequence of three fragments when discussing (in paragraph 2) how Type A has been defined. Identify these fragments. What effect do
   you think Gleick wanted the fragments to have?
3. Locate places where Gleick uses the first-person pronouns "we," "us," and "our."
   What do you think Gleick's purpose is in using these pronouns?
4. In paragraph 1, Gleick sarcastically refers to the phrase *Type A* as "magnificently
   bland." Find other places in the essay where he uses sarcasm. Why might he have
   chosen to employ such language?

Writing Assignments Using Definition
as a Pattern of Development

1. Write an essay offering a fuller definition of the Type B personality than Gleick's
   essay provides. Rather than defining Type B through negation, as Friedman and
   Rosenman do, marshal convincing evidence that illustrates the validity of the Type
   B phenomenon. Brainstorming with friends, family, and classmates will help you
   generate strong examples of this personality type. At some point in the essay, you
   might offer a brief personality sketch of the "canonical" Type B as well as discuss
   the factors that shape the Type B personality as you define it.

2. Gleick notes that, like *Type A, stress* is an ill-defined term. Brainstorm with others to identify as many examples of different kinds of stress as you can. Review the brainstormed material, and select a specific type of stress to focus on. Then write an essay providing a *clear* definition of that particular stress. Possibilities include "dating stress," "workplace stress," "online stress," "fitness stress." Near the end of the essay, you might provide concise hints for managing the stress you define. Your essay may have a humorous or a serious tone—whichever seems appropriate to your subject. Reading Alexandra Robbins and Abby Wilner's "What Is the Quarterlife Crisis?" (page 463), an essay that examines a particular kind of stress, might help you generate ideas.

Writing Assignments Combining Patterns of Development

3. Write an essay *contrasting* situations in which being Type A would be beneficial with situations in which it would be counterproductive. Under what circumstances would Type A characteristics be desirable? Under what circumstances would they be undesirable? Drawing upon your own experiences and observations, reach some conclusions about the advantages and/or limitations of the Type A personality. Along the way, you should explore the *effects* of Type A behavior in the circumstances you're addressing.

4. Gleick observes that "hurry sickness" is a trait induced by society at large. Identify a trait of yours that you think is also a reflection or *effect* of the society in which you live. You might discuss your tendency to be aggressive or nonassertive, materialistic or idealistic, studious or fun-loving. Write an essay *illustrating* this character trait at work in your everyday behavior. Explain whether you think this trait works to your advantage or disadvantage. For additional insight into how personal traits can affect one's daily life, read Barbara Ehrenreich's "What I've Learned from Men" (page 215).

Writing Assignment Using a Journal Entry as a Starting Point

5. Gleick claims that the Type A phenomenon is pervasive in our society. Write an essay of your own illustrating the extent to which your life reflects this phenomenon. Draw upon the most dramatic examples in your pre-reading journal entry. At the end of the essay, describe steps that you or anyone with similar pressures could take to slow down the frenetic pace of everyday life. Gathering information in the library and/or on the Internet might be helpful when you develop the final section of your paper.

Natalie Angier

Natalie Angier was born in 1958 and was raised in the Bronx, New York, and in Michigan. She attended Barnard College, where she studied literature, astronomy, and physics. After working for *Discover* magazine, she became a reporter for the science section of *The New York Times* in 1990. The following year she won a Pulitzer Prize for her science reporting. In addition to reporting, Angier has written several books, including *The Beauty of the Beastly* (1995), *Natural Obsessions: Striving to Unlock the Deepest Secret of the Cancer Cell* (1999), and *Woman: An Intimate Geography* (1999). Angier has always been interested in bridging the gap between science and the humanities. This article, about the scientific basis of cuteness, was published in *The New York Times* on January 3, 2006.

Pre-Reading Journal Entry

Some concepts—like beauty, elegance, and cuteness—are hard to explain, although people usually believe they understand what those concepts are. Take a moment to reflect in your journal on what *you* mean when you say something is "cute." What qualities come to mind? Consider the kinds of things that you would deem cute, and list as many as you can think of in your journal.

The Cute Factor

If the mere sight of Tai Shan, the roly-poly, goofily gamboling masked 1 bandit of a panda cub now on view at the National Zoo isn't enough to make you melt, then maybe the crush of his human onlookers, the furious flashing of their cameras and the heated gasps of their mass rapture will do the trick.

Awww. . . . Scientists who study the evolution of visual signaling have 2 identified a wide and still-expanding assortment of features and behaviors that make something look cute.

Cute cues are those that indicate extreme youth, vulnerability, harmless- 3 ness and need, scientists say.

"Omigosh, look at him! He is too cute!" 4

"How adorable! I wish I could just reach in there and give him a big 5 squeeze!"

"He's so fuzzy! I've never seen anything so cute in my life!"   6

A guard's sonorous voice rises above the burble. "OK, folks, five oohs   7
and aahs per person, then it's time to let someone else step up front."

The 6-month-old, 25-pound Tai Shan—whose name is pronounced tie-   8
SHON and means, for no obvious reason, "peaceful mountain"—is the first
surviving giant panda cub ever born at the Smithsonian's zoo. And though
the zoo's adult pandas have long been among Washington's top tourist
attractions, the public debut of the baby in December has unleashed an
almost bestial frenzy here. Some 13,000 timed tickets to see the cub were
snapped up within two hours of being released, and almost immediately
began trading on eBay for up to $200 a pair.

Panda mania is not the only reason that 2005 proved an exceptionally   9
cute year. Last summer, a movie about another black-and-white charmer, the
emperor penguin, became one of the highest-grossing documentaries of all
time.[1] Sales of petite, willfully cute cars like the Toyota Prius and the Mini
Cooper soared, while those of noncute sport utility vehicles tanked.

Women's fashions opted for the cute over the sensible or glamorous,   10
with low-slung slacks and skirts and abbreviated blouses contriving to present a customer's midriff as an adorable preschool bulge. Even the too big
could be too cute. King Kong's newly reissued face has a squashed baby-doll
appeal, and his passion for Naomi Watts ultimately feels like a serious case of
puppy love—hopeless, heartbreaking, cute.[2]

Scientists who study the evolution of visual signaling have identified a   11
wide and still expanding assortment of features and behaviors that make
something look cute: bright forward-facing eyes set low on a big round face,
a pair of big round ears, floppy limbs and a side-to-side, teeter-totter gait,
among many others.

Cute cues are those that indicate extreme youth, vulnerability, harmless-   12
ness and need, scientists say, and attending to them closely makes good Darwinian sense. As a species whose youngest members are so pathetically helpless they can't lift their heads to suckle without adult supervision, human
beings must be wired to respond quickly and gamely to any and all signs of
infantile desire.

The human cuteness detector is set at such a low bar, researchers said,   13
that it sweeps in and deems cute practically anything remotely resembling a
human baby or a part thereof, and so ends up including the young of virtually every mammalian species, fuzzy-headed birds like Japanese cranes, wool-
ly bear caterpillars, a bobbing balloon, a big round rock stacked on a smaller rock, a colon, a hyphen and a close parenthesis typed in succession.

---

[1]A reference to *March of the Penguins* (2005), directed by Luc Jacquet (editors' note).
[2]A reference to the 2005 version of *King Kong*, directed by Peter Jackson and starring Naomi
Watts as Ann Darrow, the oversized ape's female human ally (editors' note).

The greater the number of cute cues that an animal or object happens to possess, or the more exaggerated the signals may be, the louder and more italicized are the squeals provoked.

Cuteness is distinct from beauty, researchers say, emphasizing rounded over sculptured, soft over refined, clumsy over quick. Beauty attracts admiration and demands a pedestal; cuteness attracts affection and demands a lap. Beauty is rare and brutal, despoiled by a single pimple. Cuteness is commonplace and generous, content on occasion to cosegregate with homeliness.

Observing that many Floridians have an enormous affection for the manatee, which looks like an overfertilized potato with a sock puppet's face, Roger L. Reep of the University of Florida said it shone by grace of contrast. "People live hectic lives, and they may be feeling overwhelmed, but then they watch this soft and slow-moving animal, this gentle giant, and they see it turn on its back to get its belly scratched," said Dr. Reep, author with Robert K. Bonde of *The Florida Manatee: Biology and Conservation.*

"That's very endearing," said Dr. Reep. "So even though a manatee is 3 times your size and 20 times your weight, you want to get into the water beside it."

Even as they say a cute tooth has rational roots, scientists admit they are just beginning to map its subtleties and source. New studies suggest that cute images stimulate the same pleasure centers of the brain aroused by sex, a good meal or psychoactive drugs like cocaine, which could explain why everybody in the panda house wore a big grin.

At the same time, said Denis Dutton, a philosopher of art at the University of Canterbury in New Zealand, the rapidity and promiscuity of the cute response makes the impulse suspect, readily overridden by the angry sense that one is being exploited or deceived.

"Cute cuts through all layers of meaning and says, Let's not worry about complexities, just love me," said Dr. Dutton, who is writing a book about Darwinian aesthetics. "That's where the sense of cheapness can come from, and the feeling of being manipulated or taken for a sucker that leads many to reject cuteness as low or shallow."

Quick and cheap make cute appealing to those who want to catch the eye and please the crowd. Advertisers and product designers are forever toying with cute cues to lend their merchandise instant appeal, mixing and monkeying with the vocabulary of cute to keep the message fresh and fetching.

That market-driven exercise in cultural evolution can yield bizarre if endearing results, like the blatantly ugly Cabbage Patch dolls, Furbies, the figgy face of E.T., the froggy one of Yoda. As though the original Volkswagen Beetle wasn't considered cute enough, the updated edition was made rounder and shinier still.

"The new Beetle looks like a smiley face," said Miles Orvell, professor of American studies at Temple University in Philadelphia. "By this point its origins in Hitler's regime, and its intended resemblance to a German helmet, is totally forgotten."

Whatever needs pitching, cute can help. A recent study at the Veterans   24
Affairs Medical Center at the University of Michigan showed that high school students were far more likely to believe antismoking messages accompanied by cute cartoon characters like a penguin in a red jacket or a smirking polar bear than when the warnings were delivered unadorned.

"It made a huge difference," said Sonia A. Duffy, the lead author of the   25
report, which was published in *The Archives of Pediatrics and Adolescent Medicine*. "The kids expressed more confidence in the cartoons than in the warnings themselves."

Primal and widespread though the taste for cute may be, researchers say   26
it varies in strength and significance across cultures and eras. They compare the cute response to the love of sugar: everybody has sweetness receptors on the tongue, but some people, and some countries, eat a lot more candy than others.

Experts point out that the cuteness craze is particularly acute in Japan,   27
where it goes by the name "kawaii" and has infiltrated the most masculine of redoubts. Truck drivers display Hello Kitty–style figurines on their dashboards. The police enliven safety billboards and wanted posters with two perky mouselike mascots, Pipo kun and Pipo chan.

Behind the kawaii phenomenon, according to Brian J. McVeigh, a schol-   28
ar of East Asian studies at the University of Arizona, is the strongly hierarchical nature of Japanese culture. "Cuteness is used to soften up the vertical society," he said, "to soften power relations and present authority without being threatening."

In this country, the use of cute imagery is geared less toward blurring the   29
line of command than toward celebrating America's favorite demographic: the young. Dr. Orvell traces contemporary cute chic to the 1960's, with its celebration of a perennial childhood, a refusal to dress in adult clothes, an inversion of adult values, a love of bright colors and bloopy, cartoony patterns, the Lava Lamp.

Today, it's not enough for a company to use cute graphics in its adver-   30
tisements. It must have a really cute name as well. "Companies like Google and Yahoo leave no question in your mind about the youthfulness of their founders," said Dr. Orvell.

Madison Avenue may adapt its strategies for maximal tweaking of our   31
inherent baby radar, but babies themselves, evolutionary scientists say, did not really evolve to be cute. Instead, most of their salient qualities stem from the demands of human anatomy and the human brain, and became appealing to a potential caretaker's eye only because infants wouldn't survive otherwise.

Human babies have unusually large heads because humans have unusual-   32
ly large brains. Their heads are round because their brains continue to grow

throughout the first months of life, and the plates of the skull stay flexible and unfused to accommodate the development. Baby eyes and ears are situated comparatively far down the face and skull, and only later migrate upward in proportion to the development of bones in the cheek and jaw areas.

Baby eyes are also notably forward-facing, the binocular vision a likely legacy of our tree-dwelling ancestry, and all our favorite Disney characters also sport forward-facing eyes, including the ducks and mice, species that in reality have eyes on the sides of their heads.

The cartilage tissue in an infant's nose is comparatively soft and unde-veloped, which is why most babies have button noses. Baby skin sits relatively loose on the body, rather than being taut, the better to stretch for growth spurts to come, said Paul H. Morris, an evolutionary scientist at the Univer-sity of Portsmouth in England; that lax packaging accentuates the overall roundness of form.

Baby movements are notably clumsy, an amusing combination of jerky and delayed, because learning to coordinate the body's many bilateral sets of large and fine muscle groups requires years of practice. On starting to walk, toddlers struggle continuously to balance themselves between left foot and right, and so the toddler gait consists as much of lateral movement as of any forward momentum.

Researchers who study animals beloved by the public appreciate the human impulse to nurture anything even remotely babylike, though they are at times taken aback by people's efforts to identify with their preferred species. . . .

The giant panda offers . . . [a] case study in accidental cuteness. Although it is a member of the bear family, a highly carnivorous clan, the giant panda specializes in eating bamboo.

As it happens, many of the adaptations that allow it to get by on such a tough diet contribute to the panda's cute form, even in adulthood. Inside the bear's large, rounded head, said Lisa Stevens, assistant panda curator at the National Zoo, are the highly developed jaw muscles and the set of broad, grinding molars it needs to crush its way through some 40 pounds of fibrous bamboo plant a day.

When it sits up against a tree and starts picking apart a bamboo stalk with its distinguishing pseudo-thumb, a panda looks like nothing so much like Huckleberry Finn shucking corn. Yet the humanesque posture and paws again are adaptations to its menu. The bear must have its "hands" free and able to shred the bamboo leaves from their stalks.

The panda's distinctive markings further add to its appeal: the black patches around the eyes make them seem winsomely low on its face, while the black ears pop out cutely against the white fur of its temples.

As with the penguin's tuxedo, the panda's two-toned coat very likely serves a twofold purpose. On the one hand, it helps a feeding bear blend peace-fully into the dappled backdrop of bamboo. On the other, the sharp contrast between light and dark may serve as a social signal, helping the solitary bears locate each other when the time has come to find the perfect, too-cute mate.

Questions for Close Reading

1. What is the selection's thesis? Locate the sentence(s) in which Angier states her main idea. If she doesn't state her thesis explicitly, express it in your own words.
2. Angier uses the scientific term *visual signaling* (paragraphs 2, 11). What is visual signaling? Give some examples from the article of the visual signaling of "cute."
3. In paragraph 13, Angier quotes researchers as saying that the "human cuteness detector is set at . . . a low bar." What does Angier assert is the underlying reason that people respond so strongly to cuteness?
4. In paragraph 26, Angier indicates that cute varies from culture to culture. How does the significance of cute in Japan differ from its significance in the United States? Give some examples of the differences between the two cultures.
5. Refer to your dictionary as needed to define the following words used in the selection: *gamboling* (paragraph 1), *rapture* (1), *sonorous* (7), *despoiled* (15), *cosegregate* (15), *homeliness* (15), *aesthetics* (20), *blatantly* (22), *unadorned* (24), *primal* (26), *redoubts* (27), *hierarchical* (28), *inherent* (31), *salient* (31), and *winsomely* (40).

Questions About the Writer's Craft

1. The opening of a newspaper article is called a *lead*, and its purpose is to hook the reader and set up a framework for the story. Analyze the lead of Angier's article (paragraphs 1–3). How does she try to engage your interest (the hook)? How does this lead frame the contents of the remainder of the article? How are the lead and the thesis statement related in this article?
2. **The pattern.** What is the tone of Angier's article? Why did she adopt this tone? Do you think her tone is appropriate given her objective of defining the term *cuteness*? Explain your answer.
3. **Other patterns.** In paragraph 15, Angier contrasts cuteness with beauty. What are some transitional words and phrases that help sharpen this contrast?
4. **Other patterns.** Paragraphs 32 through 35 contain a lengthy description of a baby's appearance. What is the purpose of this description? Is the description mostly objective or subjective? Support your answer with examples.

Writing Assignments Using Definition as a Pattern of Development

1. In paragraph 15, Angier briefly characterizes beauty as sculptured, refined, and quick. She also contrasts beauty with cuteness. Do you agree with Angier's characterization of beauty? What are some words you would use to characterize beauty? Using Angier's characterization of beauty as a starting point, write an extended definition of beauty. Your essay can be serious, lighthearted, humorous, or satiric. For some insights on beauty, read "Beauty: When the Other Dancer Is the Self" by Alice Walker (page 408).

2. Angier indicates that the American view of cuteness is closely related to our celebration of youth (paragraph 29). Write an extended definition of youth in American culture. Consider actual youthfulness (children), the effort of mature adults
to appear younger than they are, the efforts of young people to appear older than
they are, youthful fashions, and other cultural manifestations of youth in America.
For a view of changing youth culture, you might read "Tweens: Ten Going on
Sixteen" by Kay S. Hymowitz (page 202).

Writing Assignments Combining
Patterns of Development

3. Angier gives examples of cuteness in movies (*March of the Penguins,* the 2005 version of *King Kong,* the characters E.T. and Yoda), product design (the VW Beetle),
and advertising (an antismoking campaign aimed at teens). Select one of these
examples of cuteness—or another of your own choosing—and do some research on
it. For example, if you choose a character in a movie or TV show, watch the movie
or show; if you choose a product, do research on it and use it if possible; and if you
choose an ad campaign, collect examples of the ads. Then write an essay in which
you *describe* the item, explain how it is an *example* of cuteness, and recount the
effect it has on you.

4. Angier's article suggests that all humans respond to cuteness, although there are
cultural differences in these responses. Are there other differences as well? For
example, do men and women respond differently to cuteness? Teenagers and
senior citizens? Parents and nonparents? Reflect on your own experiences with
cuteness, and inquire into the experiences of your friends, family members, and
others. Then write an essay *comparing* and *contrasting* your responses with those
of someone who differs from you in gender, age, or parental status. Explain the
possible *causes* and *effects* of your different responses to cuteness. For one man's
take on some differences between men and women, read "The Ugly Truth About
Beauty" by Dave Barry (page 368).

Writing Assignment Using a Journal
Entry as a Starting Point

5. Review the cute things you listed in your pre-reading journal. Do these things fall
into categories, such as toys, cartoons, or animals? Which of them, if any, are cute
according to the extended definition in Angier's article? Write an essay in which
you *classify* your cute things and explain how they *exemplify* (or do not exemplify) Angier's definition of cute. If your items present different characteristics from
those outlined by Angier, offer your own definition of cuteness.

Alexandra Robbins
Abby Wilner

A contributing editor at *Mademoiselle* magazine, Alexandra Robbins (1976–) has written for such publications as *The New Yorker, The Atlantic Monthly, The Washington Post, Salon,* and *USA Today.* Soon after graduating from Yale University, she began to work on the book *Quarterlife Crisis: The Unique Challenges of Life in Your Twenties* (2001) with her high school friend Abby Wilner (1976–), a Washington University of St. Louis alumna. The book, which became a *New York Times* best-seller, grew out of the two authors' own post-college experiences as well as interviews with several hundred peers. The success of *Quarterlife Crisis* led to its authors' appearing on national and international television and radio programs, including *The Today Show, The Oprah Winfrey Show, CNN Daybreak,* and *BBC Breakfast News.* Abby Wilner has since developed a series of quarterlife crisis workshops and seminars and serves as administrator of the www.quarterlifecrisis.com website. Alexandra Robbins went on to write *Secrets of the Tomb: Skull and Bones, the Ivy League, and the Hidden Paths of Power* (2002), an investigative report on Yale University's infamous secret society, and *Pledged: The Secret Life of Sororities* (2004). Both women live in Washington, D.C. The following essay is the first chapter of *Quarterlife Crisis.*

Pre-Reading Journal Entry

When you look ahead to your future after graduation, what are some of the things you fear? In your pre-reading journal, brainstorm a list of the various concerns you see looming on the horizon. Once you've completed your list, create categories grouping together similar kinds of fears. What are the resulting categories?

What Is the Quarterlife Crisis?

Jim, the neighbor who lives in the three-story colonial down the block, has recently turned 50. You know this because Jim's wife threw him a surprise party about a month ago. You also know this because, since then, Jim has dyed his hair blond, purchased a leather bomber jacket, traded in his Chevy Suburban for a sleek Miata, and ditched the wife for a girlfriend half her size and age.

Yet, aside from the local ladies' group's sympathetic clucks for the scorned wife, few neighbors are surprised at Jim's instant lifestyle change. Instead, they nod their heads understandingly. "Oh, Jim," they say. "He's just going through a midlife crisis. Everyone goes through it." Friends, colleagues, and family members excuse his weird behavior as an inevitable effect of reaching this particular stage of life. Like millions of other middle-aged people, Jim has reached a period during which he believes he must ponder the direction of his life—and then alter it.

Chances are . . . you're not Jim. You know this because you can't afford   3
a leather bomber jacket, you drive your parents' Volvo (if you drive a car at all), and, regardless of your gender, you would happily marry Jim's wife if she gets to keep the house. But Jim's midlife crisis is relevant to you nonetheless, because it is currently the only age-related crisis that is widely recognized as a common, inevitable part of life. This is pertinent because, despite all of the attention lavished on the midlife crisis, despite the hundreds of books, movies, and magazine articles dedicated to explaining the sometimes traumatic transition through middle age and the ways to cope with it, the midlife crisis is not the only age-related crisis that we experience. As Yoda whispered to Luke Skywalker, "There is another."

This other crisis can be just as, if not more, devastating than the midlife   4
crisis. It can throw someone's life into chaotic disarray or paralyze it completely. It may be the single most concentrated period during which individuals relentlessly question their future and how it will follow the events of their past. It covers the interval that encompasses the transition from the academic world to the "real" world—an age group that can range from late adolescence to the mid-thirties but is usually most intense in twentysomethings. It is what we call the quarterlife crisis, and it is a real phenomenon.

The quarterlife crisis and the midlife crisis stem from the same basic   5
problem, but the resulting panic couldn't be more opposite. At their cores, both the quarterlife and the midlife crisis are about a major life change. Often, for people experiencing a midlife crisis, a sense of stagnancy sparks the need for change. During this period, a middle-aged person tends to reflect on his past, in part to see if his life to date measures up to the life he had envisioned as a child (or as a twentysomething). The midlife crisis also impels a middle-aged person to look forward, sometimes with an increasing sense of desperation, at the time he feels he has left.

In contrast, the quarterlife crisis occurs precisely because there is none of   6
that predictable stability that drives middle-aged people to do unpredictable things. After about twenty years in a sheltered school setting—or more if a person has gone on to graduate or professional school—many graduates undergo some sort of culture shock. In the academic environment, goals were clear-cut and the ways to achieve them were mapped out distinctly. To get into a good college or graduate school, it helped if you graduated with honors; to graduate with honors, you needed to get good grades; to get good grades, you had to study hard. If your goals were athletic, you worked your way up from junior varsity or walk-on to varsity by practicing skills, working out in the weightroom, and gelling with teammates and coaches. The better

you were, the more playing time you got, the more impressive your statistics could become.

But after graduation, the pathways blur. In that crazy, wild nexus that people like to call the "real world," there is no definitive way to get from point A to point B, regardless of whether the points are related to a career, financial situation, home, or social life (though we have found through several unscientific studies that offering to pay for the next round of drinks can usually improve three out of the four). The extreme uncertainty that twentysomethings experience after graduation occurs because what was once a solid line that they could follow throughout their series of educational institutions has now disintegrated into millions of different options. The sheer number of possibilities can certainly inspire hope—that is why people say that twentysomethings have their whole lives ahead of them. But the endless array of decisions can also make a recent graduate feel utterly lost.

So while the midlife crisis revolves around a doomed sense of stagnancy, of a life set on pause while the rest of the world rattles on, the quarterlife crisis is a response to overwhelming instability, constant change, too many choices, and a panicked sense of helplessness. Just as the monotony of a lifestyle stuck in idle can drive a person to question himself intently, so, too, can the uncertainty of a life thrust into chaos. The transition from childhood to adulthood—from school to the world beyond—comes as a jolt for which many of today's twentysomethings simply are not prepared. The resulting overwhelming senses of helplessness and cluelessness, of indecision and apprehension, make up the real and common experience we call the quarterlife crisis. Individuals who are approaching middle age at least know what is coming. Because the midlife crisis is so widely acknowledged, people who undergo it are at the very least aware that there are places where they can go for help, such as support groups, books, movies, or Internet sites. Twentysomethings, by contrast, face a crisis that hits them with a far more powerful force than they ever expected. The slam is particularly painful because today's twentysomethings believe that they are alone and that they are having a much more difficult transition period than their peers—because the twenties are supposed to be "easy," because no one talks about these problems, and because the difficulties are therefore so unexpected. And at the fragile, doubt-ridden age during which the quarterlife crisis occurs, the ramifications can be extremely dangerous.

Why Worry About a Quarterlife Crisis?

The whirlwind of new responsibilities, new liberties, and new choices can be entirely overwhelming for someone who has just emerged from the shelter of twenty years of schooling. We don't mean to make graduates sound as if they have been hibernating since they emerged from the womb; certainly it is not as if they have been slumbering throughout adolescence (though some probably tried). They have in a sense, however, been encased in a bit of a cocoon, where someone or something—parents or school, for example—has protected them from a lot of the scariness of their surroundings. As a result, when graduates are let loose into the world, their dreams and desires can be tinged with trepidation. They are hopeful, but at the same time they are also, to put it simply, scared silly.

Some might say that because people have had to deal with the rite of passage from youth to adulthood since the beginning of time, this crisis is not really a "crisis" at all, given that historically this transitional period has, at various times, been marked with ceremonial rituals involving things like spears and buffalo dung. Indeed, it may not always have been a crisis.

But it has become one . . .

Although hope is a common emotion for twentysomethings, hopelessness has become just as widespread. The revelation that life simply isn't easy—a given for some twentysomethings, a mild inconvenience for others, but a shattering blow for several—is one of the most distressing aspects of the quarterlife crisis, particularly for individuals who do not have large support networks or who doubt themselves often. It is in these situations that the quarterlife crisis becomes not just a common stage—it can become hazardous. Not everyone at the age of the quarterlife encounters some sort of depression. . . . But we are addressing depression as one common result of the quarterlife crisis here so that we can illustrate why it is so important to acknowledge this transition period.

After interviewing dozens of twentysomethings who said they were depressed because of the transition, we ran our conclusions by Robert DuPont, a Georgetown Medical School professor of psychology who wrote *The Anxiety Cure.* "Based on my experience," DuPont said, "I have found that there is a high rate of all forms of disorder in this age group, including addiction, anxiety, depression, and many other kinds of problems because of the high stress associated with the transition from being a child to being an adult. And that has gotten more stressful as the road map has become less used. The old way of doing this was to get out and get it done right away. There was an economic imperative to doing it. It's not like that anymore. And as the road map has disappeared, the stress has gone up. People have to invent their own road map. It used to be that it came with the college graduation. Now you have to go out and figure it out yourself."

These high rates of disorders, however, have gone virtually unacknowledged. That's why we can't bog you down with statistics on this age group. They don't exist. Psychological research on twentysomethings, including statistics on depression and suicide, has not been performed. We asked major national mental health associations such as the National Institutes of Mental Health, the American Psychiatric Association, and the National Depressive and Manic Depressive Association for any information they had on people in their twenties. They didn't have any. As one psychologist told us, associations don't cut the data to incorporate this age group. "It's not a subject that's interesting to them. They just lump everybody together," he said. . . .

Another way the quarterlife crisis can show up, particularly in the mid- 15 to late twenties, is in a feeling of disappointment, of "This is all there is?" Maybe the job turns out to be not so glamorous after all, or maybe it just doesn't seem to lead anywhere interesting. Perhaps the year of travel in Europe was more of a wallet buster than previously imagined—even with nights in youth hostels and meals of ramen. Or maybe the move to a hip, new city just didn't turn out to be as fabulous a relocation as expected.

While these are, according to older generations, supposed to be the best 16 years of their lives, twentysomethings also feel that the choices they make during this period will influence their thirties, forties, fifties, and on, in an irreparable domino effect. As a result, twentysomethings frequently have the unshakable belief that this is the time during which they have to nail down the meaning in their lives, which explains why they often experience a nagging feeling that somehow they need to make their lives more fulfilling. This is why there are so many drastic life changes at this point in life: an investment banker breaks off his engagement and volunteers for the Peace Corps; a consultant suddenly frets that consulting may not really have that much influence on other people's lives; a waiter chucks the steady paycheck to live in his car and try to make it in Hollywood; a law school graduate decides she doesn't want to be a lawyer after all and seeks a job in technology.

The changes hurtling toward a young adult, as well as the potential for 17 more changes ahead, can be excruciatingly overwhelming for someone who is trying so hard to figure out how to feel fulfilled. A lot of people don't realize just how suffocating this pressure can be. The prevalent belief is that twentysomethings have it relatively easy because they do not have as many responsibilities as older individuals. But it is precisely this reduced responsibility that renders the vast array of decisions more difficult to make. For instance, if there were, say, a family to consider, a mother might not be as inclined to take a risk on the stock market. If a guy's elderly father were sick, he probably wouldn't take that year off to travel in South America. Twentysomethings, for the most part, just aren't at those stages yet, which is why they are sometimes envied. But because their choices aren't narrowed down for them by responsibilities, they have more decisions to make. And while this isn't necessarily bad, it can make things pretty complex. Figuring out which changes to make in order to make life more fulfilling is hard enough. But deciding to make a change and then following through with it requires an extraordinary amount of strength, which is sometimes hard to come by for a recent graduate who has not had to rely solely on himself for very long.

The most widespread, frightening, and quite possibly the most difficult 18 manifestation of the quarterlife crisis is a feeling that can creep up on a twentysomething whether he is unemployed, living at home, and friendless, or in an interesting job, with a great apartment, and dozens of buddies. Regardless of their levels of self-esteem, confidence, and overall well-being, twenty-somethings are particularly vulnerable to doubts. They doubt their decisions, their abilities, their readiness, their past, present, and future . . . but most of all, they doubt themselves. The twenties comprise a period of intense questioning—of introspection and self-development that young adults often feel they are not ready for. The questions can range from seemingly trivial choices—"Should I really have spent $100 to join that fantasy base-ball league?"—to irrefutably mammoth decisions—"When is the right time for me to start a family?" It is healthy, of course, for people to question themselves some; an occasional self-assessment or life inventory is a natural part of the quest for improvement. But if the questioning becomes constant and the barrage of doubts never seems to cease, twentysomethings can feel as if it is hard to catch their breath, as if they are spiraling downward. Many times the doubts increase because twentysomethings think it is abnormal to have them in the first place. No one talks about having doubts at this age, so when twentysomethings do find that they are continuously questioning themselves, they think something is wrong with them.

Questions for Close Reading

1. What is the selection's thesis? Locate the sentence(s) in which Robbins and Wilner state their main idea. If they don't state the thesis explicitly, express it in your own words.
2. People can be affected by the quarterlife crisis when they are in what age range? What age group is typically most vulnerable to it?
3. According to the authors, how is the quarterlife crisis similar to its midlife coun-terpart? How is it different?
4. At the end of the essay, Robbins and Wilner discuss the "most difficult manifesta-tion" of the quarterlife crisis. What is this manifestation? What is so bad about it?
5. Refer to your dictionary as needed to define the following words used in the selec-tion: *pertinent* (paragraph 3), *chaotic* (4), *disarray* (4), *interval* (4), *phenomenon* (4), *stagnancy* (5), *nexus* (7), *monotony* (8), *ramifications* (8), *trepidation* (9), *vir-tually* (14), *ramen* (15), *excruciatingly* (17), *manifestation* (18), and *barrage* (18).

Questions About the Writer's Craft

1. **The pattern.** What is Robbins and Wilner's underlying purpose in defining the term *quarterlife crisis?* Is their purpose mainly informative, speculative, or persua-sive? How do you know?
2. **Other patterns.** The essay opens with a *narrative* anecdote about "Jim." Why do you think the authors chose to begin the essay this way? How does this anec-dote relate to the paragraphs that follow it?
3. **Other patterns.** A central component in Robbins and Wilner's definition of the quarterlife crisis is a *causal analysis* of this phenomenon. What are the causes and effects they identify? How does this causal analysis contribute to the shaping of their definition?

4. Other patterns. In developing their definition of *quarterlife crisis,* the authors *compare* and *contrast* it to midlife crisis. What signal devices do they use to organize and clarify the comparisons and contrasts they identify?

Writing Assignments Using Definition as a Pattern of Development

1. In their essay and in the book in which it appears, Robbins and Wilner coin and define a kind of crisis they've observed or even experienced. Write an essay in which you coin the term for and define another kind of crisis. You might, for example, discuss the exam-cram crisis, the blind-date crisis, or the empty-fridge crisis. Be sure you give an "official" name to your crisis, and go on to develop your definition with specific examples and illustrations. A humorous or a mock-serious tone is likely to be most appropriate for your essay.

2. Underlying the quarterlife crisis, Robbins and Wilner imply, is a young person's anxiety about having to "grow up." But the meaning of growing up can vary widely from person to person. Write an essay in which you define what you think it means to "grow up." Here are some key questions you might ask yourself in formulating your definition: What new concerns and responsibilities are involved in growing up? What old priorities are left behind? At what point should people grow up? Is growing up a desirable objective? Do you feel you've reached this stage yet? Discussing these issues with friends and family before you begin writing might help you clarify your ideas. And for additional perspectives on the subject of growing up—especially growing up *too soon*—you should consult Ellen Goodman's "Family Counterculture" (page 6) and Kay S. Hymowitz's "Tweens: Ten Going on Sixteen" (page 202).

Writing Assignments Combining Patterns of Development

3. The classic definition of the word *crisis* is "turning point," though today the word generally carries the connotation of "distressing event." Think about a significant crisis you experienced at some point in your life, and write an essay *narrating* this event. Be sure in the course of your essay to examine the *causes* and *effects* of the crisis, paying special attention to whether and how you still feel its effects. Other accounts of personal crisis you might want to read before you write include any of the following: Audre Lorde's "The Fourth of July" (page 137), George Orwell's "Shooting an Elephant" (page 143), Langston Hughes's "Salvation" (page 155), Adam Mayblum's "The Price We Pay" (page 159), Beth Johnson's "Bombs Bursting in Air" (page 209), and Joseph H. Suina's "And Then I Went to School" (page 354).

4. One of the causes of the quarterlife crisis, according to the authors, is that the single clear path of education has "disintegrated into millions of different options." Write an essay in which you *divide* and *classify* three options for your future that you have considered (or are still considering). For instance, you might discuss becoming a teacher, going to law school, pursuing a performance art, enlisting in the military, creating an Internet start-up—any three possibilities you have envisioned, no matter how impractical. Discuss each career option in at least one

separate paragraph, detailing your *causes* for considering that career and speculating on the possible *effects* of selecting that path. If appropriate, you might consider doing some research in the library and/or on the Internet into projected trends—economic, social, and so on—regarding your career choices as a way of helping explain your selections.

Writing Assignment Using a Journal Entry as a Starting Point

5. Write an essay in which you identify the three main *categories* of worries you have about the future. Such categories might include career, relationship, environmental, geopolitical, and so on. For each category of worry, be sure to present a variety of specific *examples* and explanations of why these issues concern you. For instance, if you discuss the category of economic worries, you might explain that your anxiety stems from having to pay off student loans and other debts, not earning enough money in your job, needing to support a family, and so on. For additional perspectives on this issue, you might also consider talking about these issues with friends and family.

William Raspberry

Journalist William Raspberry was born in 1935 in Okolona, Mississippi. From his mother, an English teacher and poet, Raspberry learned to care "about the rhythm and grace of words." His father, a shop teacher, taught him "that neither end tables nor arguments are worthwhile unless they stand solidly on all four legs." Raspberry graduated from Indiana Central College and later joined the staff of the Indianapolis *Recorder* as a reporter and editor. Following a two-year stint in the army, he was hired by *The Washington Post,* where his nationally syndicated column ran from 1971 to 2005. His coverage of the Watts race riots in 1965 won him the Capital Press Club Journalist of the Year award, and he later went on to win the Pulitzer Prize for commentary in 1994. *Looking Backward at Us,* a collection of Raspberry's columns, was published in 1991. He currently teaches Communication and Journalism at Duke University. He and his wife live in Washington, D.C., and have three children. The following selection appeared in Raspberry's *Washington Post* column in 1982.

Pre-Reading Journal Entry

Which do you think plays a more important role in determining what a person accomplishes: innate talent or belief in oneself? Take a few minutes to respond to this question in your journal, jotting down examples drawn from your experiences and observations.

The Handicap of Definition

I know all about bad schools, mean politicians, economic deprivation and racism. Still, it occurs to me that one of the heaviest burdens black Americans—and black children in particular—have to bear is the handicap of definition: the question of what it means to be black. 1

Let me explain quickly what I mean. If a basketball fan says that the Boston Celtics' Larry Bird plays "black," the fan intends it—and Bird probably accepts it—as a compliment. Tell pop singer Tom Jones he moves "black" and he might grin in appreciation. Say to Teena Marie or the Average White Band that they sound "black" and they'll thank you. 2

But name one pursuit, aside from athletics, entertainment or sexual performance, in which a white practitioner will feel complimented to be told he does it "black." Tell a white broadcaster he talks "black" and he'll sign up 3 for diction lessons. Tell a white reporter he writes "black" and he'll take a writing course. Tell a white lawyer he reasons "black" and he might sue you for slander.

What we have here is a tragically limited definition of blackness, and it isn't only white people who buy it.

Think of all the ways black children can put one another down with charges of "whiteness." For many of these children, hard study and hard work are "white." Trying to please a teacher might be criticized as acting "white." Speaking correct English is "white." Scrimping today in the interest of tomorrow's goals is "white." Educational toys and games are "white."

An incredible array of habits and attitudes that are conducive to success in business, in academia, in the nonentertainment professions are likely to be thought of as somehow "white." Even economic success, unless it involves such "black" undertakings as numbers banking, is defined as "white."

And the results are devastating. I wouldn't deny that blacks often are better entertainers and athletes. My point is the harm that comes from too narrow a definition of what is black.

One reason black youngsters tend to do better at basketball, for instance, is that they assume they can learn to do it well, and so they practice constantly to prove themselves right.

Wouldn't it be wonderful if we could infect black children with the notion that excellence in math is "black" rather than white, or possibly Chinese? Wouldn't it be of enormous value if we could create the myth that morality, strong families, determination, courage and love of learning are traits brought by slaves from Mother Africa and therefore quintessentially black?

There is no doubt in my mind that most black youngsters could develop their mathematical reasoning, their elocution and their attitudes, the way they develop their jump shots and their dance steps: by the combination of sustained, enthusiastic practice and the unquestioned belief that they can do it.

In one sense, what I am talking about is the importance of developing positive ethnic traditions. Maybe Jews have an innate talent for communication; maybe the Chinese are born with a gift for mathematical reasoning; maybe blacks are naturally blessed with athletic grace. I doubt it. What is at work, I suspect, is assumption, inculcated early in their lives, that this is a thing our people do well.

Unfortunately, many of the things about which blacks make this assumption are things that do not contribute to their career success—except for that handful of the truly gifted who can make it as entertainers and athletes. And many of the things we concede to whites are the things that are essential to economic security.

So it is with a number of assumptions black youngsters make about what it is to be a "man": physical aggressiveness, sexual prowess, the refusal to submit to authority. The prisons are full of people who, by this perverted definition, are unmistakably men.

But the real problem is not so much that the things defined as "black"   14
are negative. The problem is that the definition is much too narrow.

Somehow, we have to make our children understand that they are intel-   15
ligent, competent people, capable of doing whatever they put their minds to
and making it in the American mainstream, not just in a black subculture.

What we seem to be doing, instead, is raising up yet another generation   16
of young blacks who will be failures—by definition.

Questions for Close Reading

1. What is the selection's thesis? Locate the sentence(s) in which Raspberry states his main idea. If he doesn't state the thesis explicitly, express it in your own words.
2. In paragraph 14, Raspberry emphasizes that the word *black* presents a problem not because it's negative but because it has become "much too narrow." According to Raspberry, what limitations have become associated with the term *black*? What negative consequences does he see resulting from these limitations?
3. In paragraph 11, Raspberry talks about "positive ethnic traditions." What does he mean by this term? What examples does he provide?
4. In Raspberry's opinion, what needs to be done to ensure the future success of African-American children?
5. Refer to your dictionary as needed to define the following words used in the selection: *diction* (paragraph 3), *scrimping* (5), *array* (6), *quintessentially* (9), *elocution* (10), *inculcated* (11), and *concede* (12).

Questions About the Writer's Craft

1. **The pattern.** Raspberry is primarily concerned with showing how limited the definition of *black* has come to be in our society. In the course of the essay, though, he also defines three other terms. Locate these terms and their definitions. How do the definitions and the effects of the definitions help Raspberry make his point about the narrowness of the term *black?*
2. **Other patterns.** In his opening paragraph, Raspberry uses the *argumentation* technique of refutation. What does he refute? What does he achieve by using this strategy at the very beginning of the essay?
3. A black journalist, Raspberry wrote, for many years, a nationally syndicated column that originated in *The Washington Post,* a major newspaper serving the nation's capital and the nation as a whole. Consider these facts when examining Raspberry's use of the pronouns *I, we,* and *our* in the essay. What do these pronouns seem to imply about Raspberry's intended audience? What is the effect of these pronouns?
4. Raspberry has chosen a relatively abstract topic to write about—the meaning of the term *black.* What techniques does he use to draw in readers and keep them engaged? Consider his overall tone, choice of examples, and use of balanced sentence structure.

Writing Assignments Using Definition as a Pattern of Development

1. Raspberry points out how restrictive the definitions of *black* and *white* can be. Do you think that the definitions of *male* and *female* can be equally restrictive?

Focusing on the term *male* or *female,* write an essay showing how the term was defined as you were growing up. Considering the messages conveyed by your family, the educational system, and society at large, indicate whether you came to perceive the term as limiting or liberating. Before planning your paper, you may want to read one or more of the following essays, all of which deal with the way gender roles influence behavior: Barbara Ehrenreich's "What I've Learned From Men" (page 215) and Virginia Woolf's "Professions for Women" (page 588).

2. In paragraph 15, Raspberry seems to define *success* as "making it in the American mainstream," but not everyone would agree that this is what constitutes success. Write an essay in which you offer your personal definition of *success.* One way to proceed might be to contrast what you consider success with what you consider failure. Or you might narrate the success story of a person you respect highly. No matter how you proceed, be sure to provide telling specifics that support your definition.

Writing Assignments Combining Patterns of Development

3. Like most people, you've probably had a "defining" term applied to you at one time or another. Perhaps you've been called "shy" or "stubborn" or "the class clown" or "the athlete in the family." Focusing on one such label that's been applied to you, write an essay showing the *effect* of this term on your life. Be sure to explain why you got the label and how you felt about it. The following essays will give you additional perspectives on the ways that labels and names affect people's lives and self-image: Joseph H. Suina's "And Then I Went to School" (page 354), Alice Walker's "Beauty: When the Other Dancer Is the Self" (page 408), and Roberto Rodriguez's "The Border on Our Backs" (page 562).

4. In his conclusion, Raspberry makes a plea for providing the younger generation with a more positive, more expansive definition of *black.* Consider the beliefs and principles that today's older generation seems to impart to the younger generation. Write an essay *arguing* which aspects of this value system seem helpful and valid and which do not. Also explain what additional values and convictions the older generation should be passing on, providing *examples* along the way. How should parents, teachers, and others convey these precepts? For a discussion of some obstacles to children's moral instruction, read Ellen Goodman's "Family Counterculture" (page 6) and Kay S. Hymowitz's "Tweens: Ten Going on Sixteen (page 202).

Writing Assignment Using a Journal Entry as a Starting Point

5. Developing the material in your pre-reading journal entry, write an essay arguing that an individual's innate talent *or* self-confidence is the critical factor in determining achievement. Consider brainstorming with others to generate examples in support of your contention. At some point in the essay, you should acknowledge the opposing viewpoint, dismantling as much of it as you can. For an inspirational account of personal achievement despite the odds, read Jacques D'Amboise's "Showing What Is Possible" (page 402).

Additional Writing Topics

DEFINITION

General Assignments

Use definition to develop any of the following topics. Once you fix on a limited subject, decide if the essay has an informative or a persuasive purpose. The paper might begin with the etymology of the term, a stipulative definition, or a definition by negation. You may want to use a number of writing patterns—such as description, comparison, narration, process analysis—to develop the definition. Remember, too, that the paper doesn't have to be scholarly and serious. There is no reason it can't be a lighthearted discussion of the meaning of a term.

1. Fads
2. A family fight
3. Helplessness
4. An epiphany
5. A workaholic
6. A Pollyanna
7. A con artist
8. A stingy person
9. A team player
10. A Yiddish term like *mensch, klutz,* or *chutzpah,* or a term from some other ethnic group
11. Adolescence
12. Fast food
13. A perfect day
14. Hypocrisy
15. Inner peace
16. Obsession
17. Generosity
18. Exploitation
19. Depression
20. A double bind

Assignments With a Specific Purpose, Audience, and Point of View

On Campus

1. You've been asked to write part of a pamphlet for students who come to the college health clinic. For this pamphlet, define *one* of the following conditions and its symptoms: *depression, stress, burnout, test anxiety, addiction* (to alcohol, drugs, or TV), *workaholism.* Part of the pamphlet should describe ways to cope with the condition described.

2. One of your responsibilities as a peer counselor in the student counseling center involves helping students communicate more effectively. To assist students, write a definition of some term that you think represents an essential component of a strong interpersonal relationship. You might, for example, define *respect, sharing, equality,* or *trust.* Part of the definition should employ definition by negation, a discussion of what the term is *not.*

At Home or in the Community

3. *Newsweek* magazine runs a popular column called "My Turn," consisting of readers' opinions on subjects of general interest. Write a piece for this column defining *today's college students.* Use the piece to dispel some negative stereotypes (for example, that college students are apathetic, ill-informed, self-centered, and materialistic).

4. In your apartment building, several residents have complained about their neighbors' inconsiderate and rude behavior. You're president of the Residents' Association, and it's your responsibility to address this problem at your next meeting. Prepare a talk in which you define *courtesy,* the quality you consider most essential to neighborly relations. Use specific examples of what courtesy is and isn't to illustrate your definition.

On the Job

5. You're an attorney arguing a case of sexual harassment—a charge your client has leveled against an employer. To win the case, you must present to the jury a clear definition of exactly what *sexual harassment* is and isn't. Write such a definition for your opening remarks in court.

6. A new position has opened in your company. Write a job description to be sent to employment agencies that will screen candidates. Your description should define the job's purpose, state the duties involved, and outline essential qualifications.

ARGUMENTATION-PERSUASION

WHAT IS ARGUMENTATION-PERSUASION?

"You can't possibly believe what you're saying."
"Look, I know what I'm talking about, and that's that."

Does this heated exchange sound familiar? Probably. When we hear the word *argument,* most of us think of a verbal battle propelled by stubbornness and irrational thought, with one person pitted against the other.

Argumentation in writing, though, is a different matter. Using clear thinking and logic, the writer tries to convince readers of the soundness of a particular opinion on a controversial issue. If, while trying to convince, the writer uses emotional language and dramatic appeals to readers' concerns, beliefs, and values, then the piece is called *persuasion.* Besides encouraging acceptance of an opinion, persuasion often urges readers (or another group) to commit themselves to a course of action. Assume you're writing an essay protesting the federal government's policy of offering aid to those suffering from hunger in other countries while many Americans go hungry. If your purpose is to document, coolly and objectively, the presence of hunger in the United States, you would prepare an argumentation essay.

Such an essay would be filled with statistics, report findings, and expert opinion to demonstrate how widespread hunger is nationwide. If, however, your purpose is to shake up readers, even motivate them to write letters to their congressional representatives and push for a change in policy, you would write a persuasive essay. In this case, your essay might contain emotional accounts of undernourished children, ill-fed pregnant women, and nearly starving elderly people.

Because people respond rationally *and* emotionally to situations, argumentation and persuasion are usually *combined*. Suppose you decide to write an article for the campus newspaper advocating a pre–Labor Day start for the school year. Your audience includes the college administration, students, and faculty. The article might begin by *arguing* that several schools starting the academic year earlier were able to close for the month of January and thus reduce heating and other maintenance expenses. Such an argument, supported by documented facts and figures, would help convince the administration. Realizing that you also have to gain student and faculty support for your idea, you might argue further that the proposed change would mean that students and faculty could leave for winter break with the semester behind them—papers written, exams taken, grades calculated and recorded. To make this part of your argument especially compelling, you could adopt a *persuasive* strategy by using emotional appeals and positively charged language: "Think how pleasant it would be to sleep late, spend time with family and friends, toast the New Year—without having to worry about work awaiting you back on campus."

When argumentation and persuasion blend in this way, emotion *supports* rather than *replaces* logic and sound reasoning. Although some writers resort to emotional appeals to the exclusion of rational thought, when you prepare argumentation-persuasion essays, you should advance your position through a balanced appeal to reason and emotion.

HOW ARGUMENTATION-PERSUASION FITS YOUR PURPOSE AND AUDIENCE

You probably realize that argumentation, persuasion, or a combination of the two is everywhere: an editorial urging the overhaul of an ill-managed literacy program; a commercial for a new shampoo; a scientific report advocating increased funding for AIDS research. Your own writing involves argumentation-persuasion as well. When you prepare a *causal analysis, descriptive piece, narrative,* or *definition essay,* you advance a specific point of view: MTV has a negative influence on teens' view of sex; Cape Cod in winter is imbued with a special kind of magic; a disillusioning experience can teach people much about themselves; *character* can be defined as the willingness to take unpopular positions on difficult issues. Indeed, an essay organized around any of the patterns of development described in this book may have a persuasive intent. You might, for example, encourage readers to try out a *process* you've explained, or to see one of the two movies you've *compared*.

Argumentation-persuasion, however, involves more than presenting a point of view and providing evidence. Unlike other forms of writing, it assumes controversy and addresses opposing viewpoints. Consider the following assignments, all of which require the writer to take a position on a controversial issue:

> In parts of the country, communities established for older citizens or childless couples have refused to rent to families with children. How do you feel about this situation? What do you think are the rights of the parties involved?

> Citing the fact that the highest percentage of automobile accidents involve young men, insurance companies consistently charge their highest rates to young males. Is this policy fair? Why or why not?

> Some colleges and universities have instituted a "no pass, no play" policy for athletes. Explain why this practice is or is not appropriate.

It's impossible to predict with absolute certainty what will make readers accept the view you advance or take the action you propose. But the ancient Greeks, who formulated our basic concepts of logic, isolated three factors crucial to the effectiveness of argumentation-persuasion: *logos, pathos,* and *ethos.*

Your main concern in an argumentation-persuasion essay should be with the *logos,* or soundness, of your argument: the facts, statistics, examples, and authoritative statements you gather to support your viewpoint. This supporting evidence must be unified, specific, adequate, accurate, and representative (see pages 33–37). Imagine, for instance, you want to convince people that a popular charity misappropriates the money it receives from the public. Your readers, inclined to believe in the good works of the charity, will probably dismiss your argument unless you can substantiate your claim with valid, well-documented evidence that enhances the *logos* of your position.

Sensitivity to *pathos,* or the emotional power of language, is another key consideration for writers of argumentation-persuasion essays. *Pathos* appeals to readers' needs, values, and attitudes, encouraging them to commit themselves to a viewpoint or course of action. The *pathos* of a piece derives partly from the writer's language. *Connotative* language—words with strong emotional overtones—can move readers to accept a point of view and may even spur them to act.

Advertising and propaganda generally rely on *pathos* to the exclusion of logic, using emotion to influence and manipulate. Consider the following pitches for a man's cologne and a woman's perfume. The language—and the attitudes to which it appeals—is different in each case:

> Brawn: Experience the power. Bold. Yet subtle. Clean. Masculine. The scent for the man who's in charge.

> Black Lace is for you—the woman who dresses for success but who dares to be provocative, slightly naughty. Black Lace. Perfect with pearls by day and with diamonds by night.

The appeal to men plays on the impact that terms like *Brawn, bold, power,* and *in charge* may have for some males. Similarly, the charged words *Black Lace, provocative, naughty,* and *diamonds* are intended to appeal to business women who—in the advertiser's mind, at least—may be looking for ways to reconcile sensuality and professionalism. (For more on slanted language, read Ann McClintock's "Propaganda Techniques in Today's Advertising," page 270.)

Like an advertising copywriter, you must select language that reinforces your message. In a paper supporting an expanded immigration policy, you might use evocative phrases like "land of liberty," "a nation of immigrants," and "America's open-door policy." However, if you were arguing for strict immigration quotas, you might use language like "save jobs for unemployed Americans," "flood of unskilled labor," and "illegal aliens." Remember, though: Such language should support, not supplant, clear thinking.

Finally, whenever you write an argumentation-persuasion essay, you should establish your *ethos,* or credibility and integrity. You cannot expect readers to accept or act on your viewpoint unless you convince them that you know what you're talking about and that you're worth listening to. Be sure, then, to tell readers about any experiences you've had that make you knowledgeable about the issue being discussed. You will also come across as knowledgeable and trustworthy if you present a logical, reasoned argument that takes opposing views into account. And make sure that your appeals to emotion aren't excessive. Overwrought emotionalism undercuts credibility. Remember, too, that *ethos* isn't constant. A writer may have credibility on one subject but not on another: An army general might be a reliable source for information on military preparedness but not for information on federal funding of day care.

Writing an effective argumentation-persuasion essay involves an interplay of *logos, pathos,* and *ethos.* The exact balance among these factors is determined by your audience and purpose (that is, whether you want the audience simply to agree with your view or whether you also want them to take action). More than any other kind of writing, argumentation-persuasion requires that you *analyze your readers* and tailor your approach to them. You need to determine how much they know about the issue, how they feel about you and your position, what their values and attitudes are, what motivates them.

In general, most readers will fall into one of three broad categories: supportive, wavering, or hostile. Each type of audience requires a different blend of *logos, pathos,* and *ethos* in an argumentation-persuasion essay.

1. A supportive audience.   If your audience agrees with your position and trusts your credibility, you don't need a highly reasoned argument dense with facts, examples, and statistics. Although you may want to solidify support by providing additional information (*logos*), you can rely primarily on *pathos*—a strong emotional appeal—to reinforce readers' commitment to your shared viewpoint. Assume that you belong to a local fishing club and have volunteered to write an article encouraging members to support threatened fishing rights in state parks. You might begin by stating that fishing strengthens the fish population by thinning out overcrowded streams. Since your audience would certainly be familiar with this idea, you wouldn't need to devote much discussion to it. Instead, you would attempt to move them emotionally. You might evoke the camaraderie in the sport, the pleasure of a perfect cast, the beauty of the outdoors, and perhaps conclude with "If you want these enjoyments to continue, please make a generous contribution to our fund."

2. A wavering audience.   At times, readers may be open to what you have to say but may not be committed fully to your viewpoint. Or perhaps they're not as informed about the subject as they should be. In either case, you don't want to risk alienating them with a heavy-handed emotional appeal. Concentrate instead on *ethos* and *logos,* bolstering your image as a reliable source and providing the evidence needed to advance your position. If you want to convince an audience of high school seniors to take a year off to work between high school and college, you might establish your credibility by recounting the year you spent working and by showing the positive effects it had on your life (*ethos*). In addition, you could cite studies indicating that delayed entry into college is related to higher grade point averages. A year's savings, you would explain, allows students to study when they might otherwise need to hold down a job to earn money for tuition (*logos*).

3. A hostile audience.   An apathetic, skeptical, or hostile audience is obviously most difficult to convince. With such an audience, you should avoid emotional appeals because they might seem irrational, sentimental, or even comical. Instead, weigh the essay heavily in favor of logical reasoning and hard-to-dispute facts (*logos*). Assume your college administration is working to ban liquor from the student pub. You plan to submit to the campus newspaper an open letter supporting this generally unpopular effort. To sway other students, you cite the positive experiences of schools that have gone dry. Many colleges, you explain, have found their tavern revenues actually increase because all students—not just those of drinking age—can now support the pub. With the greater revenues, some schools have upgraded the food served in the pubs and have hired disc jockeys or musical groups to provide entertainment. Many schools have also seen a sharp reduction in alcohol-related vandalism. Readers may not be won over to your side, but your sound, logical argument may encourage them to be more tolerant of your viewpoint. Indeed, such increased receptivity may be all you can reasonably expect from a hostile audience. (For more help in analyzing your audience, see pages 17–18.)

At this point, you have a good sense of the way writers use argumentation-persuasion to achieve their purpose and to connect with their readers. Take a moment to look closely at the website screen shot at the beginning of this chapter. The sponsoring organization is SADD, Students Against Destructive Decisions. Imagine you're writing an article, linked to this website, about the single most destructive decision made by young people today. Jot down some ideas you might cover when *arguing* that this problem merits serious consideration.

SUGGESTIONS FOR USING ARGUMENTATION-PERSUASION IN AN ESSAY

1. At the beginning of the paper, identify the controversy surrounding the issue and state your position in the thesis.   Your introduction should clarify the controversy about the issue. In addition, it should provide as much background information as your readers are likely to need.

The thesis of an argumentation-persuasion paper is often called the *assertion* or *proposition*. Occasionally, the proposition appears at the paper's end, but it is usually stated at the beginning. If you state the thesis right away, your audience knows where you stand and is better able to evaluate the evidence presented.

Remember: Argumentation-persuasion assumes conflicting viewpoints. Be sure your proposition focuses on a controversial issue and indicates your view. Avoid a proposition that is merely factual; what is demonstrably true allows little room for debate. To see the difference between a factual statement and an effective thesis, examine the two statements that follow:

Fact: In the past decade, the nation's small farmers have suffered financial hardships.

Thesis: Inefficient management, rather than competition from agricultural conglomerates, is responsible for the financial plight of the nation's small farmers.

The first statement is certainly true. It would be difficult to find anyone who believes that these are easy times for small farmers. Because the statement invites little opposition, it can't serve as the focus of an argumentation-persuasion essay. The second statement, though, takes a controversial stance on a complex issue. Such a proposition is a valid starting point for a paper intended to argue and persuade. However, don't assume that such advice means that you should take a highly opinionated position in your thesis. A dogmatic, overstated proposition ("Campus security is staffed by overpaid, badge-flashing incompetents") is bound to alienate some readers.

Remember also to keep the proposition narrow and specific, so you can focus your thoughts in a purposeful way. Consider the following statements:

Broad thesis: The welfare system has been abused over the years.

Narrow thesis: Welfare payments should be denied to unmarried teenage girls who have more than one child out of wedlock.

If you tried to write a paper based on the first statement, you would face an unmanageable task—showing all the ways that welfare has been abused. Your readers would also be confused about what to expect in the paper: Will it discuss unscrupulous bureaucrats, fraudulent bookkeeping, dishonest recipients? In contrast, the revised thesis is limited and specific. It signals that the paper will propose severe restrictions on welfare payments. Such a proposal will surely have opponents and is thus appropriate for argumentation-persuasion.

The thesis in an argumentation-persuasion essay can simply state your opinion about an issue, or it can go a step further and call for some action:

Opinion: The lack of affordable day care centers discriminates against lower-income families.

Call for action: The federal government should support the creation of more day care centers in low-income neighborhoods.

In either case, your stand on the issue must be clear to your readers.

2. Provide readers with strong support for the thesis. Finding evidence that relates to the readers' needs, values, and experience is a crucial part of

writing an effective argumentation-persuasion essay. Readers will be respon-
sive to evidence that is *unified, adequate, specific, accurate,* and *representative*
(see pages 33–37). It might consist of personal experiences or observations.
Or it could be gathered from outside sources—statistics; facts; examples; or
expert authority taken from books, articles, reports, interviews, and documentaries. A paper arguing that elderly Americans are better off than they
used to be might incorporate the following kinds of evidence:

- *Personal observation or experience:* A description of the writer's grandparents who are living comfortably on Social Security and pensions.
- *Statistics from a report:* A statement that the per capita after-tax
  income of older Americans is $335 greater than the national average.
- *Fact from a newspaper article:* The point that the majority of elderly
  Americans do not live in nursing homes or on the streets; rather, they
  have their own houses or apartments.
- *Examples from interviews:* Accounts of several elderly couples living
  comfortably in well-managed retirement villages in Florida.
- *Expert opinion cited in a documentary:* A statement by Dr. Marie
  Sanchez, a specialist in geriatrics: "An over-sixty-five American today
  is likely to be healthier, and have a longer life expectancy, than a fifty-
  year-old living only a decade ago."

As you seek outside evidence, you may—perhaps to your dismay—come
across information that undercuts your argument. Resist the temptation to
ignore such material; instead, use the evidence to arrive at a more balanced,
perhaps somewhat qualified viewpoint. Conversely, don't blindly accept
points made by sources agreeing with you. Retain a healthy skepticism, analyzing the material as rigorously as if it were advanced by the opposing side.

Also, keep in mind that outside sources aren't infallible. They may have
biases that cause them to skew evidence. So be sure to evaluate your sources.
If you're writing an essay supporting a woman's right to abortion, the
National Abortion Rights Action League (NARAL) can supply abundant statistics, case studies, and reports. But realize that NARAL most likely won't
give you the complete picture; it will probably present evidence that supports
its "pro-choice" position only. To counteract such bias, you should review
what those with differing opinions have to say. You should, for example,
examine material published by such "pro-life" organizations as the National
Right-to-Life Committee—keeping in mind, of course, that this material is
also bound to present support for its viewpoint only. Remember, too, that
there are more than two sides to a complex issue. To get as broad a perspective as possible, you should also track down sources that have no axe to
grind—that is, sources that make a deliberate effort to examine all sides of
the issue. For example, published proceedings from a debate on abortion or

an in-depth article that aims to synthesize various views on abortion would broaden your understanding of this controversial subject.

Whatever sources you use, be sure to *document* (give credit to) that material. Otherwise, readers may dismiss your evidence as nothing more than your subjective opinion, or they may conclude that you have *plagiarized*—tried to pass off someone else's ideas as your own. (Documentation isn't necessary when material is commonly known or is a matter of historical or scientific record.) In brief informal papers, documentation may consist of simple citations like "Psychologist Aaron Beck believes depression is the result of distorted thoughts" or "*Time* (Dec. 4, 2000) reports a decline in the enrollment of male students in colleges across the country." In longer, more formal papers, documentation is more detailed (see Appendix A, "A Concise Guide to Finding and Documenting Sources"). One additional point: Because documentation lends a note of objectivity to writing, it may not be appropriate in a paper that cites sources to use the first-person point of view ("I, like many college students, agree with the government report that . . ."). To be on the safe side, check with your instructor to see if you should use the third-person point of view ("Many college students agree with the government report that . . .") instead.

3. Seek to create goodwill.   To avoid alienating readers with views different from your own, stay away from condescending expressions like "Anyone can see that . . ." or "It's obvious that . . ." Also, guard against personalizing the debate and being confrontational: "*My opponents* find the law ineffective" sounds adversarial, whereas "*Those opposed* to the law find it ineffective" or "*Opponents* of the law find it ineffective" is more evenhanded. The last two statements also focus—as they should—on the issue, not on the people involved in the debate.

Goodwill can also be established by finding a *common ground*—some points on which all sides can agree, despite their differences. Assume a township council has voted to raise property taxes. The additional revenues will be used to preserve, as parkland, a wooded area that would otherwise be sold to developers. Before introducing its tax-hike proposal, the council would do well to remind homeowners of everyone's shared goals: maintaining the town's beauty and preventing the community's overdevelopment. This reminder of the common values shared by the town council and homeowners will probably make residents more receptive to the tax hike. (For more on establishing common ground, see pages 488–489.)

4. Organize the supporting evidence.   The support for an argumentation-persuasion paper can be organized in a variety of ways. Any of the patterns of development described in this book (description, narration, definition, causal analysis, and so on) may be used—singly or in combination—to develop the essay's proposition. Imagine you're writing a paper arguing that car racing should be banned from television. Your essay might contain a *description* of a horrifying accident that was televised in graphic detail; you might devote part of the paper to a *causal analysis* showing that the broadcast of such races encourages teens to drive carelessly; you could include a *process analysis* to explain how young drivers "soup up" their cars in a dangerous attempt to imitate the racers seen on television. If your essay includes several patterns, you may need a separate paragraph for each.

When presenting evidence, arrange it so you create the strongest possible effect. In general, you should end with your most compelling point, leaving readers with dramatic evidence that underscores your proposition's validity.

5. Use Rogerian strategy to acknowledge differing viewpoints.   If your essay has a clear thesis and strong logical support, you've taken important steps toward winning readers over. However, because argumentation-persuasion focuses on controversial issues, you should also consider contrary points of view. A good argument seeks out and acknowledges conflicting viewpoints. Such a strategy strengthens your argument in several ways. It helps you anticipate objections, alerts you to flaws in your own position, and makes you more aware of the other sides' weaknesses. Further, by acknowledging dissenting views, you come across as reasonable and thorough—qualities that may disarm readers and leave them more receptive to your argument. You may not convince them to surrender their views, but you can enlarge their perspectives and encourage them to think about your position.

Psychologist Carl Rogers took the idea of acknowledging contrary viewpoints a step further. He believed that argumentation's goal should be to *reduce conflict,* rather than to produce a "winner" and a "loser." But he recognized that people identify so strongly with their opinions that they experience any challenge to those opinions as highly threatening. Such a challenge feels like an attack on their very identity. And what's the characteristic response to such a perceived attack? People become defensive; they dig in their heels and become more adamant than ever about their position. Indeed, when confronted with solid information that calls their opinion into question, they devalue that evidence rather than allow themselves to be persuaded. The old maxim about the power of first impressions demonstrates this point. Experiments show that after people form a first impression of another person, they are unlikely to let future conflicting information affect that impression. If, for example, they initially perceive someone to be unpleasant and disagreeable, they tend to reject subsequent evidence that casts the person in a more favorable light.

Taking into account this tendency to cling tenaciously to opinions in the face of a challenge, Rogerian strategy rejects the adversarial approach that often characterizes argumentation. It adopts, instead, a respectful, conciliatory posture—one that demonstrates a real understanding of opposing views, one that emphasizes shared interests and values. Such an approach makes it easier to negotiate differences and arrive at—ideally—a synthesis: a new position that both parties find at least as acceptable as their original positions.

How can you apply Rogerian strategy in your writing? Simply follow the steps in the following checklist.

☑ USING ROGERIAN STRATEGY: A CHECKLIST

❑ Begin by making a conscientious effort to *understand* the viewpoints of those with whom you disagree. As you listen to or read about their opinions, try to put yourself in their shoes; focus on *what they believe* and *why they believe* it, rather than on how you will challenge their beliefs.

❑ Open your essay with an unbiased, even-handed *restatement of opposing points of view.* Such an objective summary shows that you're fair and open-minded—and not so blinded by the righteousness of your own position that you can't consider any other. Typically, people respond to such a respectful approach by lowering their defenses. Because they appreciate your ability to understand what they have to say, they become more open to your point of view.

❑ When appropriate, *acknowledge the validity* of some of the arguments raised by those with differing views. What should you do if they make a well-founded point? You'll enhance your credibility if you concede that point while continuing to maintain that, overall, your position is stronger.

❑ Point out areas of *common ground* (see page 485) by focusing on interests, values, and beliefs that you and those with opposing views share. When you say to them, "Look at the beliefs we share. Look at our common concerns," you communicate that you're not as unlike them as they first believed.

❑ Finally, *present evidence* for your position. Since those not agreeing with you have been "softened up" by your non-combative stance and disarmed by the realization that you and they share some values and beliefs, they're more ready to consider your point of view.

Let's consider, more specifically, how you might draw upon essentially Rogerian strategy when writing an argumentation-persuasion essay. In the following paragraphs, we discuss three basic strategies. As you read about each strategy, keep in mind this key point: The earlier you acknowledge alternate viewpoints, the more effective your argument will be. Establishing—right at the outset—your awareness of opposing positions shows you to be fair-minded and helps reduce resistance to what you have to say.

First, you may acknowledge the opposing viewpoint in a two-part proposition consisting of a subordinate clause followed by a main clause. The *first part of the proposition* (the subordinate clause) *acknowledges opposing opinions;* the *second part* (the main clause) *states your opinion* and implies that your view stands on more solid ground. (When using this kind of proposition, you may, but don't have to, discuss opposing opinions.) The following thesis illustrates this strategy (the opposing viewpoint is underlined once; the writer's position is underlined twice):

> <u>Although some instructors think that standardized finals restrict academic freedom,</u> <u><u>such exams are preferable to those prepared by individual professors.</u></u>

Second, *in the introduction,* you may provide—separate from the proposition—a *one- or two-sentence summary of the opposing viewpoint.* Suppose you're writing an essay advocating a ten-day waiting period before an individual can purchase a handgun. Before presenting your proposition at the end of the introductory paragraph, you might include sentences like these: "Opponents of the waiting period argue that the ten-day delay is worthless without a nationwide computer network that can perform background checks. Those opposed also point out that only a percentage of states with a waiting period have seen a reduction in gun-related crime."

Third, you can take *one or two body paragraphs* near the beginning of the essay to *present in greater detail arguments raised by opposing viewpoints.* After that, you *grant* (when appropriate) the validity of some of those points ("It may be true that . . . ," "Granted, . . ."). Then you go on to *present evidence* for your position ("Even so . . . ," "Nevertheless . . ."). Imagine you're preparing an editorial for your student newspaper arguing that fraternities and sororities on your campus should be banned. Realizing that many students don't agree with you, you "research" the opposing viewpoint by seeking out supporters of Greek organizations and listening respectfully to the points they raise. When it comes time to write the editorial, you decide not to begin with arguments for your position; instead, you start by summarizing the points made by those supporting fraternities and sororities. You might, for example, mention their argument that Greek organizations build college spirit, contribute to worthy community causes, and provide valuable contacts for entry into the business world. Following this summary of the opposing viewpoint, you might concede that the point about the Greeks' contributions to community causes is especially valid; you could then reinforce this conciliatory stance by stressing some common ground you share—perhaps you acknowledge that you share your detractors' belief that enjoyable social activities with like-minded people are an important part of campus life. Having done all that, you would be in a good position to present arguments why you nevertheless think fraternities and sororities should be banned. Because you prepared readers to listen to your opinion, they would tend to be more receptive to your argument.

6. Refute differing viewpoints.   There will be times, though, that acknowledging opposing viewpoints and presenting your own case won't be enough. Particularly when an issue is complex and when readers strongly disagree with your position, you may have to refute all or part of the *dissenting views. Refutation* means pointing out the problems with opposing viewpoints, thereby highlighting your own position's superiority. You may focus on the opposing sides' inaccurate or inadequate evidence, or you may point to their faulty logic. (Some common types of illogical thinking are discussed on pages 490–495, and 497–498.)

Let's consider how you could refute a competing position in an essay you're writing that supports sex education in public schools. Adapting the Rogerian approach to suit your purposes, you might start by acknowledging the opposing viewpoint's key argument: "Sex education should be the prerogative of parents." After granting the validity of this view in an ideal world, you might show that many parents don't provide such education. You could present statistics on the number of parents who avoid discussing sex with their children because the subject makes them uncomfortable; you could cite studies revealing that children in single-parent homes are apt to receive even less parental guidance about sex; and you could give examples of young people whose parents provided sketchy, even misleading information.

There are various ways to develop a paper's refutation section. The best method to use depends on the paper's length and the complexity of the issue. Two possible sequences are outlined here:

First Strategy	Second Strategy
• State your proposition.	• State your proposition.
• Cite opposing viewpoints and the evidence for those views.	• Cite opposing viewpoints and the evidence for those views.
• Refute opposing viewpoints by presenting counterarguments.	• Refute opposing viewpoints by presenting counterarguments.
	• Present additional evidence for your proposition.

In the first strategy, you simply refute all or part of the opposing positions' arguments. The second strategy takes the first one a step further by presenting *additional evidence* to support your proposition. In such a case, the additional evidence *must be different* from the points made in the refutation. The additional evidence may appear at the essay's end (as in the preceding outline), or it may be given near the beginning (after the proposition); it may also be divided between the beginning and end.

No matter which strategy you select, you may refute opposing views *one side at a time* or *one point at a time*. When using the one-side-at-a-time approach, you cite all the points raised by the opposing side and then present your counterargument to each point. When using the one-point-at-a-time strategy, you mention the first point made by the opposing side, refute that point, then move on to the second point and refute that, and so on. (For more on comparing and contrasting the sides of an issue, see pages 337–342.)

Throughout the essay, be sure to provide clear signals so that readers can distinguish your arguments from the other side's: "Despite the claims of those opposed to the plan, many think that . . ." and "Those not in agreement think that. . . ."

7. Use induction or deduction to think logically about your argument.

The line of reasoning used to develop an argument is the surest indicator of how rigorously you have thought through your position. There are two basic ways to think about a subject: *inductively* and *deductively.* Though the following discussion treats induction and deduction as separate processes, the two often overlap and complement each other.

Inductive reasoning involves examination of specific cases, facts, or examples. Based on these specifics, you then draw a conclusion or make a generalization. This is the kind of thinking scientists use when they examine evidence (the results of experiments, for example) and then draw a *conclusion:* "Smoking increases the risk of cancer." All of us use inductive reasoning in everyday life. We might think the following: "My head is aching" (evidence); "My nose is stuffy" (evidence); "I'm coming down with a cold" (conclusion). Based on the conclusion, we might go a step further and take some action: "I'll take an aspirin."

With inductive reasoning, the conclusion reached can serve as the proposition for an argumentation essay. (Of course, the essay will most likely include elements of persuasion since strict argumentation—with no appeal to emotions—is uncommon.) If the paper advances a course of action, the proposition often mentions the action, signaling an essay with a distinctly persuasive purpose.

Let's suppose that you're writing a paper about a crime wave in the small town where you live. You might use inductive thinking to structure the essay's argument:

Several people were mugged last month while shopping in the center of town. (*evidence*)

Several homes and apartments were burglarized in the past few weeks. (*evidence*)

Several cars were stolen from people's driveways over the weekend. (*evidence*)

The police force hasn't adequately protected town residents. (*conclusion, or proposition, for an argumentation essay with probable elements of persuasion*)

The police force should take steps to upgrade its protection of town residents. (*conclusion, or proposition, for an argumentation essay with a clearly persuasive intent*)

This inductive sequence highlights a possible structure for the essay. After providing a clear statement of your proposition, you might detail recent muggings, burglaries, and car thefts. Then you could move to the opposing viewpoint: a description of the steps the police say they have taken to protect town residents. At that point, you would refute the police's claim, citing additional evidence that shows the measures taken have not been sufficient. Finally, if you wanted your essay to have a decidedly persuasive purpose, you could end by recommending specific action the police department should take to improve its protection of the community.

As in all essays, your evidence should be *specific, unified, adequate,* and *representative* (see pages 33–37). These last two characteristics are critical when you think inductively; they guarantee that your conclusion would be equally valid even if other evidence were presented. Insufficient or atypical evidence often leads to *hasty generalizations* that mar the essay's logic. For example, you might think the following: "Some elderly people are very wealthy and do not need Social Security checks" (evidence), and "Some Social Security recipients illegally collect several checks" (evidence). If you then conclude, "Social Security is a waste of taxpayers' money," your conclusion is invalid and hasty because it's based on only a few atypical examples. Millions of Social Security recipients aren't wealthy and don't abuse the system. If you've failed to consider the full range of evidence, any action you propose ("The Social Security system should be disbanded") will probably be considered suspect by thoughtful readers. It's possible, of course, that Social Security should be disbanded, but the evidence leading to such a conclusion must be sufficient and representative.

When reasoning inductively, you should also be careful that the evidence you collect is both *recent* and *accurate*. No valid conclusion can result from dated or erroneous evidence. To ensure that your evidence is sound, you also need to evaluate the reliability of your sources. When a person who is legally drunk claims to have seen a flying saucer, the evidence is shaky, to say the least. But if two respected scientists, both with 20/20 vision, saw the saucer, their evidence is worth considering.

Finally, it's important to realize that there's always an element of uncertainty in inductive reasoning. The conclusion can never be more than an *inference,* involving what logicians call an *inductive leap.* There could be other explanations for the evidence cited and thus other positions to take and actions to advocate. For example, given a small town's crime wave, you might conclude not that the police force has been remiss but that residents are careless about protecting themselves and their property. In turn, you might call for a different kind of action—perhaps that the police conduct public workshops in self-defense and home security. In an inductive argument, your task is to weigh the evidence, consider alternative explanations, then choose the conclusion and course of action that seem most valid.

Unlike inductive reasoning, which starts with a specific case and moves toward a generalization or conclusion, *deductive reasoning* begins with a generalization that is then applied to a specific case. This movement from general to specific involves a three-step form of reasoning called a *syllogism.* The first part of a syllogism is called the *major premise,* a general statement about an entire group. The second part is the *minor premise,* a statement about an individual within that group. The syllogism ends with a *conclusion* about that individual.

Just as you use inductive thinking in everyday life, you use deductive thinking—often without being aware of it—to sort out your experiences. When trying to decide which car to buy, you might think as follows:

Major premise: In an accident, large cars are safer than small cars.

Minor premise: The Turbo Titan is a large car.

Conclusion: In an accident, the Turbo Titan will be safer than a small car.

Based on your conclusion, you might decide to take a specific action, buying the Turbo Titan rather than the smaller car you had first considered.

To create a valid syllogism and thus arrive at a sound conclusion, you need to avoid two major pitfalls of deductive reasoning. First, be sure not to start with a *hasty generalization* (see page 491) as your *major premise.* Second, don't accept as truth a *faulty conclusion.* Let's look at each problem.

Sweeping major premise.   Perhaps you're concerned about a trash-to-steam incinerator scheduled to open near your home. Your thinking about the situation might follow these lines:

Major premise: Trash-to-steam incinerators have had serious problems and pose significant threats to the well-being of people living near the plants.

Minor premise: The proposed incinerator in my neighborhood will be a trash-to-steam plant.

Conclusion: The proposed trash-to-steam incinerator in my neighborhood will have serious problems and pose significant threats to the well-being of people living near the plant.

Having arrived at this conclusion, you might decide to join organized protests against the opening of the incinerator. But your thinking is somewhat illogical. Your *major premise* is a *sweeping* one because it indiscriminately groups all trash-to-steam plants into a single category. It's unlikely that you're familiar with the operations of all trash-to-steam incinerators in this country and abroad; it's probably not true that *all* such plants have had serious difficulties that endangered the public. For your argument to reach a valid conclusion, the major premise must be based on repeated observations or verifiable facts. You would have a better argument, and thus reach a more valid conclusion, if you restricted or qualified the major premise, applying it to some, not all, of the group.

Major premise: A number of trash-to-steam incinerators have had serious problems and posed significant threats to the well-being of people living near the plants.

Minor premise: The proposed incinerator in my neighborhood will be a trash-to-steam plant.

Conclusion: It's possible that the proposed trash-to-steam incinerator in my neighborhood will run into serious problems and pose significant threats to the well-being of people living near the plant.

This new conclusion, the result of more careful reasoning, would probably encourage you to learn more about trash-to-steam incinerators in general and about the proposed plant in particular. If further research still left you feeling uncomfortable about the plant, you would probably decide to join the protest. On the other hand, your research might convince you that the plant has incorporated into its design a number of safeguards that have been successful at other plants. This added information could reassure you that your original fears were unfounded. In either case, the revised deductive process would lead to a more informed conclusion and course of action.

Faulty conclusion.   Your syllogism—and thus your reasoning—would also be invalid if your *conclusion reverses the "if . . . then" relationship implied in the major premise.* Assume you plan to write a letter to the college newspaper urging the resignation of the student government president. Perhaps you pursue a line of reasoning that goes like this one:

Major premise: Students who plagiarize papers must appear before the Faculty Committee on Academic Policies and Procedures.

Minor premise: Yesterday, Jennifer Kramer, president of the student government, appeared before the Faculty Committee on Academic Policies and Procedures.

Conclusion: Jennifer must have plagiarized a paper.

Action: Jennifer should resign her position as president of the student government.

Such a chain of reasoning is illogical and unfair. Here's why. *If* students plagiarize their papers and are caught, *then* they must appear before the committee. However, the converse isn't necessarily true—that *if* students appear before the committee, *then* they must have plagiarized. In other words, not *all* students appearing before the committee have been called up on plagiarism charges. For example, Jennifer could have been speaking on behalf of another student; she could have been protesting some action taken by the committee; she could have been seeking the committee's help on an article she plans to write about academic honesty. The conclusion doesn't allow for these other possible explanations.

Now that you're aware of potential problems associated with deductive reasoning, let's look at the way you can use a syllogism to structure an argumentation-persuasion essay. Suppose you decide to write a paper advocating support for a projected space mission. You know that controversy surrounds the manned space program, especially since seven astronauts died in a 1986 launch and another crew of seven died in a shuttle reentry accident in 2003. Confident that these tragedies have led to more rigorous controls, you want to argue that the benefits of an upcoming mission outweigh its risks. A deductive pattern could be used to develop your argument. In fact, outlining your thinking as a syllogism might help you formulate a proposition, organize your evidence, deal with opposing viewpoints, and—if appropriate—propose a course of action:

Major premise: Space programs in the past have led to important developments in technology, especially in medical science.

Minor premise: The Cosmos Mission is the newest space program.

Proposition (essay might be persuasive): The Cosmos Mission will most likely lead to important developments in technology, especially in medical science.

Proposition (essay   Congress should continue its funding of the
clearly is persuasive):   Cosmos Mission.

Having outlined the deductive pattern of your thinking, you might begin by stating your proposition and then discuss some new procedures developed to protect the astronauts and the rocket system's structural integrity. With that background established, you could detail the opposing claim that little of value has been produced by the space program so far. You could then move to your refutation, citing significant medical advances derived from former space missions. Finally, the paper might conclude on a persuasive note, with a plea to Congress to continue funding the latest space mission.

8. Use Toulmin logic to establish a strong connection between your evidence and your thesis.   Whether you use an essentially inductive or deductive approach, your argument depends on strong evidence. In *The Uses of Argument,* Stephen Toulmin describes a useful approach for strengthening the connection between evidence and thesis. Toulmin divides a typical argument into three parts:

- **Claim**—The thesis, proposition, or conclusion.
- **Data**—The evidence (facts, statistics, examples, observations, expert opinion) used to convince readers of the claim's validity.
- **Warrant**—The underlying assumption that justifies moving from evidence to claim.

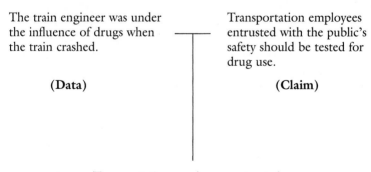

The train engineer was under the influence of drugs when the train crashed.

(Data)

Transportation employees entrusted with the public's safety should be tested for drug use.

(Claim)

Transportation employees entrusted with the public's safety should not be allowed on the job if they use drugs.

(Warrant)

As Toulmin explains in his book, readers are more apt to consider your argument valid if they know what your warrant is. Sometimes your warrant will be so obvious that you won't need to state it explicitly; an *implicit warrant* will be sufficient. Assume you want to argue that the use of live animals to test product toxicity should be outlawed. To support your claim, you cite the following evidence: first, current animal tests are painful and usually result in the animal's death; second, human cell cultures frequently offer more reliable information on how harmful a product may be to human tissue; and third, computer simulations often can more accurately rate a substance's toxicity. Your warrant, although not explicit, is nonetheless clear: "It is wrong to continue product testing on animals when more humane and valid test methods are available."

Other times, you'll do best to make your warrant *explicit*. Suppose you plan to argue that students should be involved in deciding which faculty members are granted tenure. To develop your claim, you present some evidence. You begin by noting that, currently, only faculty members and administrators review candidates for tenure. Next, you call attention to the controversy surrounding two professors, widely known by students to be poor teachers, who were nonetheless granted tenure. Finally, you cite a decision, made several years ago, to discontinue using student evaluations as part of the tenure process; you emphasize that since that time complaints about teachers' incompetence have risen dramatically. Some readers, though, still might wonder how you got from your evidence to your claim. In this case, your argument could be made stronger by stating your warrant explicitly: "Since students are as knowledgeable as the faculty and administrators about which professors are competent, they should be involved in the tenure process."

The more widely accepted your warrant, Toulmin explains, the more likely it is that readers will accept your argument. If there's no consensus about the warrant, you'll probably need to *back it up*. For the preceding example, you might mention several reports that found students evaluate faculty fairly (most students don't, for example, use the ratings to get back at professors against whom they have a personal grudge); further, students' ratings correlate strongly with those given by administrators and other faculty.

Toulmin describes another way to increase receptivity to an argument: *qualify the claim*—that is, explain under what circumstances it might be invalid or restricted. For instance, you might grant that most students know little about their instructors' research activities, scholarly publications, or participation in professional committees. You could, then, qualify your claim this way: "Because students don't have a comprehensive view of their instructors' professional activities, they should be involved in the tenure process but play a less prominent role than faculty and administrators."

As you can see, Toulmin's approach provides strategies for strengthening an argument. So, when prewriting or revising, take a few minutes to ask yourself the questions listed below.

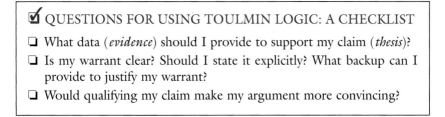

Your responses to these questions will help you structure a convincing and logical argument.

9. Recognize logical fallacies. When writing an argumentation-persuasion essay, you need to recognize *logical fallacies* both in your own argument and in points raised by opposing sides. Work to eliminate such gaps in logic from your own writing and, when they appear in opposing arguments, try to expose them in your refutation. Logicians have identified many logical fallacies—including the sweeping or hasty generalization and the faulty conclusion discussed on pages 491 and 493. Other logical fallacies are described in Ann McClintock's "Propaganda Techniques in Today's Advertising" (page 270) and in the paragraphs that follow.

The *post hoc fallacy* (short for a Latin phrase meaning "after this, therefore because of this") occurs when you conclude that a cause-effect relationship exists simply because one event preceded another. Let's say you note the growing number of immigrants settling in a nearby city, observe the city's economic decline, and conclude that the immigrants' arrival caused the decline. Such a chain of thinking is faulty because it assumes a cause-effect relationship based purely on co-occurrence. Perhaps the immigrants' arrival was a factor in the economic slump, but there could also be other reasons: the lack of financial incentives to attract business to the city, restrictions on the size of the city's manufacturing facilities, citywide labor disputes that make companies leery of settling in the area. Your argument should also consider these possibilities. (For more on the *post hoc* fallacy, see pages 385–386.)

The *non sequitur fallacy* (Latin for "it does not follow") is an even more blatant muddying of cause-effect relationships. In this case, a conclusion is drawn that has no logical connection to the evidence cited: "Millions of Americans own cars, so there is no need to fund public transportation." The faulty conclusion disregards the millions of Americans who don't own cars; it also ignores pollution and road congestion, both of which could be reduced if people had access to safe, reliable public transportation.

An *ad hominem argument* (from the Latin meaning "to the man") occurs when someone attacks a person rather than a point of view. Suppose your college plans to sponsor a physicians' symposium on the abortion controversy. You decide to write a letter to the school paper opposing the symposium. Taking swipes at two of the invited doctors who disapprove of abortion, you mention that one was recently involved in a messy divorce and that the other is alleged to have a drinking problem. By hurling personal invective, you avoid discussing the issue. Mudslinging is a poor substitute for reasoned argument.

Appeals to questionable or faulty authority also weaken an argument. Most of us have developed a healthy suspicion of phrases like *sources close to, an unidentified spokesperson states, experts claim,* and *studies show.* If these people and reports are so reliable, they should be clearly identified.

Begging the question involves failure to establish proof for a debatable point. The writer expects readers to accept as given a premise that's actually controversial. For instance, you would have trouble convincing readers that prayer should be banned from public schools if you based your argument on the premise that school prayer violates the U.S. Constitution. If the Constitution does, either explicitly or implicitly, prohibit prayer in public education, your essay must demonstrate that fact. You can't build a strong argument if you pretend there's no controversy surrounding your premise.

A *false analogy* wrongly implies that because two things share *some* characteristics, they are therefore *alike in all respects.* You might, for example, compare nicotine and marijuana. Both, you could mention, involve health risks and have addictive properties. If, however, you go on to conclude, "Driving while smoking a cigarette isn't illegal, so driving while smoking marijuana shouldn't be illegal either," you're employing a false analogy. You've overlooked a major difference between nicotine and marijuana: Marijuana impairs perception and coordination—important aspects of driving—while there's no evidence that nicotine does the same.

The *either/or fallacy* occurs when you assume that a particular viewpoint or course of action can have only one of two diametrically opposed outcomes—either totally this or totally that. Say you argue as follows: "Unless colleges continue to offer scholarships based solely on financial need, no one who is underprivileged will be able to attend college." Such a statement ignores the fact that bright, underprivileged students could receive scholarships based on their potential or their demonstrated academic excellence.

Finally, a *red herring argument* is an intentional digression from the issue—a ploy to deflect attention from the matter being discussed. Imagine that you're arguing that condoms shouldn't be dispensed to high school students. You would introduce a red herring if you began to rail against parents who fail to provide their children with any information about sex. Most people would agree that parents *should* provide such information. However, the issue being discussed is not parents' irresponsibility but the pros and cons of schools' distributing condoms to students.

REVISION STRATEGIES

Once you have a draft of the essay, you're ready to revise. The following checklist will help you and those giving you feedback apply to argumentation-persuasion some of the revision techniques discussed on pages 60–62.

☑ ARGUMENTATION-PERSUASION: A REVISION/PEER REVIEW CHECKLIST

Revise Overall Meaning and Structure

❏ What issue is being discussed? What is controversial about it?

❏ What is the essay's thesis? How does it differ from a generalization or mere statement of fact?

❏ What is the essay's purpose—to win readers over to a point of view, to spur readers to some type of action?

❏ For what audience is the essay written? What strategies are used to make readers receptive to the essay's thesis?

❏ What tone does the essay project? Is the tone likely to win readers over?

❏ If the essay's argument is essentially deductive, is the major premise sufficiently restricted? What evidence is the premise based on? Are the minor premise and conclusion valid? If not, how could these problems be corrected?

❏ Where is the essay weakened by hasty generalizations, a failure to weigh evidence honestly, or a failure to draw the most valid conclusion?

❏ Where does the essay commit any of the following logical fallacies: Concluding that a cause-effect relationship exists simply because one event preceded another? Attacking a person rather than an issue? Drawing a conclusion that isn't logically related to the evidence? Failing to establish proof for a debatable point? Relying on questionable or vaguely specified authority? Drawing a false analogy? Resorting to *either/or* thinking? Using a *red herring* argument?

Revise Paragraph Development

❏ How apparent is the link between the evidence (data) and the thesis (claim)? How could an explicit warrant clarify the connection? How would supporting the warrant or qualifying the claim strengthen the argument?

❏ Which paragraphs lack sufficient evidence (facts, examples, statistics, and expert opinion)?

❏ Which paragraphs lack unity? How could they be made more focused? In which paragraph(s) does evidence seem bland, overly general, unrepresentative, or inaccurate?

❏ Which paragraphs take opposing views into account? Are these views refuted? How? Which counterarguments are ineffective?

❏ Where do outside sources require documentation?

Revise Sentences and Words

❏ What words and phrases help readers distinguish the essay's arguments from those advanced by the opposing side?

❏ Which words carry strong emotional overtones? Is this connotative language excessive? Where does emotional language replace rather than reinforce clear thinking?

❏ Where might dogmatic language ("Anyone can see that . . ." and "Obviously, . . .") alienate readers?

STUDENT ESSAY

The following student essay was written by Mark Simmons in response to this assignment:

> Mary Sherry's "In Praise of the 'F' Word" invites controversy by attacking the popular notion that failing students is a harmful practice. Select another controversial issue, one that you feel strongly about. Conduct library research to gather evidence in support of your position, and brainstorm with others to identify some points that might be raised by those who oppose your view. Then, using logic and formal, documented evidence, convince readers that your viewpoint is valid.

Your instructor may not ask you to include research in your essay. But, if you're asked—as Mark was—to research your paper and to provide *formal documentation,* you'll want to pay special attention to the way Mark credits his sources. (In *your* paper, the Works Cited list should be double-spaced—along with the rest of the paper—and placed at the end on a separate page.) You'll also find it helpful to refer to Appendix A, "A Concise Guide to Finding and Documenting Sources" (page 607). If your instructor wants you to research your paper but will accept *informal documentation,* the material on pages 484–485 should come in handy.

Whether or not you include research in your paper, the annotations on Mark's essay and the comments following it will help you determine how well it applies the principles of argumentation-persuasion.

Compulsory National Service
by Mark Simmons

Beginning of two-paragraph introduction

Our high school history class spent several weeks studying the events of the 1960s. The most interesting thing about that decade was the spirit of service and social commitment among young people. In the '60s, young people thought about issues beyond themselves; they joined the Peace Corps, worked in poverty-stricken Appalachian communities, and participated in freedom marches against segregation. Most young people today, despite their concern with careers and getting ahead, would also like an opportunity to make a worthwhile contribution to society.   1

Common knowledge: No need to document

Convinced that many young adults are indeed eager for such an opportunity, President Bill Clinton implemented in 1994 a pilot program of voluntary national service. The following year, the program was formalized, placed under the management of the Corporation for National Service (CNS), and given the name AmeriCorps. In the years 1994–2003, approximately 250,000 AmeriCorps volunteers provided varied assistance in communities across the country ("AmeriCorps: 2

Parenthetic citation of unpaged anonymous material obtained through the Internet

Who We Are"). Such voluntary national service was also endorsed by President George W. Bush. Following the devastating terrorist attacks on September 11, 2001, President Bush urged Americans to volunteer as a way of assisting in the nation's recovery and of demonstrating a spirit of national unity. He issued an executive order in early 2002 establishing USA Freedom Corps, an organization seeking to persuade Americans to perform 4,000 hours of volunteer service over a lifetime (Hutcheson A2). In general, programs such as USA Freedom Corps and the more established AmeriCorps hold out so much promise that it seems only natural to go one step further and make young people's participation in these

Start of two-sentence thesis

programs or some kind of national service mandatory. By instituting a program of compulsory national service, the country could tap youth's idealistic desire to make a difference. Such a system would yield significant benefits.

Definition paragraph

What exactly is meant by compulsory national service? Traditionally, it has tended to mean that everyone between the ages of seventeen and twenty-five would serve the country for two years. These young people could choose between two major options: military service or a public-service corps. They could serve their time at any point within an eight-year span. The unemployed or the uncertain could join immediately after high school; college-bound students could complete their education before joining the national service. Years ago, Senator   3

Beginning of summary of a source's ideas

Sam Nunn and Representative Dave McCurdy gave a new twist to the definition of compulsory national service. They proposed a plan that would require all high school graduates applying for federal aid for college tuition to serve either in the military or in a Citizens Corps. Anyone in the Citizens Corps would be required to work full-time at public-service duties for one or two years. During that time, participants would receive a weekly stipend, and, at the end, be given a voucher worth $10,000 for each year of civilian service. The voucher could then be applied toward college credit, employment training, or a down payment on a house (Sudo 9).

Parenthetic citation—page number and author are given since the author is not cited earlier in the sentence

The traditional plan for compulsory national service and the one proposed by Nunn and McCurdy are just two of many variations that have been discussed over the years. While this country debates the concept, some nations such as France have gone ahead and accepted it enthusiastically. The idea could be workable in this country too. Unfortunately, opponents are doing all they can to prevent the idea from taking hold. They contend, first of all, that the program would cost too much. A great deal of money, they argue, would be spent administering the program, paying young people's wages, and providing housing for participants. Another argument against compulsory national service is that it would demoralize young people; supposedly, the plan would prevent the young from moving ahead with their careers and would make them feel as though they were engaged in work that offered no personal satisfaction. A third argument is that compulsory service would lay the groundwork for a dictatorship. The picture is painted of an army of young people, controlled by the government, much like the Hitler Youth of World War II.

Topic sentence

Beginning of summary of three points made by the opposing viewpoint

Topic sentence: Refutation of first point

Despite opponents' claims that compulsory national service would involve exorbitant costs, the program would not have to be that expensive to run. AmeriCorps has already provided an excellent model for achieving substantial benefits at reasonable cost. For example, a study conducted by universities in Iowa and Michigan showed that each dollar spent on AmeriCorps programs yielded $2.60 in reduced welfare costs, increased earnings, and other benefits (Garland 120). Also, the sums required for wages and housing could be reduced considerably through payments made by the towns, cities, and states using the corps's services. And the economic benefits of the program could be significant. AmeriCorps's official website gives an idea of the current scope of the program's activities. Volunteers provide crucial services including building affordable homes for families, improving health services, responding to natural disasters, and tutoring children ("AmeriCorps"). A compulsory national corps could also clean up litter, provide day care services, staff libraries, immunize children, and care for the country's growing elderly population (Clinton; Eng). All these projects would help solve

Information comes from two sources. Sources, separated by a semicolon, are given in the order they appear in the Works Cited list. First source is unpaged electronic text. No page given for second source because it runs only one page.

Topic sentence: Refutation of second point	many of the problems that plague our nation, and they would probably cost less than if they were handled by often inefficient government bureaucracies.
Attribution giving author's full name and area of expertise	Also, rather than undermining the spirit of young people, as opponents contend, the program would probably boost their morale. Many young people feel enormous pressure and uncertainty; they are not sure whether they want to find a job or further their education. Compulsory national service could give these young people much-needed breathing space. As Edward Lewis, president of St. Mary's College, says, "Many students are not ready for college at seventeen or eighteen. This kind of program responds to that need" (qtd. in Fowler 3). Robert Coles, psychiatrist and social activist, argues that a public service stint enriches participants' lives in yet another way. Coles points out that young people often have little sense of the job market. When they get involved in community service, though, they frequently "discover an area of interest . . . that launches them on a career" (93). Equally important, compulsory national service can provide an emotional boost for the young; all of them would experience the pride that comes from working hard, reaching goals, acquiring skills, and handling responsibilities (Waldman and Wofford). A positive mind-set would also result from the sense of community that would be created by serving in the national service. All young people--rich or poor, educated or not, regardless of sex and social class--would come together and perceive not their differences but their common interests and similarities (Waldman and Wofford). As President Clinton proclaimed at the Year 2000 swearing-in of AmeriCorps's recruits in Philadelphia, AmeriCorps gives volunteers a chance "to tear down barriers of distrust and misunderstanding and old-fashioned ignorance, and build a genuine American community" (Clinton).
Full-sentence quotation is preceded by a comma and begins with a capital letter	
Where secondary source was quoted	
Quotation is blended into the sentence (no comma and the quotation begins with a lowercased word)	
Quotation with ellipsis	
Just the page number is provided because the author's name is cited in the preceding attribution	
Parenthetic citation for electronic source having two authors. No page given since electronic text is unpaged.	
Topic sentence: Refutation of third point	Finally, in contrast to what opponents claim, compulsory national service would not signal the start of a dictatorship. Although the service would be required, young people would have complete freedom to choose any two years between the ages of seventeen and twenty-five. They would also have complete freedom to choose the branch of the military or public service corps that suits them best. And the corps would not need to be outfitted in military uniforms or to live in barrack-like camps. It could be set up like a regular job, with young people living at home as much as possible, following a nine-to-five schedule, enjoying all the personal freedoms that would ordinarily be theirs. Also, a dictatorship would no more likely emerge from compulsory national service than it has from our present military system. We would still have a series of checks and balances to prohibit the taking of power by one group or individual. We should also

6

7

keep in mind that our system is different from that of fascist regimes; our long tradition of personal liberty makes improbable the seizing of absolute power by one person or faction. A related but even more important point to remember is that freedom does not mean people are guaranteed the right to pursue only their individual needs. That is mistaking selfishness for freedom. And, as everyone knows, selfishness leads only to misery. The national service would not take away freedom. On the contrary, serving in the corps would help young people grasp this larger concept of freedom, a concept that is badly needed to counteract the deadly "look out for number one" attitude that is spreading like a poison across the nation.

Beginning of two-paragraph conclusion

Attribution leading to a long quotation. Attribution is followed by a colon since the lead-in is a full sentence. If the lead-in isn't a full sentence, use a comma after the attribution.

Long quotation is indented ten spaces. Don't leave any extra space within, above, or below the quotation.

For an indented quotation, the period is placed *before* the parenthetic citation.

Perhaps there will never be a time like the 1960s when so many young people were concerned with remaking the world. Still, a good many of today's young people want meaningful work. They want to feel that what they do makes a difference. A program of compulsory national service would harness this idealism and help young people realize the best in themselves. Such a program would also help resolve some of the country's most critical social problems.

Almost two decades ago, political commentator Donald Eberly expressed his belief in the power of national service. Urging the inauguration of such a program, Eberly wrote the following:

> The promise of national service can be manifested in many ways: in cleaner air and fewer forest fires; in well-cared-for infants and old folks; in a better-educated citizenry and better-satisfied work force; perhaps in a more peaceful world. National service has a lot of promise. It's a promise well worth keeping. (651)

Several years later, President Clinton took office, gave his support to the concept, and AmeriCorps was born. This advocacy of public service was then championed, at least in word, by President Bush. During his administration, however, AmeriCorps was threatened by deep budget cuts advocated by opponents of the program and its Clintonian legacy. Fortunately, despite these measures, Congress voted in 2003 with overwhelming bipartisan support to save AmeriCorps and salvage a portion of its budget ("Timely Help"). In the words of a Philadelphia Inquirer editorial, "The civic yield from that investment is incalculable" ("Ill Served"). An efficient and successful program of voluntary service, AmeriCorps has paved the way. Now seems to be the perfect

In *your* paper, the Works Cited list would be double-spaced like the rest of the paper, with no extra space after the heading or between entries. Also, in *your* paper, the Works Cited would start on a *separate* page.

Anonymous material obtained on the Internet. Names of website and of sponsoring organization appear. Electronic text is 5 paragraphs long. Web address always required.

Authored material on the Internet. Dates the material was published and accessed, respectively, are provided.

Book by one author

Published speech

Newspaper article whose text is only one page

Article from weekly magazine

Internet article with unnumbered paragraphs or pages

time to expand the concept and make compulsory national service a reality.

Works Cited

"AmeriCorps: Who We Are." AmeriCorps. A Program for
    the Corporation of National and Community Service.
    11 July 2003: 5 pars. 26 Jan. 2004 <http://
    www.americorps.org/whoweare.html>.

Clinton, William. "Remarks by the President to AmeriCorps."
    AmeriCorps. The Corporation for National Service.
    11 Oct. 2000: 28 pars. 7 Jan. 2004 <http://
    www.americorps.org/news/pr/
    potus_remarks101100.html>.

Coles, Robert. The Call of Service. Boston: Houghton Mifflin,
    1993.

Eberly, Donald. "What the President Should Do About
    National Service." Vital Speeches of the Day 15 Aug.
    1989: 561–63.

Eng, Lily. "Congressional Pressure Puts AmeriCorps Under
    the Gun." Philadelphia Inquirer 18 Apr. 1996, late
    ed.: B1.

Fowler, Margaret. "New Interest in National Youth Corps."
    New York Times 16 May 1989, natl. ed.: A25.

Garland, Susan B. "A Social Program CEOs Want to Save."
    Business Week 19 June 1996: 120–21.

Hutcheson, Ron. "Bush Moves to Establish His New
    Volunteer Program." Philadelphia Inquirer 31 Jan.
    2002: A2.

"Ill Served." Editorial. Philadelphia Inquirer Online 27 June
    2003. 1 Mar. 2004 <http://www.philly.com/mld/inquirer/
    news/editorial/6180250.htm>.

Sudo, Phil. "Mandatory National Service?" Scholastic Update
    23 Feb. 1990: 9.

"Timely Help for AmeriCorps." Editorial. New York Times
    Online 17 July 2003: 4 pars. 28 Feb 2004
    <http://www.nytimes.com/2003/07/17/
    opinion/17THU4.html>.

Article (by two authors) from scholarly journal on CD-ROM——

Waldman, Steven, and Harris Wofford. "AmeriCorps the Beautiful? Habitat for Conservative Values." <u>Policy Review</u> Sept.–Oct. 1997: 49 pars. CD-ROM. EBSCOhost.

COMMENTARY

Blend of argumentation and persuasion.   In his essay, Mark tackles a controversial issue. He takes the position that compulsory national service would benefit both the country as a whole and its young people in particular. Mark's essay is a good example of the way argumentation and persuasion often mix: Although the paper presents Mark's position in a logical, well-reasoned manner (argumentation), it also appeals to readers' personal values and suggests a course of action (persuasion).

Audience analysis.   When planning the essay, Mark realized that his audience—his composition class—would consist largely of two kinds of readers. Some, not sure of their views, would be inclined to agree with him if he presented his case well. Others would probably be reluctant to accept his view. Because of this mixed audience, Mark knew he couldn't depend on *pathos* (an appeal to emotion) to convince readers. Rather, his argument had to rely mainly on *logos* (reason) and *ethos* (credibility). So Mark organized his essay around a series of logical arguments—many of them backed by expert opinion—and he evoked his own authority by drawing on his knowledge of history and his "inside" knowledge of young people.

Introduction and thesis.   Mark introduces his subject by discussing an earlier decade when large numbers of young people worked for social change. Mark's references to the Peace Corps, community work, and freedom marches reinforce his image as a knowledgeable source and establish a context for his position. These historical references, combined with the comments about AmeriCorps, the program of voluntary national service, lead into the two-sentence thesis at the end of the two-paragraph introduction: "By instituting a program of compulsory national service, the country could tap youth's idealistic desire to make a difference. Such a system would yield significant benefits."

The second paragraph in the introduction also illustrates Mark's first use of outside sources. Because the assignment called for research in support of an argument, Mark went to the library and online and identified sources that helped him defend his position. If Mark's instructor had required extensive investigation of an issue, Mark would have been obligated both to dig more deeply into his subject and to use more scholarly and specialized sources. But given the instructor's requirements, Mark proceeded just as he should have: He searched out expert opinion that supported his viewpoint; he presented that evidence clearly; he documented his sources carefully.

Background paragraph and use of outside sources.   The third paragraph provides a working *definition* of compulsory national service by presenting two common interpretations of the concept. Such background information guarantees that Mark's readers will share his understanding of the essay's central concept.

Acknowledging the opposing viewpoint.   Having explained the meaning of compulsory national service, Mark is now in a good position to launch his argument. Even though he wasn't required to research the opposing viewpoint, Mark wisely decided to get together with some friends to brainstorm some issues that might be raised by the dissenting view. He acknowledges this position in the *topic sentence* of the essay's fourth paragraph: "Unfortunately, opponents are doing all they can to prevent the idea from taking hold." Next he summarizes the main points the dissenting opinion might advance: compulsory national service would be expensive, demoralizing to young people, and dangerously authoritarian. Mark uses the rest of the essay to counter these criticisms.

Refutation.   The next three paragraphs (5–7) *refute* the opposing stance and present Mark's evidence for his position. Mark structures the essay so that readers can follow his *counterargument* with ease. Each paragraph argues against one opposing point and begins with a *topic sentence* that serves as Mark's response to the dissenting view. Note the way the italicized portion of each topic sentence recalls a dissenting point cited earlier: "Despite opponents' claims that *compulsory national service would involve exorbitant costs,* the program would not have to be that expensive to run" (paragraph 5); "Also, rather than *undermining the spirit of young people,* as opponents contend, the program would probably boost their morale" (6); "Finally, in contrast to what opponents claim, *compulsory national service would not signal the start of a dictatorship*" (7). Mark also guides the reader through the various points in the refutation by using *transitions* within paragraphs: "*And* the economic benefits . . . could be significant" (5); "*Equally important,* compulsory national service could provide an emotional boost . . ." (6); "*Also,* a dictatorship would no more likely emerge . . ." (7).

Throughout the three-paragraph refutation, Mark uses outside sources to lend power to his argument. If the assignment had called for in-depth research, he would have cited facts, statistics, and case studies to develop this section of his essay. Given the nature of the assignment, though, Mark's reliance on expert opinion is perfectly acceptable.

Mark successfully incorporates material from these outside sources into his refutation. He doesn't, for example, string one quotation numbingly after another; instead he usually develops his refutation by *summarizing* expert opinion and saves *direct quotations* for points that deserve emphasis. Moreover, whenever Mark quotes or summarizes a source, he provides clear signals to indicate that the material is indeed borrowed. (If you'd like some suggestions for citing outside sources in an essay of your own, see pages 484–485 and 607–633.)

Some problems with the refutation.   Overall, Mark's three-paragraph refutation is strong, but it would have been even more effective if the paragraphs had been resequenced. As it now stands, the last paragraph in the refutation (7) seems anticlimactic. Unlike the preceding two paragraphs, which are developed through fairly extensive reference to outside sources, paragraph 7 depends entirely on Mark's personal feelings and interpretations for its support. Of course, Mark was under no obligation to provide research in all sections of the paper. Even so, the refutation would have been more persuasive if Mark had placed the final paragraph in the refutation in a less emphatic position. He could, for example, have put it first or second in the sequence, saving for last either of the other two more convincing paragraphs.

You may also have felt that there's another problem with the third paragraph in the refutation. Here, Mark seems to lose control of his counterargument. Beginning with "And, as everyone knows . . . ," Mark falls into the *logical fallacy* called *begging the question*. He shouldn't assume that everyone agrees that a selfish life inevitably brings misery. He also indulges in charged emotionalism when he refers—somewhat melodramatically—to the "deadly 'look out for number one' attitude that is spreading like a poison across the nation."

Inductive reasoning.   In part, Mark arrived at his position *inductively,* through a series of *inferences* or *inductive leaps.* He started with some personal *observations* about the nation and its young people. Then, to support those observations, he added his friends' insights as well as information gathered through research. Combined, all this material led him to the general *conclusion* that compulsory national service would be both workable and beneficial.

Combining patterns of development.   To develop his argument, Mark draws on several patterns of development. The third paragraph relies on *definition* to clarify what is meant by compulsory national service. The first paragraph of both the introduction and conclusion *compares* and *contrasts* young people of the 1960s with those of today. And, to support his position, Mark uses a kind of *causal analysis;* he both speculates on the likely consequences of compulsory national service and cites expert opinion to illustrate the validity of some of those speculations.

Conclusion.   Despite some problems in the final section of his refutation, Mark comes up with an effective two-paragraph conclusion for his essay. In the first closing paragraph, he echoes the point made in the introduction about the 1960s and restates his thesis. That done, he moves to the second paragraph of his conclusion. There, he quotes a dramatic statement from a knowledgeable source, cites efforts to undermine AmeriCorps, and ends by pointing out that AmeriCorps has earned the respect of some unlikely supporters. All that Mark does in this final paragraph lends credibility to the crisp assertion and suggested course of action at the very end of his essay.

Revising the first draft.   Given the complex nature of his argument, Mark found that he had to revise his essay several times. One way to illustrate some of the changes he made is to compare his final introduction with the original draft reprinted here:

Original Version of the Introduction

"There's no free lunch." "You can't get something for nothing." "You have to earn your way." In America, these sayings are not really true. In America, we gladly take but give back little. In America, we receive economic opportunity, legal protection, the right to vote, and, most of all, a personal freedom unequaled throughout the world. How do we repay our country for such gifts? In most cases, we don't. This unfair relationship must be changed. The best way to make a start is to institute a system of national compulsory service for young people. This system would be of real benefit to the country and its citizens.

When Mark met with a classmate for a peer review session, he found that his partner had a number of helpful suggestions for revising various sections of the essay. But Mark's partner focused most of her comments on the essay's introduction because she felt it needed special attention. Following his classmate's suggestion, Mark deleted the original introduction's references to Americans in general. He made this change because he wanted readers to know—from the very start of the essay—that the paper would focus not on all Americans but on American youth. To reinforce this emphasis, he also added the point about the social commitment characteristic of young people in the 1960s. This reference to an earlier period gave the discussion an important historical perspective and lent a note of authority to Mark's argument. The decision to mention the '60s also helped Mark realize that his introduction should point out more recent developments—specifically, the promise of AmeriCorps. Mark was pleased to see that adding this new material not only gave the introduction a sharper focus, but it also provided a smoother lead-in to his thesis.

These are just a few of the many changes Mark made while reworking his essay. Because he budgeted his time carefully, he was able to revise thoroughly. With the exception of some weak spots in the refutation, Mark's essay is well-reasoned and convincing.

ACTIVITIES: ARGUMENTATION-PERSUASION

Prewriting Activities

1. Imagine you're writing two essays: One *defines* hypocrisy; the other *contrasts* license and freedom. Identify an audience for each essay (college students, professors, teenagers, parents, employers, employees, or some other group). Then jot down how each essay might argue the merits of certain ways of behaving.

2. Following are several thesis statements for argumentation-persuasion essays. For each thesis, determine whether the three audiences indicated in parentheses are apt to be supportive, wavering, or hostile. Then select *one* thesis and use group brainstorming to identify, for each audience, specific points you would make to persuade each group.

   a. Students should not graduate from college until they have passed a comprehensive exam in their majors (*college students, their parents, college officials*).

   b. Abandoned homes owned by the city should be sold to low-income residents for a nominal fee (*city officials, low-income residents, general citizens*).

   c. The town should pass a law prohibiting residents who live near the reservoir from using pesticides on their lawns (*environmentalists, homeowners, members of the town council*).

   d. Faculty advisors to college newspapers should have the authority to prohibit the publication of articles that reflect negatively on the school (*alumni, college officials, student journalists*).

Revising Activities

3. Each set of statements that follows contains at least one of the logical fallacies described earlier in the chapter and in Ann McClintock's essay "Propaganda Techniques in Today's Advertising" (page 270). Identify the fallacy or fallacies in each set and explain why the statements are invalid.

   a. Grades are irrelevant to learning. Students are in college to get an education, not good grades. The university should eliminate grading altogether.

   b. The best policy is to put juvenile offenders in jail so that they can get a taste of reality. Otherwise, they will repeat their crimes again and again.

   c. So-called sex education programs do nothing to decrease the rate of teenage pregnancy. Further expenditures on these programs should be curtailed.

    d. If we allow abortion, people will think it's acceptable to kill the homeless or pull the plug on sick people—two groups that are also weak and frail.

    e. The curfews that some towns impose on teenagers are as repressive as the curfews in totalitarian countries.

4. Following is the introduction from the first draft of an essay advocating the elimination of mandatory dress codes in public schools. Revise the paragraph, being sure to consider these questions: How effectively does the writer deal with the opposing viewpoint? Does the paragraph encourage those who might disagree with the writer to read on? Why or why not? Do you see any logical fallacies in the writer's thinking? Where? Does the writer introduce anything that veers away from the point being discussed? Where? Before revising, you may find it helpful to do some brainstorming—individually or in a group—to find ways to strengthen the paragraph.

    After reworking the paragraph, take a few minutes to consider how the rest of the essay might unfold. What persuasive strategies could be used? How could Rogerian argument win over readers? What points could be made? What action could be urged in the effort to build a convincing argument?

    In three nearby towns recently, high school administrators joined forces to take an outrageously strong stand against students' constitutional rights. Acting like fascists, they issued an edict in the form of a preposterous dress code that prohibits students from wearing expensive jewelry, designer jeans, leather jackets--anything that the administrators, in their supposed wisdom, consider ostentatious. Perhaps the next thing they'll want to do is forbid students to play rock music at school dances. What prompted the administrators' dictatorial prohibition against certain kinds of clothing? Somehow or other, they got it into their heads that having no restrictions on the way students dress creates an unhealthy environment, where students vie with each other for the flashiest attire. Students and parents alike should protest this and any other dress code. If such codes go into effect, we might as well throw out the Constitution.

Mary Sherry

Following her graduation from Dominican University in 1962 with a degree in English, Mary Sherry (1940–) wrote freelance articles and advertising copy while raising her family. Over the years, a love of writing and an interest in education have been integral to all that Sherry does professionally. Founder and owner of a small research and publishing firm in Minnesota, she has taught creative and remedial writing to adults for more than twenty years. The following selection first appeared as a 1991 "My Turn" column in *Newsweek*.

Pre-Reading Journal Entry

Imagine you had a son or daughter who didn't take school seriously. How would you go about motivating the child to value academic success? Would your strategies differ depending on the age and gender of the child? If so, how and why? What other factors might influence your approach? Use your journal to respond to these questions.

In Praise of the "F" Word

Tens of thousands of 18-year-olds will graduate this year and be handed meaningless diplomas. These diplomas won't look any different from those awarded their luckier classmates. Their validity will be questioned only when their employers discover that these graduates are semiliterate. 1

Eventually a fortunate few will find their way into educational repair shops—adult-literacy programs, such as the one where I teach basic grammar and writing. There, high-school graduates and high-school dropouts pursuing graduate-equivalency certificates will learn the skills they should have learned in school. They will also discover they have been cheated by our educational system. 2

As I teach, I learn a lot about our schools. Early in each session I ask my students to write about an unpleasant experience they had in school. No writers' block here! "I wish someone would have had made me stop doing drugs and made me study." "I liked to party and no one seemed to care." "I was a good kid and didn't cause any trouble, so they just passed me along even though I didn't read well and couldn't write." And so on. 3

I am your basic do-gooder, and prior to teaching this class I blamed the poor academic skills our kids have today on drugs, divorce and other impediments to concentration necessary for doing well in school. But, as I 4 rediscover each time I walk into the classroom, before a teacher can expect students to concentrate, he has to get their attention, no matter what distractions may be at hand. There are many ways to do this, and they have much to do with teaching style. However, if style alone won't do it, there is another way to show who holds the winning hand in the classroom. That is to reveal the trump card[1] of failure.

I will never forget a teacher who played that card to get the attention of   5
one of my children. Our youngest, a world-class charmer, did little to develop his intellectual talents but always got by. Until Mrs. Stifter.

Our son was a high-school senior when he had her for English. "He sits   6
in the back of the room talking to his friends," she told me. "Why don't you move him to the front row?" I urged, believing the embarrassment would get him to settle down. Mrs. Stifter looked at me steely-eyed over her glasses. "I don't move seniors," she said. "I flunk them." I was flustered. Our son's academic life flashed before my eyes. No teacher had ever threatened him with that before. I regained my composure and managed to say that I thought she was right. By the time I got home I was feeling pretty good about this. It was a radical approach for these times, but, well, why not? "She's going to flunk you," I told my son. I did not discuss it any further. Suddenly English became a priority in his life. He finished out the semester with an A.

I know one example doesn't make a case, but at night I see a parade of   7
students who are angry and resentful for having been passed along until they could no longer even pretend to keep up. Of average intelligence or better, they eventually quit school, concluding they were too dumb to finish. "I should have been held back" is a comment I hear frequently. Even sadder are those students who are high-school graduates who say to me after a few weeks of class, "I don't know how I ever got a high-school diploma."

Passing students who have not mastered the work cheats them and the   8
employers who expect graduates to have basic skills. We excuse this dishonest behavior by saying kids can't learn if they come from terrible environments. No one seems to stop to think that—no matter what environments they come from—most kids don't put school first on their list unless they perceive something is at stake. They'd rather be sailing.

Many students I see at night could give expert testimony on unemploy-   9
ment, chemical dependency, abusive relationships. In spite of these difficulties, they have decided to make education a priority. They are motivated by the desire for a better job or the need to hang on to the one they've got. They have a healthy fear of failure.

People of all ages can rise above their problems, but they need to have a   10
reason to do so. Young people generally don't have the maturity to value education in the same way my adult students value it. But fear of failure, whether economic or academic, can motivate both.

---

[1]In cards, an advantage held in reserve until it's needed (editors' note).

Flunking as a regular policy has just as much merit today as it did two   11
generations ago. We must review the threat of flunking and see it as it really
is—a positive teaching tool. It is an expression of confidence by both teachers and parents that the students have the ability to learn the material
presented to them. However, making it work again would take a dedicated,
caring conspiracy between teachers and parents. It would mean facing the
tough reality that passing kids who haven't learned the material—while it
might save them grief for the short term—dooms them to long-term illiteracy. It would mean that teachers would have to follow through on their
threats, and parents would have to stand behind them, knowing their children's best interests are indeed at stake. This means no more doing Scott's
assignments for him because he might fail. No more passing Jodi because
she's such a nice kid.

This is a policy that worked in the past and can work today. A wise   12
teacher, with the support of his parents, gave our son the opportunity to succeed—or fail. It's time we return this choice to all students.

Questions for Close Reading

1. What is the selection's thesis? Locate the sentence(s) in which Sherry states her
   main idea. If she doesn't state the thesis explicitly, express it in your own words.
2. Sherry opens her essay with these words: "Tens of thousands of 18-year-olds will
   graduate this year and be handed meaningless diplomas." Why does Sherry consider these diplomas meaningless?
3. According to Sherry, what justification do many teachers give for "passing students who have not mastered the work" (paragraph 8)? Why does Sherry think
   that it is wrong to pass such students?
4. What does Sherry think teachers should do to motivate students to focus on
   school despite the many "distractions . . . at hand" (4)?
5. Refer to your dictionary as needed to define the following words used in the selection: *validity* (paragraph 1), *semiliterate* (1), *equivalency* (2), *impediments* (4),
   composure (6), *radical* (6), *priority* (6), *resentful* (7), *testimony* (9), *motivate* (10),
   merit (11), *conspiracy* (11), and *illiteracy* (11).

Questions About the Writer's Craft

1. **The pattern.** To write an effective argumentation-persuasion essay, writers need
   to establish their credibility. How does Sherry convince readers that she is qualified to write about her subject? What does this attempt to establish credibility say
   about Sherry's perception of her audience's point of view?
2. Sherry's title is deliberately misleading. What does her title lead you to believe the
   essay will be about? Why do you think Sherry chose this title?
3. Why do you suppose Sherry quotes her students rather than summarizing what
   they had to say? What effect do you think Sherry hopes the quotations will have
   on readers?

4. **Other patterns.** What *example* does Sherry provide to show that the threat of failure can work? How does this example reinforce her case?

Writing Assignments Using Argumentation-Persuasion as a Pattern of Development

∞ 1. Like Sherry, write an essay arguing your position on a controversial school-related issue. Possibilities include but need not be limited to the following: College students should *or* should not have to fulfill a physical education requirement; high school students should *or* should not have to demonstrate computer proficiency before graduating; elementary school students should *or* should not be grouped according to ability; a course in parenting should *or* should not be a required part of the high school curriculum. Once you select a topic, brainstorm with others to gather insight into varying points of view. When you write, restrict your argument to one level of education, and refute as many opposing arguments as you can. The following essays will help you identify educational issues worth writing about: Charles Sykes's "The 'Values' Wasteland" (page 184), William Zinsser's "College Pressures" (page 250), Clifford Stoll's "Cyberschool" (page 308), Paul Roberts's "How to Say Nothing in 500 Words" (page 314), Joseph H. Suina's "And Then I Went to School" (page 354), Jacques D'Amboise's "Showing What Is Possible" (page 402), William Raspberry's "The Handicap of Definition" (page 471), Buzz Bissinger's "Innocents Afield" (page 424), and James Barszcz's "Can You Be Educated From a Distance?" (page 522).

2. Sherry acknowledges that she used to blame students' poor academic skills on "drugs, divorce and other impediments." To what extent should teachers take these and similar "impediments" into account when grading students? Are there certain situations that call for leniency, or should out-of-school forces affecting students not be considered? To gain perspective on this issue, interview several friends, classmates, and instructors. Then write an essay in which you argue your position. Provide specific examples to support your argument, being sure to acknowledge and—when possible—to refute opposing viewpoints.

Writing Assignments Combining Patterns of Development

∞ 3. You probably feel, as Sherry does, that Mrs. Stifter is a strong, committed professional. Write an essay *illustrating* the qualities you think a teacher needs to have to be effective. Ask friends, classmates, family members, and instructors for their opinions; however, in your paper, focus on only those attributes you believe are most critical. To highlight the importance of these qualities, begin with a dramatic *contrasting* example of an ineffective teacher—someone who lacks the attributes you consider most important. To gain insight into some of the factors that make teachers effective or ineffective, read Jacques D'Amboise's "Showing What Is Possible" (page 402).

∞ 4. Where else, besides in the classroom, do you see people acting irresponsibly, expending little effort, and taking the easy way out? You might consider the workplace, a school-related club or activity, family life, or interpersonal relationships.

Select *one* area and write an essay *illustrating* the *effects* of this behavior on everyone concerned. For a broader perspective on the issue of personal responsibility, read Charles Sykes's "The 'Values' Wasteland" (page 184), John M. Darley and Bibb Latané's "Why People Don't Help in a Crisis" (page 417), William Raspberry's "The Handicap of Definition" (page 471), and Star Parker's "*Se Habla* Entitlement" (page 567).

Writing Assignment Using a Journal Entry as a Starting Point

5. Write the text for a brochure presenting parents with a step-by-step guide for dealing with academically unmotivated students. Focus your discussion on a specific level of schooling. From your pre-reading journal entry, select those strategies you consider most realistic and productive. When presenting your ideas, take into account children's likely resistance to the strategies described, and instruct parents how to deal with this resistance. Interviewing others (especially parents) and doing some research in the library and/or on the Internet will broaden your understanding of the issues involved.

Yuh Ji-Yeon

At the age of five, Yuh Ji-Yeon (1965–) immigrated from Seoul, Korea, to the United States, settling in Chicago with her parents. After graduating from Stanford University, she worked as a reporter for the *Omaha World-Herald* and *New York Newsday*. She received a doctorate from the University of Pennsylvania following her dissertation examining the experiences of Korean women immigrating to the United States as wives of U.S. soldiers, which she expanded into her book *Beyond the Shadow of Camptown* (2002). Nearly all of Yuh's writing reflects the concerns of people struggling for liberation in the face of oppression. She currently teaches history at Northwestern University. The following selection first appeared in *The Philadelphia Inquirer* in 1991.

Pre-Reading Journal Entry

Which events in American history do you consider shameful? List these events in your journal. For each, jot down what your teachers taught you about the event when you were a child. Does what you were taught as a child differ from what you know now? In what way? If you did later on learn harsher truths about these events, how did you feel? Do you believe that you should have been told the truth from the beginning? Why or why not?

Let's Tell the Story of All America's Cultures

I grew up hearing, seeing and almost believing that America was white— 1 albeit with a little black tinge here and there—and that white was best.

The white people were everywhere in my 1970s Chicago childhood: 2 Founding Fathers, Lewis and Clark, Lincoln, Daniel Boone, Carnegie, presidents, explorers and industrialists galore. The only black people were slaves. The only Indians were scalpers.

I never heard one word about how Benjamin Franklin was so impressed 3 by the Iroquois federation of nations that he adapted that model into our system of state and federal government. Or that the Indian tribes were systematically betrayed and massacred by a greedy young nation that stole their land and called it the United States.

I never heard one word about how Asian immigrants were among the 4 first to turn California's desert into fields of plenty. Or about Chinese immigrant Ah Bing, who bred the cherry now on sale in groceries across the nation. Or that plantation owners in Hawaii imported labor from China, Japan, Korea and the Philippines to work the sugar cane fields. I never learned that Asian immigrants were the only immigrants denied U.S. citizenship, even though they served honorably in World War I. All the immigrants in my textbook were white.

I never learned about Frederick Douglass, the runaway slave who   5
became a leading abolitionist and statesman, or about black scholar W.E.B. Du Bois. I never learned that black people rose up in arms against slavery. Nat Turner wasn't one of the heroes in my childhood history class.

I never learned that the American Southwest and California were already   6
settled by Mexicans when they were annexed after the Mexican-American War. I never learned that Mexico once had a problem keeping land-hungry white men on the U.S. side of the border.

So when other children called me a slant-eyed chink and told me to go   7
back where I came from, I was ready to believe that I wasn't really an American because I wasn't white.

America's bittersweet legacy of struggling and failing and getting another   8
step closer to democratic ideals of liberty and equality and justice for all wasn't for the likes of me, an immigrant child from Korea. The history books said so.

Well, the history books were wrong.   9

Educators around the country are finally realizing what I realized as a   10
teenager in the library, looking up the history I wasn't getting in school. America is a multicultural nation, composed of many people with varying histories and varying traditions who have little in common except their humanity, a belief in democracy and a desire for freedom.

America changed them, but they changed America too.   11

A committee of scholars and teachers gathered by the New York State   12
Department of Education recognizes this in their recent report, "One Nation, Many Peoples: A Declaration of Cultural Interdependence."

They recommend that public schools provide a "multicultural educa-   13
tion, anchored to the shared principles of a liberal democracy."

What that means, according to the report, is recognizing that America   14
was shaped and continues to be shaped by people of diverse backgrounds. It calls for students to be taught that history is an ongoing process of discovery and interpretation of the past, and that there is more than one way of viewing the world.

Thus, the westward migration of white Americans is not just a heroic set-   15
tling of an untamed wild, but also the conquest of indigenous peoples. Immigrants were not just white, but Asian as well. Blacks were not merely passive slaves freed by northern whites, but active fighters for their own liberation.

In particular, according to the report, the curriculum should help children   16
"to assess critically the reasons for the inconsistencies between the ideals of the U.S. and social realities. It should provide information and intellectual tools that can permit them to contribute to bringing reality closer to the ideals."

In other words, show children the good with the bad, and give them the   17
skills to help improve their country. What could be more patriotic?

Several dissenting members of the New York committee publicly worry   18
that America will splinter into ethnic fragments if this multicultural curriculum is adopted. They argue that the committee's report puts the focus on
ethnicity at the expense of national unity.

But downplaying ethnicity will not bolster national unity. The history of   19
America is the story of how and why people from all over the world came to
the United States, and how in struggling to make a better life for themselves,
they changed each other, they changed the country, and they all came to call
themselves Americans.

E pluribus unum. Out of many, one.   20

This is why I, with my Korean background, and my childhood tormentors,   21
with their lost-in-the-mist-of-time European backgrounds, are all Americans.

It is the unique beauty of this country. It is high time we let all our chil-   22
dren gaze upon it.

Questions for Close Reading

1. What is the selection's thesis? Locate the sentence(s) in which Yuh states her main
   idea. If she doesn't state the thesis explicitly, express it in your own words.
2. Yuh makes the rather shocking claim that "the history books were wrong" (paragraph 9). Why does she make this statement? What evidence does she offer to support it?
3. According to Yuh, what changes are needed in U.S. history courses?
4. Why does Yuh feel it is critical that U.S. students receive more than the traditional whites-only version of our nation's history? Who will be served by making history books more multicultural?
5. Refer to your dictionary as needed to define the following words used in the selection: *albeit* (paragraph 1), *tinge* (1), *galore* (2), *multicultural* (10, 13, 18), *interdependence* (12), *indigenous* (15), *dissenting* (18), *ethnicity* (18), and *bolster* (19).

Questions About the Writer's Craft

1. **The pattern.** Where in her argument does Yuh present the opposing viewpoint?
   Why do you suppose she waits so long to deal with the dissenting opinion? What
   effect does this delay have on her argument's effectiveness?
2. **Other patterns.** Why might Yuh have decided to use so many *examples* in paragraphs 2 through 6? How do these examples contribute to the persuasiveness of her
   position? Why might she have placed these examples before her thesis statement?
3. Yuh mixes the subjective and the objective in her argument. Where does she use
   specifics from her own life? How do these personal details help persuade readers
   to accept her viewpoint?
4. Yuh often uses parallelism and repetition of phrases, particularly in paragraphs 1
   through 6 and paragraph 15. What effect do you think she intended these two
   stylistic devices to have on her readers?

Writing Assignments Using Argumentation-Persuasion as a Pattern of Development

1. Using the resources of the library and/or Internet, read several articles about the ongoing debate over multiculturalism's role in contemporary education. In addition to locating coverage of the 1991 New York State Department of Education Study (cited by Yuh in paragraph 12) and historian Arthur Schlesinger's *Time* essay "The Cult of Ethnicity: Good and Bad" (July 8, 1991), you should review many more recent sources on this issue. Review your research, and decide whether or not you support the idea of a multicultural curriculum. Then write an essay in which you argue your position, refuting as many of the opposing views as possible. Draw upon your own experiences as well as your research when developing your point of view.

2. Yuh cites a problem she encountered in her education. What problems or insufficiencies have you found in your own education? Perhaps you perceive an overemphasis on athletics, a reliance on rote memorization, a tendency to discourage female students from pursuing an interest in math and science. Select a single problem at one level of education, and brainstorm with others to gather material about the problem. Then write an essay directed at those who think all is well in our educational system. Be sure your argument illustrates the inaccuracy of these individuals' overly positive view. Before writing your paper, you may want to read Charles Sykes's "The 'Values' Wasteland" (page 184), William Zinsser's "College Pressures" (page 250), Clifford Stoll's "Cyberschool" (page 308), Joseph H. Suina's "And Then I Went to School" (page 354), Buzz Bissinger's "Innocents Afield" (page 424), Mary Sherry's "In Praise of the 'F' Word" (page 512), and James Barszcz's "Can You Be Educated From a Distance?" (page 522) because they offer critiques of U.S. education.

Writing Assignments Combining Patterns of Development

3. Because the mainstream culture they lived in didn't recognize the presence of minorities, the author's classmates considered Yuh an outsider, almost a nonbeing. To what extent, in your opinion, does television contribute to the dehumanization of minorities? For several days, watch a variety of television shows, noting how a particular ethnic or minority group (such as African-Americans, Hispanic-Americans, or the elderly) is portrayed. Then write an essay *arguing* that the depiction of this group on television is either accurate *or* distorted. Support your main idea with plentiful *examples* of specific television shows, including newscasts, situation comedies, talk shows, and so forth.

4. In her essay, Yuh refers to a report issued by the New York State Department of Education. The report argues that curriculum should encourage students to examine "the reasons for the inconsistencies between the ideals of the U.S. and social realities." Like most people, you probably detected such disparities when you were growing up. Perhaps as a youngster, you heard an admired neighbor brag about "scamming" the government or a business of owed money. As a high school student, you might have learned that an esteemed coach took kickbacks from college recruiters. Focus on one such clash between the ethical ideal and the

everyday reality, and write about the incident's *effect* on you. Provide dramatic *details* to show how you reacted, what you did to explain the discrepancy to yourself, and whether you asked adults to help you understand the situation. At the end, reach some conclusions about the way children can be helped to deal with such collisions between ideals and reality. Before writing your paper, you may want to read Audre Lorde's "The Fourth of July" (page 137) and Langston Hughes's "Salvation" (page 155), two powerful essays that explore a child's disillusionment with adult realities.

Writing Assignment Using a Journal Entry as a Starting Point

∞ **5.** Write an essay in which you argue for *or* against schools' revealing harsh historical realities to children. Review your pre-reading journal entry, and select *one* historical event to focus on. Provide plentiful reasons to support your position, whenever possible pointing out weaknesses in opposing viewpoints. To deepen your understanding of the issue, consider reading Audre Lorde's "The Fourth of July" (page 137) and Beth Johnson's "Bombs Bursting in Air" (page 209), essays exploring parents' quandary between protecting their children and educating them about life's painful realities.

James Barszcz

After earning his doctoral degree in English at Rutgers University, James Barszcz (1955–) taught college for several years. He is now employed at a major telecommunications company and pursues writing and independent scholarship in his spare time. In addition to issues related to technology and the classroom, his research interests include nineteenth-century American literature, especially Hawthorne, Melville, and Emerson. He lives with his wife and two children in Maplewood, New Jersey.

Pre-Reading Journal Entry

While many students readily acknowledge the practical reasons for attending college, fewer consider the intangible opportunity for personal development that higher education can provide. Take a few moments to consider what personal qualities you seek to cultivate in the course of your college education. Freewrite about this subject in your pre-reading journal, listing the various characteristics you hope to develop by the time you get your diploma. Discussing your thoughts with peers might help broaden your perspective on this question.

Can You Be Educated From a Distance?

By almost any measure, there is a boom in Internet-based instruction. In just a few years, thirty-four percent of American colleges and universities have begun offering some form of what's called "distance learning" (DL), and among the larger schools, it's closer to ninety percent. If you doubt the popularity of the trend, you probably haven't heard of the University of Phoenix. It grants degrees entirely on the basis of online instruction. It enrolls 90,000 students, a statistic used to support its claim to be the largest private university in the country. 1

While the kinds of instruction offered in these programs will differ, DL usually signifies a course in which the instructors post syllabi, reading assignments, and schedules on websites, and students send in their written assignments by e-mail. Other forms of communication often come into play, such as threaded messaging, which allows for posting questions and comments that are publicly viewable, as a bulletin board would, as well as chat rooms for real-time interchanges. Generally speaking, face-to-face communication with an instructor is minimized or eliminated altogether. 2

The attraction for students might at first seem obvious. Primarily, there's 3
the convenience promised by courses on the Net: you can do the work, as
they say, in your pajamas. But figures indicate that the reduced effort results
in a reduced commitment to the course. While the attrition rate for all
freshmen at American universities is around twenty percent, the rate for online students is thirty-five percent. Students themselves seem to understand
the weaknesses inherent in the setup. In a survey conducted for eCornell, the
DL division of Cornell University, less than a third of the respondents expected the quality of the online course to be as good as the classroom course.

Clearly, from the schools' perspective, there's a lot of money to be saved. 4
Although some of the more ambitious programs require new investments in
servers and networks to support collaborative software, most DL courses can
run on existing or minimally upgraded systems. The more students who
enroll in a course but don't come to campus, the more the school saves on
keeping the lights on in the classrooms, paying custodians, and maintaining
parking lots. And, while there's evidence that instructors must work harder
to run a DL course for a variety of reasons, they won't be paid any more, and
might well be paid less.

But as a rule, those who champion distance learning don't base their 5
arguments on convenience or cost savings. More often, they claim DL signals
an advance in the effectiveness of education. Consider the vigorous case made
by Fairleigh Dickinson University (FDU), in Madison, New Jersey, where
students—regardless of their expectations or desires—are now required to
take one DL course per year. By setting this requirement, FDU claims that
it recognizes the Internet as "a premier learning tool" of the current technological age. Skill in using online resources "prepares our students, more
than others, for life-long learning—for their jobs, their careers, and their personal growth." Moreover, Internet-based courses will connect FDU students
to a "global virtual faculty," a group of "world-class scholars, experts, artists,
politicians, and business leaders around the world."

Sounds pretty good. But do the claims make much sense? First, it should 6
be noted that students today and in the future might well use the Internet
with at least as much facility as the faculty. It's not at all clear that they need
to be taught such skills. More to the point, how much time and effort do you
suppose "world-class scholars" (much less politicians and business leaders)
will expend for the benefit of students they never meet or even see? Probably
a lot less than they're devoting to the books, journal articles, and position
papers that are already available to anyone with access to a library.

Another justification comes from those who see distance learning as the 7
next step in society's progress toward meritocracy. A recent article in *Forbes*
magazine cites Professor Roger Schank of Northwestern University, who
predicts that soon "students will be able to shop around, taking a course
from any institution that offers a good one. . . . Quality education will be

available to all. Students will learn what they want to learn rather than what some faculty committee decided was the best practical compromise." In sum, says Professor Schank, who is also chairman of a distance-learning enterprise called CognitiveArts, "Education will be measured by what you know rather than by whose name appears on your diploma."

Statements like these assume education consists in acquiring information ("what you know"). Accept that and it's hard to disagree with the conclusions. After all, what does it matter how, or through what medium, you get the information? But few truly educated people hold such a mechanistic view. Indeed, traditionally, education was aimed at cultivating intellectual and moral values, and the "information" you picked up was decidedly secondary. It was commonplace for those giving commencement speeches to note that, based on etymology, education is a drawing out, not a putting in. That is, a true education *educes,* or draws out, from within a person qualities of intellect and character that would otherwise have remained hidden or dormant. 8

Exactly how this kind of educing happens is hard to pin down. Only in part does it come from watching professors in the classroom present material and respond to student questions, the elements of education that can be translated to the Net with reasonable fidelity. Other educational experiences include things like watching how professors joke with each other (or not!) in the hallways, seeing what kinds of pictures are framed in a professor's office, or going out for coffee after class with people in your dorm. Such experiences, and countless others, are sometimes labeled (and dismissed) as "social life on campus." But they also contribute invaluably to education. Through them, you learn a style, in the noblest sense of that term, a way of regarding the information you acquire and the society you find yourself in. This is what the philosopher Alfred North Whitehead meant when he called style the ultimate acquisition of a cultivated mind. And it's the mysterious ways of cultivating that style that the poet Robert Frost had in mind when he said that all that a college education requires is that you "hang around until you catch on." Hang around campus, that is, not lurk on the Net. 9

Questions for Close Reading

1. What is the selection's thesis? Locate the sentence(s) in which Barszcz states his main idea. If he doesn't state the thesis explicitly, express it in your own words.
2. According to Barszcz, what primarily attracts students and schools to distance learning?
3. What does Barszcz say are the most common arguments made by proponents of distance learning?
4. How does Barszcz define *education?* Do you agree with his definition, or do you see education functioning in a different way? Explain.
5. Refer to your dictionary as needed to define the following words used in the selection: *attrition* (3), *virtual* (5), *facility* (6), *meritocracy* (7), *mechanistic* (8), *etymology* (8), *dormant* (8), and *fidelity* (9).

Questions About the Writer's Craft

1. **The pattern.** What sort of audience—supportive, wavering, or hostile (see page 481)—does Barszcz seem to have geared his argument toward? How can you tell?
2. **Other patterns.** Barszcz develops paragraph 2 through *division-classification*. What larger topic does he divide into categories? What are these categories? What organizational order does he use in this paragraph?
3. Barszcz quotes literature from Fairleigh Dickinson University (FDU) in some detail. Considering that FDU's position represents an opposing point of view, why do you think he quotes FDU at such length? What is the effect of this quoting?
4. **Other patterns.** In paragraphs 2 and 8, Barszcz provides two *definitions* that fundamentally differ in purpose and tone. Describe the differences.

Writing Assignments Using Argumentation-Persuasion as a Pattern of Development

1. Barszcz posits that a central component of education should be the cultivation of "moral values." Do you agree? Take the case of public elementary schools. Write an essay in which you argue that these schools should *or* should not instruct students in morality as part of the curriculum. Be sure as you develop your argument to acknowledge and refute opposing points of view. You might benefit from reading Yuh Ji-Yeon's "Let's Tell the Story of All America's Cultures" (page 517), in which the author advocates a certain type of moral education.
2. Barszcz suggests that the true motivation of some who champion distance learning is financial. Think of some other phenomenon—say, the invasion of one country by another, the marketing of a new medication, advertisements for life insurance—and write an essay *arguing* that a financial motive underlies lofty rhetoric ("We will liberate the people of . . . ," "We care about your health," "Invest in your children's future"). Support your case with at least three major *examples* that *illustrate* your assertion. You should also consider citing facts, statistics, and/or expert opinions derived from visiting the library and/or going online to lend additional authority to your position.

Writing Assignments Combining Patterns of Development

3. In Barszcz's view, educated people are intellectually and morally cultivated. Write an essay *describing* someone you know (or know of) who, in your view, epitomizes an educated person. What are the person's intellectual qualities? What are his or her character traits? What are his or her moral values and tastes? As you answer these questions about the person, provide vivid *examples* to *illustrate* the characteristics you're describing. You might begin by reading "Sister Flowers" (page 100), in which Maya Angelou lovingly conveys the portrait of a very cultivated lady.
4. As Barszcz indicates, on-campus experiences contribute to college students' education. In an essay of your own, *narrate* a school-related experience from any time in your life that left you significantly better educated. The experience you describe, though school-related, need not be strictly academic. For example, you

might discuss developing a friendship with someone from a different culture, coming to appreciate an initially disliked instructor, participating in an inspiring class, and so on. *Describe* those details that convey what made the experience so enlightening. How did the experience make you more understanding, aware, critical, sensitive, or appreciative? How did it alter your worldview?

Writing Assignment Using a Journal
Entry as a Starting Point

∞ 5. A "true education," according to Barszcz, "*educes,* or draws out, from within a person qualities of intellect and character that would otherwise have remained hidden or dormant" (paragraph 8). What personal qualities do you hope a college education will educe from you? Reviewing what you wrote in your pre-reading journal entry, write an essay in which you identify at least two or three qualities you hope to nurture during your college years and explain why you hope to do so. For instance, you might discuss your aspiration to become more intellectually objective, more assertive, more articulate, and so on. And, in order to demonstrate the progress you hope to make, for each quality, you should *contrast* yourself at the outset of your college education with where you hope to be by the end. For some general reflections on the role of education in students' lives, read any of the following: William Zinsser's "College Pressures" (page 250), Clifford Stoll's "Cyberschool" (page 308), Joseph H. Suina's "And Then I Went to School" (page 354), Mary Sherry's "In Praise of the 'F' Word" (page 512), and Yuh Ji-Yeon's "Let's Tell the Story of All America's Cultures" (page 517).

Mark Twain

Mark Twain is a central figure in American literature. Published in 1884, *The Adventures of Huckleberry Finn*, Twain's finest work, recounts a journey down the Mississippi by two memorable figures: a white boy and a black slave. Twain was born Samuel Langhorne Clemens in 1835 and was raised in Hannibal, Missouri. During his early years, he worked as a riverboat pilot, newspaper reporter, printer, and gold prospector. Although his popular image is as the author of such comic works as *The Adventures of Tom Sawyer* (1876), *Life on the Mississippi* (1883), and *The Prince and the Pauper* (1882), Twain had a darker side that may have resulted from the bitter experiences of his life: financial failure and the deaths of his wife and daughter. His last writings are savage, satiric, and pessimistic. The following selection is taken from *Letters From the Earth*, one of Twain's later works.

Pre-Reading Journal Entry

What would you identify as the major differences between human beings and other animals? What are the similarities? In your journal, list as many items for each as you can, from the obvious to the subtle. Be as specific as you can.

The Damned Human Race

I have been studying the traits and dispositions of the "lower animals" (so-called), and contrasting them with the traits and dispositions of man. I find the result humiliating to me. For it obliges me to renounce my allegiance to the Darwinian theory of the Ascent of Man from the Lower Animals; since it now seems plain to me that the theory ought to be vacated in favor of a new and truer one, this new and truer one to be named the *Descent* of Man from the Higher Animals.

In proceeding toward this unpleasant conclusion I have not guessed or speculated or conjectured, but have used what is commonly called the scientific method. That is to say, I have subjected every postulate that presented itself to the crucial test of actual experiment, and have adopted it or rejected it according to the result. Thus I verified and established each step of my course in its turn before advancing to the next. These experiments were made in the London Zoological Gardens, and covered many months of painstaking and fatiguing work.

Before particularizing any of the experiments, I wish to state one or two   3
things which seem to more properly belong in this place than further along.
This in the interest of clearness. The massed experiments established to my
satisfaction certain generalizations, to wit:

1. That the human race is of one distinct species. It exhibits slight variations—in color, stature, mental caliber, and so on—due to climate,
   environment, and so forth; but it is a species by itself, and not to be
   confounded with any other.
2. That the quadrupeds are a distinct family, also. This family exhibits
   variations—in color, size, food preferences and so on; but it is a family by itself.
3. That the other families—the birds, the fishes, the insects, the reptiles,
   etc.—are more or less distinct, also. They are in the procession. They
   are links in the chain which stretches down from the higher animals
   to man at the bottom.

Some of my experiments were quite curious. In the course of my reading   4
I had come across a case where, many years ago, some hunters on our Great
Plains organized a buffalo hunt for the entertainment of an English earl—
that, and to provide some fresh meat for his larder. They had charming sport.
They killed seventy-two of those great animals; and ate part of one of them
and left the seventy-one to rot. In order to determine the difference between
an anaconda and an earl—if any—I caused seven young calves to be turned
into the anaconda's cage. The grateful reptile immediately crushed one of
them and swallowed it, then lay back satisfied. It showed no further interest
in the calves, and no disposition to harm them. I tried this experiment with
other anacondas; always with the same result. The fact stood proven that the
difference between an earl and an anaconda is that the earl is cruel and the
anaconda isn't; and that the earl wantonly destroys what he has no use for,
but the anaconda doesn't. This seemed to suggest that the anaconda was not
descended from the earl. It also seemed to suggest that the earl was descended from the anaconda, and had lost a good deal in the transition.

I was aware that many men who have accumulated more millions of   5
money than they can ever use have shown a rabid hunger for more, and have
not scrupled to cheat the ignorant and the helpless out of their poor servings
in order to partially appease that appetite. I furnished a hundred different
kinds of wild and tame animals the opportunity to accumulate vast stores of
food, but none of them would do it. The squirrels and bees and certain birds
made accumulations, but stopped when they had gathered a winter's supply,
and could not be persuaded to add to it either honestly or by chicanery. In
order to bolster up a tottering reputation the ant pretended to store up supplies, but I was not deceived. I know the ant. These experiments convinced

me that there is this difference between man and the higher animals: he is avaricious and miserly, they are not.

In the course of my experiments I convinced myself that among the animals man is the only one that harbors insults and injuries, broods over them, waits till a chance offers, then takes revenge. The passion of revenge is unknown to the higher animals.   6

Roosters keep harems, but it is by consent of their concubines; therefore no wrong is done. Men keep harems, but it is by brute force, privileged by atrocious laws which the other sex were allowed no hand in making. In this matter man occupies a far lower place than the rooster.   7

Cats are loose in their morals, but not consciously so. Man, in his descent from the cat, has brought the cat's looseness with him but has left the unconsciousness behind—the saving grace which excuses the cat. The cat is innocent, man is not.   8

Indecency, vulgarity, obscenity—these are strictly confined to man; he invented them. Among the higher animals there is no trace of them. They hide nothing; they are not ashamed. Man, with his soiled mind, covers himself. He will not even enter a drawing room with his breast and back naked, so alive are he and his mates to indecent suggestion. Man is "The Animal that Laughs." But so does the monkey, as Mr. Darwin pointed out; and so does the Australian bird that is called the laughing jackass. No—Man is the Animal that Blushes. He is the only one that does it—or has occasion to.   9

At the head of this article[1] we see how "three monks were burnt to death" a few days ago, and a prior "put to death with atrocious cruelty." Do we inquire into the details? No; or we should find out that the prior was subjected to unprintable mutilations. Man—when he is a North American Indian—gouges out his prisoner's eyes; when he is King John, with a nephew to render untroublesome, he uses a red-hot iron; when he is a religious zealot dealing with heretics in the Middle Ages, he skins his captive alive and scatters salt on his back; in the first Richard's time he shuts up a multitude of Jew families in a tower and sets fire to it; in Columbus's time he captures a family of Spanish Jews and—but *that* is not printable; in our day in England a man is fined ten shillings for beating his mother nearly to death with a chair, and another man is fined forty shillings for having four pheasant eggs in his possession without being able to satisfactorily explain how he got them. Of all the animals, man is the only one that is cruel. He is the only one that inflicts pain for the pleasure of doing it. It is a trait that is not known to the higher animals. The cat plays with the frightened mouse; but she has this excuse, that she does not know that the mouse is suffering. The cat is moderate—unhumanly moderate: she only scares the mouse, she does not hurt   10

[1]Twain originally began his article with newspaper clippings containing telegrams that reported atrocities in Crete (editors' note).

it; she doesn't dig out its eyes, or tear off its skin, or drive splinters under its nails—man-fashion; when she is done playing with it she makes a sudden meal of it and puts it out of its trouble. Man is the Cruel Animal. He is alone in that distinction.

The higher animals engage in individual fights, but never in organized masses. Man is the only animal that deals in that atrocity of atrocities, War. He is the only one that gathers his brethren about him and goes forth in cold blood and with calm pulse to exterminate his kind. He is the only animal that for sordid wages will march out, as the Hessians did in our Revolution, and as the boyish Prince Napoleon did in the Zulu war, and help to slaughter strangers of his own species who have done him no harm and with whom he has no quarrel.

Man is the only animal that robs his helpless fellow of his country—takes possession of it and drives him out of it or destroys him. Man has done this in all the ages. There is not an acre of ground on the globe that is in possession of its rightful owner, or that has not been taken away from owner after owner, cycle after cycle, by force and bloodshed.

Man is the only Slave. And he is the only animal who enslaves. He has always been a slave in one form or another, and has always held other slaves in bondage under him in one way or another. In our day he is always some man's slave for wages, and does that man's work; and this slave has other slaves under him for minor wages, and they do *his* work. The higher animals are the only ones who exclusively do their own work and provide their own living.

Man is the only Patriot. He sets himself apart in his own country, under his own flag, and sneers at the other nations, and keeps multitudinous uniformed assassins on hand at heavy expense to grab slices of other people's countries, and keep *them* from grabbing slices of *his*. And in the intervals between campaigns he washes the blood off his hands and works for "the universal brotherhood of man"—with his mouth.

Man is the Religious Animal. He is the only Religious Animal. He is the only animal that has the True Religion—several of them. He is the only animal that loves his neighbor as himself, and cuts his throat if his theology isn't straight. He has made a graveyard of the globe in trying his honest best to smooth his brother's path to happiness and heaven. He was at it in the time of the Caesars, he was at it in Mahomet's time, he was at it in the time of the Inquisition, he was at it in France a couple of centuries, he was at it in England in Mary's day, he has been at it ever since he first saw the light, he is at it today in Crete—as per the telegrams quoted above[2]—he will be at it somewhere else tomorrow. The higher animals have no religion. And we are told that they are going to be left out, in the Hereafter. I wonder why? It seems questionable taste.

[2]See note, page 529 (editors' note).

Man is the Reasoning Animal. Such is the claim. I think it is open to dis-   16
pute. Indeed, my experiments have proven to me that he is the Unreasoning
Animal. Note his history, as sketched above. It seems plain to me that whatever he is he is *not* a reasoning animal. His record is the fantastic record of a
maniac. I consider that the strongest count against his intelligence is the fact
that with that record back of him he blandly sets himself up as the head animal of the lot: whereas by his own standards he is the bottom one.

In truth, man is incurably foolish. Simple things which the other animals   17
easily learn, he is incapable of learning. Among my experiments was this. In
an hour I taught a cat and a dog to be friends. I put them in a cage. In another hour I taught them to be friends with a rabbit. In the course of two days
I was able to add a fox, a goose, a squirrel and some doves. Finally a monkey. They lived together in peace; even affectionately.

Next, in another cage I confined an Irish Catholic from Tipperary, and   18
as soon as he seemed tame I added a Scotch Presbyterian from Aberdeen.
Next a Turk from Constantinople; a Greek Christian from Crete; an Armen-
ian; a Methodist from the wilds of Arkansas; a Buddhist from China; a Brah-
man from Benares. Finally, a Salvation Army Colonel from Wapping. Then I
stayed away two whole days. When I came back to note results, the cage of
Higher Animals was all right, but in the other, there was but a chaos of gory
odds and ends of turbans and fezzes and plaids and bones and flesh—not a
specimen left alive. These Reasoning Animals had disagreed on a theological
detail and carried the matter to a Higher Court.

One is obliged to concede that in true loftiness of character, Man can-   19
not claim to approach even the meanest of the Higher Animals. It is plain
that he is constitutionally incapable of approaching that altitude; that he is
constitutionally afflicted with a Defect which must make such approach forever impossible, for it is manifest that this defect is permanent in him, indestructible, ineradicable.

I find this Defect to be *the Moral Sense*. He is the only animal that has it.   20
It is the secret of his degradation. It is the quality *which enables him to do
wrong*. It has no other office. It is incapable of performing any other function.
It could never have been intended to perform any other. Without it, man
could do no wrong. He would rise at once to the level of the Higher Animals.

Since the Moral Sense has but the one office, the one capacity—to enable   21
man to do wrong—it is plainly without value to him. It is as valueless to him
as is disease. In fact, it manifestly *is* a disease. *Rabies* is bad, but it is not so bad
as this disease. Rabies enables a man to do a thing which he could not do
when in a healthy state: kill his neighbor with a poisonous bite. No one is the
better man for having rabies: The Moral Sense enables a man to do wrong. It
enables him to do wrong in a thousand ways. Rabies is an innocent disease,
compared to the Moral Sense. No one, then, can be the better man for having the Moral Sense. What, now, do we find the Primal Curse to have been?

Plainly what it was in the beginning: the infliction upon man of the Moral Sense; the ability to distinguish good from evil; and with it, necessarily, the ability to *do* evil; for there can be no evil act without the presence of consciousness of it in the doer of it.

And so I find that we have descended and degenerated, from some far   2 ancestor—some microscopic atom wandering at its pleasure between the mighty horizons of a drop of water perchance—insect by insect, animal by animal, reptile by reptile, down the long highway of smirchless innocence, till we have reached the bottom stage of development—namable as the Human Being. Below us—nothing.

Questions for Close Reading

1. What is the selection's thesis? Locate the sentence(s) in which Twain states his main idea. If he doesn't state the thesis explicitly, express it in your own words.
2. Because of their intelligence, humans are usually called the highest animal. What, according to Twain, are the specific traits that make humans the lowest animal?
3. How does the story of the earl who hunted down seventy-two buffalo show that an anaconda is superior to an earl?
4. What does Twain mean when he points out that humankind is the only animal that "has occasion to" blush? What are some of the occasions for blushing that he highlights in the essay?
5. Refer to your dictionary as needed to define the following words used in the selection: *confounded* (paragraph 3), *anaconda* (4), *wantonly* (4), *chicanery* (5), *heretics* (10), *constitutionally* (19), *ineradicable* (19), and *smirchless* (22).

Questions About the Writer's Craft

1. **The pattern.** Most writers don't tell the reader outright the reasoning process they used to arrive at their essay's proposition. But Twain claims that he reached his conclusion about human beings inductively—through the use of the "scientific method." Why does Twain make this claim?
2. Where in the essay does Twain try to shock the audience? Why do you think he adopts this technique?
3. **Other patterns.** In some paragraphs, Twain provides numerous *examples* of political and religious atrocities. Why do you suppose he supplies so many examples?
4. Black humor is defined as "the use of the morbid and the absurd for comic purposes." What elements of the morbid and the absurd do you find in Twain's essay? Would you say "The Damned Human Race" is an example of black humor? Explain.

Writing Assignments Using Argumentation-Persuasion as a Pattern of Development

1. In an essay, argue that human beings are worthy of being considered the "highest animal." The paper should acknowledge and then refute Twain's charges that people

are miserly, vengeful, foolish, and so on. To support your proposition, use specific examples of how human beings can be kind, caring, generous, and peace-loving.

2. Write an essay agreeing with Twain that it is our everyday meannesses, unkindnesses, and cruelties that make us the "lowest animal." Use compelling examples to support your argument, including description and dialogue whenever appropriate. You might focus on one of the following topics:

> Violence toward children
> Abuse of animals
> Hurtful sarcasm
> Insults of a racial, sexist, or religious nature
> Indifference to the unfortunate

Somewhere in the essay, you should acknowledge the view that humans are capable of considerable kindness and compassion. For more perspectives like Twain's, read Stephanie Ericsson's "The Ways We Lie" (page 240) and Stephen King's "Why We Crave Horror Movies" (page 397).

Writing Assignments Combining Patterns of Development

3. What failings of human decency do you see around you every day in your town, on your campus, or at your job? Write an essay *arguing* that inhumanity resides not just in atrocities but also in ordinary acts of indifference. Providing compelling *examples* or *anecdotes* will be crucial as you make your argument. In your essay, you may use Twain's kind of bitter sarcasm, or you may adopt a more objective, less vitriolic tone. You might also read John M. Darley and Bibb Latané's "Why People Don't Help in a Crisis" (page 417), another essay specifically exploring the causes of inhumanity.

4. How could humans become less cruel? Write an essay outlining a new *process* for raising children or "re-civilizing" adults—a process that, if instituted, would have a clearly beneficial *effect* on human morality.

Writing Assignment Using a Journal Entry as a Starting Point

5. Write an essay in which, unlike Twain, you illustrate the *similarities* between human beings and other species of animals. Using your pre-reading journal entry, select the most compelling similarities. Try to explore likenesses that go beyond such obvious ones as eating, sleeping, reproduction, etc.; focus instead on behaviors and traits that are elusive but telling. Your essays, which may be humorous or serious, should reveal your attitude toward the similarities you discuss. Do they reflect favorably or negatively on the human species?

Stanley Fish

Stanley Fish is best known as a scholar of the English poet John Milton and as a literary theorist. He was born in Providence, Rhode Island, in 1938, and grew up in Philadelphia, Pennsylvania. After earning his bachelor's degree from the University of Pennsylvania, he went on to receive a Ph.D. from Yale University in 1962. Fish has taught English at the University of California at Berkeley, Johns Hopkins University, and Duke University. From 1999 to 2004 he was dean of the College of Liberal Arts and Sciences at the University of Illinois at Chicago, and in 2005 he became a professor of humanities and law at Florida International University. His best-known work on Milton is *Surprised by Sin: The Reader in Paradise Lost* (1967). In addition to his distinguished academic career and many scholarly publications, Fish has also had a career as a public intellectual. He has written and lectured about many issues, including the politics of the university. His books on current political and cultural issues include *There's No Such Thing as Free Speech . . . and It's a Good Thing, Too* (1994) and *The Trouble With Principle* (1999). This article was published in *The Chronicle of Higher Education,* for which Fish writes a regular column on campus politics and academic careers, on June 13, 2003.

Pre-Reading Journal Entry

The issue of freedom of speech on campus is a topic that never seems to go away, maintaining relevance from generation to generation of college students. How do you feel about freedom of speech on campus? In your journal, list several controversial issues that might be debated in a college setting. For each issue, indicate whether you feel that divergent, even inflammatory views should have an opportunity to be heard on campus—for example, in class, in the college newspaper, or in a lecture series. Reflect in your journal on why you feel as you do.

Free-Speech Follies

The modern American version of crying wolf is crying First Amendment.[1] If you want to burn a cross on a black family's lawn or buy an election by contributing millions to a candidate or vilify Jerry Falwell and his

---

[1]The relevant part of the First Amendment of the U.S. Constitution reads: "Congress shall make no law . . . abridging the freedom of speech, or of the press; or the right of the people peaceably to assemble, and to petition the Government for a redress of grievances" (editors' note).

mother in a scurrilous "parody," and someone or some government agency tries to stop you, just yell "First Amendment rights" and you will stand a good chance of getting to do what you want to do.

In the academy,[2] the case is even worse: Not only is the First Amend- 2 ment pressed into service at the drop of a hat (especially whenever anyone is disciplined for anything), it is invoked ritually when there are no First Amendment issues in sight.

Take the case of the editors of college newspapers who will always cry 3 First Amendment when something they've published turns out to be the cause of outrage and controversy. These days the offending piece or editorial or advertisement usually involves (what is at least perceived to be) an attack on Jews. In January of this year, the *Daily Illini*, a student newspaper at the University of Illinois at Urbana-Champaign, printed a letter from a resident of Seattle with no university affiliation. The letter ran under the headline "Jews Manipulate America" and argued that because their true allegiance is to the state of Israel, the president should "separate Jews from all government advisory positions"; otherwise, the writer warned, "the Jews might face another Holocaust."

When the predictable firestorm of outrage erupted, the newspaper's edi- 4 tor responded by declaring, first, that "we are committed to giving all people a voice"; second, that, given this commitment, "we print the opinions of others with whom we do not agree"; third, that to do otherwise would involve the newspaper in the dangerous acts of "silencing" and "self-censorship"; and, fourth, that "what is hate speech to one member of a society is free speech to another."

Wrong four times. 5

I'll bet the *Daily Illini* is not committed to giving all people a voice—the 6 KKK? man-boy love? advocates of slavery? would-be Unabombers? Nor do I believe that the editors sift through submissions looking for the ones they disagree with and then print those. No doubt they apply some principles of selection, asking questions like, Is it relevant, or Is it timely, or Does it get the facts right, or Does it present a coherent argument?

That is, they exercise judgment, which is quite a different thing from 7 silencing or self-censorship. No one is silenced because a single outlet declines to publish him; silencing occurs when that outlet (or any other) is forbidden by the state to publish him on pain of legal action; and that is also what censorship is.

As for self-censoring, if it is anything, it is what we all do whenever we 8 decide it would be better not to say something or cut a sentence that went just a little bit too far or leave a manuscript in the bottom drawer because it is not yet ready. Self-censorship, in short, is not a crime or a moral failing; it is a responsibility.

---

[2]Refers to institutions of higher learning (editors' note).

And, finally, whatever the merits of the argument by which all assertions are relativised—your hate speech is my free speech—this incident has nothing to do with either hate speech or free speech and everything to do with whether the editors are discharging or defaulting on their obligations when they foist them off on an inapplicable doctrine, saying in effect, "The First Amendment made us do it."

More recently, the same scenario played itself out at Santa Rosa Junior College. This time it was a student who wrote the offending article. Titled "Is Anti-Semitism Ever the Result of Jewish Behavior?" it answered the question in the affirmative, creating an uproar that included death threats, an avalanche of hate mail, and demands for just about everyone's resignation. The faculty adviser who had approved the piece said, "The First Amendment isn't there to protect agreeable stories."

He was alluding to the old saw that the First Amendment protects unpopular as well as popular speech. But what it protects unpopular speech *from* is abridgment by the government of its free expression; it does not protect unpopular speech from being rejected by a newspaper, and it confers no positive obligation to give your pages over to unpopular speech, or popular speech, or any speech.

Once again, there is no First Amendment issue here, just an issue of editorial judgment and the consequences of exercising it. (You can print anything you like; but if the heat comes, it's yours, not the Constitution's.)

In these controversies, student editors are sometimes portrayed, or portray themselves, as First Amendment heroes who bravely risk criticism and censure in order to uphold a cherished American value. But they are not heroes; they are merely confused and, in terms of their understanding of the doctrine they invoke, rather hapless.

Not as hapless, however, as the Harvard English department, which made a collective fool of itself three times when it invited, disinvited and then reinvited poet Tom Paulin to be the Morris Gray lecturer. Again the flash point was anti-Semitism. In his poetry and in public comments, Paulin had said that Israel had no right to exist, that settlers on the West Bank "should be shot dead," and that Israeli police and military forces were the equivalent of the Nazi SS. When these and other statements came to light shortly before Paulin was to give his lecture, the department voted to rescind the invitation. When the inevitable cry of "censorship, censorship" was heard in the land, the department flip-flopped again, and a professor-spokesman declared, "This was a clear affirmation that the department stood strongly by the First Amendment."

It was of course nothing of the kind; it was a transparent effort of a bunch that had already put its foot in its mouth twice to wriggle out of trouble and regain the moral high ground by striking the pose of First Amendment defender. But, in fact, the department and its members were not First Amendment defenders (a religion they converted to a little late), but serial bunglers.

What should they have done? Well, it depends on what they wanted to   16
do. If they wanted to invite this particular poet because they admired his
poetry, they had a perfect right to do so. If they were aware ahead of time of
Paulin's public pronouncements, they could have chosen either to say something by way of explanation or to remain silent and let the event speak for
itself; either course of action would have been at once defensible and productive of risk. If they knew nothing of Paulin's anti-Israel sentiments (difficult to believe of a gang of world-class researchers) but found out about
them after the fact, they might have said, "Oops, never mind" or toughed it
out—again alternatives not without risk. But at each stage, whatever they did
or didn't do would have had no relationship whatsoever to any First Amendment right—Paulin had no right to be invited—or obligation—there was no
obligation either to invite or disinvite him, and certainly no obligation to
reinvite him, unless you count the obligations imposed on yourself by a succession of ill-thought-through decisions. Whatever the successes or failures
here, they were once again failures of judgment, not doctrine.

In another case, it looked for a moment that judgment of an appropriate   17
kind was in fact being exercised. The University of California at Berkeley
houses the Emma Goldman Papers Project, and each year the director sends
out a fund-raising mailer that always features quotations from Goldman's
work. But this January an associate vice chancellor edited the mailer and
removed two quotations that in context read as a criticism of the Bush administration's plans for a war in Iraq. He explained that the quotations were not
randomly chosen and were clearly intended to make a "political point, and
that is inappropriate in an official university situation."

The project director (who acknowledged that the quotes were selected   18
for their contemporary relevance) objected to what she saw as an act of censorship and a particularly egregious one given Goldman's strong advocacy of
free expression.

But no one's expression was being censored. The Goldman quotations   19
are readily available and had they appeared in the project's literature in a setting that did not mark them as political, no concerns would have been raised.
It is just, said the associate vice chancellor, that they are inappropriate in this
context, and, he added, "It is not a matter of the First Amendment."

Right, it's a matter of whether or not there is even the appearance of the   20
university's taking sides on a partisan issue; that is, it is an empirical matter
that requires just the exercise of judgment that associate vice chancellors are
paid to perform. Of course he was pilloried by members of the Berkeley faculty and others who saw First Amendment violations everywhere.

But there were none. Goldman still speaks freely through her words.   21
The project director can still make her political opinions known by writing
letters to the editor or to everyone in the country, even if she cannot use the
vehicle of a university flier to do so. Everyone's integrity is preserved. The

project goes on unimpeded, and the university goes about its proper academic business. Or so it would have been had the administration stayed firm. But it folded and countermanded the associate vice chancellor's decision.

At least the chancellor had sense enough to acknowledge that no one's speech had been abridged. It was just, he said, an "error in judgment." Aren't they all?

Are there then no free-speech issues on campuses? Sure there are; there just aren't very many. When Toni Smith, a basketball player at Manhattanville College, turned her back to the flag during the playing of the national anthem in protest against her government's policies, she was truly exercising her First Amendment rights, rights that ensure that she cannot be compelled to an affirmation she does not endorse. . . . And as she stood by her principles in the face of hostility, she truly was (and is) a First Amendment hero, as the college newspaper editors, the members of the Harvard English department, and the head of the Emma Goldman Project are not. The category is a real one, and it would be good if it were occupied only by those who belong in it.

Questions for Close Reading

1. What is the selection's thesis? Locate the sentence(s) in which Fish states his main idea. If he doesn't state his thesis explicitly, express it in your own words.
2. What does Fish mean by "Self-censorship, in short, is not a crime or a moral failing; it is a responsibility" (paragraph 8)?
3. In paragraph 15, Fish refers to the Harvard English department as "serial bunglers." What does he mean by this?
4. According to Fish, why aren't the editors of student newspapers that publish inflammatory material First Amendment heroes? Who does he believe are the true First Amendment heroes?
5. Refer to your dictionary as needed to define the following words used in the selection: *vilify* (paragraph 1), *scurrilous* (1), *firestorm* (4), *coherent* (6), *abridgment* (11), *hapless* (13), *rescind* (14), *chancellor* (17), *egregious* (18), *partisan* (20), *empirical* (20), *pilloried* (20), *countermanded* (21).

Questions About the Writer's Craft

1. **The pattern.** Writing on a complex and controversial issue, Fish presents the opposing viewpoint—that self-censorship is not a violation of the First Amendment. What strategies does Fish use to deal with this view and to present his own argument?
2. **Other patterns.** All the examples that Fish uses to support his argument are related to anti-Semitism. If Fish had broadened the examples to include instances of speech that defamed groups other than Jews, would the essay have been more or less effective? Support your answer.
3. Paragraph 5 has only three words, "Wrong four times." What is the effect of this brevity?
4. Most readers of *The Chronicle of Higher Education*, where this essay was first published, are academics—administrators, faculty, and graduate students—or those

with a professional interest in higher education. They are likely to know Fish by reputation, especially since he publishes a regular column. Given this, how would you assess Fish's *ethos*? How effective is his use of *logos* in this argument? How effective is his use of *pathos*?

Writing Assignments Using Argumentation-Persuasion as a Pattern of Development

1. Fish gives an example of a controversy surrounding an anti-Semitic letter to the editor published in a campus student newspaper. Since publications print letters to the editor to open up their pages to public opinion and dissent, one might argue that the criteria for printing letters to the editor should be quite broad—much broader than the criteria the publication uses for its own articles—in order to give members of the public an opportunity to air their views. Write an essay in which you *argue* that letters to the editor should (or should not) be printed with the aim of giving all readers an opportunity to state their opinions. Don't forget to acknowledge (and, if possible, to refute) opposing viewpoints—perhaps including Fish's—at some point in your paper.

2. Many colleges and universities have tried to compromise on the free-speech issue by limiting controversial speech to designated "free-speech zones," areas on campus where speeches, rallies, and pamphleteering are permitted. Elsewhere on such a campus, free speech is subject to tight administration control. Proponents of free-speech zones argue that universities have a right to control activities that interfere with their operation; opponents argue that free-speech zones are unconstitutional. Do some research about free-speech zones on the Internet or in the library. Write an essay *arguing* that free-speech zones are (or are not) a legitimate way to manage free-speech issues on campus. If your own campus has free-speech zones, use it as an example to support your argument. Use other colleges and universities as examples as well. Conclude your essay with a call to action.

Writing Assignments Combining Patterns of Development

3. What procedures has your college or university established so that people on campus—faculty, staff, and/or students—can file grievances if they feel they have been the targets of hate speech or have been discriminated against in some way? In an essay, describe this *process* and indicate whether you feel it is adequate and appropriate. If it isn't, explain what steps need to be taken to improve the procedures. No matter what position you take, you should provide *examples* to illustrate your point of view.

4. Stereotyping isn't restricted to minorities. Most of us have felt unfairly stereotyped at some time or another, perhaps because of gender, physical or intellectual abilities, or even a hobby or interest. Write an essay *recounting* a time you were treated unfairly or cruelly because of some personal characteristic. Be sure to show how the event *affected* you. The following essays will provide insight into the potentially corrosive effect of labels and stereotypes: Audre Lorde's "The Fourth of July" (page 137), Charmie Gholson's "Charity Display?" (page 151), Alice Walker's "Beauty: When the Other Dancer Is the Self" (page 408), William Raspberry's

"The Handicap of Definition" (page 471), and Roberto Rodriguez's "The Border on Our Backs" (page 562).

Writing Assignment Using a Journal
Entry as a Starting Point

5. Write an editorial for your college newspaper arguing that a college campus is *or* is not the place to air conflicting, even inflammatory views about *one* of the controversial issues listed in your pre-reading journal entry. Perhaps you feel that the issue warrants a public forum in one campus setting but not another. If so, explain why. To lend authority to your position, interview students who don't share your point of view. Be sure to acknowledge their position in your editorial.

Camille Paglia

Before 1990, Camille Paglia, professor of humanities at Philadelphia's University of the Arts, was known primarily for her electrifying performance in the classroom. Then came the publication of Paglia's *Sexual Personae: Art and Decadence From Nefertiti to Emily Dickinson,* a sweeping book that moves with dizzying speed from the days of cave art to the nineteenth century. *Sexual Personae* makes the case that men create art as a defensive response to woman's terrifying cosmic power—specifically, her sexual and procreative force. Suddenly Paglia became an international celebrity and had many opportunities to express her controversial views. She has been both revered and reviled for making statements like these: "Male aggression and lust are the energizing factors in culture" and "If I ever got into a dating situation where I was overpowered and raped, I would say, 'Oh well, I misread the signals.'" Born in 1947, Paglia earned her doctorate from Yale University, where her Ph.D. thesis was an early version of *Sexual Personae. Sex, Art, and American Culture: Essays* (1992), *Vamps and Tramps: New Essays* (1994), *Alfred Hitchcock's "The Birds"* (1998), and *Break, Burn, Blow,* a critical anthology of forty-three poems by various poets, are among Paglia's latest works. Formerly a columnist for *Salon* online magazine, she is a contributing editor to *Interview* magazine and appears frequently on television programs to provide commentary on pop culture and gender issues. The following selection, written in Paglia's characteristically provocative style, first appeared in *New York Newsday* in 1991.

Pre-Reading Journal Entry

How would you define "date rape"? Use your journal to formulate a preliminary definition. Working as quickly as you can, jot down your preliminary thoughts about what it is and what it isn't.

Rape: A Bigger Danger Than Feminists Know

Rape is an outrage that cannot be tolerated in civilized society. Yet feminism, which has waged a crusade for rape to be taken more seriously, has put young women in danger by hiding the truth about sex from them. 1

In dramatizing the pervasiveness of rape, feminists have told young women that before they have sex with a man, they must give consent as explicit as a legal contract's. In this way, young women have been convinced 2 that they have been the victims of rape. On elite campuses in the Northeast and on the West Coast, they have held consciousness-raising sessions, petitioned administrations, demanded inquests. At Brown University, outraged, panicky "victims" have scrawled the names of alleged attackers on the walls of women's rest rooms. What marital rape was to the '70s, "date rape" is to the '90s.

The incidence and seriousness of rape do not require this kind of exaggeration. Real acquaintance rape is nothing new. It has been a horrible problem for women for all of recorded history. Once, father and brothers protected women from rape. Once, the penalty for rape was death. I come from a fierce Italian tradition where, not so long ago in the motherland, a rapist would end up knifed, castrated, and hung out to dry.   3

But the old clans and small rural communities have broken down. In our cities, on our campuses far from home, young women are vulnerable and defenseless. Feminism has not prepared them for this. Feminism keeps saying the sexes are the same. It keeps telling women they can do anything, go anywhere, say anything, wear anything. No, they can't. Women will always be in sexual danger.   4

One of my male students recently slept overnight with a friend in a passageway of the Great Pyramid in Egypt. He described the moon and sand, the ancient silence and eerie echoes. I am a woman. I will never experience that. I am not stupid enough to believe I could ever be safe there. There is a world of solitary adventure I will never have. Women have always known these somber truths. But feminism, with its pie-in-the-sky fantasies about the perfect world, keeps young women from seeing life as it is.   5

We must remedy social injustice whenever we can. But there are some things we cannot change. There are sexual differences that are based in biology. Academic feminism is lost in a fog of social constructionism. It believes we are totally the product of our environment. This idea was invented by Rousseau.[1] He was wrong. Emboldened by dumb French language theory, academic feminists repeat the same hollow slogans over and over to each other. Their view of sex is naive and prudish. Leaving sex to the feminists is like letting your dog vacation at the taxidermist's.   6

The sexes are at war. Men must struggle for identity against the overwhelming power of their mothers. Women have menstruation to tell them they are women. Men must do or risk something to be men. Men become masculine only when other men say they are. Having sex with a woman is one way a boy becomes a man.   7

College men are at their hormonal peak. They have just left their mothers and are questing for their male identity. In groups, they are dangerous. A woman going to a fraternity party is walking into Testosterone Flats, full of prickly cacti and blazing guns. If she goes, she should be armed with resolute   8

---

[1] A French political writer and philosopher (1712–78) (editors' note).

alertness. She should arrive with girlfriends and leave with them. A girl who lets herself get dead drunk at a fraternity party is a fool. A girl who goes upstairs alone with a brother at a fraternity party is an idiot. Feminists call this "blaming the victim." I call it common sense.

For a decade, feminists have drilled their disciples to say, "Rape is a crime   9 of violence but not of sex." This sugar-coated Shirley Temple nonsense has exposed young women to disaster. Misled by feminism, they do not expect rape from the nice boys from good homes who sit next to them in class.

Aggression and eroticism, in fact, are deeply intertwined. Hunt, pursuit   10 and capture are biologically programmed into male sexuality. Generation after generation, men must be educated, refined, and ethically persuaded away from their tendency toward anarchy and brutishness. Society is not the enemy, as feminism ignorantly claims. Society is woman's protection against rape. Feminism, with its solemn Carry Nation[2] repressiveness, does not see what is for men the eroticism or fun element in rape, especially the wild, infectious delirium of gang rape. Women who do not understand rape cannot defend themselves against it.

The date-rape controversy shows feminism hitting the wall of its own   11 broken promises. The women of my '60s generation were the first respectable girls in history to swear like sailors, get drunk, stay out all night—in short, to act like men. We sought total sexual freedom and equality. But as time passed, we woke up to cold reality. The old double standard protected women. When anything goes, it's women who lose.

Today's young women don't know what they want. They see that femi-   12 nism has not brought sexual happiness. The theatrics of public rage over date rape are their way of restoring the old sexual rules that were shattered by my generation. Yet nothing about the sexes has really changed. The comic film *Where the Boys Are* (1960), the ultimate expression of '50s man-chasing, still speaks directly to our time. It shows smart, lively women skillfully anticipating and fending off the dozens of strategies with which horny men try to get them into bed. The agonizing date-rape subplot and climax are brilliantly done. The victim, Yvette Mimieux, makes mistake after mistake, obvious to the other girls. She allows herself to be lured away from her girlfriends and into isolation with boys whose character and intentions she misreads. *Where the Boys Are* tells the truth. It shows courtship as a dangerous game in which the signals are not verbal but subliminal.

Neither militant feminism, which is obsessed with politically correct lan-   13 guage, nor academic feminism, which believes that knowledge and experience are "constituted by" language, can understand preverbal or nonverbal communication. Feminism, focusing on sexual politics, cannot see that sex exists in and through the body. Sexual desire and arousal cannot be fully translated into verbal terms. This is why men and women misunderstand each other.

[2]A nineteenth-century reformer who advocated the abolition of alcohol (editors' note).

Trying to remake the future, feminism cut itself off from sexual history.   14
It discarded and suppressed the sexual myths of literature, art and religion.
Those myths show us the turbulence, the mysteries and passions of sex. In
mythology we see men's sexual anxiety, their fear of woman's dominance.
Much sexual violence is rooted in men's sense of psychological weakness
toward women. It takes many men to deal with one woman. Woman's vorac-
ity is a persistent motif. Clara Bow,[3] it was rumored, took on the USC[4] football team on weekends. Marilyn Monroe, singing "Diamonds Are a Girl's
Best Friend," rules a conga line of men in tuxes. Half-clad Cher, in the video
for "If I Could Turn Back Time," deranges a battleship of screaming sailors
and straddles a pink-lit cannon. Feminism, coveting social power, is blind to
woman's cosmic sexual power.

To understand rape, you must study the past. There never was and never   15
will be sexual harmony. Every woman must be prudent and cautious about
where she goes and with whom. When she makes a mistake, she must accept
the consequences and, through self-criticism, resolve never to make that mistake again. Running to mommy and daddy on the campus grievance committee is unworthy of strong women. Posting lists of guilty men in the toilet is cowardly, infantile stuff.

The Italian philosophy of life espouses high-energy confrontation. A   16
male student makes a vulgar remark about your breasts? Don't slink off to
whimper with the campus shrinking violets. Deal with it. On the spot. Say,
"Shut up, you jerk! And crawl back to the barnyard where you belong!" In
general, women who project this take-charge attitude toward life get
harassed less often. I see too many dopey, immature, self-pitying women
walking around like melting sticks of butter. It's the Yvette Mimieux syn-
drome: make me happy. And listen to me weep when I'm not.

The date-rape debate is already smothering in propaganda churned out   17
by the expensive Northeastern colleges and universities, with their over-
concentration of boring, uptight academic feminists and spoiled, affluent
students. Beware of the deep manipulativeness of rich students who were
neglected by their parents. They love to turn the campus into hysterical psy-
chodramas of sexual transgression, followed by assertions of parental authority and concern. And don't look for sexual enlightenment from academe,
which spews out mountains of books but never looks at life directly.

As a fan of football and rock music, I see in the simple, swaggering mas-   18
culinity of the jock and in the noisy posturing of the heavy-metal guitarist
certain fundamental, unchanging truths about sex. Masculinity is aggressive,
unstable, combustible. It is also the most creative cultural force in history.
Women must reorient themselves toward the elemental powers of sex, which
can strengthen or destroy.

[3]A movie star from the Roaring Twenties era (editors' note).
[4]University of Southern California (editors' note).

The only solution to date rape is female self-awareness and self-control. A   19
woman's number-one line of defense against rape is herself. When a real rape
occurs, she should report it to the police. Complaining to college committees
because the courts "take too long" is ridiculous. College administrations are
not a branch of the judiciary. They are not equipped or trained for legal
inquiry. Colleges must alert incoming students to the problems and dangers
of adulthood. Then colleges must stand back and get out of the sex game.

Questions for Close Reading

1. What is the selection's thesis? Locate the sentence(s) in which Paglia states her
   main idea. If she doesn't state the thesis explicitly, express it in your own words.
2. In Paglia's opinion, why are women more "vulnerable and defenseless" now than
   in the past?
3. According to Paglia, what "truth about sex" has feminism hidden from young
   women?
4. What does Paglia believe is "the only solution to date rape"?
5. Refer to your dictionary as needed to define the following words used in the selection: *inquests* (paragraph 2), *testosterone* (8), *constituted* (13), *grievance* (15), and
   judiciary (19).

Questions About the Writer's Craft

1. **The pattern.**   Examine the way Paglia develops her argument in paragraphs 6
   and 8. Which of her assertions in these paragraphs can be assumed to be true without further proof? Why do you think Paglia includes these essentially incontestable
   statements? Conversely, which of her assertions in paragraphs 6 and 8 require further proof before their truth can be demonstrated? Does Paglia provide such support? Explain.
2. **Other patterns.**   How does Paglia use the *comparison-contrast* pattern to develop her argument?
3. Paglia's style is frequently characterized by short sentences strung together with
   few transitions. Locate some examples of this style. Why might Paglia have chosen this style? What is its effect?
4. Where does Paglia use emotional, highly connotative language? Where does she
   employ strongly worded absolute statements? Do you think that this use of *pathos*
   makes Paglia's argument more or less convincing? Explain.

Writing Assignments Using Argumentation-Persuasion
as a Pattern of Development

∞ 1. Read Susan Jacoby's "Common Decency" (page 547), an essay that takes exception to Paglia's view of date rape. Decide which writer presents her case more convincingly. Then write an essay arguing that the *other writer* has trouble making a
   strong case for her position. Consider the merits and flaws (including any logical
   fallacies) in the argument, plus such issues as the writer's credibility, strategies
   for dealing with the opposing view, and use of emotional appeals. Throughout,

support your opinion with specific examples drawn from the selection. Keep in mind that you're critiquing the effectiveness of the writer's argument. It's not appropriate, then, simply to explain why you agree or disagree with the writer's position or merely to summarize what the writer says.

2. Paglia criticizes those who claim that the environment, or social climate, is primarily responsible for shaping gender differences. She believes that such differences "are based in biology." Write an essay arguing your own position about the role that environment and biology play in determining sex-role attitudes and behavior. Remembering to acknowledge opposing views, defend your own viewpoint with plentiful examples based on your experiences and observations. You may also need to conduct some library research to gather support for your position. The following essays will provide insights that you may want to draw upon in your paper: Barbara Ehrenreich's "What I've Learned From Men" (page 215) and Dave Barry's "The Ugly Truth About Beauty" (page 368).

Writing Assignments Combining Patterns of Development

3. Paglia writes in paragraph 7 that "men become masculine only when other men say they are. Having sex with a woman is one way a boy becomes a man." Write an essay constructing your own *definition* of masculinity. Comment on the extent to which you feel being sexually active is an important criterion, but also include other hallmarks and *examples* of masculinity.

4. Date rape seems to be on the rise. Brainstorm with others to identify what may be leading to its growing occurrence. Focusing on several related *factors,* write an essay showing how these factors contribute to the problem. Possible factors include the following: the way males and females are depicted in the media (advertisements, movies, television, rock videos); young people's use of alcohol; the illicit use of "date rape drugs"; the emergence of coed college dorms. At the end of the essay, offer some recommendations about *steps* that can be taken to create a safer climate for dating. You should consider supporting your speculations with information about date rape gathered in the library and/or on the Internet.

Writing Assignment Using a Journal Entry as a Starting Point

5. Drawing upon the material in your pre-reading journal entry, write an essay in which you present a carefully considered definition of the term "date rape." Explain clearly what constitutes date rape and what doesn't. To deepen your understanding of this thorny issue, consider brainstorming with others as well as conducting research in the library and/or on the Internet. One issue to consider: Do males and females define the term differently? If so, how do they define it, and why might their definitions differ?

Susan Jacoby

In her first job as a newspaper reporter, Susan Jacoby (1945–) carefully avoided doing "women's stories," believing that such features weren't worthy of a serious journalist. However, Jacoby's opinion changed with the times, especially as women's issues began to gain increasing attention. Indeed, many of her essays—including those in *The New York Times* and *McCall's*—have dealt with women's concerns. Several of Jacoby's essays have been collected in *The Possible She* (1979) and *Money, Manners, and Morals* (1993). In 1994, she coauthored the biography *Soul to Soul: A Black Russian American Family 1865–1992.* Jacoby's most recent books include *Body* and *Geotrivia Sports,* both published in 1996; *Half-Jew: A Daughter's Search for Her Family's Buried Past* (2000); and *Freethinkers: A History of American Secularism* (2004). The following selection, published in *The New York Times* in April 1991, was written in response to the book *Sexual Personae* by Camille Paglia (see page 541).

Pre-Reading Journal Entry

The phrase "boys will be boys" is often cited to explain certain types of male behavior. What kinds of actions typically fall into this category? List a few of these in your journal. Which behaviors are positive? Why? Which are negative? Why?

Common Decency

She was deeply in love with a man who was treating her badly. To assuage 1 her wounded ego (and to prove to herself that she could get along nicely without him), she invited another man, an old boyfriend, to a dinner *à deux* in her apartment. They were on their way to the bedroom when, having realized that she wanted only the man who wasn't there, she changed her mind. Her ex-boyfriend was understandably angry. He left her apartment with a not-so-politely phrased request that she leave him out of any future plans.

And that is the end of the story—except for the fact that he was eventu- 2 ally kind enough to accept her apology for what was surely a classic case of "mixed signals."

I often recall this incident, in which I was the embarrassed female par- 3 ticipant, as the controversy over "date rape"—intensified by the assault that

William Kennedy Smith[1] has been accused of—heats up across the nation. What seems clear to me is that those who place acquaintance rape in a different category from "stranger rape"—those who excuse friendly social rapists on grounds that they are too dumb to understand when "no" means no—are being even more insulting to men than to women.

These apologists for date rape—and some of them are women—are really saying that the average man cannot be trusted to exercise any impulse control. Men are nasty and men are brutes—and a woman must be constantly on her guard to avoid giving a man any excuse to give way to his baser instincts.   4

If this view were accurate, few women would manage to get through life without being raped, and few men would fail to commit rape. For the reality is that all of us, men as well as women, send and receive innumerable mixed signals in the course of our sexual lives—and that is as true in marital beds at age fifty as in the back seats of cars at age fifteen.   5

Most men somehow manage to decode these signals without using superior physical strength to force themselves on their partners. And most women manage to handle conflicting male signals without, say, picking up carving knives to demonstrate their displeasure at sexual rejection. This is called civilization.   6

Civilized is exactly what my old boyfriend was being when he didn't use my muddleheaded emotional distress as an excuse to rape me. But I don't owe him excessive gratitude for his decent behavior—any more than he would have owed me special thanks for not stabbing him through the heart if our situations had been reversed. Most date rapes do not happen because a man honestly mistakes a woman's "no" for a "yes" or a "maybe." They occur because a minority of men—an ugly minority, to be sure—can't stand to take "no" for an answer.   7

This minority behavior—and a culture that excuses it on grounds that boys will be boys—is the target of the movement against date rape that has surfaced on many campuses during the past year.   8

It's not surprising that date rape is an issue of particular importance to college-age women. The campus concentration of large numbers of young people, in an unsupervised environment that encourages drinking and partying, tends to promote sexual aggression and discourage inhibition. Drunken young men who rape a woman at a party can always claim they didn't know what they were doing—and a great many people will blame the victim for having been there in the first place.   9

That is the line adopted by antifeminists like Camille Paglia,[2] author of the controversial *Sexual Personae: Art and Decadence From Nefertiti to*   10

---

[1]William Kennedy Smith, the nephew of John, Robert, and Edward Kennedy, was accused of raping a woman in 1991. Kennedy was acquitted, but the trial, broadcast on television, created a national furor and generated heated debate on the issue of date rape (editors' note).

[2]For information on Camille Paglia, see page 541 (editors' note).

Emily Dickinson. Paglia, whose views strongly resemble those expounded twenty years ago by Norman Mailer[3] in *The Prisoner of Sex,* argues that feminists have deluded women by telling them they can go anywhere and do anything without fear of rape. Feminism, in this view, is both naïve and antisexual because it ignores the power of women to incite uncontrollable male passions.

Just to make sure there is no doubt about a woman's place, Paglia also   11
links the male sexual aggression that leads to rape with the creative energy of art. "There is no female Mozart," she has declared, "because there is no female Jack the Ripper." According to this "logic," one might expect to discover the next generation of composers in fraternity houses and dorms that have been singled out as sites of brutal gang rapes.

This type of unsubtle analysis makes no distinction between sex as an   12
expression of the will to power and sex as a source of pleasure. When domination is seen as an inevitable component of sex, the act of rape is defined not by a man's actions but by a woman's signals.

It is true, of course, that some women (especially the young) initially   13
resist sex not out of real conviction but as part of the elaborate persuasion and seduction rituals accompanying what was once called courtship. And it is true that many men (again, especially the young) take pride in the ability to coax a woman a step further than she intended to go.

But these mating rituals do not justify or even explain date rape. Even   14
the most callow youth is capable of understanding the difference between resistance and genuine fear; between a halfhearted "no, we shouldn't" and tears or screams; between a woman who is physically free to leave a room and one who is being physically restrained.

The immorality and absurdity of using mixed signals as an excuse for   15
rape is cast in high relief when the assault involves one woman and a group of men. In cases of gang rape in a social setting (usually during or after a party), the defendants and their lawyers frequently claim that group sex took place but no force was involved. These upright young men, so the defense invariably contends, were confused because the girl had voluntarily gone to a party with them. Why, she may have even displayed sexual interest in *one* of them. How could they have been expected to understand that she didn't wish to have sex with the whole group?

The very existence of the term "date rape" attests to a slow change in   16
women's consciousness that began with the feminist movement of the late 1960s. Implicit in this consciousness is the conviction that a woman has the right to say no at any point in the process leading to sexual intercourse—and that a man who fails to respect her wishes should incur serious legal and social consequences.

---

[3]An American essayist and novelist (editors' note).

The other, equally important half of the equation is respect for men. If   17
mixed signals are the real cause of sexual assault, it behooves every woman
to regard every man as a potential rapist.

In such a benighted universe, it would be impossible for a woman (and,   18
let us not forget, for a man) to engage in the tentative emotional and physical
exploration that eventually produces a mature erotic life. She would have to
make up her mind right from the start in order to prevent a rampaging male
from misreading her intentions.

Fortunately for everyone, neither the character of men nor the general   19
quality of relations between the sexes is that crude. By censuring the minority of men who use ordinary socializing as an excuse for rape, feminists insist
on sex as a source of pure pleasure rather than as a means of social control.
Real men want an eager sexual partner—not a woman who is quaking with
fear or even one who is ambivalent. Real men don't rape.

Questions for Close Reading

1. What is the selection's thesis? Locate the sentence(s) in which Jacoby states her
   main idea. If she doesn't state the thesis explicitly, express it in your own words.
2. Why does Jacoby feel that she doesn't owe her old boyfriend a great deal of gratitude, even though she sent mixed signals about what type of relationship she
   wanted?
3. What does Jacoby mean in paragraph 6 by her comment, "This is called civilization"? How does this comment support her thesis?
4. Why does Jacoby think that it's insulting to men to accept Paglia's notion that
   men are ruled by uncontrollable passions?
5. Refer to your dictionary as needed to define the following words used in the selection: *apologists* (paragraph 4), *deluded* (10), *unsubtle* (12), *implicit* (16), *benighted* (18), *erotic* (18), *rampaging* (18), and *ambivalent* (19).

Questions About the Writer's Craft

1. **The pattern.** One way to refute an idea is to carry it to its logical extreme, thus
   revealing its inherent falsity or absurdity. This technique is called *reduction ad
   absurdum*. Examine paragraphs 4–5 and 15 and explain how Jacoby uses this technique to refute Paglia's position on date rape.
2. **Other patterns.** Locate places in the essay where Jacoby *compares* and *contrasts*
   male and female behavior or the behavior of rapists and nonrapists. How does her
   use of comparison-contrast help her build her argument?
3. What introduction technique (see pages 53–55) does Jacoby use to begin the
   essay? How does this type of introduction help her achieve her persuasive goal?
4. How would you characterize Jacoby's tone? Identify specific sentences and words
   that convey this tone. What effect might Jacoby have hoped this tone would have
   on readers?

Writing Assignments Using Argumentation-Persuasion as a Pattern of Development

1. Jacoby feels that Camille Paglia and others "excuse . . . rapists." If you haven't already done so, read "Rape: A Bigger Danger Than Feminists Know" (page 541) to see what Paglia says about who bears primary responsibility for preventing rape. Then decide to what degree you feel men who commit date rape should be held accountable for their actions. Argue your position in an essay, making reference to both Jacoby's and Paglia's ideas to support your case. Also include reasons and evidence of your own.

2. Determine what your campus is doing about date rape. Does it have a formal policy defining date rape, a hearing process, ongoing workshops, discussions during orientation for incoming students? Write a paper explaining how your college deals with date rape. Then argue either that more attention should be devoted to this issue or that your college has adopted fair and comprehensive measures to deal with the problem. If you feel the college should do more, indicate what additional steps should be taken.

Writing Assignments Combining Patterns of Development

3. Jacoby acknowledges that males and females often send "mixed signals" and cause each other confusion. Select one time that you found "mixed signals" with a person of the opposite sex to be a problem. For example, you might have conflicted because of different ways of expressing anger or because of dissimilar styles in asking for support. In an essay of your own, *recount* what happened and explore the *reason(s)* why you think such mixed signals occurred. Before writing the paper, consider reading Dave Barry's "The Ugly Truth About Beauty" (page 368) for a humorous take on the differences between men and women.

4. Interview some people, both males and females, to determine their *definition* of date rape. In an essay, discuss any *differences* between the two sexes' perspectives. That done, present your own definition of date rape, explaining what it is and what it isn't.

Writing Assignment Using a Journal Entry as a Starting Point

5. Some people believe that "boys-will-be-boys" behavior is potentially dangerous and therefore not acceptable. Others argue that it is perfectly innocent and therefore permissible. What do you think? Drawing upon your pre-reading journal entry, write an essay taking a position on this issue. Provide persuasive examples to support your viewpoint, refuting as much of the opposing argument as you can. Discussing the topic with others and doing some research in the library and/or on the Internet will broaden your understanding of this complex issue.

Jonathan Alter

Chicago native Jonathan Alter (1957–) has been a senior editor and columnist at *Newsweek* magazine since 1991. His widely acclaimed "Between the Lines" column examines politics, the media, and society at large, and in his "Conventional Wisdom/watch" column, he comments irreverently on the weekly news. Since 1996, Alter has also been a contributing correspondent for NBC News, appearing regularly on *Today*, *NBC Nightly News*, and MSNBC. Alter's reporting on the death penalty earned him the John Bartlow Martin Award in 2001. Prior to joining *Newsweek*, Alter was an editor at *The Washington Monthly*. His work has also been published in *The New Republic*, *Esquire*, *Slate*, *Rolling Stone*, and *The New York Times*. A graduate of Harvard University, Alter most recently authored a book about Franklin D. Roosevelt (2004). He lives in New Jersey with his wife and three children. The following essay appeared in the November 5, 2001, issue of *Newsweek*.

Pre-Reading Journal Entry

The terrorist attacks of September 11, 2001, have had a significant impact on society. What are those effects, tangible and otherwise? Use your pre-reading journal to freewrite about the various consequences of the 9/11 tragedy. Discussing your ideas with friends and family might help give you a broader perspective on these effects.

Time to Think About Torture[1]

In this autumn of anger, even a liberal can find his thoughts turning to . . . torture. OK, not cattle prods or rubber hoses, at least not here in the United States, but *something* to jump-start the stalled investigation of the greatest crime in American history. Right now, four key hijacking suspects aren't talking at all.

Couldn't we at least subject them to psychological torture, like tapes of dying rabbits or high-decibel rap? (The military has done that in Panama and elsewhere.) How about truth serum, administered with a mandatory IV? Or deportation to Saudi Arabia, land of beheadings? (As the frustrated FBI has been threatening.) Some people still argue that we needn't rethink any

[1]This selection and the one that follows it were written *prior to* public discovery of the Abu Ghraib Prison incidents, in which Iraqi prisoners were subjected to abuse by U.S. military personnel (editors' note).

of our old assumptions about law enforcement, but they're hopelessly "Sept. 10"—living in a country that no longer exists.

One sign of how much things have changed is the reaction to the anti- 3
terrorism bill, which cleared the Senate last week by a vote of 98–1. While the ACLU[2] felt obliged to quibble with a provision or two, the opposition was tepid, even from staunch civil libertarians. That great quote from the late Chief Justice Robert Jackson—"The Constitution is not a suicide pact"—is getting a good workout lately. "This was incomparably more sober and sensible than what some of our revered presidents did," says Floyd Abrams, the First Amendment lawyer, referring to the severe restrictions on liberty imposed during the Civil War and World War I.

Fortunately, the new law stops short of threatening basic rights like free 4
speech, which is essential in wartime to hold the government accountable. The bill makes it easier to wiretap (under the old rules, you had to get a warrant for each individual phone, an anachronism in a cellular age), easier to detain immigrants who won't talk and easier to follow money through the international laundering process. A welcome "sunset" provision means the expansion of surveillance will expire after four years. That's an important precedent, though odds are these changes will end up being permanent. It's a new world.

Actually, the world hasn't changed as much as we have. The Israelis have 5
been wrestling for years with the morality of torture. Until 1999 an interrogation technique called "shaking" was legal. It entailed holding a smelly bag over a suspect's head in a dark room, then applying scary psychological torment. (To avoid lessening the potential impact on terrorists, I won't specify exactly what kind.) Even now, Israeli law leaves a little room for "moderate physical pressure" in what are called "ticking time bomb" cases, where extracting information is essential to saving hundreds of lives. The decision of when to apply it is left in the hands of law-enforcement officials.

For more than 20 years Harvard Law School professor Alan Dershowitz[3] 6
has argued to the Israelis that this is terribly unfair to the members of the security services. In a forthcoming book, "Shouting Fire," he makes the case for what he calls a "torture warrant," where judges would balance competing claims and make the call, as they do in issuing search warrants. Dershowitz says that as long as the fruits of such interrogation are used for investigation, not to convict the detainee (a violation of the Fifth Amendment right against self-incrimination), it could be constitutional here, too. "I'm not in favor of torture, but if you're going to have it, it should damn well have court approval," Dershowitz says.

Not surprisingly, judges and lawyers in both Israel and the United States 7
don't agree. They prefer looking the other way to giving even mild torture

---

[2]The ACLU (American Civil Liberties Union) is a nonprofit organization that opposes violations of Americans' civil liberties (editors' note).
[3]Renowned criminal defense and civil liberties attorney (editors' note).

techniques the patina of legality. This leaves them in a strange moral position. The torture they can't see (or that occurs after deportation) is harder
on the person they claim to be concerned about—the detainee—but easier
on their consciences. Out of sight, out of mind.

Short of physical torture, there's always sodium pentothal ("truth   8
serum"). The FBI is eager to try it, and deserves the chance. Unfortunately,
truth serum, first used on spies in World War II, makes suspects gabby but
not necessarily truthful. The same goes for even the harshest torture. When
the subject breaks, he often lies. Prisoners "have only one objective—to end
the pain," says retired Col. Kenneth Allard, who was trained in interrogation.
"It's a huge limitation."

Some torture clearly works. Jordan broke the most notorious terrorist of   9
the 1980s, Abu Nidal, by threatening his family. Philippine police reportedly helped crack the 1993 World Trade Center bombings (plus a plot to crash
11 U.S. airliners and kill the pope) by convincing a suspect that they were
about to turn him over to the Israelis. Then there's painful Islamic justice,
which has the added benefit of greater acceptance among Muslims.

We can't legalize physical torture; it's contrary to American values. But   10
even as we continue to speak out against human-rights abuses around the
world, we need to keep an open mind about certain measures to fight terrorism, like court-sanctioned psychological interrogation. And we'll have to
think about transferring some suspects to our less squeamish allies, even if
that's hypocritical. Nobody said this was going to be pretty.

Questions for Close Reading

1. What is the selection's thesis? Locate the sentence(s) in which Alter states his main
   idea. If he doesn't state the thesis explicitly, express it in your own words.
2. In the course of his essay, Alter provides examples of the kinds of torture he would
   find acceptable. What are they? Conversely, what are the methods of torture that
   he dismisses?
3. In paragraph 2, Alter refers to people who are "hopelessly 'Sept. 10'—living in a
   country that no longer exists." What does he mean by this?
4. What is the "strange moral position" that Alter describes in paragraph 7? What
   commentary do you think he's making about the "judges and lawyers in both
   Israel and the United States"?
5. Refer to your dictionary as needed to define the following words used in the selection: *stalled* (paragraph 1), *decibel* (2), *serum* (2), *deportation* (2), *quibble* (3), *provision* (3), *tepid* (3), *staunch* (3), *anachronism* (4), *laundering* (4), *extracting* (5),
   detainee (6), *patina* (7), *sanctioned* (10), and *squeamish* (10).

Questions About the Writer's Craft

1. **The pattern.** The technique of acknowledging and refuting opposing points of
   view is an important means of reinforcing one's argument. Where does Alter

employ this technique? Does his use of this strategy contribute to the effectiveness of his argument? Explain.

2. In the sentences comprising paragraph 2, Alter employs two distinct stylistic techniques that depart from typical sentence format. What are these two techniques? What effect do you think they are meant to have on readers?

3. **Other patterns.** In paragraphs 6 and 7, Alter provides a *contrast* between two points of view. Whom and what does he contrast? What do you think is his purpose in doing so?

4. **Other patterns.** In the process of setting forth his argument, Alter *divides* torture into the categories of "psychological" and "physical." How does he *define* each? Are his distinctions adequate, and do they reinforce his central assertion? Explain.

Writing Assignments Using Argumentation-Persuasion as a Pattern of Development

1. Since the publication of Alter's essay, many new developments have evolved in the U.S. government's methods for dealing with people suspected of terrorist involvement—most notoriously, the Abu Ghraib Iraqi prisoner abuse scandal. Investigate these developments by visiting the library and/or going online. Using this information, write an essay in which you argue for *or* against the U.S. government's current practices and procedures regarding the treatment of terrorism suspects. As you formulate your argument, provide actual examples, based on your research, to support your position. And be sure to acknowledge and logically dismantle opposing points of view along the way.

2. In his essay, Alter makes a case in favor of using torture as one means of fighting terrorism. Consider his arguments, as well as those in Henry Porter's "Now the Talk Is About Bringing Back Torture" (page 557), an essay that takes a very different position from Alter's. Then write an essay in which you agree or disagree with the following statement: "Torture is never justified under any circumstances."

Writing Assignments Combining Patterns of Development

3. Alter uses the term "hopelessly 'Sept. 10'" to refer to a mind-set predating the events of 9/11. Consider your own experience since the 9/11 tragedy. What has changed in your life—from abstract ideas and feelings to more tangible lifestyle adjustments—since the attacks? Take some time to brainstorm ideas in your journal and to discuss this topic with peers. Then write an essay in which you *compare* and *contrast* your September 10th and September 11th mind-sets, focusing on at least two or three different elements. For example, you might contrast a new anxiety about airplane travel with a formerly carefree attitude. Or you might admit to now holding cultural prejudices that you had never held before. In order to convey the differences, you'll need to provide vivid *examples* throughout of your behavior and beliefs pre- and post-9/11.

4. Torture in the context of Alter's discussion is no laughing matter. But people sometimes use the term *torture* informally to refer to something that they really can't stand being around or doing. For example, one person's torture might be

listening to "elevator music" or looking at photo albums of a friend's cat, while another's might be enduring a tedious first-period lecture in history class or the company of a self-righteous relative. Brainstorm about things that you find "torturous" in a humorous kind of way. Then write a lighthearted essay in which you discuss two or three things that you consider "torture." Be sure, in the process, to provide vivid, *descriptive examples* to *illustrate* to readers exactly what your torturous experiences entail and why each is so unbearable.

Writing Assignment Using a Journal Entry as a Starting Point

5. As the Alter essay makes clear, one of the unfortunate results of the 9/11 tragedy is the need to discuss whether torture is an acceptable means of extracting information viable to national security. Is that need among the most significant effects of the attack? Refer to your pre-reading journal entry, and select what *you* believe are the three most important effects of the terrorist attack on the United States. Write an essay in which you explore these effects and the impact they're having on society. You might consider doing some research in the library and/or on the Internet in order to gather information and analysis about these consequences.

Henry Porter

Born in 1953, Henry Porter is the London editor of *Vanity Fair* magazine as well as a regular contributor to London's *Observer, Guardian, Evening Standard,* and *Sunday Telegraph* newspapers. In addition to his journalistic achievements, he has earned success as a novelist, about which he has commented, "Writing fiction is like working in technicolour compared to the black and white of journalism." His political thrillers include *Remembrance Day* (1999), *A Spy's Life* (2001), and most recently, *Empire State* (2003). Porter lives in London with his wife and two daughters. The following essay originally appeared in the November 11, 2001, issue of *The Observer.*

Pre-Reading Journal Entry

Because of its prominent influence on world politics, economics, and culture, the United States is subject to a great deal of criticism by people around the world. How do you feel, in general, about people outside the United States criticizing America? Is your reaction usually positive, negative, or neutral when you hear such criticism? Take some time to freewrite on this subject in your pre-reading journal. Then exchange your thoughts with friends and family to gauge what others think about this topic.

Now the Talk Is About Bringing Back Torture

For America's supporters, the blind cohesion of the United States is impressive but also worrying. Two months after the attacks there is still no real debate about the fundamentals of U.S. policy or any real criticism of the way the Bush White House conducted itself prior to the September attacks. More surprising is that the country appears nowhere near ready for the total review and overhaul of the institutions—the FBI, CIA and State Department—which failed the people so drastically.

If these things were discussed as vigorously as they are here,[1] the U.S. would be stronger and able to present a more convincing case to the world about its current action. Instead much necessary self-examination is suppressed in the cause of unity and to reassure a president whose lack of rhetorical subtlety and modulation does seem to betray a pretty basic intellect—even to Americans.

---

[1] In England (editors' note).

It is in this fiercely uncritical mood that the issue of torture has been   3
raised. Columnists and TV discussion shows have begun to ask at what stage
the authorities might consider torturing suspects who have information vital
to the security of the American people. *Newsweek*'s Jonathan Alter wrote that
in this "autumn of anger" even a liberal wondered whether torture would
"jump-start the stalled investigation into the greatest crime in American history." He refers to the wall of silence which has met investigators questioning
the small number of material witnesses among the 1,147 suspects currently
held by the U.S. in connection with the attacks. Little has been learnt about
al-Qaeda from them and nothing about future attacks on America and its
overseas assets.

Similar frustrations surfaced on the Fox and CNN TV networks and   4
in the *Wall Street Journal,* where the academic Jay Winick explained how a
terrorist named Abdul Hakim Murad had been tortured by the Philippine
authorities in 1995 and revealed a plot to crash 11 U.S. airliners into the
Pacific and one into the CIA headquarters at Langley, Virginia. He went on
to wonder what would have happened if Murad had been held by the U.S.
authorities, his implication being that hundreds, maybe thousands, of lives
might have been lost because of the U.S.'s respect for human rights.

Today, when a sealed container of smallpox virus or a nuclear suitcase   5
bomb are seen as real threats in the U.S., the case of Abdul Murad seems
especially relevant. What if one of these suspects or some future detainee is
thought to know about plans to cause thousands of American deaths? Surely the nation should steel itself to do anything necessary to avert the deaths?

A round-up of these speculations in the *New York Times* made plain that   6
torture was still unthinkable to commentators and to most of the American
public: the U.S. is still a long way off using torture in its war against terrorism, was the conclusion. But how true is that? After all, America is capable
of inflicting great pain and fear in the execution of convicted murderers.
There are now about 70 executions a year in the U.S. This is despite the
anguish of the people placed on a gurney to wait for, and sometimes hear
about, temporary reprieves; despite the reports which show that those who
are executed are almost always unable to afford the best legal representation;
despite the UN convention that prohibits the execution of people who committed their crimes when they were under 18 years of age. (Only Somalia and
the U.S. refused to sign.)

This inadvertent torture, delivered as a by-product of the people's   7
vengeance, is nothing like the act which sets out to inflict pain in order to
extract information or to terrorise a section of the population. There is a
world of difference in the intention, if not in some cases, the effect, and that
makes a lot of difference to the American conscience.

Even if this was so, America has in the last few decades been remarkably   8
close to regimes which routinely practise torture. The U.S. Ambassador to
the United Nations, John Negroponte, is someone who could testify to this,

but he won't because as Ambassador to Honduras between 1981 and 1985 he was involved with the fight against communist insurgents in neighbouring countries.

This included the torture of more than 100 women who fled El Salvador   9 and were disposed of by being thrown from helicopters. The U.S. also supported General Pinochet's regime in Chile where the socialist opposition was terrorised with unbelievable barbarity. This is to say nothing of the torture used in Saudi Arabia and to a lesser degree in Israel, both countries which enjoy U.S. support.

To the perversely legal mind, torture could be regarded as morally less of   10 a crime than state-sponsored killing, because the victim stands a chance of surviving the ordeal. The targets of the CIA, which is armed with new authority from President Bush and is contemplating clandestine operations aimed at killing specific members of al-Qaeda, will not live. If you have authorised assassinations, then why not torture? The first is final; the second is not— necessarily.

The legal answer to this, as Amnesty International points out, is that   11 America ratified the UN convention against torture and it would be impossible to derogate from that stand. But this answer assumes that the American authorities would feel compelled to admit that they had used torture when faced with a suspect who possessed information crucial to the safety of large numbers of U.S. citizens. They wouldn't because it has been the wisdom of successive administrations that the American people would often prefer to be kept in the dark about what has been done in their interests.

So in a way it is good that the issue of torture has been raised in the U.S.   12 for at least the issue is not being consigned to that area of affairs where Americans prefer not to go. But it is not encouraging that American commentators have so little grasp of the profound and terrible concession which is made to bin Laden if a single person is tortured during the prosecution of the war against him. Torture is an absolute evil and there can be no allowances, especially in a country which stands for liberty and spends a good deal of time distinguishing itself from the Taliban and al-Qaeda on those grounds.

Americans have broadly shown indifference to the violated human rights   13 of the majority of the 1,147 people detained, often without charge, since 11 September. It is to be hoped that their very understandable fears do not lead to a further deterioration of human rights.

Questions for Close Reading

1. What is the selection's thesis? Locate the sentence(s) in which Porter states his main idea. If he doesn't state the thesis explicitly, express it in your own words.

2. What does Porter mean when he refers to the "blind cohesion" (paragraph 1) and the "fiercely uncritical mood" (3) in the United States? Do you agree with his evaluation?

3. In paragraphs 6 and 7, Porter deviates from his main topic to discuss what he believes is a related issue. What is the issue that Porter discusses in these paragraphs? How does he connect it to his larger argument? Do you agree with his reasoning?

4. Neither Porter nor Jonathan Alter (see page 552), to whom Porter is responding, presents a clear definition of "torture" in his essay. Why do you think that both of these authors fail to define the central term about which they're arguing?

5. Refer to your dictionary as needed to define the following words used in the selection: *cohesion* (paragraph 1), *overhaul* (1), *vigorously* (2), *suppressed* (2), *rhetorical* (2), *modulation* (2), *assets* (3), *steel* (5), *avert* (5), *speculations* (6), *gurney* (6), *reprieves* (6), *inadvertent* (7), *routinely* (8), *insurgents* (8), *barbarity* (9), *clandestine* (10), *derogate* (11), *consigned* (12), and *concession* (12).

Questions About the Writer's Craft

1. The pattern. Given Porter's main objective of refuting the opposing point of view about torture, Rogerian method (pages 486–489) plays a central role in his argument. Where does Porter employ this technique? Does his use of Rogerian strategy contribute to the effectiveness of his argument? Explain.

2. The pattern. How would you characterize the tone of Porter's argument? Is his language objective and neutral, or is it subjective and passionate—or somewhere in between? Cite examples to support your opinion.

3. Other patterns. In his essay, Porter implies a *contrast* between the United States and England. What are the differences he suggests? How does this contrast contribute to his thesis?

4. Other patterns. Where in the selection does Porter use *examples* to support his claims? How do the examples help him reinforce his case?

Writing Assignments Using Argumentation-Persuasion as a Pattern of Development

1. Near the end of his essay, Porter forcefully pronounces that "[t]orture is an absolute evil." What is something that you feel you can unequivocally declare is absolutely evil? Take some time to brainstorm your ideas on this question. Then write an essay in which you argue that one particular thing is an absolute evil. Your essay might adopt a serious tone and discuss something like racism, cruelty, war, or so on. Or you might opt for a more lighthearted approach and identify something such as dieting, term papers, or getting old. Either way, provide abundant examples to illustrate your point about that absolute evil.

2. Although some of the political conditions Porter discusses have changed since his essay's publication, his broader critique of Americans' "blind cohesion" and "fiercely uncritical mood" remains at issue. Do you agree with his perspective? Write an essay in which you argue that, in general, Americans have *or* haven't become less questioning of authority since the 9/11 attacks. In addition to conducting research on this topic in the library and/or on the Internet, you might also conduct an informal poll of friends and family regarding this question. In concluding your essay, provide your thoughts as to whether people's propensity—or lack thereof—to question authority in these circumstances is a positive or negative phenomenon.

Writing Assignments Combining Patterns of Development

3. When Porter observes that "the blind cohesion of the United States is impressive but also worrying," he implicitly points to the issue of patriotism. Since 9/11, the question of what qualifies as patriotic and unpatriotic thought and behavior has been a highly debated topic in the United States. What do you think about this issue? Freewrite for a few moments on the subject of patriotism, and share your ideas with peers when you're done. Then write an essay in which you *define* what you believe true patriotism is. You might choose to develop your definition, in part, through negation—discussing what patriotism *isn't*. But no matter how you develop your definition, be sure to provide abundant *examples* to help *illustrate* what you mean.

4. One of the more biting accusations Porter makes is that the U.S. government assumes Americans "would often prefer to be kept in the dark about what has been done in their interests." Consider this claim, but on a more personal level: When was a time you wish you hadn't known about something that had happened? Or, conversely, when was a time you didn't know about something but wish you had? Write an essay *narrating* the incident about which you wish you had *or* hadn't known. You might write, for example, about wishing you *hadn't* learned that a beloved relative was unfaithful to a spouse, or how you wish you *had* known sooner that a friend was terminally ill. Part of your essay should address why you feel as you do, as well as how the opposite set of circumstances would have *caused* you to behave differently. In "Bombs Bursting in Air" (page 209), Beth Johnson discusses the impact of learning news she'd rather not have to confront.

Writing Assignment Using a Journal Entry as a Starting Point

5. In the course of his essay, Porter attacks the U.S. government and, to an extent, the American people. In general, how do you feel about people outside the United States criticizing America? Do you find these outside perspectives instructive or intrusive? Refer to the thoughts you recorded in your pre-reading journal entry on this subject. Then write an essay in which you argue that it is *or* isn't productive to consider what outsiders have to say about the United States and its policies. In order to reinforce your position, you might want to do some research in the library and/or on the Internet into times in the past when there have been significant foreign demonstrations opposing or supporting U.S. policies.

Roberto Rodriguez

Roberto Rodriguez was born in 1954 in Aguacalientes, Mexico, and raised in East Los Angeles. In 1972, he began his journalism career at *La Gente,* a newspaper at the University of California, Los Angeles. He has written for many publications, including *Black Issues in Higher Education, Lowrider* magazine, the *Eastside Sun* (Los Angeles), and *La Opinion,* the largest Spanish-language daily newspaper in the United States. In addition, Rodriguez's columns have been syndicated in *The Washington Post, The Los Angeles Times,* and *USA Today.* Since 1994, he and his wife, Patrisia Gonzales, have written "Column of the Americas," a weblog that focuses on current issues from the perspective of indigenous peoples. Two books he wrote about police brutality were published under one title, *Justice: A Question of Race* (1997). In 2002, Rodriguez and Gonzales were named Distinguished Community Scholars at the Cesar Chavez Center at UCLA, where they are establishing the discipline of indigenous studies. The following article was posted on the "Column of the Americas" website, www.voznuestra.com/Americas, on April 17, 2006.

Pre-reading Journal Entry

Do you think that schools should engage in discussions of immigration, ethnicity, and racism, which can be sensitive and painful topics? Why do you feel as you do? Would such discussions be appropriate at some levels of school but not at others? Take some time to explore these questions in your journal.

The Border on Our Backs

Look up the word *Mexican* or *Central American* in any U.S. political 1 dictionary and you will find these definitions:

> 1) people who are illegal, or are treated as such, no matter how long they've been living in this country; 2) the nation's number one threat to homeland security; 3) people who do the jobs no Americans want and who threaten the American Way of Life; 4) as a result of extremist politicians, the nation's favorite scapegoats; and 5) people, who due to vicious anti-immigrant hysteria, are prone to become Democrats.

By next year, there may be two new entries: 6) Peoples who carry the   2
border on their backs, and 7) peoples not afraid to stand up for their rights.

Who could have predicted that millions of peoples would be taking to   3
the streets nationwide to protest draconian immigration bills that call for the
building of Berlin-style walls, more *migra*,[1] massive repatriations, the crimi-
nalization of human beings and the creation of a new anti-family apartheid-
style Bracero[2] or Guest Worker program? Beyond the bills, the protests are
actually about asserting the right—virtually a cry—to be treated as full
human beings.

How long was this community supposed to remain in silence?   4

Perhaps it is racial/cultural fatigue.   5

Let's not pretend that this hysteria is not about race, color and dehu-   6
manization. It's not even anti-immigrant or even anti-Latino/Hispanic
bigotry. It's the exploitation of a deep-seated fear and loathing of Mexicans
and Central Americans by shameless politicians. Why? Because of what our
color represents. Otherwise, how and why do government agents single us
out at lines, borders and internal checkpoints? Otherwise, why do dragnet
immigrant raids always target brown peoples? Why is all the hate and vilification directed at brown peoples and the southern border? Otherwise,
why are these politicians also not bothered by the millions of Canadians,
Europeans or Russians who overstay their visas? (No one should hate them
either.)

Just what does brown represent in this country? Shall we delude our-   7
selves like the Census Bureau and pretend that we're actually White?

Or should we simply stop speaking our languages, stop eating our own   8
foods . . . and stop identifying with our home countries of Mexico, El Salvador, Guatemala, Peru, Colombia, etc. In other words, we're OK if we
stop being who we are—if we culturally deport ourselves and conduct auto
ethnic cleansing campaigns (we're also OK if we fight their illegal permanent wars).

And yet, there's that small matter of our red-brown skin. Just what could   9
it possibly represent? A reminder? Memory? Might it be our thousands-of-
years old Indigenous cultures—the ones that were supposedly obliterated—
the ones we were supposed to reject?

We deny the nopal[3] no longer. We know full well we're not on foreign   10
soil, but on Indian lands. (Were we supposed to forget that too?) So there's
no going back. If anything, we are back. The whole continent, the whole
earth—which our ancestors have traversed for thousands of years—is our

[1]Mexican term for "immigration police" (editors' note).
[2]Latin American migrant worker (editors' note).
[3]Literally, "prickly pear." There is a common Mexican expression, "Pareces que tienes el nopal
en la frente," which literally translated means "It appears you have a prickly pear on your forehead." Idiomatically, the meaning is "You appear to be Indian, yet you deny it" (editors' note).

mother. Meanwhile, we watch Congress and the president do a dance about not pardoning or not granting amnesty to those who've been remanded to live in shadows. Sinverguenzas![4] Just who precisely needs to be pardoned? Those who are exploited and who've been here forever . . . or those who've been complicit in our dehumanization?

Through all this, we've been baited into fighting with African Americans, American Indians, Asians, Mexican Americans, and poor and white middle class workers—because Mexicans supposedly steal their jobs and are ruining the quality of life.   11

The truth is, American Indians, African Americans and Asians should be at the head of our protests—for it is they and their struggles against dehumanization that we draw inspiration from. But in the end, it is those who allow extremists to speak in their name, who must also step forward and tell their representatives that a society divided into legal and illegal human beings is no longer acceptable.   12

Every cell in our bodies tells us this. And the unprecedented protests have created the consciousness that a two-tiered society—the definition of apartheid—is intolerable.   13

A flawed bill will pass—many bills will pass—yet some sectors of the population will continue to view and treat Mexicans/Central Americans as illegal, unwanted and subhuman.   14

But enough. Ya Basta! IKUALI![5] As is said at the rallies: Nosotros no somos ilegales ni inmigrantes. Somos de este continente.[6] We are neither illegal nor even immigrants. Tojuan Titehuaxkalo Panin Pacha Mama.[7]   15

---

[4]Mexican expression meaning "Scoundrels!" (editors' note).
[5]*Ya basta* is Spanish and *ikuali* is Nahuatl (the Aztec language) for "enough" (editors' note).
[6]Spanish for "We are neither illegal nor immigrants. We are from this continent" (editors' note).
[7]Nahuatl for "We are from this earth" (editors' note).

Questions for Close Reading

1. What is the selection's thesis? Locate the sentence(s) in which Rodriguez states his main idea. If he doesn't state his thesis explicitly, express it in your own words.
2. What is the meaning of the essay's title, "The Border on Our Backs"?
3. According to Rodriguez, how are American policies on illegal immigrants similar to apartheid?
4. According to Rodriguez, who should be the inspiration for illegal Mexican and Central American immigrants in the United States? Why?
5. Refer to your dictionary as needed to define the following words used in the selection: *scapegoats* (paragraph 1), *draconian* (3), *repatriations* (3), *apartheid* (3), *bigotry* (6), *dragnet* (6), *vilification* (6), *delude* (7), *indigenous* (9), *obliterated* (9), *traversed* (10), *amnesty* (10), *remanded* (10), and *complicit* (10).

Questions About the Writer's Craft

1. Rodriguez opens his essay with some definitions of *Mexican* and *Central American* that he claims can be found in any U.S. political dictionary. How effective is this opening? What tone does it set for the remainder of the essay?
2. **The pattern.** What evidence does Rodriguez cite to support his claim that American attitudes toward immigrants from Mexico and Central America are fundamentally racist? How effective is this evidence and the way it is presented? What is the balance between *logos* and *pathos* here?
3. Rodriguez uses many words and phrases in Spanish and Nahuatl throughout the essay without translating them. How effective is this use of language? What does it suggest about the audience for which he is writing?
4. **The pattern.** What fallacies, if any, are in this argument? Explain the nature of the fallacy or fallacies.

Writing Assignments Using Argumentation-Persuasion as a Pattern of Development

1. Rodriguez argues that the struggle of illegal immigrants is similar to the struggle of American Indians, African Americans, Mexican Americans, and other American groups who have fought against dehumanization (paragraphs 11 and 12). Do you agree? Focusing on a specific group of disadvantaged Americans, write an essay in which you support or challenge Rodriguez's argument. To ensure that your position is more than a reflexive opinion, conduct some library research on the group in question, and read Star Parker's "*Se Habla* Entitlement" (page 567), an essay that is in sharp opposition to Rodriguez's. No matter which side you take, assume that some readers are opposed to your point of view. Acknowledge and try to dismantle as many of their objections as possible. Refer, whenever it's relevant, to Parker's argument in your paper.
2. Rodriguez suggests that racial profiling at the U.S. borders unfairly targets people of color and is used by politicians to exploit whites' fears (paragraph 6). In recent years, racial profiling has been used by many law enforcement agencies to identify suspected criminals and terrorists as well as illegal immigrants, although many people dispute both the fairness and the effectiveness of the technique. Do some research on racial profiling and then write an essay arguing that racial profiling is (or is not) a fair and effective method of identifying people who are likely to be criminals. Your essay can focus on the issue of racial profiling in general, or it can focus on a particular use of racial profiling. In your essay, you should acknowledge and refute as many opposing arguments as possible.

Writing Assignments Combining Patterns of Development

3. Rodriguez believes that illegal immigrants should stand up for their right to be treated as "full human beings." Select a group that you believe is disadvantaged and should stand up for its rights. Possibilities include a specific racial, ethnic, or religious group; the disabled; the overweight; those in abusive relationships. Write

an essay explaining some specific *steps* these groups could take to secure their rights. Conclude your paper by discussing the *effects* of winning such rights. What would be gained? What, if anything, would be lost? Before writing, read one or more of the following essays to sharpen your understanding of disadvantaged people and the struggle for human rights: "The Fourth of July" by Audre Lorde (page 137), "Charity Display?" by Charmie Gholson (page 151), "Workers" by Richard Rodriguez (page 361), "The Handicap of Definition" by William Raspberry (page 471), and "Let's Tell the Story of All America's Cultures" by Yuh Ji-Yeon (page 517).

4. Rodriguez refers to Mexicans and Central Americans as threatening the American Way of Life (paragraph 1). Write an essay in which you *define* what the American Way of Life means to you. Along the way, *compare* and/or *contrast* your definition with what you think is the prevailing definition of this term. To illustrate your definition, provide *examples* and/or *stories*. Your essay can be serious, humorous, or satiric in tone.

Writing Assignment Using a Journal Entry as a Starting Point

∞ 5. Write an essay arguing that schools should or should not encourage students to discuss immigration, ethnicity, and racism. Review your pre-reading journal entry, and select a specific level of schooling to focus on before taking a position. Supplement the material in your journal by gathering the opinions, experiences, and observations of friends, family, and classmates. No matter which position you take, remember to cite opposing arguments, refuting as many of them as you can. Before writing, consider reading "Let's Tell the Story of All America's Cultures" (page 517) in which Yuh Ji-Yeon forcefully argues in favor of the need for honest discussion of race and ethnicity in the classroom.

Star Parker

Star Parker, born in 1957, is the founder and leader of the Coalition on Urban Renewal and Education, a nonprofit organization that advocates on issues of race, poverty, education, and inner-city neighborhoods. At one time a single mother living on welfare in Los Angeles, Parker eventually returned to college for a bachelor's degree in marketing. She went on to establish an urban Christian magazine and become a strong advocate for conservative Christian political views. In 1992, her business was destroyed in the Los Angeles riots. This experience intensified her focus on faith-based and free-market approaches to solving the problems of poverty. As a social policy consultant, Parker frequently appears on national television and radio stations, including CNN, MSNBC, and Fox, and she often testifies before Congress. Parker has published three books: *Pimps, Whores, and Welfare Brats: From Welfare Cheat to Conservative Messenger* (1998), *Uncle Sam's Plantation: How Big Government Enslaves American's Poor and What We Can Do About It* (2003), and *White Ghetto: How Middle Class America Reflects Inner City Decay* (2006). This opinion piece was published on WorldNetDaily.com, an independent news website, on April 18, 2006.

Pre-Reading Journal Entry

The issue of immigration—especially questions of who should be permitted into the country and who should be permitted to stay—has recently been hotly debated both by politicians and pundits and by everyday people. What do you think would happen if U.S. immigration laws were strictly enforced and those who were here illegally were sent back to their home countries? What positive effects would there be? What negative effects would there be? What do you think would happen if all immigrants who were here illegally were allowed to stay and start the process of becoming citizens? Take some time to respond to these questions in your journal.

Se Habla[1] Entitlement

When it comes to matters of economy, I think of myself as libertarian. I   1
believe in free markets, free trade and limited government. But I must confess, our Latino neighbors are challenging my libertarian instincts regarding our immigration conundrum.

The recent pro-immigration demonstrations around the country have   2
been a major turnoff.

[1]Spanish for "is spoken" (editors' note).

There is something not convincing about illegal immigrants demonstrating to claim they have inalienable rights to come here, be here, work here, become citizens here—and make all these claims in Spanish.

Hearing "We Shall Overcome" in Spanish just doesn't provoke my sympathies. I don't buy that, along with life, liberty and the pursuit of happiness, our Creator endowed anyone with the right to sneak into the United States, bypass our laws and set up shop. Maybe our immigration laws do need fixing. But this is a discussion for American citizens. In English.

This could be the finest hour for the political left if we really can be convinced that illegal immigration is a right, that those here illegally are innocent victims, and that the real guilt lies with U.S. citizens who believe our laws mean something and should be enforced.

Draping these bogus claims in the garb of the civil-rights movement is particularly annoying.

The civil-rights movement was about enforcing the law, not breaking it. The Civil War amendments to the Constitution were not getting the job done in what has been a long struggle in this country to treat blacks as human beings. If Americans were kidnapping Mexicans and selling them into slavery here, I might see the equivalence. But these are free people, who chose to come here and chose to do so illegally.

Just considering Mexicans, how can we understand their taking to the streets of our country to demand rights and freedom when they seem to have little interest in doing this where they do have rights, which is in Mexico? There is no reason why Mexico, a country rich in beauty and natural resources, cannot be every bit as prosperous as the United States.

It's not happening because of a long history of mismanagement, corruption and excessive government. Although Mexico is a democracy, for some reason Mexicans seem to need to be north of the Rio Grande to get politically active and demand the benefits of a free society.

Last year the Pew Hispanic Center surveyed adults in Mexico and asked them if they would come to the United States if they had the means and opportunity to do so. Forty-six percent responded yes. Almost half of Mexican adults said they'd rather live here! When asked if they would do it illegally, more than 20 percent said yes.

Yet in the contest for the Mexican presidency, the leading candidate is a leftist former mayor of Mexico City who is polling in the high 30s.[2]

Maybe you can figure out why almost half of Mexican adults say they would rather live in the United States, presumably because of the opportunities our free society affords, yet vote for a leftist candidate who will continue policies in Mexico that choke off any prospect for growth, prosperity and opportunity.

---

[2]With a very narrow margin, the more conservative Felipe Calderon ultimately defeated the leftist Andres Manuel Lopez Obrador in the Mexican presidential election of 2006.

So forgive me for being a little suspicious of the wholesome picture   13
being painted of these folks who are pouring across our border allegedly just
to be free, work and maintain traditional families.

Anyone who lives in Southern California, as I do, knows that the Latino-   14
immigrant community is far from the paragon of virtue that the forces who
want to encourage open borders would have us believe. I see much of the
same troubling behavior that blacks get tarred with. Much of the gang
behavior in Los Angeles, unfortunately, is Latino-related. The L.A. Unified
School District is over three-quarters Latino, who drop out at the same
alarming 50 percent rate as inner-city blacks. Out-of-wedlock births among
Hispanic women approach 50 percent.

Those who want to hoist the banner of the Statue of Liberty, Ellis Island   15
and the American tradition of immigration should remember that when
immigrants were passing through Ellis Island at the early part of the last century, the federal government accounted for about 3 percent of the American
economy. Today it is 25 percent.

Part of the package deal that comes with showing up in the United   16
States today is our welfare state as well as our free economy. Illegal status is
really a temporary situation, anyway. Illegal immigrants' children who are
born here are U.S. citizens. Significant demands are being made on our tax
dollars in the way of schools, health care and government services, including
law enforcement.

Yes, let's encourage freedom. But freedom is a privilege and a responsibility.   17
We have enough people already here who think it's all about entitlement.   18

Questions for Close Reading

1. What is the selection's thesis? Locate the sentence(s) in which Parker states her
   main idea. If she doesn't state her thesis explicitly, express it in your own words.
2. Why does Parker object to pro-immigration demonstrators adopting the strategies
   of the American civil rights movement?
3. In paragraph 15, Parker contrasts the size of the federal government a hundred
   years ago with its size now. To what does she attribute its increase?
4. Why does Parker object to the feeling of entitlement that she claims immigrants have?
5. Refer to your dictionary as needed to define the following words used in the selection: *entitlement* (title), *libertarian* (paragraph 1), *conundrum* (1), *inalienable*
   (3), *provoke* (4), *bogus* (6), *garb* (6), and *paragon* (14).

Questions About the Writer's Craft

1. **The pattern.** Which of the two possible strategies for organizing a refutation (see
   pages 489–490) does Parker use in her essay? Do you consider the points she
   makes in the refutation sufficiently persuasive? Explain.
2. **Other patterns.** In paragraph 14, Parker compares and contrasts the Latino and
   African American communities of southern California. What is the purpose of this
   comparison? How effective is it?

3. The second paragraph of the Declaration of Independence begins: "We hold these truths to be self-evident, that all men are created equal, that they are endowed by their Creator with certain unalienable Rights, that among these are Life, Liberty and the pursuit of Happiness." There are echoes of this sentence in paragraphs 3 and 4 of Parker's essay. What is the effect of her adopting this vocabulary?

4. Throughout the essay, Parker uses language that describes her reactions to pro-immigration demonstrations and arguments: "a major turnoff" (paragraph 2), "not convincing" (3), "doesn't provoke my sympathies" (4), "particularly annoying" (6), and "a little suspicious" (13). What do these phrases contribute to the tone of the essay? How do they help Parker communicate her argument more convincingly?

Writing Assignments Using Argumentation-Persuasion as a Pattern of Development

1. Parker, an African American, claims to have been "turned off" by the pro-immigration demonstrations that took place in spring of 2006 in an attempt to influence immigration legislation pending in Congress. She objects to the pro-immigration movement's adoption of the strategies of the American civil rights movement—the language, the demonstrations, and the songs sung in Spanish. In contrast, in "The Border on Our Backs" (page 562), Roberto Rodriguez, a Mexican American, is elated by these demonstrations, claiming that immigrants are finally asserting their human rights in the great tradition of the civil rights movement. What do you think of demonstrations in the United States by illegal immigrants? Do you sympathize with the immigrants' arguments? Do you think their demonstrations further the immigrants' cause, or set it back? Write an essay in which you argue that demonstrations by illegal immigrants are (or are not) justified and appropriate, citing at least two or three reasons for your position. Be sure to support your reasons with examples wherever possible.

2. Parker characterizes herself as a libertarian in matters of economics. Libertarians advocate that individuals should be free to do whatever they wish with themselves and their property, as long as they do not infringe on the liberty of others. Libertarians also believe that people are responsible for their own actions. They strongly oppose welfare programs, which they believe forces taxpayers to provide aid to others. In fact, Parker's final reason for opposing illegal immigrants is that they contribute to the growth of the welfare state (paragraph 15 and 16). Write an essay supporting or opposing the libertarian position on the welfare state. Argue that government does (or does not) have the responsibility to help individuals in times of need (poor economic conditions, disability, and natural disasters, for example). Be sure to address whether the effect on individuals of such government assistance is empowering—or whether it perpetuates dependence. Use specific examples to support your position.

Writing Assignments Combining Patterns of Development

3. Imagine what your life would be like if you moved to another state or country alone or just with your immediate family. Then write an essay in which you provide *examples* showing how your life would or would not change if you moved to

a strange place. Consider the language barrier, if any, in your education, your work, your friendships, and your family life. Reach some conclusions about the overall *effect* of making this move, including whether life would be easier or more difficult.

4. Choose a social program or common practice that involves the concept of entitlement. For example, among social programs you could choose affirmative action, Medicaid, Medicare, welfare, or unemployment insurance. Among common practices you might select nepotism (favoring relatives or friends when hiring), legacy admissions to colleges (admitting the children of alumni), or illegal campaign contributions. Research the program or practice on the Internet or in the library. Write an essay in which you explain the *effects* of such a program or practice on recipients. *Compare* and *contrast* the benefits and drawbacks of receiving such an entitlement. Finally, *argue* that the program or practice should be continued or abolished.

Writing Assignment Using a Journal Entry as a Starting Point

5. Review your journal entries about the possible effects of deporting illegal immigrants or allowing them to stay, also called *amnesty*. The last amnesty in the United States took place in 1986 and was granted to immigrants who could prove they had resided here for five years or more. Amnesty is always controversial. Some argue that granting amnesty rewards illegal behavior and encourages more illegal immigration. Others argue that regularizing the status of long-time illegal residents simply provides them with a path for becoming full citizens, upholding the ideals of an open and democratic society. Write an essay in which you *argue* either in favor of or against an amnesty for current illegal immigrants who have resided in the United States for at least five years. In addition to discussing the *effects* of allowing immigrants to stay that you outlined in your journal entry, do some research on the 1986 amnesty to understand its *effects*. If they are still relevant today, use them to support your point of view about amnesty.

Additional Writing Topics

ARGUMENTATION-PERSUASION

General Assignments

Using argumentation-persuasion, develop one of the topics below in an essay. After choosing a topic, think about your purpose and audience. Remember that the paper's thesis should state the issue under discussion as well as your position on the issue. As you work on developing evidence, you might want to do some outside research. Keep in mind that effective argumentation-persuasion usually means that some time should be spent acknowledging and perhaps refuting opposing points of view. Be careful not to sabotage your argument by basing your case on a logical fallacy.

1. Euthanasia
2. Hiring or college-admissions quotas
3. Giving birth-control devices to teenagers
4. Prayer in the schools
5. Living at home after college
6. The drinking age
7. Spouses sharing housework equally
8. Smoking in public places
9. Big-time sports in college
10. Pornography on the Internet
11. Single parents with young children
12. Global warming
13. Legalizing marijuana
14. Political campaigns
15. Requiring college students to pass a comprehensive exam in their majors before graduating
16. Reinstating the military draft
17. Putting elderly parents in nursing homes
18. An optional pass-fail system for courses
19. The homeless
20. Nonconformity in a neighborhood: allowing a lawn to go wild, keeping many pets, painting a house an odd color, or some other atypical behavior

Assignments With a Specific Purpose, Audience, and Point of View

On Campus

1. Your college's Financial Aid Department has decided not to renew your scholarship for next year, citing a drop in your grades last semester and an unenthusiastic recommendation from one of your instructors. Write a letter to the director of financial aid arguing for the renewal of your scholarship.

2. You strongly believe that a particular policy or regulation on campus is unreasonable or unjust. Write a letter to the dean of students (or other appropriate administrator) arguing that the policy needs to be, if not completely revoked, amended in some way. Support your contention with specific examples showing how the regulation has gone wrong. End by providing constructive suggestions for how the policy problem can be solved.

At Home or in the Community

3. You and one or more family members don't agree on some aspect of your romantic life (you want to live with your boyfriend/girlfriend and they don't approve; you want to get married and they want you to wait; they simply don't like your partner). Write a letter explaining why your preference is reasonable. Try hard to win your family member(s) over to your side.

4. Assume you're a member of a racial, ethnic, religious, or social minority. You might, for example, be a Native American, an elderly person, a female executive. On a recent television show or in a TV commercial, you saw something that depicts your group in an offensive way. Write a letter (to the network or the advertiser) expressing your feelings and explaining why you feel the material should be taken off the air.

On the Job

5. As a staff writer for an online pop-culture magazine, you've been asked to nominate the "Most Memorable TV Moment of the Last 50 Years" to be featured as the magazine's lead article. Write a letter to your supervising editor in support of your nominee.

6. As a high school teacher, you support some additional restriction on students. The restriction might be "no cell phones in school," "no T-shirts," "no food in class," "no smoking on school grounds." Write an article for the school newspaper, justifying this new rule to the student body.

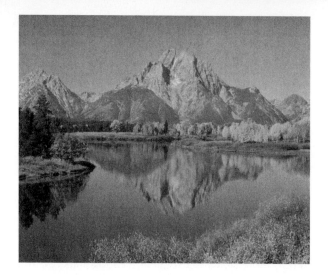

COMBINING THE PATTERNS

Throughout this book, you've studied the patterns of development—narration, process analysis, definition, and so on—in depth. You've seen how the patterns are used as strategies for generating, developing, and organizing ideas for essays. You've also learned that, in practice, most types of writing combine two or more patterns. The two sections that follow provide additional information about these important points. The rest of the chapter then gives you an opportunity to look more closely at the way several writers use the patterns of development in their work.

THE PATTERNS IN ACTION: DURING THE WRITING PROCESS

The patterns of development come into play throughout the composing process. In the prewriting stage, awareness of the patterns encourages you to think about your subject in fresh, new ways. Assume, for example, that you've been asked to write an essay about the way children are disciplined in school. However, you draw a blank as soon as you try to limit this general subject. To break the logjam, you could apply one or more patterns of development to your subject. *Comparison-contrast* might prompt you to write an essay investigating the differences between your parents' and your own feelings about school discipline. *Division-classification* might lead you to another paper—one that categorizes the kinds of discipline used in school. And *cause-effect* might point to still another essay—one that explores the way students react to being suspended.

Further along in the writing process—after you've identified your limited subject and your thesis—the patterns of development can help you generate your paper's evidence. Imagine that your thesis is "Teachers shouldn't discipline students publicly just to make an example of them." You're not sure, though, how to develop this thesis. Calling upon the patterns might spark some promising possibilities. *Narration* might encourage you to recount the disastrous time you were singled out and punished for the misdeeds of an entire class. Using *definition,* you might explain what is meant by an *autocratic* disciplinary style. *Argumentation-persuasion* might prompt you to advocate a new plan for disciplining students fairly and effectively.

The patterns of development also help you organize your ideas by pointing the way to an appropriate framework for a paper. Suppose you plan to write an essay for the campus newspaper about the disturbingly high incidence of shoplifting among college students; your purpose is to persuade young people not to get involved in this tempting, supposedly victimless crime. You believe that many readers will be deterred from shoplifting if you tell them about the harrowing *process* set in motion once a shoplifter is detected. With this step-by-step explanation in mind, you can now map out the essay's content: what happens when a shoplifter is detained by a salesperson, questioned by store security personnel, led to a police car, booked at the police station, and tried in a courtroom.

THE PATTERNS IN ACTION: IN AN ESSAY

Although this book devotes a separate chapter to each of the nine patterns of development, all chapters emphasize the same important point: Most writing consists of several patterns, with the dominant pattern providing the piece's organizational framework. To reinforce this point, each chapter contains a section, "How [the Pattern] Fits Your Purpose and Audience," that shows how a writer's purpose often leads to a blending of patterns. Also, the commentary following each student essay talks about the way the paper mixes patterns. Similarly, at least one of the questions in the "Questions About the Writer's Craft" section following each professional selection asks you to analyze the piece's combination of patterns. Further, the assignments in "Writing Assignments Combining Patterns of Development" encourage you to experiment with mixing patterns in your own writing. In short, all through *The Longman Reader* we emphasize that the patterns of development are far from being mechanical formulas. On the contrary: They are practical strategies that open up options in every stage of the composing process.

Now you'll have a chance to focus on the way student and professional writers combine patterns in their essays. In the pages ahead, you'll find one student essay and six professional selections, two by each of the following three writers: Virginia Woolf; Martin Luther King, Jr.; and Joan Didion. As you read each essay, ask yourself these questions:

1. What are the writer's *purpose* and *thesis?*

2. What *pattern of development dominates* the essay? How does this pattern help the writer support the essay's thesis and fulfill the essay's purpose?

3. What *other patterns appear* in the essay? How do these secondary patterns help the writer support the essay's thesis and fulfill the essay's purpose?

Your responses to these three questions will reward you with a richer understanding of the way writers work. To give you an even clearer sense of how writers mix patterns, we have annotated the student essay (Tasha Walker's "The Super-Sizing of America's Kids" below) and the first professional essay (Virginia Woolf's "The Death of the Moth" on page 582). The preceding three questions served as our guide when we prepared the annotations. By making your own annotations on these essays and then comparing them to ours, you can measure your ability to analyze writers' use of the patterns. You can further evaluate your analysis of the pieces by answering the three questions on your own and then comparing your responses to ours on pages 580–581 and 585–587.

STUDENT ESSAY

The following student essay was written by Tasha Walker in response to this assignment:

In the essay "Tweens: Ten Going on Sixteen," Kay S. Hymowitz explores an alarming trend among children: the tendency of preteens to act much older than they are. Write an essay analyzing the causes and effects of another significant problem among young people today. Conclude your essay by offering possible solutions for the problem you've examined.

The annotations on the essay will help you look at the way Tasha uses various patterns of development to achieve her purpose and develop her thesis.

Introduction has *narrative* and *descriptive* elements	The Super-Sizing of America's Kids by Tasha Walker
Examples of foods *contrast* with *examples* later in ¶	Picture this scene from the 1950s. A couple of kids wake up, get dressed, and sit down for breakfast before leaving for school. They're greeted by an array of healthy choices: a glass of orange juice, a bowl of cornflakes or oatmeal with a healthy serving of milk, perhaps a plateful of scrambled eggs and toast.
Contrast between average breakfast in the 1950s and today	Now fast-forward a few decades to the present. The situation is very different. If kids sit down for breakfast at all, they gulp down a bowl of rainbow-colored sugary bits with a dollop

1

of milk. Or, racing out the door, they grab a syrupy jumbo cinnamon bun or a glazed, fudge-filled toaster tart.

What's the harm, you might ask, in giving kids tasty, convenient food options? After all, kids burn so much energy; they shouldn't have to worry about their diet until they're adults. Right? Wrong, says the latest information on obesity in the United States. According to several recent studies cited by the magazine Children's Health (October 2003), the number of overweight American kids has more than doubled in the last thirty years. As many as 22 percent of today's children are considered dangerously obese. Many are developing diet-related diabetes, a disease that used to be seen almost exclusively in adults. When California's students (grades 5 through 12) were given a basic fitness test, almost eight out of ten failed. These statistics point to a clear conclusion: There's a growing problem of childhood obesity in this country, a dire trend that must be stopped in its tracks.

Exemplification in the form of facts and statistics

Causal analysis (main pattern) begins with *effects* of problem

Statement of purpose/thesis: Need to end increasing childhood obesity; emotional language urging action reinforces essay's *persuasive* intent

Causal analysis shifts to several *causes* of problem

Transition signals first *cause* of problem

Whether they're called big-boned, chubby, husky, or plus-sized, kids are becoming heavier at younger ages and less physically fit than ever before. But why? Like most serious problems, this one has a number of causes. One factor is the massive impact of electronic entertainment on kids' lives. Kids used to go outside to play because that was more fun than sitting around the house. Today, kids at home have access to cable TV channels, the Internet, DVD players, and a dizzying assortment of video games, all of which diminish the lure of outdoor play.

Transition signals second *cause* of problem

Another cause is the lack of parental supervision. Decades ago, most kids had an adult at home encouraging them to play outdoors. Now, a large number of American families have two working parents or a working single parent. For most of the daylight hours, parents aren't around to make sure their kids get some exercise. Parents who can't be home may feel guilty; one way to relieve this guilt is to buy kids the game system of their dreams and a nice wide-screen TV to play it on, almost guaranteeing that kids will sit idle rather than participate in vigorous physical activity.

Transition signals most important *cause* of problem

But more than any other factor, fast-food restaurants and other sources of calorie-laden junk have dramatically contributed to the fattening of America's kids. In Super Size Me, director Morgan Spurlock, dismayed by American obesity statistics (particularly among children), decided to eat nothing but McDonald's fast food for a month and film the experience. To many of today's kids, normal dinnertime equals McDonald's, Domino's, Taco Bell, or Kentucky Fried Chicken. And increasingly, lunchtime at school means those foods too since a good number of schools have sold chain restaurants the right to put their food items on the lunch line. Many schools also allow candy and soft-drink vending machines on their campuses. Given the choice between an apple and a candy bar, how many kids would choose the apple?

Start of secondary causal analysis (effects of fast food on kids)

Exemplification in the form of facts and statistics

Whether for breakfast, lunch, or dinner, when fast food   6 becomes the staple of young people's diets, it's the kids who become Whoppers. And it has become the staple for many. Children's Health reports that nationwide, kids get 40 percent of their meals from fast-food chains and convenience stores. And what makes the situation even worse is the increasingly huge portions sold by fast-food restaurants. In the 1950s, the standard meal at McDonald's consisted of a hamburger, two ounces of French fries, and a 12-ounce Coke. That meal provided 590 calories. But today's customers are encouraged to say "Super-size that!" For very little extra money, diners end up with a quarter-pound burger, extra-large fries, and a gigantic cup of Coke, all adding up to 1,550 calories. A whole generation of kids is growing up believing that this massive shot of fat, sugar, and sodium equals a "normal portion." Kids' perception of what's normal is also distorted by the size of the drinks sold by fast-food and convenience stores. The drinks, often sporting names like the "Big Gulp" or "Super Thirst Quencher," are huge in both size and popularity. Every day, the average adolescent chugs enough soda and fruit beverages to equal the sugar content of fifty chocolate-chip cookies. No wonder kids are becoming "super-sized" themselves.

Emotional language reinforces essay's persuasive intent

Exemplification in the form of facts and statistics

The fast-food franchises push youngsters to overeat in   7 other ways too. Plunking themselves down in front of the TV to watch after-school and Saturday-morning cartoons, children see at least an hour of commercials for every five hours of programming. On Saturday mornings, nine out of ten of those TV ads are for sugary cereals, fast foods, and other non-nutritious junk. Watching those commercials makes the kids hungry--or at least makes them think they are. So they snack as they sit in front of the TV set. Then at mealtime, they beg for the junk food they've seen televised all day long. The result? Kids get bigger, and bigger, and bigger.

End of secondary causal analysis

Emotional language reinforces essay's persuasive intent

Argumentation presents several possible solutions to problem

Transitions signal several solutions

There's no overnight solution to the problem of American   8 children's increasing weight. But there are some remedies that could be put into place easily. To begin, fast-food meals and junk-food vending machines should be banned from schools, as some states have started to do. Second, food companies should reduce serving sizes and lower the fat and sugar content of the snack items that children eat most often.

(Kraft Foods has recently begun to take such steps.) Third, commercials for junk food should be prohibited from being aired on TV during children's viewing time, specifically Saturday mornings. Fourth, parents and schools need to educate kids about the benefits of healthy foods and moderate portion size--and about the drawback of huge meals of junk food. Schools could, for example, mount an educational effort equivalent to the school-based anti-smoking campaign of the 1980s and 1990s. Fifth, fast-food restaurants should be required to do something like what tobacco companies have to do: clearly display health warnings on their products. If young people learned in school and at home about healthy eating, they might think twice about ordering a Double Whopper with cheese, an extra-large order of fries and a king-sized Dr. Pepper, especially if they read something like this:

Exemplification in the form of hypothetical situation

- Your meal provides 2030 calories, 860 of those calories from fat.
- Your recommended daily intake is 2000 calories, with no more than 600 of those calories coming from fat.

At a glance, they could see that in one fast-food meal, they would be taking in more calories and fat than they should consume in an entire day.

Transition signals last solution

Finally, parents need to curb their reliance on fast food to nourish their children. Making fast food an occasional treat rather than an everyday habit can make a significant difference. Parents may argue that they simply don't have time to cook healthy, well-balanced meals, particularly during the week. The answer may be to get the whole family involved in preparing meals ahead of time. (Younger kids, whose attitudes are still in the formative stage, love helping out in the kitchen.) Letting kids assist in preparing, packaging, and freezing their own nutritious, reasonably sized individual servings for later use can go a long way toward helping youngsters develop more healthy attitudes toward food.

9

Restatement of purpose/thesis; emotional language urging action reinforces essay's persuasive intent

Such efforts, challenging as they may be, are well worth the trouble. Why? Because overweight kids today become overweight adults tomorrow. Overweight adults are at increased risk for heart disease, diabetes, stroke, and cancer. Schools, fast-food restaurants, and the media are contributing to a public-health disaster in the making. Anything that decreases the role that super-sized junk food plays in kids' lives needs to be done, and done quickly.

10

The following answers to the questions on pages 575–576 will help you analyze Tasha Walker's use of the patterns of development in her essay "The Super-Sizing of America's Kids."

1. *What are the writer's purpose and thesis?*

   Tasha's general purpose, clearly indicated in the assignment, is to explore the causes and effects of a significant problem among young people today. Tasha chooses to address the problem of increasing obesity among children. She expresses her thesis in the final sentence of paragraph 2: "There's a growing problem of childhood obesity in this country, a dire trend that must be stopped in its tracks." Over the course of her essay, Tasha marshals compelling evidence of the obesity problem, explores its causes and effects, and concludes with thoughts on how this problem might be rectified.

2. *What pattern of development dominates the essay? How does this pattern help the writer support the essay's thesis and fulfill the essay's purpose?*

   As the assignment required, Tasha uses *causal analysis* as her essay's principal pattern of development. To establish the severity of the childhood obesity problem, Tasha presents, in paragraph 2, a battery of statistics pointing to obesity's dire and pervasive *effects*. She then shifts gears in paragraph 3 to consider the *causes* of this obesity. The phrase "Like most serious problems, this one has a number of causes" announces that Tasha will discuss a series of causes. She uses various signal phrases, including "One factor" (3), "Another cause" (4), and "But more than any other factor" (5), to direct readers' attention to each factor under consideration. This clear, easy-to-follow presentation—first of effects and then of causes—allows Tasha to develop her thesis and meet her writing objectives. Along the way, several *secondary causal analyses* buttress her overarching examination of causes and effects. Consider paragraphs 5–7. There, Tasha begins by citing fast-food restaurants as the most significant cause of kids' poor eating habits; that done, she examines how the fast-food industry affects kids—how it distorts their perception of portion size and uses enticing commercials to increase their reliance on "calorie-laden junk" (5).

3. *What other patterns appear in the essay? How do these secondary patterns help the writer support the essay's thesis and fulfill the essay's purpose?*

   Although Tasha's essay is primarily a causal analysis, it contains a strong element of *argumentation-persuasion*. For one thing, Tasha's thesis takes the form of an *argument:* The "dire trend [of childhood obesity] . . . must be stopped in its tracks" (paragraph 2). Careful to support her argument with solid reasoning, Tasha uses facts and statistics throughout the essay. She also employs strong language to enhance the argument's *persuasiveness*. Note, for example, the way she's worded her thesis to convey a sense of urgency. Note, too, the way she forcefully restates her core argument at various points in the essay. In paragraph 3, she asserts that "kids are becoming heavier at younger ages and less physically fit than ever before," and later she argues, "No wonder kids are becoming 'super-sized' themselves" (6) and "Kids get bigger, and bigger, and bigger" (7). The essay's last sentence ("Anything that decreases the role that super-sized junk food plays in kids' lives needs to be done, and done quickly") echoes the feeling of urgency expressed in the thesis.

Tasha's essay draws upon other patterns of development as well. The introductory anecdote, *narrative* and *descriptive* in structure, *contrasts* kids' waking up to breakfast in the 1950s with what happens nowadays. Vivid contrasting *examples* ("a bowl of . . . oatmeal" versus a "bowl of rainbow-colored sugary bits") help Tasha establish her key point: that childhood obesity is a contemporary trend that didn't exist in the past. Tasha continues to use exemplification in the form of facts (6 and 8), statistics (2 and 7), and hypothetical situations (8 and 9). Taken together, all these patterns help Tasha make her point about the importance of reversing the dangerous trend of childhood obesity.

Now that you've seen the way one student writer brings together several patterns of development in an essay, it will be helpful to look at the way a renowned prose stylist, Virginia Woolf, does the same in her classic essay "The Death of the Moth."

Virginia Woolf

Virginia Woolf is considered one of the most innovative writers of the twentieth century. Born in 1882 in London, Woolf was educated at home by her father, Leslie Stephen, a well-known biographer, critic, and scholar. Along with her sister, Woolf became a key member of the Bloomsbury Group, a circle of writers and artists committed to the highest standards in art and literature. Woolf married a fellow Bloomsbury member, author and publisher Leonard Woolf. Together, they established Hogarth Press, which went on to publish Woolf's ground-breaking writings, including the novels *Mrs. Dalloway* (1923) and *To the Lighthouse* (1927), as well as the collection of essays *A Room of One's Own* (1920). Woolf's experimentation with point of view and her use of stream of consciousness earned her a place as a pivotal figure in English literature. Although Woolf's work met with critical acclaim and her collaboration with her husband was productive, Woolf was troubled all her life by severe depression. She committed suicide in 1941. The first of the following two selections by Woolf, "The Death of the Moth," appeared in the volume *The Death of the Moth and Other Essays* (1948); the second, "Professions for Women," was delivered as a speech to the Women's Service League in 1931.

The Death of the Moth

Description of the moth

Definition (by negation): How this moth differs from the usual kind

Part of implied purpose/thesis: Nature's energy

Description of nature's energy here *contrasts* with *description* of nature in ¶5 (part of purpose/thesis)

Moths that fly by day are not properly to be called   1
moths; they do not excite that pleasant sense of dark autumn nights and ivy-blossom which the commonest yellow-underwing asleep in the shadow of the curtain never fails to rouse in us. They are hybrid creatures, neither gay like butterflies nor sombre like their own species. Nevertheless the present specimen, with his narrow hay-coloured wings, fringed with a tassel of the same colour, seemed to be content with life. It was a pleasant morning, mid-September, mild, benignant, yet with a keener breath than that of the summer months. The plough was already scoring the field opposite the window, and where the share had been, the earth was pressed flat and gleamed with moisture. Such vigour came rolling in from the fields and the down beyond that it was difficult to keep the eyes strictly turned upon the book. The rooks too were keeping one of their annual

festivities; soaring round the tree tops until it looked as if a vast net with thousands of black knots in it had been cast up into the air; which, after a few moments, sank slowly down upon the trees until every twig seemed to have a knot at the end of it. Then, suddenly, the net would be thrown into the air again in a wider circle this time, with the utmost clamour and vociferation, as though to be thrown into the air and settle slowly down upon the tree tops were a tremendously exciting experience.

The same energy which inspired the rooks, the ploughmen, the horses, and even, it seemed, the lean bare-backed downs, sent the moth fluttering from side to side of his square of the window-pane. One could not help watching him. One was, indeed, conscious of a queer feeling of pity for him. The possibilities of pleasure seemed that morning so enormous and so various that to have only a moth's part in life, and a day moth's at that, appeared a hard fate, and his zest in enjoying his meagre opportunities to the full, pathetic. He flew vigorously to one corner of his compartment, and, after waiting there a second, flew across to the other. What remained for him but to fly to a third corner and then to a fourth? That was all he could do, in spite of the size of the downs, the width of the sky, the far-off smoke of houses, and the romantic voice, now and then, of a steamer out at sea. What he could do he did. Watching him, it seemed as if a fibre, very thin but pure, of the enormous energy of the world had been thrust into his frail and diminutive body. As often as he crossed the pane, I could fancy that a thread of vital light became visible. He was little or nothing but life.

Yet, because he was so small, and so simple a form of the energy that was rolling in at the open window and driving its way through so many narrow and intricate corridors in my own brain and in those of other human beings, there was something marvellous as well as pathetic about him. It was as if someone had taken a tiny bead of pure life and decking it as lightly as possible with down and feathers, had set it dancing and zigzagging to show us the true nature of life. Thus displayed one could not get over the strangeness of it. One is apt to forget all about life, seeing it humped and bossed and garnished and cumbered so that it has to move with the greatest circumspection and dignity. Again, the thought of all that life might have been had he been born in any other shape caused one to view his simple activities with a kind of pity.

Comparison between nature's energy and the moth's strong life force (part of purpose/thesis)

Start of *narrative* (main pattern) about the moth's plight

Start of *narrative* about Woolf's reaction to the moth's plight

Description of moth's strong life force—despite its small size (these two contrasting qualities are part of purpose/thesis)

Part of purpose/thesis: The moth represents life

Narrative about Woolf's reaction continues

Restatement of part of purpose/thesis: The moth's two contrasting qualities

Restatement of part of purpose/thesis: The moth represents life

2

3

Narrative about the moth's plight continues; tension builds —

Narrative about Woolf's reaction continues

Hint of the resolution of the *narrative* about the moth —

Narrative about Woolf's reaction continues —

Description of nature's indifference here *contrasts* with *description* of nature in ¶1 (part of purpose/thesis) —

Restatement of part of purpose/thesis: The strength of the moth's life force—despite small size —

Part of purpose/thesis: Death's inevitability —

Narrative about moth continues —

Narrative about Woolf's reaction continues —

Restatement of part of purpose/thesis: The strength of the moth's life force—despite its size

After a time, tired by his dancing apparently, he settled   4
on the window ledge in the sun, and, the queer spectacle
being at an end, I forgot about him. Then, looking up, my
eye was caught by him. He was trying to resume his dancing, but seemed either so stiff or so awkward that he could
only flutter to the bottom of the window-pane; and when he
tried to fly across it he failed. Being intent on other matters
I watched these futile attempts for a time without thinking,
unconsciously waiting for him to resume his flight, as one
waits for a machine, that has stopped momentarily, to start
again without considering the reason of its failure. After perhaps a seventh attempt he slipped from the wooden ledge
and fell, fluttering his wings, on to his back on the window
sill. The helplessness of his attitude roused me. It flashed
upon me that he was in difficulties; he could no longer raise
himself; his legs struggled vainly. But, as I stretched out a
pencil, meaning to help him to right himself, it came over
me that the failure and awkwardness were the approach of
death. I laid the pencil down again.

The legs agitated themselves once more. I looked as if   5
for the enemy against which he struggled. I looked out of
doors. What had happened there? Presumably it was midday,
and work in the fields had stopped. Stillness and quiet had
replaced the previous animation. The birds had taken themselves off to feed in the brooks. The horses stood still. Yet
the power was there all the same, massed outside, indifferent, impersonal, not attending to anything in particular.
Somehow it was opposed to the little hay-coloured moth. It
was useless to try to do anything. One could only watch the
extraordinary efforts made by those tiny legs against an
oncoming doom which could, had it chosen, have submerged an entire city, not merely a city, but masses of human
beings; nothing, I knew, had any chance against death. Nevertheless after a pause of exhaustion the legs fluttered again.
It was superb, this last protest, and so frantic that he succeeded at last in righting himself. One's sympathies, of
course, were all on the side of life. Also, when there was
nobody to care or to know, this gigantic effort on the part
of an insignificant little moth, against a power of such magnitude, to retain what no one else valued or desired to keep,
moved one strangely. Again, somehow, one saw life, a pure
bead. I lifted the pencil again, useless though I knew it to
be. But even as I did so, the unmistakable tokens of death

showed themselves. The body relaxed, and instantly grew

Resolution of the *narrative* about the moth

stiff. The struggle was over. The insignificant little creature now knew death. As I looked at the dead moth, this minute wayside triumph of so great a force over so mean an antagonist filled me with wonder. Just as life had been strange a

Restatement of part of purpose/ thesis: Death's inevitability

few minutes before, so death was now as strange. The moth having righted himself now lay most decently and uncomplainingly composed. O yes, he seemed to say, death is stronger than I am.

The following answers to the questions on pages 575–576 will help you analyze Virginia Woolf's use of the patterns of development in the essay "The Death of the Moth."

1. *What are the writer's purpose and thesis?*

Woolf's *purpose* is to show that the tiny moth's courageous but ultimately futile battle to cling to life embodies the struggle at the very heart of all existence. Woolf achieves her purpose by relating the story of the moth's efforts to resist death. Her *thesis* might be expressed this way: Although living creatures may make "extraordinary efforts" (paragraph 5) to hold onto life, these attempts aren't strong enough to defy death. Nothing, Woolf writes, has "any chance against death" (5).

Woolf's purpose and thesis first become apparent at the end of paragraph 2. There she shows that the moth, with his "frail and diminutive body," represents "nothing but life." Although "small . . . and . . . simple" (3), the moth is suffused with the same extraordinary energy that is evident in the natural world beyond Woolf's window. This energy, combined with the moth's tiny size, makes the creature both "marvellous" and "pathetic" (3)—two qualities that are particularly apparent during the moth's final struggles. During those moments, the moth makes a final "superb" (5) protest against death, but ultimately the "insignificant" (5) creature—like all forms of life—must cease his valiant struggle and die.

2. *What pattern of development dominates the essay? How does this pattern help the writer support the essay's thesis and fulfill the essay's purpose?*

Although the essay's first paragraph is largely descriptive, it becomes clear by paragraph 2 that the description is in service of a larger narrative about the moth's struggles. It's this narrative that dominates the essay.

At the beginning, the moth is imbued with vitality, as he flies "vigorously" (paragraph 2) and with "zest" (2) from one side of the window to the other. But narrative tension begins to build in paragraph 4. There Woolf writes that the moth tries once again to cross the windowpane, fails repeatedly, and slips "on to his back," seemingly defeated. However, even then, the moth doesn't abandon his hold on life, for—as Woolf relates in paragraph 5—he tries, despite exhaustion, to right himself. Against all odds, he finally succeeds, but his frantic struggle to hold onto life takes its toll, and the tiny creature soon dies. This detailed story of the moth's futile battle against death is presented as an emblem of the fate of all life. Through this narrative, Woolf achieves her purpose and thesis: to convey the power of nature and the inability of living creatures—despite heroic efforts—to defy this power.

Paralleling the tale of the moth's struggle is another *narrative*: the story of Woolf's changing understanding of the event that unfolds before her. When the moth is "dancing" (3), energetic, and vital, Woolf "could not help watching him" (2) and feels a kind of wonderment at this "tiny bead of pure life" (3). Then in paragraph 4, Woolf writes that she forgets about the moth for a while until she happens to look up and see his "futile attempts" to "resume . . . dancing." For a few moments, she watches the moth's "stiff" and "awkward" efforts to fly, expecting him to demonstrate the same vitality as before. Suddenly, she understands that the moth is "in difficulties" and can no longer lift himself up. She tries to help but abandons her efforts when she realizes that the moth's labored efforts signify the "approach of death." Paragraph 5 presents the final stage of Woolf's interior narrative. She looks outside her window for an explanation of the moth's plight. But now she finds that the forces of nature—earlier so exuberant and vibrant—are, if anything, "opposed to the little hay-coloured moth." With that, her attention is once again drawn to the moth and the fluttering of his legs. Although drained, the tiny creature makes one last effort to resist death—and, improbably enough, picks himself up one more time. Struck by the sheer power of the moth's life force, Woolf is prompted, as before, to help the creature, even though she recognizes the futility. But then the "unmistakable tokens of death" appear, and the moth gives up his struggle, succumbing—as all forms of life must—to the forces of nature. With the moth lying "uncomplainingly composed," Woolf comes to accept the fact that death is stronger than life.

3. *What other patterns appear in the essay? How do these secondary patterns help the writer support the essay's thesis and fulfill the essay's purpose?*

Although the essay is predominantly a narrative, it also contains other patterns. The *descriptive* passage at the beginning of the essay includes a brief *definition by negation* in which Woolf explains how the creature she is observing differs from the usual, more colorful night moth. The rest of paragraph 1 draws upon description to evoke the sense of early autumn and nature's extraordinary energy. This description of the natural world's vibrancy and abundance, exemplified by the rooks and plowed earth, *contrasts* with Woolf's later characterization of the natural world in paragraph 5. There she writes, "Stillness and quiet . . . replaced the previous animation," and she senses not that nature fosters vitality, but that it is "indifferent, impersonal, not attending to anything in particular."

Shifting her focus in paragraph 2 from the natural world to the moth, Woolf exercises her *descriptive* powers to convey the moth's extraordinary zest as he flies across the windowpane. In this paragraph, Woolf also draws upon *comparison-contrast* to show that despite *differences* in their sizes, the tiny moth and the vast natural world embody the *same* primal energy. Woolf's consideration of this elemental similarity leads her to the basic *contrast* at the heart of the essay: While the moth's tiny size makes him "pathetic," his formidable life spirit makes him "marvellous." He may be small and lightweight, but he is abuzz with vitality. When contrasted to the enormous power of nature, the moth—like all forms of life—may be puny, but his impulse to defy such power inspires awe and reverence.

Virginia Woolf

Professions for Women[1]

When your secretary invited me to come here, she told me that your Society is concerned with the employment of women and she suggested that I might tell you something about my own professional experiences. It is true I am a woman; it is true I am employed; but what professional experiences have I had? It is difficult to say. My profession is literature; and in that profession there are fewer experiences for women than in any other, with the exception of the stage—fewer, I mean, that are peculiar to women. For the road was cut many years ago—by Fanny Burney, by Aphra Behn, by Harriet Martineau, by Jane Austen, by George Eliot[2]—many famous women, and many more unknown and forgotten, have been before me, making the path smooth, and regulating my steps. Thus, when I came to write, there were very few material obstacles in my way. Writing was a reputable and harmless occupation. The family peace was not broken by the scratching of a pen. No demand was made upon the family purse. For ten and sixpence one can buy paper enough to write all the plays of Shakespeare—if one has a mind that way. Pianos and models, Paris, Vienna and Berlin, masters and mistresses, are not needed by a writer. The cheapness of writing paper is, of course, the reason why women have succeeded as writers before they have succeeded in the other professions.

But to tell you my story—it is a simple one. You have only got to figure to yourselves a girl in a bedroom with a pen in her hand. She had only to move that pen from left to right—from ten o'clock to one. Then it occurred to her to do what is simple and cheap enough after all—to slip a few of those pages into an envelope, fix a penny stamp in the corner, and drop the envelope into the red box at the corner. It was thus that I became a journalist; and my effort was rewarded on the first day of the following month—a very

1

2

[1]The following is a speech delivered by Woolf to the Women's Service League in 1931 (editors' note).
[2]Fanny Burney (1752–1840), Aphra Behn (1640–89), Harriet Martineau (1802–76), Jane Austen (1775–1817), and Marian Evans (1819–80), whose pen name was George Eliot, were all English women of letters (editors' note).

glorious day it was for me—by a letter from an editor containing a cheque for one pound ten shillings and sixpence. But to show you how little I deserve to be called a professional woman, how little I know of the struggles and difficulties of such lives, I have to admit that instead of spending that sum upon bread and butter, rent, shoes and stockings, or butcher's bills, I went out and bought a cat—a beautiful cat, a Persian cat, which very soon involved me in bitter disputes with my neighbors.

What could be easier than to write articles and to buy Persian cats with the profits? But wait a moment. Articles have to be about something. Mine, I seem to remember, was about a novel by a famous man. And while I was writing this review, I discovered that if I were going to review books I should need to do battle with a certain phantom. And the phantom was a woman, and when I came to know her better I called her after the heroine of a famous poem, "The Angel in the House." It was she who used to come between me and my paper when I was writing reviews. It was she who bothered me and wasted my time and so tormented me that at last I killed her. You who come of a younger and happier generation may not have heard of her—you may not know what I mean by the Angel in the House. I will describe her as shortly as I can. She was intensely sympathetic. She was immensely charming. She was utterly unselfish. She excelled in the difficult arts of family life. She sacrificed herself daily. If there was chicken, she took the leg; if there was a draught she sat in it—in short she was so constituted that she never had a mind or a wish of her own, but preferred to sympathize always with the minds and wishes of others. Above all—I need not say it—she was pure. Her purity was supposed to be her chief beauty—her blushes, her great grace. In those days—the last of Queen Victoria—every house had its Angel. And when I came to write I encountered her with the very first words. The shadow of her wings fell on my page; I heard the rustling of her skirts in the room. Directly, that is to say, I took my pen in hand to review that novel by a famous man, she slipped behind me and whispered: "My dear, you are a young woman. You are writing about a book that has been written by a man. Be sympathetic; be tender; flatter; deceive; use all the arts and wiles of our sex. Never let anybody guess that you have a mind of your own. Above all, be pure." And she made as if to guide my pen. I now record the one act for which I take some credit to myself, though the credit rightly belongs to some excellent ancestors of mine who left me a certain sum of money—shall we say five hundred pounds a year?—so that it was not necessary for me to depend solely on charm for my living. I turned upon her and caught her by the throat. I did my best to kill her. My excuse, if I were to be had up in a court of law, would be that I acted in self-defence. Had I not killed her she would have killed me. She would have plucked the heart out of my writing. For, as I found, directly I put pen to paper, you cannot review even a novel without having a mind of your own, without expressing what you think to be the truth about human relations, morality, sex. And all these

3

questions, according to the Angel in the House, cannot be dealt with freely and openly by women; they must charm, they must conciliate, they must—to put it bluntly—tell lies if they are to succeed. Thus, whenever I felt the shadow of her wing or the radiance of her halo upon my page, I took up the inkpot and flung it at her. She died hard. Her fictitious nature was of great assistance to her. It is far harder to kill a phantom than a reality. She was always creeping back when I thought I had despatched her. Though I flatter myself that I killed her in the end, the struggle was severe; it took much time that had better have been spent upon learning Greek grammar; or in roaming the world in search of adventures. But it was a real experience; it was an experience that was bound to befall all women writers at that time. Killing the Angel in the House was part of the occupation of a woman writer.

But to continue my story. The Angel was dead; what then remained?   4 You may say that what remained was a simple and common object—a young woman in a bedroom with an inkpot. In other words, now that she had rid herself of falsehood, that young woman had only to be herself. Ah, but what is "herself"? I mean, what is a woman? I assure you, I do not know. I do not believe that you know. I do not believe that anybody can know until she has expressed herself in all the arts and professions open to human skill. That indeed is one of the reasons why I have come here—out of respect for you, who are in process of showing us by your experiments what a woman is, who are in process of providing us, by your failures and successes, with that extremely important piece of information.

But to continue the story of my professional experiences. I made one   5 pound ten and six by my first review; and I bought a Persian cat with the proceeds. Then I grew ambitious. A Persian cat is all very well, I said; but a Persian cat is not enough. I must have a motor car. And it was thus that I became a novelist—for it is a very strange thing that people will give you a motor car if you will tell them a story. It is a still stranger thing that there is nothing so delightful in the world as telling stories. It is far pleasanter than writing reviews of famous novels. And yet, if I am to obey your secretary and tell you my professional experiences as a novelist, I must tell you about a very strange experience that befell me as a novelist. And to understand it you must try first to imagine a novelist's state of mind. I hope I am not giving away professional secrets if I say that a novelist's chief desire is to be as unconscious as possible. He has to induce in himself a state of perpetual lethargy. He wants life to proceed with the utmost quiet and regularity. He wants to see the same faces, to read the same books, to do the same things day after day, month after month, while he is writing, so that nothing may break the illusion in which he is living—so that nothing may disturb or disquiet the mysterious nosings about, feelings round, darts, dashes and sudden discoveries of that very shy and illusive spirit, the imagination. I suspect that this state is the same both for men and women. Be that as it may, I want you to imagine me writing a novel in a state of trance. I want you to figure to yourself a girl sitting with a pen in her hand, which for minutes, and indeed for hours, she never dips into the inkpot. The image that comes to my mind when I think of this girl is the image of a fisherman lying sunk in dreams on the verge of a deep lake with a rod held out over the water. She was letting her imagination sweep unchecked round every rock and cranny of the world that lies submerged in the depths of our unconscious being. Now came the experience, the experience that I believe to be far commoner with women writers than with men. The line raced through the girl's fingers. Her imagination had rushed away. It had sought the pools, the depths, the dark places where the largest fish slumber. And then there was a smash. There was an explosion. There was foam and confusion. The imagination had dashed itself against something hard. The girl was roused from her dream. She was indeed in a state of the most acute and difficult distress. To speak without figure she had thought of something, something about the body, about the passions which it was unfitting for her as a woman to say. Men, her reason told her, would be shocked. The consciousness of what men will say of a woman who speaks the truth about her passions had roused her from her artist's state of unconsciousness. She could write no more. The trance was over. Her imagination could work no longer. This I believe to be a very common experience with women writers—they are impeded by the extreme conventionality of the other sex. For though men sensibly allow themselves great freedom in these respects, I doubt that they realize or can control the extreme severity with which they condemn such freedom in women.

These then were two very genuine experiences of my own. These were two of the adventures of my professional life. The first—killing the Angel in the House—I think I solved. She died. But the second, telling the truth about my own experiences as a body, I do not think I solved. I doubt that any woman has solved it yet. The obstacles against her are still immensely powerful—and yet they are very difficult to define. Outwardly, what is simpler than to write books? Outwardly, what obstacles are there for a woman rather than for a man? Inwardly, I think, the case is very different: she has still many ghosts to fight, many prejudices to overcome. Indeed it will be a long time still, I think, before a woman can sit down to write a book without finding a phantom to be slain, a rock to be dashed against. And if this is so in literature, the freest of all professions for women, how is it in the new professions which you are now for the first time entering? 6

Those are the questions that I should like, had I time, to ask you. And indeed, if I have laid stress upon these professional experiences of mine, it is because I believe that they are, though in different forms, yours also. Even when the path is nominally open—when there is nothing to prevent a woman from being a doctor, a lawyer, a civil servant—there are many phantoms and obstacles, as I believe, looming in her way. To discuss and define 7 them is, I think, of great value and importance; for thus only can the labour be shared, the difficulties be solved. But besides this, it is necessary also to discuss the ends and the aims for which we are fighting, for which we are doing battle with these formidable obstacles. Those aims cannot be taken for granted; they must be perpetually questioned and examined. The whole position, as I see it—here in this hall surrounded by women practicing for the first time in history I know not how many different professions—is one of extraordinary interest and importance. You have won rooms of your own in the house hitherto exclusively owned by men. You are able, though not without great labor and effort, to pay the rent. You are earning your five hundred pounds a year. But this freedom is only a beginning; the room is your own, but it is still bare. It has to be furnished; it has to be decorated; it has to be shared. How are you going to furnish it, how are you going to decorate it? With whom are you going to share it, and upon what terms? These, I think, are questions of the utmost importance and interest. For the first time in history you are able to ask them; for the first time you are able to decide for yourselves what the answers should be. Willingly would I stay and discuss those questions and answers—but not tonight. My time is up; and I must cease.

Martin Luther King, Jr.

More than thirty years after his assassination, Martin Luther King, Jr. (1929–68), is still recognized as the towering figure in the struggle for civil rights in the United States. Born in Atlanta, Georgia, King earned doctorates from Boston University and Chicago Theological Seminary and served as pastor of a Baptist congregation in Montgomery, Alabama. Advocating a philosophy of nonviolent resistance to racial injustice, he led bus boycotts, marches, and sit-ins that brought about passage of the 1964 Civil Rights Act and the Voting Rights Act of 1965. Dr. King was awarded the Nobel Peace Prize in 1964. The following two selections by King are taken from *Where Do We Go From Here: Community or Chaos?* (1967).

Where Do We Go From Here: Community or Chaos?

A final problem that mankind must solve in order to survive in the world 1
house that we have inherited is finding an alternative to war and human destruction. Recent events have vividly reminded us that nations are not reducing but rather increasing their arsenals of weapons of mass destruction. The best brains in the highly developed nations of the world are devoted to military technology. The proliferation of nuclear weapons has not been halted, in spite of the limited-test-ban treaty.

In this day of man's highest technical achievement, in this day of daz- 2
zling discovery, of novel opportunities, loftier dignities and fuller freedoms for all, there is no excuse for the kind of blind craving for power and resources that provoked the wars of previous generations. There is no need to fight for food and land. Science has provided us with adequate means of survival and transportation, which make it possible to enjoy the fullness of this great earth. The question now is, do we have the morality and courage required to live together as brothers and not be afraid?

One of the most persistent ambiguities we face is that everybody talks 3
about peace as a goal, but among the wielders of power peace is practically nobody's business. Many men cry "Peace! Peace!" but they refuse to do the things that make for peace.

The large power blocs talk passionately of pursuing peace while expand- 4
ing defense budgets that already bulge, enlarging already awesome armies

and devising ever more devastating weapons. Call the roll of those who sing the glad tidings of peace and one's ears will be surprised by the responding sounds. The heads of all the nations issue clarion calls for peace, yet they come to the peace table accompanied by bands of brigands each bearing unsheathed swords.

The stages of history are replete with the chants and choruses of the con-   5 querors of old who came killing in pursuit of peace. Alexander, Genghis Khan, Julius Caesar, Charlemagne and Napoleon were akin in seeking a peaceful world order, a world fashioned after their selfish conceptions of an ideal existence. Each sought a world at peace which would personify his egotistic dreams. Even within the life span of most of us, another megalomaniac strode across the world stage. He sent his blitzkrieg-bent legions blazing across Europe, bringing havoc and holocaust in his wake. There is grave irony in the fact that Hitler could come forth, following nakedly aggressive expansionist theories, and do it all in the name of peace.

So when in this day I see the leaders of nations again talking peace while   6 preparing for war, I take fearful pause. When I see our country today intervening in what is basically a civil war, mutilating hundreds of thousands of Vietnamese children with napalm, burning villages and rice fields at random, painting the valleys of that small Asian country red with human blood, leaving broken bodies in countless ditches and sending home half-men, mutilated mentally and physically; when I see the unwillingness of our government to create the atmosphere for a negotiated settlement of this awful conflict by halting bombings in the North and agreeing unequivocally to talk with the Vietcong—and all this in the name of pursuing the goal of peace—I tremble for our world.[1] I do so not only from dire recall of the nightmares wreaked in the wars of yesterday, but also from dreadful realization of today's possible nuclear destructiveness and tomorrow's even more calamitous prospects.

Before it is too late, we must narrow the gaping chasm between our   7 proclamations of peace and our lowly deeds which precipitate and perpetuate war. We are called upon to look up from the quagmire of military programs and defense commitments and read the warnings on history's signposts.

One day we must come to see that peace is not merely a distant goal that   8 we seek but a means by which we arrive at that goal. We must pursue peaceful ends through peaceful means. How much longer must we play at deadly war games before we heed the plaintive pleas of the unnumbered dead and maimed of past wars?

President John F. Kennedy said on one occasion, "Mankind must put an   9 end to war or war will put an end to mankind." Wisdom born of experience should tell us that war is obsolete. There may have been a time when war

---

[1]Only after more than 58,000 Americans had been killed did the United States withdraw from Vietnam. The war then continued until the North Vietnamese, aided by the Vietcong, took over all of Vietnam (editors' note).

served as a negative good by preventing the spread and growth of an evil force, but the destructive power of modern weapons eliminates even the possibility that war may serve any good at all. If we assume that life is worth living and that man has a right to survive, then we must find an alternative to war. In a day when vehicles hurtle through outer space and guided ballistic missiles carve highways of death through the stratosphere, no nation can claim victory in war. A so-called limited war will leave little more than a calamitous legacy of human suffering, political turmoil and spiritual disillusionment. A world war will leave only smoldering ashes as mute testimony of a human race whose folly led inexorably to ultimate death. If modern man continues to flirt unhesitatingly with war, he will transform his earthly habitat into an inferno such as even the mind of Dante[2] could not imagine.

Therefore I suggest that the philosophy and strategy of nonviolence become immediately a subject for study and for serious experimentation in every field of human conflict, by no means excluding the relations between nations. It is, after all, nation-states which make war, which have produced the weapons that threaten the survival of mankind and which are both genocidal and suicidal in character.   10

We have ancient habits to deal with, vast structures of power, indescribably complicated problems to solve. But unless we abdicate our humanity altogether and succumb to fear and impotence in the presence of the weapons we have ourselves created, it is as possible and as urgent to put an end to war and violence between nations as it is to put an end to poverty and racial injustice.   11

The United Nations is a gesture in the direction of nonviolence on a world scale. There, at least, states that oppose one another have sought to do so with words instead of with weapons. But true nonviolence is more than the absence of violence. It is the persistent and determined application of peaceable power to offenses against the community—in this case the world community. As the United Nations moves ahead with the giant tasks confronting it, I would hope that it would earnestly examine the uses of nonviolent direct action.   12

I do not minimize the complexity of the problems that need to be faced in achieving disarmament and peace. But I am convinced that we shall not have the will, the courage and the insight to deal with such matters unless in this field we are prepared to undergo a mental and spiritual re-evaluation, a change of focus which will enable us to see that the things that seem most real and powerful are indeed now unreal and have come under sentence of death. We need to make a supreme effort to generate the readiness, indeed the eagerness, to enter into the new world which is now possible, "the city which hath foundation, whose Building and Maker is God."   13

---

[2]In *The Divine Comedy* (1321), Italian poet Dante depicts the burning torments of hell endured by a lost soul before it can attain salvation (editors' note).

It is not enough to say, "We must not wage war." It is necessary to love   14
peace and sacrifice for it. We must concentrate not merely on the eradication
of war but on the affirmation of peace. A fascinating story about Ulysses and
the Sirens[3] is preserved for us in Greek literature. The Sirens had the ability
to sing so sweetly that sailors could not resist steering toward their island.
Many ships were lured upon the rocks, and men forgot home, duty and honor
as they flung themselves into the sea to be embraced by arms that drew them
down to death. Ulysses, determined not to succumb to the Sirens, first decided to tie himself tightly to the mast of his boat and his crew stuffed their ears
with wax. But finally he and his crew learned a better way to save themselves:
They took on board the beautiful singer Orpheus, whose melodies were
sweeter than the music of the Sirens. When Orpheus sang, who would bother
to listen to the Sirens?

So we must see that peace represents a sweeter music, a cosmic melody   15
that is far superior to the discords of war. Somehow we must transform the
dynamics of the world power struggle from the nuclear arms race, which no
one can win, to a creative contest to harness man's genius for the purpose of
making peace and prosperity a reality for all the nations of the world. In
short, we must shift the arms race into a "peace race." If we have the will and
determination to mount such a peace offensive, we will unlock hitherto
tightly sealed doors of hope and bring new light into the dark chambers of
pessimism.

[3]Ulysses and the Sirens, as well as Orpheus (mentioned later in the paragraph), are all figures in
Greek mythology (editors' note).

Martin Luther King, Jr.

The World House

Some years ago a famous novelist died. Among his papers was found a list   1
of suggested plots for future stories, the most prominently underscored being
this one: "A widely separated family inherits a house in which they have to live
together." This is the great new problem of mankind. We have inherited a
large house, a great "world house" in which we have to live together—black
and white, Easterner and Westerner, Gentile and Jew, Catholic and Protes-
tant, Moslem and Hindu—a family unduly separated in ideas, culture and
interest, who, because we can never again live apart, must learn somehow to
live with each other in peace.

However deeply American Negroes are caught in the struggle to be at last   2
at home in our homeland of the United States, we cannot ignore the larger
world house in which we are also dwellers. Equality with whites will not solve
the problems of either whites or Negroes if it means equality in a world society stricken by poverty and in a universe doomed to extinction by war.

All inhabitants of the globe are now neighbors. This worldwide neigh-   3
borhood has been brought into being largely as a result of the modern scientific and technological revolutions. The world of today is vastly different from
the world of just one hundred years ago. A century ago Thomas Edison had
not yet invented the incandescent lamp to bring light to many dark places of
the earth. The Wright brothers had not yet invented that fascinating mechanical bird that would spread its gigantic wings across the skies and soon dwarf
distance and place time in the service of man. Einstein had not yet challenged
an axiom and the theory of relativity had not yet been posited.

Human beings, searching a century ago as now for better understand-   4
ing, had no television, no radios, no telephones and no motion pictures
through which to communicate. Medical science had not yet discovered the
wonder drugs to end many dread plagues and diseases. One hundred years
ago military men had not yet developed the terrifying weapons of warfare
that we know today—not the bomber, an airborne fortress raining down
death; nor napalm, that burner of all things and flesh in its path. A century
ago there were no skyscraping buildings to kiss the stars and no gargantuan

bridges to span the waters. Science had not yet peered into the unfathomable ranges of interstellar space, nor had it penetrated oceanic depths. All these new inventions, these new ideas, these sometimes fascinating and sometimes frightening developments came later. Most of them have come within the past sixty years, sometimes with agonizing slowness, more characteristically with bewildering speed, but always with enormous significance for our future.

The years ahead will see a continuation of the same dramatic develop-   5
ments. Physical science will carve new highways through the stratosphere. In a few years astronauts and cosmonauts will probably walk comfortably across the uncertain pathways of the moon. In two or three years it will be possible, because of the new supersonic jets, to fly from New York to London in two and one-half hours. In the years ahead medical science will greatly prolong the lives of men by finding a cure for cancer and deadly heart ailments. Automation and cybernation will make it possible for working people to have undreamed-of amounts of leisure time. All this is a dazzling picture of the furniture, the workshop, the spacious rooms, the new decorations and the architectural pattern of the large world house in which we are living.

Along with the scientific and technological revolution, we have also wit-   6
nessed a worldwide freedom revolution over the last few decades. The present upsurge of the Negro people of the United States grows out of a deep and passionate determination to make freedom and equality a reality "here" and "now." In one sense the civil rights movement in the United States is a special American phenomenon which must be understood in the light of American history and dealt with in terms of the American situation. But on another and more important level, what is happening in the United States today is a significant part of a world development.

We live in a day, said the philosopher Alfred North Whitehead, "when   7
civilization is shifting its basic outlook; a major turning point in history where the presuppositions on which society is structured are being analyzed, sharply challenged, and profoundly changed." What we are seeing now is a freedom explosion, the realization of "an idea whose time has come," to use Victor Hugo's[1] phrase. The deep rumbling of discontent that we hear today is the thunder of disinherited masses, rising from dungeons of oppression to the bright hills of freedom. In one majestic chorus the rising masses are singing, in the words of our freedom song, "Ain't gonna let nobody turn us around." All over the world like a fever, freedom is spreading in the widest liberation movement in history. The great masses of people are determined to end the exploitation of their races and lands. They are awake and moving toward their goal like a tidal wave. You can hear them rumbling in every village street, on the docks, in the houses, among the students, in the churches and at political meetings. For several centuries the direction of history flowed from the nations and societies of Western Europe out into the rest of

[1]Victor Hugo (1802–85) was a French poet, dramatist, and novelist (editors' note).

the world in "conquests" of various sorts. That period, the era of colonialism, is at an end. East is moving West. The earth is being redistributed. Yes, we are "shifting our basic outlooks."

These developments should not surprise any student of history. Oppressed   8
people cannot remain oppressed forever. The yearning for freedom eventually manifests itself. The Bible tells the thrilling story of how Moses stood in Pharaoh's court centuries ago and cried, "Let my people go." This was an opening chapter in a continuing story. The present struggle in the United States is a later chapter in the same story. Something within has reminded the Negro of his birthright of freedom, and something without has reminded him that it can be gained. Consciously or unconsciously, he has been caught up by the spirit of the times, and with his black brothers of Africa and his brown and yellow brothers in Asia, South America and the Caribbean, the United States Negro is moving with a sense of great urgency toward the promised land of racial justice.

Nothing could be more tragic than for men to live in these revolutionary   9
times and fail to achieve the new attitudes and the new mental outlooks that the new situation demands. In Washington Irving's familiar story of Rip Van Winkle, the one thing that we usually remember is that Rip slept twenty years. There is another important point, however, that is almost always overlooked. It was the sign on the inn in the little town on the Hudson from which Rip departed and scaled the mountain for his long sleep. When he went up, the sign had a picture of King George III of England. When he came down, twenty years later, the sign had a picture of George Washington. As he looked at the picture of the first President of the United States, Rip was confused, flustered and lost. He knew not who Washington was. The most striking thing about this story is not that Rip slept twenty years, but that he slept through a revolution that would alter the course of human history.

One of the great liabilities of history is that all too many people fail to   10
remain awake through great periods of social change. Every society has its protectors of the status quo and its fraternities of the indifferent who are notorious for sleeping through revolutions. But today our very survival depends on our ability to stay awake, to adjust to new ideas, to remain vigilant and to face the challenge of change. The large house in which we live demands that we transform this worldwide neighborhood into a worldwide brotherhood. Together we must learn to live as brothers or together we will be forced to perish as fools.

We must work passionately and indefatigably to bridge the gulf between   11
our scientific progress and our moral progress. One of the great problems of mankind is that we suffer from a poverty of the spirit which stands in glaring contrast to our scientific and technological abundance. The richer we have become materially, the poorer we have become morally and spiritually.

Every man lives in two realms, the internal and the external. The internal   12
is that realm of spiritual ends expressed in art, literature, morals, and religion.

The external is that complex of devices, techniques, mechanisms, and instrumentalities by means of which we live. Our problem today is that we have allowed the internal to become lost in the external. We have allowed the means by which we live to outdistance the ends for which we live. So much of modern life can be summarized in that suggestive phrase of Thoreau:[2] "Improved means to an unimproved end." This is the serious predicament, the deep and haunting problem, confronting modern man. Enlarged material powers spell enlarged peril if there is not proportionate growth of the soul. When the external of man's nature subjugates the internal, dark storm clouds begin to form.

Western civilization is particularly vulnerable at this moment, for our   1.
material abundance has brought us neither peace of mind nor serenity of spirit. An Asian writer has portrayed our dilemma in candid terms:

> You call your thousand material devices "labor-saving machinery," yet you are forever "busy." With the multiplying of your machinery you grow increasingly fatigued, anxious, nervous, dissatisfied. Whatever you have, you want more; and wherever you are you want to go somewhere else . . . your devices are neither time-saving nor soul-saving machinery. They are so many sharp spurs which urge you on to invent more machinery and to do more business.

This tells us something about our civilization that cannot be cast aside   1.
as a prejudiced charge by an Eastern thinker who is jealous of Western prosperity. We cannot escape the indictment.

This does not mean that we must turn back the clock of scientific prog-   1.
ress. No one can overlook the wonders that science has wrought for our lives. The automobile will not abdicate in favor of the horse and buggy, or the train in favor of the stagecoach, or the tractor in favor of the hand plow, or the scientific method in favor of ignorance and superstition. But our moral and spiritual "lag" must be redeemed. When scientific power outruns moral power, we end up with guided missiles and misguided men. When we foolishly minimize the internal of our lives and maximize the external, we sign the warrant for our own day of doom.

Our hope for creative living in this world house that we have inherited   1.
lies in our ability to reestablish the moral ends of our lives in personal character and social justice. Without this spiritual and moral reawakening we shall destroy ourselves in the misuse of our own instruments.

---

[2]Henry David Thoreau (1817–62) was an American philosopher and essayist (editors' note).

Joan Didion

Known for her taut prose style and sharp social commentary, Joan Didion (1934–) graduated from the University of California at Berkeley. Her essays have appeared in the *Saturday Evening Post,* the *American Scholar,* and the *National Review,* as well as in three collections: *Slouching Towards Bethlehem* (1969), *The White Album* (1979), and *After Henry* (1992). *Salvador* (1983) is a book-length essay about a 1982 visit to Central America. The coauthor of several screenplays (including *A Star Is Born* in 1976 and *Up Close and Personal* in 1996), Didion has also written novels, including *Run River* (1963), *A Book of Common Prayer* (1977), *Democracy* (1984), *The Last Thing He Wanted* (1996), and *Where I Was From* (2003), as well as *Fixed Ideas: America Since 9.11* (2003), a book of political commentary. Most recently, Didion published *The Year of Magical Thinking* (2005), a memoir. "The Santa Ana" and "Marrying Absurd" are both from *Slouching Towards Bethlehem.*

The Santa Ana

There is something uneasy in the Los Angeles air this afternoon, some unnatural stillness, some tension. What it means is that tonight a Santa Ana will begin to blow, a hot wind from the northeast whining down through the Cajon and San Gorgonio Passes, blowing up sandstorms out along Route 66, drying the hills and the nerves to the flash point. For a few days now we will see smoke back in the canyons, and hear sirens in the night. I have neither heard nor read that a Santa Ana is due, but I know it, and almost everyone I have seen today knows it too. We know it because we feel it. The baby frets. The maid sulks. I rekindle a waning argument with the telephone company, then cut my losses and lie down, given over to whatever is in the air. To live with the Santa Ana is to accept, consciously or unconsciously, a deeply mechanistic view of human behavior.

I recall being told, when I first moved to Los Angeles and was living on an isolated beach, that the Indians would throw themselves into the sea when the bad wind blew. I could see why. The Pacific turned ominously glossy during a Santa Ana period, and one woke in the night troubled not only by the peacocks screaming in the olive trees but by the eerie absence of surf. The heat was surreal. The sky had a yellow cast, the kind of light sometimes called "earthquake weather." My only neighbor would not come out

1

2

of her house for days, and there were no lights at night, and her husband roamed the place with a machete. One day he would tell me that he had heard a trespasser, the next a rattlesnake.

"On nights like that," Raymond Chandler[1] once wrote about the Santa Ana, "every booze party ends in a fight. Meek little wives feel the edge of the carving knife and study their husbands' necks. Anything can happen." That was the kind of wind it was. I did not know then that there was any basis for the effect it had on all of us, but it turns out to be another of those cases in which science bears out folk wisdom. The Santa Ana, which is named for one of the canyons it rushes through, is a *foehn* wind, like the *foehn* of Austria and Switzerland and the *hamsin* of Israel. There are a number of persistent malevolent winds, perhaps the best known of which are the mistral of France and the Mediterranean sirocco, but a *foehn* wind has distinct characteristics: it occurs on the leeward slope of a mountain range and, although the air begins as a cold mass, it is warmed as it comes down the mountain and appears finally as a hot dry wind. Whenever and wherever a *foehn* blows, doctors hear about headaches and nausea and allergies, about "nervousness," about "depression." In Los Angeles some teachers do not attempt to conduct formal classes during a Santa Ana, because the children become unmanageable. In Switzerland the suicide rate goes up during the *foehn,* and in the courts of some Swiss cantons the wind is considered a mitigating circumstance for crime. Surgeons are said to watch the wind, because blood does not clot normally during a *foehn.* A few years ago an Israeli physicist discovered that not only during such winds, but for the ten or twelve hours which precede them, the air carries an unusually high ratio of positive to negative ions. No one seems to know exactly why that should be; some talk about friction and others suggest solar disturbances. In any case the positive ions are there, and what an excess of positive ions does, in the simplest terms, is make people unhappy. One cannot get much more mechanistic than that.

Easterners commonly complain that there is no "weather" at all in Southern California, that the days and the seasons slip by relentlessly, numbingly bland. That is quite misleading. In fact the climate is characterized by infrequent but violent extremes: two periods of torrential subtropical rains which continue for weeks and wash out the hills and send subdivisions sliding toward the sea; about twenty scattered days a year of the Santa Ana, which, with its incendiary dryness, invariably means fire. At the first prediction of a Santa Ana, the Forest Service flies men and equipment from northern California into the southern forests, and the Los Angeles Fire Department cancels its ordinary non-firefighting routines. The Santa Ana caused Malibu to burn the way it did in 1956, and Bel Air in 1961, and Santa Barbara in 1964. In

[1]Raymond Chandler (1888–1959) was an American novelist, best known for his detective novels featuring the character of Philip Marlowe (editors' note).

the winter of 1966–67 eleven men were killed fighting a Santa Ana fire that spread through the San Gabriel Mountains.

Just to watch the front-page news out of Los Angeles during a Santa Ana is to get very close to what it is about the place. The longest single Santa Ana period in recent years was in 1957, and it lasted not the usual three or four days but fourteen days, from November 21 until December 4. On the first day 25,000 acres of the San Gabriel Mountains were burning, with gusts reaching 100 miles an hour. In town, the wind reached Force 12, or hurricane force, on the Beaufort Scale; oil derricks were toppled and people ordered off the downtown streets to avoid injury from flying objects. On November 22 the fire in the San Gabriels was out of control. On November 24 six people were killed in automobile accidents, and by the end of the week the Los Angeles *Times* was keeping a box score of traffic deaths. On November 26 a prominent Pasadena attorney, depressed about money, shot and killed his wife, their two sons, and himself. On November 27 a South Gate divorcée, twenty-two, was murdered and thrown from a moving car. On November 30 the San Gabriel fire was still out of control, and the wind in town was blowing eighty miles an hour. On the first day of December four people died violently, and on the third the wind began to break.

It is hard for people who have not lived in Los Angeles to realize how radically the Santa Ana figures in the local imagination. The city burning is Los Angeles's deepest image of itself: Nathanael West perceived that, in *The Day of the Locust;* and at the time of the 1965 Watts riots what struck the imagination most indelibly were the fires.[2] For days one could drive the Harbor Freeway and see the city on fire, just as we had always known it would be in the end. Los Angeles weather is the weather of catastrophe, of apocalypse, and, just as the reliably long and bitter winters of New England determine the way life is lived there, so the violence and the unpredictability of the Santa Ana affect the entire quality of life in Los Angeles, accentuate its impermanence, its unreliability. The wind shows us how close to the edge we are.

[2]Set in Hollywood, West's 1939 novel, *The Day of the Locust,* ends with a description of Los Angeles engulfed in flames. In 1965, the Watts section of Los Angeles experienced widespread riots, leaving much of the area devastated by fire (editors' note).

Joan Didion

Marrying Absurd

To be married in Las Vegas, Clark County, Nevada, a bride must swear 1
that she is eighteen or has parental permission and a bridegroom that he is
twenty-one or has parental permission. Someone must put up five dollars for
the license. (On Sundays and holidays, fifteen dollars. The Clark County
Courthouse issues marriage licenses at any time of the day or night except
between noon and one in the afternoon, between eight and nine in the
evening, and between four and five in the morning.) Nothing else is required.
The State of Nevada, alone among these United States, demands neither a
premarital blood test nor a waiting period before or after the issuance of a
marriage license. Driving in across the Mojave from Los Angeles, one sees
the signs way out on the desert, looming up from that moonscape of rattle-
snakes and mesquite, even before the Las Vegas lights appear like a mirage on
the horizon: "GETTING MARRIED? Free License Information First Strip Exit."
Perhaps the Las Vegas wedding industry achieved its peak operational efficiency between 9:00 P.M. and midnight of August 26, 1965, an otherwise
unremarkable Thursday which happened to be, by Presidential order,[1] the last
day on which anyone could improve his draft status merely by getting married. One hundred and seventy-one couples were pronounced man and wife
in the name of Clark County and the State of Nevada that night, sixty-seven
of them by a single justice of the peace, Mr. James A. Brennan. Mr. Brennan
did one wedding at the Dunes and the other sixty-six in his office, and
charged each couple eight dollars. Once bride lent her veil to six others. "I
got it down from five to three minutes," Mr. Brennan said later of his feat.
"I could've married them *en masse,* but they're people, not cattle. People
expect more when they get married."

What people who get married in Las Vegas actually do expect—what, in 2
the largest sense, their "expectations" are—strikes one as a curious and self-
contradictory business. Las Vegas is the most extreme and allegorical of

[1]Refers to a declaration made by President Lyndon Johnson regarding the draft for the Vietnam
conflict (editors' note).

American settlements, bizarre and beautiful in its venality and in its devotion to immediate gratification, a place the tone of which is set by mobsters and call girls and ladies' room attendants with amyl nitrite poppers[2] in their uniform pockets. Almost everyone notes that there is no "time" in Las Vegas, no night and no day and no past and no future (no Las Vegas casino, however, has taken the obliteration of the ordinary time sense quite so far as Harold's Club in Reno, which for a while issued, at odd intervals in the day and night, mimeographed "bulletins" carrying news from the world outside); neither is there any logical sense of where one is. One is standing on a highway in the middle of a vast hostile desert looking at an eighty-foot sign which blinks "STARDUST" or "CAESAR'S PALACE." Yes, but what does that explain? This geographical implausibility reinforces the sense that what happens there has no connection with "real" life; Nevada cities like Reno and Carson City are ranch towns, Western towns, places behind which there is some historical imperative. But Las Vegas seems to exist only in the eye of the beholder. All of which makes it an extraordinarily stimulating and interesting place, but an odd one in which to want to wear a candlelight satin Priscilla of Boston wedding dress with Chantilly lace insets, tapered sleeves and a detachable modified train.

And yet the Las Vegas wedding business seems to appeal to precisely that impulse. "Sincere and Dignified Since 1954," one wedding chapel advertises. There are nineteen such wedding chapels in Las Vegas, intensely competitive, each offering better, faster, and, by implication, more sincere services than the next: Our Photos Best Anywhere, Your Wedding on A Phonograph Record, Candlelight with Your Ceremony, Honeymoon Accommodations, Free Transportation from Your Motel to Courthouse to Chapel and Return to Motel, Religious or Civil Ceremonies, Dressing Rooms, Flowers, Rings, Announcements, Witnesses Available, and Ample Parking. All of these services, like most others in Las Vegas (sauna baths, payroll-check cashing, chinchilla coats for sale or rent) are offered twenty-four hours a day, seven days a week, presumably on the premise that marriage, like craps, is a game to be played when the table seems hot. 3

But what strikes one most about the Strip chapels, with their wishing wells and stained-glass paper windows and their artificial bouvardia, is that so much of their business is by no means a matter of simple convenience, of late-night liaisons between show girls and baby Crosbys. Of course there is some of that. (One night about eleven o'clock in Las Vegas I watch a bride in an orange minidress and masses of flame-colored hair stumble from a Strip chapel on the arm of her bridegroom, who looked the part of the expendable nephew in the movies like *Miami Syndicate*.[3] "I gotta get the kids," the bride 4

---

[2]An illegal liquid drug, inhaled through the nose, that originally came in small capsules that would "pop" upon opening. Known for heightening sexual arousal, it also causes dizziness and sometimes a blackout (editors' note).

[3]The actual title is *The Miami Story*, a 1954 film about a group of citizens destroying a crime syndicate with the help of a reformed criminal (editors' note).

whimpered. "I gotta pick up the sitter, I gotta get to the midnight show." "What you gotta get," the bridegroom said, opening the door of a Cadillac Coupe de Ville and watching her crumple on the seat, "is sober.") But Las Vegas seems to offer something other than "convenience"; it is merchandising "niceness," the facsimile of proper ritual, to children who do not know how else to find it, how to make the arrangements, how to do it "right." All day and evening long on the Strip, one sees actual wedding parties, waiting under the harsh lights at a crosswalk, standing uneasily in the parking lot of the Frontier while the photographer hired by The Little Church of the West ("Wedding Place of the Stars") certifies the occasion, takes the picture: the bride in a veil and white satin pumps, the bridegroom usually in a white dinner jacket, and even an attendant or two, a sister or a best friend in hot-pink *peau de soie*, a flirtation veil, a carnation nosegay. "When I Fall in Love It Will Be Forever," the organist plays, and then a few bars of *Lohengrin*. The mother cries; the stepfather, awkward in his role, invites the chapel hostess to join them for a drink at the Sands. The hostess declines with a professional smile; she has already transferred her interest to the group waiting outside. One bride out, another in, and again the sign goes up on the chapel door: "One moment please—Wedding."

I sat next to one such wedding party in a Strip restaurant the last time I   5 was in Las Vegas. The marriage had just taken place; the bride still wore her dress, the mother her corsage. A bored waiter poured out a few swallows of pink champagne ("on the house") for everyone but the bride, who was too young to be served. "You'll need something with more kick than that," the bride's father said with heavy jocularity to his new son-in-law; the ritual jokes about the wedding night had a certain Panglossian character, since the bride was clearly several months pregnant. Another round of pink champagne, this time not on the house, and the bride began to cry. "It was just as nice," she sobbed, "as I hoped and dreamed it would be."

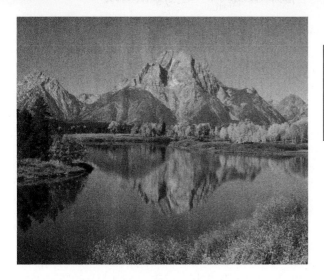

Appendix

A

A CONCISE GUIDE
TO FINDING AND
DOCUMENTING SOURCES

Many assignments in *The Longman Reader* suggest that you might want to do some research in the library and/or on the Internet. Such research enlarges your perspective and enables you to move beyond off-the-top-of-your-head opinions to those that are firmly supported. This appendix will be useful if you do decide to draw upon outside sources when preparing a paper. The appendix explains how to (1) use the library to find books, reference works, and periodicals on a subject; (2) research a topic using the Internet; and (3) document print and electronic sources.

USING THE LIBRARY TO FIND
BOOKS ON YOUR SUBJECT

To locate books on a specific topic, go to your college's *library catalog,* which lists all the books in the library. Although most college libraries have a *computerized catalog* of their book holdings, some use a *card catalog,* a list of alphabetically arranged cards in a series of drawers. Library technology is changing rapidly. With each passing year, a greater number of college (and local) libraries can be accessed online. That means that you can check—at any time of the day or night—a library's book holdings from your home or dorm computer.

Searching the Library Catalog
by Author, Title, or Subject

Whether you use your own computer to visit a library's holdings online or use the library's computerized (or card) catalog, you need to familiarize yourself with the three ways to look up a book: by author, title, or subject. To locate a specific book, you can do either an *author* or a *title search*. To search by author, look up the book under the author's last name; to search by title, use the first word in the title, or the second word if the first is *A*, *An*, or *The*. To identify books on a specific topic, do a *subject search*. Following are some strategies for searching a computerized catalog by subject. (If your library's holdings aren't computerized, it's easy to adapt the suggestions to card-catalog research.) For a subject search, type in a word or phrase that summarizes your topic. You may have to try several key terms to discover under which term(s) the computer lists sources on your topic. Assume you're conducting research to identify classroom strategies that undermine student success. You might start by typing the word "Education." But that word would probably yield so many possibilities that you wouldn't know where to start. You might narrow your search by entering "teaching techniques," "classroom practices," or "academic failure." For help in identifying appropriate key terms, speak with your college librarian. He or she will probably have you consult the *Library of Congress Subject Headings* or a bound or on-screen thesaurus of headings used in your library's database.

When you search for a book by subject, the screen usually indicates narrower subheadings under that topic. When you click on one of those subheads, a list of books on that subject will appear. To get complete bibliographic information about a specific book, follow the computer's instructions. The book's publisher, publication date, call number (see below), and so on will then appear on the screen. Most computerized catalogs also indicate the status of a book—whether it is available, on reserve, out on loan, overdue, lost, or available through an interlibrary loan system. (If all copies of the book are checked out, fill out a form to be notified when the book is returned.) On the next page is one college's computerized catalog display for a book on how bias in educational materials affects students' education.

Once the computer identifies books on your subject, you can copy down the authors, titles, and call numbers of promising books; or, in many libraries, you can direct the computer to print out a list. Mastering your library's computerized catalog enables you to identify in minutes sources that once might have taken you several hours to track down.

Locating Books in the Stacks

Most college libraries contain several floors of bookshelves (called *stacks*). There you'll find fiction, nonfiction, periodicals, microfilm and microfiche

Computerized card catalog display

Other subject headings to look under to find additional relevant books. The underlining indicates that these are links to related subjects in the computerized catalog.

AUTHOR:	**Noguera, Pedro**
TITLE:	**City schools and the American dream: Reclaiming the promise of public education**
PUBLICATION INFO:	**New York: Teachers College Press, 2003**
PHYSICAL DESCRIP:	**xvi, 189 p. ; 24 cm.**
SUBJECTS:	**Urban schools–United States.**
	Educational equalization–United States.
	School improvement programs–United States.

1. CALL NUMBER: LC5131.N64 2003—STACKS—Checked Out

2. CALL NUMBER: LC5131.N64 2003—STACKS—Available

Indicates the book's call number, location, and availability in the library. In this case, the library owns two copies, one checked out, the other available.

files, reserved books, government documents, reference works (see page 610), and special collections. To locate a book in the stacks, use its *call number* (a number used to classify a book and indicate its location in the library). The call number appears both in the catalog entry and on the spine of the book. There are two major systems of call numbers in use in the United States— the *Dewey Decimal* and the *Library of Congress*. Once you have a book's call number, consult a map or list (usually posted near the front desk) to see where in the library you'll find the book. For example, to track down Pedro Noguera's *City Schools and the American Dream,* you'd need to find where the library shelves books with the call number *LC5131.N64 2003.* If your library has closed stacks, make out a call slip, and a member of the staff will get the book for you.

USING THE LIBRARY TO FIND REFERENCE WORKS ON YOUR SUBJECT

Though they present highly condensed information, *reference works* can be helpful, especially in the early stages of your research. Some reference volumes cover a wide range of subjects (*Encyclopaedia Britannica* and the *World Almanac and Book of Facts*), while others are more specialized (*Mathematics Dictionary* and *Dance Encyclopedia*). Many reference volumes are available on CD-ROM or can be accessed online. Those that aren't are most likely arranged on library shelves alphabetically by subject ("Art," "Economics," "History"), which makes it easy to browse for useful reference volumes. Keep in mind that reference materials can't be checked out; you must consult them while in the library. The following box lists representative reference books found in most college libraries. Check with the librarian to see if any you're interested in are available electronically.

Representative Reference Works

Biography: *International Who's Who, Who's Who in America*

Business/Economics: *Dictionary of Banking and Finance, Encyclopedia of Economics*

Ethnic/Feminist Studies: *Encyclopedia of Feminism, Harvard Encyclopedia of American Ethnic Groups*

Fine Arts: *New Grove Dictionary of American Music, The New Harvard Dictionary of Music, The Oxford Companion to Art, The Thames and Hudson Dictionary of Art Terms*

History/Political Science: *Editorials on File, Encyclopedia of American Political History, Facts on File, A Political Handbook of the World*

Literature/Film: *The Oxford Companion to American Literature, The Oxford Companion to English Literature, World Encyclopedia of the Film*

Philosophy/Religion: *A Dictionary of Non-Christian Religions, The Encyclopedia of American Religions, An Encyclopedia of Philosophy*

Psychology/Education: *Encyclopedia of Education, Encyclopedia of Psychology, Encyclopedia of Special Education*

Science/Technology/Mathematics: *A Dictionary of Mathematics, Encyclopedia of Medical History, McGraw-Hill Encyclopedia of Science and Technology, The Merck Index of Chemicals and Drugs*

Social Sciences: *Dictionary of Anthropology, Encyclopedia of Crime and Justice, International Encyclopedia of the Social Sciences*

USING THE LIBRARY TO FIND ARTICLES ON YOUR SUBJECT

Periodicals are publications issued at intervals throughout the year. Generally, periodicals contain material that is more recent than that found in books or reference works. There are three broad types of periodicals: general, scholarly, and serious. Written for the average reader, *general periodicals* (daily newspapers and magazines such as *Time* and *Newsweek*) contain articles that provide background information rather than comprehensive coverage of a subject. Intended for readers with specialized knowledge, *scholarly publications* (such as the *Journal of Experimental Child Psychology* and the *Journal of Renaissance Drama*) provide in-depth analyses written by authorities in the field. Designed for well-educated laypeople rather than those having specialized knowledge, *serious publications* (for example, *Scientific American* and *Smithsonian*) develop subjects with less depth than scholarly publications.

Using Periodical Indexes, Abstracts, and Bibliographies

Periodical indexes are cumulative directories that list articles published in specific journals, newspapers, and magazines. (Major newspapers, such as *The New York Times*, publish their own directories.) Most periodical indexes list articles under subject headings. Beneath the headings, individual articles are organized alphabetically by authors' last names.

When you were in high school, you may have used the *Readers' Guide to Periodical Literature* or *InfoTrac*, which list highly accessible, general-interest articles published by popular newsstand magazines such as *U.S. News & World Report* and *Sports Illustrated*. The college equivalents of the *Readers' Guide* and *InfoTrac* are the *Humanities Index* and the *Social Sciences Index*. To locate articles appropriate for college-level research, you'll need to consult these indexes as well as those listing articles from more academic, professional, and specialized publications.

Some specialized indexes provide brief descriptions of the articles they list. These indexes are usually called *abstracts*. Examples are *Abstracts of Folklore Studies* and *Criminal Justice Abstracts*. Abstracts usually contain fewer listings than other types of indexes and are restricted to a limited field. In contrast to indexes that list only articles, *bibliographies* like the *Modern Language Association International Bibliography* list books as well as articles.

You shouldn't end your search for appropriate material until you've consulted the most pertinent indexes and bibliographies. For a paper on the psychology of child abuse, you might start with *The New York Times Index* and then move to more specialized volumes, such as *Psychological Abstracts, Child Development Abstracts,* and *Mental Health Book Review Index*. To ensure that you don't miss current developments in your subject area, start with the most recent years and work your way back.

Most college libraries offer computerized databases of the major periodical indexes, abstracts, and bibliographies. The databases, which group directories alphabetically by subject, can be accessed through the library's computer terminals—and often through a campus-wide computer network; this makes it possible for you to conduct part of your research from your own room. In most libraries, periodical databases are maintained in the same system as the computerized catalog for books. (If your school library isn't computerized, you'll probably find the periodical indexes located in the periodicals section, arranged alphabetically by title. Simply scan the shelves to find the index you want.)

The following box lists a small sample of the indexes, abstracts, and bibliographies found in most college libraries. Check with the librarian to see which can be accessed electronically.

Representative Indexes, Abstracts, and Bibliographies

General: *Academic Search FullTEXT, EBSCOhost, Humanities Index, InfoTrac Academic Index, Magazine Index Plus, National Newspaper Index, NewsBank, Readers' Guide to Periodical Literature, Social Sciences Index*

Arts/Literature: *Art Index, Book Review Digest, Film International Index, Modern Language Association (MLA) International Bibliography, Music Catalogue, The New York Times Book Review Index, Play Index*

Education: *Education Abstracts, Education Index, ERIC (Educational Resources Information Center)*

Ethnic/Feminist Studies: *Bibliography on Women, Black Studies Database, Ethnic Newswatch, Hispanic American Periodicals Index*

History/Political Science/Government: *Catalog of U.S. Government Publications, Historical Abstracts, Political Science Bibliographies, Public Affairs Information Service*

Philosophy/Religion: *Philosopher's Index, Religion Index*

Psychology/Sociology: *PsychArticles, SocioFile*

Sciences: *Applied Science and Technology Index, Biological Abstracts, Computer Database, Engineering & Applied Science Index, Environment Index, Health Index, Medline*

Whether a periodicals directory is in computerized or print form, you identify titles of relevant articles by looking under keywords that describe your subject. If you don't find your subject listed in a printed index, or if a computerized database yields no titles when you type in keywords, try alternate terms for your topic. Suppose you're researching the subject of business ethics. In addition to using "Business ethics" as keywords, you might try "Bribery" or "Fraud" to find relevant articles. Computerized and print indexes also show cross-references. By looking under "Business ethics," you might see suggested search terms such as "Advertising ethics," "Banking, ethical aspects," and "Commercial crime." In many libraries, the computer terminals at which you view database listings are hooked up to printers. So you can print out the listings rather than record them from the screen, or you can e-mail listings to yourself. Some online and CD-ROM databases offer access to the full text of selected articles or books. These texts may be read on screen and, if the computer terminal connects to a printer, printed out.

Below is an entry from the computerized database EBSCOhost. The entry gives all the information you need to track down the article in the library.

In the event of any puzzling abbreviations or symbols in computerized guides, ask your librarian either to explain their meaning or to direct you to a printed key for an explanation.

Locating a Specific Issue of a Periodical

If you don't have the option of printing out the text of relevant online articles, you'll need to obtain the original text. To do so, you have to determine whether the library owns the specific periodicals and issues you want. If your library catalogs its periodicals online, search for a periodical by typing in its name. Does that particular name appear on screen? If it does, your library owns issues of that publication. With a few additional keystrokes, you can obtain more detailed information—such as which issues of the periodical the library holds and their location in the library.

EBSCOhost entry

If your library doesn't catalog its periodicals online, look for a card catalog of holdings. The library probably has a separate periodicals card catalog in the periodicals section. Look up the periodicals by name. A periodical card will usually tell you the issues owned by the library and their location.

Recent issues of magazines, newspapers, and journals are kept in the library's periodicals section, where they are arranged alphabetically by title. Less current issues can be found in bound volumes in the periodicals section, in the stacks, or on microfilm. Usually, periodicals must be read in the library. Back issues of major newspapers are generally stored on microfilm filed in cabinets in a separate location.

USING THE INTERNET TO RESEARCH YOUR SUBJECT

Computer technology isn't, of course, limited to college libraries. It's everywhere. Nothing demonstrates the staggering impact of the computer revolution more powerfully than the growth of the Internet. This global network of interlinked computer systems puts a massive storehouse of information within the reach of anyone with access to a personal computer and an Internet connection. Such a wealth of material presents obvious research benefits to you as a student. However, when faced with the task of using the Internet, you may feel overwhelmed and unsure of how to proceed. The following pages will introduce you to the Internet, show you how to access its resources, and offer pointers on evaluating the material you find there.

The Internet is the catch-all term for the global network that links individual computers throughout the world. The *World Wide Web* refers to a global information system existing *within* the Internet. The Web consists of uncounted millions of *websites.* Some websites feature text only; others also contain graphics; still others include audio and video components. Although there's great variation in the content and design of websites, all contain a *home page* that provides the site's title, descriptive material about the site, and a menu consisting of *links* to the information that can be accessed at the site. A link is a stepping stone to other pages on the site or to a related website. You can jump from the first location to the next just by clicking on the link. (For more on links, see page 617.)

Accessing the Web

Access to the Web is provided through a software program called a *Web browser.* Internet Explorer, Netscape, and Apple Safari are several widely used browsers. If you attend one of the many colleges or universities providing Web access to students, you'll probably use one of these browsers. At these schools, you can do your research online by accessing the library's catalog of holdings, its databases, and other resources. If your school doesn't offer Web access and you have a computer and Internet connection at home, you can subscribe to a commercial online service, such as America Online or Earthlink, both of which have their own browsers.

The Advantages and Limitations of the Web

The World Wide Web offers a collection of data that surpasses anything else the world has seen. With the click of a mouse, you can read electronic versions of *The Washington Post* or *The Times of London;* you can check the temperature in Cairo or get up-to-the-minute stock quotes; you can read reviews of a best-selling novel or learn about alternative treatments for arthritis. Because the Web (unlike a library) *doesn't have a centralized organizational structure,* you're automatically—and somewhat haphazardly—exposed to this staggering array of material.

Keep in mind, too, that anyone—from Nobel Prize winners to members of extreme fringe groups—can post material on the Web at any time. Not surprisingly, then, the quality of information found on the Web ranges from authoritative to speculative to fraudulent. Unlike sources in the library, which may be dated or even no longer accurate, online material is generally up-to-date because it can be posted on the Web as soon as it's created (though, increasingly, online materials can also be outdated). Yet the instantaneous nature of Web postings can create problems. Library materials certainly aren't infallible, but most have gone through a process of editorial review before being published. This is often *not* the case with material on the Web. Given this basic limitation, it's not a good idea to rely solely on the Web when you research a topic. Consider using the Web as a supplement to, rather than a substitute for, library research. (For more about evaluating the currency and validity of material on the Web, see page 620.)

Using Online Time Productively

Whether you access the Web through a university service or a commercial provider, the following suggestions will help you use online time productively. First, just as you do when conducting library research (see pages 607–614), be sure to record accurate and sufficient information about your online source so you can provide full documentation when it comes time to write your paper. Specifically, be sure to record the material's title and date, as well as the date of your retrieval. You also need to copy the source's full *URL (uniform resource locator),* or Internet *address.* Here, for example, is the address for *The Boston Globe,* a newspaper: *www.boston.com.* Having the address makes it possible for you—and the reader of your research paper—to return to this page in the future. Type the address *exactly* as it appears on the website's home page. Don't capitalize something that originally was in lowercase letters, and don't leave extra space between elements in the address. Typing even slight changes in the address usually makes it impossible to access the site. Second, when you find a helpful website that you may want to visit again, use your browser's *Bookmark* or *Favorite Places* option. After you "bookmark" a site, its address is saved in your personal file, so you can click on its name and instantly return to the site, without having to remember (or type) its address.

Using the Internet to Find Books on Your Topic

Assume that you've used your library's computerized catalog to track down several books on your subject. Now you'd like to go online to see if there are additional books—especially brand-new or forthcoming releases— you might find helpful. In such a case, you could access the site of one or both of the following national booksellers: Amazon (at *www.amazon.com*) and Barnes and Noble (at *www.bn.com*). At either site, you would use the "Browse Books" feature on the bookseller's home page to identify relevant books. Let's say you want to investigate how the experience of childhood poverty affected the politics of certain American presidents. Using the "Browse Subjects" box on the Books page, you note that one of the subject listings is a term like "Biography." Clicking on that term, you see that one of the subcategories is a term like "Leaders and Notable People" or "Political Biographies." Click on the appropriate links as they appear, and eventually a list of books on American presidents appears. By clicking on specific titles from the list, you obtain information about each book, including reviewer and reader comments. With this information, you can usually determine which books are appropriate for your purpose. At that point, you check the availability of those books in the library or, if you wish, purchase them online.

Online booksellers can also help you narrow your topic. Perhaps you want to research the topic of illiteracy. As soon as you type the word "illiteracy" in the "Search" box on the bookseller's Books page, you receive a long list of books on the subject. Simply looking at the range of titles can help you narrow your research. You might, for example, decide to focus on illiteracy in the workplace, teenagers' declining reading scores, or programs that teach marginally literate parents how to read to their children.

Using the Internet to Find Articles and Other Materials on Your Topic

What do you do if you want to go online to track down articles, speeches, legislation, TV transcripts, and so on about your subject? How, given the array of online material, can you identify pertinent sources? Search directories and search engines will help.

Google directory page

Search Directories.   A *search directory*, a service that organizes websites by subject categories, will point you in the right direction. If you're not sure how to narrow your topic, seeing the search directory's categories may help you by identifying directions you wouldn't have thought of on your own. New search directories crop up regularly, but one of the most popular and user-friendly is Google. When you go to Google's home page and click on "More" and then "Even More," you will eventually get to a page where you can click on "Directory." That will take you to the Google Directory page, illustrated above. (Because websites change constantly, what appears on your computer screen may not be identical to what's shown here.)

As you see, Google divides websites into a number of categories: Arts, Business, and so on. Each category is presented as a *link* (see page 614). Typically, a link shows up as an underlined word or phrase that's a different color from the type elsewhere on the page. When you click on a link, you're automatically transported to a related site. There you're presented with a more focused list of websites to choose from. As you move from link to link, you go from the general topic to more specific aspects of the topic. For example, say you're researching how product recalls are communicated to consumers. You notice that there's a section titled "Consumers" under the category "Home." Click on "Consumers" and you're presented with a screen that lists several dozen consumer-related links, from "Advocacy and Protection" to "Travel." When you see the link "Recalls," you know you're on the right track. As soon as you click on "Recalls," links to related sites appear on screen. From those, you select the sites you think will be most useful in your research.

Search Engines.   Search directories are wonderful tools when you begin exploring your topic. But when you're refining your investigation, you'll want to use another kind of resource—the *search engine.* Search engines comb through the vast amount of information on the Web for sites that match your research needs. You activate a search engine by entering key words or phrases that tell the engine what to look for. Increasingly, search engines and search directories are combined, which makes it possible to access both from the site's home page. The following box lists some popular search directories and search engines and their addresses.

Popular Search Directories and Engines

About at *www.about.com*

AltaVista at *www.altavista.com*

Excite! at *www.excite.com*

Google at *www.google.com*

Lycos at *www.lycos.com*

Refdesk at *www.refdesk.com*

Yahoo! at *www.yahoo.com*

Tips for Using Search Engines.   When you reach the home page of a search engine, it's a good idea to click on the "Help" or "Tips" button. When you do, you'll receive specific guidelines for using that particular search engine efficiently. As you proceed, don't forget to "bookmark" (see page 616) the search engines you use so you can return to them easily at a later date.

If you look at a Google home page, you'll see that at the top, there's an empty box above the words "Google Search." That's where you enter in keyword(s) describing your research topic. After you click on "Google Search" (or whatever your search engine calls its "Search" command), the engine scans the Web for your keyword(s). It then provides you with a list of "hits," or links, to websites where your keyword is found. Most search engines also provide a brief description of each site.

The success of your search depends on how carefully you follow your search engine's guidelines and on how specific and descriptive your search terms are. For example, say you're doing research on college financial aid. Depending upon your search engine, if you simply enter the words *college financial aid* in the search box, the engine may provide a list of *every* document that contains the word *college* or *financial* or *aid*—hundreds of thousands of hits. To limit the number of hits you get, follow with great care your search engine's specific guidelines. If no guidelines are provided or if the guidelines are confusing, try the suggestions described below.

☑ FOCUSING A WEB SEARCH: A CHECKLIST

❑ Put quotation marks around the phrase you are searching for—in this case, "college financial aid." Many search engines interpret the quotation marks to mean you want only those documents that include the complete phrase *college financial aid*. If you don't include the quotation marks, you may receive listings for each word.

❑ To focus your search further, use the plus (+) and minus (−) signs, leaving no space before or after the signs. Say you're interested in college financial aid as it applies to grants. Try typing this in the search box:

"college financial aid" + grants

The + sign between *college financial aid* and *grants* instructs the search engine to locate items that contain both sets of keywords. A minus (−) sign has the opposite effect. If you want information about college financial aid, *excluding* information about grants, you would type your search phrase like this:

"college financial aid" − grants

❑ Use the Boolean[1] operative words AND, OR, and NOT to limit your search. When you investigate a topic via a search engine that recognizes Boolean logic (the search tips will indicate if it does, or you can experiment on your own as you type in search phrases), using these operatives between key terms broadens or narrows the range of your search. For example, assume you typed the following: reggae music AND Rastafarians AND Jamaica. Using the operative AND instructs the search engine to return only those documents containing all three search terms.

---

[1]Named for George Boole, a nineteenth-century mathematician, Boolean logic modifies search items through the use of the "operators" AND, OR, and NOT.

Evaluating Internet Materials

You need to take special care to evaluate the worth of material you find on the Web. Electronic documents often seem to appear out of nowhere and can disappear without a trace. And anyone—from scholar to con artist—can create a Web page. How, then, do you know if an Internet source is credible? The following checklist provides some questions to ask when you work with online material.

☑ EVALUATING INTERNET MATERIALS: A CHECKLIST

❑ Who is the author of the material? Does the author offer his or her credentials in a résumé or biographical note? Do these credentials qualify the author to provide reliable information on the topic? Does the author provide an e-mail address so you can request more information? The less you know about an author, the more suspicious you should be about using the data.

❑ Can you verify the accuracy of the information presented? Does the author refer to studies or to other authors you can investigate? If the author doesn't cite other works or other points of view, that may suggest the document is opinionated and one-sided. In such a case, it's important to track down material addressing alternative points of view.

❑ Who's sponsoring the website? Many sites are established by organizations—businesses, agencies, lobby groups—as well as by individuals. If a sponsor pushes a single point of view, you should use the material with great caution. Once again, make an extra effort to locate material addressing other sides of the issue.

❑ Is the cited information up-to-date? Being on the Internet doesn't guarantee that information is current. To assess the timeliness of Internet materials, check at the top or bottom of the document for copyright date, publication date, and/or revision date. Those dates will help you determine whether the material is recent enough for your purposes.

DOCUMENTING SOURCES

In Chapter 11, you learned the importance of *documentation*—giving credit to the print and electronic sources whose words and ideas you borrow in an essay (see page 485). That earlier discussion showed you how to document sources in informal papers. The following pages will show you how to use the documentation system of the Modern Language Association (MLA)[2] when citing sources in more formal papers.

The discussion here covers key features of the MLA system. For more detailed coverage, you may want to consult a recent composition handbook or the latest edition of the *MLA Handbook for Writers of Research Papers*. For a sample paper that uses MLA documentation, turn to the student essay on pages 501–506.

WHAT TO DOCUMENT

You may inadvertently fall into the trap of *plagiarizing*—passing off someone else's ideas as your own—if you're not sure when you need to acknowledge outside sources in an essay. To avoid plagiarism, you must provide documentation in the following situations:

- When you include *word-for-word quotations* from a source.
- When you *summarize or restate in your own words* ideas or information from a source, unless that material is *commonly known* or is a *matter of historical or scientific record*.
- When you *combine a summary and a quotation*.

An important note: On the whole, you should try to state borrowed material in your own words. A string of quotations signals that you haven't sufficiently evaluated and distilled your sources. Use quotations sparingly; draw upon them only when they dramatically illustrate key points you want to make. Also, keep in mind that quotations won't, by themselves, make your case for you. You need to interpret and comment on them, showing how they support your points.

HOW TO DOCUMENT

The MLA documentation system uses the *parenthetic reference,* a brief note in parentheses inserted into the text after borrowed material. The parenthetic reference doesn't provide full bibliographic information, but it presents enough so that readers can turn to the Works Cited list (see page 627) at the end of the paper for complete information. If the method of documentation

---

[2]MLA documentation is appropriate in papers written for humanities courses, such as your composition class. If you're writing a paper for a course in the social sciences (for example, psychology, economics, or sociology), your professor will probably expect you to use the citation format developed by the American Psychological Association (APA). For information about APA documentation, consult *The Longman Writer* or the most recent edition of the *Publication Manual of the American Psychological Association.*

you learned in high school involved footnotes or endnotes, you will be happy to know that parenthetic documentation—currently the preferred method—is much easier to use. While it is now accepted by most college professors, be sure to check with your professors to determine their documentation preferences.

Whenever you quote or summarize material from an outside source, you must do two things: (1) *identify the author* and (2) *specify the page(s)* in your source on which the material appears. The author's name may be given *either* in a lead-in sentence (often called the *attribution*) *or* in the parentheses following the borrowed material. The page number *always* appears in parentheses. The examples below illustrate the MLA documentation style and are based on the following excerpt from page 8 of Julian Stamp's book *The Homeless and History:*

> The key to any successful homeless program requires a clear understanding of just who are the homeless in our country. Since fifty percent of shelter residents have drug and alcohol addictions, programs need to provide not only a place to sleep but also comprehensive substance-abuse treatment. Since roughly one-third of the homeless population is mentally ill, programs need to offer psychiatric care, even institutionalization, not just housing subsidies. Since the typical head of a homeless family often lacks the know-how needed to maintain a job and a home, programs need to supply employment and life skills training.
>
> When we switch our focus to larger *economic* issues, we see that homelessness cannot be resolved solely at the level of the individual. Since the 1980s, the gap between the rich and the poor has widened, buying power has stagnated, jobs have fled overseas, and funding for low-cost housing has been almost eliminated. Given these developments, homelessness begins to look like a product of history, and only by addressing shifts in the American economy can we begin to find effective solutions.

Using Parentheses Only

Counseling and support services are not enough to solve the problem of homelessness; proposed solutions must also address the complex economic issues at the heart of homelessness (Stamp 8).

If we look beyond the problems of homelessness, to "larger economic issues, we see that homelessness cannot be resolved solely at the level of the individual" (Stamp 8).

Given the fact that a significant percentage of the homeless suffer from mental illness, "programs need to offer psychiatric care . . ., not just housing subsidies" (Stamp 8).

Using Parentheses and Attributions

Julian Stamp argues that homelessness must be addressed in terms of economics, not simply in terms of individual counseling, addiction therapy, or job training (8).

As Stamp explains, "The key to any successful homeless policy requires a clear understanding of just who are the homeless. . . ." (8).

Because half of those taking refuge in shelters have problems with drugs and alcohol, Stamp reasons that "programs need to provide not only a place to sleep but also comprehensive substance-abuse treatment" (8).

One historian points out that "homelessness cannot be resolved solely at the level of the individual" (Stamp 8).

According to statistics, half of the homeless individuals living in shelters are substance abusers (Stamp 8).

In The Homeless and History, Stamp maintains that economic issues, rather than difficulties in people's personal lives, are at the core of the homeless problem (8).

Glance back at the above examples and note the following:

- An attribution may specify the author's name (*Julian Stamp argues that; As Stamp explains*) or it may refer to a source more generally (*One historian points out; According to statistics*). If you want to call attention to a specific author, use an attribution indicating the author's name. Otherwise, use a more general attribution and a parenthetic citation that includes the name along with the page number (as in the fourth and fifth examples above).
- The first time an author is referred to in the text, the author's full name is provided; afterward, only the last name is given.
- When the author's name is provided in the text, the name is not repeated in the parentheses. (Later nonparenthetic references to the same author give only the last name.)

Sometimes, to inform readers of an author's expertise, you may identify that person by profession (*The historian Julian Stamp*). Don't, however, use such personal titles as *Mr.* or *Ms.* And as part of an attribution, you may mention your source's title (*In The Homeless and History, Stamp maintains that . . .*).

   When providing the necessary information, try to avoid such awkward constructions as these: "According to Julian Stamp, he says that . . ." and "In the book by Julian Stamp, he argues that . . ." Instead, follow these hints for writing smooth, graceful attributions. First, don't always place attributions at the beginning of the sentence; experiment by placing them in the middle (*The key to any successful homeless policy,* **Stamp explains,** *"requires a clear under-standing of just who are the homeless"*) or at the end (*Half of homeless individuals living in shelters are substance abusers,* **according to statistics.**) Second, try not to use a predictable subject-verb sequence (*Stamp argues that, Stamp explains that*) in all your attributions. Aim for variations like the following:

> The information compiled by Stamp shows . . .
>
> In Stamp's opinion, . . .
>
> Stamp's study reveals that . . .

Finally, rather than repeatedly using the verbs *says* or *writes* in your attributions, seek out more vigorous verbs, making sure the verbs you select are appropriate to the tone and content of the piece you're quoting. The boxed list that follows offers a number of options.

acknowledges	demonstrates	reports
adds	endorses	responds
admits	grants	reveals
argues	implies	says
asserts	insists	shows
believes	maintains	speculates
compares	notes	states
confirms	points out	suggests
contends	questions	wonders
declares	reasons	writes

Key Points to Remember

Take a moment to look again at the preceding examples and note the points presented in the following checklist.

☑ CITING SOURCES: A CHECKLIST

❑ The parenthetic reference is placed *immediately after* the borrowed material, at a natural pause in the sentence or at the end of the sentence.

❑ The parenthetic reference is placed *before* any *internal punctuation* (a comma or semicolon) as well as *before* any *terminal punctuation* (a period or question mark).

❑ If you want to call attention to a specific author, use an attribution indicating the author's name.

- ❏ When the author's name is provided in the attribution, the name is *not* repeated in the parentheses.
- ❏ The first time an author is referred to in an attribution, the author's *full name* is given; afterwards, only the *last name* is provided.
- ❏ Sometimes, to inform readers of an author's area of expertise, the person may be identified by profession ("the historian Julian Stamp argues that . . ."), title, or affiliation.
- ❏ When the author's name is provided in the parentheses, only the last name is given.
- ❏ The page number comes directly after the author's name. (If the source is only one page long, only the author's name is needed.)
- ❏ There is no punctuation between the author's name and the page number.
- ❏ There is no *p.* or *page* preceding the page number.
- ❏ Words may be deleted from a quotation as long as the author's original meaning isn't changed. In such a case, three spaced periods—called an *ellipsis* (. . .)—are inserted in place of the deleted words.[3] An ellipsis is not needed when material is omitted from the start of a quotation.

Three Other Important Points

Here are three additional situations you may encounter when documenting sources.

1. More than one source by the same author. When your paper includes references to more than one work by the same author, you must specify—either in the parentheses or in the attribution—the particular work being cited. You do this by providing the *title*, as well as the author's name and the page(s). As with the author's name, the title may be given in *either* the attribution *or* the parenthetic citation. Here are some examples:

In The Language and Thought of the Child, Jean Piaget states that "discussion forms the basis for a logical point of view" (240).

Piaget considers dialogue essential to the development of logical thinking (Language and Thought 240).

The Child's Conception of the World shows that young children think that the name of something can never change (Piaget 81).

---

[3]The 1999 edition of the *MLA Handbook for Writers of Research Papers* called for the use of brackets with ellipsis points. Earlier editions and the current require only the ellipses. Check with your instructors to see which guidelines they want you to follow.

Young children assume that everything has only one name and that no others are possible (Piaget, <u>Child's Conception</u> 81).

Notice that when a work is named in the attribution, the full title appears; when a title is given in the parenthetic citation, though, only the first few significant words appear. (However, don't use the ellipsis to indicate that some words have been omitted from the title; the ellipsis is used only in actual quotations.)

2. Long quotations.   A quotation extending beyond four typed lines starts on a new line and is indented ten spaces from the left margin throughout. Since this *block format* already indicates a quotation, quotation marks are not used. Double-space the block quotation, as you do the rest of your paper. Don't leave extra space above or below the quotation. Long quotations, which should be used sparingly, require a lead-in. A lead-in that *isn't* a full sentence is followed by a comma, while a lead-in that *is* a full sentence (as in the following example) is followed by a colon.

Stamp cites changing economic conditions as the key to a national homeless policy:

> Since the 1980s, the gap between the rich and the poor has widened, buying power has stagnated, jobs have fled overseas, and funding for low-cost housing has been almost eliminated. Given these developments, homelessness begins to look like a product of history, and only by addressing shifts in the American economy can we begin to find effective solutions. (8)

Notice that the page number appears in parentheses, just as in a short quotation. But in a long quotation, the parenthetic citation is placed one space *after* the period that ends the quotation.

3. Quoting or summarizing a source within a source.   If you quote or summarize a *secondhand source* (someone whose ideas come to you only through another source), you need to make this clear. The parenthetic documentation should indicate "as quoted in" with the abbreviation *qtd. in:*

According to Sherman, "Recycling has, in several communities, created unanticipated expenses" (qtd. in Pratt 3-4).

Sherman explains that recycling can be surprisingly costly (qtd. in Pratt 3-4).

Your Works Cited list would include the source you actually read (Pratt), rather than the source you refer to secondhand (Sherman).

LIST OF WORKS CITED

A documented paper ends with a list of Works Cited, which includes only those sources you actually acknowledge in the paper. Placed on its own page, the Works Cited list provides the reader with full bibliographic information about the sources cited in the parenthetic references (see pages 621–624). By referring to the Works Cited list that appears at the end of the student essay on pages 501–506, you will notice the following:

- The list is organized alphabetically by authors' last names. Entries without an author are alphabetized by the first major word in the title (that is, not *A, An,* or *The*).
- Entries are not numbered.
- If an entry runs longer than one line, each additional line is indented five spaces. Entries are double-spaced with no extra space between entries.

Sample Works Cited Entries

Listed here are sample Works Cited entries for the most commonly used kinds of sources. Refer to these samples when you prepare your own Works Cited list, taking special care to reproduce the punctuation and spacing exactly. If you don't spot an entry for the kind of source you need to document, consult the latest edition of the *MLA Handbook* for more comprehensive examples.

CITING BOOKS

Book by One Author

List the author's last name followed by a comma, the first name, and a period. Then give the title (underlined),[4] followed by a period, and city of publication, followed by a colon and the shortened version of the publisher's name (for example, use UP for "University Press" and Norton for "W.W. Norton & Co."). End with the year of publication and a period.

McDonnell, Lorraine M. Politics, Persuasion, and Educational Testing. Cambridge: Harvard UP, 2004.

---

[4] *Important note:* According to MLA guidelines, underlining titles is generally preferred to italicizing them because of the greater visibility of underlines; if you'd like to use italics instead, check with your instructor. (For a review of when titles should be underlined and when they should appear in quotation marks, see pages 645–646, the "Misuse of Italics and Underlining" section of Appendix B.)

Book by Two or Three Authors

Provide all the authors' names in the order they appear on the title page of the book, but reverse only the first author's name.

Douglas, Susan, and Meredith Michaels. The Mommy Myth: The Idealization of Motherhood and How It Has Undermined Women. New York: Free Press, 2004.

Gunningham, Neil A., Robert Kagan, and Dorothy Thornton. Shades of Green: Business, Regulation, and Environment. Palo Alto: Stanford UP, 2003.

Book by Four or More Authors

For a work by four or more authors, give only the first author's name followed by a comma and *et al.* (Latin for "and others").

Brown, Michael K., et al. Whitewashing Race: The Myth of a Color-Blind Society. Berkeley: U of California P, 2003.

Two or More Works by the Same Author

If you use more than one work by the same author, list each book separately. Give the author's name in the first entry only; begin the entries for other books by that author with three hyphens followed by a period. Arrange the works alphabetically by title.

McChesney, Robert W. The Problem of the Media: U.S. Communication Politics in the 21st Century. New York: Monthly Review, 2004.

- - - . Rich Media, Poor Democracy: Communication Politics in Dubious Times. Champaign: U of Illinios P, 1999.

Revised Edition

Indicate a revised edition (*Rev. ed., 2nd ed., 3rd ed., 4th ed.*, and so on) after the title.

Weiss, Thomas G., David P. Forsythe, and Roger A. Coate. The United Nations and Changing World Politics. 3rd ed. Boulder: Westview, 2001.

Zinn, Howard. A People's History of the United States: 1492–Present. Rev. ed. New York: Perennial, 2003.

Book With an Editor or Translator

Following the title, type *Ed.* or *Trans.*, followed by the name of the editor or translator.

Douglass, Frederick. My Bondage and My Freedom. Ed. John David Smith. New York: Penguin, 2003.

Anthology or Compilation of Works by Different Authors

List anthologies according to the editor or editors' names, followed by *ed.*

Kasser, Tim, and Allen D. Kanner, eds. Psychology and Consumer Culture: The Struggle for a Good Life in a Materialistic World. Washington, DC: American Psychological Association, 2004.

Section of an Anthology or Compilation

Begin this entry with the author and title of the selection (in quotation marks), followed by the title of the anthology. The editors' names are listed after the anthology title and are preceded by *Ed.* Note that the entry ends with the page numbers on which the selection appears.

Levin, Diane E., and Susan Linn. "The Commercialization of Childhood: Understanding the Problem and Finding Solutions." Psychology and Consumer Culture: The Struggle for a Good Life in a Materialistic World. Eds. Tim Kasser and Allen D. Kanner. Washington, DC: American Psychological Association, 2004. 212–28.

Section or Chapter in a Book by One Author

Wolfson, Evan. "Is Marriage Equality a Question of Civil Rights?" Why Marriage Matters: America, Equality, and Gay People's Right to Marry. New York: Simon & Schuster, 2004. 242-69.

Reference Work

"Temperance Movements." Columbia Encyclopedia. 6th ed. New York: Columbia UP, 2000.

Book by an Institution or Corporation

Give the name of the institution or corporation in the author position, even if the same institution is the publisher.

United Nations. Department of Economic and Social Affairs. <u>Human Development,</u>
  <u>Health, and Education: Dialogues at the Economic and Social Council.</u>
  New York: United Nations, 2004.

CITING PERIODICALS

Article in a Weekly or Biweekly Magazine

Provide the author's name (if the article is signed), article title (in quotation marks), periodical name (underlined and with *no* period), and date of publication, followed by a colon and page number(s) of the article.

Leo, John. "Campus Censors in Retreat." <u>U.S. News & World Report</u> 16 Feb.
  2004: 64-65.

Article in a Monthly or Bimonthly Magazine

Wheeler, Jacob. "Outsourcing the Public Good." <u>Utne</u> Sept.-Oct. 2004: 13-14.

Article in a Daily Newspaper

If the article is printed on multiple, nonconsecutive pages, simply list the first page (including both section and page numbers or letters) followed by a plus sign (+). (Note: Omit the initial *The* from newspaper names.)

Doolin, Joseph. "Immigrants Deserve a Fair Deal." <u>Boston Globe</u> 19 Aug. 2003:
  A19+.

Editorial, Letter to the Editor, or Reply to a Letter

List as you would any signed or unsigned article, but indicate the type of piece after the article's title.

Johnson, Paul. "Want to Prosper? Then Be Tolerant." Editorial. <u>Forbes</u> 21 June
  2004: 41.

"Playing Fair with Nuclear Cleanup." Editorial. <u>Seattle Times</u> 5 Oct. 2003: D2.

Article in a Scholarly Journal

Some journals are paged continuously; the first issue of each year starts with page 1, and each subsequent issue picks up where the previous one left off. For such journals, use numerals to indicate the volume number after the title, and then indicate the year in parentheses. Note that neither *volume* nor *vol.* is used. The article's page(s) appear at the end, separated from the year by a colon.

Manning, Wendy D. "Children and the Stability of Cohabiting Couples." Journal of Marriage & Family 66 (2004): 674-89.

For a journal that pages each issue separately, use numerals to indicate the *volume and issue numbers;* separate the two with a period but leave no space after the period.

Chew, Cassie. "Achieving Unity Through Diversity." Black Issues in Higher Education 21.5 (2004): 8-11.

CITING ELECTRONIC SOURCES

Article in an Online Periodical

For an article obtained online, supply the same information you would for printed text: author's name, selection's title, source, and (when available) publication date and page or paragraph numbers. When page or paragraph numbers are provided, list them after the date of publication (using *pp.* for "pages" or *par.* for "paragraphs").

Complete your listing with the date on which you accessed the material, followed by the exact address of the website (in angle brackets) and then a final period. (Since online material can be revised at any time, it's critical that you provide your date of access to identify the version you retrieved.) Note that long Web addresses should be broken up only after slashes.

Orecklin, Michele. "Stress and the Superdad." Time Online. 16 Aug. 2004. 19 May 2005 <http://www.time.com/time/magazine/article/ 0,9171,1101040823-682260,00.html>.

Nachtigal, Jeff. "We Own What You Think." Salon 18 Aug. 2004. 17 Mar. 2005 <http://www.salon.com/tech/feature/2004/08/18/evan_brown/>.

Article in a Full-Text Online Periodicals Index

For full-text articles accessed through an online index (generally only available to libraries by subscription), begin with the same information as for online periodicals. After the publication information (issue, date, and page numbers), list the title of the index (underlined), its vendor, and the library through which you gained access to it. Complete the entry with the date you accessed the index and the index's Web address.

Weiler, Angela M. "Using Technology to Take Down Plagiarism." Community College Week 16.16 (2004): 4-6. EBSCOhost. MasterFILE Premier. Camden County Lib., Voorhees. 17 Apr. 2005 <http://web5.epnet.com>.

Online Book

When it's available, include the book's original publication information between the book's title and the underlined database name. Also include (when available) the name of the site's editor, its electronic publication date, its sponsoring organization, your date of access, and the Web address.

Franklin, Benjamin. The Autobiography of Benjamin Franklin. London, 1793.
    Electronic Text Center. Ed. Judy Boss. 1995. U of Virginia Lib.
    16 Jan. 2005 <http://etext.lib.virginia.edu/toc/modeng/public/
    Fra2Aut.html>.

Online Reference Work

"Salem Witch Trials." Encyclopaedia Britannica Online. 2004. Encyclopaedia
    Britannica Premium Service. 8 June 2005 <http://www.britannica.com/
    ebc/article?eu=402856&query=salem%20witch%20trials&ct=>.

Professional or Personal Website

You'll note that in the second entry below, *Uncle Tom's Cabin* is *not* underlined. It's a title that would ordinarily be underlined, but since the rest of the website title is underlined, the book title is set off by a *lack* of underlining.

Finney, Dee. Native American Culture. 21 July 2003. 17 Feb. 2006
    <http://www.greatdreams.com/native.htm>.

Harriet Beecher Stowe's Uncle Tom's Cabin & American Culture: A Multi-Media
    Archive. Ed. Stephen Railton. 20 Jan. 2003. Dept. of English, U of Virginia.
    2 Apr. 2006 <http://www.iath.virginia.edu/utc/>.

Computer Software

Cite the following information (when available): author of the software, title (underlined), medium (CD-ROM or diskette), version, publication city, publisher, and year of publication.

World Book Encyclopedia 2004 Premier Edition. CD-ROM. 2004 ed. Renton:
    Topics Entertainment, 2004.

E-mail Message

Mack, Lynn. "New Developments in Early Childhood Education." E-mail to the
    author. 30 Aug. 2006.

CITING OTHER NONPRINT SOURCES

Television or Radio Program

"A Matter of Choice? Gay Life in America." <u>Nightline</u>. Narr. Ted Koppel. Part 4 of 5. ABC. WPVI-TV, Philadelphia. 23 May 2002.

Movie, Recording, Videotape, DVD, Filmstrip, or Slide Program

Provide the author or composer of the piece (if appropriate); title (underlined); director, conductor, or performer; medium; distributor; and year of release.

<u>Fahrenheit 911</u>. Dir. Michael Moore. 2004. DVD. Columbia Tristar, 2004.

Personal or Phone Interview

Langdon, Paul. Personal interview. 26 Jan. 2006.

Lecture

Blacksmith, James. "Urban Design in the New Millennium." <u>Cityscapes Lecture Series</u>. Urban Studies Institute. Metropolitan College, Washington, DC. 18 Apr. 2005.

Papa, Andrea. "Reforming the Nation's Tax Structure." Lecture. Accounting 302, Cypress College. Astoria, NY. 3 Dec. 2004.

AVOIDING TEN COMMON
WRITING ERRORS

Many students consider grammar a nuisance. Taking the easy way out, they cross their fingers and hope they haven't made too many mistakes. They assume that their meaning will come across, even if their writing contains some errors—perhaps a misplaced comma here or a dangling modifier there. Not so. Surface errors annoy readers and may confuse them. Such errors also weaken a writer's credibility because they defy language conventions, customs that readers expect writers to honor. By mastering grammar, punctuation, and spelling conventions, students can increase their power and versatility as writers.

This concise appendix, "Avoiding Ten Common Writing Errors," will help you brush up on the most useful rules and conventions of writing. It's organized according to the broad skill areas, listed below, that give writers the most trouble. (For more extensive instruction in grammar and style, refer to the Handbook section of *The Longman Writer.*) Throughout this appendix, grammatical terminology is kept to a minimum. Although we assume that you know the major parts of speech (noun, verb, pronoun, and so on), we do, when appropriate, provide on-the-spot definitions of more technical grammatical terms.

Here are the ten common writing errors covered:

1. Fragments
2. Comma Splices and Run-ons
3. Faulty Subject-Verb Agreement

4. Faulty Pronoun Agreement
5. Misplaced and Dangling Modifiers
6. Faulty Parallelism
7. Comma Misuse
8. Apostrophe Misuse
9. Confusing Homonyms
10. Misuse of Italics and Underlining

1 FRAGMENTS

A full *sentence* satisfies two conditions: (1) it has a subject and a verb, and (2) it can stand alone as a complete thought. Although a *fragment* is punctuated like a full sentence, it doesn't satisfy these two requirements.

NO   Meteorologists predict a drought this summer. *In spite of heavy spring rains.*

NO   *A victim of her own hypocrisy.* The senator lost the next election.

Some Easy Ways to Correct Fragments

A. Attach the fragment to the beginning or end of the preceding (or following) sentence, changing punctuation and capitalization as needed.

YES   In spite of heavy spring rains, meteorologists predict a drought this summer.
or
Meteorologists predict a drought this summer, in spite of heavy spring rains.

B. Attach the fragment to a newly created sentence.

YES   Meteorologists predict a drought this summer. *They do so* in spite of heavy spring rains.

C. Insert the fragment into the preceding (or following) sentence, adding commas as needed.

YES   The senator, *a victim of her own hypocrisy,* lost the next election.

D. Supply the missing subject and/or verb, changing other words as necessary.

YES   *The senator became* a victim of her own hypocrisy. *She* lost the next election.

2 COMMA SPLICES AND RUN-ONS

Consider the following faulty sentences:

> **NO**   The First Amendment cannot be taken for granted, it is the bedrock of our democracy.
>
> **NO**   The First Amendment cannot be taken for granted it is the bedrock of our democracy.

The first example is a *comma splice:* a comma used to join, or splice together, two complete thoughts, even though the comma alone is not strong enough to connect the two independent ideas. The second example is a *run-on,* or fused, sentence: two sentences run together without any punctuation indicating where the first sentence ends and the second begins.

Some Easy Ways to Correct Comma Splices and Run-ons

A. Place a period, question mark, or exclamation point at the end of the first sentence, and capitalize the first letter of the second sentence.

> **YES**   The First Amendment cannot be taken for *granted. It* is the bedrock of our democracy.

B. Use a semicolon to mark where the first sentence ends and the second begins.

> **YES**   The First Amendment cannot be taken for *granted; it* is the bedrock of our democracy.

C. Turn one of the sentences into a dependent phrase.

> **YES**   *Because* it is the bedrock of our democracy, the First Amendment cannot be taken for granted.

D. Keep or add a comma at the end of the first sentence, but follow the comma with a coordinating conjunction (*and, but, for, nor, or, so, yet*).

> **YES**   The First Amendment cannot be taken for granted, *for* it is the bedrock of our democracy.

3 FAULTY SUBJECT-VERB AGREEMENT

A verb should match its subject in number. If the subject is singular (one person, place, or thing), the verb should have a singular form. If the subject is plural (two or more persons, places, or things), the verb should have a plural form. Always determine the verb's subject and make sure that the verb agrees with it, rather than with some other word in the sentence.

NO   The *documents* from the court case *was* unsealed for the first time in three decades.

YES   The *documents* from the court case *were* unsealed for the first time in three decades.

Some Easy Ways to Correct Faulty Subject-Verb Agreement

A. When there are two or more singular subjects (joined by *and*) in a sentence, use a plural verb. (However, when the word *or* joins the subjects, use a *singular* verb.)

YES   A sprawling maple *and* a lush rose bush *flank* [not *flanks*] my childhood home.

B. When the subject and verb are separated by a prepositional phrase, be sure to match the verb to its subject—not to a word in the prepositional phrase that comes between them.

YES   The *quality* of student papers *has* [not *have*] been declining over the past semester.

C. When the words *either . . . or* or *neither . . . nor* connect two subjects, use the verb form (singular or plural) that agrees with the subject *closer* to the verb.

YES   *Neither* the employees *nor* the store *owner was* [not *were*] aware of the theft.

YES   *Neither* the store owner *nor* her *employees were* [not *was*] aware of the theft.

D. When using the indefinite pronouns *anybody, anyone, anything, each, either, everyone, everybody, everyone, everything, neither, nobody, none, no one, nothing, one, somebody, someone,* or *something,* use a *singular* verb.

YES   *Neither* of the candidates *is* [not *are*] willing to address the issue.

When you use the indefinite pronouns *all, any, most, none,* or *some,* use a *singular* or a *plural* verb, depending on whether the pronoun refers to one thing or to a number of things.

YES   The spokesperson announced that only *some* of the *report has* been confirmed.

In the preceding sentence, *some* refers to a single report and therefore takes a *singular* verb. In the following sentence, *some* refers to *multiple* reports and therefore takes a *plural* verb.

> YES   The spokesperson announced that only *some* of the *reports have* been confirmed.

E. When the subject of a sentence refers to a group acting as a unit, use a *singular* verb.

> YES   The local baseball *team is* [not *are*] boycotting the new sports stadium.

F. When words such as *here, there, how, what, when, where, which, who,* and *why* invert normal sentence order—so that the verb comes before the subject—look ahead for the subject and make sure that it and the verb agree.

> YES   There *is* [not *are*] a *series* of things to consider before deciding on a college major.
> YES   What *are* [not *is*] the *arguments* against energy conservation?

4 FAULTY PRONOUN AGREEMENT

A *pronoun* must agree in number with its *antecedent*—the noun or pronoun it replaces or refers to. If the antecedent is singular, the pronoun must be singular. If the antecedent is plural, the pronoun must be plural.

Some Easy Ways to Correct Faulty Pronoun Agreement

A. A compound subject (two or more nouns joined by *and*) requires plural pronouns.

> YES   Both the car *manufacturers* and the tire *company* had trouble restoring *their* reputations after losing the class-action lawsuit.

However, when the nouns are joined by *or* or *nor,* the pronoun form (singular or plural) should agree with the noun that is *closer* to the verb.

> YES   Neither the car manufacturers *nor* the tire *company* restored *its* reputation after losing the class-action lawsuit.
> YES   Neither the tire company *nor* the car *manufacturers* restored *their* reputations after losing the class-action lawsuit.

B. A subject that is a *collective noun* (referring to a group that acts as a unit) takes a singular pronoun.

YES   The *orchestra* showed *its* appreciation by playing a lengthy encore.

Or, if a singular pronoun sounds awkward, simply make the antecedent plural.

YES   The orchestra *members* showed *their* appreciation by playing a lengthy encore.

C. The indefinite pronouns *anybody, anyone, anything, each, either, everybody, everyone, everything, neither, nobody, no one, nothing, one, somebody, someone,* and *something* are singular and therefore take singular pronouns.

YES   *Each* of the buildings had *its* [not *their*] roof replaced.
YES   *Neither* of the executives resigned *his* [not *their*] position after the revelations.

Using the singular form with indefinite pronouns can be awkward or sexist when the pronoun encompasses both male and female. To avoid these problems, you can make the antecedent plural and use a plural pronoun.

AWK   *Anyone* who exhibits symptoms should see her or his doctor immediately.
YES   *Individuals* who exhibit symptoms should see *their* doctor immediately.

D. Within a sentence, pronouns should be in the same *person* (point of view) as their antecedents.

NO   To register to vote, *citizens* [third person] can visit the state government's website, where *you* [second person] can download the appropriate forms.
YES   To register to vote, *citizens* [third person] can visit the state government's website, where *they* [third person] can download the appropriate forms.

5 MISPLACED AND DANGLING MODIFIERS

A *modifier* is a word or group of words that describes something else. Sometimes sentences are written in such a way that modifiers are misplaced. Here is an example of a *misplaced modifier:*

NO   Television stations carried the story of the disastrous tornado *throughout the nation.* [The tornado was throughout the nation?]
YES   Television stations *throughout the nation* carried the story of the disastrous tornado.

Modifiers are commonly misused in another way. An introductory modifier must modify the subject of the sentence. If it doesn't, it may be a **dangling modifier.** Here's an example:

> **NO** *Faded and brittle with age,* archaeologists unearthed a painted clay pot near the riverbank. [The archaeologists were faded and brittle with age?]
>
> **YES** Archaeologists unearthed a painted clay pot, *faded and brittle with age,* near the riverbank.
> *or*
> *Faded and brittle with age,* a painted clay pot was unearthed near the riverbank by archaeologists.

An Easy Way to Correct Misplaced Modifiers

A. Place the modifier next to the word(s) it describes.

> **NO** Passengers complained about the flight at the customer service desk, *which was turbulent and delayed.* [The customer service desk was turbulent and delayed?]
>
> **YES** Passengers complained about the flight, *which was turbulent and delayed,* at the customer service desk.

> **NO** Because he repeatedly failed, the judge's son *almost* retook the bar exam ten times. [He nearly retook the exam but didn't actually do so at all?]
>
> **YES** Because he repeatedly failed, the judge's son retook the bar exam *almost* ten times.

Some Easy Ways to Correct Dangling Modifiers

The following dangling modifier can be corrected in one of two ways, discussed below.

> **NO** *Leaping gracefully across the stage,* spectators were in awe of the agile dancer.

A. Rewrite the sentence by adding to the modifying phrase the word that is being described.

> **YES** *As the agile dancer leaped* gracefully across the stage, spectators were in awe of him.

B. Rewrite the sentence so that the word being modified becomes the subject.

> **YES** Leaping gracefully across the stage, *the agile dancer awed* the spectators.

6 FAULTY PARALLELISM

Words in a pair or in a series should be phrased in *parallel* (matching) grammatical structures. Otherwise, *faulty parallelism* results.

NO	After hiking all day, the campers were *exhausted, hungry,* and *experienced soreness.* [Of the three items in the series, the first two are adjectives, but the last is a verb plus a noun.]
YES	After hiking all day, the campers were *exhausted, hungry,* and *sore.*

Words that follow *correlative conjunctions—either . . . or, neither . . . nor, both . . . and, not only . . . but also*—should also be parallel.

NO	Every road to the airport is **either** *jammed* **or** *is closed* for repairs. [The word *either* is followed by an adjective (*jammed*), but *or* is followed by a verb and adjective (*is closed*).]
YES	Every road to the airport is **either** *jammed* **or** *closed* for repairs.

An Easy Way to Correct Faulty Parallelism

A. Use the *same grammatical structure* for each item in a pair or series.

NO	The finalists for the sales job possess *charismatic personalities, excellent references,* and *they are extensively experienced.*
YES	The finalists for the sales job possess *charismatic personalities, excellent references,* and *extensive experience.*

NO	We knew that autumn was on its way because *the leaves were changing color, the sun was setting earlier,* and *there was a chill in the air.*
YES	We knew that autumn was on its way because *the leaves were changing color, the sun was setting earlier,* and *the air was becoming chillier.*

NO	The romantic comedy that premiered last night was neither *romantic* nor *was it funny.*
YES	The romantic comedy that premiered last night was neither *romantic* nor *funny.*

7 COMMA MISUSE

The *comma* is so frequent in writing that mastering its use is essential. By dividing a sentence into its parts, commas clarify meaning.

Most Common Uses of the Comma

A. When two complete sentences are joined with a coordinating conjunction (*and, but, for, nor, or, so, yet*), a comma is placed *before* the conjunction.

> YES   Many attended the political rally, *but* few demonstrated enthusiasm for the cause.

B. Introductory material, which precedes a sentence's main subject and verb, usually is followed by a comma.

> YES   *Like most kids,* the children in the study were powerfully influenced by TV advertisements.

Similarly, material attached to the *end* of a sentence may be preceded by a comma.

> YES   The children in the study were powerfully influenced by TV advertisements, *which peddled expensive toys and unhealthy snacks.*

C. When a word or phrase describes a noun but isn't crucial for identifying that noun, it is set off from the rest of the sentence with a comma.

> YES   First-year film students are required to analyze *Metropolis,* a late-1920s film that exhibited important artistic innovations.

D. When words or phrases inserted into the body of a sentence can be removed without significant loss of meaning, such elements are considered *interrupters*. Interrupters should be preceded and followed by commas when they occur midsentence.

> YES   Dr. Gene Nome, *a leading genetic researcher,* testified before Congress on the need for increased funding.

E. In a list of *three or more* items in a series, the items should be separated by commas.

> YES   The writing process usually entails *prewriting, drafting,* and *revising.*

F. A comma should be inserted between a short quotation and a phrase that indicates the quotation's source.

YES One voter commented, "This is the first candidate I've voted for enthusiastically."
or
"This is the first candidate I've voted for enthusiastically," one voter commented.
or
"This is the first candidate," one voter commented, "I've voted for enthusiastically."

G. Commas are placed between the numbers in a date and between the elements of the address with the exception that no comma precedes a zip code.

YES On November 17, 2006, the fourth graders mailed "Dear President" letters to The White House, 1600 Pennsylvania Avenue, Washington, DC 20500.

8 APOSTROPHE MISUSE

Like the comma, the *apostrophe* is a commonly used—and misused—punctuation mark.

Most Common Uses of the Apostrophe

A. In standard contractions, an apostrophe replaces any omitted letters.

YES can't, don't, I'm, she's, we've

B. The possessive form of most singular nouns requires adding *'s*.

YES Senator Ross's position is that health care is every person's right.

For *plural nouns* ending in *s,* an apostrophe only is added to show possession.

YES The twelve senators' position on Native Americans' rights is clear.

Plural nouns that do not end in *s* need *'s* to show possession.

YES Improvement in the children's test scores enabled the school to rise in rank.

However, an apostrophe is *not* used to form the simple plural of a noun.

NO The central role of *radio's* in American homes has declined in recent decades.

YES The central role of *radios* in American homes has declined in recent decades.

C. Beware of confusing possessive pronouns with contractions. The possessive forms of personal pronouns do *not* include an apostrophe. Here are the correct forms:

YES mine, yours, his, hers, its, ours, theirs

Note that *its* (*without* an apostrophe) is the possessive form of *it*, whereas *it's* (*with* an apostrophe) means "it is" or "it has."

YES The factory closed *its* [not *it's*] doors last week.

YES The company president determined that *it's* [for it *is*] time to close down the factory.

Similarly, *whose* (*without* an apostrophe) is the possessive form of *who*, whereas *who's* (*with* an apostrophe) means "who is" or "who has."

YES The sculptor *whose* [not *who's*] work is being exhibited just arrived at the gallery.

YES The sculptor *who's* [for *who is*] exhibiting his work just arrived at the gallery.

---

9 CONFUSING HOMONYMS

Homonyms are words that sound alike but have different spellings and meanings. Here are some of the most troublesome.

Accept means "receive" or "agree to." **Except** means "but" or "excluding."

YES *Except* for your position on mandatory school uniforms, I *accept* your ideas about changing the education system.

Affect means "influence" (verb). **Effect** means "result" (noun) or "bring about" (verb).

YES It's amazing how much a hurricane's *effects* can *affect* a region's economy.

Its means "belonging to it." **It's** means "it is" or "it has."

YES *It's* been years since the factory produced *its* last car.

Principal means either "main" or "the person in charge of a school." **Principle** means "a law or concept."

YES   The *principal* topic you should study for your midterm is the *principle* of gravity.

Than is a word used in comparisons. **Then** means "at that time."

YES   The insurance agent assessed the house and *then* wrote a report stating that the damage was worse *than* expected.

Their means "belonging to them." **There** refers to a place other than "here." **They're** means "they are."

YES   *They're* planning to drop off *their* donations for the food drive in the bin over *there*.

To can be part of a verb (as in *to smile* or *came to*) or a preposition meaning "toward." **Too** means "overly" (as in *too hot*) or "also." **Two** refers to the number 2.

YES   *Two* of my coworkers go outside *to* eat lunch every day; today they invited me, *too*.

Whose means "belonging to someone or something." **Who's** means "who is" or "who has."

YES   We're trying to determine *who's* going to call my aunt, *whose* son was injured in an accident.

Your means "belonging to you." **You're** means "you are."

YES   When *your* mother calls you by *your* first, middle, and last name, you know *you're* in trouble.

10 MISUSE OF ITALICS AND UNDERLINING

Computers and other printing innovations have allowed italics (*slanted type*) to replace underlining (underlined type) in printed text. The following are the most common uses of italics (or of underlining, if you're writing by hand or using a typewriter).

A. The titles of works that are published (or, in the case of visual works, displayed) individually should be italicized or underlined. Such works, which are often lengthy, include books, magazines, journals, newspapers, movies, TV programs, musical recordings, plays, paintings, and sculptures.

Note: The titles of shorter works—such as poems, short stories, articles, essays, songs, and TV episodes—published as part of a magazine, anthology, or other collection are *not* italicized; use quotation marks for such titles.

> YES   After reading Anne Sexton's poem "The Starry Night" from the collection *All My Pretty Ones,* the students went online to look at Van Gogh's painting *The Starry Night.*
>
> YES   The Discovery Channel program *The Beatles: The Later Years* focused primarily on the band's albums *Sgt. Pepper's Lonely Hearts Club Band* and *Abbey Road.*

B. Foreign words not fully incorporated into mainstream English should be italicized or underlined.

> YES   The labor union leaders sought a *tête-à-tête* with the company's executives in order to resolve a work strike.

C. Words that you wish to emphasize should be italicized or underlined. However, this should be done sparingly at the risk of actually *weakening* emphasis.

> YES   Users of the new computer program report that they don't like it. They *love* it.

D. When a word is being referred to *as a word* or as a *defined term,* it should be italicized or underlined.

> YES   When writing, avoid using a word like *conflagration* when *fire* will do.
> YES   The word *conflagration* actually means "fire."

GLOSSARY

Abstract and concrete language refers to two different qualities of words. Abstract words and phrases convey concepts, qualities, emotions, and ideas that we can think and talk about but not actually see or experience directly. Examples of abstract words are *conservatism, courage, avarice, joy,* and *hatred.* Words or phrases whose meanings are directly seen or experienced by the senses are concrete terms. Examples of phrases using concrete words are *split-level house, waddling penguin,* and *short pink waitress uniform.*

Adequate—see *Evidence.*

Ad hominem **argument**—see *Logical fallacies.*

Analogy refers to an imaginative comparison between two subjects that seem to have little in common. Often a writer can make a complex idea or topic understandable by comparing it to a more familiar subject, and such an analogy can be developed over several paragraphs or even an entire essay. For example, to explain how the economic difficulties of farmers weaken an entire nation, a writer might create an analogy between failing farms and a cancer that slowly destroys a person's life.

Argumentation-persuasion tries to encourage readers to accept a writer's point of view on some controversial issue. In *argumentation,* a writer uses objective reasoning, facts, and hard evidence to demonstrate the soundness of a position. In *persuasion,* the writer uses appeals to the emotions and value systems, often in the hope of encouraging readers to take a specific action. Argumentation and persuasion are frequently used together in an essay. For example, a writer might argue for the construction of a highway through town by pointing out that the road would bring new business, create new jobs, and lighten traffic. The writer also might try to persuade readers to vote for a highway appropriations bill by appealing to their emotions, claiming that the highway would allow people to get home faster, thus giving them more time for family life and leisure activities. A whole essay can be organized around argumentation-persuasion, or an essay developed chiefly through another pattern may contain elements of argumentation-persuasion.

Assertion refers to the *thesis* of an *argumentation-persuasion* essay. The assertion, or *proposition,* is a point of view or opinion on a controversial issue or topic. The assertion cannot be merely a statement of a fact. Such statements as "Women still experience discrimination in the job market," "General Rabb would make an ideal mayor for our town," and "This university should devote more funds to raising the quality of the food services" are examples of assertions that could serve as theses for argumentation-persuasion essays.

Audience refers to a writer's intended readers. In planning the content and tone of an essay, you should identify your audience and consider its needs. How similar are the members of your audience to you in knowledge and point of view? What will they need to know for you to achieve your *purpose?* What *tone* will make them open to receiving your message? For example, if you were to write a description of a trip to Disney World, you would have to explain a lot more to an eighty-year-old grandmother who had never seen a theme park than to a young parent who has probably visited several. If you wrote about the high cost of clothing for an economics professor, you would choose a serious, analytic tone and supply statistical evidence for your points. If you wrote about the same topic for the college newspaper, you might use a tone tinged with humor and provide helpful hints on finding bargain clothing.

Begging the question—see *Logical fallacies.*

Brainstorming is a technique used in the *prewriting* stage. It helps you discover the limited subject you can successfully write about and also generates raw material—ideas and details—to develop that subject. In brainstorming, you allow your mind to play freely with the subject. You try to capture fleeting thoughts about it, no matter how random, minor, or tangential, and jot them down rapidly before they disappear from your mind.

Causal analysis—see *Cause-effect.*

Causal chain refers to a series of causes and effects, in which the result or effect of a cause becomes itself the cause of a further effect, and so on. For example, a person's alarm clock failing to buzz might begin a causal chain by causing the person to oversleep. Oversleeping then causes the person to miss the bus, and missing the bus causes the person to arrive late to work. Arriving late causes the person to miss an important phone call, which causes the person to lose a chance at a lucrative contract.

Cause-effect, sometimes called *causal analysis,* involves analyzing the reasons for or results of an event, action, decision, or phenomenon. Writers develop an essay through an analysis of causes whenever they attempt to answer such questions as "Why has this happened?" or "Why does this exist?" When writers explore such questions as "What happens or would happen if a certain change occurs?" or "What will happen if a condition continues?" their essays involve a discussion of effects. Some cause-effect essays concentrate on the causes of a situation, some focus on the effects, and others present both causes and effects. Causal analysis can be an essay's central pattern, or it can be used to help support a point in an essay developed primarily through another pattern.

Characteristics—see *Formal definition.*

Chronological sequence—see *Narrative sequence* and *Organization.*

Circularity is an error in *formal definition* resulting from using variations of the to-be-defined word in the definition. For example, "A scientific hypothesis is a hypothesis made by a scientist about the results of an experiment" is circular because the unknown term is used to explain itself.

Class—see *Formal definition.*

Coherence refers to the clear connection among the various parts of an essay. As a writer, you can draw upon two key strategies to make writing coherent. You can use a clear *organizational format* (for example, a chronological, spatial, emphatic, or simple-to-complex sequence). You can also provide *appropriate signaling* or *connecting devices* (transitions, bridging sentences, repeated words, synonyms, and pronouns).

Comparison-contrast means explaining the similarities and/or differences between events, objects, people, ideas, and so on. The comparison-contrast format can be used to meet a purely factual purpose ("This is how A and B are alike or different"). But usually writers use comparison-contrast to make a judgment about the relative merits of the subjects under discussion. Sometimes a writer will concentrate solely on similarities *or* differences. For instance, when writing about married versus single life, you would probably devote most of your time to discussing the differences between these lifestyles. Other times, comparison and contrast are found together. In an essay analyzing two approaches to U.S. foreign policy, you would probably discuss the similarities *and* the differences in the goals and methods characteristic of each approach. Comparison-contrast can be the dominant pattern in an essay, or it can help support a point in an essay developed chiefly through another pattern.

Conclusion refers to the one or more paragraphs that bring an essay to an end. Effective conclusions give the reader a sense of completeness and finality. Writers often use the conclusion as a place to reaffirm the *thesis* and to express a final thought about the subject. Methods of conclusion include summarizing main points, using a quotation, predicting an outcome, and recommending an action.

Conflict creates tension in the readers of a *narration*. It is produced by the opposition of characters or other forces in a story. Conflict can occur between individuals, between a person and society or nature, or within a person. Readers wonder how a conflict will be resolved and read on to find out.

Connotative and denotative language refers to the ability of language to emphasize one or another aspect of a word's range of meaning. *Denotative language* stresses the dictionary meaning of words. *Connotative language* emphasizes the echoes of feeling that cluster around some words. For example, the terms *weep, bawl, break down,* and *sob* all denote the same thing: to cry. But they have different associations and call up different images. A writer employing the connotative resources of language would choose the term among these that suggested the appropriate image.

Controlling idea—see *Thesis.*

Deductive reasoning is a form of logical thinking in which general statements believed to be true are applied to specific situations or cases. The result of deduction is a conclusion or prediction about the specific situation. Deduction is often expressed in a three-step pattern called a *syllogism.* The first part of the syllogism is a general statement about a large class of items or situations, the *major premise.* The second part is the *minor premise,* a more limited statement about a specific item or case. The third part is the *conclusion,* drawn from the major premise, about that specific case or item. Deductive reasoning is very common in everyday thinking. For example, you might use deduction when car shopping:

In an accident, large cars are safer than small cars. (*major premise*)

The Turbo Titan is a large car. (*minor premise*)

In an accident, the Turbo Titan will be safer than a small car. (*conclusion*)

Definition explains the meaning of a word or concept. The brief formal definitions found in the dictionary can be useful if you need to clarify or restrict the meaning of a term used in an essay. In such cases, the definition is short and to the point. But you may also use an *extended definition* in an essay, taking several paragraphs, even the entire piece, to develop the meaning of a term. You may use extended definition to convey a personal slant on a well-known term, to refute a commonly held interpretation of a word, or to dissect a complex or controversial issue. Definition can be the chief method of development in an essay, or it can help support a point in an essay organized around another pattern.

Definition by negation is a method of defining a term by first explaining what the term is *not,* and then going on to explain what it is. For example, you might begin a critical essay about television with a definition by negation: "Television, far from being a medium that dispenses only light, insubstantial fare, actually disseminates a dangerously distorted view of family life." Definition by negation can provide a stimulating introduction to an essay.

Denotative language—see *Connotative and denotative language.*

Description involves the use of vivid word pictures to express what the five senses have experienced. The subject of a descriptive essay can be a person, a place, an object, or an event. Description can be the dominant pattern in an essay, or it can be used as a supplemental method in an essay developed chiefly through another pattern.

There are two main types of description. In an *objective description,* a writer provides details about a subject without conveying the emotions the subject arouses. For example, if you were involved in a traffic accident, your insurance agent might ask you to write an objective description of the events leading up to and during the crash. But in a *subjective description,* the writer's goal is to evoke in the reader the emotions felt during the experience. For example, in a cautionary letter to a friend who has a habit of driving dangerously, you might write a subjective description of your horrifyingly close call with death during a car accident.

Development—see *Evidence.*

Dialogue is the writer's way of directly presenting the exact words spoken by characters in a *narration.* By using dialogue, writers can convey people's individuality and also add drama and immediacy to an essay.

Directional process analysis—see *Process analysis.*

Division-classification refers to a logical method for analyzing a single subject or several related subjects. Though often used together in an essay, division and classification are separate processes. *Division* involves breaking a subject or idea into its component parts. For instance, the concept "an ideal vacation" could be divided according to its destination, accommodations, or cost. *Classification* involves organizing a number of related items into categories. For example, in an essay about the overwhelming flow of paper in our everyday lives, you might classify the typical kinds of mail most people receive: personal mail (letters, birthday cards, party invitations), business mail (bills, bank statements, charge-card receipts), and junk mail (flyers about bargain sales, solicitations to donate, contest announcements). Division-classification can be the dominant pattern in a paper, or it may be used to support a point in an essay organized chiefly around another pattern of development.

Dominant impression refers to the purpose of a descriptive essay. While some descriptive essays have a thesis, others do not; instead, they convey a dominant impression or main point. For example, one person writing a descriptive essay about New York City might use its architectural diversity as a focal point. Another person writing a description of Manhattan might concentrate on the overpowering sense of hustle and speed about everyone and everything in the city. Both writers would select only those details that supported their dominant impressions.

Dramatic license refers to the writer's privilege, when writing a narrative, to alter facts or details to strengthen the support of the *thesis* or *narrative point*. For example, a writer is free to flesh out the description of an event whose specific details may be partially forgotten or to modify or omit details of a narrative that do not contribute to the meaning the writer wishes to convey.

Either-or fallacy—see *Logical fallacies.*

Emphatic sequence—see *Organization.*

Ethos refers to a writer's reliability or credibility. Such an image of trustworthiness is particularly important to readers of an *argumentation-persuasion* essay or piece. Writers establish their *ethos* by using reason and logic, by being moderate in their appeals to emotions, by avoiding a hostile tone, and by demonstrating overall knowledgeability of the subject. The most effective argumentation-persuasion involves an interplay of *ethos, logos,* and *pathos.*

Etymology refers to the history of a word or term. All English words have their origins in other, often ancient, languages. Giving a brief etymology of a word can help a writer establish the context for developing an *extended definition* of the word. For example, the word *criminal* is derived from a Latin word meaning "accusation" or "accused." Today, our word *criminal* goes beyond the concept of "accused" to mean "guilty."

Evidence lends substance, or support, to a writer's main ideas and thus helps the reader to accept the writer's viewpoint. Evidence should meet several criteria. First of all, it should be *unified,* in the sense that all supporting ideas and details should relate directly to the key point the writer is making. Second, evidence should be *adequate;* there should be enough evidence to convince the reader to agree with the thesis. Third, evidence should be *specific;* that is, vivid and detailed rather than vague and general. Fourth, evidence must be *accurate* and not overstate or understate information. Fifth, evidence should be *representative,* relying on the typical rather than the atypical to make a point. The bulk of an essay is devoted to supplying evidence. Supporting the thesis with solid evidence is the third stage in the writing process.

Exemplification, at the heart of all effective writing, involves using concrete specifics to support generalizations. In exemplification, writers provide examples or instances that support or clarify broader statements. You might support the thesis statement "I have a close-knit family" by using such examples as the following: "We have a regular Sunday dinner at my grandmother's house with at least ten family members present"; "My sisters and brothers visit my parents every week"; "I spend so much time on the phone talking with my sisters that sometimes I have trouble finding time for my new college friends." Exemplification may be an essay's central pattern, or it may supplement another pattern.

Extended definition—see *Definition.*

Fallacies—see *Logical fallacies.*

False analogy—see *Logical fallacies.*

Figures of speech are imaginative comparisons between two things usually thought of as dissimilar. Some major figures of speech are *simile, metaphor,* and *personi-fication. Similes* are comparisons that use the signal words *like* or *as:* "Superman was as powerful as a locomotive." *Metaphors,* which do not use signal words, directly equate unlike things: "The boss is a tiger when it comes to landing a contract"; "The high-powered pistons of the boxer's arms pummeled his oppo-nent." *Personification* attributes human characteristics to inanimate things or nonhuman beings: "The angry clouds unleashed their fury on the town"; "The turtle shyly poked his head out of his shell."

First draft refers to the writer's first try at producing a basic, unpolished version of the whole essay. It is often referred to as the "rough" draft, and nothing about it is final or unchangeable. The process of writing the first draft often brings up new ideas or details. Writers sometimes break off writing the draft to *brainstorm* or *freewrite* as new ideas occur to them and then return to the draft with new inspiration. You shouldn't worry about spelling, grammar, or style in the first-draft stage; instead, you should keep focused on casting your ideas into sentence and paragraph form. Writing the first draft is the fifth stage in the writing process.

Flashback—see *Narrative sequence.*

Flashforward—see *Narrative sequence.*

Formal definition involves stating a definition in a three-part pattern of about one sentence in length. In presenting a formal definition, a writer puts the *term* in a *class* and then lists the *characteristics* that separate the term from other members of its class. For example, a formal definition of a word processor might be "A word processor (term) is an electronic machine (class) that is used to write, edit, store, and produce typewritten documents (characteristics)." Writers often use a formal definition to prepare a reader for an extended definition that follows.

Freewriting is most often used during the *prewriting* stage to help writers generate ideas about a limited topic. To use this method, write nonstop for five or ten minutes about everything your topic brings to mind. Disregard grammar, spelling, and organization as you keep your pen and mind moving. Freewriting is similar to *brainstorming,* except that the result is a rambling, detail-filled para-graph rather than a list. Freewriting can also be used to generate ideas during later stages of the writing process.

Gender-biased language gives the impression that one sex is more important, pow-erful, or valuable than the other. When writing, you should work to replace such sexist language with *gender-neutral* or *nonsexist* terms that convey no sex-ual prejudice. First of all, try to avoid *sexist vocabulary* that demeans or excludes one of the sexes: *stud, jock, chick, fox,* and so on. Also, just as adult males should be called *men,* adult females should be referred to as *women,* not *girls.* And men shouldn't be empowered with professional and honorary titles (*President* George W. Bush) while professional women—such as congressional representa-tives—are assigned only personal titles (*Ms.* Gwen Moore). Here are some examples of the way you can avoid words that exclude women: Change "chair-man" to *chairperson,* "layman" to *layperson,* "congressman" to *congressional representative,* "workmen" to *workers,* the "average guy" to the *average person.* Second, be aware of the fact that indefinite singular nouns—those representing a general group of people consisting of both genders—can lead to *sexist pronoun use:* for example, "On *his* first day of school, a young child often experiences separation anxiety." This sentence appears to exclude female children from consideration, although the situation being described applies equally to them. Third, recognize that indefinite pronouns like *anyone, each,* and *everybody* may also pave the way to sexist pronoun use. Although such pronouns often refer to a number of individuals, they're considered singular. So, wanting to be grammatically correct, you may write a sentence like the following: "Everybody wants *his* favorite candidate to win." The sentence, however, is sexist because *everybody* is certainly not restricted to men. One way to avoid this type of sexist construction is to use both male and female pronouns: "Everybody wants *his* or *her* favorite candidate to win." Another approach is to use the gender-neutral pronouns *they, their,* or *themselves:* "Everybody wants *their* favorite candidate to win." Be warned, though. Some people object to using these plural pronouns with singular indefinite pronouns, even though the practice is common in everyday speech. Two alternative strategies enable you to eliminate the need for *any* gender-marked singular pronouns. First, you can change singular general nouns or indefinite pronouns to their plural equivalents and then use plural pronouns, which are not gender-specific. For example, you may change "A *workaholic* feels anxious when *he* isn't busy" to "*Workaholics* feel anxious when *they're* not busy" and "*Everyone* in the room expressed *his* opinion freely" to "*Those* in the room expressed *their* opinions freely." Second, you can recast the sentence to omit the singular pronoun: For instance, you may change "A *manager* usually spends part of each day settling squabbles among *his* staff" to "A manager usually spends part of each day settling *staff squabbles*" and "No *one* wants *his* taxes raised" to "No one wants *to pay more taxes.*"

Hasty generalization—see *Logical fallacies.*

Inductive reasoning is a form of logical thinking in which specific cases and facts are examined to draw a wider-ranging conclusion. The result of inductive reasoning is a generalization that is applied to situations or cases similar to the ones examined. Induction is typical of scientific investigation and of everyday thinking. For example, on the basis of specific experiences, you may have concluded that when you feel chilly in a room where everyone else is comfortable, you are likely to develop a cold and fever in the next day or two. In an *argumentation-persuasion* essay, the conclusion reached by induction would be your *assertion* or *thesis.*

Inference is the term for a conclusion based on *inductive reasoning.* Because the reasoning behind specific cases may not be simple, there is usually an element of uncertainty in an inductive conclusion. Choosing the correct explanation for specific cases is a matter of carefully weighing and selecting alternative conclusions.

Informational process analysis—see *Process analysis.*

Introduction refers to the first paragraph or several paragraphs of an essay. The introduction serves three purposes. It informs readers of the general subject of the essay, it catches their attention, and it presents the controlling idea or thesis. The methods of introducing an essay include the use of an anecdote, a quotation or surprising statistic or fact, and questions. Or you may narrow your discussion down from a broad subject to a more limited one.

Irony occurs when a writer or speaker implies (rather than states directly) a discrepancy or incongruity of some kind. *Verbal irony,* which is often tongue-in-cheek, involves a discrepancy between the literal words and what's actually meant ("I know you must be unhappy about receiving the highest grade in the course"). If the ironic comment is designed to be hurtful or insulting, it qualifies as *sarcasm* ("Congratulations! You failed the final exam"). In *situational irony,* the circumstances are themselves incongruous. For example, although their constitutional rights were violated when the federal government detained them in internment camps, Japanese-Americans nevertheless played American football, sang American songs, and saluted the American flag during their imprisonment.

Journal writing is a form of prewriting in which writers make daily entries in a private journal, much as they would in a diary. Whether they focus on one topic or wander freely, journal writers jot down striking incidents, images, and ideas encountered in the course of a day. Such journal material can produce ideas for future essays.

Logical fallacies are easily committed mistakes in reasoning that writers must avoid, especially when writing *argumentation-persuasion* essays. There are many kinds of logical fallacies. Here are several:

Ad hominem argument occurs when someone attacks another person's point of view by criticizing that person, not the issue. Often called "mudslinging," *ad hominem* arguments try to invalidate a person's ideas by revealing unrelated, past or present, personal or ethical flaws. For example, to claim that a person cannot govern the country well because it can be proven he or she has little sense of humor is to use an *ad hominem* argument.

Begging the question is a fallacy in which the writer assumes the truth of something that needs to be proven. Imagine a writer argues the following: "A law should be passed requiring dangerous pets like German shepherds and Doberman pinschers to be restrained by fences, leashes, and muzzles." Such an argument begs the question since it assumes readers will automatically accept the view that such dogs are indeed dangerous.

Either-or fallacies occur when it's argued that a complex situation can be resolved in only one of two possible ways. Here's an example: "If the administration doesn't grant striking professors more money, the college will never be able to attract outstanding teachers in years ahead." Such an argument oversimplifies matters. Excellent teachers might be attracted to a college for a variety of reasons, not just because of good salaries: the school's location, research facilities, reputation for scholarship, hardworking students, and so on.

False analogy erroneously suggests that because two things are alike in some regards, they are similar in all ways. In the process, significant differences between the two are disregarded. If you argue that a woman prosecuting a rapist is subjected to a second rape in court, you're guilty of a false analogy. As embarrassing, painful, and hurtful as the court proceedings may be, the woman is not physically assaulted, as she was when she was raped. Also, as difficult as her decision to seek justice might be, she's in court by choice and not against her will.

Hasty generalizations are unsound *inductive inferences* based on too few instances of a behavior, situation, or process. For example, it would be a hasty generalization to conclude that you're allergic to a food such as curry because you once ate it and became ill. There are several other possible explanations for your illness, and only repetitions of this experience or a lab test could prove conclusively that you're allergic to this food.

Non sequiturs are faulty conclusions about cause and effect. Here's an example: "Throughout this country's history, most physicians have been male. Women apparently have little interest in becoming doctors." The faulty conclusion accords one factor—the possible vocational preferences of women—the status of sole cause. The conclusion fails to consider pressures on women to devote themselves to homemaking and to avoid an occupation sexually stereotyped as "masculine."

Post hoc thinking results when it's presumed that one event caused another just because it occurred first. For instance, if your car broke down the day after you lent it to your brother, you would be committing the *post hoc* fallacy if you blamed him, unless you knew he did something to your car's engine.

Questionable authority, revealed by such phrases as "studies show" and "experts claim," undercuts a writer's credibility. Readers become suspicious of such vague and unsubstantial appeals to authority. Writers should demonstrate the reliability of their sources by citing them specifically.

Red herring arguments are deliberate attempts to focus attention on a peripheral matter rather than examine the merits of the issue under discussion. Imagine that a local environmental group advocates stricter controls for employees at a nearby chemical plant. The group points out that plant employees are repeatedly exposed to high levels of toxic chemicals. If you respond, "Many of the employees are illegal aliens and shouldn't be allowed to take jobs from native-born townspeople," you're throwing in a red herring. By bringing in immigration policies, you sidetrack attention from the matter at hand: the toxic level to which plant employees—illegal aliens or not—are exposed.

Logos is a major factor in creating an effective argument. It refers to the soundness of *argumentation,* as created by the use of facts, statistics, information, and commentary by authoritative sources. The most effective arguments involve an interplay among *logos, pathos,* and *ethos.*

Major premise—see *Deductive reasoning.*

Minor premise—see *Deductive reasoning.*

MLA documentation is the system developed by the Modern Language Association for citing sources in a paper. When you quote or summarize source material, you must do two things within your paper's text: (1) identify the author and (2) specify the pages on which the material appears. You may provide the author's name in a lead-in sentence or within parentheses following the borrowed material; the page number always appears in parentheses, inserted in the text after the borrowed material. The material in the parentheses is called a *parenthetic reference.* A paper using MLA documentation ends with a *Works Cited* list, which includes only those sources actually acknowledged in the paper. Entries are organized alphabetically by authors' last names. Entries without an author are alphabetized by the first major word in the title.

Narration means recounting an event or a series of related events to make a point. Narration can be an essay's principal pattern of development, or it can be used to supplement a paper organized primarily around another pattern. For instance, to persuade readers to avoid drug use, a writer might use the narrative pattern by recounting the story of an abuser's addiction and recovery.

Narrative point refers to the meaning the writer intends to convey to a reader by telling a certain story. This narrative point might be a specific message, or it might be a feeling about the situation, people, or place of the story. This under-lying meaning is achieved by presenting details that support it and eliminating any that are nonessential. For example, in an essay about friendship, a writer's point might be that friendships change when one of the friends acquires a sig-nificant partner of the opposite sex. The writer would focus on the details of how her close female friend had less time for her, changed their usual times of getting together, and confided in her less. The writer would omit judgments of the friend's choice of boyfriend and her friend's declining grades because these details, while real for the writer, would distract the reader from the essay's narrative point.

Narrative sequence refers to the order in which a writer recounts events. When you follow the order of the events as they happened, you're using *chronological sequence*. This sequence, in which you begin at the beginning and end with the last event, is the most basic and commonly used narrative sequence. If you inter-rupt this flow to present an event that happened before the beginning of the narrative sequence, you're employing a *flashback*. If you skip ahead to an event later than the one that comes next in your narrative, you're using the *flash-forward* technique.

Non sequiturs—see *Logical fallacies.*

Objective description—see *Description.*

One-side-at-a-time method refers to one of the two techniques for organizing a *comparison-contrast* essay. In using this method, a writer discusses all the points about one of the compared and contrasted subjects before going on to the other. For example, in an essay titled "Single or Married?" a writer might first discuss single life in terms of amount of independence, freedom of career choice, and companionship. Then the writer would, within reason, discuss mar-ried life in terms of these same three subtopics. The issues the writer discusses in each half of the essay would be identical and presented in the same order. See also *Point-by-point method.*

Organization refers to the process of arranging evidence to support a thesis in the most effective way. When organizing, a writer decides what ideas come first, next, and last. In *chronological* sequence, details are arranged according to occurrence in time. In *spatial* sequence, details appear in the order in which they occur in space. In *emphatic* order, ideas are sequenced according to impor-tance, with the most significant, outstanding, or convincing evidence being reserved for last. In *simple-to-complex* order, easy-to-grasp material is presented before more-difficult-to-comprehend information. Organizing is the fourth stage of the writing process.

Outlining involves making a formal plan before writing a *first draft*. Writing an outline helps you determine whether your supporting evidence is logical and adequate. As you write, you can use the outline to keep yourself on track. Many writers use the indentation system of Roman numerals, letters, and Arabic num-bers to outline; sometimes writers use a less formal system.

Paradox refers to a statement that seems impossible, contrary to common sense, or self-contradictory, yet that can—after consideration—be seen to be plausible or true. For example, Oscar Wilde produced a paradox when he wrote "When the gods wish to punish us, they answer our prayers." The statement doesn't contradict itself because often, Wilde believes, that which we wish for turns out to be the very thing that will bring us the most pain.

Parenthetic reference—see *MLA documentation.*

Pathos refers to the emotional power of an *argumentation-persuasion* essay. By appealing to the needs, values, and attitudes of readers and by using *connotative language,* writers can increase the chances that readers will come to agree with the ideas in an essay. Although *pathos* is an important element of persuasion, such emotional appeals should reinforce rather than replace reason. The most effective argumentation-persuasion involves an interplay among *pathos, logos,* and *ethos.*

Peer review is the critical reading of another person's writing with the intention of suggesting changes. To be effective, peer review calls for readers who are objective, skilled, and tactful enough to provide useful feedback. Begin by giving your readers a clear sense of what you expect from the review. To promote specific responses, ask the reviewers targeted (preferably written) questions. Following the review, rank the problems and solutions that the reviewers identified. Then enter your own notes for revising in the margins of your draft so that you'll know exactly what changes need to be made in your draft as you rework it.

Plan of development refers to a technique whereby the writer supplies the reader with a brief map of the main points to be covered in an essay. If used, the plan of development occurs as part of the *thesis* or in a sentence following the thesis. In it, the main ideas are mentioned in the order in which they'll appear in the supporting paragraphs. Longer essays and term papers usually need a plan of development to maintain unity, but shorter papers may do without one.

Point-by-point method refers to one of the two techniques for organizing a *comparison-contrast* essay. A writer using this method moves from one aspect of one subject to the same aspect of another subject before going on to the second aspect of each subject. For example, in an essay titled "Single or Married?" a writer might first discuss the amount of independence a person has when single and when married. Then, the writer might go on to discuss how much freedom of career choice a person has when single and when married. Finally, the writer might discuss, in turn, the amount of companionship available in each of the two lifestyles. See also *One-side-at-a-time method.*

Point of view refers to the perspective a writer chooses when writing about a subject. If you narrate events as you experience them, you're using the *first-person* point of view. You might say, for example, "*I* noticed jam on the child's collar and holes in her shirt." If you relate the events from a distance—as if you observed them but did not experience them personally—you're using the *third-person* point of view; for instance, "Jam splotched the child's collar, and her shirt had several holes in it." The point of view should be consistent throughout an essay.

Post hoc **thinking**—see *Logical fallacies.*

Prewriting is the first stage of the writing process. During prewriting, you jot down rough ideas about your subject without yet moving to writing a draft of your essay. Your goals at this stage are to (1) understand the boundaries of the assignment, (2) discover the limited subject you could write about, (3) generate raw material about the limited subject, and (4) organize the raw material into a very rough *scratch outline.* If you keep in mind that prewriting is "unofficial," it can be a low-pressure, even enjoyable activity.

Process analysis refers to writing that explains the steps involved in doing something or the sequence of stages in an event or behavior. There are two types of process analysis. In *directional process analysis,* readers are shown how to do something step by step. Cookbook recipes, tax form instructions, and how-to books are some typical uses of directional process analysis. In *informational process analysis,* the writer explains how something is done or occurs, without expecting the reader to attempt the process. "A Senator's Road to Political Power," "How a Bee Makes Honey," and "How a Convict Gets Paroled" would be titles of essays developed through informational process analysis. Process analysis can be the dominant mode in an essay, as in these examples, or it may help make a point in an essay developed chiefly through another pattern. For example, in a cause-effect essay that explores the impact of the two-career family, process analysis might be used to explain how parents arrange for day care.

Proofreading involves rereading a final draft carefully to catch any errors in spelling, grammar, punctuation, or typing that have slipped by. While such errors are minor, a significant number of them can seriously weaken the effectiveness of an essay. Proofreading is the last stage in the writing process.

Proposition—see *Assertion.*

Purpose is the reason a writer has for preparing a particular essay. Usually, writers frame their purposes in terms of the effect they wish to have on their *audience.* They may wish to explore the personal meaning of a subject or experience, explain an idea or process, provide information, influence opinion, or entertain. Many essays combine purposes, with one purpose predominating and providing the essay's focus.

Red herring argument—see *Logical fallacies.*

Refutation is an important strategy in *argumentation-persuasion.* In refutation, writers acknowledge that there are opposing views on the subject under discussion and then go on to do one of two things. Sometimes they may admit that the opposing views are somewhat valid but assert that their own position has more merit and devote their essay to demonstrating that merit. For example, a writer might assert, "Business majors often find interesting and lucrative jobs. However, in the long run, liberal arts graduates have many more advantages in the job market because the breadth of their background helps them think better, learn faster, and communicate more effectively." This writer would concentrate on proving the advantages that liberal arts graduates have. At other times, writers may choose to argue actively against an opposing position by dismantling that view point by point. Such refutation of opposing views can strengthen the writer's own arguments.

Repeated words, synonyms, and pronouns—see *Signaling devices.*

Revision means, literally, "reseeing" a *first draft* with a fresh eye, as if the writer had not actually prepared the draft. When revising, you move from more global issues (like clarifying meaning and organization) to more specific matters (like fine-tuning sentences and word choice). While revising, you make whatever changes are necessary to increase the essay's effectiveness. You might strengthen your thesis, resequence paragraph order, or add more transitions. Such changes often make the difference between mediocre and superior writing. Revision, itself a multi-stage process, is the last stage of the writing process.

Satire is a humorous form of social criticism usually aimed at society's institutions or human behavior. Often irreverent as well as witty, satire is serious in purpose: to point out evil, injustice, and absurdity and bring about change through an increase in awareness. Satire ranges widely in tone: it may be gentle or biting; it may sarcastically describe a real situation or use fictional characters and events to spoof reality. Satire often makes use of *irony.*

Scratch outline refers to your first informal plan for an essay, devised at the end of the *prewriting* stage. In making a scratch outline, you select ideas and details from your raw material for inclusion in your essay and discard the rest. You also arrange these ideas in an order that makes sense and that will help you achieve your *purpose.* A scratch outline is tentative and flexible, and can be reshaped as needed.

Sensory description vividly evokes the sights, smells, tastes, sounds, and physical feelings of a scene or event. For example, if a writer carefully chooses words and images, readers can see the vibrant reds and oranges of falling leaves, taste the sourness of an underripe grapefruit, hear the growling of motorcycles as a gang sweeps through a town, smell the spicy aroma of a grandmother's homemade tomato soup, and feel the pulsing pain of a jaw after Novocain wears off. Sensory description is particularly important in writing *description* or *narration.*

Sentence variety adds interest to the style of an essay or paragraph. In creating sentence variety, writers mix different kinds of sentences and sentence patterns. For example, you might vary the way your sentences open or intersperse short sentences with long ones, simple sentences with complex ones. Repetitive sentence patterns tend to make readers lose interest.

Signaling devices indicate the relationships among ideas in an essay. They help the reader follow the train of thought from sentence to sentence and from paragraph to paragraph. There are three types of connectives. *Transitions* are words that clarify flow of meaning. They can signal an additional or contrasting point, an enumeration of ideas, the use of an example, or other movement of ideas. *Linking sentences* summarize a point just made and then introduce a follow-up point. *Repeated words, synonyms,* and *pronouns* create a sense of flow by keeping important concepts in the mind of the reader.

Spatial sequence—see *Organization.*

Specific—see *Evidence.*

Stipulative definition is a way of restricting a term for the purposes of discussion. Many words have multiple meanings that can get in the way of clarity when a writer is creating an *extended definition.* For example, you might stipulate the following definition of *foreign car:* "While many American automobiles use parts or even whole engines made by foreign car manufacturers, for the purposes of discussion, 'foreign car' refers only to those automobiles designed and manufactured wholly by a company based in another country. By this definition, a European vehicle made in Pennsylvania is *not* a foreign car."

Subjective description—see *Description.*

Support—see *Evidence.*

Syllogism—see *Deductive reasoning.*

Term—see *Formal definition.*

Thesis is the central idea in any essay, usually expressed in a one- or two-sentence *thesis statement.* Writers accomplish two things by providing a thesis statement in an essay: They indicate the essay's limited subject and express an attitude about that subject. Also called the *controlling idea,* the thesis statement consists of a particular slant, angle, or point of view about the limited subject. Stating the thesis is the second stage of the writing process.

Tone conveys your attitude toward yourself, your purpose, your topic, and your readers. As in speaking, tone in writing may be serious, playful, sarcastic, and so on. Generally, readers detect tone more by how you say something (that is, through your sentence structure and word choice) than by what you say.

Topic sentence is the term for the sentence(s) that convey the main idea of a paragraph. Such sentences are often, but not always, found at the start of a paragraph. They provide a statement of the subject to be discussed and an indication of the writer's attitude toward that subject. Writers usually concern themselves with topic sentences during the writing of the first draft, the fifth stage of the writing process.

Transitions—see *Signaling devices.*

Unified—see *Evidence.*

Works Cited—see *MLA documentation.*

ACKNOWLEDGMENTS

Alter, Jonathan, "Time to Think About Torture." From *Newsweek*, November 5, 2001. Copyright © 2001. Newsweek, Inc. All rights reserved.

Angelou, Maya, "Sister Flowers." From *I Know Why the Caged Bird Sings* by Maya Angelou. Copyright © 1969 and renewed 1997 by Maya Angelou. Used by permission of Random House, Inc.

Angier, Natalie, "The Cute Factor." Copyright © by The New York Times Co. Reprinted with permission.

Barry, Dave, "The Ugly Truth About Beauty." © Tribune Media Services, Inc. All rights reserved. Reprinted with permission.

Barszcz, James, "Can You Be Educated From a Distance?" Reprinted by permission of James Barszcz.

Bissinger, Buzz, "Innocents Afield." From *The New York Times* op-ed, December 16, 2004. Reprinted with permission.

Brooks, David, "Psst! 'Human Capital.'" Originally published in *The New York Times*, November 13, 2005.

Carson, Rachel, "A Fable for Tomorrow." From *Silent Spring* by Rachel Carson. Copyright © 1962 by Rachel L. Carson, renewed 1990 by Roger Christie. Reprinted by permission of Houghton Mifflin Company. All rights reserved.

Chapman, Stephen, "The Prisoner's Dilemma." From *The New Republic*, March 8, 1980. Reprinted by permission of *The New Republic*. Copyright © 1980. *The New Republic*, LLC.

Cofer, Judith Ortiz, "A Partial Remembrance of a Puerto Rican Childhood." "Casa" is reprinted with permission from the publisher of *Silent Dancing: A Partial Remembrance of a Puerto Rican Childhood* by Judith Ortiz Cofer (Houston: Arte Publico Press—University of Houston, 1991.)

Cole, K. C., "Entropy." From *The New York Times*, March 18, 1982. Copyright © 1982 by The New York Times Co. Reprinted by permission.

D'Amboise, Jacques, "Showing What Is Possible." From *Parade*, August 6, 1989. Reprinted with permission of Jacques d'Amboise.

Darley, John M., and Bibb Latané, "Why People Don't Help in a Crisis?" Reprinted with permission from *Psychology Today* Magazine, copyright © (1968) Sussex Publishers, Inc.

Didion, Joan, "The Santa Ana" (excerpt from "Los Angeles Notebook") and "Marrying Absurd" from *Slouching Towards Bethlehem* by Joan Didion. Copyright © 1966, 1968, renewed 1996 by Joan Didion. Reprinted by permission of Farrar, Straus and Giroux, LLC.

Ehrenreich, Barbara, "What I've Learned From Men." From *Ms.* Magazine, August 1985. Reprinted by permission of *Ms.* Magazine, © 1985.

Ericsson, Stephanie, "The Ways We Lie." From *The Utne Reader*, 1992. Copyright © 1992 by Stephanie Ericsson. Reprinted by permission of Dunham Literary as agents for the author. Originally published in *The Utne Reader*.

Fish, Stanley, "Free-Speech Follies." From *The Chronicle of Higher Education*, March 13, 2003. © 2003, Stanley Fish, Davidson-Kahn Distinguished University Professor of Humanities and Law, Florida International University, College of Law. Reprinted with permission.

Gholson, Charmie, "Charity Display?" From *The New York Times*, January 2, 2005. Reprinted with permission.

Gleick, James, "Life as Type A." From *Faster* by James Gleick. Copyright © 1999 by James Gleick. Used by permission of Pantheon Books, a division of Random House, Inc.

Goodman, Ellen, "Family Counterculture." From *Value Judgments* (originally appeared in *The Boston Globe*, August 16, 1991). © 1991, The Washington Post Writers Group. Reprinted with permission.

Helvarg, David, "The Storm This Time." Reprinted with permission from *Multinational Monitor*, Sept./Oct. 2005, pp. 9–18.

Hughes, Langston, "Salvation." From *The Big Sea* by Langston Hughes. Copyright © 1940 by Langston Hughes. Copyright renewed © 1968 by Arna Bontemps and George Houston Bass. Reprinted by permission of Hill and Wang, a division of Farrar, Straus and Giroux, LLC.

Hymowitz, Kay S., "Tweens: Ten Going on Sixteen." From *City Journal*, Autumn 1998, Vol. 8, No. 4. Reprinted with permission of City Journal/Manhattan Institute.

Jacoby, Susan, "Common Decency." Copyright © 1991 by Susan Jacoby. Originally appeared in *The New York Times* (1991). Reprinted by permission of Georges Borchardt, Inc. on behalf of the author.

Johnson, Beth, "Bombs Bursting in Air." Reprinted by permission of the author. Beth Johnson lives in Lederach, PA.

King, Martin Luther, Jr., "Where Do We Go From Here: Community or Chaos?" and "The World House." Reprinted by arrangement with the Estate of Martin Luther King, Jr., c/o Writers House as agent for the proprietor New York, NY. Copyright © 1967 Martin Luther King, Jr., copyright renewed 1995 Coretta Scott King.

King, Stephen, "Why We Crave Horror Movies." Originally appeared in *Playboy*, 1982. Reprinted with permission. © Stephen King. All rights reserved.

Lorde, Audre, "The Fourth of July." Reprinted with permission from *Zami: A New Spelling of My Name* by Audre Lorde. Copyright 1982 by Audre Lorde. The Crossing Press, an imprint of Ten-Speed Press, Berkeley, CA, www.tenspeed.com.

Lutz, William, "Doublespeak." From *Doublespeak: From Revenue Enhancement to Terminal Living* by William Lutz, Harper Collins. Copyright © 1989 by William D. Lutz.

Mayblum, Adam, "The Price We Pay." From *Doubletake Magazine*, Special Edition, 2001. Reprinted by permission of the author.

McClintock, Ann, "Propaganda Techniques in Today's Advertising." Reprinted by permission of the author.

Mitford, Jessica, "The American Way of Death." Reprinted by permission of the Estate of Jessica Mitford. Copyright © 1998 by the estate of Jessica Mitford, all rights reserved.

Orwell, George, "Shooting an Elephant." From *Shooting an Elephant and Other Essays* by George Orwell, copyright 1950 by Sonia Brownell Orwell and renewed 1978 by Sonia Pitt-Rivers, reprinted by permission of Harcourt, Inc.

Paglia, Camille, "Rape: A Bigger Danger Than Feminists Know." Reprinted with permission of the author.

Parker, Star, "*Se Habla* Entitlement." Posted on worldnetdaily.com, April 18, 2006. Reprinted with permission.

Parks, Gordon, "Flavio's Home." From *Voices in the Mirror* by Gordon Parks. Copyright © 1990 by Gordon Parks. Used by permission of Doubleday, a division of Random House, Inc.

Porter, Henry, "Now the Talk Is About Bringing Back Torture." From *The Guardian*, November 11, 2001. Reprinted by permission of the author.

Raspberry, William, "The Handicap of Definition." © 1982, The Washington Post Writers Group. Reprinted with permission.

Rego, Caroline, "The Fine Art of Complaining." Reprinted by permission of the author.

Robbins, Alexandra, and Abby Wilner, "What Is the Quarterlife Crisis?" Introduction from *Quarterlife Crisis* by Alexandra Robbins and Abby Wilner, Copyright © 2001 by Alexandra Robbins and Abby Wilner. Used by permission of Jeremy P. Tarcher, an imprint of Penguin Group (USA), Inc.

Roberts, Paul, "How to Say Nothing in 500 Words." From *Understanding English* by Paul Roberts. Copyright © 1951 by Paul Roberts. (Boston: David Godine, 1981.) Reprinted by permission of Pearson Education, Inc.

Rodriguez, Richard, "Workers." From *Hunger of Memory* by Richard Rodriguez. Copyright © 1981 by Richard Rodriguez. (Boston: David Godine, 1981.) Reprinted by permission of Georges Borchardt, Inc., on behalf of the author.

Rodriguez, Roberto, "The Border on Our Backs." From "Column of the Americas." Reprinted with permission of the author.

Savan, Leslie, "Black Talk and Pop Culture." From *Slam Dunks and No Brainers* by Leslie Savan. Used by permission of Alfred A. Knopf, a Division of Random House, Inc.

Sherry, Mary, "In Praise of the 'F' Word." From *Newsweek*, May 6, 1991. Reprinted with permission of the author.

Shipley, David, "Talk About Editing." Originally published in *The New York Times*, July 31, 2005.

Stoll, Clifford, "Cyberschool." From *High-Tech Heretic* by Clifford Stoll, © 1990 by Clifford Stoll. Used by permission of Doubleday, a division of Random House, Inc.

Suina, Joseph H., "And Then I Went to School." From Suina, J. (n.d.). "And Then I Went to School," *Linguistic and Cultural Influences on Learning Mathematics.* Mahwah, NJ: Lawrence Erlbaum Associates, Inc. Reprinted with permission.

Sykes, Charles, "The 'Values' Wasteland." From *Dumbing Down Our Kids* by Charles Sykes, copyright © 1995 by the author and reprinted with permission of St. Martin's Press, LLC.

Twain, Mark, "The Damned Human Race." From *Letters from the Earth by Mark Twain.* Edited by Bernard DeVoto. Copyright © 1938, 1944, 1946, 1959, 1962 by The Mark Twain Company. Copyright 1942 by The President and Fellows of Harvard College. Reprinted by permission of HarperCollins Publishers.

Walker, Alice, "Beauty: When the Other Dancer Is the Self." From *In Search of Our Mothers' Gardens: Womanist Prose.* Copyright © 1983 by Alice Walker. Reprinted by permission of Harcourt, Inc.

White, E. B., "Once More to the Lake." From *One Man's Meat* by E. B. White. Text copyright © 1941 by E. B. White. Copyright renewed. Reprinted by permission of Tilbury House, Publishers, Gardiner, Maine.

Woolf, Virginia, "The Death of the Moth" and "Professions for Women." From *The Death of the Moth and Other Essays* by Virginia Woolf. Copyright © 1942 by Harcourt, Inc., and renewed 1970 by Marjorie T. Parsons, Executrix, reprinted by permission of the publisher.

Yuh, Ji-Yeon, "Let's Tell the Story of All America's Cultures." From *The Philadelphia Inquirer,* June 30, 1991. Reprinted by permission of the author.

Zinsser, William, "College Pressures." From *Blair & Ketchums Country Journal,* April 1979. Copyright © 1979 by William K. Zinsser. Reprinted by permission of the author.

Cover, pages iii, 1, 6, 12, 84, 92, 100, 107, 114, 137, 143, 151, 155, 159, 184, 193, 202, 209, 215, 240, 250, 259, 263, 270, 296, 301, 308, 314, 327, 350, 354, 361, 368, 372, 397, 402, 408, 417, 424, 445, 450, 456, 463, 471, 512, 517, 522, 527, 534, 541, 547, 552, 557, 562, 567, 574, 582, 588, 593, 597, 601, 604, 607, 634: ©Joseph Sohm; ChromoSohm Inc./Corbis

71, 73: ©Rudi Von Briel/PhotoEdit, Inc.

94, 95: ©David Helvarg/Blue Frontier Campaign

123, 124: ©Bill Pugliano/Getty Images

169, 172: ©Bill Arnon/PhotoEdit, Inc.

223, 227: ©LWA-Dann Tardiff/Corbis

280, 282: ©Angelo Cavalli/Getty Images

335, 337: ©The Advertising Archive Ltd.

381, 383: ©Ken McGraw/Index Stock Imagery, Inc.

432, 434: ©Donald Miralle/Getty Images

477, 482: Homepage reprinted with permission from Students Against Destructive Decisions.

617: Screenshot © Google Inc. and are used with permission.

INDEX

To the Student
From the Authors

By now, you realize that almost all writing goes through a series of revisions. The same was true for this book. *The Longman Reader*, Eighth Edition, has been reworked a number of times, with each revision taking into account students' and instructors' reactions to drafts of material.

Before we prepare the ninth edition of *The Longman Reader*, we'd like to know how you, the student, feel about the book. We hope you'll spend a few minutes completing this brief questionnaire. You can be sure that your responses will help shape subsequent editions. Please send your completed survey to the College English Editor, Longman Publishers, 1185 Avenue of the Americas, New York, NY 10036.

Thanks for your time.

College _____ City and state _____

Course title _____ Instructor _____

DESCRIPTION	I really liked it.	It was okay.	I didn't like it.	I didn't read it.
Parks, *Flavio's Home*	____	____	____	____
Helvarg, *The Storm This Time*	____	____	____	____
Angelou, *Sister Flowers*	____	____	____	____
White, *Once More to the Lake*	____	____	____	____
Cofer, *A Partial Remembrance of a Puerto Rican Childhood*	____	____	____	____

NARRATION				
Lorde, *The Fourth of July*	____	____	____	____
Orwell, *Shooting an Elephant*	____	____	____	____
Gholson, *Charity Display?*	____	____	____	____
Hughes, *Salvation*	____	____	____	____
Mayblum, *The Price We Pay*	____	____	____	____

EXEMPLIFICATION

	I really liked it.	It was okay.	I didn't like it.	I didn't read it.
Sykes, *The "Values" Wasteland*	___	___	___	___
Savan, *Black Talk and Pop Culture*	___	___	___	___
Hymowitz, *Tweens: Ten Going on Sixteen*	___	___	___	___
Johnson, *Bombs Bursting in Air*	___	___	___	___
Ehrenreich, *What I've Learned From Men*	___	___	___	___

DIVISION-CLASSIFICATION

Ericsson, *The Ways We Lie*	___	___	___	___
Zinsser, *College Pressures*	___	___	___	___
Brooks, *Psst! "Human Capital"*	___	___	___	___
Lutz, *Doublespeak*	___	___	___	___
McClintock, *Propaganda Techniques in Today's Advertising*	___	___	___	___

PROCESS ANALYSIS

Shipley, *Talk About Editing*	___	___	___	___
Mitford, *The American Way of Death*	___	___	___	___
Stoll, *Cyberschool*	___	___	___	___
Roberts, *How to Say Nothing in 500 Words*	___	___	___	___
Rego, *The Fine Art of Complaining*	___	___	___	___

COMPARISON-CONTRAST

Carson, *A Fable for Tomorrow*	___	___	___	___
Suina, *And Then I Went to School*	___	___	___	___
Rodriguez, *Workers*	___	___	___	___
Barry, *The Ugly Truth About Beauty*	___	___	___	___
Chapman, *The Prisoner's Dilemma*	___	___	___	___

CAUSE-EFFECT

	I really liked it.	It was okay.	I didn't like it.	I didn't read it.
King, *Why We Crave Horror Movies*	____	____	____	____
D'Amboise, *Showing What Is Possible*	____	____	____	____
Walker, *Beauty: When the Other Dancer Is the Self*	____	____	____	____
Darley & Latané, *Why People Don't Help in a Crisis*	____	____	____	____
Bissinger, *Innocents Afield*	____	____	____	____

DEFINITION

Cole, *Entropy*	____	____	____	____
Gleick, *Life as Type A*	____	____	____	____
Angier, *The Cute Factor*	____	____	____	____
Robbins & Wilner, *What Is the Quarterlife Crisis?*	____	____	____	____
Raspberry, *The Handicap of Definition*	____	____	____	____

ARGUMENTATION-PERSUASION

Sherry, *In Praise of the "F" Word*	____	____	____	____
Yuh, *Let's Tell the Story of All America's Cultures*	____	____	____	____
Barszcz, *Can You Be Educated From a Distance?*	____	____	____	____
Twain, *The Damned Human Race*	____	____	____	____
Fish, *Free-Speech Follies*	____	____	____	____
Paglia, *Rape: A Bigger Danger Than Feminists Know*	____	____	____	____
Jacoby, *Common Decency*	____	____	____	____
Alter, *Time to Think About Torture*	____	____	____	____
Porter, *Now the Talk Is About Bringing Back Torture*	____	____	____	____
Rodriguez, *The Border on Our Backs*	____	____	____	____
Parker, *Se Habla Entitlement*	____	____	____	____

COMBINING THE PATTERNS

	I really liked it.	It was okay.	I didn't like it.	I didn't read it.
Woolf, *The Death of the Moth*	____	____	____	____
Woolf, *Professions for Women*	____	____	____	____
King, *Where Do We Go From Here: Community or Chaos?*	____	____	____	____
King, *The World House*	____	____	____	____
Didion, *The Santa Ana*	____	____	____	____
Didion, *Marrying Absurd*	____	____	____	____

Any general comments or suggestions?

Name _____ Date _____

Address _____

THANKS AGAIN!